Trimble Families of America

John Farley Trimble

Trimble Families of America

Stanley Barry Trimble

The Trimble
Families of America
2021 Edition

Volume 1

By

John Farley Trimble
and
Stanley Barry Trimble

1973 - 2021

Trimble Families of America

ISBN 978-1-6780-2942-5
Printed in the United States of America

Trimble Families of America

Trimble Families of America

Trimble Families of America

Explanation of Numbering System

The progenitor of each family is given a letter of the alphabet, his children are given numbers after the letter symbol, such as A310. The children are indented under the father, then later in the book when that child's lineage is given, his number is brought to the left margin. The page on which the child's lineage is given could appear as far as ten or fifteen pages after the father's lineage, for example:

A6–Moses Trimble.

    The children of Moses Trimble:

  + **A13–James Trimble.**
   A14–Susanna Trimble.
   A15–Elizabeth Trimble.
   A16–Sally Trimble.

Moses Trimble is the father, and his four children follow his letter of A, and each are numbered. the small + in front of the child number indicates that James has a parent record in the book. To follow James Trimble, A13, as he is the only child we follow in this case

A13–James Trimble. Son of Moses Trimble.

Here you will find the family lineage and short biography of James Trimble. Then you follow his children as you did to find James.

Most of the data about an individual is in their parent entry if they have children. If the individual does not have children, all the data is in their child entry.

Original Preface

By John Farley Trimble

The purpose of this book is not to present a cut-and-dried family lineage of "who begat whom," but a record, at least in a limited measure, the invaluable role of the Scotts-Irish in the building of America, with a brief necessary glimpse at the background of this hardy race which began in Scotland and Ireland; using one family as an example. The Trimble genealogy, while admittedly incidental to the basic subject, becomes an integral element in the record as it relates to contemporary places, events, and other family groups.

It is this writer's opinion that without the contributions of the Scotts-Irish to our nation, the history of America would have to be rewritten. Always pioneers, they served notably and well. It was they who pushed the American boundary ever westward, fighting Native Americans and settling land. It was they whose farsighted realization of the necessity of education with its higher institutions of learning led them to establish colleges on the frontier lines. It was they who presented themselves as a constant bulwark of defense against tyranny and oppression, specifically-and magnificently-in the War for Independence. It was they who demanded, and eventually secured, absolute religious freedom for America, not willing to settle for mere token toleration, a people marked by a history of glorious and unfaltering loyalty to their religious convictions, whether in Ireland or America.

This work was written as a labor of love, with the hope that present and succeeding generations of Trimbles will find in their ancestry a cause for inspiration and expression in the Psalm: "The lines are fallen unto me in pleasant places; yea, I have a goodly heritage" (Psalm 16:6). And may they discover, as I (John Farley Trimble) have done in my years of research, that true success of man, while determined no little by environmental conditions, is for the most part born and nourished by these values implanted by his forefathers: an abiding trust in his Creator; a love and loyalty for his country; a desire to improve himself through education; a deep sense of moral integrity; and a commitment to the quest of finding a way to better his own and his neighbor's surroundings.

Furthermore, I (John Farley Trimble) am of the deep conviction that the young people of today who are in rebellion for rebellion's sake against the "status quo" would change their thinking if they could but envision the sacrifices and sufferings of their ancestors, in whose daily grim game of hide-and-seek with death found themselves unequally pitted against disease and pestilence,

Trimble Families of America

floods and famine, Native Americans and wild animals, and all sorts of extreme privations. Yet they sought to establish institutions of civilization, a government to insure a law-abiding orderly community of people; homes and villages to grow into future thriving cities; churches and schools to develop man's spiritual and cultural being, roads, waterways, and eventually railroads to pave the way for sophisticated modes of travel and communication that would promote industry and expansion; these, and countless other contributions. If the young protestors could but picture the severe hardships entailed in laying the foundation upon which this great nation of ours stands, they would not take lightly or for granted their rich inheritance. Instead of advocating anarchy and violence through wanton destruction of property or by escape from society in withdrawal, they would, I (John Farley Trimble) feel certain, strive by an orderly, legal approach to effect what changes in the establishment they deem necessary; and this, too, with educated, temperate reasoning.

Two great truths these angry young people could learn from the study of the evolvement of our nation. First, that enraged and impatient demands accomplish little toward the betterment of our society, being by nature destructive and negative. It is only through selfless dedication to a cause, with much hard work and perseverance, that an improvement is brought about. Secondly, they would do well to bear in mind that America was founded by displaced races such as the Scotts-Irish, who were invariably a minority group in a strange land amid alien unfriendly peoples. However, it is the constant desire for reform that has made America great and will continue to make America greater.

The most rewarding primary trait in all the Trimbles I (John Farley Trimble) have contacted in America, Ireland, and England is the expression of one thing in common, the integrity of all the Trimbles they knew.

I wish to express my thanks to the many people without whose assistance I could never have compiled the information contained in this book. To the following I am deeply indebted: Eugene E. Trimble of Kensington, Maryland, for permission to use his book, The Trimble Families, from which I have gained an immense amount of material especially concerning the North Mountain (Augusta County, Virginia) branch of Trimbles. His record I have quoted almost verbatim. Ruth E. Frey of Paris, Illinois, whose record on her branch of the family I consider to be the best documented in the field. Okey Bailes, genealogist, of Parkersburg, West Virginia, whose pioneer findings encouraged me to do a more extensive search. Mrs. Carl Boyd, historian and genealogist, of Mount Sterling, Kentucky. Mrs. Lillian Bush, a grand lady of the

3

Trimble Families of America

Original Preface

South who, despite her advanced age of ninety years, gave me abundant accurate data pertaining to our mutual Trimble family line. Dr. John F. Trimble, eminent psychiatrist of Washington, D.C., and his wife Peggy, assistant comptroller of The Washington Star newspaper, William Cattell Trimble, retired U.S. Foreign Service officer of Brooklandville, Maryland. He is a direct descendant of the illustrious Confederate general, Isaac Ridgeway Trimble. And to the many other individuals who gave freely of their time and resources to facilitate publication of this manuscript.

I must acknowledge a debt of gratitude to the authors, compilers, and publishers of the numerous books, periodicals, and other historical papers from which I have drawn generously for much of my information. Proper credit has been given to these authors and their works in the Bibliography of this book. Old courthouse, church, and other records across the country have spoken from the past to aid me in my search.

An explanation by way of an apology is here proffered to future readers of this book who may not find mention of their line of Trimbles. Scarcity of early records makes it a virtual impossibility to furnish a perfect genealogy for each various branch of the family tree down through the generations for two hundred fifty years. The reader may be confident that all data has been documented where possible. Also, this is the most nearly complete work in all facts pertaining to the Trimble genealogy assembled in book form thus far.

In the process of compiling information for my book, I have corresponded with Trimbles all over the United States. Many responses have included important facts dealing with their lineage. Each genealogical offering regardless of how fragmentary has been incorporated into that representative section of the book. Those whom I have been unable to contact, as well as the people who have failed to answer my correspondence, will be able, with the information they have concerning their ancestry and the resources of this book, to trace their line of descent.

The Trimbles in the United States have sprung from Scotts-Irish immigrants who came to this country direct from Northern Ireland. Numerous other families of Scotts-Irish descent came to America about the same time; to name a few: Bell, McClure, McDowell, Breckenridge, Houston, and Moffitt, etc.

We quote from Boogher's Gleanings of Virginia History, "When the Revolution ended, these brave and enterprising men began the march of civilization westward, and the first settlers of Kentucky were almost entirely from the upper portion of the Virginia Valley. The Prestons, Breckenridges, Logans, Allens, Trimbles, Andersons, McDowells, and many others, sought

4

Trimble Families of America

their fortunes in the new lands west of the Allegheny Mountains, and from these pioneer settlers has descended a race of people unsurpassed by any in the world for chivalry, courage, eloquence, and statesmanship. They have been found in every station of life, filling well the place which destiny has assigned to them, and the highest tribute which could be paid to the Scotts-Irish pioneers of Augusta County would be the roster of distinguished men who trace their ancestry to this section of the Valley of Virginia."

Update Preface

By Stanley Barry Trimble

This is an updated of John Farley Trimble's book. Michael Anthony Trimble, John Farley Trimble's son gave me permission to reprint and update The Trimble Families of America. It has been no small task. I (Stanley Trimble) have found references to this book in ancestry data. John did not provide references in his book because he wanted it more readable. He had a difficult task to gather information. No e-mail, no internet. Finding a descendent to correspond with to gather update information. Now there is abundant ancestry information, so much that the sorting false from true is difficult. On ancestry.com, one person could enter inaccurate data in their family tree and this inaccuracy could be duplicated in more family trees. I am including references for some of people that have been added.

I have access to more information and easier access with the internet. If someone in the future wants to add the next generation of Trimbles. you have my permission.

Our Trimble reunion started back in the 1940s on Labor Day at my Grandfather Conroy Trimble's house in Barnett's Creek, Johnson County, Kentucky. Everyone had to walk the last mile or so to get there. My grandfather, Conroy Trimble moved the reunion to Armco Park in Ashland, Kentucky in the mid-1960s because his siblings were getting too old to make the trip. My father, Clifford Trimble was president of the reunion for 20 years. The meals that were served were feasts. Simple country cooking made by the best cooks. In the 1990s I was the president of this reunion for several years before moving to Florida for work.

John Farley Trimble came to our reunion twice. He mentioned both in his book. I remember him coming to our Trimble Reunion at Armco Park in Ashland, Kentucky in the early 1970s. They stayed in motel the first trip and stayed at our house during the second visit. I had to give up my room for a night.

One of the first years the reunion was in Ashland a prize of a silver cup was given to the youngest child. It was engraved with Trimble Reunion Youngest Child and the year. These cups are really treasured by the recipients as heir looms. Trimble Child Cups were given away for over 40 years.

During the time of my working on this update has been interesting and will probably be mentioned in our history. President Donald Trump was elected, served and defeated while I was working on this book. The COVID 19 virus pandemic occurred during this period. The vaccines are being given now. Hopefully, it will be gone by the time this is published. The summer riots occurred last summer with BLM and Antifa.

Several people that I know have gotten COVID 19 and survived and died. Everyone has learned to wear a face mask in public. Indoor dining was prohibited. Restaurants were all closed for several months, then take-out only was allowed, home delivery became popular. Many restaurants have closed permanently. For a month toilet paper disappeared from store shelves. I still have no idea what they were doing with all that toilet paper. We were all quarantined at home. All but essential workers stayed at home. Students did remote learning. All elective medical procedures were postponed. Family gathering were restricted. Life will return to normal, but I think what normal is has changed.

At the front of this book, I gather the names of all individuals that served in the military. They are grouped by the period of wars and alphabetized within those periods.

In America, we express a location by writing City, County State. My address is Ashland, Boyd County, Kentucky. In the United Kingdom, they express their location with six or so names in a row. I had one Trimble that I corresponded with explained them to me, it was a little confusing for me. In some of the family trees individuals start in the United Kingdom, so they have a longer list for their location.

In John Farley Trimble's book, he put the father's last name last on the children of line. As an example, my parents would be "The children of Clifford Eldon and Doris Deloris Price Trimble:" I have changed this to "The children of Clifford Eldon Trimble and Doris Deloris Price:" There is one exception to this, if the wife's maiden name is not known I place the husband's last name last, "The children of Clifford and Doris Trimble:"

And the sons become the fathers and their daughters will be wives
As the torch is passed from hand to hand
And we struggle through our lives
Though the generations wander, the lineage survives
And all of us, from dust to dust, we all become forefathers by and by

From Forefathers by Dan Fogelberg

For my son Houston and my daughter Shellie.

List of Trimbles Military Service.

I added this section. I found so many that had military service listed in their individual listing that they need gathered in one place. Several of my proof readers really liked it.   Enjoy   Stanley Trimble

- **James Trimble.** (H6) Born on June 1, 1746 and died October 10, 1774. He died in the Battle of Point Pleasant. This was the major action of Dunmore's War. The only war declared by a state, Virginia, against Shawnee and Mingo tribes.
- **George Trimble.** (D7) Born on January 1, 1756, in Augusta County Virginia. George served as a private in the company of his brother Captain James Trimble (B2) of the Augusta County, Virginia Militia.
- **James Trimble.** (B2) Born on February 25, 1753 in Augusta County, Virginia. He was a Captain in the Virginia Militia.

War of the American Revolution.
- **John Linn.** (G17) Born on April 2, 1754. Married Ann Fleming.
- **Moses Trimble.** (J4) Born in Virginia about 1754 and died in 1828 in Newton County, Georgia, served in the American Revolution from which service he received several grants of land in Georgia.
- **Robert Trimble.** (I2) Born in 1739 in Virginia was a Captain during the American Revolution.
- **William Trimble, II.** (G5) Born in 1736 at Newberry, Cumberland County, Kentucky and died in 1798. Served in the Revolutionary War as a private in the First Battalion from 1777 to 1779.
- **Reverend William Trimble Linn.** (G16) Born on February 27, 1752, in Lurgan Township, Franklin County, Pennsylvania, and died in 1808 in Albany, New York. He was ordained in the ministry at Philadelphia in 1775 and was appointed chaplain in the War of the Revolution, serving in the fifth and sixth battalions, February 15, 1776.
- **William Trimble.** (D10) Born in 1760 in Augusta County, Virginia. William was given his pension as a Revolutionary War soldier on December 2, 1835.

War of 1812.
- **John Graham.** (D76) Lived to be eighty-three years of age He was a captain in the War of 1812.

- **Judge William McClung.** (G29) Born in 1787 and died 1876. He was a soldier in the War of 1812.
- **William McClure.** (A12) Born in 1764 in Augusta County, Virginia. A veteran's mark at his grave says he served in the Revolutionary War and enlisted in Washington County, Virginia for the War of 1812 under Lieutenant William Huston and was killed at the battle of Norfolk, Virginia in 1814.
- **Abner Trimble.** (AH1) Born in 1795 in England and died in 1819 in Franklin County, Ohio. He served in the War of 1812, from Ohio in the company Captain Bartholomew Fryatt.
- **Governor Hugh Allen Trimble.** (B5) Allen and the General MacArthur became close friends and in the War of 1812. Allen rose to rank of general in the Ohio Militia under General Harrison, who after the war persuaded Allen to run for public office. Thus, started his political career. Allen was governor of the state of Ohio.
- **Capt John Trimble.** (C7) John Trimble organized a company of volunteers and went to Norfolk in the War of 1812.
- **John Trimble.** (G21) Born on May 23, 1780 and died July 26, 1845. John was a soldier in the War of 1812.
- **Mark Trimble.** (D48) Born in 1782 in Greenbrier County, now West Virginia and died on August 2, 1861, in Johnson County, Kentucky. He fought in the war of 1812.
- **Senator William Allen Trimble.** (B6) Born on April 4, 1786, died December 12, 1821, in Washington, D.C. He died from wounds received when he was Brevet Colonel in the War of 1812. He was a national hero at the Battle of Lake Erie in the War of 1812 where he received the wound which was to later cause his death.
- **William Trimble.** (D51) Born in 1787 in what Monroe County is now, West Virginia. was a bugle boy in the War of 1812 and he was an eyewitness to the killing of Native American leader Tecumseh.
- **William Clark Trimble.** (D62) Born in 1794. He was in the War of 1812, in Captain W. Bott's company, Second Regiment, Kentucky Mounted Volunteer Militia. He appears on the company payroll for August 27 to November 3, 1813.

Mexican American War.

- **William James Trimble** (AJ2) Born on November 16, 1795 in Lexington, Fayette County, Kentucky and died on January 5, 1844 in

Trimble Families of America

Perote Prison, Mexico. He was captured in the Dawson Massacre on September 18, 1842 at Salado, Texas. He was then marched to the Perote Prison. His name is listed on the on the memorial for Dawson Men Captured at the Salado, Texas.

He became the self-appointed morale officer of the captives, being dubbed "Tecolote" (Screech Owl) by his captors because he was able to mimic the owl. Trimble went out of his way to humorously harass his captors and thereby entertain his fellow captives.

- **Edward (Ned) Trimble.** (AJ4) Born in 1810 in Kentucky and died September 18, 1842 in San Antonio, Texas. He was killed in the Dawson Massacre on September 18, 1842 at Salado, Texas. His name is listed on the memorial for Dawson Men Killed at the Salado, Texas as Ned Trimble.

Civil War.

- **Francis J. Baily.** (AM260) Born on September 27, 1836 and died on March 18, 1865. He was with the Union army during the late Civil War and died of sickness in a wagon in the South.

- **William Thomas Harper.** (AM647) Born on June 20, 1835 and died on October 8, 1864. He was in the Union army during the Civil War, was taken prisoner and died in the Confederate prison at Florence, South Carolina to which place he had been transferred from Andersonville, Georgia, where he had first been incarcerated.

- **Benjamin Henry Downing.** (AM575) Born on October 17, 1842 and died in November 1908. He enlisted in the Forty-ninth Regiment Pennsylvania Volunteers, entered the service on April 19, 1861, participated in many of the important battles—McClellan's seven days' campaign in front of Richmond, Antietam, Fredericksburg, Grant's Campaign through the Wilderness to Richmond, Sheridan's campaign in the Shenandoah Valley, the fighting in front of Petersburg, Virginia, and many other battles and skirmishes. He was wounded, disabled, and mustered out of service March 1, 1865.

- **James Dennis Downing.** (AM523) Born on March 15, 1840. He was a private during the Civil War in Company F, 9th Regiment, Pennsylvania Volunteer Infantry and in Company A, 43rd Regiment, Pennsylvania Infantry.

- **Joseph B. Downing.** (AM197) Born on November 14, 1843. He enlisted in the army from August 15, 1861 to July 15, 186- and was promoted to Captain of Company F, 49 Regiment, Pennsylvania. Volunteers during the Civil War.

- **William Downing.** (AM196) Born on February 17, 1842 and died on May 10, 1864 in Battle of Spotsylvania Court House. He enlisted in Company D, 49 Regiment, Pennsylvania, Volunteers during the Civil War.
- **Paschell Evans.** (AM431) Born on February 17, 1835 He enlisted during the Civil War in Company C, 175 Regiment Pennsylvania Volunteer Infantry.
- **Schyler V. Fiske.** (AL313) He died in November 1863, in the army.
- **Edward Freeman.** (AL315) He enlisted in the army during the Civil War and was never heard from, probably killed.
- **George Washington Jobe.** (AM446) Born on December 4, 1837 and died on July 1, 1864. He enlisted in the Fifth Pennsylvania Cavalry during the Civil War. He was wounded whilst on a raid at Roanoke River, and his companions being unable to rescue him, he fell into the enemy's hands, who stripped him of clothing and left him to suffer and perish alone.
- **George Mechem Halsted.** (AL330) Born on September 14, 1845. He was in the telegraph service during the Civil War.
- **Milton Arnold Halsted.** (AL327) Born on September 12, 1838. He entered the army as assistant surgeon of the 15th New York Calvary and saw hard service and mustered out in 1865.
- **Stanley Mechem Halsted.** (AL329) Born on October 18, 1843. He was a member of 71st New York Infantry and afterwards a captain in another regiment.
- **Nathan Hollen.** (C35) He was Private in 144th Regiment, Indiana Infantry of Union Army during the Civil War.
- **Peter Lamb.** (G110) He served in the Civil War.
- **John Litzenberg McClellan.** (AM688) Born on September 17, 1840 and died on March 7, 1862. He was quartermaster on Gen. George B. McCall's staff during the Civil War.
- **Green McGuire.** (D426) A Confederate soldier killed in battle. Older brother of Simpson McGuire and Felix McGuire.
- **Simpson McGuire.** (D427) He died of injuries received in the Civil War. He was the brother of Green McGuire and Felix McGuire.
- **Felix McGuire.** (D428) Born on August 13, 1840 in Hazel Green,

Trimble Families of America

Kentucky He fought with John Hunt Morgan in the Civil War. He was the brother of Green McGuire and Simpson McGuire.

- **George W. Morton.** (A131) Born in 1837 in Mississippi and died on September 17, 1862 in Battle of Antietam at Sharpsburg, Maryland. George as selected Second Lieutenant of the Coahoma Invincibles Company B, 11th Regiment, Mississippi Infantry of the Confederate Army.

- **James Keeport Morton.** (A132) Born in 1840 in Grenada, Mississippi and died on September 17, 1862 in Battle of Antietam at Sharpsburg, Virginia. J. K. Morton was selected captain in Coahoma Invincibles, Company B, 11th Regiment, Mississippi Infantry of the Confederate Army.

- **Samuel E. Nealis.** (AM484) Born on March 6, 1843. Married Mary Emma White on December 22, 1884. He was a carpenter. He enlisted on May 21, 1861, in Company A, 2nd Delaware Regiment, discharged July 1864, re-enlisted for a short term.

- **Clarence Peters.** (AM400) Born on November 18, 1843, He was active in the military service of Maryland. National Guard, 1867-77. In July 1877, he was Colonel Sixth Regiment Infantry, during the "railroad riot" and under orders sent 3 companies to reinforce Fifth Regiment Infantry, leaving himself and 32 men to defend the Armory at Front and Fayette Streets, containing 2 Gatling guns, 500 rifles and 10,000 cartridges against the mob. The three companies marching through the streets were assailed by the mob, and fired upon them, causing some causalities, but checking the rioters. Colonel Peters resigned after he had spent 8 years in perfecting his regiment, because of not being sustained by the Governor of Maryland and quit the military service.

- **George Peters.** (AM127) Born on February 21, 1808. At the beginning of the Civil War, he enlisted as a Colonel of the First Maryland Rifle Raiment. He recruited from same into the Confederate Maryland line at Harper's Ferry, Virginia in May 1861. After much peril he reached the Confederacy in October 1862. He was appointed as an officer in the Confederate States' service and under Surgeon General S. P. Moore oversaw the department for the transportation of the sick and wounded of the armies in Virginia. He also served under Brigadier General John H. Winder, Commanding Department of Richmond, Virginia. Colonel Peters organized and commanded the first troops (infantry) for the defense of Richmond. He was in service from in November 1861, until on April 3, 1865, and was paroled in Richmond, Virginia in May 1865. He died on August 29, 1865 in Richmond of disease contracted in the service. His wife and younger children joined her husband under a flag of truce in January 1863.

- **George H. Peters.** (AM402) Born on May 30, 1848. In January 1863, he accompanied by his mother and went into the Confederacy; in 1863-64 he was courier to Medical Director Cavrington, Richmond, Virginia. In September 1864, enlisted in Company G., 3rd Battalion Res. Troops, under Brigadier General George C. Lee. and served in the lines in front of Fort Harrison until April 1865.

- **Winfield Peters.** (AM399) Born on July 8, 1841. He was a soldier in the Maryland Line, 1st Regt. Infantry, 1861-62, and an officer, 1862-65, in the army of Northern Virginia, C. S. A. He began service under Johnston at Harper's Ferry, Virginia, followed Gen. Lee from June 1862 to Appomattox; withdrawing prior to the surrender; with his men joined Johnston at Greensboro, North Carolina; rode with Calvary. escort of President. Davis to Charlotte, North Carolina, thence started with others for Trans-Mississippi Dept.; was captured at Athens, Georgia, by Stoneman's Federal cavalry; escaped and was paroled in Opelika, Alabama on June 21, 1865, and returned to Baltimore, Maryland, October 5, 1865, having been absent 4 years, 4 months and 4 days.

- **Edgar Ward Prewitt.** (F61). He enlisted in Union 40th Regiment, Missouri Infantry Company: K in 1863.

- **James Moss Prewitt.** (F62) He enlisted in Union 11th Regiment, Missouri Cavalry Company: A as a Private.

- **Paul Jones Prewitt.** (F63) Born on January 10, 1830 in Howard County, Missouri and died on June 21, 1895 in Garland, Dallas County, Texas. He enlisted in the Missouri State Guard 7th Regiment 8th Division for the Confederacy.

- **Beale Howard Richardson.** (AM412) Born on October 11, 1843. In Virginia in September, 1862, and joined the Fourth Virginia Cavalry; at the battle of Sharpsburg in September 17, 1862, was captured and taken to Fort Delaware; exchanged in November 19; returned to Virginia; appointed to a position in the War Department under

Trimble Families of America

Colonel George Peters; in June 1863 joined the First Maryland Cavalry as a private, and remained in the field until November, 1864, when he was transferred to Gulf Department, and appointed purchasing agent at Mobile; on the evacuation of that place on April 12, 1865, took charge of steamer *Cherokee*, loaded with $250,000 worth of government freight; proceeded to Macon, Mississippi; here surrender was announced; returned to Mobile penniless; on June 9, 1865.

- **Joseph Trimble Rothrock.** (AL285) Born on April 9, 1839. They lived at Wilkes-Barre, Pennsylvania, for some time moved thence to West Chester, 428 N. Church Street, where they continue. He was a Captain in Co. E, 20th Pennsylvania. Cavalry in the Civil War and wounded at Fredericksburg, Virginia.

- **Edward A. Thomas.** (AL301) Born on April 27, 1888 and died on September 2, 1890 He raised a company of volunteers for the Civil War known as Company C, 111th Regiment, New York Volunteers, of which he was captain. He was taken prisoner at Harper's Ferry and was later exchanged.

- **Armon D. Trimble.** (AM383) He entered the army during the Civil War and rose to the ranks of lieutenant.

- **Asa Mahan Trimble.** (G131) Born on September 30, 1836 and died on May 21, 1903. Asa was a member of the Sixty-fifth Ohio Infantry in the War Between the States.

- **Charles William Trimble.** (B32) Born on December 21, 1841. He was killed at the Second Battle of Bull Run of the Civil War on August 29, 1862, Seventy-third Regiment, Ohio Volunteer Infantry.

- **Christopher Columbus Trimble.** (C69) Born on August 10, 1842 Private, Company C, 8th Calvary. Enlisted on April 27, 1862. AWOL for 85 days on October 31, 1864.

- **Cyrenius Wait Trimble.** (D227) Born on February 23, 1834 in Pulaski County, Kentucky and died on June 6, 1908. He was in the Nineteenth Infantry Kentucky for the Union, enlisted in 1862.

- **Ebenezer Trimble.** (G82) Born in 1837. During the Civil War he died in prison camp.

- **Edwin Trimble, Jr.** (F82) Died in 1862. He was killed in the Civil War. He was a colonel in the Fourteenth Cavalry of the Confederate Army.

- **Francis Marion Trimble.** (AJ13) Born on May 29, 1841 in Fayette

County, Texas and died on October 8, 1923 in Menard, Texas. He enlisted on January 28, 1861 as a Private in Company D, 5th Regiment, Texas Calvary, Confederate States Army.

- **General Isaac Ridgeway Trimble.** (F26) Born on May 20, 1804, in Culpeper County, Virginia. In 1818 Isaac Ridge way Trimble secured, through his half-brother David, who was then a congressman, an appointment to the Military Academy at West Point, from which he graduated in 1822 in the top section of his class and received his commission as second lieutenant. He transferred to the Corps of Engineers. He was a civil engineer with the construction of roads, canals and railroads.

Although a Southerner in sympathy and Marylander by adoption (he took up residence in Baltimore shortly after leaving the army), Isaac Ridgeway Trimble was initially opposed to secession, believing that the differences between the states should be settled by peaceful means. However, an order for his arrest issued by the Federal authorities on April 19, 1861, because of his action in destroying, on the orders of the governor of Maryland and the mayor of Baltimore, several bridges on the railroad line to Wilmington, led him to offer his services to the Confederacy. He was appointed brigadier general, Confederate States of America, and subsequently was promoted to major general. Isaac Ridgeway Trimble's war record is mentioned in several books on the War Between the States and are available to the reader at any library. Following the war, Isaac lived in Baltimore with a country home, Ravenshurst, in Baltimore County. He died on January 10, 1888, and is buried in Greenmount Cemetery, Baltimore.

General Trimble was nearing sixty years of age at the beginning of the Civil War. In the war, officers of his rank were generally young men who had shortly before graduated from West Point, such as J. E. B. Stuart, the latter upon resigning from the Union Army and joining the Confederate forces were usually given much higher ranks. General Trimble appeared to be a favorite of Stonewall Jackson, as when Jackson was given a higher promotion, he had Trimble promoted also, under him, to assume the command of Jackson's former troops. General Trimble was wounded and during his recuperation period was taken out of actual combat, thus being given command of troops in the Shenandoah Valley.

Trimble Families of America

On the eve of the Battle of Little Round Top (Pickett's Charge) General Trimble rejoined Lee at Gettysburg. Lee replaced another general with Isaac Trimble and he commanded one of the three divisions that were in Pickett's Charge. According to one version of later history, Pickett was not in this charge, the account said he was AWOL and was scheduled for court martial but that the trial was never held as Lee was on the defensive the remainder of the war and needed all his general officers as now, he had lost Stonewall Jackson, General Isaac R. Trimble, and later, J. E. B. Stuart. General Lee in his memoirs says that had he not lost so many of his best generals the outcome might have been different.

During the charge at Gettysburg, General Trimble was again wounded resulting in the loss of a leg. He spent the next two years as a prisoner of war in a Union prison camp. Upon his release, now past sixty years of age, the "old warrior" single leggedly set out once more to join General Lee in Virginia. It was in Lynchburg, Virginia, that he received word of Lee's surrender. On September 22, 1862, Stonewall Jackson wrote the adjutant general: "I respectfully recommend that Brig. General I. R. Trimble be appointed to Major General. It is proper, in this connection, to state that I do not regard him as a good disciplinarian, but his success in battle has induced me to recommend his promotion. I will mention but one instance, though several might be named, in which he rendered distinguished service. After a day's march of over 30 miles, he ordered his command, consisting of two small Regiments, the 21st of Georgia and the 21st of North Carolina to charge the enemy's position at Manassas Junction. This charge resulted in the capture of several prisoners and 8 pieces of artillery. I regard that day's achievement as the most brilliant that has come under my observation during the present war."

- **James M. Trimble.** (D191) Born on January 1, 1825 in Barnett's Creek, Johnson County, Kentucky. He server in the Confederate Army during the Civil War, in the First Battalion, Kentucky Mounted Rifles as a Private.
- **James Trimble.** (AM123) Born on November 28, 1819. During the Civil War he was in the commissary department of the army.
- **John Joseph Trimble.** (AM375) Born on September 27, 1841. During the Civil War he enlisted in Company G, 91st Regiment,

Trimble Families of America

Pennsylvania. Infantry, as corporal on November 1, 1861 and discharged on August 12, 1862 to accept promotion as First Lieutenant in Company F, 12th Regiment. New Jersey Infantry: resignation accepted on account of poor health on October 31, 1863. He was engaged in the two great battles of Chancellorsville and Gettysburg, in the latter of which he was wounded. He lived at the National Home for Disabled Volunteer Soldiers, Danville, Illinois.

- **John N. Trimble.** (AN9) Born in 1838 in Crawford, Ohio and died April 4, 1863 in Overton Hospital, Memphis, Tennessee as a Union soldier the Civil War.
- **John N. Trimble.** (AM101) Born on February 6, 1834 and died October 25, 1866. He enlisted in Company I, 160th Regular, O. Volunteer Infantry as a corporal, May 1864 and was discharged September 12, 1864.
- **John Thomas Trimble.** (J130) Born in 1836 and died in 1865. John Thomas was a soldier of the Confederacy and died at Petersburg, Virginia.
- **Moses Jackson Trimble.** (C6) He was a private in Company of Rifleman in 105th Regiment of the Militia of Virginia from March 8, 1814 to July 5, 1814.
- **Moses Marion Trimble.** (J131) Born in 1836 and died on July 1, 1862, in the Civil War in Virginia.
- **Nelson Trimble.** (AN5) Born on July 4, 1832 in Bucyrus, Crawford County, Ohio. He was a Union soldier during the Civil War.
- **Richard Menifee Trimble.** (D200) Born on August 12, 1837, died February 21, 1909, in Montgomery County, Kentucky. He served in the Confederate Army under General Buell.
- **Samuel Walker Trimble.** (I42) Born on August 20, 1838 in San Antonio, Bexar, Texas and died on February 21, 1915 in Del Rio, Texas. Samuel was a private in Company E Texas Calvary of Confederate States during the Civil War.
- **Thomas Heber Trimble.** (G141) Born in 1841. He served in the Civil War.
- **Thomas Jefferson White.** (AM481) Born on September 17, 1848 near "Steamboat," Chester County, Pennsylvania. He enlisted during the Civil War on July 19, 1864, in Company P, 192nd Regiment. Penna. Volunteers and was mustered out with his regiment on

November 15, 1864, at Philadelphia, Pennsylvania.

- **George Washington White.** (AM494) Born on January 22, 1832. He enlisted on December 26, 1863, in Battery C, 2nd Pennsylvania. Volunteers Heavy Artillery. He was honorably discharged on January 29, 1866.

Spanish American War.

- **Charles S. Finley.** (AM856) Born on December 17, 1873. He was in the Spanish-American war, came home sick and died at Missoula, Montana.
- **Robert H. Henderson** (AL654) was in the Canadian Army.
- **John M. McClellan.** (AL575) Born on June 33, 1877 and died on December 23, 1902. Never married. He served in the army during the Spanish-American War and died of fever contracted in the service. He was enlisted in Company E, 36th Regiment U. S. Volunteers.
- **Oscar Sarke Miles.** (AM1648) Born on June 8, 1887. He was in the U. S. Marine Service.
- **Albert Gorham Thomas.** (AL550) Born on July 19, 1876. He served in the U. S. Navy during the war with Spain.
- **John Trimble.** (A221) In 1897 he received an A.B. degree at the University of Alabama. He was captain of the Third Alabama Infantry Volunteers in the Spanish-American War of 1898.

Cuban War

- **Charles A. Downing.** (AM1306) Born on October 20, 1880. He enlisted during the Cuban War in April 1898, in Company B, 3rd Regiment, Illinois Infantry, at Springfield, and was mustered out in January 1899 at Joliet, Illinois.
- **Allen O. Evans.** (AM1347) Born on September 12, 1878 and died on October 10, 1900. He was in the Cuban War and died in the service, buried at Clarksville, Tennessee.
- **John Walter Lemaster.** (D737) Died in the army.

World War I

- **George Halcomb Allen.** (AM1843) Born in May 1896 in Columbus, Muscogee County, Georgia and died on October 12, 1918 in Meuse-Argonne, Romagne, France. He was a Second Lieutenant in 4th Infantry Regiment, 3rd Infantry Division during World War I.

Trimble Families of America

- **Clayton Trimble, Jr.** (N24) He was killed while serving in the armed forces.
- **J. Smith Trimble.** (D820) Born on January 10, 1892. He served in World War I.
- **Leroy Chester Trimble.** (AM304) Born on March 7, 1889 in St. Louis, Missouri. Died on September 5, 1976 in Wynnewood, Montgomery County, Pennsylvania. He was a veteran of the Army during World War I from April 27, 1918 to May 3, 1919. He was a Sergeant in the Medical Corps.
- **Palmer Trimble.** (D797) Born on August 9, 1901 in Johnson County, Kentucky. He enlisted in the Army on November 3, 1919 and was discharged on November 2, 1920. He enlisted the second time December 5, 1920 and was discharged on December 4, 1923. He enlisted the third time on May 23, 1928 and was discharged on January 29, 1930.
- **James Archibald Trimble.** (A265) Born on May 7, 1894. He served in the army in World War I.
- **James William Trimble.** (Q11) During the First World War, he served in the United States Army as a private and was assigned to the Adjutant General's Office, Little Rock, Arkansas.

World War II

- **Larry G. Arrowood.** (D1211) Enlisted in the Air force on March 19, 1954 in Ashland, Kentucky. He took basic training in Sampson Air Force Base, New York. He was discharged from active duty in October 1957 at Maxwell Air Force base in Alabama. "President Eisenhower cut back on the Armed Forces at that time and every one that would be discharged in the next 6 months had a choice to get out early, so I took it."
- **Okey Lester Bailes.** (D1393) Born on March 14, 1918. Okey has two years of college and armed force duty of five years in World War II and two years in the Korean Conflict.
- **Frank Alien Carroll.** (D1275) His career was in the United States Air Force. They live in California.
- **William Allen "Bill" Caudill.** (D1197) Born on August 10, 1914 in Johnson County, Kentucky. Enlisted on May 18, 1944 in the Army and discharged in 1945.
- **Billy Joe Haney.** (AJ95) Born on July 31, 1924 in Menard, Menard

County, Texas. Billy Joe was a military veteran serving in United States Navy during WWII. He was Sheriff of Menard County for 24 years.

- **Robert Draper Hill.** (D1270) Born on January 12, 1920. He was a veteran of World War II.
- **Wilbur Marks Hill.** (D1272) Born on July 3, 1927. He was a veteran of World War II.
- **Guy McLaughlin.** (A246) Born on March 1885 in Lynchburg, Virginia. In 1915 was a member of naval aviator Bluejackets in Pensacola, Escambia County, Florida and in 1919 was an assistant supervisor at Navy flight school in San Diego, California. He was with second group that began training on March 21, 1917.
- **Herman June Roberts.** (C245) He served during World War II.
- **Billy Rogers. (**D1763) He was a veteran of the U.S. Army.
- **Hoy Preston.** (D811) Born on February 14, 1918 in Kentucky and died on June 3, 1999 in Kentucky. Hoy enlisted during World War II on January 26, 1943.
- **Robert Carl Staley.** (G317) Born on November 3, 1916 in Walnut Township, Marshall County, Indiana and died on May 14, 1999 in Indianapolis, Marion County, Indiana. Bob was a World War II veteran. He landed in Liverpool on his birthday on November 3, 1943. He was assigned to General Eisenhower's headquarters, where he was to serve as a jeep driver. Except for the nightly buzz bombs which flew overhead at 2 am and for one 100-pound bomb that landed in camp but failed to explode, things were calm. Even Ike was calm and talked freely with his men when he had the time. Bob even got invited to the wedding of Ike's aide. Bob's primary responsibility was to drive an orderly down to headquarters twice a day. In his leisure time he discovered the game of golf (but some of the fairways had big divots - where bombs had hit). He was later stationed in Frankfort, Germany.
- **J. Edward Toy, Jr.** (D1263) He was in World War II from November 1943 to June 1946.
- **John Crittenden Toy.** (D1264) John was in World War II from June 1941 to May 1945 and was at Schofield Barrack when Pearl Harbor was Bombed.
- **Bruce Trimble.** (O21) In the U.S. Air Force.
- **Christian Van Trimble.** (AJ34) Born on July 14, 1921 in Menard,

Menard County, Texas and died on June 11, 2016 in Menard, Texas. He served in World War II enlisted on July 18, 1942. He was discharged from the US Army on October 20, 1945, in Santa Barbara, California. He was in the United States Army as Technician 4th Grade, Battery A, 461st anti-aircraft artillery air-craft warning battalion. He went to England and then France and saw combat in the Normandy Campaign and Battle of the Bulge. He received the European, African, Middle Eastern Theater medal. His feet were frozen in the Battle of the Bulge, and he had to be evacuated. He endured several surgeries on his feet in England before returning home for discharge. His feet gave him problems the rest of his life. He was Honorably Discharged on October 20, 1945.

- **Claude Trimble.** (D1226) He enlisted in the army infantry on December 19, 1940 at Fort Thomas Newport, Kentucky. He was discharged on November 4, 1945.
- **Claude Mack Trimble.** (Q15) Born on December 8, 1903. Graduated from the University of Arkansas and attended Purdue University. He retired a lieutenant colonel after thirty years in the service of his country.
- **Clifford Eldon Trimble.** (D1200) Born on September 3, 1926 in Paintsville, Kentucky. He was drafted into the Army when he was 18 while still in high school. He took his physical in Huntington, West Virginia. He was then allowed to complete high school. He went to basic training in Texas. When he reported for basic training, they had too many recruits, so the bottom of the alphabetic list was placed on KP for 13 weeks. He took basic training during the next class. World War II ended before he got out of basic training. He served as a guard at a prison for American soldiers in New York.
- **Earl Anson Trimble.** (AJ35) Born on April 21, 1923 in Menard, Menard County, Texas and died on January 4, 2021 in Fort McKavett, Texas. He enlisted on February 10, 1943 in the United States Army as a Technician 4th Grade in Company A 110th Regiment 28th Division. He served in Rhineland and Ardennes and was in the Battle of the Bulge, received American Theater of Operations, Europe/African/Middle Eastern Theater of Operations, WWII Victory, and Good Conduct Medals. The 28th Division was one of the most decorated infantry divisions in its 140-year history.

Trimble Families of America

- **Emmett Ryan Trimble.** (D1260) Born on July 24, 1923 and died on December 21, 1962. Emmett was a veteran of the U.S. Army.

- **Francis Ford Trimble.** (F88) Born on October 31, 1898 in Seattle, Washington and died after 1943. He graduated from West Point U.S. Military Academy in New York in 1920. Served as a Lieutenant aide-de-camp to General Douglas MacArthur for 7 years in Philippines.

- **Isaac Ridgeway Trimble, Jr.** (F111) He was commissioned lieutenant colonel in the U.S. Army Medical Corps in 1941 and subsequently promoted to colonel. His entire military service during World War II was in the Pacific area where he was appointed chief surgical consultant on the staff of General MacArthur.

- **James Trimble.** (F133) He was killed on Iwo Jima at age of eighteen.

- **James Guy Trimble.** (AH47) Enlisted in the aircraft mechanic working at the NAS in Navy on March 12, 1941 at 17. He was an aircraft mechanic. Discharged in 1958. He continued as an aircraft mechanic in Pensacola, Florida until 1984.

- **Jerry E. Trimble.** (O18) Captain in the U.S. Air Force.

- **John Thomas Trimble.** (D1256) Born on November 8, 1912 and died on March 11, 1959. John Thomas was a veteran of World War II.

- **Kenny James Trimble.** (AG4) He was born March 1, 1919 in International Falls, Koochiching, Minnesota and died May 8, 1991 Reno, Washoe County, Nevada. He served in the Army playing trombone during World War II.

- **Oral C. Trimble.** (D1177) Killed in World War II in U.S. Navy.

- **Paul Crittenden Trimble.** (D829) Born on November 20, 1911. He served in World War II.

- **Paul Edwin Trimble (Admiral, Retired).** (K32) Born on March 24, 1913, at Agenda, Kansas. This author (John Farley Trimble) has had extensive communication in the past few years with Paul E. Trimble and considers him to be a man of rare intellect and congenial personality.

    His military career began with his appointment as cadet to the U.S. Coast Guard Academy at New London, Connecticut, on August 13, 1932. He was graduated with a B.S. degree and a commission as ensign in the Coast Guard on June 8, 1936.

    Subsequently he advanced to lieutenant (j.g.) on June 8, 1939;

lieutenant on February 25, 1942; lieutenant commander on December 8, 1942; commander on April 15, 1949; captain on July 1, 1958; rear admiral on July 1, 1964; and vice-admiral on July 27, 1966.

After leaving the academy he served six years of sea duty on board various Coast Guard cutters stationed on the coast of New England: the cutter *Mojave, Algonquin, Chelan, Tahoe,* and *Cayuga*. In August 1940, he was ordered to a postgraduate training course at the Harvard School of Business Administration, where he was graduated with a master's degree (MBA) with distinction in June 1942; he was named a Baker Scholar in 1941.

With the service's World War II expansion program underway, he resumed regular military duties at the Third Coast Guard District office in New York as finance officer. From August 1943 to August 1945 he commanded, respectively, the patrol frigates, U.S.S. *Hoquiam*, operations. While with the Sausalito he also commanded, Escort Division Twenty-seven, which ultimately was turned over to Russia under the lend-lease program.

After the war he was assigned as assistant chief, Budget Division, at Coast Guard Headquarters, Washington, D.C. From October 1951 to July 1953, he commanded the *Starts (WAG-83),* a multi-function (search and rescue, logistics, law enforcement, buoy tending, icebreaking) vessel then stationed at Juneau, Alaska. Following that tour of. duty, he was returned to Coast Guard Headquarters to serve, successively, as chief, Budget and Cost Analysis Division, until September 1955, as assistant comptroller until August 1957, and as comptroller of the Coast Guard until August 1959.

After commanding the 327-foot *Duane* on ocean station patrol and search and rescue in the North Atlantic for two years, he became commanding officer of the Coast Guard base at Boston, Massachusetts in July 1961.

On July 13, 1966, the president named Rear Admiral Trimble to the post of assistant commandant of the U.S. Coast Guard with the rank of vice-admiral (succeeding retiring VADM William D. Shields, USCG).

In December 1966, VADM Trimble received the Distinguished Service Medal from the secretary of the treasury for his service from June 1964 to November 1966.

23

Trimble Families of America

In June 1967 he was presented the Legion of Merit Medal by the secretary of transportation, Alan S. Boyd, for his performance as chairman of the Interagency Task Force.

In June 1970, he was presented the Distinguished Service Medal by Secretary John A. Volpe for his performance as assistant commandant of the Coast Guard.

- **Richard George Trimble.** (G288) Born on July 25, 1927 in Cleveland, Ohio. He served in the navy and the air force.
- **Robert Trimble.** (O20) In the U.S. Air Force.
- **Robert Finley Trimble.** (H62) Born in 1924 (twin) Brigadier General He was born in Boligee, Alabama on July 26, 1924. Robert entered the United States Military Academy at West Point, New York in July 1942 and graduated in June 1945, with a B.S. degree and a commission in the Air Corps of the U.S. Army. Later during the years from 1949 to 51, he attended the University of Michigan and obtained an M.A. in business administration. As a pilot, Robert initially trained in B-25 and B-17 aircraft. However, changes in requirements resulted in his flying RF-51 and RB-26 photo reconnaissance aircraft in Europe, special air mission VC-47 aircraft in the States, and F-48 fighter Bomber aircraft in Korea. After rising to the level of "Command Pilot," his assignment to procurement duties resulted in the discontinuance of his regular flying duties.

  He was appointed director of Procurement Policy of Headquarters, U.S. Air Force, and in December 1970 he was selected for promotion to the rank of brigadier general with promotion to become effective in August 1971.

- **Robert Marshall Trimble.** (AK16) Born about 1920 in Philadelphia, Pennsylvania and died on May 12, 2009 in Pennsylvania. Married Eleanor on September 15, 1917 in Chester, Pennsylvania. Robert was a Captain flying B-24 Liberators at first, later B-17 Flying Fortresses in WW II. He completed thirty missions over Germany. He was then giving a secret mission behind the eastern front. His listed mission was to retrieve aircraft that had to landed in the Soviet East due to a shortage of fuel to fly back to England. His unlisted mission was to retrieve prisoners of war that Russia had freed but not given transportation back to England. He also helped French girls that Germany had forced to work in the east and Jews that were freed but also abandoned. He received many medals: Bronze Star,

Distinguished Flying Cross, French Croix de Guerre, and a letter from the Russian dated 1996 with a commemorative medal awarded for participation in the "Great Patriotic War." He had declined an invitation to an award ceremony for the Russian medal because of that mistrust. He is the most heroic of everyone in the book.

- **Wayne Trimble.** (O19) Works with guided missiles.
- **Webb Ware Trimble.** (F92) Born on March 10, 1906 and died after 1943. He was a Captain at Fort Sills, Oklahoma.
- **William Albert Trimble.** (AH48) Born on August 21, 1928 in Wanblee, South Dakota and died on November 8, 1982 in Rapid City, Pennington County, South Dakota. Enlisted in the US Army during World War II on February 1, 1946 served through 1949 attaining the rank of Corporal.
- **Raymond Edwin Trimble.** (AJ39) Born on November 24, 1931 in Menard County, Texas and died on April 27, 2008 in London, Kimble, Texas. He enlisted on March 17, 1955 as a paratrooper in the 80th Airborne, Fort Bragg, North Carolina. He was SP3, He was dropped onto a moving train and was dragged between two cars and had lifelong back problems, He was discharged on March 15, 1957.
- **Ronald Welch.** (D1930) He was in the U.S. Navy.

Korea Conflict

- **Gene Paul Carroll.** (D1279) Born on November 20, 1932. He is a veteran of the U.S. Air Force from 1951 to 1955. He was in the European theater and Korean Conflict.
- **Byron Douglas Trimble.** (D1139) Born on May 27, 1931 and died December 29, 2018 in Beavercreek, Ohio. He served in the United States Air Force, stationed at Yokota Air Force Base in Japan.
- **Eugene Louis Trimble.** (AJ57) Born on March 13, 1940 in Menard County, Texas and died on July 29, 2007 in San Antonio, Bexar County, Texas. He served as MM3 (Machinists Mate Petty Officer Third Class) in US Navy from 1957 to 1961.
- **Thomas Lee Tremble.** (AO84) Born on September 2, 1946 in Statesboro, Bulloch County, Georgia and died on February 24, 2018 in Walterboro, Colleton County, South Carolina. He retired from the United States Air Force Reserves.
- **Gary Lee Trimble.** (D1286) Born on September 13, 1932. A veteran of the Korean Conflict, he was in the U.S. Air Force from 1951 to

Trimble Families of America

1955.

- **William Cattell Trimble, Jr.** (F127) Born on February 7, 1935, graduated from Princeton, A.B., in 1958, the University of Maryland Law School in 1964, ensign and subsequently lieutenant (j.g.), USNR, from 1958 to 1961.
- **William Houston Yeary, Jr.** (D1274) Born on December 25, 1932. He is a veteran of the Korean Conflict, enlisting in the U.S. Air Force in 1951, serving until 1955.

Vietnam War

- **Phillip Hager Caudill.** (D1676) Born on January 20, 1944 served in the US Army as a Specialist 5th Class. He was stationed as a driver. He enlisted on June 25, 1965 and was discharged on June 15, 1967.
- **James E. Foels.** (K99) Born on July 22, 1960, at Boston, Massachusetts. He is a graduate of the U.S. Coast Guard Academy, class of 1959, and is now operations officer with the Coast Guard at Saint Petersburg, Florida.
- **George Edward Montgomery, Jr.** (A314) Born on November 6, 1947. He graduated from West Virginia University in 1968 and served in Vietnam as an observer and received an appointment as first lieutenant. For outstanding achievements, he was awarded three Bronze Star Medals, the Distinguished Flying Cross and the Army Commendations Medal.
- **Alex Allen McCarty.** (D1668) Born on January 6, 1936. was in the Air Force from 1954 to 1960. He was stationed at Wright Patterson Air Force Base, Greenland, and Saudi Arabia.
- **John Eldon Neel.** (AJ74) Born on May 13, 1948 in Tarrant, Texas and died on October 21, 1998 in Virginia. He is buried in Arlington National Cemetery He was an Air Traffic Controller in the United States Navy in Vietnam.
- **Martha Ann Patton.** (AJ70) Born on May 3, 1951 in San Antonio, Texas. She was in the Supply Corps as a Lieutenant Junior Grade in the United States Navy on November 20, 1981.
- **Richard Carl Staley.** (G347) Born on March 6, 1943. He served 5 years in the Navy and served in Vietnam. He retired from the Central Intelligence Agency.
- **Glenn Earl Trimble.** (AJ68) Born on November 1, 1950 in Tyler, Smith County, Texas. He served in the United States Marine Corps

Trimble Families of America

from February 1970 to November 1971 with 2nd Combined Action Group in Vietnam Nam in August 1970 to April 1971. He was wounded by land mine in March 1971. His stateside service with 1st Division Headquarters Battalion at Camp Pendleton. He attained the rank of Corporal. He received these awards: Vietnam Service medal; Combat Action medal, Purple Heart; Navy Commendation Medal. He has military disability.

- **William Bradley Trimble, Jr**. (S51) Born on October 19, 1940. He was a lieutenant in the United States Navy.
- **Ray Trimble.** (AG2) Recently (the printing date of the first edition date 1975) retired from the U.S. Navy as a full commander.
- **Bradley Alan Trimble.** (D2167) Born on October 17, 1964 in Tacoma, Washington. Enlisted in the Reserve National Guard of Virginia in July 1983 to July 1986 He was on Active Duty in Fort Lewis Washington from 1986 to 1989 as a Corporal.
- **Darrell Conard Trimble.** (D1671) Born on March 9, 1947 served as Sergeant E5 in the US Army stationed in Germany. He enlisted on September 20, 1966 and discharged September 1, 1968.
- **David Carroll Trimble.** (D1672) Born on August 23, 1949 served as Specialist 4th Class Medical Specialist in the US Army serving at Fort Rucker, Alabama. He enlisted on May 12, 1969 and was discharged on May 11, 1971.
- **Joseph Finch Trimble.** (S52) Born on December 3, 1942. Joseph has a B.A. in political science and was a captain in the U.S. Army, with the 101st Airborne, Green Beret. Has three Silver Stars, and three Bronze USA.
- **Larry Allen Trimble.** (D1673) was stationed in the Air Force stationed Guam while in the army.
- **Theodore Ridgeway Trimble.** (F129) Born on May 12, 1945. Graduated from Randolph-Macon College, A.B. in 1968, U.S. Army in 1968, commissioned second lieutenant, infantry in June 1969 and assigned with U.S. forces in Korea in 1973.

- **Jeffery Carlton Bingham.** (D1688) After graduating from Anderson University, Jeffery enlisted in the Marines in October 1989 as a Second Lieutenant to learn to fly. He attended flight school in Pensacola, Florida. He was assigned to fly CH-46 helicopter. He was stationed in North Carolina and Okinawa, Japan. He was discharged in June 2000. After leaving the marines Jeffery started flying for NetJets.

- **Reason Seth Trimble.** (AJ56) Born on January 23, 1938 in Kimble, Texas and died on September 22, 1983 in San Antonio, Bexar, Texas. He served in the Army in the Military Police as a SP4 in Korea. He is buried in Fort Sam Houston national cemetery in San Antonio, Texas.

Iraq and Afghanistan

- **Jacob Carlton Bingham.** (D2127) Born on May 4, 1993. Enlisted in the Marines.
- **James Robert Green.** (AJ165) Born on May 25, 1993 in San Antonio, Bexar County, Texas. Married Jessica Lerma. He enlisted in 2012 in the United States Air Force. He is a Staff Sergeant serving in Guam.
- **Jacob Daniel Hedtke.** (AJ241) Born on June 12, 2001 in Syracuse, Onondaga County, New York. He enlisted in the United States Army in 2020. He is now Private First Class, stationed at Fort Campbell, Kentucky.
- **Smith Harper** (AJ138) Born on October 3, 1976 in Portsmouth, Norfolk County, Virginia. He served in the United States Air Force from July 1994 to September 9, 1999 and was discharged as a Staff Sergeant. He was stationed in Pensacola, Florida and Ramstein Air Force Base in Germany. In 2002 to 2006 he served in the Pennsylvania Air National Guard at the 171st refueling wing in Pittsburgh.
- **Samantha Ayla-May Mullins.** (AJ235) Born on August 26, 1996 in Saginaw County, Michigan. Married Michael Reinert. She enlisted in the United States Navy for four years from 2014 to 2018. Served in Norfolk and Oceania, Virginia. She was an E-4 when she was discharged.
- **Tyler D'Artagnan Mullins.** (AJ234) He is currently Senior Airman (E4) in the United States Air Force. Enlisted in 2014, basic training at Lackland Air Force Base in San Antonio, Texas from February 2014 to April 2014. Then on to technical training at Keesler Air Force Base, Mississippi. He was at Cannon Air Force Base, New Mexico from August 2014 to May 2021. Currently in South Korea.
- **Jason Charles Shevokas.** (AJ129) Born on October 30, 1977 on

Trimble Families of America

Andrews Air Force Base, Prince George's County, Maryland. Married Stacie Oliver on November 26, 2005 in Ohio. He is serving as a Major in the United States Marine Corps.

- **Lori Ann Shevokas.** (AJ128) Born on July 11, 1976 in Arlington County, Virginia. She enlisted in the United States Army National Guard in April, 2002 and transferred to active-duty United States Army in January, 2003. She served in South Korea in 2005-2006. She received four Army Achievement medals and a Good Conduct Medal. She received an Honorable Discharge at Fort Derrick, Maryland, in January, 2007 as an E-4.
- **Jaymes Eric "Jaymie" Trimble.** (AJ158) Born on January 11, 1989 in San Angelo, Tom Green County, Texas. He was commissioned Second Lieutenant in the United States Air Force in May, 2013, when he got his pilot's wings. In 2021, he is serving as a Captain in the United States Air Force at Fort MacDill Air Force Base, Tampa, Florida.
- **Michael Kevin Trimble.** (AJ105) Born on August 24, 1961 in Long Beach, California and died on April 3, 2010 in Riverside, Sacramento County, California. He served in the United States Marine Corp in the Persian Gulf as Staff Sergeant about 1978-1992.
- **Nickolas Adam Trimble.** (D2127) Born on January 5, 1985 Nick was a Marine, he enlisted January 26, 2003 and was discharged January 21, 2007. He was deployed to Iraq for seven months.
- **Travis Seth Trimble.** (AJ146) Born on January 26, 1982 in Austin, Travis County, Texas. He enlisted on June 11, 2001 in the United States Marine Corp he attained the rank of Lance Corporal (E-3) as a Vehicular Diesel Mechanic. He was discharged on June 11, 2005.
- **Robert Wayne Trimble.** (AJ102) Born on July 9, 1966 in Houston, Texas. Married twice. He was in the United States Army from 1988 to 2008 plus 4 years in the Texas Army National Guard. He served during the Bosnian War from June of 1992 through December of 1992. His stateside duty station were Fort Hood, Texas, Fort Huachuca, Arizona, Fort Belvoir, Virginia, and Fort Bliss, Texas. Retired as Sergeant First Class from the United States Army in September of 2008 with 20 years and 3 months of service.

Historical Background

Historical Background

The Trimble family in America is of Scotts-Irish descent. When we use the term Scotts-Irish, we are not speaking of a people of mixed Scotch and Irish blood, rather we are alluding to the Scotch who were transplanted into Northern Ireland by King James I as a buffer against the Celtic Irish.

English soldiers were sent into Northern Ireland to drive out the Celtic earls who had been rebelling against English rule. After which, King James I implanted the region mainly with Lowland Scots and some English, as he felt the Lowland Scots were the people with the courage to withstand attacks from (as King James I described) the "heathen Irish" and he felt the English were too gentle a people. They were given rich lands. He barred from this implantation the Highland Scots, the Celts, and the border tribes who were of the Lowland Scots but known as the "Robber Knights" due to their pillaging across the English border. The Turnbulls fall into this latter category because they were from Roxburghshire, a border county, and their castle was named Bedrule.

The Turnbulls and Armstrongs were two great clans of the border counties. According to the great historian Charles Wareing Bardsley, the names Trimble and Trumbull are derived from the Scottish border clan of Turnbull. The Turnbulls who migrated to England changed their name to Trumbull and the Turnbulls who migrated to Northern Ireland changed their name to Trimble. This is established by the fact that both families used the Turnbull coat of arms as their identification.

Turnbull

Now let us go back to how the name Turnbull originated. In the beginning surnames were generally given people for a deed well done, or an occupation, or the locality in which they lived, etc. The name Turnbull originated from a deed of valor by a young man who was in the company of King Robert Bruce. This is authenticated in several places but the source I (John Farley Trimble) will quote is in the Library of Congress in Washington, D.C., namely Bellenden's (sixteenth century) translation of Boece's *Scotorum History*. I quote:

It is said, King Bruce, eftir his coronatioun, went to ane hunting in this wod, haven bot ane quiet cumpanie with him, and eschapit narowlie of his lef; for one of the bullis, eftir that he wes sair woundit be the untaris, ruschit feirslie on the King, howebeit he had no wapinnis in his hand to debait himself fra the dint thairof. Incontinent, ane man of gret spreit, quhilk wes standing neir by, lap

31

Trimble Families of America

afore the king; and nocht allanerlie (only) kest the bull be manifest force to the erd, bot held him, guhill the remanent huntaris slew him with thair wappinis. This man that rescoursit the king wes callit "Turnbull", and wes rewardit with riche landis be the king.

The following episode is depicted in the Trimble also Turnbull and Trumbull coat of arms found in the book Americans of Gentle Birth, a copy of which is in the Library of Congress.

During a hunting trip King Robert Bruce had dismounted and was resting when attacked by a wild bull. A young companion threw himself between King Bruce and killed the bull. Thus, became knighted by the King as Sir Turnbull and given rich lands for this deed of valor.

Presbyterianism

Due to the influence of Calvin and Knox the Lowland Scots were primarily Presbyterian. This religious factor created tension between the Scots and English and was the direct cause of several wars between the two nations.

In the earlier centuries Scotland and Ireland were both inhabited by the Celts. Then as the Scandinavians began plundering and settling the coast of Europe, scores of families began settling on the coastal regions of Scotland driving the Celts back into the highlands. These became known as the Highland Scots. The Lowland Scots as an ethnic group were largely Scandinavian. The first settlement of this type on record was Loarn More, who with his brothers Angus and Fergus and a company of followers effected a coastal settlement in the year A.D. 503.

As they spread farther inland to the borders of England they were largely ruled by separate clans. Most renowned of the early Scotch Turnbulls seems to have been William Turnbull. He went into the ministry in the early fifteenth century and was made lord keeper of the Privy Seal of Scotland in 1442, made bishop of Glasgow in 1447, and founded the University of Glasgow in 1450.

In the eleventh century Malcolm I was the first man to partly organize the Scots into a nation. He was followed in the latter part of the thirteenth and early part of the fourteenth century by King Robert Bruce, the greatest king Scotland ever knew. He organized Scotland into a nation equal to England in power. Then his descendant, Mary Queen of Scots, was for a short time a ruler of the British Empire. Her descendant, King James I, who was also a Scot, ruled the British Empire during this implantation of Northern Ireland.

Ireland Records

Records in early Ireland are very scant and many were destroyed by fire.

Trimble Families of America

Therefore, it is impossible to connect family genealogy by means of early Irish records. I (John Farley Trimble) have corresponded with several historical societies in Ireland but to no avail. However, the letters of early immigrants to America reveal that many Trimbles called each other 'cousin'. They were in all probability descended from John, a tenant of Sir Archibald Atcheson, as James, one of the five brothers, brought to America a certificate from a later Sir Archibald Atcheson recommending him as a surveyor.

Early Trimble Settlers in America

Of the Trimbles who settled in America prior to the Revolutionary War, records show Joseph Trimble settling in Pennsylvania about 1730. He worked for and later was a partner of a quaker minister who owned a mill. He is the progenitor of a famous line of Trimbles. Joseph was the grandfather of Robert Trimble, a justice of the Supreme Court, and Major General Isaac Ridgeway Trimble, the famous Confederate general in the Civil War.

Also, around 1730 William and James Trimble migrated to Pennsylvania and married the Palmer sisters. They became Quakers and had full rights to citizenship. Pennsylvania was still under the Penns. The compiler did not work on this line as it is complete in the Palmer & Trimble Genealogy. The Palmer & Trimble genealogy is complete in the 2021 edition.

Five brothers, James, John, Moses, David, and Alexander, in the early 1730s migrated to Pennsylvania but did not become Quakers. When the governor of Virginia opened the Shenandoah Valley for settlement to the Scotts-Irish allowing them religious toleration, this created a mass migration to the valley including the four oldest of the Five Trimble Brothers. The youngest brother Alexander, still a small boy, stayed in Philadelphia with his cousin Gilbert Tennent, a minister of the Second Presbyterian Church of Philadelphia. The Tennents were instrumental in establishing Presbyterianism in America. Their father, William Tennent, was founder of the "log colleges" which were later twelve important colleges, greatest of which is Princeton University.

There were four more Trimbles who migrated to the United States in the 1730s. The compiler believes they were also brothers but has no definite data to confirm this belief. They were John, whom we will name North Mountain John. He settled in the North Mountain area of Virginia. He had children by 1740 when he proved his importation at Orange, Virginia. James and his wife Grace settled first in the North Mountain area of Virginia but later moved to South Carolina. Walter, his wife was Rosanna. They, too, settled first in the North Mountain area of Virginia later moving to South Carolina. William, who settled in Carlisle, Pennsylvania.

Trimble Families of America

Historical Background

This genealogy deals in length with the descendants of the above Trimble families. If there were other pre-Revolution immigrants, the compiler has found no records.

In my research of the early Trimble families, it is interesting to note the emphasis placed on marriage partners for the young folk. One such incident tells of Jane Allen Trimble, widow of James Trimble, a son of John of the five brothers. They had settled in Hillsboro, Ohio, yet Jane traveled by horseback to Staunton, Virginia, with her daughter in search of a suitable husband for the girl. The widow felt that on the frontier of Ohio there was not a suitable eligible bachelor for her daughters. This was a journey of about two weeks. One of her daughters married a young attorney in Staunton by the name of McCue.

Migration Westward

At the close of the Revolutionary War, Kentucky war opened for settlement to the white man as most of the hostile Native Americans had been driven out. The Revolutionary War veterans were given lands in Kentucky provided they settled the land. There was in 1783 a mass migration from the Valley of Virginia to Kentucky because of richer lands.

A party of 300 people on horseback formed at Staunton, Virginia. They were led by Captain James Trimble, son of John of the five brothers. (James, in my estimation, is the greatest of all the early Trimbles in America.) They could not travel the nearer route through the mountains (now West Virginia) because of the hostile Native Americans. Instead, they traveled south through Tennessee and the Cumberland Gap and north into Kentucky. They settled near what is now Lexington, Kentucky.

As the West was further opened, several of the Scotts-Irish in Kentucky migrated more westward. The Trimbles kept pushing to the West and settling lands with some ending up on the West Coast in Washington, Oregon, and California. I will not go into detail of their movement westward as the reader can see in the genealogy section where his forbearers and relatives settled. Yet tracing the Trimble family westward is the same story as the settling of the West. I will briefly give an illustration of my grandfather's family that will give an example of this movement of the mid-nineteenth century. (Families were parted never to see one another again.) Also, of the importance of good rich land for farming in the eighteenth and nineteenth centuries and of those who possessed such land many became prosperous.

My grandfather (John Farley Trimble), David Franklin Trimble, was sheriff of Montgomery County, Kentucky (Mount Sterling, Kentucky), in the 1850s and was quite a large landowner. He was bushwhacked (ambushed) in 1865, and killed by an unknown assassin, leaving a large family. My father, the youngest, was two years old. He was succeeded as sheriff by his brother Harvey. My grandmother remarried and taking two boys, my father included, moved to Nicholas County, West Virginia. Here she bought a large tract of land. The other seven children went westward in a covered wagon, the eldest being a girl aged eighteen who was married. The oldest boy, John, then sixteen, left the wagon in Indiana near Crawfordsville because he said it was the richest soil he had ever seen. He became a large farmer and landowner. I visited him in Indiana in 1933. The remaining children moved on as three settled in Missouri, one in Nebraska, one in Kansas, and one moved even farther and settled in the state of Washington. More on these and their descendants will be in the genealogy section. My grandmother never saw her children again. My father only knew John, whom he met after their mother's death.

The movement westward meant separation of families such as would be unfamiliar in our day of rapid transportation and communication.

Religion's Influence in Settling America

The two basic factors in the eighteenth-century migration to America were religious freedom and the opportunity for economic growth.

As the later Stuarts came to the throne of England, they ruled that no one in North Ireland could hold public office unless he belonged to the Church of England and put a high tariff on linen exports from this area, linen being the principal industry. This caused many to become dissatisfied with conditions in Ireland and thus created the stage for mass migration to America.

When the French persecuted the Huguenots, this became reason for their migration from that area into the Carolinas.

In the early seventeenth century when the Puritans were denied religious freedom in England and Holland and conditions became intolerable, they, too, began the journey to America.

Under William Penn, the Quakers settled Pennsylvania to form a state religion as they thought best.

The Catholics came to Maryland under Lord Baltimore for freedom to express their religious beliefs.

Only the English, who settled in Virginia and the southern states, came for economic reason alone. They continued to practice the religion of their mother country, the Church of England.

A vast majority of the Scotts-Irish came to Pennsylvania as the William Penn family offered settlers religious toleration. Many Scotts-Irish came to New England and some to the Carolinas, also several families settled in Bermuda.

Trimble Families of America

However, in this country, until the time of Thomas Jefferson, George Washington, and James Madison, and the Revolutionary War, the Presbyterians did not find religious freedom. They found a vast difference between religious toleration and religious freedom.

Under the Quakers in Pennsylvania, they were really counted as second-class citizens and had to bear the burden of fighting the Native Americans and pushing ever westward. The primary cause of their trouble was that the lands were owned by the Penn family and settlers had to buy or rent from them. This the Scotts-Irish were opposed to doing. Through the Declaration of Independence, the Continental Congress declared void the Penn Charter which in turn brought about great rebellion from the Quakers, a majority of whom then became Tories and did not fight for independence from England.

Through the passage of this legislation came a great controversy in the Continental Congress between the Scotts-Irish and the Quakers. In May 1776 Congress voted to establish state governments replacing colonial governments. The act immediately cancelled the Penn Family Charter.

The famous historian, Joseph Galloway, who was a member of the Continental Congress and intimate friend of Benjamin Franklin, said, "the underlying cause of the American revolution was the activity and influence of the Presbyterian interests." Galloway himself did not vote for independence and returned to England where he served in the House of Commons. Galloway said, "It was the Presbyterians who supplied to Colonial resistance a lining without which it would have collapsed. The revolt got its formidable character from the organized activities of the Presbyterians."

English historian Lecky said, "Scotts-Irish went with hearts burning with indignation and in the War of Independence, they were almost to a man on the side of the insurgents." This historian in his History of England in the eighteenth century repeatedly refers to the hundreds of years of the Scotts-Irish fighting against the yoke of English domination.

We have quoted from two English historians who were opposed to the revolution instead of our own historians to make a more unbiased statement.

Washington said that the turning point of the war was the victories at Trenton and Princeton, and he gave credit for the victories to the support given him by the Presbyterians in his army. After these two victories, Franklin and Jefferson were in France trying to enlist the aid of France to our cause. As they showed the results of Trenton and Princeton, France decided that we had a chance of victory and moved in with aid to our cause, after which England began to lose the war.

Trimble Families of America

Our historians of the Revolutionary War period seem to play down the role of the French in our winning the struggle. The fact is that had not the French entered to aid our cause, the Colonists would have had no chance of winning this war. In fact, after the French intervention, the French troops far outnumbered the colonial troops, and supplied the aid of their tremendous sea power and supplies.

It was the Presbyterians that suffered through Valley Forge with Washington. There were so many Tories in the area that Washington knew his chief support lay within the Presbyterians. In fact, when the Continental Congress fled Philadelphia and English General Howe captured the city, his welcome was almost like that offered a conquering hero by the inhabitants as the Loyalist sentiment was very strong there.

As America grew, the three major Protestant denominations were Presbyterian, Lutheran, and Episcopalian (Anglican). These remained prominent until the early nineteenth century at which time the Methodists and Baptists started their spiritual revivals. These methods of reform were not acceptable to the existing major denominations due to the lack of liturgical order of service.

This type of religious expression by the Methodists was started by George Wakefield and John and Charles Wesley. They had been ordained in the Church of England, yet their procedures were not compatible with the mother church. These three men were students together at Oxford University in England where they formed a small club among students., John Wesley wrote a paper called The Methods concerning the reforms needed in the church. Hence the name Methodist was created and became a separate church with pro-Calvinistic beliefs.

George Wakefield made eight trips to America and died after preaching in a service in the New England area. The Wesley brothers also made several trips to America.

The Methodists along with the Baptists made great inroads into the religious culture of the time. Especially was this true on the frontiers with their camp-meeting-evangelistic approaches. The Methodists had tremendous influence on the frontiers with their circuit-rider preachers, who rode horseback from farm to farm holding meetings in the homes.

The untold influence of these circuit-rider preachers can well be brought to light with the following example: Jane Allen Trimble was the widowed mother of two sons, one who later became a governor of Ohio and one a United States Senator and whose families on both sides had been for two centuries ardent

37

Presbyterians. There was no Presbyterian church near enough to the Trimble farm in Ohio for them to attend. A circuit rider called regularly at this home to hold religious services. From these services the family became such ardent converts to Methodism that one son became a minister of the church and he and his brothers were instrumental in founding the Ohio Wesleyan University. Jane's youngest daughter was so strong in the Methodist belief of total abstinence of alcoholic drink that she became "Mother Thompson," the famous leader of the temperance movement of 1874.

However, regardless of all the frontier proselyting by the evangelistic churches, Presbyterianism remains one of the leading denominations in America today. The rigid requirement of this church that its clergy be formally educated caused some defection to the evangelistic-type church. Here the ministry did not require education or deem it a necessity for those who felt "called" into the church clergy.

This author (John Farley Trimble) sincerely believes that man finds happiness mainly through his belief in a Supreme Being greater than himself, namely God, whose compassion will remise his transgressions and bring purpose to our lives.

Education

Great emphasis has been placed by the Scotts-Irish on the role of education in the life of the individual. This has been exemplified by the early establishment of the University of Glasgow and the University of Edinburgh. In America this was carried out through the "log colleges" from Princeton in New Jersey to Transylvania, the first college in Kentucky. The early settlers on the frontiers, before the establishment of schools, sought ways to ensure tutors from the East to educate their children as did James Trimble, who settled in Lexington, Kentucky.

It has been interesting to note, in my research, the emphasis placed upon religion and education by Trimbles from early Ireland to present-day America.

We see in the 1740s the establishment of the schools formed by the Presbyterians which were the roots its religious aftermath.

Princeton University was the fourth college in America with Harvard being first. William and Mary came second and Yale third.

The forerunner of Princeton was the first "log college" founded by William Tennent in 1728. Probably no other school produced so many eminent men according to the number of its students. His four sons became ministers. Other "log colleges" were founded by the following men: Samuel Blair, John Rowland, James McCrea, William Robinson, John Blair, Samuel Finley, John Roan,

Daniel Lawrence, and William Dean. Some of these colleges were the forerunners of our colleges today. In fact, Aaron Burr, father of the vice-president, was a graduate of these "log colleges," and later president of Princeton University. The second trustees of Princeton University were all graduates of these "log colleges" but one.

These pupils of William Tennent established other "log colleges." Samuel Finley established one at Nottingham, Maryland, who was famous in its time. Among its pupils were Governor Martin of North Carolina, Dr. Tennent of Abindon, Pennsylvania, and the famous Reverend Waddell, a blind preacher of Virginia.

Princeton University has had the distinction of being the father of an illustrious breed of institutions of learning along the track of the Scotts-Irish immigration to the South and West. Among them was Hampden-Sydney in Virginia, 1776. It served the Presbyterians in southwestern Virginia and North Carolina with its first president being a Princeton tutor, the Reverend Sam S. Smith. Established in 1749 was what is now Washington and Lee in Lexington, Virginia. Its first president was William Graham. This school was later called Washington Academy because of a large donation to it by George Washington. Then later the name became Washington and Lee in honor of Robert E. Lee. George Moffitt, stepson of immigrant John Trimble who was murdered by the Native Americans in 1764, was one of the first trustees of this school.

Joseph Alexander opened the first college in Upper Carolina which was called Liberty Hall, later Queens College, and still later the University of North Carolina.

The first school of classical learning in the Mississippi Valley was a "log college." In 1785 Samuel Doak from Princeton established Martin Academy, later called Washington College, in Washington County, Tennessee.

Robert Trimble's uncle, a Mr. McMillion, was the first president of Washington and Jefferson College in Pennsylvania. Transylvania College near Lexington, Kentucky, was the first college west of the Allegheny Mountains.

There were many other colleges established by the Presbyterians and they are too numerous to mention in this brief sketch. As the reader can see in education alone, the contribution of the Presbyterian church has been tremendous.

Scotts-Irish

By Stanley Trimble

John in his historical background, he arranged it by topic. I have chosen to arrange mine is chronological.

Prior to the Roman invasion of British Isles in 43 AD, those that lived in Caledonia (Scotland) were the same as those that lived in the south of the British Isle. They were the same culture, the same language, the same military prowess. They were both Celts. What changed to make the Scotts different from the Britts.

Scotland was never ruled by a foreign power. Even when the Kingdom of Scotland merged with the Kingdom of England and Ireland, it was James VI King of Scotland that became James I King of England and Ireland. There was more to the difference than just Caledonia not being part of the Roman Empire.

The British Isle has been inhabited for thousands of years They traded with the Phoenicians. There was trade between the British Isle and the mainland of Europe. The island was known as a source of tin and copper used to make bronze which was traded for wine from France and other items

The recorded history of the British Isle started some 2,000 years ago with Roman documents. Roman General Gaius Julius Caesar was nearing the end of his northern campaign. He had defeated the Gaels or Celts of France and Spain. He thought that Celts from the British Isle had assisted the mainland Celts in the battles with the Roman Legions. So, he wanted to investigate what there was to the land (Dover) that was visible from Calais, France. In 55 and 54 BC, Caesar launched two separate invasions of the British Isles, though neither resulted in a full Roman occupation of the island. With his complete conquest of the tribes of northern France and Spain, he had a secure base to attack England.

The first invasion was in late 55 BC. Caesar had spent a few weeks planning the invasion. Caesar did not have enough ships, so he leased ships from France. They all sailed at the different time expecting to arrive at the same time. The unexpected tides and rough seas caused the ships to not arrive together. The first landing site was Dover, but the chalk cliffs prevented a safe landing with narrow beaches at the foot of the cliffs. He had questioned traders about the British island before the invasion. Continental land the traders had informed their trading partners in Britain, so the Celts of Britain were expecting them. The Celts launched an arrow attack from the tops of the cliffs. When the ships attempted to land, they were too close causing some to collide. The Celts of

Britain attacked the ships that did land. After repelling the Celts and repairing enough ships, they loaded the ships and sailed back to France.

The next year in 54 BC, Caesar was better prepared. He had more soldiers He had enough ships ready earlier in the year. They all sailed from the same port together. Landed where there was no British force waiting and spaced out the landing sites and got enough troops on shore before the fighting started. After several battles, Caesar had received tribute from several tribes and formed alliance with several tribes, so he boarded his ships and returned to the mainland.

Rome left the British Isle alone for a century until 43 AD. Roman Emperor Claudius directed four legions to invade the British Island. Gnaeus Julius Agricola was appointed governor of Britain in 78 AD. He started a series of major engagements. He defeated the northern Celtic tribes in the Battle at Mons Graupius in 84 AD. But holding the north against the Celts in the rock mountains of northwestern Caledonia was challenging so they retreated to the middle of Britain.

In 122 AD the Romans built Hadrian's Wall on a line was between the River Tyne and the Solway Firth (a firth is like a bay) to keep the northern Celts out. This is near the border between Scotland and England now. There were forts evenly spaced along the wall to house Roman troops. The forts were also used to conduct trade between Caledonia and Roman Britain. Rome defended their position at Hadrian's wall until they withdrew from Britain.

The Celts living south of Hadrian's Wall became Romanized. Rome supplied security. They forgot how to fight. They used Roman coins instead of barter. Wealthy Romans built estates in southeastern Britain. A Roman bath was built in Bath, England. Rome built roads between the largest settlements in Britain. The British Celts became civilized.

Early in the fifth century the Roman Empire started declining. After an attack from the Visigoths, Rome permanently withdrew its army from the British Island to reinforce troops in Rome under attack by Visigoths. With Roman soldiers gone, the Celts of Britain were unprepared for their own defense.

The Anglos and Saxons; Germanic tribes invaded eastern England. This is the origin of the name England and the English language. Over the next several centuries the Germanic tribes pushed the Brittani of southern England into western reaches of England into Wales and Cornwall. This was by use of force and assimilation as the Angles migrated the locals were assimilated into the Germanic culture. In the middle of the fifth century, the Germanic raiders

Trimble Families of America

settled. In a few generations the future English language won out over the Brittani's Gaelic.

The Northern part of Scotland was inhabited by Picts. We do not know what they called themselves, but the Roman writers named them Picts. Most descriptions of them in Roman documents say they were large, tattooed, with red hair and beards. In the rocky northern part of Scotland, the Picts would just meld into forests and hid from their enemies.

Because Ireland was never captured by Rome, their culture had not been influenced by Rome. Daniel Binchy, an early Irish Historian, wrote that the Irish were "*tribal, rural, hierarchical and familiar.*" I will explain each in a slightly different order.

Tribal, this is the origin for the clan system of Scotland. Everyone belonged to a local tribe and there were over a hundred tribes at any time in Ireland and a tribe could be made of a few thousand individuals. Ireland was also divided into five providences. They are Ulster, Connacht, Meath, Leinster, and Munster. They did not have a fixed border. The clan was the source Scotland's power. Every member of the clan owed allegiance to the clan leader. Even after the kingdom of Scotland was set up. A Scott owed more allegiance to his clan leader than the king.

Rural, there were no cities in Ireland until the late Middle Ages. So, it was all rural. People lived in widely scattered small settlements. These were usually in ring forts a bank surrounded by a ditch or was on an island in a lake. These were round and made of wood and wicker and connected with the land with a pathway that could be removed for defense. These were the center of the clan.

Familiar, as in family was the basic root of society not the individual. There was legal definition of family. Who was a member of your family was not just for social gathering but was legally defined. It gave you rights. The right to how land was inherited or sold. The *Derbfine* "certain kin" were those individuals descended from a common great grandfather. That is four generations. They had to confer with each other on how to distribute funds from the sale of land or to sell land you had to have consensus from the *Derbfine.*

Irish legal system was entirely based on civil law as opposed to criminal law. Murder or assault became matters of a civil lawsuit. The *Derbfine* would be parties to the lawsuit because the losing party's kin may have to pay the debt. On the winning side you may receive payment for the loss of an uncle. There were set percentages for closeness of a kin, a child received a full share, a half share for a paternal uncle or a maternal aunt, a third share for a cousin.

Hierarchical, the value of individual families varied just as other early societies. An individual's value was determined by two factors: wealth and status. In a murder the amount you must pay was determined by the victim's status. The value was in units of *Cumal*. A *Cumal* was one slave girl or three cows. Insulting someone's honor was also a reason for a lawsuit.

How many *Cumals* an individual was worth was decided by their status. At the top tier were kings, bishops, and poets. The second tier were nobles and learned classes. The third tier were farmers. And at the bottom were slaves who had no honor value. Most of learned the class were the lawyers and you can surmise from the above description that they were quite valued. Lawyers and Poets were the only ones free to travel throughout Ireland.

The method of forcing someone to obey the law was Distraint. If someone owed money you could take some of his cattle through Distraint. This would explain some of the cattle raiding. This will come into context when mentioning *reiving* later.

The northeastern Ulster in Ireland can be seen from eastern shore of the western isles of Scotland. The social structure of Ireland is important in our understanding of Scottish society because after Rome withdrew from Britain, the Scotti tribe of Ulster Ireland slowly started migrating across the Irish Sea to Caledonia. These Scotti created the Kingdom of Scotti in the Ulster of Ireland and the western isles of Scotland. The culture of the Scotti from Ireland became the culture of medieval Scotland.

Jim Webb wrote in his book Born Fighting: "Although some historians mention Viking invasions from Norway and possible early forays from Spain, Scotland was principally inhabited by four different early peoples, and it would take nearly a thousand years for these peoples to finally cohere into a true Scottish nation. The strongest of them, and the oldest inhabitants of the land, were the Picts, a Celtic people who believed in matrilineal descent and whose origins will probably never be fully known. These were the wild, combative tribes who stood so strongly against the Romans, entering their journals as large-limbed, tattooed, red-haired madmen, which probably was not much of an exaggeration.*

The most learned and diplomatic of the four peoples were the Scots, or Scotti, a powerful Irish tribe that had gained ascendance in Northern Ireland. By the fifth century the Scotti were joining a larger Irish migration across the narrow sea into western Scotland. Nora Chadwick mentions this 'invasion from Ireland which, beginning in a small way, grew in importance till it imposed the Irish language on the whole of the Highlands in what is known today as Gaelic, and gradually extended its political sway over the Picts.' In the southwest of Scotland were the Britons, a Celtic tribe that once had dominated England itself and now straddled the border roughly created by Hadrian's Wall. And in the southeast, in an area below modern-day Edinburgh called the Lothians, were the Angles, a largely Germanic tribe that had swept northward from the border areas during the seventh century.

It was the Scotti who were principally responsible for the union of the different kingdoms, beginning in the ninth century when they defeated the Picts and united their peoples into a single kingdom called Alba. Over the next two centuries the Scots continued their consolidation through warfare and intermarriage, and by 1034 "the Picts, the Scots, the Lothian Angles and the Strathclyde [southwestern Scotland] Britons owed common allegiance to an Alban king.". [1]

What was it like in Scotland during the tenth through the twelfth century? There were two small kingdoms at the beginning of this period: Dal Riata and Fortriu. Dal Riata or kingdom of Scotti was a Gaelic kingdom of western Scotland and the northern part of Ulster Ireland. The inhabitants of Dal Riata were the Scotti from Ulster Ireland who had been there for centuries before the Romans. Southwestern Scotland can be seen from Ireland, so the Scotti sailed across the narrow Irish Sea.

The other kingdom was Fortriu or Pictland. The inhabitants of Fortriu were the Picts. They had no written language. Most of what is known came from the writings of their enemies. Their name Picts or their latin name Picti refers to the tattoos that they were covered with. They were further described as large framed with red hair. These two kingdoms fought each other. Dál Riata and Pictland merged to form the Kingdom of Alba or Scotland.

Scotland had developed as tribal or clan. A Scotsman owed loyalty to the clan not necessarily to the king. Every clan occupied a distinct territory and most had a defendable fortress. Every member of the clan would defend the clan like their life depended on it. As Scotland developed into a nation, affiliation to the clan had greater loyalty than being a citizen of Scotland. This affiliation to the clan stayed with the Scott-Irish when they moved to America. The Scott-Irish in America considered being in the military not only a duty but also an honor.

---

[1] Born Fighting: How the Scots Irish Shaped America, Jim Webb, Broadway Books, a Division of Random House, Inc., 2004, Chapter 2.

Trimble Families of America

Scott-Irish

The clan chief was the military leader as well as the community leader. The chief decided where members lived as well as which field, they farmed. This could change every year. The best field or place to live usually went to the best soldier not the best farmer.

The fields surrounding the hill fort ran up and down the slope. The fields were not plowed going around the hill, but up and down the hill. So, rain would drain through the plowed field draining away loose soil. The fields had no fixed boundary. So, the exact location of a field or the size could change. The fields closest to the fort were smaller and were planted with vegetables. The further away fields were larger and used to raise oats or barley. The fields furthest away were used as pasture for the long hair cattle or sheep.

In the morning, the livestock would be drove to the fields away from the fort then in the evening they would be driven back to their homes where the sheep and cattle would be sheltered in their homes. Having no fence or hedge row to separate the gardens from the fields meant that sheep or cattle could eat your crop if the herder did keep them away.

To keep cattle out of the fields and to find better grazing. During the warmer months, the cattle and sheep would be driven up the hills and mountains to new pasture at higher elevations. The weather was nice enough to camp at night. This allowed the fields at lower levels to grow back. They would keep them on summer pasture until fall weather. They would drive the cattle and goats back to the area around the fort.

Farming in Scotland was very primitive. The plow being used was crude. It was a large a slab from a straight log with a large branch sticking out at a 45-degree angle. The branch was capped with a wrap of iron, and it was used to stir the soil. The plow was pulled by a team of six oxen and took six to eight men to manage. The resulting plowed field only had the rows where the seeds were planted was disturbed and the balk (the area between the rows) was undisturbed.

They depended on another animal the Galloway Nag. It was more a pony than a horse. It was sturdy, sure footed in the rough territory even in icy conditions. It could keep a fast pace for hours. Even though the rider's feet would dangle below the animal's belly. This breed is now extinct. The need for the sturdy nag was no longer needed so breeders stopped breeding them.

Another thing that hurt farming was frequent wars between Britain and Scotland. These wars took place in warmer weather while crops were growing. An army would travel from one country to the other. Troops would eat some of the crops. Troops, horses and wagons would also trample on the crops as they

45

traveled to and from the battle.

Housing in Scotland was crude. The walls of dwellings were short made of posts drove in the ground spaced around the wall. Wove between the posts were branches or reeds. These were covered with clay. It had a thatched roof supported on small tree trunks for beams. Because of the shortage of trees, when they moved, they would take the beams and move them to the next home. A hole was left in the middle to let the smoke out. The entrance door was just a hide hung to keep the wind out. A fire was open in the center of the room. There was an iron pot hanging near the fire in which almost anything could be cooking in the stew. This primitive form of construction was necessary because homes would be burned by troops traveled through the area.

At night, the family would sleep on the floor on one side of the room. On the other side of the room was where the livestock slept. The sheep and cattle were safer inside at night. In the early centuries of Scotland, the threat was predatory animal. In the 1400's and 1500's the threat was reivers (raiders) from across border. The smell and flies were considered normal. English travelers thought that the Scotts were dirty, and their food was nasty.

Scotts owed the clan leader two weeks military service. They would carry one weaving (eight feet) of wool, a small wooden shield, a short sword, a thin iron plate, and a leather pouch which held oats. At night they would wrap themselves in the wool to sleep. In the morning they would take a handful of oats, mix it with water to form a paste which they would roast on the iron plate over a fire. The interruptions in the care of crops for military service and the infrequent destruction of crops slowly changed the Scottish culture away from raising crops.

The Scotts were Celtic Druids. They had no written language, so little is known about them. They were oracles and advisers for kings. As the Roman Catholic Church expanded after the removal of Rome, brave priests evangelized the Celtic Kings. Saint Patrick converted Ireland to Christian. Saint Columba came to Scotland and settled on Iona Island. Where he built a church and monastery. By the early middle age, the British Isles were Christian. But Scottish farmers were not deeply religious. They were much more superstitious. They believed in fairies, elves, ghost, banshees, and luck. All were beliefs from Druids.

The early medieval Scottish farmer was considered prosperous from the sales of wool and leather. The mountainous landscape of Scotland is perfect for sheep, goats and the long-haired cattle. During the tenth through the thirteenth century wool and leather were shipped down the Tweed and Teviot Rivers to

Trimble Families of America

Scott-Irish

Roxburgh Castle where buyers from across Europe owned and shipped on small boats down the River Tweed to Berwick upon Tweed. There it was shipped to France and Belgium and fabricated into clothing. This income allowed the farmers to buy things that made life easier. For decades Scotland collected more than a fourth of their budget from tax collected from wool and leather trading.

Scotland was a remote corner on western and northern Europe. New farming methods, better care of individual health and rights of individuals took a while to meander to Scotland. It also took a long time for the fidelity to the king to reach Scotland.

The history of England and for that matter Scotland and Ireland transformed in 1066. It is one date you should remember from history class. This is when William of Normandy concurred England. William the illegitimate son of the Duke of Normandy ascended to Duke as a child. He was controlled by different members of the Norman aristocracy. In 1047 he suppressed a rebellion and gained control of the duchy. In 1050 he married Matilda of Flounders; this gave him more power. In the early 1060's William was a contender for the English throne held by Edward the Confessor. He was his first cousin once removed. Edward died on January 5, 1066. Harold Godwinson his brother-in-law was appointed King. William built a fleet and invaded England in September 1066. He defeated and killed Harold in the Battle of Hastings. William was crowned King of England on Christmas 1060.

The entire kingdom of England spoke English, but their new king spoke French and he ruled in the French language. William appointed all new Earls and Dukes which spoke French. All proclamations were in French. All the aristocracy now were speaking French. The courts of Scotland were suddenly out of date speaking English. This changed the future of England for not only were the new rulers speaking French, but they were practicing French customs.

Scotland did not change to French. A key moment, indeed, in this transformation of Scottish society took place in the middle of the twelfth century during the reign of King David I (1124–1153). Although descended from the Celtic dynasty that had ruled in central Scotland since the late eighth century, David had grown up at the court of Henry I of England (1100 – 1135), where he received what contemporaries regarded as the benefits of a civilized education. Exposed in his youth to European cultural norms - modes and morals of warfare, methods of government, and manners in general - David returned home to Scotland as king and began the business of acquainting his

47

subjects with these new customs. In this he was helped by several friends he had made during his time in England, who went with him on his return, and whom he rewarded with lands and honors north of the Border. To take just one obvious example, David brought with him a certain Robert de Brus, a man who originally hailed from Brix in Normandy, and who was the forefather of the Robert Bruce who claimed the Scottish throne in 1290.[2]

John was crowned King of England in 1199. There was baronial revolt at the end of John's reign led to the signing of *Magna Carta*, a document sometimes considered an early step in the evolution of the constitution of the United Kingdom.

John's son Henry was crowned King of England in 1216 as Henry III. Henry III had a rough start. Louis VIII of France was proclaimed King of England by some of the rebellious barons, but the Pope excommunicated Louis Henry settled with Earls in the Barons War. He agreed to the *Magna Carta* and returned their land to settle. Henry III later underwent a second coronation at Westminster Abbey on 17 May 1220.

In Scotland, Alexander II was born 1198 and died 1249. He spent time in England with John of England. He was knighted by John in 1214. He was crowned King of Scotland in 1214 on the Stone of Scones. Alexander joined the English baron in revolt against John of England. He led an army into England. In retaliation English forces sacked Berwick-on-the-Tweed. Alexander's forces reached Dover where Alexander paid homage to the invader Prince Louis of France. But John died and the Pope excommunicated Louis, so he and his army withdrew, and Alexander II and his army returned to Scotland. Henry III became King. Henry III and Alexander II reconciled with each other signing the Treaty of York, which established the border between England and Scotland, which is mostly where it is today. Alexander II married Henry III sister, Joan of England. Alexander II having been in court of England reformed the Scottish court became more French.

Henry III was not an aggressive King. He was easy to forgive aggressions and debts. In 1236 he married Eleanor of Provence. She persuaded Henry III to grant positions to members of her family mostly in 1263, one of the more radical barons, Simon de Montfort, seized power, resulting in the Second

---

[2] Morris, Marc. *A Great and Terrible King*: Edward I and the Forging of Britain (p. 242). Pegasus Books. Kindle Edition.

Trimble Families of America

Barons' War. In the Battle of Lewes, Henry III was defeated and taken prisoner. Henry III's oldest son Edgar I met Montfort in battle the next year and defeated him freeing his father.

Edward I of England was born 1239 and died 1307. He was crowned King of England in 1272. Edward I was on his way to Middle East on a Crusade when he received word that his father had died in 1272. He made a slow return to England. Making his way through his holdings in eastern France arriving in England and being crowned at Westminster Abbey in 1274. He was nicknamed "Longshanks" for he was 6 ft. 2 in. He married Eleanor of Castile in 1254. They had many children but only six lived to adulthood, five girls and one son, Edward II.

Edward I restored royal authority of the crown after the rule of Henry III. Edward I established Parliament as a permanent institution Edward I reformed the royal administration and common law. He suppressed two rebellions in Wales, one in 1276-1277 the second 1282-1283 with a full invasion. Wales became subject to English rule. Castles were built in the countryside and towns and were settled with Englishmen.

The first five brothers in this book are James, John, Moses, David, and Alexander. I can understand how the first four got their name. They all came from the Bible. But where did Alexander come from? It did not make sense that he was named for Alexander the Great. Then I started reading up on Scott-Irish history. I found Alexander III of Scotland; I understand why Alexander was included with the Bible names.

In Scotland, Alexander III was born at Roxburgh in 1241, the only son of Alexander II by his second wife Marie de Coucy. Alexander's father died on July 8, 1249 and he became king at the age of seven, crowned at Scone on July 13, 1249 at eight. All the kings of Scotland were crowned while sitting on the Stone of Scone. Alexander III married Margaret of England in 1251. He was ten and she was eleven. She was the second daughter of Henry III of England. He seized the opportunity to demand his son-in-law pay homage, but Alexander did not comply. He replied favorably without swearing fealty to Henry III. They had three children: Margaret, Alexander, and David. Margaret born 1261 and died 1283 married King Eric II of Norway. Alexander was born 1264 and died 1284. David was born 1272 and died 1281.

Alexander III and Edward I were in-laws. They visited often and were friendly. In 1275 Alexander's wife Margaret of England died leaving Alexander a widow. In 1281, the youngest of Alexander's children David died. Two years later in 1283, Alexander's oldest Margaret died during childbirth of Alexander's granddaughter, Margaret, Maid of Norway. The next year in 1284, Alexander's last living child, Alexander died. This left Alexander with only the Maid of Norway as heir to the throne. It was not easy for a female to assume the throne and she was being raised in Norway.

This is where Edward I of England came up with an idea for the ruler of England and Ireland to also become ruler of Scotland. This would enable Edward I to achieve one of his desires to rule all the British Isles. Edward I of England proposed to Alexander that Edward's son Edward II to wed Margaret the Maid of Norway which would make Edward II ruler of all. Alexander had not spent his decade as a widower alone but now he needed an heir, so he wed Yolande de Dreux on November 1, 1285.

Yolinda's birthday was March 19th. On March 18, 1286 Alexander spent the evening at Edinburgh Castle celebrating his second marriage and overseeing a meeting with royal advisors. He was cautioned against making the journey to Fife because of weather conditions but crossed the Forth from Dalmeny to Inverkeithing anyway. On arriving in Inverkeithing, he insisted on not stopping for the night, despite the pleas of the nobles accompanying him and the master of the Inverkeithing saltpans. Alexander again dismissed concerns about travelling in a storm and set off with three local guides. The king became separated from his guides near Kinghorn and was found dead with a broken neck near the shore the following morning. It is assumed that his horse lost its footing in the dark.[3] Yolande was said to be pregnant, but she lost the child. So, the Maid of Norway was now the queen of Scotland. She was still in Norway. Her father and Scottish leaders finalized plans for her marriage to Edward's Son Edward II. Finally, in September 1290, she boarded a ship for Britain. On the trip she became sick, so they stopped in Orkney where she died.

Now Scotland had a succession problem There was no living descendents of King William the Lion. This began a two-year process to choose the new King. The Guardians of Scotland feared a civil war, so they asked Edward I of England help them choose the next king. Edward I saw a second chance to rule Scotland. He agreed.

"Edward I promised the previous year that Scotland would remain 'free in itself, and without subjection.' Guardians of Scotland meet in May 1291 in Berwick upon the Tweed, which is in Scotland. Edward I however went to

---

[3] https://en.wikipedia.org/wiki/Alexander_III_of_Scotland, Succession

Trimble Families of America

Norham across the Tweed River in England and a few miles upstream and demanded that the Guardians meet him there. The Guardian complied.

It was, in fact, far worse than they had feared. Once inside the castle at Norham, the Scottish delegates were treated to an introductory speech by Roger Brabazon, an English royal justice. After a lot of flowery rhetoric about the beauty of peace and so on, they were told that Edward I had come north to do right to anybody who had a claim to the Scottish throne. This implied that the king envisaged other candidates besides Bruce and Balliol, which would, in turn, alter the nature of his intervention. With more than two claimants, a straightforward arbitration of the kind anticipated by the Scots would become impossible. Edward I was therefore proposing an alternative arrangement, namely that he should act, not as arbiter, but as judge. This was a role that he naturally felt entitled to assume, given the fact that he was Scotland's rightful overlord.

The Scots were stupefied. It was surprising enough to discover that there were apparently other claimants besides Bruce and Balliol, but the corollary was outrageous. The king of England their overlord? They protested, with pardonable exaggeration, that they had never heard of such a novelty.

Edward I had expected such a reaction – he had, after all, received a similar response from his late brother-in-law in 1278. Accordingly, he had taken the trouble on this occasion to prepare his ground thoroughly in advance. Two months earlier, a search of the archives had been ordered – and not just the royal ones. In abbeys and priories all over England, monks had been made to ferret through their chronicles and muniments to build the king's case. Given that the trawl was so extensive, the haul was disappointing (inevitably, of course, given that the superiority that Edward I took for granted was built on exceedingly week, and for the most part fantastical, foundations). Nevertheless, in the days before the Scots had crossed to Norham, a crowd of clerics had told the king what he wanted to hear: his was indeed the superior right. This enabled Edward I to present the Scots with a two-fold challenge. If they would not concede his overlordship as a matter of course, he said, they should disprove the facts set out in his new dossier. Or, as an alternative to both these options, they could decide the matter by force.

It was Robert Wishart, bishop of Glasgow and Guardian, who recovered himself sufficiently to respond on behalf of the startled Scots. In the first place, he said, it did not matter what they, as temporary custodians, might or might not concede: only a king of Scotland could answer such a momentous demand. Secondly, the bishop took Edward I to task over his reasoning: they were not obliged to prove him wrong; rather he should prove himself right. Thirdly, and more caustically, Wishart reminded the English king that he was supposed to be a crusader and observed that a threat to unleash war against a defenseless people did him no credit. At this last Edward I was predictably enraged and prompted to issue a new threat. He would indeed lead a crusading army, he declared – against the Scots!" [4]

Thirteen candidates submitted claims for the crown, but really there were just two Robert De Bruce and John Balliol. Edward I postponed his decision for two years. It was reported that when he was near the end of his analysis his vicar ask him who was thinking about selecting. He replied that Robert De Bruce was the best candidate. The vicar asked which candidate would be the best one that would be best at controlling Scotland or the one that Edward I could control the best. Edward I select John Balliol. John swore fealty to Edward I.

John Baliol was crowned in 1292. He was summoned by Edward I to appear before the English court. As king of Scotland, he appeared. John signed a mutual Protection treaty with France. In 1296, England declared war on France. So, John Balliol invaded England sacking Cumberland. Edward I in turn invaded Scotland destroying Berwick. English troops spent four days massacring more than 16,000 citizens. Somewhere, it was written that Edward I only ordered them to stop after seeing a solder murder a pregnant woman in labor and her child. There was a fortified building in Berwick built by Henry III and given to foreign wool trader with the stipulation that they defend it and never surrender. They did just that as it was burned. John finally stood up to Edward I pushed by Scottish lords. Edward I arrested John and imprisoned him in the Tower of London. For years as Scotts were facing English troops, they were spurred on by remembering the slaughter at Berwick.

Edward I took his army of 30,000 and captured every castle in Scotland and replaced every Scottish sheriff with an Englishman. He had every landowner swear fealty to Edward I. Then he withdrew. The new sheriffs were killed or run out of Scotland, most before Edward I had left Scotland.

Andrew Moray, a Scottish esquire from northern Scotland lead a revolt

---

[4] Morris, Marc. A Great and Terrible King: Edward I and the Forging of Britain (p. 250). Pegasus Books. Kindle Edition.

against Edward's troops and joined forces with another esquire from the middle of Scotland, William Wallace. They began making raids against the English and retreating to hide in forests. In September 1296, they had assembled an army at Stirling, north of the river. The bridge over the Stirling River was a small wooden structure that could only handle two mounted soldiers at a time. Edward I was involved with the French and sent John de Warenne, 6th Earl of Surrey, and Hugh de Cressingham to take care of the revolt. On September 11, 1296, two nuns meet with William Wallace to negotiate terms. Wallace reputedly responded with, "We are not here to make peace but to do battle to defend ourselves and liberate our kingdom. Let them come on and we shall prove this to their very beards."

Moray and Wallace were camped on Abbey Craig north of the Stirling River. They dominated the soft flat ground north of the river. The English force of English, Welsh and Scots knights, bowmen and foot soldiers camped south of the river. Sir Richard Lundie, a Scots knight who joined the English after the Capitulation of Irvine, offered to outflank the enemy by leading a cavalry force over a ford two miles upstream, where sixty horsemen could cross at the same time. Hugh de Cressingham, King Edward's treasurer in Scotland, persuaded the Earl to reject that advice and ordered a direct attack across the bridge.

The English soldiers began crossing the bridge two at a time. The Scotts waited till about 2,000 soldiers had crossed. Then they attacked. The knights that had crossed were too close together spread out on soft soil. The Scotts were armed long pikes which would keep the knights from reaching the foot soldiers. They came down from the high ground in rapid advance and fended off a charge by the English heavy cavalry and then counterattacked the English infantry. They gained control of the east side of the bridge and cut off the chance of English reinforcements to cross. Caught on the low ground in the loop of the river, which was marshy gives horses no footing, with no chance of relief or of retreat, most of the outnumbered English on the east side were killed. A few hundred may have escaped by swimming across the river. Most that tried to swim drown weighted down with armor.

Marmaduke Thweng managed to fight his way back across the bridge with some of his men. After the escape of Sir Marmaduke Thweng, Surrey ordered the bridge to be destroyed, retreated towards Berwick, leaving the garrison at Stirling Castle isolated and abandoning the Lowlands to the rebels. James Stewart, the High Steward of Scotland, and Malcolm, Earl of Lennox, whose forces had been part of Surrey's army, observed the carnage to the north of the bridge, withdrew. Then, the English supply train was attacked at *The Pows*, a wooded marshy area, by James Stewart and the other Scots lords, killing many of the fleeing soldiers.[5] During the battle Andrew Moray was wounded and died by November. This is the battle of Stirling Bridge. Not the same as Braveheart.

In 1298, Edward I invaded Scotland with over 25,000 foot-soldiers, most were from Wales. They failed to bring William Wallace to battle. The Scotts shadowed the English intending to avoid battle until Edward I ran short of money and withdrew. While returning to Edinburgh, they received intelligence that the Scotts were camped nearby at Falkirk. Edward I quickly moved engage the Scottish army.

Wallace arranged his spearmen in four schiltrons—circular, defensive hedgehog formations, surrounded by wooden stakes connected with ropes, to keep the infantry in formation. The English, however, employed Welsh longbowmen, who swung tactical superiority in their favor. The English proceeded to attack with cavalry and put the Scottish archers to flight. The Scottish cavalry withdrew as well, due to its inferiority to the English heavy horses. Edward's men began to attack the schiltrons, which were still able to inflict heavy casualties on the English cavalry. It remains unclear whether the infantry shooting bolts, arrows, and stones at the spearmen proved the deciding factor, although it is highly likely that it was the arrows of Edward's bowmen. Gaps in the schiltrons soon appeared, and the English exploited these to crush the remaining resistance. The Scots lost many men, including John de Graham. Wallace escaped, though his military reputation suffered badly. [6] In 1296, the Stone of Scones was taken by Edward I as spoils of war and removed to Westminster Abbey, where it was fitted into a wooden chair—known as King Edward's Chair—on which most subsequent English and then British sovereigns have been crowned.

September 1298, Wallace resigned as Guardian of Scotland in favor of Robert the Bruce, Earl of Carrick and future king. Wallace evaded capture by the English until August 5, 1305 when John de Menteith, a Scottish knight loyal to Edward I, turned Wallace over to English soldiers at Robroyston near Glasgow. William was taken to London. He was tried for treason. He replied that he could not be guilty of treason for he was never his subject. He was found guilty He taken to the Tower of London, dragged naked through London,

---

[5] https://en.wikipedia.org/wiki/Battle_of_Stirling_Bridge

[6] https://en.wikipedia.org/wiki/William_Wallace, Battle of Falkirk

hanged, drawn, and quartered.

In 1307, Edward I again started north to subdue the Scotts. On the way Edward I developed dysentery. He was forced ride in a wagon. They camped just south of the border. Edward's servants went to lift him up so he could eat, and he died in their arms. Edward I was returned to England and buried in Westminster. Edward II was crowned King of England.

Edward II ignored Scotland while he consolidated power. Edward had a close and controversial relationship with Piers Gaveston, who had joined his household in 1300. The precise nature of their relationship is uncertain; they may have been friends, lovers or sworn brothers. Edward's relationship with Gaveston inspired Christopher Marlowe's 1592 play *Edward II*, along with other plays, films, novels and media. Gaveston's power as Edward II's favorite provoked discontent both among the barons and the French royal family, and Edward was forced to exile him. On Gaveston's return, the barons pressured the king into agreeing to wide-ranging reforms, called the Ordinances of 1311. The newly empowered barons banished Gaveston, to which Edward responded by revoking the reforms and recalling his favorite. Led by Edward's cousin Thomas, 2nd Earl of Lancaster, a group of the barons seized and executed Gaveston in 1312, beginning several years of armed confrontation.

In February 1306, Robert Bruce wounded his chief rival for the Scottish throne John III Comyn, Lord of Badenoch. He rushed from the church where they had met and encountered his attendants outside. He told them what had happened and said, "I must be off, for I doubt I have slain the Red Comyn." "Doubt?" Roger de Kirkpatrick of Closeburn answered. "I mak sikker" ("I'll make sure,"). Kirkpatrick then rushed into the church and killed Comyn. Five weeks later Robert De Bruce had himself crowned King of Scotland on the stone of Scones on March 25, 1306. He still had to get the barons of Scotland to agree.

Edward I's forces defeated Robert in the battle of Methven, forcing him to flee into hiding before re-emerging in 1307 to defeat an English army at Loudoun Hill and wage a phenomenally successful guerrilla war against the English. Bruce defeated his other Scots enemies, destroying their strongholds and devastating their lands, and in 1309 held his first parliament. A series of military victories between 1310 and 1314 won him control of much of Scotland.[7]

---

[7] https://en.wikipedia.org/wiki/Robert_the_Bruce

Trimble Families of America

By 1314, Robert the Bruce had recaptured most of the castles in Scotland once held by Edward II, pushing raiding parties into northern England as far as Carlisle. In response, Edward II planned a major military campaign with the support of Lancaster and the barons, mustering a large army between 15,000 and 20,000 strong. Meanwhile, Robert had besieged Stirling Castle, a key fortification in Scotland; its English commander had stated that unless Edward II arrived by June 24, 1314, he would surrender. News of this reached the king in late May, and he decided to speed up his march north from Berwick-upon-Tweed to relieve the castle. Robert, with between 5,500 and 6,500 troops, predominantly spearmen, prepared to prevent Edward II's forces from reaching Stirling.

King Edward II invaded Scotland after Bruce demanded that all supporters still loyal to ousted Scottish king John Balliol acknowledge Bruce as their king or lose their lands. Stirling Castle, a Scottish royal fortress occupied by the English, was under siege by the Scottish army. King Edward II assembled a formidable force of soldiers from England, Ireland and Wales to relieve it – the largest army ever to invade Scotland.[8] Robert De Bruce had captured many castles consolidating his control of Scotland. Every Castle he captured he tore down, so it could not be used against Scotland later.

King Edward II was certain that the English army would be successful. The Barons that went with the English army brought wagon of treasures, paintings, and furniture. They were accompanied by their families. They were ready to take possession of the castles that were promised by Edward II. Edward had taken too much time prepare his army. He planned to be in Stirling before the date his Stirling commander had given for their surrender, June 24, 1314. This attempt failed when he found his path blocked by a smaller army commanded by Bruce. When he found Robert's army, the train was stretched out behind the English army and the train was not in a location to camp or near water. The English troops had marched most of the night to reach Sterling.

The Scottish army was divided into three divisions of schiltrons commanded by Bruce, his brother Edward Bruce, and his nephew, the Earl of Moray. Conventional knowledge at that time was that infantry could not defeat mounted knights, but Robert did. After Robert Bruce killed Sir Henry de Bohun on the first day of the battle, the English were forced to withdraw for the night. Sir Alexander Seton, a Scottish noble serving in Edward's army, defected to the

---

[8] https://en.wikipedia.org/wiki/Battle_of_Bannockburn

Trimble Families of America

Scottish side informing them of the English camp's position and low morale.

Edward II's army was tired from long marches when they started fighting on the first day. At the end of the day, they could not rest for there was no camp site at their location. Edward moved his army about seven miles to a better camp site with water nearby. This took most of the night and his army was even more exhausted.

Robert Bruce decided to launch a full-scale attack on the English forces and to use his schiltrons again as offensive units, a strategy his predecessor, William Wallace, had not used. The English army was defeated in a pitched battle which resulted in the deaths of several prominent commanders, including the Earl of Gloucester and Sir Robert Clifford, and the capture of many others.

Robert defeated a much larger English army under Edward II of England, confirming the re-establishment of an independent Scottish kingdom. The battle marked a significant turning point, with Robert's armies now free to launch devastating raids throughout northern England, while also extending his war against the English to Ireland by sending an army to invade there and by appealing to the Irish to rise against Edward II's rule.

Despite Bannockburn and the capture of the final English stronghold at Berwick in 1318, Edward II refused to renounce his claim to the overlordship of Scotland. In 1320, the Scottish nobility submitted the Declaration of Arbroath to Pope John XXII, declaring Robert as their rightful monarch and asserting Scotland's status as an independent kingdom. In 1324, the Pope recognized Robert I as king of an independent Scotland, and in 1326, the Franco-Scottish alliance was renewed in the Treaty of Corbeil. In 1327, the English deposed Edward II in favor of his son, Edward III, and peace was concluded between Scotland and England with the Treaty of Edinburgh–Northampton in 1328, by which Edward III renounced all claims to sovereignty over Scotland. Scotland had defeated the English Army.

When the War of Independence began the Borders had been moving forward towards civilization; when they ended the people of the Marches had returned to something like the cave ages. Centuries of progress had been destroyed in a generation, and the natives, to quote Scott, had been carried back in every art except those which concerned the destruction of each other. Partly this arose from the type of war prescribed, says Fordun, by Bruce for the defeat of the invading English.[9]

It was an uneasy time and both governments, with an eye to defense, encouraged settlers into the border area with the offer of either land or low rents as an incentive.

The area became overpopulated because of this generous offer, and this problem was further compounded by a system of partible inheritance known as 'gavelkind'. Property was divided equally among all heirs This had a profound effect on Border economy. The land owned by a father was shared among his sons and divided and subdivided with each subsequent generation, and the holdings eventually became too small to provide a living for their owners – the difficult situation was further exacerbated by poor soil quality and outdated farming methods, not to mention the waves of war that were being waged constantly. Although some of the gentry owned large extents of land and thousands of sheep, many of the peasants struggled to survive and were forced to the edge of starvation, and consequently raiding became a part-time occupation necessary to supplement the family income.[10]

All the movement of troops during the Scottish Wars of Independence had a negative effect on farming. Planting a field of vegetables then having an army trample the crops. cattle, goats, and sheep could be slaughtered to feed troops.

There were three counties in England and three counties in Scotland next to the border these were called marches, which is an old English word for boundary. West, middle, and east marches in both England and Scotland. There was no marked border and no fence. A Scott could cross the border into England steal cattle and drive them back across the border to Scotland or reverse. The English officials had no authority in Scotland to arrest the thief or reverse.

England and Scotland had a treaty just to handle this. There was a Warden appointed in each March in Scotland and England. These Wardens were to bring justice in dealing with across the border offences. This did not work very smoothly. The best protection from those across the border was those in your own clan.

---

[9] Fraser, George MacDonald. The Steel Bonnets: The Story of the Anglo-Scottish Border Reivers (p. 28). Skyhorse Publishing.

[10] Nixon, Philip. *Exploring Border Reivers History* (Kindle Locations 125-131). JMD Media Ltd. Kindle Edition.

Trimble Families of America

These raiders were called reivers. Early in this article in the part I mentioned about Irish law, distraint if someone owed you money you could take some of their cattle as payment. Reivers claimed that what they stole on the raids was their inheritance.

Reivers would make most of their raids in the cooler months when the cattle were brought back from their summer pasture. They would travel in a group usually around fifteen but there have been raids of over 200. All the reivers on a raid would be from the same clan or related clans. Raids would start after dark leaving their home area. Reivers would travel overnight then camp and sleep during the day then at dark they would steal the cattle, rape, steal valuable, and burn homes, then drive the cattle back to their homes. Sometimes the reivers would be detected then alarm was raised. A group would give chase trying to catch the reivers before they crossed the border.

Both sides would be riding their Galloway Nags. This was a short sturdy horse, not much larger than a pony. They are very sure footed and seem to know the trails in the dark. They were quiet when traveling and able to travel far distances. Reivers would at times depend on their ride to find the trail going and returning.

The Border robber was a specialist, and needed special equipment, the most important part of which was his horse, a Galloway Nag. "They reckon it a great disgrace for anyone to make a journey on foot," wrote Leslie, and Froissart had noted two centuries earlier how the Scots at war "are all a-horseback. the common people on little hackneys and geldings." The Border horses, called hobblers or hobbys, were small and active, and trained to cross the most difficult and boggy country, "and to get over where our footmen could scarce dare to follow." Such precious animals naturally attracted legislation, particularly in England, where horses were in short supply. In the late 1500s their export to Scotland was strictly banned; Hunsdon "condemde sundry" for this treason in 1587 and complained that English gentlemen were involved in the illicit trade. It was a well-broken law in both directions, for Scotland had banned horse export twenty years earlier, with no great success.[11]

The Border rider, as he sat his hobbler, was a most workmanlike figure, far more streamlined than the ordinary cavalryman of his time. His appearance was "base and beggarly" by military standards, and this applied to the lords as well

---

[11] *Fraser, George MacDonald.* The Steel Bonnets: The Story of the Anglo-Scottish Border Reivers (p. 85). *Skyhorse Publishing.*

59

as to the lowly. "All clad a like in jacks covered with white leather, dooblettes of the same or of fustian, and most commonly all white hosen," Patten noted after Pinkie (1547). "Not one with either chain, brooch, ring or garment of silk that I could see. This vileness of port was the cause that so many of their great men and gentlemen were killed and so few saved. The outward show. whereby a stranger might discern a villain from a gentleman, was not among them to be seen." On his head the rider wore the steel bonnet, which in the early part of the century was usually the salade hat, basically a metal bowl with or without a peak, or the burgonet, a rather more stylish helmet which, in its lightest form, was open and peaked. These headpieces, many of which would be home-made by local smiths, were gradually replaced in Elizabethan times by the morion, with its curved brim, comb, and occasional earpieces. Over his shirt the rider might wear a mail coat, but the more normal garment was the jack, a quilted coat of stout leather sewn with plates of metal or horn for added protection. It was far lighter than armor, and almost as effective against cuts and thrusts; backs and breasts of steel might be worn by the wealthier Borderers, but for horsemen whose chief aim was to travel light they were a mixed blessing. The Scots Borderers were officially recognized by the Privy Council as "light horsemen" who were not obliged to serve in heavy armor during war; the English Borderers, when employed on campaigns, were similarly used as scouts and "prickers". Leather boots and breeches completed the clothing, which was without badges except in wartime, when the riders wore kerchiefs tied round their arms as signs of recognition, as well as the crosses of St George or St Andrew, according to their nationality—or their allegiance. [12]

The raids were more than cattle rustling. There were many murders, kidnaps, rapes, and black mail. It was called black mail in all the references that I have read, it was really ransom.

The economy of the Marches has dramatically changed. During the reign of Alexander III and Edward I. In Scotland, the herding of cattle and sheep for the sale of wool and leather, they did well. After raiding started farming fell way slowly. No one grew anything. A steer born one side of the border could travel back and forth across the border several times before being slaughtered. The total economic value in Marches decreased every year.

---

[12] Fraser, George MacDonald. *The Steel Bonnets: The Story of the Anglo-Scottish Border Reivers* (pp. 86-87). Skyhorse Publishing. Kindle Edition.

Trimble Families of America

Scott-Irish

Another feature of clans which was brought to America was feuds. It took only the slightest infraction to start a feud. Feuds between clans made no difference whether they both were on the same side of the border or not. Feuds could last for decades. Some families were involved many feuds Armstrong, Grahams, Irvines, Kerrs, and Elliots. The two clans the Turnbulls had feuds with were the Armstrong and Kerrs. One story I read, one clan was planning an attack on another clan. They sent an envoy to ask the Turnbulls if they would help. The envoy returned with the Turnbulls reply, "we have nothing against the clan but if it is a good fight, we are in." Reiving started in the early fourteenth century and continued into the early sixteenth century. The longer it went the more violent it became.

On a September night in 1596 Jock and Geordie Burn were returning from a routine raid across the Cheviot tops. Driving cattle before them, the Scots reivers were very unlucky. Riding through the gloaming they were intercepted by Sir Robert Carey, the Warden of the English East March, who was out on patrol with 20 troopers at his back. Hopelessly outnumbered, Geordie Burn, his uncle and their two henchmen fought ferociously. One escaped, two were killed, and Geordie was overpowered and taken prisoner.

Probably at Harbottle Castle, Carey had Burn quickly tried, convicted and condemned to death. But sentence was delayed while the news of the reiver's capture could reach the ears of his patron, Sir Robert Kerr of Cessford. Perhaps there would be an advantageous negotiation, perhaps an attempted reprisal which might deliver more prisoners to Carey. In the event there was silence. No word came over the hill trails and Geordie Burn realized that he had been abandoned and was likely to hanged.

Sir Robert Carey's curiosity was stirred. It is said that the warden disguised himself and with two companions went to Burn's cell to talk with the condemned man. The swagger had gone, and in his resignation, the reiver reviewed the life he had led. Carey later wrote down what he remembered. It amounts to the only authentic testament left by a Border Reiver.

He voluntarily of himself said that he had lived long enough to do so many villainies as he had done; and told us that he had lain with about 40 men's wives, some in England, some in Scotland, and that he had killed seven Englishmen with his own hands, cruelly murdering them; that he had spent his whole time in whoring, drinking, stealing, and taking deep revenge for slight offences. He seemed to be very penitent, and much desired a minister for the comfort of his soul.[13] After hearing all Geordie offenses Sir Robert moved the hanging up to the next day.

In 1517, Martin Luther in Germany posted his *Ninety-five Theses.* This was the beginning of the Protestant reformation.

Henry VIII in 1525 wanted an annulment from Catherine his wife who had not had him a son. The Pope Clement VII refused. So, Henry VIII initiated the English Reformation, separating the Church of England from papal authority. He appointed himself Supreme Head of the Church of England and dissolved convents and monasteries, for which he was excommunicated. He annulled his marriage to Catherine and married Anne Boleyn. He was the first English King that was not Catholic. Henry VIII also made a large profit for the confiscation of churches and monasteries which included several wineries.

Edward VI became King of England when he was nine. During his reign, the Church of England became more like a protestant church. Edward fell ill in 1553. His sickness was found to be terminal. He set up a will to have his cousin Lady Jane Grey to become Queen, ignoring his two sisters Mary and Elizabeth. Edward VI died in February. Jane became queen but was deposed by Mary nine days after becoming queen in 1553.

Mary became Queen of England. She at first ruled that her subject did not have to follow her religion, but by the end of September 1553, leading Protestant churchmen—including John Bradford, John Rogers, John Hooper, Hugh Latimer, and Thomas Cranmer—were imprisoned. Mary's first Parliament, which assembled in early October, declared the marriage of her parents valid and abolished Edward's religious laws. Church doctrine was restored to the form it had taken in the 1539 Six Articles of Henry VIII, which (among other things) re-affirmed clerical celibacy. Married priests were deprived of their benefices.

Mary had always rejected the break with Rome instituted by her father and the establishment of Protestantism by her brother's regents. Philip persuaded Parliament to repeal Henry's religious laws, thus returning the English church to Roman authority. Reaching an agreement took months and Mary and Pope Julius III had to make a major concession: the confiscated monastery lands

---

[13] Moffat, Alistair. The Reivers: The Story of the Border Reivers (Kindle Locations 399-410). Birlinn.

were not returned to the church but remained in the hands of their influential new owners. By the end of 1554, the pope had approved the deal, and the Heresy Acts were revived.

Under the Heresy Acts, many Protestants were executed in the Marian persecutions. Around 800 rich Protestants, including John Foxe, fled into exile. In total, 283 were executed, most by burning. The burnings proved so unpopular that even Alfonso de Castro, one of Philip's own ecclesiastical staff, condemned them and another adviser, Simon Renard, warned him that such "cruel enforcement" could "cause a revolt". Mary persevered with the policy, which continued until her death and exacerbated anti-Catholic and anti-Spanish feeling among the English people. The victims of the persecutions became lauded as martyrs.

Mary was weak and ill from May 1558. In pain, possibly from ovarian cysts or uterine cancer, she died on November 17, 1558, aged 42, at St James's Palace.

Elizabeth I became Queen of England in 1558. Elizabeth was protestant. Elizabeth's personal religious convictions have been much debated by scholars. She was a Protestant but kept Catholic symbols (such as the crucifix) and downplayed the role of sermons in defiance of a key Protestant belief.

In terms of public policy, she favored pragmatism in dealing with religious matters. The question of her legitimacy was a key concern: although she was technically illegitimate under both Protestant and Catholic law, her retroactively declared illegitimacy under the English church was not a serious bar compared to having never been legitimate as the Catholics claimed she was. For this reason alone, it was never in serious doubt that Elizabeth would embrace Protestantism.

Elizabeth and her advisers perceived the threat of a Catholic crusade against heretical England. Elizabeth therefore sought a Protestant solution that would not offend Catholics too greatly while addressing the desires of English Protestants; she would not tolerate the more radical Puritans though, who were pushing for far-reaching reforms. As a result, the parliament of 1559 started to legislate for a church based on the Protestant settlement of Edward VI, with the monarch as its head, but with many Catholic elements, such as vestments.

The House of Commons backed the proposals strongly, but the bill of supremacy met opposition in the House of Lords, particularly from the bishops. Elizabeth was fortunate that many bishoprics were vacant at the time, including the Archbishopric of Canterbury. This enabled supporters amongst peers to outvote the bishops and conservative peers. Nevertheless, Elizabeth was forced to accept the title of Supreme Governor of the Church of England rather than the more contentious title of Supreme Head, which many thought unacceptable for a woman to bear. The new Act of Supremacy became law on 8 May 1559. All public officials were to swear an oath of loyalty to the monarch as the supreme governor or risk disqualification from office; the heresy laws were repealed, to avoid a repeat of the persecution of dissenters practiced by Mary.

In Scotland, James V (April 10, 1512 –December 14, 1542) was King of Scotland from 9 September 1513 until his death, which followed the Scottish defeat at the Battle of Solway Moss. His only surviving legitimate child, Mary, Queen of Scots, succeeded him when she was just six days old. During the reign of Henry VIII and Mary I of England, Scotland remain Catholic. Mary Queen of Scots was six when she became Queen. Mary of Guise was Regent for Mary Queen of Scots.

John Knox (c. 1514 – 24 November 1572) was a Scottish minister, theologian, and writer who was a leader of the country's Reformation. He was the founder of the Presbyterian Church of Scotland.

Born in Giffordgate, a street in Haddington, East Lothian, Knox is believed to have been educated at the University of St Andrews and worked as a notary-priest. Influenced by early church reformers such as George Wishart, he joined the movement to reform the Scottish church. He was caught up in the ecclesiastical and political events that involved the murder of Cardinal David Beaton in 1546 and the intervention of the regent Mary of Guise. He was taken prisoner by French forces the following year and exiled to England on his release in 1549.

While in exile, Knox was licensed to work in the Church of England, where he rose in the ranks to serve King Edward VI of England as a royal chaplain. He exerted a reforming influence on the text of the *Book of Common Prayer*. In England, he met and married his first wife, Margery Bowes. When Mary I ascended the throne of England and re-established Roman Catholicism, Knox was forced to resign his position and leave the country. Knox moved to Geneva and then to Frankfurt. In Geneva, he met John Calvin, from whom he gained experience and knowledge of Reformed theology and Presbyterian polity. He created a new order of service, which was eventually adopted by the reformed church in Scotland. He left Geneva to head the English refugee church in Frankfurt, but he was forced to leave over differences concerning the liturgy, thus ending his association with the Church of England.

On his return to Scotland, Knox led the Protestant Reformation in Scotland, in partnership with the Scottish Protestant nobility. The movement may be a revolution, since it led to the ousting of Mary of Guise, who governed the country in the name of her young daughter Mary, Queen of Scots. Knox helped write the new confession of faith and the ecclesiastical order for the newly created reformed church, the Kirk. He continued to serve as the religious leader of the Protestants throughout Mary's reign. In several interviews with the Queen, Knox admonished her for supporting Catholic practices. After she was imprisoned for her alleged role in the murder of her husband Lord Darnley, and King James VI was enthroned in her stead, Knox openly called for her execution. He continued to preach until his final days. [14]

Presbyterian church was organized democratically. The session (local congregation) had a committee which ran the church. They were elected from the session by the members by the session members. Sessions elected members of presbytery in a geographic area. Presbyteries were organized by geography in areas in a Synod. Synods were members of general assembly. In all this the Sessions, presbytery, synods, and general assembly elected those to represent them in the next level up. This was started in the sixteenth century. It was democratic representation.

The accession of the Protestant Elizabeth in England in 1558 stirred the hopes and fears of Scottish Protestants. Elizabeth came to secretly support the Lords of the Congregation. In January 1559, the anonymous *Beggars' Summons* threatened friars with eviction in favour of beggars. This was calculated to appeal to the passions of the populace of towns who appeared to have complaints against friars. Fearing disorder and now determined by circumstance to show less tolerance, the Regent summoned the reformed preachers to appear before her at Stirling on 10 May. Insurrection followed. The men of Angus assembled in Dundee to accompany the preachers to Stirling, and on 4 May they were joined by John Knox, who had recently arrived from France. Stirred by Knox's sermons in Perth and Dundee, the mob sacked religious houses (including the tomb of James I in Perth). In response, the Regent marched on Perth, but was forced to withdraw and negotiate when another reformed contingent arrived from the west at Cupar Muir.

Among the Regent's ambassadors were the Earl of Argyll and Lord James Stewart, Earl of Moray, both professed Protestants. When the Regent stationed French mercenaries in Perth, both abandoned her and joined the Lords of the Congregation at St Andrews, where they were also joined by John Knox. Even

---

[14] https://en.wikipedia.org/wiki/John_Knox#Knox_and_Queen_Mary,_1561 - 1564

Trimble Families of America

Edinburgh soon fell to them in July, as Mary retreated to Dunbar. The Congregation Lords made a truce with Guise and signed the Articles of Leith at Leith Links on 25 July 1559 which promised religious tolerance, then withdrew to Stirling.

In September, the earlier regent, the 2nd Earl of Arran, with the safe return of his son, accepted the leadership of the Lords of the Congregation and set up a provisional government. However, Mary of Guise was reinforced by professional French troops. Some of these troops set up themselves at Kinghorn in Fife, and after they destroyed the house of William Kirkcaldy of Grange, according to Knox, Mary declared, "Where is now John Knox's God? My God is now stronger than his, yea, even in Fife." In November, the rebels were driven back to Stirling. Fighting continued in Fife. All seemed lost for the Protestant side until an English fleet arrived in the Firth of Forth in January 1560, which caused the French to retreat to Leith.

Negotiations with England then began, from which Knox was excluded; his earlier tract *The First Blast of the Trumpet Against the Monstrous Regiment of Women*, although it had been aimed at Mary Tudor, made him unacceptable to the female English monarch. The resulting Treaty of Berwick in February was an agreement between the Earl of Arran and the English to act jointly to expel the French. As a result, the newly crowned Queen of England, Elizabeth I, sent an English land army into Scotland to join their Scottish allies in besieging the French at Leith. As the fighting continued the English ambassador in France Nicholas Throckmorton praised Guise for having the "hart of a man of warre" and the English bishop John Jewel described her as "a woman with a man's courage."

After an English assault on Leith was repulsed with heavy losses, some of the leaders of the Lords of the Congregation came to Edinburgh Castle on May 12, 1560 and had dinner with Mary and the keeper of the castle, Lord Erskine. They discussed a plan that had been made before the troubles, in which Mary would have travelled to France and met Elizabeth in England, and her brother would have been made Viceroy in Scotland. The Lords again complained about Frenchmen being appointed to Scottish government posts. Negotiations to end the siege of Leith and demolish new fortifications at Dunbar Castle continued. But the next day, the talks ended when permission was refused for the French commanders in Leith to come to the castle to discuss the proposals with Mary.

While continuing to fortify Edinburgh Castle, Mary became seriously ill, and over the course of the next eight days her mind began to wander; some days she could not even speak. On 8 June she made her will. She died of dropsy on 11

Trimble Families of America

Scott-Irish

June 1560. [15]

At the start of the sixteenth century 80 percent of Scots could not read. Scots seldom attended church or Mass. They were still not that sanitary. There were very few schools for children and few schools of higher education. There were lots of places to buy liquor. Books were a rarity to find. Parents expectation for their children was low.

After the Presbyterian Church of Scotland was established by John Knox things changed quick. Within ten years 90 percent of Scots were christians and belonged to the local Presbyterian Kirk (Church). All Presbyterian Kirks had a minister with five years of college and had a local public school. The schools were free to anyone. This meant that clan leaders son attended the same class as the farmer's children. More than 80 percent of the members of Presbyterian Kirk could read. Several colleges opened to educate the ministers for Presbyterian Kirks. Drinking liquor was discouraged. Presbyterian Kirk service could be expected to last most of the day. Scots had developed a monstrous thirst for knowledge of the Bible. Books could be found in most homes.

Mary, the only surviving legitimate child of King James V of Scotland, was six days old when her father died, and she acceded to the throne. She spent most of her childhood in France while Scotland was ruled by regents, and in 1558, she married Francis, the Dauphin of France. Mary was queen consort of France from his accession in 1559 until his death in December 1560. Widowed, Mary returned to Scotland, arriving in Leith on August 19, 1561. Four years later, she married her half-cousin, Henry Stuart, Lord Darnley, and in June 1566 they had a son, James.

In February 1567, Darnley's residence was destroyed by an explosion, and he was found murdered in the garden. James Hepburn, 4th Earl of Bothwell, was generally believed to have orchestrated Darnley's death, but he was acquitted of the charge in April 1567, and the following month he married Mary. Following an uprising against the couple, Mary was imprisoned in Loch Leven Castle. On 24 July 1567, she was forced to abdicate in favour of her one-year-old son. After an unsuccessful attempt to regain the throne, she fled southward seeking the protection of her first cousin once removed, Queen Elizabeth I of England.

Mary had once claimed Elizabeth's throne as her own and was considered the legitimate sovereign of England by many English Catholics, including

---

[15] https://en.wikipedia.org/wiki/Mary_of_Guise

67

participants in a rebellion known as the Rising of the North. Perceiving Mary as a threat, Elizabeth had her confined in various castles and manor houses in the interior of England. After eighteen and a half years in custody, Mary was found guilty of plotting to assassinate Elizabeth in 1586 and was beheaded the following year at Fotheringhay Castle. [16]

John VI King of Scotland was at thirteen months on July 24, 1567. He was raised Protestant. James was the son of Mary, Queen of Scots, and a great-great-grandson of Henry VII, King of England and Lord of Ireland, and thus a potential successor to all three thrones.

Elizabeth I was getting on in age. She was born on September 7, 1533. She was almost 65 when Elizabeth's senior adviser, William Cecil, 1st Baron Burghley, died on August 4, 1598. His political mantle passed to his son, Robert Cecil, who soon became the leader of the government. One task he addressed was to prepare the way for a smooth succession. Since Elizabeth would never name her successor, Cecil was obliged to continue in secret. He therefore entered a coded negotiation with James VI of Scotland, who had a strong but unrecognized claim. Cecil coached the impatient James to humor Elizabeth and "secure the heart of the highest, to whose sex and quality nothing is so improper as either needless expostulations or over much curiosity in her own actions". The advice worked. James's tone delighted Elizabeth, who responded: "So trust I that you will not doubt but that your last letters are so acceptably taken as my thanks cannot be lacking for the same but yield them to you in grateful sort". In historian J. E. Neale's view, Elizabeth may not have declared her wishes openly to James, but she made them known with "unmistakable if veiled phrases".

The Queen's health remained fair until the autumn of 1602, when a series of deaths among her friends plunged her into a severe depression. In February 1603, the death of Catherine Carey, Countess of Nottingham, the niece of her cousin and close friend Lady Knollys, came as a particular blow. In March, Elizabeth fell sick and remained in a "settled and unremovable melancholy" and sat motionless on a cushion for hours on end. When Robert Cecil told her that she must go to bed, she snapped: "Must is not a word to use to princes, little man." She died on 24 March 1603 at Richmond Palace, between two and three in the morning. A few hours later, Cecil and the council set their plans in

---

[16] https://en.wikipedia.org/wiki/Mary,_Queen_of_Scots

motion and proclaimed James King of England. [17]

At last England and Ireland was united with Scotland, but not under an English King instead under a Scottish King. King James VI of Scotland also became James I of England and Ireland. James hired scholars to translate the bible to English, The King James Bible. He also funded a colony in America.

James survived two conspiracies in the first year of his reign, despite the smoothness of the succession and the warmth of his welcome: The Bye Plot and Main Plot, which led to the arrest of Lord Cobham and Sir Walter Raleigh, among others. Those hoping for a change in government from James were disappointed at first when he kept Elizabeth's Privy Councilors in office, as secretly planned with Cecil, but James soon added long-time supporter Henry Howard and his nephew Thomas Howard to the Privy Council, as well as five Scottish nobles.

Reivers were suddenly under the same king on both sides of the border. Rustling cattle and crossing the border to evade chasers no longer worked, chasers just followed. After a few years of securing his hold on the crown, James acted. He marched into the main hold of the McDonalds. And hung them all.

In the Nine Years' War of 1594-1603, an alliance of northern Gaelic chieftains—led by Hugh O'Neill of Tír Eoghain, Hugh Roe O'Donnell of Tyrconnell, and Hugh Maguire of Fermanagh—resisted the imposition of English government in Ulster. Following an extremely costly series of campaigns by the English, including massacre and use of ruthless scorched earth tactics, the war ended in 1603 with the surrender of the Gaelic alliance and the Treaty of Mellifont. The terms of surrender granted to the rebels were considered generous at the time.

After the Treaty of Mellifont, the northern chieftains tried to consolidate their positions, and the English administration attempted to undermine them. In 1607, the chieftains left Ireland to seek Spanish help for a new rebellion, in the Flight of the Earls. King James issued a proclamation declaring their action to be treason, paving the way for the forfeiture of their lands and titles.

A colonization of Ulster had been proposed since the end of the Nine Years' War. The original proposals were smaller, involving planting settlers around key military posts and on church land, and would have included large land grants to native Irish lords who sided with the English during the war, such as Niall Garve O'Donnell. However, in 1608 Sir Cahir O'Doherty of Inishowen

---

[17] https://en.wikipedia.org/wiki/Elizabeth_I#Accession

launched a rebellion, capturing and burning the town of Derry. The brief rebellion was ended by Sir Richard Wingfield at the Battle of Kilmacrennan. The rebellion prompted Arthur Chichester, the Lord Deputy of Ireland, to plan a much bigger plantation and to expropriate the legal titles of all native landowners in the province. John Davies, the Attorney-General for Ireland, used the law as a tool of conquest and colonization. Before the Flight of the Earls, the English administration had sought to minimize the personal estates of the chieftains, but now they treated the chieftains as sole owners of their whole territories, so that all the land could be confiscated. Most of this land was deemed to be forfeited (or escheated) to the Crown because the chieftains were declared to be attainted. English judges had also declared that titles to land held under gavelkind, the native Irish custom of inheriting land, had no standing under English law. Davies used this to confiscate land when other means failed.

The Plantation of Ulster was presented to James VI & I as a joint "British", or English and Scottish, venture to 'pacify' and 'civilize' Ulster, with at least half the settlers to be Scottish. James had been King of Scotland before he also became King of England and needed to reward his subjects in Scotland with land in Ulster to assure them, they were not being neglected now that he had moved his court to London. In addition, long-standing contact and settlement between Ulster and the west of Scotland meant that Scottish participation was a practical necessity.[18]

At first land was given to Londoners. They settled, but it became rough as there were Irish nearby that had been forced off their land. At the first trouble most of the Londoners gave up and went back to London. Then James VI & I decided to select a tougher group. He selected several of the rowdiest clans and moved most of the clan on to a land grant in Ireland. When the Turnbull clan migrated to Ireland, they changed their name to Trimble.

The Scotts brought along their Presbyterian Kirk (Church).

By the 1630s it is suggested that the plantation was settling down with "tacit religious tolerance", and in every county Old Irish were serving as royal officials and members of the Irish Parliament. However, in the 1640s, the Ulster Plantation was thrown into turmoil by civil wars that raged in Ireland, England and Scotland. The wars saw Irish rebellion against the planters, twelve years of bloody war, and ultimately the re-conquest of the province by the English parliamentary New Model Army that confirmed English and Protestant

---

[18] https://en.wikipedia.org/wiki/Plantation_of_Ulster

dominance in the province.

After 1630, Scottish migration to Ireland waned for a decade. In the 1630s, Presbyterians in Scotland staged a rebellion against Charles I for trying to impose Anglicanism. The same was attempted in Ireland, where most Scots colonists were Presbyterian. Many of them returned to Scotland as a result. Charles I subsequently raised an army largely composed of Irish Catholics and sent them to Ulster in preparation to invade Scotland. The English and Scottish parliaments then threatened to attack this army. Amid this, Gaelic Irish landowners in Ulster, led by Felim O'Neill and Rory O'More, planned a rebellion to take over the administration in Ireland.

On 23 October 1641, the Ulster Catholics staged a rebellion. The mobilized natives turned on the British colonists, massacring about 4,000 and expelling about 8,000 more. Marianne Elliott believes that "1641 destroyed the Ulster Plantation as a mixed settlement". The initial leader of the rebellion, Felim O'Neill, had been a beneficiary of the Plantation land grants. Most of his supporters' families had been dispossessed and were likely motivated by the desire to recover their ancestral lands. Many colonists who survived rushed to the seaports and went back to Great Britain.

The massacres made a lasting impression on psyche of the Ulster Protestant population. A.T.Q. Stewart states that "The fear which it inspired survives in the Protestant subconscious as the memory of the Penal Laws or the Famine persists in the Catholic." He also believed that "Here, if anywhere, the mentality of siege was born, as the warning bonfires blazed from hilltop to hilltop, and the beating drums summoned men to the defense of castles and walled towns crowded with refugees."

In the summer of 1642, the Scottish Parliament sent some 10,000 soldiers to quell the Irish rebellion. In revenge for the massacres of Scottish colonists, the army committed many atrocities against the Catholic population. Based in Carrickfergus, the Scottish army fought against the rebels until 1650. In the northwest of Ulster, the colonists around Derry and east Donegal organized the Laggan Army in self-defense. The British forces fought an inconclusive war with the Ulster Irish led by Owen Roe O'Neill. All sides committed atrocities against civilians in this war, exacerbating the population displacement begun by the Plantation.

In addition to fighting the Ulster Irish, the British settlers fought each other in 1648–49 over the issues of the English Civil War. The Scottish Presbyterian army sided with the King and the Laggan Army sided with the English Parliament. In 1649–50, the New Model Army, along with some of the British colonists under Charles Coote, defeated both the Scottish forces and the Ulster Irish.

The English Civil War (1642–1651) was a series of civil wars and political machinations between Parliamentarians ("Roundheads") and Royalists ("Cavaliers"), mainly over the manner of England's governance and issues of religious freedom.

Unlike other civil wars in England, which were mainly fought over *who* should rule, these conflicts were also concerned with *how* the three kingdoms of England, Scotland, and Ireland were to be governed. The outcome was threefold: the trial and execution of Charles I (1649); the exile of his son, Charles II (1651); and the replacement of English monarchy with the Commonwealth of England, which from 1653 (as the Commonwealth of England, Scotland, and Ireland) unified the British Isles under the personal rule of Oliver Cromwell (1653–58) and briefly his son Richard (1658–59). The execution of Charles I was particularly notable given that an English king had never been executed before. In England, the monopoly of the Church of England on Christian worship was ended, while in Ireland the victors consolidated the established Protestant Ascendancy. Constitutionally, the wars established the precedent that an English monarch cannot govern without Parliament's consent, although the idea of Parliamentary sovereignty was only legally established as part of the Glorious Revolution in 1688 covers events leading to the deposition of James II and VII, and replacement by his daughter Mary II, and her Dutch husband, William III of Orange. William and Mary supported Protestants James II and VII retreated to France where he received an army of 6,000.

Derry Ireland was changed by Presbyterian during the plantation. They changed the name to Londonderry. The worst conflict between the Irish Catholics and the Scottish Presbyterian was at Londonderry During the Jacobite War.

James II doubted the loyalty of his English troops. He therefore asked Tyrconnell to send him reliable Irish troops. These units sailed to Chester in September and early October 1688. To replace them Tyrconnell ordered four new regiments to be raised, one for each Irish province. He ordered Alexander MacDonnell, Earl of Antrim, a Catholic nobleman of Scottish origin, to raise the Ulster regiment. Antrim, already in his seventies, hired 1,200 Scottish mercenaries (called redshanks), making sure they were all Catholics. The unit was supposed to be ready on November 20, but delays occurred.

At that time Tyrconnell's remodeling of the Irish army had advanced so far that few units still had significant numbers of Protestant soldiers. One of those was the regiment of Viscount Mountjoy, a Protestant loyal to James. This unit was in garrison at Derry. Tyrconnell considered this unit unreliable and on November 23 he ordered Mountjoy to march to Dublin. Mountjoy's regiment was to be replaced by Antrim's, but that was not ready, and Derry found itself without garrison.

When Antrim finally got his troops on the way, he met Colonel George Philips at Newtown Limavady, who sent a messenger to Derry to warn the city. On December 7, with Antrim's regiment ready to cross the Foyle River under Derry's Ferryquay Gate, thirteen apprentices seized the city keys and locked the gates. With this act Derry was in open rebellion against Tyrconnell and his master James II, who was already in exile in France at that time. Antrim was not strong enough to take the town by force and retreated to Coleraine. [19]

Having broken through the Passes, Hamilton reached Londonderry on April 18 and summoned the city to surrender. They refused. The castle was defended all summer. The city had endured 105 days of siege, from April 18 to August 1, 1689. Some 4,000 of its population of 8,000 are said to have died during this siege. They ate all the dogs, horses, and shoe leather. James' army refused to allow anyone to leave. It was very brutal. On August 1, 1688 those in Londonderry woke to find the sieging army had disappeared.

The Battle of the Boyne was on July 1, 1690 between the forces of the deposed King James II versus those of King William III who, with his wife Queen Mary II (his cousin and James's daughter), had acceded to the Crowns of England and Scotland in 1689. The battle took place across the river Boyne close to the town of Drogheda in the Kingdom of Ireland, modern-day Republic of Ireland, and resulted in a victory for William. This turned the tide in James's failed attempt to regain the British crown and ultimately aided in ensuring the continued Protestant ascendancy in Ireland. William's forces defeated James's army, which consisted mostly of raw recruits. Although the Williamite War in Ireland continued until October 1691, James fled to France after the Boyne, never to return.

The supporters of William III and Mary II were nicknamed "Billies" especially those in Ireland. It was meant as an insult but the protestants in Ireland liked the nickname, so it stayed around for a while. When these "Billies" moved to America they settled in the hills of Virginia, the name

---

[19] https://en.wikipedia.org/wiki/Siege_of_Derry

Scott-Irish

changed to "Hill Billies." This also was considered a compliment.

In 1700's, some Scotts had lived in Ireland for a century. The land they had moved to in Ireland was in poor condition, swamps, homes and barns in bad shape and were not defendable. They were given 31-year leases and the prices was low to entice Scotts to lease. When the leases were up. The farms were much improved so the landlord who did not live in Ireland, wanted to increase the lease payment. So, starting in early 1700, the Scotts Irish became interested in moving to America.

The Edict of Nantes signed in April 1598 by King Henry IV of France, granted the Calvinist Protestants of France (also known as Huguenots) substantial rights in the nation, which was still considered essentially Catholic at the time. In the edict, Henry aimed primarily to promote civil unity. The edict separated civil from religious unity, treated some Protestants for the first time as more than mere schismatics and heretics, and opened a path for secularism and tolerance.

The later Edict of Fontainebleau, which revoked the Edict of Nantes in October 1685, was promulgated by Louis XIV, the grandson of Henry IV. It drove an exodus of Protestants and increased the hostility of Protestant nations bordering France.[20]

There was an advertisement circulating in France, for Huguenots to come to England where they would be provided transportation to America. The advertisement was fake, but Huguenots made their way to England and Wales. In 1700 several hundred French Huguenots migrated from England to the colony of Virginia, where the King William III of England had promised them land grants in Lower Norfolk County.

---

[20] https://en.wikipedia.org/wiki/Edict_of_Nantes

Trimble Families of America

Scott-Irish

Prior to the American Revolution there really was no religious freedom. Each colony had its own religion. Virginia opened the plateau in the middle of the state to the Presbyterian from Scotland and the Huguenots from Germany to act as a buffer against the Native Americans. They would be allowed to practice their own religion.

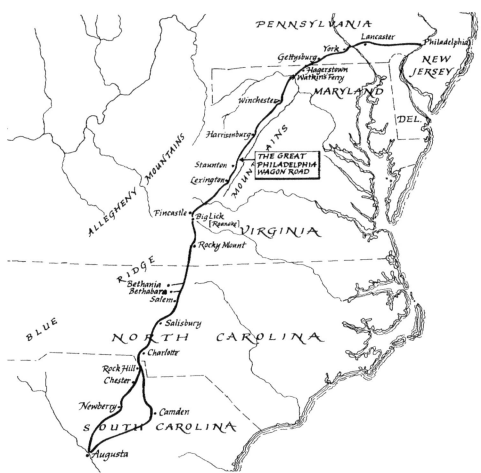

The Appalachian Mountains runs from New York to Georgia, running through Pennsylvania, Maryland, Virginia, North Carolina, and South Carolina. This range had no place to cross in a wagon. The Blue Ridge Mountains runs from Pennsylvania to Georgia and lies east of the Appalachian range, running through Maryland, Virginia, North Carolina, and South Carolina. There is a plateau that lies between these two ranges.

When the Scott-Irish and the Huguenots came from Ireland the landed in Philadelphia. They got a wagon and followed the Great Wagon Road. The road started in Philadelphia went west till it ran up against the Appalachian Mountains. Then it turned south and followed the plateau south through

75

Trimble Families of America

Maryland then Virginia. One branch went into Tennessee. Another branch went to North Carolina, South Carolina and into Georgia.

The Huguenots would travel until they found a spot and settled there and seldom moved. They would buy their property. The Scott-Irish would travel to a spot that was empty and build a home seldom even registering their property. Pennsylvania was run by the Religious Society of Friends or Quakers. They would try to acquire land from the Native Americans for settlement and did not want people to settle on un acquired land. The Scott-Irish would settle on a piece of land and build a log home without permission. Governments would come in move all the belongs out of the house then burn the house. Those whose owned the house would just watch as it burned. The next day after the government people had left, they began building a new house.

In 1700's, Scotts-Irish moved to America in 5 waves, 1717-18, 1725-29, 1740-41, 1754-55, and 1771-75, ending with start of the American Revolution.

Scotts-Irish would settle on a piece of property and build a house. After living there a few years some would sell the land and move to another place further down the Great Wagon Road and settle there, only to move again. The four brothers: G – William "The Settler" Trimble, H – "North Mountain" John Trimble, I – Walter and Rosanna Trimble, and J – James "The Plantationer" all settled in Pennsylvania first before moving to the middle of Virginia. Several of these then moved further south.

Jim Webb titled his book on the Scott-Irish *Born Fighting*. The reason is in the Marches of Scotland and England, the reivers were always prepared to fight. After moving to Ireland, they had to constantly be on watch for attacks from the Irish. Now they were on the frontier of America. acting as a buffer against attacks from Native Americans. The attitude that developed was a fierce independence and self-reliance.

When the Scott-Irish moved to America, they were still Presbyterian. But to start a church they needed to attract a presbyterian minister to America. A minister had study for five years then take a dangerous voyage across the Atlantic. They could get a minister, but they had to wait for one to come to them. The synods in America established colleges to educate ministers locally.

The democratic character of the Presbyterian Church affected the political attitude of the Scott-Irish. They were a strong supporter of independence from Britain. A majority of George Washington's army was Scott-Irish. The Battle of Kings Mountain was fought almost entirely by Scott-Irish, and they had not joined an army.

After the American Revolution, soldiers had not been paid so they were given land grants in Kentucky. There was another migration to Kentucky. When these Presbyterians moved to Kentucky, it became impossible to start a Presbyterian Church. It was too hard to get educated ministers to move to the wilderness. They either joined Baptist churches or Methodists.

When the Scott-Irish moved into an area, they hunted to put meat on the table. In Virginia, they hunted bison, they were plentiful and had lots of meat; bear, they were fatty and tasted good and could render an oil for frying; elk, they were meaty; deer, they had good meat; turkey, were and easy shot off the roast, pigs, they brought pigs with them, and the pigs were let roam the hill where they feed on acorns and plentiful chestnuts. They got the urge to move when the game got scarce meaning they would have to raise animals to place meat on the table.

The Genealogies

Five Brothers

In this section we will present the genealogy of the Five Trimble Brothers who migrated to America in the 1730s, settling first in Pennsylvania then in the late 1730s moving to the Shenandoah Valley of Virginia.

The compiler has seen several accounts of their having landed at the port of Baltimore along with the Moffitt and Hayes families in their own boat. However, there is no way to authenticate this event. They came from Armagh, Ireland, and the older brothers were surveyors by profession. They brought with them a certificate to this effect signed by Sir Archibald Atcheson.

The four oldest brothers, namely James, John, Moses, and David, came to Virginia. Alexander, being the youngest and at that time a minor, was left in Philadelphia with the Reverend Gilbert Tennent, a relative and minister of the Second Presbyterian Church of Philadelphia.

The four Trimble brothers who settled in Virginia, lived the rest of their lives and died in Virginia, except David, who in his later years was compelled to move to Montgomery County, Kentucky, with his sons and daughters. His wife and all his brothers had died. This was around 1798. A large percentage of the Trimbles in America today are the descendants of David.

A - James Trimble

James and his four brothers came to America in the 1730s, settling first near Philadelphia, Pennsylvania. As the Shenandoah Valley of Virginia was opened for settlers, the Scotts-Irish was granted the privilege of worshiping in their Presbyterian tradition by Governor William Gooch of Virginia. This settlement in the valley was to serve also as a buffer against the Native Americans for the protection of the English settlers to the east. During this time hundreds of families began migrating to the valley among which were four of the Five Trimble Brothers.

A1–James Trimble. Born in 1710 in Armagh, Ireland and died in April 1776 in Lexington, Virginia. He emigrated to Pennsylvania between 1734 and 1735. He married Sarah Kersey in 1746 in Augusta County, Virginia. He is buried Old Monmouth Graveyard, Lexington, Virginia. Sarah was born in 1716 in Cowpasture, Augusta County, Virginia and died in 1776 in Botetourt County, Virginia.[21] James was the eldest seems to have been the more affluent. He purchased several large tracts of land in Virginia and was referred to as "gentleman" in early records. This was a title given in colonial days to the landed gentry, which at that time in Great Britain would be just below that of a knight. As records in the valley were not kept before 1740, it is uncertain when James came to Virginia. Upon the formation of Augusta County, Virginia, in 1742 he was appointed deputy surveyor. From Ireland James had brought a certificate from Sir Archibald Atcheson identifying him as a surveyor and attesting to his high character.

With the formation of Botetourt County, Virginia, James was appointed one of the justices (the governing body of the county), which office he held the remainder of his life.

Holly Hill Plantation on the forks of the James River, about four miles east of what is now Lexington, Virginia, was the home of James Trimble and his wife Sarah Kersey, who came from the Cowpasture River area west of Lexington in Augusta County, Virginia. Prior to the formation of now Lexington, this area was called Monmouth. James owned several large tracts of land and was among the most prominent settlers of the valley and one of

---

[21] Joseph Addison Waddell, Annals of August County, Virginia from 1726 to 1871, by. Second Edition, Virginia, C. Russell Caldwell, Publisher, 1902, p. 178.

the largest landowners. Because James did possess such vast landholdings his several sons were not among those who found it necessary to move westward in search of land. James gave to each of his children large tracts of land acreage enough to provide for their families.

It is interesting to note that even though James Trimble had six sons there was only one grandson to carry on the family name from his issue. James had four daughters.

James and Sarah Trimble are buried in the "Old Monmouth Cemetery" outside of Lexington, Virginia, now Rockbridge County. He died in 1776. His will is recorded in *Will Book I,* page 308, Rockbridge County Courthouse, Virginia.

My wife and I (John Farley and Loretta Trimble) visited the "Old Monmouth Cemetery" and found it to be quite unkept. A partial wall of stone where the second Monmouth church had stood bears a plaque telling the history of the church and cemetery. Many of the headstones were crumbled and some had fallen. The Monmouth church was reorganized and has a new church building about two miles west of the "Old Monmouth" site. This cemetery where James is buried is located on Route 60 and a historical road marker identifies the location.

We are indebted to Mrs. W. W. McCrary, Jr., of 516 Jefferson, Lonoke, Arkansas 72086, for her contribution to the Thomas Clark Trimble II line.

The children of James Trimble and Sarah Kersey:

+ **A2–Jane (Jean) Trimble.** Born in 1747 in Rockbridge County, Virginia and died in 1781 in Virginia. Married William McClure.

+ **A3–John Trimble.** Born on August 24, 1749 and died on August 21, 1783. Married Mary Alexander.

+ **A4–Agnes Trimble.** Born on September 4, 1751, in Rockbridge County, Virginia and died in 1822 in Rockbridge County, Virginia. Married David Steele.

+ **A5–Isaac Trimble.** Born on October 24, 1753 in Augusta County, Virginia and died on November 6, 1836 in Lexington, Fayette County, Kentucky. Married Frances Matthews.

  A6–James Trimble, Jr. Born on November 20, 1755 in Augusta County, Virginia and died in 1779 in Rockbridge County, Virginia, unmarried.

+ **A7–Moses Trimble.** Born on October 2, 1757 in Augusta County, Virginia and died in 1821. Married Mary Brawley on April 9, 1793.

+ **A8–Sarah Trimble.** Born on February 15, 1760 in Augusta County, Virginia and died after 1850. Married Samuel Steele on August 15, 1782 in Rockbridge County, Virginia.

    A9—Alexander Trimble. Born on February 15, 1762, died in 1816 in Virginia. Married Martha Grigsby on December 12, 1793 and lived at Holly Hill Plantation, three miles east of Lexington, Virginia. Martha was born on September 19, 1772 and died on October 4, 1868. They had no children. His widow Martha survived him by fifty years. A woman of rare intelligence, her letters to relatives contributed greatly to the family history.

    A10—William Trimble. Born on April 4, 1764, died in 1794. William never married. He was sheriff of Rockbridge County and died at Staunton, Virginia, on his way to take taxes to Richmond, Virginia. In an old letter he was described as a very handsome man.

   + **A11—Rachel Trimble.** Born on September 8, 1765, married Joseph Caruthers.

A2—Jane (Jean) Trimble. Daughter of James Trimble and Sarah Kersey. Born in 1747 in Rockbridge County, Virginia. Married William Kelso McClure on December 26, 1769 in Rockbridge County, Virginia. William was born in 1739 in Orange County, Virginia and died in 1785 in Rockbridge County, Virginia. William was the son of Samuel McClure and Mary Bell Kelso married 1736 in County Donegal, Ireland. Samuel was born in 1709 in Raphoe, County Donegal, Ulster, Ireland and died on March 13, 1799 in Lexington, Rockbridge County, Virginia. Mary was born in 1713 in Donegal, Ireland and died 1779 in Lexington, Rockbridge County, Virginia.

    The children of William Kelso McClure and Jane (Jean) Trimble:

   + **A12—William McClure.** Born in 1764 in Augusta County, Virginia and died in 1814 in Norfolk, Virginia. Married Mary Shields.

   + **A13—Samuel McClure.** Born in 1765 in Rockbridge County, Virginia and died in February 1833 in Troy, Richland County, Ohio. Married Nancy Rutan.

    A14—Jane 'Jenny' McClure. Born in 1772 in Rockbridge County, Virginia. Married Joseph Paxton on November 22, 1792.

   + **A15—James A. McClure.** Born in 1774 in Rockbridge County, Virginia and died May 27, 1827 in Rockbridge County, Virginia. His will was probated in Lexington, Kentucky. Married Rebecca Jackson.

   + **A16—Sarah 'Sally' McClure.** Born about 1776 in Rockbridge County, Virginia. Married William Grigsby on January 7, 1790 in Rockbridge County, Virginia.

    A17—Mary McClure. Born about 1778 in Rockbridge County, Virginia and died about 1850 in Virginia. Married David Templeton on May 10, 1791 in

Trimble Families of America

Rockbridge County, Virginia. David was born about 1780 in Virginia and died about 1850 in Virginia.

+ **A18—Agnes McClure.** Born about 1780 Augusta County, Virginia and died in 1850 in Virginia. Married William Douglas on December 21, 1803 in Rockbridge County, Virginia.

+ **A19—John McClure.** Born about 1783 in Virginia and died on January 7, 1835 in Rockbridge County, Virginia. Married twice.

+ **A20—Alexander Trimble McClure.** Born on December 23, 1784 in Rockbridge County, Virginia and died on September 25, 1823 in Grant, Kentucky. Married Betsy Paxton on November 17, 1808.

A3—John Trimble. Son of James Trimble and Sarah Kersey. Born on August 12, 1749 and died on August 21, 1783, while still a young man. Married Mary Alexander on January 11, 1779 in Rockbridge County, Virginia, daughter of Archibald Alexander who was a prominent officer in the valley. She was an aunt of Dr. Alexander of Princeton University. She was born on February 4, 1760 in Augusta County, Virginia. Like his father, John was a surveyor. John left much property to his son, James.

The children of John Trimble and Mary Alexander:

+ **A21—James Trimble.** Born on July 5, 1781, in Rockbridge County, Virginia and died August 7, 1824. Married Letitia Breckenridge Clark.

A4—Agnes Trimble. Daughter of James Trimble and Sarah Kersey. Born on September 4, 1752 and died in 1822 in Rockbridge County, Virginia. Married David Steele on May 21, 1789 in Rockbridge County, Virginia,[22] and became the ancestor of the prominent Steele family. Members are still living in Rockbridge County, Virginia. David was born in 1756 in Augusta County. Virginia and died on December 12, 1812 in Jessamine, Kentucky. David's parents are Robert Steele and Maria Elizabeth Wendell Married in 1750 in Augusta County, Virginia. Robert was born in 1730 in Augusta, County, Virginia and died on April 30, 1800 in Augusta County, Virginia. Maria was born on November 15, 1748 and died on April 15, 1778 in Augusta County, Virginia.

They had five sons, two of whom died. Three lived, yet we only find record of one. His name is Joseph He lived with Alexander Trimble's widow,

---

[22] Dodd, Jordan R., et al. Early American Marriages: Virginia to 1850. Bountiful, UT, USA: Precision Indexing Publishers.

84

Martha Grigsby Trimble, and married Martha Paxton.

The child of David Steele and Agnes Trimble:

+ **A22—Joseph Steele.** Born on July 10, 1795 in Rockbridge County, Virginia and died on September 6, 1872 in Rockbridge County, Virginia. Married Martha "Patsy" Paxton on December 18, 1817.

A5—Isaac Trimble. Son of James Trimble and Sarah Kersey. Born on October 24, 1753 in Rockbridge County, Virginia and died on November 6, 1836 in Lexington, Fayette County, Kentucky. He married Frances Matthews on January 6, 1783. and is buried in Lexington, Virginia. Isaac was a very eccentric man. For the greater part of his life was intemperate. The last ten years of his life he lived with Martha Grigsby Trimble. During the last four years of his life, he read the Bible through four times. Martha believed he died a Christian. The only child that we find a record of was Sally.

The child of Isaac Trimble and Frances Matthews:

+ **A23—Sally Trimble.** Born in 1790 in Virginia and died in August 1813 in Lewisburg, Greenbrier, Virginia. Married James McLaughlin.

A7—Moses Trimble. Son of James Trimble and Sarah Kersey. Born on October 2, 1757 in Rockbridge County, Virginia and died in 1821 in Rockbridge County, Virginia. He married Mary Brawley on April 9, 1793. They lived in Rockbridge County, Virginia. Moses was a prosperous farmer and was an elder in the Falling Springs Presbyterian Church. He had one son, James and three daughters.

The children of Moses Trimble and Mary Brawley:

+ **A24—James Trimble.** Born in 1794 in Rockbridge County, Virginia and died in Kanawha County, now West Virginia.

+ **A25—Susanna Trimble.** Born in 1796 in Rockbridge County, Virginia and died in Rockbridge County, Virginia. Married Mathias Benson. He was born in 1789 in Bath County, Virginia and died in 1847.

  A26—Elizabeth Trimble. Born in 1798 in Rockbridge County, Virginia and died in Rockbridge County, Virginia.

+ **A27—Sally Trimble.** Born in 1800 in Rockbridge County, Virginia and died in Rockbridge County, Virginia. Married James Miller in 1820 in Rockbridge County, Virginia.

A8—Sarah Trimble. Daughter of James Trimble and Sarah Kersey. Born on February 15, 1760 in Rockbridge County, Virginia and died after 1850 in Monroe County, Tennessee. She married Samuel Steele on August 15, 1782 in Rockbridge County, Virginia. He was born on October 30, 1756 in Augusta County, Virginia and died on April 6, 1845 in Monroe County, Tennessee. They moved to Tennessee from the Valley at Lexington, Virginia.

The children of Samuel Steele and Sarah Trimble:

+ **A28—Jane Steele.** Born on December 10, 1784 in Rockbridge County, Virginia. Married Isaac Campbell on December 5, 1809 in Monroe County, West Virginia.

A29—James T. Steele. Born on February 10, 1786.

+ **A30—Sophia Steele.** Born on December 4, 1788 in Rockbridge County, Virginia and died August 27, 1853 in Calhoun County, Alabama. Married John Patton Montgomery.

+ **A31—Sarah Trimble 'Sally' Steele.** Born on February 15, 1790 Rockbridge County, Virginia and died on May 23, 1876 in Grayson County, Texas. Married William Montgomery in 1811 in Blount County, Texas.

A32—Rachel Steele. Born on September 15, 1792.

A33—John Steele. Born on November 19, 1794.

A34—Mary Steele. Born on May 8, 1797.

A35—Martha G. Steele. Born on March 23, 1800.

A36—David A. Steele. Born on June 18, 1802.

A11—Rachel Trimble. Daughter of James Trimble and Sarah Kersey. Born on September 8, 1765 in Lexington, Virginia and died on September 12, 1822 in Tennessee. She married Joseph Caruthers on May 7, 1785 and they moved westward. Joseph was born on February 19, 1764 in Lexington, Virginia and died in 1830 Lexington, Henderson County, Tennessee. Joseph was the son of William Caruthers and Margaret McCroskerie. William was born in 1722 in Letterkenny, Donegal County, Ireland. Margaret was born in 1718 in Virginia and died in 1758.

The children of Joseph Caruthers and Rachel Trimble:

A37—Samuel Caruthers. Born on October 30, 1784 and died on June 2, 1798 in Rockbridge, Virginia.

+ **A38—Sally Caruthers.** Born on February 12, 1787 in Rockbridge, Virginia and died in 1827 in Rockbridge County, Virginia. Married William Thompson.

A39—Peggy Caruthers. Born on January 2, 1789 in Rockbridge County, Virginia and died in 1864 in Liberty, Amite County, Mississippi.

A40—James Caruthers. Born on March 1, 1795 in Rockbridge County, Virginia and died in 1862 in Jackson, Madison County, Tennessee.

A41—Rachel Caruthers. Born on May 15, 1797 in Lexington, Virginia and died on August 22, 1804 in Lexington, Virginia.

A42—Phebe Caruthers. Born on January 10, 1799 in Lexington, Virginia and died in Henry, Henry County, Tennessee.

A43—Thomas Jefferson Caruthers. Born on February 1, 1801 in Rockbridge County, Virginia and died on August 19, 1836 in Davidson, Davidson County, Tennessee.

A44—Joseph Caruthers. Born on November 10, 1802 in Virginia and died on December 9, 1884 in Arkansas.

A45—Alexander Caruthers. Born on December 22, 1804 and died in 1866 in Holly Springs, Marshall County, Mississippi.

+ **A46—Nancy Steele Caruthers.** Born on July 22, 1807 in Lexington, Henderson County, Tennessee and died on July 14, 1846 in Grenada, Yalobusha County, Mississippi. Married George Keeport Morton on June 15, 1830 in Lexington, Henderson County, Tennessee.

A47—Elizabeth Caruthers. Born on November 20, 1809 and died in Savannah, Hardin County, Tennessee.

A48—Melinda Caruthers. Born on March 17, 1812 in Lexington, Henderson County, Tennessee.

A12—William McClure. Son of William Kelso McClure and Jane Trimble. (Third generation of James Trimble and Sarah Kersey.) Born in 1764 in Augusta County, Virginia. A veteran's mark at his grave says he served in the Revolutionary War and enlisted in Washington County, Virginia for the War of 1812 under Lieutenant William Huston and was killed at the battle of Norfolk, Virginia in 1814. Married Mary Shields. She was born in 1775 and died in 1848 in Kentucky. After William was killed Mary married Adam Surber.

The children of William McClure and Mary Shields:

A49—Mary Ann McClure. Born in 1791 in Augusta, Virginia. Married Phillip Minton in 1825 in Washington, Virginia.

+ **A50—William McClure.** Born in 1791 in Augusta County, Virginia and died on February 11, 1865. Married Sally Bennett in 1816 in Chemung, Chemung County, New York.

A51—Elizabeth McClure. Born on 1793 in Augusta County, Virginia.

A52—Polly McClure. Born on 1793 in Virginia.

A53—Jemina McClure. Born on 1795 in Augusta County, Virginia.

A54—Robert McClure. Born on 1798 in Augusta County, Virginia. Married

Trimble Families of America

Rebecca Mathias.

A55—Jane McClure. Born in 1799 in Augusta County, Virginia and died in Illinois. Married David Mitchell.

A56—Louisa Viletha McClure. Born on April 13, 1803 in Washington, Virginia. Married Adam Surber.

A57—Robert McClure. Born in 1804 in Virginia.

A58—John Shields McClure. Born on March 1, 1811 in Washington, Virginia and died on July 30, 1907 in Kentucky. Married Eliza Margaret Hubble.

+ **A59—David McClure.** Born on August 30, 1814 in Washington, Virginia and died about 1854 in Appanoose County, Iowa. Married Lavina Hubble on December 16, 1833 in Pulaski County, Kentucky.

A13—Samuel McClure. Son of William Kelso McClure and Jane Trimble. (Third generation of James Trimble and Sarah Kersey.) Born in 1765 in Rockbridge County, Virginia and died in February 1833 in Troy, Richland County, Ohio. Married Nancy Rutan on November 23, 1822. She was born in 1768 in Rockbridge County, Virginia and died on November 29, 1817 in Troy, Richland, Ohio.

The child of Samuel McClure and Nancy Rutan:

+ **A60—Hugh Rutan McClure.** Born on August 3, 1825 and died in May 1848. Married Rebecca Martillia Balch.

A15—James A. McClure. Son of William Kelso McClure and Jane Trimble. (Third generation of James Trimble and Sarah Kersey.) Born in 1774 in Rockbridge County, Virginia and died on May 27, 1830 in Rockbridge County, Virginia. His will was probated in Lexington, Kentucky. Married Rebecca Jackson. She was born in 1770 and died on August 10, 1857.

The child of James A. McClure and Rebecca Jackson:

A61—Elizabeth McClure. Born on July 31, 1785 and died on August 4, 1824.

A62—Rachel McClure. Born in 1796.

A63—Nancy McClure. Born in 1800.

A64—John McClure. Born in 1800 and died in 1849.

A65—James McClure. Born in 1805.

A66—Hugh McClure. Born in 1806 and died on August 10, 1867.

A16—Sarah 'Sally' McClure. Daughter of William Kelso McClure and Jane Trimble. (Third generation of James Trimble and Sarah Kersey.) Born about 1776 in Rockbridge County, Virginia. Married William Grigsby on January 7, 1790 in Rockbridge County, Virginia.

The child of William Grigsby and Sarah 'Sally' McClure:
A67—Caroline Grigsby. Born on May 6, 1807 in Virginia and died on January 26, 1892 in Greensburg, Decatur, Indiana.

A18—Agnes McClure. Daughter of William Kelso McClure and Jane Trimble. (Third generation of James Trimble and Sarah Kersey.) Born about 1780 Augusta County, Virginia and died in 1850 in Virginia. Married William Douglas on December 21, 1803 in Rockbridge County, Virginia.

The children of William Douglas and Agnes McClure:
A68—Hannah Douglas. Born on July 19, 1796 and died after 1870.
A69—Patsy Douglas. Born on August 14, 1798.

A19—John McClure. Son of William Kelso McClure and Jane Trimble. (Third generation of James Trimble and Sarah Kersey.) Born about 1783 in Virginia and died on January 7, 1835 in Rockbridge County, Virginia.

Married first to Jane "Jenny" McClure on June 2, 1808 in Rockbridge County, Virginia. Jenny was born on September 17, 1789 in Rockbridge, Virginia and died before 1821.

Married second to Nancy Cunningham on November 6, 1824 in Rockbridge County, Virginia. Nancy was born on December 20, 1803 and died on June 26, 1836 in Rockbridge County, Virginia.

The children of John McClure and Jane "Jenny" McClure:
A70—James Madison McClure. Born about 1810 in Rockbridge County, Virginia and died on July 28, 1829 in Rockbridge County, Virginia.
A71—John Trimble McClure. Born about 1812 in Rockbridge County, Virginia and died about 1834.
+**A72—Eglantine McClure.** Born about 1816 in Rockbridge County, Virginia. Married Addison J. Henderson on March 8, 1836 in Rockbridge County, Virginia.

A20—Alexander Trimble McClure. Son of William Kelso McClure and Jane Trimble. (Third generation of James Trimble and Sarah Kersey.) Born on December 23, 1784 in Rockbridge County, Virginia and died on September 25, 1823 in Grant, Kentucky. Married Betsy Paxton on November 17, 1808 in Rockbridge County, Virginia. She was born on July 19, 1789 in "River Vale," South of the James River, Rockbridge County, Virginia and died in 1824 in Barrens County, Kentucky.

The children of Alexander McClure and Betsy Paxton:
A73—Eliza McClure. Born in 1809 in Rockbridge County, Virginia and died in

A - James Trimble

> 1838 in Carthage, Hancock County, Illinois.
>
> **A74—William McClure.** Born on March 4, 1811 in Rockbridge County, Virginia and died in 1858.
>
> **A75—Mary Ann McClure.** Born on March 4, 1813 in Rockbridge County, Virginia and died on April 3, 1896 in Warsaw, Illinois.
>
> **A76—Tirsay McClure.** Born on 1816 in Kentucky and died on August 4, 1858 in Illinois.
>
> **A77—Phebe McClure.** Born after 1816 in Kentucky and died on November 10, 1834 in Rockbridge County, Virginia. Married Thomas Preston Paxton.
>
> **A78—Aurelia McClure.** Born in 1818 in Kentucky and died in 1898 in Rockbridge County, Virginia.

A21—James Trimble. Son of John Trimble and Mary Alexander. (Third generation of James Trimble and Sarah Kersey.) Born on July 5, 1781 in Rockbridge County, Virginia. James went with his mother to Tennessee after her second marriage to Louis Jordan on November 10, 1785. James died in Nashville, Tennessee, in July 1824. James married Letitia Breckenridge Clark, a niece of Dolly Madison. Letitia was born on September 26, 1792 and died on June 9, 1861. He was a well-educated man and became a federal judge in Tennessee in 1810. He returned to Virginia and studied law under Judge Coalter at Staunton. An example of the esteem in which he was held is exemplified by the fact that Andrew Jackson sent his young protégé, Sam Houston, to study law in James Trimble's office. Trimble was a kinsman of Houston. He was the progenitor of a long family of jurists in the South who are serving as judges to the present day. In 1807 he was appointed attorney general of east Tennessee, later commissioner of land claims for Louisiana.

> The children of James Trimble and Letitia Clark:
>
> + **A79—John Trimble.** Born on February 7, 1812 and died on February 23, 1884.
>
> + **A80—Thomas Clark Trimble.** Born in 1813 and died November 20, 1883. Married Fannie Erwin.
>
> + **A81—Eliza Melvina Trimble.** Born on July 2, 1819 in Tennessee and died on November 13, 1893 in Nashville, Davidson County, Tennessee. Married Adrian Van Sinderen Lindsley in 1838.

A22—Joseph Steele. Son of David Steele and Agnes Trimble. (Third generation of James Trimble and Sarah Kersey.) Born on July 10, 1795 in Rockbridge County, Virginia and died on September 6, 1872 in Rockbridge County, Virginia. Married Martha "Patsy" Paxton on December 18, 1817.

The children of Joseph Steele and Martha "Patsy" Paxton:

A82—Agnes Jane Steele. Born on December 19, 1820 and died on January 23, 1876 in Rockbridge County, Virginia.

A83—Elizabeth Steele. Born on August 18, 1823 in Rockbridge County, Virginia.

A84—David William Steele. Born on February 25, 1826 in Rockbridge County, Virginia and died on May 12, 1864 in Fredericksburg, Spotsylvania, Virginia.

A85—Joseph Grigsby Steele. Born on September 10, 1827 in Rockbridge County, Virginia and died on July 9, 1886 in Lexington, Virginia. Buried in Stonewall Jackson Memorial Cemetery, Lexington, Virginia.

A86—Sarah Josephine Steele. Born about 1828.

A87—Mary Ashley Steele. Born on November 23, 18311836 in Rockbridge County, Virginia and died on July 9, 1886 in Lexington, Virginia. Married Adolphus Elhart in 1855.

A88—Phebe A Steele. Born on October 6, 1836 in Rockbridge County, Virginia and died on October 10, 1920 in Memphis, Shelby, Tennessee Memphis, Shelby, Tennessee. Married John Fabian Baker on September 28, 1858 in Liberty, Georgia.

A23—Sally Trimble. Daughter of Isaac Trimble and Frances Matthews. (Third generation of James Trimble and Sarah Kersey.) Born in 1790 in Virginia and died in August 1813 in Lewisburg, Greenbrier, Virginia. Married James McLaughlin. He was born in 1790 in Ireland and died in 1830 in Greenbrier County, Virginia.

The children of James McLaughlin and Sally Trimble:

A88—Mary McLaughlin. Born in 1811 in Greenbrier County, Virginia.

+ A90—James T. McLaughlin. Born on July 28, 1813 in Greenbrier County, Virginia and died in 1902 in Lynchburg, Virginia. Married Ann Ball Miller on September 10, 1844 in Pittsylvania, Virginia.

A24—James Trimble. Son of Moses Trimble and Mary Brawley. (Third generation of James Trimble and Sarah Kersey.) Born in 1794 in Rockbridge County, Virginia and died in Kanawha County, now West Virginia. James married Rebecca Stockton, daughter of Aaron Stockton, Rebecca was born on May 22, 1813 and migrated with the Stockton family to the Falls of the Kanawha River. They installed a ferry and tavern hostel at now Gauley Bridge, West Virginia. This had become the main route westward from Virginia about the turn of the century. The Stockton family became one of the early prominent families in Kanawha County, West Virginia. James died

Trimble Families of America

young leaving small children. We have records of two sons of James.

The children of James Trimble and Rebecca Stockton:

+ **A91—Aaron Trimble.** Born about 1834 in Kanawha County, West Virginia and married Corole Bowsman.

A92—Moses Trimble. He lived in Fayette County, West Virginia which borders Nicholas. He had a daughter.

A93—Elizabeth Trimble. Married a Mr. Smith and they owned a hotel in Charleston, West Virginia.

A94—Nannie Harriman Trimble. Born on May 14, 1836 and died on January 30, 1889. Married Mordecai Levi, a Christianized Jew who was a prominent lawyer in early Charleston, West Virginia. He was born on December 11, 1835 in Brown County, Ohio and died on January 14, 1914 in Charleston, West Virginia.

A95—Sally Trimble. Married James Miller in 1820.

+ **A96—Osman Trimble.** Born in 1813 in Rockbridge County, Virginia and died on November 8, 1893, at Clifton (now Pratt), West Virginia. Married Jeanetta White.

A25—Susanna Trimble. Daughter of Moses Trimble and Mary Brawley. (Third generation of James Trimble and Sarah Kersey.) Born in 1796 in Rockbridge County, Virginia and died in Rockbridge County, Virginia. Married Mathias Benson. He was born in 1789 in Bath County, Virginia and died in 1847.

The children of Mathias Benson and Susanna Trimble:

A97—Mary A. Benson.

A98—Elizabeth Benson. Born about 1815. Married Robert Botkin.

A99—Matilda Jane Benson. Born about 1820. Married Noah Stout on April 19, 1847 in Highland County, Virginia.

A100—Susan Benson. Born about 1821.

A101—Isaac J. Benson. Born about 1824. Married Mary.

A102—Caroline Benson. Born about 1826.

A103—Lucinda Benson. Born about 1828. Married James Stevenson on February 4, 1851.

A104—Margaret Benson. Born about 1831.

A105—William W. Benson. Born about 1831.

A27—Sally Trimble. Daughter of Moses Trimble and Mary Brawley. (Third generation of James Trimble and Sarah Kersey.) Born in 1800 in Rockbridge County, Virginia and died in Rockbridge County, Virginia. Married James Miller in 1820. in Rockbridge County, Virginia. James was born in 1791 in

Virginia. His parents were Jacob Miller and Margaret Penner. They were married in 1755. Jacob was born in 1758 in Wytheville, Wythe, Virginia and died in 1833. Margaret was born in 1762 Virginia and buried Green River Union Cemetery, Richardsville, Kentucky.

The children of James Miller and Sally Trimble:

A106—Elihu Trimble Miller. Born on October 20, 1820 in Rockbridge County, Virginia and August 29, 1922 in Rockbridge County, Virginia.

A28—Jane Steele. Daughter of Samuel Steele and Sarah Trimble. (Third generation of James Trimble and Sarah Kersey.) Born on December 10, 1784 in Rockbridge County, Virginia. Married Isaac Campbell on December 5, 1809 in Monroe County, West Virginia. Isaac was born in 1790 in Monroe, Amherst County, Virginia and died on November 17, 1860 in Monroe, Amherst County, Virginia

The children of Isaac Campbell and Jane Steele:

A107—Isaac H. Campbell. Born on October 7, 1808 in Monroe, West Virginia and died on October 5, 1861 in Monroe, West Virginia.

A108—Isabella Jane Campbell. Born on September 19, 1811 in Monroe, Amherst County, Virginia and died on December 20, 1886 in Linden, Atchison County, Kansas.

+**A109—Lewis Campbell.** Born in 1813 in Monroe, Amherst County, Virginia and died 1850 in Monroe, Amherst, Virginia. Married Mary Ann Brown.

A110—Clemet Campbell. Born in 1815 in Monroe, West Virginia.

A111—Emily Campbell. Born in 1820 in Monroe, West Virginia.

A112—Calvin Campbell. Born in 1821 in Monroe, West Virginia.

A113—Elizabeth Campbell. Born in 1823 in Monroe, West Virginia.

A30—Sophia Steele. Daughter of Samuel Steele and Sarah Trimble. (Third generation of James Trimble and Sarah Kersey.) Born on December 4, 1788 in Rockbridge County, Virginia and died on August 27, 1853 in Calhoun County, Alabama. Married John Patton Montgomery.

The child of John Patton Montgomery and Sophia Steele:

+**A114—Francis Evans 'Fannie' Montgomery.** Born about 1844 in Georgia. Married Thomas Howard Clements.

A31—Sarah Trimble 'Sally' Steele. Daughter of Samuel Steele and Sarah Trimble. (Third generation of James Trimble and Sarah Kersey.) Born on February 15, 1790 Rockbridge County, Virginia and died on May 23, 1876 in

Grayson County, Texas. Married William Montgomery in 1811 in Blount County, Texas.

The child of William Montgomery and Sarah Trimble 'Sally' Steele:

A115—Sophia C. Montgomery. Born on March 24, 1812 in Blount County, Tennessee and died on April 12, 1875 in Grayson County, Texas.

A116—Thomas Emerson Montgomery. Born on August 4, 1814 in Blount County, Tennessee and died on January 11, 1874 in Bells, Grayson County, Texas.

A117—James Addison Montgomery. Born on November 25, 1820 in Blount County, Tennessee and died in 1892 in Denton County, Texas.

A118—Rachel M. Montgomery. Born on March 22, 1824, Tennessee and died on November 22, 1889, Grayson County, Texas.

A119—George H. Montgomery. Born on February 10, 1827, Monroe County, Tennessee and died on December 18, 1906, Grayson County, Texas.

A120—Lucian Pinckney Montgomery. Born on April 8, 1828 in Alabama and died on October 15, 1903 in Grayson County, Texas.

A121—Isaac Montgomery. Born on May 12, 1830, Alabama.

A122—Armina Montgomery. Born on March 20, 1832, Alabama.

A38—Sally Caruthers. Daughter of Joseph Caruthers and Rachel Trimble. (Third generation of James Trimble and Sarah Kersey.) Born on February 12, 1787 in Rockbridge, Virginia and died in 1827 in Rockbridge County, Virginia. Married William Thompson on January 16, 1806 in Rockbridge County, Virginia. William was born in August 1782 in Virginia and died on June 28, 1855 in Rockbridge County, Virginia.

The children of William Thompson and Sally Caruthers:

A123—Joseph Thompson. Born about 1808 in Rockbridge County, Virginia.

A124—Margaret Thompson. Born about 1810 in Rockbridge County, Virginia.

A125—Rachel Thompson. Born about 1813 in Rockbridge County, Virginia and died on September 30, 1882 in Tennessee.

+A126—John W. Thompson. Born on October 10, 1816 in Rockbridge County, Virginia and died on August 16, 1886 in Lower James, Botetourt County, Virginia. Married Isabella Gilmore Lackey.

A127—Phoebe Thompson. Born about 1818 in Rockbridge County, Virginia.

A128—James J. Thompson. Born about 1821 in Rockbridge County, Virginia and died on August 9, 1896 in Rockbridge County, Virginia.

A46—Nancy Steele Caruthers. Daughter of Joseph Caruthers and Rachel Trimble. (Third generation of James Trimble and Sarah Kersey.) Born on

July 22, 1807 in Lexington, Henderson County, Tennessee and died on July 14, 1846 in Grenada, Yalobusha County, Mississippi. Married George Keeport Morton on June 15, 1830 in Lexington, Henderson County, Tennessee. George was born in 1800 in Pittsburg, Mississippi.

The children of George Keeport Morton and Nancy Steele Caruthers:

A129—Catherine Elizabeth Morton. Born on April 26, 1831 in Mississippi and died on August 18, 1907 in Memphis, Shelby County, Tennessee.

A130—Joseph C. Morton. Born in 1833 in Grenada, Yalobusha County, Mississippi.

A131—George W. Morton. Born in 1837 in Mississippi and died on September 17, 1862 in Battle of Antietam at Sharpsburg, Maryland. George as selected Second Lieutenant of the Coahoma Invincibles, Company B, 11th Regiment, Mississippi Infantry of the Confederate Army. His brother, J. K. Morton was selected captain. He was promoted to Major on the day he died.

A132—James Keeport Morton. Born in 1840 in Grenada, Mississippi and died on September 17, 1862 in Battle of Antietam at Sharpsburg, Virginia. J. K. Morton was selected captain in Coahoma Invincibles, Company B, 11th Regiment, Mississippi Infantry of the Confederate Army.

+ **A133—John Paul Morton.** Born in 1840 in Mississippi. Married Ella T.

A50—William McClure. Son of William McClure and Mary Shields. (Fourth generation of James Trimble and Sarah Kersey.) Born in 1791 in Augusta County, Virginia and died on February 11, 1865. Married Sally Bennett in 1816 in Chemung, Chemung County, New York. Sally was born on November 21, 1795 in Chemung, Chemung County, New York and died on March 20, 1834 in Havana, Gadsden County, Florida.

The children of William McClure and Sally Bennett:

A134—Uriah McClure. Born in 1817 in New York.

A135—Elizabeth McClure. Born in 1819 in New York.

A59—David McClure. Son of William McClure and Mary Shields. (Fourth generation of James Trimble and Sarah Kersey.) Born on August 30, 1814 in Washington, Virginia and died about 1854 in Appanoose County, Iowa. Married Lavina Hubble on December 16, 1833 in Pulaski County, Kentucky.

The children of David McClure and Lavina Hubble:

A136—Arentha Ann McClure. Born in 1835 in Kentucky and died on October 3, 1893 in Weston, Umatilla County, Oregon.

A137—William Henry McClure. Born on January 16, 1837 in Pulaski County, Kentucky and died on January 10, 1914 in Colorado. Married Elizabeth

Trimble Families of America

Manley Cooley on June 25, 1857.

A138—John C. McClure. Born about 1840. Marriage to Hannah Horn in 1865.

A139—James E. McClure. Born on November 25, 1842 in Pulaski County, Kentucky. Married to Martha J. Warford in Centerville, Appanoose County, Iowa

A140—Cyrus McClure. Born about 1845 in Kentucky.

A60—Hugh Rutan McClure. Son of Samuel McClure and Nancy Rutan. (Fourth generation of James Trimble and Sarah Kersey.) Born on August 3, 1825 in Ohio and died in May 1848 in Grayson County, Texas. Married Rebecca Martillia Balch on December 13, 1842. Rebecca was born in 1825 and died on November 1, 1853.

The children of Hugh Rutan McClure and Martillia Balch:

A141—Joseph McClure. Born on March 10, 1844 and died February 22, 1921.

A142—Sarah Jane McClure. Born on March 7, 1846.

A72—Eglantine McClure. Daughter of John McClure and Jane "Jenny" McClure. (Fourth generation of James Trimble and Sarah Kersey.) Born about 1816 in Rockbridge County, Virginia. Married Addison J. Henderson on March 8, 1836 in Rockbridge County, Virginia. Addison was born 1810 and died on February 6, 1848.

The children of Addison J. Henderson and Eglantine McClure:

A143—Eglanatine Jane Henderson. Born in 1837.

A144—Hannah Jane Henderson. Born in 1837 in Rockbridge, Virginia.

A145—Elizabeth Henderson. Born in 1839.

A79—John Trimble. Son of James Trimble and Letitia Clark. (Fourth generation of James Trimble and Sarah Kersey.) Born on February 7, 1812, at Nashville, Tennessee and died on February 23, 1884 in Nashville, Tennessee. John was educated at Nashville University. In 1836, he was elected attorney general for the district which position he held for six years. In 1843 he was elected by the Whigs to the general assembly and in 1867 was elected to the Fortieth U.S. Congress but declined to be a candidate for reelection. He held many public offices during his career. He was a strong Unionist. (I (John Farley Trimble) have a copy of his letter to Governor Andrew Johnson in which he was strongly against Tennessee's secession from the Union.) Married Margaretta Houston Doak McEwen on September 7, 1835. She was born on August 1, 1816 in Tennessee and died on September 12, 1867 in Davidson County, Tennessee.

The children of John Trimble and Margaretta McEwen:

+ **A146—Mary Caroline Trimble.** Born on September 6, 1839 in Davidson County, Tennessee and died on October 24, 1911 in Nashville, Davidson County, Tennessee. Married James Miner Kercheval.

A147—Robert Trimble. Born in 1842 in Davidson County, Tennessee.

+ **A148—Letitia Clark Trimble.** Born on June 20, 1843 in Davidson County, Tennessee and died on April 6, 1928 in Nashville, Davidson County, Tennessee. Married Robert McPhail Smith.

A149—James Trimble. Born on September 27, 1845 in Davidson County, Tennessee and died on August 6, 1911 in Nashville, Davidson County, Tennessee. Married twice. Married first to Leticia Lindsley on October 26, 1876 in Davidson County, Tennessee. Married second to Marina Turner Woods on February 12, 1896.

A150—John Trimble Jr. Born in 1854 in Davidson County, Tennessee and died on July 17, 1899 in Nashville, Davidson County, Tennessee. Married Cornelia Ricketts on November 3, 1881 in St Louis, St Louis County, Missouri.

A80—Thomas Clark Trimble. Son of James Trimble and Letitia Clark. (Fourth generation of James Trimble and Sarah Kersey.) Born in 1813 in Nashville, Tennessee and died on November 20, 1883 in Lonoke, Arkansas. Buried Lonoke Cemetery. Thomas Clark Trimble was a lawyer Married Fannie Erwin Williams on May 23, 1837 at Davidson, Tennessee. Fannie was born in 1817 and died July 16, 1852. He lived at Holly Springs, Marshall County, Mississippi, until 1852. Thereafter in Sumner County, Tennessee.

The children of Thomas Clark Trimble and Fannie Erwin Williams:

+ **A151—Nathaniel Williams Trimble.** Born in 1842 and died in 1918. He married Jennie Robinson on March 5, 1875, at Montgomery, Alabama.

+ **A152—Thomas Clark Trimble II.** Born on July 25, 1847 and was still living around 1915.

A153—James Trimble.

A154—Penelope Trimble.

A155—John Trimble.

A156—Susan Trimble.

A157—William Trimble.

A158—Frank Trimble.

A81—Eliza Melvina Trimble. Daughter of James Trimble and Letitia Clark. (Fourth generation of James Trimble and Sarah Kersey.) Born on July 2,

Trimble Families of America

1819 in Tennessee and died on November 13, 1893 in Nashville, Davidson County, Tennessee. Married Adrian Van Sinderen Lindsley in 1838. Adrian was born on September 8, 1814 in Princeton, Mercer County, New Jersey and died on January 23, 1885 in Davidson, Davidson County, Tennessee.

The children of Adrian Van Sinderen Lindsley and Eliza Melvina Trimble:

A159—James Lindsley. Born on March 28, 1839 in Nashville, Davidson County, Tennessee and died April 3, 1893.

A160—Mary Margaret Lindsley. Born in 1841 in Tennessee and died in 1922 in Flushing, Queens County, New York.

A161—John Berrien Lindsley. Born on March 3, 1846 in Nashville, Davidson County, Tennessee and died on October 14, 1847 in Nashville, Davidson County, Tennessee.

A162—Adrian Van Sinderen Lindsley. Born on October 11, 1847 in Davidson, Davidson County, Tennessee and died in 1900 in Nashville, Davidson County, Tennessee.

A163—Philip Thomas Lindsley. Born on June 1849 in Davidson, Davidson County, Tennessee and died on October 17, 1928 in New York City, New York.

A164—Latitia Lindsley. Born on July 8, 1852 in Nashville, Davidson County, Tennessee and died on September 24, 1894 in Nashville, Davidson County, Tennessee.

A165—Louisa Reid Lindsley. Born in 1853 in Davidson, Davidson County, Tennessee.

+ **A166—Frank Lindsley.** Born on October 13, 1856 in Davidson, Davidson County, Tennessee and died in 1930 in Wilson County, Tennessee. Married twice.

A167—John Trimble Lindsley. Born on December 17, 1858 in Nashville, Davidson County, Tennessee and died in 1930 in Wilson County, Tennessee.

A168—Latitia Trimble Lindsley. Born about 1858 in Tennessee.

A169—Bessie Lindsley. Born on March 8, 1862 in Nashville, Davidson County, Tennessee Death on October 18, 1927 in Evanston, Cook County, Illinois.

A170—Webster Lindsley. Born about 1866 in Davidson, Davidson County, Tennessee and died in 1910 in Davidson County Asylum, Davidson County, Tennessee.

A90—James T. McLaughlin. Son of James McLaughlin and Sally Trimble. (Fourth generation of James Trimble and Sarah Kersey.) Born on July 28,

Trimble Families of America

1813 in Greenbrier County, Virginia and died in 1902 in Lynchburg, Virginia. Married Ann Ball Miller on September 10, 1844 in Pittsylvania, Virginia. She was born on November 28, 1818 in New London, Campbell County, Virginia and died on February 10, 1894 in Lynchburg, Campbell County, Virginia.

The children of James T. McLaughlin and Ann Ball Miller:

A171—Fannie Mclaughlin. Born in 1846 in Virginia.

A172—Sallie T. McLaughlin. Born in 1847 in Virginia.

+ **A173—James T. M. McLaughlin.** Born in September 1849 in Halifax, Virginia and died in 1918 in Lynchburg, Virginia. Married in Emma Guy in 1882 in Lynchburg, Virginia.

A174—Mary S. McLaughlin. Born in 1852 in Virginia.

A175—Cornelia D. McLaughlin. Born in 1853 in Virginia.

A176—Samuel M. McLaughlin. Born in 1855 in Virginia and died in 1888 in Virginia.

A177—William D. McLaughlin. Born in 1859 in Virginia and died in Kansas.

A91—Aaron Trimble. Son of James Trimble and Rebecca Stockton. (Fourth generation of James Trimble and Sarah Kersey.) Born in Kanawha County, West Virginia and married Corole Bowsman. They moved to Nicholas County, West Virginia, in 1878 settling on Muddlety Creek. He became a very prosperous farmer.

The children of Aaron Trimble and Carole Bowsman:

+ **A178—Elizabeth Trimble.** Born on July 13, 1860 and died on October 28, 1949. Married Arch Hill.

+ **A179—Nannie Trimble.** Married Richard McCoy of Nicholas County.

A96—Osman Trimble. Son of James Trimble and Rebecca Stockton. (Fourth generation of James Trimble and Sarah Kersey.) Born in 1813 in Rockbridge County, Virginia. He died on November 8, 1893, at Clifton (now Pratt), West Virginia. Married Jeanetta White on March 19, 1845. Osman was a brick-mason and had his own kiln at Cedar Grove, West Virginia. He migrated to Kanawha County in a covered wagon and bought a house at the mouth of Paint Creek near the C&O Bridge. He made the purchase from Van Hanna.

The children of Osman Trimble and Jeanetta White:

+ **A180—James William Trimble.** Born on January 7, 1851 and died on August 22, 1918. James married two times.

A181—Mary Trimble. Married Richard Smoot who had a general store at

Hansford, West Virginia. They had no children, but adopted a little girl named Queenie Meeks, but they changed her name to Kathleen.

A182—Lee D. Trimble. Born on June 30, 1861 and died on May 29, 1928. Married Alice Peyton, who was the first supervisor of the Old Sheltering Arms Hospital at Hansford, West Virginia. He was a brick and stone mason. They had no children.

+ **A183—Minneapolis Trimble.** Born on July 26, 1869 and died on January 5, 1942. Married on July 26, 1899, to John W. Walton, a C&O Railway employee.

A184—Elizabeth Trimble. Died young, near the age of ten years.

A185—Ida Trimble. Died in infancy.

A109—Lewis Campbell. Son of Isaac Campbell and Jane Steele. (Fourth generation of James Trimble and Sarah Kersey.) Born in 1813 in Monroe, Amherst County, Virginia and died in 1850 in Monroe, Amherst County, Virginia. Married Mary Ann Brown. Mary was born in 1821 in Kanawha County, West Virginia.

The children of Lewis Campbell and Mary Ann Brown:

+ **A186—Charles R. Campbell.** Born on 1837 in Monroe, Amherst County, Virginia.

A187—Henry B. Campbell. Born on 1840 in Monroe, Amherst County, Virginia and died in Alabama. Married Sarah Ellen Larmore in 1866 in DeKalb County, Alabama.

A188—Isaac Campbell. Born in 1847 in Virginia.

A189—Andrew L. Campbell. Born in 1850 in Monroe, Amherst County, Virginia.

A190—John C. Campbell. Born in 1853 in Virginia.

A114—Francis Evans 'Fannie' Montgomery. Daughter of John Patton Montgomery and Sophia Steele. (Fourth generation of James Trimble and Sarah Kersey.) Born about 1844 in Georgia. Married Thomas Howard Clements.

The children of Thomas Howard Clements and Francis Evens 'Fannie' Montgomery:

A191—S. Clements. Born about 1867 in Alabama.

A192—L. Clements. Born about 1869 in Alabama.

A193—F. Clements. Born about 1872 in Alabama.

A194—M. Clements. Born about 1873 in Alabama.

A195—A. Clements. Born about 1875 in Alabama.

A196—William Clements. Born about 1878 in Alabama.

A126—John W. Thompson. Son of William Thompson and Sally Caruthers. (Fourth generation of James Trimble and Sarah Kersey.) Born on October 10, 1816 in Rockbridge County, Virginia and died on August 16, 1886 in Lower James, Botetourt County, Virginia. Married Isabella Gilmore Lackey. Isabella was born on February 2, 1826 in Botetourt County, Virginia and died on May 7, 1877 in James River, Botetourt County, Virginia.

The children of John W. Thompson and Isabella Gilmore Lackey:

A197—William N. Thompson. Born on September 14, 1847 in Botetourt County, Virginia and died on December 13, 1868 in Botetourt County, Virginia.

+ **A198—Charles Frank Thompson.** Born on September 14, 1849 in Botetourt County, Virginia and died on December 15, 1899 in Sulphur, Murray County, Oklahoma. Married Martha Virginia "Jennie" Morgan.

A199—James Edgar Thompson. Born on April 6, 1852 in Botetourt County, Virginia and died on May 16, 1904 is buried in High Bridge Cemetery, Rockbridge County, Virginia.

A200—Nora J. Thompson. Born on August 9, 1856 in Botetourt County, Virginia and died on November 6, 1862 in Botetourt County, Virginia.

A201—Robert W. Thompson. Born on April 20, 1861 in Botetourt County, Virginia and died on February 1, 1930 in Botetourt County, Virginia.

A202—Kate Z. Thompson. Born on 1863 in Rocky Point, Botetourt County, Virginia and died on March 25, 1932 in Buchanan County, Virginia.

A203—Joseph Bell Thompson. Born on 1867 in Rocky Point, Botetourt County, Virginia and died on March 25, 1937 in Buchanan County, Virginia.

A133—John Paul Morton. Son of George Keeport Morton and Nancy Steele Caruthers. (Fourth generation of James Trimble and Sarah Kersey.) Born in 1840 in Mississippi. Married Ella T. Ella was born in 1848 in Tennessee.

The children of John Paul Morton and Ella T. Ella:

A204—Clara Morton. Born in 1870 in Friars Point, Coahoma County, Mississippi.

A205—Nellie Morton. Born in 1875 in Mississippi.

A146—Mary Caroline Trimble. Daughter of John Trimble and Margaretta McEwen. (Fifth generation of James Trimble and Sarah Kersey.) Born on September 6, 1839 in Davidson County, Tennessee and died on October 24, 1911 in Nashville, Davidson County, Tennessee. Married James Miner Kercheval on March 27, 1861. He was born on July 8, 1835 in Maury

County, Tennessee and died on January 3, 1911 in Tennessee.

The children of James Miner Kercheval and Mary Caroline Trimble:

A206—Mary K. Kercheval. Born in April 1863 in Tennessee.

A207—John T. Kercheval. Born in December 1866 in Tennessee.

A208—Maggie Kercheval. Born in May 1868 in Tennessee.

A209—James Miner Kercheval, Jr. Born in August 1870 in Tennessee.

A148—Letitia Clark Trimble. Daughter of John Trimble and Margaretta McEwen. (Fifth generation of James Trimble and Sarah Kersey.) Born on June 20, 1843 in Davidson County, Tennessee and died on April 6, 1928 in Nashville, Davidson County, Tennessee. Married Robert McPhail Smith. He was born on October 19, 1837 in Virginia and died on December 13, 1897.

The children of Robert McPhail Smith and Letitia Clark Trimble:

A210—Kenneth Ward-Smith.

A211—Robert T. Smith. Born about 1865 in Tennessee.

A212—William R. Smith. Born about 1868 in Tennessee.

A213—Henry Evert Smith. Born on September 25, 1870 in Nashville, Davidson, Tennessee.

A214—Henrietta Smith. Born about 1871 in Tennessee.

A215—Marian Smith. Born about 1875 in Tennessee.

A216—Hugh B. Smith. Born about 1877 in Tennessee.

A217—George McPhail Smith. Born on November 15, 1878 in Nashville, Davidson County, Tennessee.

A218—Edwin Kennedy Smith. Born about 1884 in Nashville, Davidson, Tennessee and died on April 1, 1963 in Mobile, Mobile, Alabama. Married Virginia Victoria Creary.

A151—Nathaniel Williams Trimble. Son of Thomas Clark Trimble and Fannie Erwin Williams. (Fifth generation of James Trimble and Sarah Kersey.) He was a lawyer. Born on January 4, 1842, at Holly Springs, Madison County, Mississippi and died on March 2, 1918, at Birmingham, Alabama. He was educated in the private schools of Tennessee and by tutors in his father's home and read law in the office of his uncle the Honorable John Trimble of Nashville Admitted to the bar in 1866 and practiced in Nashville, Montgomery and Birmingham. He was president of the Black Warrior Coal Company. While he was not an active church member, he was known for his Christian character, a love for all mankind and great generosity. His life was one of giving. He educated three boys in addition to his own six children and many in the legal profession of Birmingham owe much of their success to his advice and financial aid when beginning their practice. He married Jennie Robinson on March 5, 1875, at Montgomery, Alabama.

The children of Nathaniel Williams Trimble and Jennie Robinson:

+ **A219—Nathaniel Williams Trimble II.** Died in 1917 at Birmingham.

  A220—Duncan Dhu Trimble. In 1897 he received an A.B. degree at the University of Alabama. He also earned a law degree from the Law School of Lebanon, Tennessee and practiced at Birmingham, Alabama. He died in Fort Dodge, Iowa, where he had gone to live with his sister because of poor health, on October 30, 1931. He never married.

+ **A221—John Trimble.** In 1897 he received an A.B. degree at the University of Alabama. He was captain of the Third Alabama Infantry Volunteers in the Spanish-American War of 1898. He received a law degree from the University of Virginia and practiced in Birmingham, Alabama. He married Dorothy Probandt of San Angelo, Texas. His will was recorded in Atlanta, Georgia, on June 27, 1962.

  A222—Ella Dunlop Trimble. A graduate of Livingston Normal School, Livingston, Alabama, she was a portrait painter and studied art at the Corcoran Art Gallery in Washington, D.C. In New York, she studied under William Chase and studied in Rome, Italy. Ella married the Reverend Pomeroy Hickock Hartman of Lyons, New York. She died on January 15, 1933, at Horseheads, New York. They had no children.

+ **A223—Mary Erwin Trimble.** Married Dr. Howard J. Shore of Winston-Salem, North Carolina.

  A224—Jennie de Nouville Trimble. From Salem College in Winston-Salem, North Carolina, she received an A.B. degree. She was considered a beauty and belle of Alabama, spending most of her life in Birmingham. She never married and died on December 5, 1925, at Birmingham.

A152—Thomas Clark Trimble II. Son of Thomas Clark Trimble and Fannie Erwin Williams. (Fifth generation of James Trimble and Sarah Kersey.) Born on July 25, 1847, in Holly Springs, Mississippi. Married Sally (Sarah) Chapline. They moved to Lonoke County, Arkansas. He was judge of the Seventeenth Judicial Circuit Court and a law partner of U.S. Senator Joseph T. Robinson.

The children of Thomas Clark Trimble II and Sally (Sarah) Chapline:

+ **A225—Thomas Clark Trimble III.** Born on August 27, 1878. He married Elsie Walls on June 5, 1915.

  A226—Mattie Eleanor Trimble.

A227—Nellie Chapline Trimble.

A228—Bessie May Trimble. (Twin.)

A229—Robert Lee Trimble. (Twin.)

A230—Wilhelmia Trimble. Born in 1877 and died in 1904 at Lonoke, Arkansas. married William Witherspoon McCrary. They had one child, W. W. McCrary, Jr., born in 1904.

A231—George Trimble.

A232—Fannie Trimble.

A166—Frank Lindsley. Son of Adrian Van Sinderen Lindsley and Eliza Melvina Trimble. (Fifth generation of James Trimble and Sarah Kersey.) Born on October 13, 1856 in Davidson, Davidson County, Tennessee and died in 1930 in Wilson County, Tennessee. Married twice. Married first to Lucy Bruton on October 13, 1880 in Tennessee. Lucy was born in 1859 in Cincinnati, Hamilton County, Ohio and died in May 1899 in Lebanon, Wilson County, Tennessee Married second to Virginia ——— in 1916 in Wilson County, Tennessee. Virginia was born in 1898.

The children of Frank Lindsley and Lucy Bruton:

A233—Eliza Van Lindsley. Born in 1883 in Tennessee.

A234—Lucy B. Lindsley. Born in November 1884 in Tennessee.

A235—James Trimble Lindsley. Born on November 3, 1886 in Tennessee and died in July 1981 in Nashville, Davidson County, Tennessee.

A236—Alice Lindsley. Born in September 1889 in Tennessee.

A237—Mae Lindsley. Born on September 23, 1890 in Lebanon, Wilson County, Tennessee and died on March 6, 1925 in Nashville, Davidson County, Tennessee.

A238—Mary Lindsley. Born in September 1891 in Tennessee.

A239—Laetitia Lindsley. Born in August 1893 in Lebanon, Wilson County, Tennessee.

A240—Frank Lindsley Jr. Born in September 1895 in Lebanon, Wilson County, Tennessee.

A241—Halbert Lindsley. Born on September 19, 1896 in Tennessee and died on February 3, 1974 in Los Angeles, Los Angeles County, California.

A242—Albert Lindsley. Born on September 1897 in Wilson County, Tennessee and died in 1974.

A243—Emily Lindsley. Born in May 1899 in Wilson County, Tennessee and died on November 18, 1983 in Maysville, Mason County, Kentucky.

The children of Frank and Virginia Lindsley:

A244—Daniel Lindsley. Born in 1922 and died in 2010.

A173—James T. M. McLaughlin. Son of James T. McLaughlin and Ann Ball Miller. (Fifth generation of James Trimble and Sarah Kersey.) Born in September 1849 in Halifax, Virginia and died in 1918 in Lynchburg, Virginia. Married Emma Guy in 1882 in Lynchburg, Virginia. She was born in 1858 in Virginia and died 1891 in Savannah, Georgia.

The children of James T. M. McLaughlin and Emma Guy:

+ **A245—Annie McLaughlin.** Born on November 3, 1883 in Lynchburg, Virginia and died on November 10, 1956 in Charleston, Charleston County, South Carolina. Married William James Megginson.

+ **A246—Guy McLaughlin.** Born in March 1885 in Lynchburg, Virginia and died in 1959 in Roanoke, Virginia. Married Mary Eleanor Cousins. In 1915 was a member of naval aviator's blue jackets in Pensacola, Escambia County, Florida and in 1919 was an assistant supervisor at Navy flight school in San Diego, California. He was with second group that began training on March 21, 1917.

A247—Paul McLaughlin. Born about 1889 in Georgia and died in 1892 in Lynchburg, Virginia.

A248—John McLaughlin. Born about 1890 in Georgia and died on May 31, 1892 in Lynchburg, Virginia.

A178—Elizabeth Trimble. Daughter of Aaron Trimble and Corole Bowsman. (Fifth generation of James Trimble and Sarah Kersey.) Born on July 13, 1860 and died October 28, 1949. Married Arch Hill. He was born on April 8, 1867 and died on February 18, 1944. They lived on Muddlety Creek in Nicholas County, West Virginia.

The children of Arch Hill and Elizabeth Trimble:

A249—Meredith Hill. Born on February 25, 1890 and died in March 1970. He married Beulah Register and was a druggist in the state of Georgia.

Children: Meredith, Jr. and Joyce.

+ **A250—William Hill.** A farmer in Nicholas County, he died in 1970.

+ **A251—Anna Hill.** Born in January 1892. Married J. Frank Been and lives in Florida.

A252—Corile Hill. A prominent educator in the public-school system of West Virginia. She received an A.B. degree from Marshall University and a master's degree from West Virginia University. She retired as subject supervisor for Nicholas County Schools. At this time Corile is involved in community and church affairs being the superintendent of the Summersville

Trimble Families of America

Presbyterian Church School. Miss Hill is a highly respected, beautifully gracious lady of whom this author (John Farley Trimble) has known since early in life. My wife was a teacher in the Nicholas County Schools and Miss Hill was her supervisor, inspiration, and friend. Corile Hill was born on December 4, 1902 and never married. She was named after her grandmother Corole Bowsman Trimble although the spelling is different.

A179—Nannie Trimble. Daughter of Aaron Trimble and Corole Bowsman. (Fifth generation of James Trimble and Sarah Kersey.) Married Richard McCoy of Nicholas County, West Virginia

The children of Richard McCoy and Nannie Trimble:
  A253—Virginia McCoy.
  A254—Irene McCoy.
  A255—Ernest McCoy.
  A256—Ruth McCoy.
  A257—Bernice McCoy.
  A258—Harry McCoy.
  A259—Delbert McCoy.
  A260—Blanche McCoy.

A180—James William Trimble. Son of Osman Trimble and Jeanetta White. (Fifth generation of James Trimble and Sarah Kersey.) Born on January 7, 1851 and died on August 22, 1918. James married two times. Married first to Louella Huddleston in 1873. Married second to James married Nannie Belle Miller on September 28, 1892. We quote one of his daughters, Mary Trimble Baughan, "James was a good father and loved his children. He was a quiet and gentle man. His word was good as gold. He was a stone and brick mason, plasterer. He made his own brick and many of the old brick buildings still standing in Montgomery, West Virginia, are from his kiln at Cedar Grove, West Virginia. He was an industrious man and left his children a vast estate in the town of Pratt, West Virginia."

The children of James William Trimble and Louella Huddleston:
  A261—Henrietta Lillian Trimble. Born on January 23, 1875 and died on January 10, 1950. Married Alford Robert Shaw on July 23, 1900. He was a mail clerk on the K&M Railway. She attended school in Alderson, West Virginia, was a teacher, artist, and did hand painted China and excellent needlework, was a member of the Episcopal church in Hansford and a charter member of the William Morris Chapter of the D.A.R.
  +A262—Samuel Joseph Trimble. Born on November 7, 1878. Married

106

Americus Adkins. He worked with his father as a brick mason. Samuel attended Marshall College in Huntington, West Virginia. He was a great hunter and fisherman. Samuel was a member of the Old Kanawha Baptist Church.

A263—Mary Sicily Trimble. Born on December 13, 1880 and died on October 29, 1962. Married James Edward Shields on October 26, 1904. They had no children. She attended Marshall College, Huntington, West Virginia, and she enjoyed entertaining her relatives and friends. Mary liked to knit and sew and did beautiful needlework. She and her husband were members of the Old Kanawha Baptist Church. She was a charter member of the William Morris Chapter of the D.A.R.

A264—A daughter. Born on April 15, 1881 and died on July 16, 1881 at three months old.

The children of James Trimble and Nannie Miller:

A265—James Archibald Trimble. Born on May 7, 1894. He was a twin, but his twin died in infancy. Married Lessie Jarrett. He is now deceased. James was a sign painter, plasterer, paperhanger, brick mason, and songwriter. He can play a little on most any musical instrument.

He served in the army in World War I. He is an outstanding athlete in swimming and loves animals. James is a member of the Calvary Episcopal Church in Montgomery, West Virginia and a member of the American Legion Post, No. 58, in Montgomery.

He lives now in the old home in Pratt where he was born.

A266—A twin. Born on May 7, 1894, who was the twin of James Archibald (le) and died in infancy.

A267—Mary Wilson Trimble. Married William Hansford Baughan on August 12, 1931. He was a clerk for the C&O Railway and later had his own insurance agency. He was the mayor of Pratt for twelve years and a member of the Old Kanawha Baptist Church.

Mary was a teacher and principal in the public schools. Prior to teaching, she worked as a clerk in a general store in Pratt and served at Gallagher, West Virginia, as postmaster and clerked for the C&O Railway for five years.

She is a 1928 graduate of East Bank High School, graduated from West Virginia Institute of Technology at Montgomery in 1943 with an A.B. degree. She is a member of the Calvary Episcopal Church in Montgomery.

We are gratefully indebted to Mary Wilson Trimble Baughan for the

Trimble Families of America

excellent genealogy of her Trimble family. Many hours and much work has been part of the assembling of this information.

A268—**Corinne Smoot Trimble.** Born on May 7, 1898 and died on October 16, 1966. Married Leslie Nugen, a painter for Carbide in South Charleston, West Virginia, on October 26, 1929. There were no children in this marriage. She prepared for teaching and was placed up Cabin Creek, West Virginia, but her father would not let her go. She later became a clerk in a general store in Pratt. She and her husband were members of the Calvary Episcopal Church in Montgomery, West Virginia. She had poor health.

+ A269—**Osman Allen Trimble.** Born on January 30, 1901. Married Virginia White on October 26, 1929.

A270—**Margaret Miller Trimble.** Born on May 22, 1903. Married Charles W. Jarrett on August 12, 1938. He is now deceased. There were no children in this marriage. Margaret received her A.B. degree from West Virginia Tech in 1944. She taught the first grade in the public schools of Kanawha County for 46 years. She is a member of the Delta Kappa Gamma Society, likes art and China painting, and is a member of the Calvary Episcopal Church.

+ A271—**Jeanetta Shields Trimble.** Born on March 27, 1909. Married George Edward Montgomery on January 15, 1927.

A183—**Minneapolis Trimble.** Son of Osman Trimble and Jeanetta White. (Fifth generation of James Trimble and Sarah Kersey.) Born on July 26, 1869 and died on January 5, 1942. Married on July 26, 1899, to John W. Walton, a C&O Railway employee.

The children of John W. Walton and Minneapolis Trimble:

A272—**Dorothy Musgrave Walton.** Married Ballard Smith of Newark, New Jersey and had a son, John Ballard.

A273—**John Trimble Walton.** Married Marion Louise Page. John was a C&O employee and had no children.

A186—**Henry B. Campbell.** Son of Lewis Campbell and Mary Ann Brown. (Fifth generation of James Trimble and Sarah Kersey.) Born in 1840 in Monroe, Amherst County, Virginia and died in Alabama. Married Sarah Ellen Larmore in 1866 in DeKalb County, Alabama. Sarah was born in 1846 in Fort Payne, De Kalb County, Alabama and died in 1889 in Fort Payne, De Kalb, Alabama.

The children of Henry B. Campbell and Sarah Ellen Larmore:

+ A274—**Mary Nowlin Campbell.** Born on January 1867 in Fort Payne, De

Kalb, Alabama and died in Texas. Married Reuben O. Chitwood in 1882.

A275–Emma M. Campbell. Born in October 1868 in DeKalb County, Alabama and died on September 11, 1929 in Fort Payne, De Kalb County, Alabama.

A276–Laura L. Campbell. Born in 1870 in Fort Payne, DeKalb County, Alabama and died in 1873 in Fort Payne, DeKalb County, Alabama.

A277–Florence Campbell. Born in 1874 in Fort Payne, DeKalb County, Alabama.

A278–Charles O. V. Campbell. Born in 1876 in Fort Payne, DeKalb County, Alabama.

A279–John H. Campbell. Born in 1878 in Fort Payne, DeKalb County, Alabama.

A280–David L. Campbell. Born in 1880 in Fort Payne, DeKalb County, Alabama.

A281–Emma M. Campbell. Born in 1885 in Fort Payne, DeKalb County, Alabama and died in Fort Payne, DeKalb County, Alabama.

A198–Charles Frank Thompson. Son of John W. Thompson and Isabella Gilmore Lackey. (Fifth generation of James Trimble and Sarah Kersey.) Born on September 14, 1849 in Botetourt County, Virginia and died on December 15, 1899 in Sulphur, Murray County, Oklahoma. Married Martha Virginia "Jennie" Morgan. Martha was born on March 20, 1848 in Rockbridge County, Virginia and died on April 23, 1916 in Collin County, Texas.

The children of Charles Frank Thompson and Martha Virginia "Jennie" Morgan:

A282–Charles Belle Thompson. Born on January 15, 1875 in Virginia and died on June 14, 1948 in Sulpher, Murray County, Oklahoma.

+ **A283–George Morgan Thompson.** Born on September 28, 1876 in Botetourt County, Virginia and died on February 17, 1955 in Coalgate, Coal County, Oklahoma. Married Cora Olive Miller.

A284–Mary V. Thompson. Born in 1878 in Botetourt County, Virginia and died in 1952 in McKinney, Collin County, Texas.

A285–Beula Thompson. Born about December 1879 in Botetourt County, Virginia and died in 1972 in Sulphur, Murray County, Oklahoma.

A286–John S. Thompson. Born about 1885 in Texas and died on February 4, 1962 in Multnomah County, Oregon.

A287–Hugh Walter Thompson. Born on March 4, 1886 in Marietta, Love

County, Oklahoma Death on January 8, 1975 in Apache, Caddo County, Oklahoma.

A288—Josie E. Thompson. Born on January 31, 1891 in Texas and died on February 21, 1907 in Murray County, Oklahoma.

A219—Nathaniel Williams Trimble II. Son of Nathaniel Williams Trimble and Jennie Robinson. (Sixth generation of James Trimble and Sarah Kersey.) In 1895 he attended the University of Alabama. Nathaniel was deputy clerk of the U.S. Courts of Birmingham, Alabama. He was in the lumber business in Mexico City, Mexico and married Eleanor Offert of Montgomery, Alabama. He died in 1917 at Birmingham. They had two children who died in infancy.

A221—John Trimble. Son of Nathaniel Williams Trimble and Jennie Robinson. (Sixth generation of James Trimble and Sarah Kersey.) In 1897 he received an A.B. degree at the University of Alabama. He was captain of the Third Alabama Infantry Volunteers in the Spanish-American War of 1898. He received a law degree from the University of Virginia and practiced in Birmingham, Alabama. He married Dorothy Probandt of San Angelo, Texas. His will was recorded in Atlanta, Georgia, on June 27, 1962.

The child of John Trimble and Dorothy Probandt:

+ **A289—John Felix Trimble.** Born on October 25, 1926. Married Peggy Ann Boyette.

An infant daughter who died early.

A223—Mary Erwin Trimble. Daughter of Nathaniel William Trimble and Jennie Robinson. (Sixth generation of James Trimble and Sarah Kersey.) She received an A.B. degree from Salem College, Winston-Salem, North Carolina, a M.S. degree in piano at Salem College and a degree in voice from Daisy Rowley Music Studio at Birmingham, Alabama. She studied voice culture in Dresden, Germany and married Dr. Howard J. Shore of Winston-Salem, North Carolina.

The child of Dr. Howard J. Shore and Mary Erwin Trimble:

A290—Mary Trimble Shore. Daughter of Dr. Howard J. and Mary Erwin Trimble.

A225—Thomas Clark Trimble III. Son of Thomas Clark Trimble II and Sally (Sarah) Chapline. (Sixth generation of James Trimble and Sarah Kersey.) Born on August 27, 1878. He married Elsie Walls on June 5, 1915. In 1897 he attended the University of Arkansas and practiced law in the firm of Trimble, Robinson, Trimble with his father and U.S. Senator Joseph T.

Robinson, who was also the Democratic candidate for vice-president in 1928.

The children of Thomas Clark Trimble III and Elsie Walls:

A291—Thomas Clark Trimble IV.

A292—Elizabeth Jane Trimble.

A293—Walls Trimble. Attorney in Little Rock, Arkansas.

A294—Molly Ann Trimble.

A295—Susan Trimble.

A245—Annie McLaughlin. Daughter of James T. M. McLaughlin and Emma Guy. (Sixth generation of James Trimble and Sarah Kersey.) Born on November 3, 1883 in Lynchburg, Virginia and died on November 10, 1956 in Charleston, Charleston County, South Carolina. Married William James Megginson. He was born on January 13, 1884 in Lynchburg, Campbell, Virginia and died on September 2, 1954 in Charleston, South Carolina.

The children of William James Megginson and Annie McLaughlin Megginson:

A296—William James Megginson Jr. Born on February 25, 1910 in Guilford, North Carolina and died on March 16, 1958. Married Ina "Eagle" Smith. They had one child.

A297—Guy Trimble Megginson. Born in 1912 in Lynchburg, Virginia and died on September 2, 1912 in Lynchburg city, Virginia.

+ **A298—Emma Guy Megginson.** Born on July 24, 1914 in Lynchburg, Virginia and died on March 3, 2011 in Johns Island, Charleston, South Carolina. Married Howard Arthur Felder.

A299—Francis Lewis Megginson. Born on July 12, 1916 in Virginia. and died in October 1976. Married and had two children.

A246—Guy McLaughlin. Son of James T. M. McLaughlin and Emma Guy. (Sixth generation of James Trimble and Sarah Kersey.) Born in March 1885 in Lynchburg, Virginia and died in 1959 in Roanoke, Virginia. Married Mary Eleanor Cousins. She was born in June 1885 in Staunton, Halifax, Virginia and died on July 9, 1963 in Roanoke, Virginia. In 1915 was a member of naval aviator Bluejackets in Pensacola, Escambia County, Florida and in 1919 was an assistant supervisor at Navy flight school in San Diego, California. He was with second group that began training on March 21, 1917.

The children of Guy McLaughlin and Mary Eleanor Cousins:

A300—Guy McLaughlin. Born on December 14, 1915 in South Boston, Halifax County, Virginia and died on September 22, 1987 in Lancaster, Lancaster, Pennsylvania. Married Lucy Clark Staples. They have two children.

Trimble Families of America

A301—Hannah Lacy Mclaughlin. Born on August 8, 1918 in Virginia and died on October 23, 1975 in Roanoke, Roanoke, Virginia. Married Harry Figgatt Carper.

A302—Mary Miller Mclaughlin. Born on November 19, 1922 in south Boston, Halifax County, Virginia and died on December 10, 2005 in Harrisburg, Dauphin, Pennsylvania. Married Hank Withers.

A250—William Hill. A farmer in Nicholas County, he died in 1970.

The children of William Hill:

A303—James Hill.

A304—Paul Hill.

A305—Eugene Hill.

A306—Ruth Hill.

A307—William Hill.

A251—Anna Hill. Born in January 1892. Married J. Frank Been and lives in Florida.

The children of Anna Hill:

A308—Eulace Hill. Married first a Mr. Rowan and second a Mr. Rose.

A262—Samuel Joseph Trimble. Son of James William Trimble and Louella Huddleston. (Sixth generation of James Trimble and Sarah Kersey.) Born on November 7, 1878. Married Americus Adkins. He worked with his father as a brick mason. Samuel attended Marshall College in Huntington, West Virginia. He was a great hunter and fisher. Samuel was a member of the Old Kanawha Baptist Church.

The children of Samuel Joseph Trimble and Americus Adkins:

A309—Mildred Trimble. Married Frank Barkus. They have two children and two grandsons.

A310—Maxine Trimble. She is single.

A269—Osman Allen Trimble. Son of James William Trimble and Louella Huddleston. (Sixth generation of James Trimble and Sarah Kersey.) Born on January 30, 1901. Married Virginia White on October 26, 1929. He attended Morris Harvey College in Barboursville, West Virginia, where he played football. He worked in 1917 for the express on a Paint Creek passenger train and later was a fireman for the C&O. Still later, he became an engineer and retired in 1970 after serving for fifty-two years.

The children of Osman Allen Trimble and Virginia White:

A311—James MacDonald Trimble. He lives in Mexico.

A312—George David Trimble. He is a professor of English in a college.

+ **A313—Susan Beth Trimble.** A student at West Virginia Tech in Montgomery. Osman Allen Trimble has two grandsons: Kurt Holden and Stephen Carl. This entire family belongs to the Calvary Episcopal Church.

A271—Jeanetta Shields Trimble. Daughter of James William Trimble and Louella Huddleston. (Sixth generation of James Trimble and Sarah Kersey.) Born on March 27, 1909. Married George Edward Montgomery on January 15, 1927. He was the grandson of James W. Montgomery, founder of the town of Montgomery, West Virginia. They have one son. Jeanetta is a graduate of West Virginia Tech in Montgomery, received her A.B. degree in 1944. She is an outstanding athlete in swimming and is an artist, does China painting and sewing. She is in her forty-fifth year of teaching and is at the present at Pratt Elementary.

Jeanetta belongs to the Delta Kappa Gamma Society and was a C.A.R. in the William Morris Chapter of the D.A.R.

The child of George Edward Montgomery and Jeanetta Shields Trimble:

A314—George Edward Montgomery, Jr. Born on November 6, 1947. He graduated from West Virginia University in 1968 and served in Vietnam as an observer and received an appointment as first lieutenant. For outstanding achievements, he was awarded three Bronze Star Medals, the Distinguished Flying Cross, and the Army Commendations Medal.

A274—Mary Nowlin Campbell. Daughter of Henry B. Campbell and Sarah Ellen Larmore. (Sixth generation of James Trimble and Sarah Kersey.) Born in January 1867 in Fort Payne, De Kalb, Alabama and died in Texas. Married Reuben O. Chitwood in 1882. He was born in July 1866 in DeKalb County, Alabama and died in Texas.

The children of Reuben O. Chitwood and Mary Nowlin Campbell:

A315—Luther P Chitwood. Born in 1884 in Alabama. Married Krysta Chitwood.

+ **A316—Oscar C. Chitwood.** Born in June 1886 in Texas. Married Georgia O.

A317—Hugh Chitwood. Born in 1888 in Texas and died 1888 in Texas.

A318—Joe Chitwood. Born in August 1889 in Alabama. Married Cluma. She was born about 1899.

A319—Charles Madison Chitwood. Born on February 28, 1895 in Bosque County, Texas and died on January 2, 1929 in Temple, Texas. Married Mary

Nola Flinn. She was born in May 1898 in Nolan, Nolan County, Texas and died in May 1995 in Colorado Springs, Colorado.

A283—George Morgan Thompson. Son of Charles Frank Thompson and Martha Virginia "Jennie" Morgan. (Sixth generation of James Trimble and Sarah Kersey.) Born on September 28, 1876 in Botetourt County, Virginia and died on February 17, 1955 in Coalgate, Coal County, Oklahoma. Married Cora Olive Miller. She was born on December 4, 1879 in Miller County, Missouri and died on June 6, 1965 in Coalgate, Coal County, Oklahoma.

The children of George Morgan Thompson and Cora Olive Miller:

A320—Otto Franklin Thompson. Born on January 14, 1904 in Coalgate, Coal County, Oklahoma and died on March 4, 1975 in Oklahoma City, Oklahoma County, Oklahoma. Married Helen Wheeler Hughes. She was born on August 4, 1906 in Coalgate, Coal County, Oklahoma and died on October 18, 1991 in Oklahoma City, Oklahoma County, Oklahoma.

A321—Charles Thompson. Born on July 11, 1906 in Coalgate, Coal County, Oklahoma and died on July 1, 1916 in Coalgate, Coal County, Oklahoma.

A322—Gladys Alene Thompson. Born on September 10, 1909 in Coalgate, Coal County, Oklahoma and died on August 8, 2002 in Oklahoma City, Oklahoma County, Oklahoma.

A289—John Felix Trimble. Son of John Trimble and Dorothy Probandt. (Seventh generation of James Trimble and Sarah Kersey.) Born on October 25, 1926. He is a psychologist and writer. Married on April 20, 1946, to Peggy Ann Boyette of Charlotte, North Carolina. Mrs. Trimble is assistant controller with the Evening Star Newspaper Company of Washington, D.C.

The children of John Felix Trimble and Peggy Ann Boyette:

A323—John Robert Trimble. Born on February 19, 1948. Attended Virginia Polytechnic Institute, at Blacksburg, Virginia. He received a degree in economics in 1970. Married to Shirley Marie Harley on August 16, 1969, at the Campbell Memorial Presbyterian Church at Vinton, Virginia. Shirley has a degree in art from Radford College, Radford, Virginia. They have no children.

A324—Elizabeth Ann Trimble. Born on December 14, 1948. She attended the University of Virginia Extension School and is married to B. Glen Layfield. They were married on January 10, 1969, at the Marine Corps Chapel, Camp Lejeune, North Carolina. Mr. Layfield is a student at Control Data Institute, Arlington, Virginia. They have no children.

Trimble Families of America

A298—Emma Guy Megginson. Daughter of William James Megginson and Annie McLaughlin Megginson. (Seventh generation of James Trimble and Sarah Kersey.) Born on July 24, 1914 in Lynchburg, Virginia and died on March 3, 2011 in Johns Island, Charleston, South Carolina. Married Howard Arthur Felder. He was born on August 12, 1913 in South Carolina and died on September 5, 1976 in Johns Island, Charleston, South Carolina.

The children of Howard Arthur Felder and Emma Guy Megginson:

A325—Alton Hayne Felder.

A326—Ellen Elizabeth Felder.

A327—unnamed Felder. Married Patricia.

A328—Howard Arthur Felder, Jr. Born on September 1, 1939 in South Carolina.

A329—James Norwood Felder. Born on May 3, 1943. Married Ann.

A313—Charles Madison Chitwood. Son of Reuben O. Chitwood and Mary Nowlin Campbell. (Seventh generation of James Trimble and Sarah Kersey.) Born on February 28, 1895 in Bosque County, Texas and died on January 2, 1929 in Temple, Texas. Married Mary Nola Flinn.

The children of Charles Madison Chitwood and Mary Nola Flinn:

A330—Infant Chitwood. Born and died in 1818.

A331—Juanita Charlene Chitwood. Born on April 15, 1920 in Sweetwater, Nolan County, Texas and died on April 3, 2001 in Colorado Springs, El Paso County, Colorado.

A332—Infant Chitwood. Born and died in 1923.

A316—Oscar C. Chitwood. Son of Reuben O. Chitwood and Mary Nowlin Campbell. (Seventh generation of James Trimble and Sarah Kersey.) Born in June 1886 in Texas. Married Georgia O. She was born in 1887 in Texas.

The child of Oscar C. Chitwood and Georgia O:

A333—Easter Chitwood. Born in 1909 in Texas.

B - John Trimble

John was one of the original five brothers. His birth date is unknown. Mary Moffitt and John Trimble were married about November 15, 1752 at Middle River, Augusta County, Virginia, just two miles from Churchville. Her maiden name was Mary Christian. She was the widow of John Moffitt and the mother of five children. The most renowned of which was Colonel George Moffitt, a Colonial and Revolutionary War soldier and one of the founders of Washington and Lee College at Lexington, Virginia.[23]

B1—John Trimble was the last white man to be massacred by the Native Americans in the Valley of Virginia. This occurred September 13, 1764. (A historical road marker of this event has been placed eight miles west of Staunton, Virginia and two miles east of Churchville.[24]

This was during the second Kerrs Creek Massacre. The Native Americans were led by a notorious half-breed named Dickerson. They captured alive all his horses and cattle and burned and stripped his lands. The Native Americans took prisoner his son, James, then a youth of eleven and Mrs. Kitty Moffitt Estill, James's half-sister who was awaiting the birth of her child. The Native Americans, after joining two additional divisions of their party, retreated for five days and nights into the mountains. On the morning after the raid Colonel (then captain) George Moffitt was in pursuit of the enemy with twenty-five men. They had organized during the night.

Moffitt discovered the Native Americans on the morning of the fifth day in their camp on a spur of the Allegheny Mountains, near what is now White Sulphur Springs, West Virginia. During the pursuit Moffitt had nearly given up the endeavor after losing the Native Americans' trail. But one of the militia found a blue garter placed by Mrs. Estill on a bush. Upon uncovering the Native Americans' camp, Moffitt's men attacked, killing most Native Americans and wounding the rest except Dickerson who escaped.

A man named Russell was the only person in Moffitt's party to be wounded. He was carried on a litter back to Staunton. This same Russell, in the Battle of Point Pleasant, met and killed the half-breed Dickerson in hand-

---

[23] Place: Augusta Co., Virginia; Year: 1740; Page Number: 47

[24] Autobiography and Correspondence of Allen Trimble Governor of Ohio, by Allen Trimble, 1909. Page 3

to-hand combat.

The child of John Trimble and Mary Moffitt:

+ **B2–James Trimble.** Born on February 25, 1753 in Augusta County, Virginia and died on October 4, 1804. Married first, to Patsy McNair. Married, second, Jane Allen in Augusta County, Virginia.

B2–James Trimble. Son of John Trimble and Mary Moffitt. Born on February 25, 1753 and died on October 4, 1804. Married Patsy McNair at Augusta County, Virginia. Patsy died in 1774.

James married, second, Jane Allen in Augusta County, Virginia and they had seven sons and two daughters. Jane was born on March 15, 1755. She was the eldest daughter of James and Peggy Allen.

(In this author's (John Farley Trimble) opinion this James Trimble was the most outstanding of all the early Trimbles.) At an early age he was in the Battle of Point Pleasant. He was a Captain of Rifle Rangers in the Revolutionary War, being given lands in Kentucky, he led an immigration of nearly three hundred people from the Valley of Virginia westward into Kentucky, settling in the bluegrass region of now Lexington.[25]

We quote from the Days of War for Independence, 1774-1783:

There was no road, the trail being wide enough for only one horse, the emigrants went in single file, forming a line of nearly a mile long. At the eastern base of Clinch Mountain there was the first indication of Native Americans prowling near them. Clinch River was swollen by recent rains, and in crossing it Mrs. Trimble and her children came near losing their lives. A Mrs. Ervin carried two Negro children in a wallet thrown across her horse and these were washed off by the current but rescued by a Mr. Wilson.

A party of eight horsemen overtook the emigrants at Clinch River and preceded them on the route. Their bodies were found next day on the trail, killed by Native Americans. Measles broke out, and there was scarcely a family in the train that had not a patient to nurse but notwithstanding their exposure to rain during several days, no death occurred. They finally reached their destination.

Through hard work James and his sons, with their slaves, hued out of that wilderness one of the finest plantations in Kentucky. He built the first home in Kentucky out of sawn lumber.

---

[25] Sons of the American Revolution Membership Applications, 1889-1970. Louisville, Kentucky: National Society of the Sons of the American Revolution. Microfilm, 508 rolls.

Trimble Families of America

James possessed great courage and foresight and felt by his hard work and endeavor he could accomplish the goal of educating his several children. To their lives he wanted to contribute guidance for them and the welfare of this new nation.

On one of his trips to Tidewater Virginia to purchase more slaves, he spent a few days at the home of a friend on a Virginia plantation. During his visit there he saw the young affluent whites growing up in idleness, which was in his opinion, the laying of the groundwork for a decadent society. The moral issue of slavery was not only an injustice to the black man but more injurious to the slave owners themselves. This situation bore such an impact on his thinking that upon returning home he called a meeting of his slaves. He promised then that five years from that day, when his plantation was completed, he would then give them their freedom.

The Kentucky laws, at that time, allowed no man to free his slaves. Henry Clay, a young Kentucky lawyer and friend of James Trimble, petitioned the legislature of Kentucky to allow James to free his slaves. This petition was three times denied.

James Trimble concerned and more determined to remedy this slave issue decided to sell his Kentucky lands and move to the wilderness of Ohio, a free state. Here he would undertake to rebuild in order that his slaves could be freed.

He took a trip into Ohio and contacted his friend General Duncan MacArthur (the forebearer of General Douglas MacArthur). They went to an area near Hillsboro, Highland County, Ohio, and bought 6,000 acres of land. The deed was recorded on December 21, 1782. MacArthur helped him survey the land and James soon began building his new home.

But on one of his frequent trips back home to Kentucky he contracted the fever and died without seeing his dream completed. However, his sons, the oldest of which was Allen, did complete the exodus from Kentucky to Ohio. He freed the slaves even though he and his mother Jane Allen Trimble opposed the freedom for the slaves and the move to Ohio.

The Kentucky Legislature on the fourth attempt by Henry Clay gave permission for James Trimble to free his slaves. This was the first for Kentucky. But by this time James had already decided to make the move to Ohio.

The ideals and goals that James had wanted for his family and for the new nation as well did become a reality though he died before they materialized. His son, Allen, served Ohio as governor for two terms and William was U.S.

Senator, etc.

The children of James Trimble and Patsy McNair:

B3—Hanna Trimble. Born on May 22, 1774. Married Hugh Allen, nephew of James second wife Jane Allen.

The children of James Trimble and Jane Allen:

B4—John Allen Trimble. Born on January 9, 1780 was accidentally killed in childhood. He was named for his mother's brother who was killed at Grant's Defeat in the Battle of Fort Duquesne.

From the *Autobiography and Correspondence of Allen Trimble Governor of Ohio.* Allen wrote "We were in the garden with father and mother, whilst they were looking at the vegetables and flowers, we two were at play, running around the squares upon the walks. I was behind, not being able to keep up and he, running at his ease, turned his head to see how near I was. As he resumed his former movement, he came in contact with mother, who was crossing the walk before him. He carried a stick in his mouth which was very sharp at one end. The other, which was blunt, struck against mother's arm, as she stooped to examine a flower. The sad result -was a wound in the throat which caused his death."[26]

+ **B5—Hugh Allen Trimble.** Born on November 24, 1783, died on February 3, 1870. Married Margaret McDowell.

+ **B6—William Allen Trimble.** Born on April 4, 1786, died on December 12, 1821.

B7—James Allen Trimble. Born on February 25, 1788, in Woodford County, Kentucky. Died on April 14, 1866, at Hillsboro, Ohio. He married Ann Shields. They had no children.

+ **B8—Margaret Trimble.** Born on November 9, 1790.

B9—Cary Allen Trimble. Born on November 24, 1792, in Woodford County, Kentucky, died on September 10, 1821, at Hillsboro, Ohio. He was unmarried.

B10—Mary Trimble. Born on September 15, 1795, at Woodford County, Kentucky and died on August 10, 1836, at Hillsboro, Ohio. Mary rode with her mother, Jane, by horseback to Augusta County, Virginia, where she met and married John M. Nelson. They lived in Hillsboro, Highland County, Ohio. It seems Jane Allen Trimble wanted her daughters to marry men of

---

[26] Autobiography and Correspondence of Allen Trimble Governor of Ohio Reprinted from, The "Old Northwest" Genealogical Society, 1909.

Trimble Families of America

B - John Trimble

the Scotts-Irish descent.

B11—Cyrus W. Trimble. Born on December 30, 1797, in Woodford County, Kentucky and died on October 5, 1822. He was unmarried.

+ **B12—John A. Trimble.** Born on May 31, 1801, died in 1885.

B5—Hugh Allen Trimble. Son of James Trimble and Jane Allen (Third generation of John Trimble and Mary Moffitt.) Hugh Allen Trimble was called by his middle name Allen, which we will use in this genealogy. He was named after his mother's uncle, Hugh Allen who was killed in the Battle of Point Pleasant. Born on November 24, 1783 and died on February 3, 1870. Allen was governor of the state of Ohio, he married Margaret McDowell, daughter of General Joseph McDowell of North Carolina. They were married in January 1806. She died on January 21, 1809, leaving two children: Joseph and Madison. On January 10, 1811, he married the second time to Rachel Woodrow, the daughter of Joshua and Elizabeth Woodrow. Their children were William, Henry, Gary Allen, and Eliza Jane.

Allen was the second eldest son of James and grandson of John, who was killed by Native Americans in Virginia in 1764. Allen was a baby of one year at the time his father moved to Kentucky and settled the wilderness near what is now Lexington, Kentucky. At this time Kentucky had become more populated as Allen was reaching his youth and his father's estate was quite extensive.

John Allen, Allen's older brother, was killed in an accident while playing when a child. This left Allen in the eldest son's place. Allen and his father agreed that the younger boys would be educated, and Allen would help with the work and running of this vast plantation, thus his education would come later.

Allen, having studied surveying, planned on entering this profession after the family was settled in Ohio, but due to his past infirmity, his friend General MacArthur advised him against this.

We quote from the Autobiography of Allen Trimble:

So, I immediately mentioned the subject to General MacArthur, who was with father for several days surveying his Scioto and Paint Creek lands. The General said he would not advise me to engage in the laborious business of surveying in the feeble condition of my health, as a mere boy. My constitution not apparently strong and, as he had learned, somewhat injured by over-exertion, he thought the exposure to which I would be subjected as a surveyor might operate somewhat injuriously in the end, rather than acting favorably

120

Trimble Families of America

B - John Trimble

to the renewal of my health. So, I took his advice for the present, at any rate.

The overexertion, referred to by him, occurred during the previous harvest. I was one of fifteen hands reaping wheat with the old-fashioned cradle-scythe. The day was excessively hot and warm. The wheat was heavy, and you must remember I was yet in my teens, and not a first-rate reaper, and it required great exertion to keep up with the company, all of whom were first rate reapers, myself being the exception. But I could bind more rapidly than any man in the big field and took the lead in the last trial through the long rows of shocks of wheat and in the end, I won the race, ran to a cool spring near the "Outcome," and foolishly drank a hearty draught of cold water.

Not being very robust, I was taken immediately with cramps of the stomach and carried to the house speechless. But after bathing and being rubbed for some time, I recovered my speech, but my system was severely dazed, and I was threatened debility.

I recovered slowly, but when father started to Ohio, I was able to ride thirty miles each day and thus continued to improve and, on our return, could ride forty miles in a day without much difficulty.

As early Kentucky, in the bluegrass section, raised abundant quantities of corn, much was made into whiskey, hence the start of Kentucky's great whiskey distillery industry. Hogs were raised in massive numbers, fattened on this corn supply and sold rather cheaply in the state. Allen, a teenager, took a large drove of hogs, with the help of slaves and began a hog drive from Kentucky up to Richmond, Virginia. This was quite an accomplishment to drive these hogs through wilderness country, a journey of nearly six hundred miles. He went south through the Cumberland Gap in Tennessee, this being the same route his father used in the migration to Kentucky from Virginia.

After great hardships Allen reached Richmond and sold his hogs at a good profit. Upon his return home to Kentucky, he was determined to repeat this venture the coming year. As the year passed and time for the journey was nearing, he decided to find a shorter route and pioneered the passage up the Kanawha River in West Virginia to the mouth of Gauley River on to Greenbrier County and into Staunton, Virginia. Several sources of historical records tell of the streets of Staunton being lined with people cheering his tremendous success.

At the time of his father's untimely death in 1804, the year before the family was to move to Ohio, Allen at the age of nineteen found himself head

Trimble Families of America

of a family with new lands to settle. Some of their slaves chose to stay with the family, as free men, even though his father had freed all his slaves earlier.

We quote from the. Autobiography of Allen Trimble:

As before remarked, I concurred with mother upon the question of freeing the slaves and also removing to the North-western territory, but feeling it my duty to submit to the superior judgment of my father, I had concluded that, if on viewing the new country, I could see my prospect or any prospect of making a comfortable living, I would embrace it at once, for, having studied surveying at our home school, I concluded to seek employment as a Deputy-surveyor, under General Massie or General MacArthur.

With the family's move to Ohio, Allen was advised considerably by his father's friend General Duncan MacArthur. Allen devoted his next few years to getting the family and lands all settled and the younger brothers and sisters educated. Allen's son, Gary A. Trimble, married Mary, the daughter of General MacArthur. Allen and the general became very close friends and in the War of 1812. Allen rose to rank of general in the Ohio Militia under General Harrison, who after the war persuaded Allen to run for public office. Thus, started his political career.

Allen was one of the early governors of Ohio. He was appointed governor in 1820 to fill a vacancy. He was elected governor in 1826, then reelected in 1828. He is noted for forming the public-school system of Ohio and securing the canal system on which he continued working after his term as governor. It was this canal system that opened Ohio to the trade markets of the East making Ohio one of our early leading states.

Allen was a devout Methodist stemming from the influence of the services held in his home by the frontier circuit-rider preachers. In Virginia the Trimbles were Presbyterians but on the frontier, one attended the church near enough for travel. Later in Ohio, Allen was the motivating force behind the founding of Ohio Wesleyan University. He was a staunch promoter of Methodism. Perhaps he would have gone farther in politics had it not been for his Methodistic views of Freemasonry. He was violently opposed to this because of the Methodist beliefs against secret organizations. (I have read correspondence of Allen's in which he denounces Freemasonry, which was also a strong force in America. Many of our presidents belonged to the Masonry starting with George Washington.)

Allen was outstanding and has been named one of the three leading early governors of Ohio. William McKinley listed Allen among these noted early governors. William was a United States senator from the state of Ohio.

Throughout the reading of Governor Allen Trimble's memoirs, one is aware of his high value of integrity, morality, and deep religious faith. He wrote of hearing his grandmother Trimble, widow of John, tell, "after the Native Americans had killed her husband and taken all the cattle, her family became hard-pressed for food, especially milk, next morning she heard a cow mooing at the gate. Going out she tried to drive the cow away, but she came back. Finally, Mrs. Trimble milked her then the cow did go away but came daily to furnish milk for the family until they were able to secure a cow of their own. The cow then left and was never seen again, and it did not belong to any neighbor in the vicinity. She said she is sure God sent this cow and the Governor says he doesn't doubt it."

On December 4, 1822, David Trimble wrote the following letter to the then General Allen Trimble.

Dear Sir:

I have thought much about the next President; I have listened attentively to others and said nothing myself; and I am now decidedly of opinion that if Ohio recommends Mr. Clay to the other states, as the proper person, he will be the President without doubt. If you come out for him Pennsylvania will be with you. This I formerly thought doubtful, but I am now perfectly satisfied in that respect. All depends upon Ohio, but it is especially necessary that she should express her mind by some mode that will leave no doubt of her intention. A state caucus, or something like that.

Think of this seriously, and if you do anything, the sooner the better. I have very many hopes that Maryland will be for us also. She is now in a quandary, and a firm and decisive step taken by Ohio, will probably induce her to follow.

The people of Maryland are most certainly with us; and their leading men will have to try to carry them over to any other man. I say all this upon much inquiry and mature reflection, and I repeat it, if Ohio comes out for Clay, he will be the President; if not, not. Our fate is in your hands. The knowing ones here think that South Carolina will finally be for Clay. The Virginias effect to believe that you will wait to know what Pennsylvania and New York will do, and then go with them.

This is not to be read to everyone, but you may in confidence show it to a few of Clay's friends.

I am, very respectfully, David Trimble.

Trimble Families of America

(At this time David Trimble and Henry Clay were U.S. congressman from the state of Kentucky.)

On November 19, 1835, Henry Clay sent the following letter to Allen Trimble.

Maysville, 19th, November 1835

Dear Sir: When I was at Frankfort, I spoke to Mr. Brown about the price of his 1000 Acres of land on Rattlesnake, which you mentioned to me. He asks three dollars per acre. Is it worth that? Would you advise the purchase at that? and be willing to take half? Is it well watered? How much is first rate?

Be pleased to write me, addressing me at Washington City. I am now on my way there. Your friend,

H. Clay

This family was probably most prominent of all the Trimble families in America. The sad part is that no male heirs lived in the twentieth century to carry on these notable traditions.

The author (John Farley Trimble) believes, having studied all manuscripts, that Jane Allen Trimble was the guiding influence in keeping the bloodline so closely interwoven as she made several trips back to the Valley of Virginia to find suitable mates for her children. In this author's (John Farley Trimble) opinion, the fact that there were no male heirs may have been the result of very selective marriages into the Scotts-Irish elite society often distant kinsmen. Perhaps the genes were so close was the reason that so many of their descendents either died young or had no offspring. As is evidenced in the David Trimble family of whom is descended half the Trimbles of today, they took in marriage frontier men and women of the locality in which they lived.

The children of Hugh Allen Trimble and Margaret McDowell:
+ **B13—Joseph McDowell Trimble.** Born on April 15, 1807.
+ **B14—James Madison Trimble.** Born on September 27, 1808.

The children of Hugh Allen Trimble and Rachel Woodrow:
+ **B15—William Henry Trimble.** Born on September 5, 1811.
+ **B16—Cary Allen Trimble.** Born on September 13, 1813.
+ **B17—Eliza Jane Trimble.** Born on August 24, 1816.

B6—William Allen Trimble. Son of James Trimble and Jane Allen. (Third generation of John Trimble and Mary Moffitt.) Born on April 4, 1786, died on December 12, 1821, in Washington, D.C. He was a U.S. senator from Ohio, one of the youngest men ever elected to the U.S. Senate but died during his first term at the age of thirty-five. He was unmarried. He died due to wounds received when he was Brevet Colonel in the War of 1812. William Allen was a brilliant lawyer, and some historians say that had he not died so early that he would have had a promising political future. His fellow Ohio senator was William Henry Harrison who later became president of the United States.

William was born within the limits of Woodford County, Kentucky. When a lad, he was attacked by the "white swelling," which occasioned extreme suffering. The skills of the ablest physicians in the country were exhausted in attempts to effect a cure. All their endeavors proving fruitless, it was seriously feared no relief was to be had except by amputation. In the end, however, he fell into the hands of a Native American doctor, who in a few months effected a radical cure.

To this circumstance of his life, William remarked that it was singular that gentlemen of much learning and science, who made the healing art their daily study, availing themselves of the improvements and discoveries of their predecessors, should have known so little of his disease and that a man illiterate, perhaps not able to read, should have had it so perfectly under his control. But, he said, the learned physicians are too much governed in their studies and practice by books, by rule, and fear to trust their own good common sense.

William attended Transylvania University in Kentucky after having finished his studies there he entered himself as a student of law in the office of his friend Judge Robert Trimble. He studied at the school of a Mr. Neif located at the Falls of the Schuylkill, near Philadelphia. Mr. Neif had been a disciple of the celebrated Pestalozzi and was then trying to introduce into this country his method of instruction. To enable him to make the experiment, many individuals of wealth and influence were active in giving him countenance and patronage. William Trimble was forcibly struck with the superiority of the system over all others of which he had any knowledge. The usual method appeared to him essentially defective in addressing itself almost exclusively to the memory, whereas the new one looked to reason and the judgment. He believed that lessons received through the process of reasoning were more likely to remain and to enlarge those powers and capacities which elevate man so much above the brute.

From Mr. Neif's school he proceeded to Litchfield, in Connecticut and

B - John Trimble

became a pupil in the law school of Judge Reeves. Thereafter, he returned to Highland County, Ohio, which he chose as his permanent residence because of numerous relations living there and a farm which he owned.

William was a national hero at the Battle of Lake Erie in the War of 1812. Here he received the wound which was to later cause his death. William was instrumental along with his brother Allen in the recruiting of troops in Ohio for this war. This man would probably have been the most distinguished of all the Trimbles had he not met his untimely death at the age of thirty-five.

In December 1819, William Trimble took his seat in the Senate and very soon gave promise of much future usefulness. Becoming a member of one of the most august bodies in the world, under such flattering circumstances, excited him to the highest pitch of industry. Having distinguished himself in the battles of his country and obtaining an imperishable name on the pages of history, he found a new field opened.

He sought to be well versed in all the subject matters he found pertinent in his new role of politics. To reach the accuracy desirable, he found no labor more profitable than that which was bestowed upon old records, journals, and public documents, though repulsive in appearance, rich as treasures of information.

For two sessions of Congress, he was in the public spotlight for his determined interest in the situations of his state. These included the public lands, internal improvements, and domestic manufactures, all of which were exciting topics at that time.

At length, however, nature yielded to the recurring shocks of the wound and on December 12, 1821, he expired, mourned by his friends and regretted by all. The Senate and House of Representatives attended the funeral, after passing resolutions lamenting his death and to wear crape for thirty days.

As evidence of the esteem in which Colonel Trimble was held at the time of his death by the legislature of Ohio, the following account is copied from the journals:

Whereas this General Assembly have been advised of the decease of the Honorable William A. Trimble, late a Senator in the Congress of the United States from this State, after a lingering illness, produced by a wound received in the service of his country, in the late war with Great Britain: and whereas this General Assembly are desirous to manifest their sorrow and regret for the loss of this distinguished citizen, and their high sense of his public services and private virtues: Therefore,

Resolved, unanimously, by the Senate and House of Representatives, that in evidence of the deep concern and sincere regret so justly felt for the decease of the Honorable William A. Trimble, late a Senator of the United States for the State of Ohio, the members of this Legislature will wear crape on the left arm, during the remainder of the present session.

This was adopted by both Houses.

The information concerning William A. Trimble has come from Biographical Sketches with Other Literary Remains of the Late Federal Judge, by Campbell.

B8—Margaret Trimble. Daughter of James Trimble and Jane Allen. (Third generation of John Trimble and Mary Moffitt.) Born on November 9, 1790, in Woodford County, Kentucky. She married James McCue of Augusta County, Virginia. Margaret and her mother, Jane, rode horses from Hillsboro, Ohio, to Augusta County where she met and married McCue. Jane felt there was no one of such proper breeding on the frontier lands as she wanted for her daughter's husband. So, she returned to Virginia in search of a proper gentleman for her daughter.

The children of James McCue and Margaret Trimble:

  B18—J. Marshall McCue. Born in 1816 and was a member of the Virginia Legislature during the war. From an old letter written by Marshall McCue in 1874, his mother was still living and was in her eighty-fourth year.

B12—John A. Trimble. Son of James Trimble and Jane Allen. (Third generation of John Trimble and Mary Moffitt.) Born on May 31, 1801, in Woodford County, Kentucky. He died on November 5, 1885, at New Vienna, Ohio. He married Lavina Boys, the daughter of Dr. and Mrs. William Boys of Hillsboro, Ohio. All of John's children were born at Hillsboro.

The children of John Trimble and Lavina Boys:

  B19—Jane St. Clair Trimble. Born in 1830 and died in 1839.

  B20—William Boys Trimble. Born in 1833 and died in 1837.

  B21—Mary Ella Trimble. Born in 1836 died 1860, unmarried.

  B22—Rosa Augusta Trimble. Born 1838 and died in 1839.

  B23—Cyrus Boys Trimble. Born in 1841 and died in 1867, unmarried.

  B24—John Alexander Trimble. Born in 1844 and died in 1868, unmarried.

  B25—Dr. Rodney Telfair Trimble. Born in 1846 and died in 1908. Married Emma H. Smith, daughter of Dr. Samuel W. Smith of Hillsboro, on December 15, 1897. They had no children.

  B26—Alice M. Trimble. Born in 1848, unmarried. Of eight children, John A.

Trimble Families of America

and Lavina B. Trimble had no grandchildren born to carry on their name.

B13—Joseph McDowell Trimble. Son of Hugh Allen Trimble and Margaret McDowell. (Fourth generation of John Trimble and Mary Moffitt.) Born in Woodford County, Kentucky, on April 15, 1807 and died in Columbus, Ohio. He graduated in 1828 from Ohio University at Athens. He was professor of mathematics at Augusta College in Kentucky until 1835 when he was ordained by the Methodist Episcopal church and was one of the shining lights of that order. He married on September 22, 1830, Sara Ann Pearson (Trimble) Starr, a niece of General Isaac Ridgeway Trimble. They had no children.

B14—James Madison Trimble. Son of Hugh Allen Trimble and Margaret McDowell. (Fourth generation of John Trimble and Mary Moffitt.) Born on September 27, 1808 and died on February 1, 1874. He was married in October 1830 to Mary Ann Smith of Hillsboro.

The children of James Trimble and Mary Ann Smith:

+ **B27—Sara Jane Trimble.** Born on September 17, 1831, died on June 19, 1879, married Robert Lilly.

+ **B28—John Allen Trimble.** Born on September 14, 1836 and died on March 17, 1897.

  B29—Joseph McDowell Trimble. Born on June 16, 1839, died on January 28, 1842.

  B30—James Smith Trimble. Born on April 21, 1843 and died on May 17, 1884, unmarried.

+ **B31—Margaret McDowell Trimble.** Born on September 15, 1846.

  B32—Charles William Trimble. Born on December 21, 1841. He was killed at the Second Battle of Bull Run of the Civil War on August 29, 1862, Seventy-third Regiment, Ohio Volunteer Infantry.

  B33—George Smith Trimble. Born on May 4, 1847 and died on March 20, 1879, unmarried.

B15—William Henry Trimble. Son of Hugh Allen Trimble and Rachel Woodrow. (Fourth generation of John Trimble and Mary Moffitt.) Born on September 5, 1811 and died on February 7, 1883. He married Martha Hale, daughter of Ebenezer and Eunice Hale of Zanesville, Ohio.

The children of William Henry and Martha Hale Trimble:

  B34—Catherine B. Trimble. Born on July 31, 1849, died July 9, 1883, unmarried.

  B35—William Trimble. Born on July 18, 1851 and died on August 18, 1853.

B36—Clarence Trimble. Born on August 11, 1854 (twin) and died on August 20, 1854.

B37—Allen Trimble. Born on August 11, 1854 (twin) and died on July 15, 1875, unmarried.

B38—Ebenezer Trimble. Born on October 9, 1856 and died on March 13, 1876, unmarried.

B16—Cary Allen Trimble. Son of Hugh Allen Trimble and Rachel Woodrow. (Fourth generation of John Trimble and Mary Moffitt.) Born on September 13, 1813 and died on May 4, 1887. Gary was a congressman and a physician. He served as a member of the House of Representatives as a Republican from the state of Ohio from 1859 to 1863. He married two times. Married first to Mary MacArthur, the second daughter of General Duncan MacArthur of Chillicothe. Married second to Anna Porter Thompson on November 12, 1844. Gary Allen Trimble is buried at the Grandview Cemetery in Chillicothe, Ohio.

The children of Cary Allen Trimble and Mary MacArthur:

+ **B39—Nannie Trimble.** Born on September 29, 1839 and died on January 28, 1866.

The children of Cary Allen Trimble and Anna Porter Thompson:

B40—Allen Trimble. Born on January 30, 1851 and died on July 1, 1860.

B17—Eliza Jane Trimble. Daughter of Hugh Allen Trimble and Rachel Woodrow. (Fourth generation of John Trimble and Mary Moffitt.) Born on August 24, 1816 and died on November 4, 1905. Married on September 21, 1837, to James Henry Thompson of Harrodsburg, Kentucky. He was admitted to the bar in 1831 and was sheriff of Jessamine County, Kentucky, and an attorney in Versailles, Kentucky. In 1836, he moved to Batavia, Ohio, and in 1842 to Hillsboro, Ohio. He was registrar in bankruptcy in 1867 and in 1881, was a judge of common pleas. He was a Whig and then a Republican. In 1877, he published a history of Highland County. Eliza Jane was the famous Mother Thompson, leader of the famous Temperance Crusade of 1874.

The children of James Henry Thompson and Eliza Jane Trimble:

B41—Allen Trimble Thompson.

B42—Anna Porter Thompson.

B43—John Henry Thompson.

B44—Joseph Trimble Thompson.

B45—Maria Doiress Thompson.

Trimble Families of America

B - John Trimble

B46–Mary MacArthur Thompson.
B47–Henry Burton Thompson.
B48–John Burton Thompson.

B27–Sara Jane Trimble. Daughter of James Trimble and Mary Ann Smith. (Fifth generation of John Trimble and Mary Moffitt.) Married Robert Lilly.

The children of Robert Lilly and Sara Jane Trimble:
B49–Anna Lilly. Married a Mr. Yacobian.
B50–Madge Lilly. Married a Mr. Tikerian.
B51–Charles Lilly.
B52–George Lilly.

B28–John Allen Trimble. Son of James Trimble and Mary Ann Smith. (Fifth generation of John Trimble and Mary Moffitt.) Married on October 8, 1866, to Lucy G. Holloway of Henderson, Kentucky.

The children of John Allen Trimble and Lucy G. Holloway:
+ **B53–Nanny Trimble.**
B54–Tracy Trimble. Married Dr. H. M. Brown, no children.
B55–Starling Trimble. He had one son; his name is unknown.

B31–Margaret McDowell Trimble. Daughter of James Trimble and Mary Ann Smith. (Fifth generation of John Trimble and Mary Moffitt.) Born on December 11, 1867, she married Frank Wadman Armstrong of Philadelphia, Pennsylvania.

The child of Frank Wadman Armstrong and Margaret McDowell Trimble:
B56–Mary Armstrong. She married Robert Alex Swergert.

B39–Nannie Trimble. Daughter of Cary Trimble and Mary MacArthur. (Fifth generation of John Trimble and Mary Moffitt.) She married William Mederia of Chillicothe, Ohio.

The children of William Mederia and Nannie Trimble:
B57–John Mederia.
B58–Nannie Mederia. Married a Mr. Waddle.
B59–Mary MacArthur Mederia. Married a Mr. Fullerton.

B53–Nanny Trimble. Daughter of John Allen Trimble and Lucy G. Holloway. (Sixth generation of John Trimble and Mary Moffitt.) Married John Myers Clark on January 1, 1889.

The children John Myers Clark and Nanny Trimble:

130

B60—John Wessner Clark. Born on April 9, 1890.
B61—Edward Starling Clark. Born on August 7, 1892.
B62—Lucy Trimble Clark. Born on January 26, 1897.
B63—Olive Hickson Clark. Born on December 15, 1901.

C - Moses Trimble

Moses Trimble, one of the Five Trimble Brothers, settled first on the Borden tract between Lexington and Staunton, Virginia. His land neighbored that of Robert Houston. Moses was a witness to Houston's will. He later moved to Washington, Virginia, near Abingdon, and his will is recorded there in *Will Book No. 1,* page 83, May 20, 1783. It was witnessed by William Russell, a brother-in-law of Patrick Henry. Usually, a relative was witness to a will and a member of the court and a friend.

C1—Moses Trimble Born in 1718 in Armagh, Ireland and died on July 18, 1783 in Washington, Virginia. Married Jane Belcher. She was born in 1710 and died in1744.

His will reads:

IN THE NAME OF GOD AMEN, I Moses Trimble of the County of Washington and State of Virginia being of sound and disposing mind, do make and ordain this my last Will and Testament in the manner and form following viz: In the first place be collected and Debts paid, I bequeath to my Son Moses which is due to me in Rockbridge County, likewise one hundred & thirty pounds lying in the above Rockbridge out of which money he said Moses is to pay the moiety of Fifteen pounds to my loving wife and likewise Fifteen pounds to my Daughter Jain as soon as he collects the said money. I bequeath likewise to my son Moses his bed and furniture. I likewise bequeath to my loving wife her bed & furniture of likewise one large pewter dish and two Basons and the half of the small pewter. And the half of the small pewter and all my plantation utensils I bequeath to my son Moses. I bequeath to my daughter Jane a white Mare and her colt, and her saddle and two cows. I likewise bequeath to my Son Thomas Cloth to make him a suit of Cloaths and likewise I bequeath to my Wife one cow and one heifer, and the remainder of the Household furniture, which furniture at her decease is to be equally divided between Moses and Jane my Son & Daughter I likewise bequeath to my Son James the Land I now live on, and my great coat and my Hat. And lastly, I do make and constitute my son Moses & George Edgar for my Executors. IN WITNESS whereof I have hereunto set my hand and seal this third day of January in the Year of our Lord Christ one thousand seven hundred and eighty-three.

Teste:

James Berry Moses Trimble (SEAL)

William Russell

Andrew Russell

At a Court held for Washington County the 20th Day of May 1783. This last Will and Testament of Moses Trimble Deceased was showed in Court and proved by the Oaths of Jas. Berry, William Russell &: Andrew Russell, witnesses thereto & ordered to be recorded.

Teste: John Campbell, C.W.C.

The children of Moses Trimble and Jane Belcher:

+ **C2—James Trimble.** Born in 1744 in Augusta County, Virginia and died on November 9, 1823 in Virginia. Married Rachel Berry on May 28, 1806.

C3—Moses Trimble, Jr. Born in 1746 in Virginia. Married Mary Berry on January 20, 1803 in Washington County, Virginia.[27]

C4—Thomas Trimble.

C5—Jane or Jain Trimble. Born in 1750. Married on November 1, 1796 to James Tygart. They were married by Edward Crawford. Washington County, Virginia, *Marriage Record Book II*, page 465.

Also, we are uncertain if the following marriages, as recorded in Orange County, Indiana, are the children of Moses, Jr., or of George Trimble, son of the first David, who was born in 1814 in Kentucky, and his widow Jean Armstrong Trimble and children moved to Orange County, Indiana.

Marriages in Orange County, Indiana

Vol. 1, page 167-Dickson Trimble and Edith Weeks January 29, 1843 by Bailey Leonard.

Vol. 1, page 199-Elizabeth Trimble and William Mitchell February 29, 1843 by Wm. W. Martin.

Vol. 6, page 21-James J. Trimble and Emily Kitner April 9, 1854.

Vol. 6, page 60-Nancy Trimble and Lomax Wellington November 2,

---

[27] Dodd, Jordan R., et al. *Early American Marriages: Virginia to 1850*. Bountiful, UT, USA: Precision Indexing Publishers

Trimble Families of America

C - Moses Trimble

1862.

C2–James Trimble. Son of Moses Trimble and Jane Belcher. He was born in 1744 in Virginia and died on November 9, 1823 in Virginia. Married Rachel Berry on May 28, 1773. Rachel was born in 1744 and died in 1820 in Washington County, Virginia. She was the daughter of Frances Berry Sr. and Isabel. Deed Book No. 3, page 546, of Washington County, Virginia, records transactions for James and Rachel Trimble. James's will is recorded in Will Book No. 5, page 143, at Washington County, Virginia. This was probated on November 19, 1823. Administrator was William Trimble. It included: "$29.00 in silver, livestock, farm tools, kitchen furniture, 1 confession of faith and 11 other books, 1 bed, 1 dresser, 1 old chest." The appraisers were: John Reid, Jacob Miclele, Isaac McGown.

The child of James Trimble and Rachel Berry:

+ **C6–Moses Jackson Trimble.** Born on September 28, 1775 in Virginia and died on June 11, 1850 in French Lick, Orange County, Indiana. Married on January 20, 1803, to Mary Polly Berry in Washington County, Virginia. The marriage was performed by Edward Crawford in Washington County, Virginia, *Marriage Record Book II,* page 465.

+ **C7–Capt. John Trimble.** Born on February 2, 1779 in Augusta, Virginia and died on May 1, 1865 in Galax, Grayson County, Virginia. He married Susan Jane Nuckolls on May 24, 1808 in Carrol County, Virginia.

+ **C8–Isabella Trimble.** Born on February 2, 1779 in Virginia and died in 1847 in Kentucky. Married John Tigert on January 28, 1800 in Washington County, Virginia.

C9–James Alexander Trimble. Born in 1785 and died in 1863.

C10–Mary E. Trimble. Born in 1785 in Washington County, Virginia and died on March 20, 1806. Married Welcome Martin on March 20, 1806.

C11–Hanna Trimble. Born in 1788 in Washington County, Virginia. Married Thomas Rhea on March 24, 1808.

C12–William Trimble. Born in 1790 in Washington County, Virginia and died 1846. Married Elizabeth.

C6–Moses Jackson Trimble. Son of James Trimble and Rachel Berry. (Third generation of Moses Trimble and Jane Belcher) Born on September 28, 1775 in Virginia and died on June 11, 1850 in French Lick, Orange County, Indiana. Married on January 20, 1803, to Mary Berry in Washington County, Virginia. The marriage was performed by Edward Crawford. Washington

134

County, Virginia, *Marriage Record Book II*, page 465.

Moses was a private in Company of Rifleman in 105th Regiment of the Militia of Virginia from March 8, 1814 to July 5, 1814.

The children of Moses Jackson Trimble and Mary Berry:

+ **C13—Jane Trimble.** Born in 1804 in Washington County, Virginia and died on August 17, 1837 in Lawrence, Lawrence County, Illinois. Married Berry Belcher on March 11, 1824, Orange County, Indiana Marriage Records Vol. 1, page 17.

C14—Isabella Trimble. Born in 1806 in Washington County, Virginia. Married David W. Wolfington on May 20, 1824 in Orange County, Indiana. He was born about 1800 in Guilford County, North Carolina and died in 1850.

+ **C15—Lucinda Trimble.** Born on April 30, 1810 in Washington County, Virginia and died on December 10, 1855 in Orange County, Indiana. Married Bailey Leonard on October 6, 1827, Orange County, Indiana Marriage Records Vol. 1, page 92.

+ **C16—William B. Trimble.** Born in 1812 in Washington County, Virginia and died on April 19, 1857. Married Susannah Clark in December 1837 by William C. Walls, Orange County, Indiana Marriage Records Vol. 1, page 138.

+ **C17—James Jackson Trimble.** Born on November 1, 1814 in Washington County, Virginia and died on August 31, 1876 in French Lick, Orange County, Indiana. Married to Emily Willyard on April 3, 1854 in Orange County, Indiana.

C18—John Dixon Trimble. Born on February 19, 1817 in Washington County, Virginia and died on November 23, 1853 in Orange County, Indiana.

C7—Capt. John Trimble. Son of James Trimble and Rachel Berry. (Third generation of Moses Trimble and Jane Belcher.) Born on February 2, 1779 in Augusta, Virginia and died on May 1, 1865 in Galax, Grayson County, Virginia. He married Susan Jane Nuckolls in 1808. Susan was born in 1788 in Hanover, Virginia and died on August 30, 1833 in Galax, Grayson County, Virginia. Susanna Nuckolls was the daughter of Charles Nuckolls and Mary Black Hix and is buried with her husband John in the Trimble Cemetery, Galax, Virginia. Mary born in 1753 in Virginia. John and Susannah had 7 boys and 6 girls most of whom went to Illinois or Indiana.

When John Trimble and Susan Nuckolls were married, Susan's father, Charles Nuckolls, gave John several slaves to have as his own and do with as he might wish. John said to his father-in-law "And you give these negroes to do with as I choose?" and he said, "Yes, to do with as you choose." John said to them. "You are all free, I wouldn't own the soul off any man." This did not promote a very friendly feeling between John, who preferred to do his own work, and his father-in-law who never would let you forget he belonged to Aristocracy.

John Trimble organized a company of volunteers and went to Norfolk in the War of 1812. He acquired 1300 acres on Meadow Creek where he operated a grist mill and worked as a carpenter and mason. John Trimble worked for James Toncry, contractor for the construction of the Court House at Greenville (Old Town) as a carpenter and brick mason. Susannah, John's wife, came to view the work, and fell near the doorway with an apparent heart attack. She was carried across the street to the Dickenson Ordinary where she died in a matter of hours on August 30, 1833. John lived, at the time of his death, with daughter Rachel Trimble (C20) and her husband John Foster.

The children of John Trimble and Susan Nuckolls:

+ **C19—Charles Nuckolls Trimble.** Born on June 16, 1809 in Grayson County, Virginia and died on December 31, 1896 in Vermilion County, Illinois. Married three times.

+ **C20—Rachel Berry Trimble.** Born on December 21, 1810 in Galax, Grayson County, Virginia and died on October 25, 1883. Married John Foster.

   C21—Polly Hix Trimble. Born on March 28, 1812 in Galax, Grayson County, Virginia and died September m14, 1860. Married Burr Wright.

+ **C22—James Harrison Trimble.** Born on July 16, 1813 in Galax, Grayson County, Virginia and died after 1830 and before 1903 in Independence, Missouri. Married Nancy Welch on October 25, 1838.

+ **C23—William Jackson Trimble.** Born on May 20, 1815 in Grayson County, Virginia and died on September 14, 1860 in Galax, Grayson County, Virginia. Married Elizabeth Rector on December 17, 1839 in Grayson County, Virginia

+ **C24—Nancy Franklin Trimble.** Born on August 11, 1816 in Galax, Grayson County, Virginia. Married William Kain on November 19, 1844.

+ **C25—John Bobbitt Trimble.** Born on January 11, 1818 in Grayson County, Virginia and died on August 24, 1907 in Decatur, Indiana. Married Adelaide Owens who was born in 1818 in Virginia.

+ **C26—Sally Nuckolls Trimble.** Born on August 13, 1819 in Galax, Grayson County, Virginia and died in 1842. Married a Sharp in 1855 in

Greensburg, Decatur, Indiana.

C27—Martin Isom Trimble. Born in 1821 in Galax, Grayson County, Virginia and died in infancy.

C28—Caroline Ward Trimble. Born on December 11, 1821 in Grayson County, Virginia and died on May 24, 1888 in Oldtown, Grayson County, Virginia and is buried Meadow Creek Baptist Church, Grayson County, Virginia.

+ **C29—Jane Clements Trimble.** Born on November 20, 1823 in Virginia and died between 1891 and 1917. Married Ovid McCracken on April 10, 1845.

+ **C30—George Washington Trimble.** Born on July 13, 1825 in Virginia and died on March 28, 1914 in Tipton County, Indiana. Married Mary Barclay.

+ **C31—Christopher Columbus Trimble.** Born on February 27, 1828 in Virginia and on died December 23, 1913. Married Twice.

C8—Isabella Trimble. Daughter of James Trimble and Rachel Berry. (Third generation of Moses Trimble and Jane Belcher.) Born on February 2, 1779 in Virginia and died in 1847 in Warren County, Kentucky. Married John Tigert on January 28, 1800 in Washington County, Virginia, married by Edward Crawford. John was born in 1798 in Virginia and died in 1820 in Warren County, Kentucky.

The children of John Tigert and Isabella Trimble:

C32—Hannah Tigert.

C33—John Tigert.

+ **C34—James Tigert.** Born in 1819 in Warren County, Kentucky. Married Emelia Hendrick on June 7, 1838.

C13—Jane Trimble. Daughter of Moses Jackson Trimble and Mary Berry. (Fourth generation of Moses Trimble and Jane Belcher.) Born in 1804 in Washington County, Virginia and died on August 17, 1837. Married Berry Belcher on March 11, 1824 in Orange County, Indiana. In 1830 census Jane lived in Orange County, Indiana.

The children of Berry Belcher and Jane Trimble:

+ **C35—Martha Jane Belcher.** Born on October 25, 1825 in Orange County, Indiana and died on June 7, 1898 in Crawford County, Indiana. Married Nathan Hollen on May 31, 1849 in Crawford County, Indiana.

+ **C36—Jeremiah Belcher.** Born on December 20, 1821 in Orange County, Indiana and died on September 18, 1905. Married Nancy Jane Pace on

C - Moses Trimble

January 18, 1860. She was born on August 6, 1830 in Tennessee and died on February 15, 1885 in Knox, Indiana.

C37—Mary Ann Belcher. (twin) Born on June 1828 in Orange County, Indiana.

C38—Jesse Belcher. (twin) Born in June on 1828 in Orange County, Indiana and died on January 20, 1908.

C39—Moses Jackson Belcher. Born in June 1829 in Patoka, Crawford County, Indiana and died on August 17, 1896 in Norman, Cleveland County, Oklahoma.

C40—Lucinda Belcher. Born in 1834 Lawrence, Lawrence County, Illinois died in 1882 in Rush, Texas and died in 1882 in Rusk, Texas.

C41—Rebecca Emaline Belcher. Born on March 23, 1836 in Lawrence, Lawrence County, Illinois died on February 16, 1901 in Taswell, Crawford County, Indiana.

+ **C42—John Wesley Belcher.** Born on November 26, 1839 in Jackson, Orange County, Indiana and died on April 6, 1910 in Taswell, Crawford County, Indiana. Married Sarah Victoria Suddarth in 1861.

C15—Lucinda Trimble. Daughter of Moses Jackson Trimble and Mary Berry. (Fourth generation of Moses Trimble and Jane Belcher) Born on April 30, 1810 in Washington County, Virginia and died on December 10, 1855 in Orange County, Indiana. Married Bailey Leonard, born on February 2, 1806 in Guilford County, North Carolina and died on February 27, 1874 in Franklin, Franklin County, Kansas.

The child of Bailey Leonard and Lucinda Trimble:

+ **C43—Emeline Leonard.** Born on June 6, 1846 to Terre Haute, Vigo County, Indiana and died on March 30, 1933 in Nevada, Vernon, Missouri. Married John Bailey Hobson on February 5, 1862.

C16—William B. Trimble. Son of Moses Jackson Trimble and Mary Berry. (Fourth generation of Moses Trimble and Jane Belcher) Born in 1812 in Washington County, Virginia and died on April 19, 1857. Married Susannah Clark in December 1837. She was born on August 27, 1815 in Pennsylvania and died on December 19, 1888.

The children of William B. Trimble and Susannah Clark:

C44—Mary Trimble. Born on November 12, 1838 and died in 1904.

+ **C45—Martin V. Trimble.** Born on August 7, 1840 in Indiana and died on June 26, 1917. Married Katherine Mary Williams on April 21, 1882 in Keokuk, Lee, Iowa.

+ **C46—Nancy Ann Trimble.** Born on February 2, 1842 in Indiana and died on September 12, 1920 in Keokuk, Lee County, Iowa. Married Ralph Remson Teller.

C47—Jasper Trimble. Born on August 1, 1844.

C48—Benjamin Trimble. Born on November 26, 1846.

C49—William Owen Trimble. Born on May 1, 1848.

C50—Lucinda Trimble. Born on July 12, 1853.

C51—Robert Trimble. Born on October 20, 1854.

C52—Rebecca Ann Trimble. Born on February 24, 1856 in Indiana. She was residing in Montrose, Lee, Iowa.

C17—James Jackson Trimble. Son of Moses Jackson Trimble and Mary Berry. (Fourth generation of Moses Trimble and Jane Belcher.) Born on November 1, 1814 in Washington County, Virginia and died on August 31, 1876 in French Lick, Orange County, Indiana, buried in Moore's Ridge Cemetery, Orange County, Indiana. Married to Emily Willyard on April 3, 1854 in Orange County, Indiana. She was born on July 25, 1824 in, Stokes County, North Carolina. Her parents were Daniel Willyard and Mary Ledford.

The children of James Jackson Trimble and Emily Willyard:

+ **C53—Volney Thorton Trimble.** Born on January 9, 1855 in French Lick Township, Orange County, Indiana and died on March 7, 1929 in New Albany, Floyd County, Indiana. Married Anna L. Snipes on February 15, 1877 in Orange County, Indiana.

C54—William E. Trimble. Born on September 17, 1856 in French Lick Township, Orange County, Indiana.

C55—Charles S. Trimble. Born on November 1, 1858 in French Lick Township, Orange County, Indiana.

C56—Mary J. Trimble. Born about 1860 in French Lick Township, Orange County, Indiana.

C19—Charles Nuckolls Trimble. Son of John Trimble and Susan Nuckolls. (Fourth generation of Moses Trimble and Jane Belcher.) Born on June 16, 1809 in Galax, Grayson County, Virginia and died on December 31, 1896 in Vermilion County, Illinois. Married the first time to Frances Preston in 1835 and. Frances was born in 1810 in Virginia and died between 1835 and 1848 in Virginia. Married the second time to Sarah Jane Doran on January 14, 1849. Sarah was born on May 8, 1818 in Hardy County, Virginia and died on July 11, 1873 in Virginia. Married Charlottie Mills on April 18, 1874 in Catlin, Vermilion County, Illinois. Charlottie was born on November 26, 1843 in Old Bluff, Mercer County, Virginia and died on March 23, 1911 in

Trimble Families of America

C - Moses Trimble

Laurens, Pocahontas County, Iowa. In the 1850 census Charles' occupation was carpenter.

The children of Charles Nuckolls Trimble and Frances Preston:

C57—Franklin Preston Trimble. Born on October 6, 1835 in Virginia and died on June 24, 1922 in Oakwood, Vermillion County, Illinois.

The children of Charles Nuckolls Trimble and Sarah Doran:

C58—Sarah Ann Trimble. Born on February 15, 1850 in Vermilion County, Illinois and died on December 18, 1934.

+ **C59—Charles Columbus Trimble.** Born on August 23, 1854 in Vermilion County, Illinois and died on April 3, 1939 in Oakwood, Vermilion County, Illinois.

C60—John William Trimble. Born on August 31, 1856 in Vermilion County, Illinois and died on February 4, 1930 in Oakwood Village, Vermilion, Illinois.

The children of Charles Trimble and Charlottie Mills:

C61—Malinda Trimble. Born on March 18, 1877 and died in 1958.

C62—Lucinda Trimble. Born on September 23, 1878 in Oakwood, Illinois and died on May 3, 1942 in Palo Alto, Iowa. Married Emory Kirby

C63—Perry Otto Trimble. Born in 1880 in Hillery, Vermilion County, Illinois.

C20—Rachel Berry Trimble. Daughter of John Trimble and Susan Nuckolls. (Fourth generation of Moses Trimble and Jane Belcher.) Born on December 21, 1810 in Galax, Grayson County, Virginia and died on October 25, 1883. Married John Foster.

The child of John Foster and Rachel Berry Trimble:

C64—Martin Trimble.

C22—James Harrison Trimble. Son of John Trimble and Susan Nuckolls. (Fourth generation of Moses Trimble and Jane Belcher.) Born on July 16, 1813 in Galax, Grayson County, Virginia and died after 1838 and before 1903 in Independence, Missouri. Practice medicine for a short time. Contracted TB which was his cause of death. Married Nancy Welch on October 25, 1838.

The children of James Harrison Trimble and Nancy Welch:

C65—James H. Trimble.

C66—John A. Trimble. Died in 1887 in Algiers, Africa.

C67—Sarah Nuckolls Trimble.

C23—William Jackson Trimble. Son of John Trimble and Susan Nuckolls.

140

(Fourth generation of Moses Trimble and Jane Belcher.) Born on May 20, 1815 in Grayson County, Virginia and died on September 14, 1860 in Galax, Grayson County, Virginia. Married Elizabeth Rector on December 17, 1839 in Grayson County, Virginia. Elizabeth was born in 1817 in Virginia and died in 1887. Elizabeth was the daughter of Bennett Rector and Nancy Conley. Bennett was born on January 3, 1782 in Germantown, Fauquier County, Virginia and died on December 25, 1866 in Grayson County, Virginia. Nancy was born in 1780 in Ashe, North Carolina and died in 1819 in Delhart, Grayson County, Virginia. Bennett and Nancy were married in 1800.

The children of William Jackson Trimble and Elizabeth Rector:

C68—Garland Trimble. Born in 1841.

+ **C69—Christopher Columbus Trimble.** Born on August 10, 1842 and died June 17, 1929. Married Elizabeth Rector December 17, 1839 in Grayson County, Virginia.

+ **C70—Susan Jane Trimble.** Born on December 1, 1844 in Grayson County, Virginia and died on July 13, 1929 in Grayson County, Virginia. Married James M. Mooney on July 21, 1870 in Alleghany County, North Carolina.

C71—Jasper Trimble. Born on November 30, 1846 and died on September 26, 1862.

+ **C72—Evaline Trimble.** Born on July 5, 1850 and died on January 17, 1903 in Grayson, Virginia. Married Logan Roberts.

C73—Elbert Trimble. Born on September 7, 1853. Married Almeda Calloway and died on May 9, 1933. They had one child, Jimmie Trimble born in 1884 and died in 1885.

C74—Melviny Caroline Trimble. Born on June 9, 1857 in Virginia and died on February 22, 1938.

C24—Nancy Franklin Trimble. Daughter of John Trimble and Susan Nuckolls. (Fourth generation of Moses Trimble and Jane Belcher.) Born on August 11, 1816 in Galax, Grayson County, Virginia. Married William Kain on November 19, 1844 in Surry County, North Carolina.

The children of William Kain and Nancy Franklin Trimble:

C75—Martin M. Kain. Born in 1839 and died in 1874.

C76—Sally Ann Kain. Born about 1846.

+ **C77—Eli Franklin Kain.** Born in November 1855 in Virginia and died on February 21, 1923 in Virginia. Married to Matilda Nations on October

12, 1876 in Surry County, North Carolina.

C78—Susan Kain. Born about 1858.

C79—Jennie Kain.

C25—John Bobbitt Trimble. Son of John Trimble and Susan Nuckolls. (Fourth generation of Moses Trimble and Jane Belcher.) Born on January 11, 1818 in Grayson County, Virginia and died on August 24, 1907 in Decatur, Indiana. Married Adelaide Owens on February 4, 1836 in Fayette, Indiana.

The children of John Bobbitt Trimble and Adelaide Owens:

C80—Myra Bell Trimble. Born in 1854 in Indiana. Married William Morse.

C81—Fred Trimble. Born in 1855 in Indiana.

+ **C82—Oscar Bobbitt Trimble.** Born on August 19, 1859 in Indiana and died on May 30, 1934. Married to Ida Mary Butler born in June 1860 in Indiana and died after 1930.

C83—Arthur B. Trimble. Born in January 1862 in Indiana. Married Mary ———. Mary was born about 1899 in Indiana and died before 1930.

C84—Carrie Alice Trimble. Born on January 12, 1864 in Greensburg Indiana. Married Curtis McCoy, born on May 2, 1863 in Washington, Decatur County, Indiana.

C26—Sally Nuckolls Trimble. Son of John Trimble and Susan Nuckolls. (Fourth generation of Moses Trimble and Jane Belcher.) Born on August 13, 1819 in Galax, Grayson County, Virginia and died in 1842. Married a Mr. Sharp in 1855 in Greensburg, Decatur County, Indiana.

The children of Mr. Sharp and Sally Nuckolls Trimble:

C85—Martha Sharp.

C86—Mary Sharp.

C87—Charles Sharp.

C88—Lucille Sharp.

C29—Jane Clements Trimble. Daughter of John Trimble and Susan Nuckolls. (Fourth generation of Moses Trimble and Jane Belcher.) Born on November 20, 1823 in Virginia and died between 1891 and 1917. Married Ovid McCracken on April 10, 1845. Ovid born in 1819.

The children of Ovid McCracken and Jane Clements Trimble:

C89—George McCracken. Born between 1841 and 1864. Married Elizabeth Harley.

C90—Caroline McCracken. Born in 1847 in Indiana.

C91—Virginia McCracken. Born on December 29, 1842 in Indiana and died on

August 28, 1848 in Indiana. Buried Wesley Cemetery, Decatur County, Indiana.

C92—Virgil McCracken. Born on January 16, 1850 Jackson township, Decatur, Indiana and died on November 25, 1922 in Billings, Yellowstone, Montana. Married Susan Matilda Hornaday on February 13, 1879.

C30—George Washington Trimble. Son of John Trimble and Susan Nuckolls. (Fourth generation of Moses Trimble and Jane Belcher.) Born on July 13, 1825 in Virginia and died on March 28, 1914 in Tipton County, Indiana. Married Mary Barclay.

The children of George Washington Trimble and Mary Barclay:

C93—Bertha Trimble.

C94—Jessie Trimble.

C95—Charles Nuckolls Trimble.

C96—Adolphus Trimble.

C97—Edward Trimble.

C31—Christopher Columbus Trimble. Son of John Trimble and Susan Nuckolls. (Fourth generation of Moses Trimble and Jane Belcher.) Born on February 27, 1828 in Virginia and died on December 23, 1913. Married first time to Lydia McCormick on April 14, 1850 in Sardin, Decatur County, Indiana. Lydia born on August 4, 1829 in Franklin County, Ohio and died on June 14, 1880 in Windfall, Tipton County, Indiana.

Married second time to Julia F. Jackson on June 26, 1881 married by Reverend Garrett White in Windfall, Tipton County, Indiana. Julia born on January 3, 1843 in Pope County, Illinois died on April 15, 1909 in Windfall, Tipton County, Indiana.

The children of Christopher Trimble and Lydia McCormick:

C98—John Columbus Trimble. Born on July 18, 1851 and died on August 16, 1852.

C99—William Scott Trimble. Born on April 14, 1853 in Scipio, Jennings, Indiana and died on March 17, 1918. Married Sarah Elizabeth Mooney on April 1, 1883.

C100—James Monroe Trimble. Born on September 7, 1855 and died on May 2, 1929. Married Rose May Harley. Rose born on November 17, 1867 and died on January 21, 1928.

C101—Courtland Prentice Trimble. Born on May 13, 1858 and died on January 28, 1881.

C102—Lincoln Trimble. Born on June 25, 1860 and died on March 4, 1866 at the age of 5.

C103—Elmer Ellsworth Trimble. Born on November 9, 1862 in Sardina, Decatur County, Indiana and died on September 13, 1930. Married Luella Blanche Allen on February 24, 1889.

C104—Charles Nuckolls Trimble. Born on May 8, 1865.

C105—Aldie Eugene Trimble. Born on September 20, 1866 and died in 1947.

C106—Alma Eugenia Trimble. Born on September 20, 1868 and died on May 12, 1927. Married Louis Delos Platt.

C107—Benjamin Franklin Trimble. Born on February 23, 1870 and died on October 13, 1904. Married Myrtle Kinder.

The children of Christopher Trimble and Julia Jackson:

C108—Martha Louise Trimble. Born on July 18, 1883 in Richmond, Indiana and died on April 11, 1973. Married Fred J. Allen on August 6, 1904.

C109—Kenneth Blaine Trimble. Born on September 8, 1885 and died in 1958.

C110—Charles Mercer Trimble. Born on July 16, 1886 and died in 1944.

C34—James Tigert. Son of John Tigert and Isabella Trimble. (Fourth generation of Moses Trimble and Jane Belcher.) Born in 1819 in Warren County, Kentucky. Married Emelia Hendrick on June 7, 1838. Emelia born in 1819.

The children of James Tigert and Emelia Hendrick:

C111—Samuel T. Tigert. Born about 1839 in Warren County, Kentucky. Married Charlotte. Her last name was not found.

C112—John W. Tigert. Born about 1841 in Warren County, Kentucky.

+ **C113—Sarah Elizabeth Tigert.** Born about 1842 in Warren County, Kentucky and died on December 30, 1922. Several places have her birth date in 1852, but she is list in the 1850 census as age 8. Married John Wesley Kennedy.

C114—Susan A. Tigert. Born about 1845 in Warren County, Kentucky.

C115—James W. Tigert. Born about 1848 in Warren County, Kentucky.

+ **C116—Joseph H. Tigert.** Born on February 26, 1851 in Warren County, Kentucky and died on July 13, 1911 in Warren County, Kentucky.

C117—Squire Ewing Tigert. Born on January 13, 1852 in Warren County, Kentucky and died on April 3, 1900 in Warren County, Kentucky. Married Elizabeth A. Gott on March 28, 1876.

C118—Franklin P. Tigert. Born on October 2, 1853 in Warren County, Kentucky.

C35—Martha Jane Belcher. Daughter of Berry Belcher and Jane Trimble. (Fifth generation of Moses Trimble and Jane Belcher.) Born on October 25, 1825 in Orange County, Indiana and died on June 7, 1898 in Crawford County, Indiana. Married Nathan Hollen on May 31, 1849 in Crawford County, Indiana. Nathan was Private in 144th Regiment, Indiana Infantry of Union Army during the Civil War.

The children of Nathan Hollen and Martha Jane Belcher:

C119—William K. Hollen. Born about 1860.

C120—Jasoh Hollen. Born about 1862.

C121—Nathan M.E. Hollen. Born about 1865.

C122—Lean Hollen. Born about 1867.

C123—Ruthie E. Collins. Born about 1868. She was adopted.

C36—Jeremiah Belcher. Son of Berry Belcher and Jane Trimble (Fifth generation of Moses Trimble and Jane Belcher.) Born on December 20, 1821 in Orange County, Indiana and died on September 18, 1905. Married three times. First to Rebecca Brock born on March 10, 1830 in Knox County, Kentucky and died on June 4, 1859 in Patoka, Crawford County, Indiana. Second to Nancy Jane Pace on January 18, 1860. She was born on August 6, 1830 in Tennessee and died on February 15, 1885 in Knox, Indiana. Third to Elizabeth Tevebaugh on July 26, 1884. She was born on February 1825 in Indiana and died in 1900 in Indiana.

The children of Jeremiah Belcher and Rebecca Brock:

C124—John Belcher. Born in 1849.

C125—Francis Belcher. Born in 1852 and died in 1819.

C126—Nancy Belcher. Born in 1854 and died in 1920.

C127—Joseph Mason Belcher. Born in 1856 and died in 1926.

C128—Martha J. Belcher. Born in 1856 and died in 1880.

C129—Rebecca S. Belcher. Born in 1859 and died in 1887.

Children of Jeremiah Belcher and Nancy Jane Pace.

C130—Elizabeth Belcher. Born in 1862 and died in 1900.

C131—George W. Belcher. Born in 1863 and died in 1876.

C42—John Wesley Belcher. Son of Berry Belcher and Jane Trimble (Fifth generation of Moses Trimble and Jane Belcher.) Born on November 26, 1839 in Jackson, Orange County, Indiana and died on April 6, 1910 in Taswell, Crawford County, Indiana. Married Sarah Victoria Suddarth in 1861. Sarah was born on January 31, 1842 in Marengo, Crawford County, Indiana and died on December 31, 1922 in Taswell, Crawford County, Indiana.

The children of John Wesley Belcher and Sarah Victoria Suddarth:

C132—Charles Belcher. Born in 1854.

C133—Laura Belcher. Born in 1859.

C134—Lydia Belcher. Born about 1862 in Indiana and died on March 26, 1898 in Layton, Graham County, Arizona.

C135—Mary Frances Belcher. Born on June 27, 1864 in Patoka, Crawford County, Indiana and died on June 27, 1864 in Crawford County, Indiana.

C136—George W. Belcher. Born about 1865 in Indiana and died on February 18, 1931 in Princeton, Gibson County, Indiana.

C137—Mary J. Belcher. Born in 1868 in Crawford County, Indiana.

C138—Martha A. Belcher. Born about 1870 in Indiana.

+ **C139—John Henry Belcher.** Born on April 6, 1871 in Indiana and died on March 17, 1938 in South Haven, Van Buren, Michigan. Married Emily S. Highfill on June 22, 1892 in Taswell, Crawford County, Indiana.

C140—Manda J. Belcher. Born in 1872 in Indiana and died in July 1899 in Crawford County, Indiana.

C141—William L. Belcher. Born about 1878 in Indiana and died on September 17, 1949 in Crawford, Indiana.

C142—Lucinda Belcher. Born on January 13, 1880 in Crawford County, Indiana and died on May 1, 1954 in Van Buren, Michigan.

C143—James N. Belcher. Born in May 1883 in Indiana and died on June 11, 1938 in Indiana.

C144—Sarah Elizabeth Belcher. Born on July 1, 1885 in Crawford County, Indiana and died in July 1885 in Crawford County, Indiana.

C43—Emeline Leonard. Daughter of Bailey Leonard and Lucinda Trimble. (Fifth generation of Moses Trimble and Jane Belcher.) Born on June 6, 1846 to Terre Haute, Vigo, Indiana and died on March 30, 1933 in Nevada, Vernon, Missouri. Married John Bailey Hobson on February 5, 1862. He was born on August 24, 1864 in Orange County, Indiana and died on July 7, 1925 in Ottawa, Franklin, Kansas.

The child of John Bailey Hobson and Emeline Leonard:

C145—Ida Viola Hobson. Born on November 29, 1863 in Orange, Indiana and died on July 18, 1949 in Gainesville, Forsyth County, Georgia.

C45—Martin V. Trimble. Son of William B. Trimble and Susannah Clark. (Fifth generation of Moses Trimble and Jane Belcher.) Born on August 7, 1840 in Indiana and died on June 26, 1917. Married Katherine Mary Williams on April 21, 1882 in Keokuk, Lee, Iowa. Katherine born in August 1862.

The children of Martin Trimble and Katherine Williams:

C146—Myrtle M. Trimble. Born in March 1885 in Jackson, Lee County, Iowa.

C147—Howard Trimble. Born on August 26, 1887 in Jackson, Lee County, Iowa Death in October 1979 in Hesperia, Oceana County, Michigan.

C148—Chester Trimble. Born on September 10, 1889 in Jackson, Lee County, Iowa and died on January 30, 1967 in Keokuk, Lee County, Iowa.

C149—Sadie E. Trimble. Born in June 1891 in Jackson, Lee County, Iowa.

C150—Jessie Trimble. Born in September 1894 in Jackson, Lee County, Iowa.

C46—Nancy Ann Trimble. Daughter of William B. Trimble and Susannah Clark. (Fifth generation of Moses Trimble and Jane Belcher.) Born on February 2, 1842 in Indiana and died on September 12, 1920 in Keokuk, Lee County, Iowa. Married Ralph Remson Teller born on January 29, 1827 in New York, New York and died on March 10, 1893 in Jacksonville, Florida.

The children of Ralph Remson Teller and Nancy Ann Trimble:

C151—William Harley Teller. Born on July 15, 1900 in Keokuk, Lee County, Iowa and died in May 1980 in Anniston, Calhoun County, Alabama.

C152—Flossie Mildred Teller. Born on October 11, 1902 in Keokuk, Lee County, Iowa and died in Loveland, Colorado.

C153—Ralph Hartwig Teller. Born on March 12, 1905 in Keokuk, Lee County, Iowa and died on July 31, 1987 in Richmond City, Virginia.

C154—Ruth Elizabeth Teller. Born on November 25, 1906 in Keokuk, Lee County, Iowa and died on May 29, 1949 in Keokuk, Lee County, Iowa.

C155—Clyde Elsworth Teller. Born on May 31, 1909 in Keokuk, Lee County, Iowa and died on November 18, 1966 in Keokuk, Lee County, Iowa. Married Thelma Azilene Smith on July 22.

C156—Laurence Leslie Teller. Born on October 10, 1911 in Keokuk, Lee County, Iowa and died on September 5, 1990 in Keokuk, Lee County, Iowa. Married Margaret Walte in 1947 in Keokuk, Lee, Iowa.

C157—Etta Audrey Teller. Born on October 23, 1913 in Keokuk, Lee County, Iowa and died in March 1995 in Keokuk, Lee County, Iowa.

C158—Carl Morrel Teller. Born on September 23, 1915 in Keokuk, Lee County, Iowa and died on April 5, 1990 in Wayland, Clark County, Missouri. Married Neleene B. Bollin on September 14, 1935.

C159—Katherine Teller. Born on January 8, 1919 in Keokuk, Lee County, Iowa and died on September 30, 2003 in Melrose Park, Cook County, Illinois Married Mr. Jakubec.

Trimble Families of America

C53—Volney Thorton Trimble. Son of James Jackson Trimble and Emily Willyard. (Fifth generation of Moses Trimble and Jane Belcher.) Born on January 9, 1855 in French Lick Township, Orange County, Indiana and died on March 7, 1929 in New Albany, Floyd County, Indiana. Married Anna L. Snipes on February 15, 1877 in Orange County, Indiana. Anna was born on November 15, 1858 in North Carolina and died July 15, 1920 in Indiana.

The children of Volney Thorton Trimble and Anna L. Snipes:

+ **C160—James J. Trimble.** Born on December 1877 in Indiana and died in July 1974 in Roberts, Ford County, Illinois. Married Mabel Hahn.

C161—Ora A. Trimble. Born on March 1882 in Orange County, Indiana.

C162—Bex A. Trimble. Born on April 1884 in Indiana and died on September 19, 1965 in Mt Vernon, Posey County, Indiana.

C163—Sampson O. Trimble. Born on October 1886 in Indiana in Orange County, Indiana.

C164—Rufus A. Trimble. Born on May 1889 in Indiana and died on March 21, 1971 in San Francisco, San Francisco County, California

C165—Emma B. Trimble. Born on July 1891 in Indiana and died in 1945 in Indiana.

C166—Sott S. Trimble. Born on May 1894 in Indiana and died in April 1984 in Frankfort, Clinton County, Indiana.

C59—Charles Columbus Trimble. Son of Charles Nuckolls Trimble and Sarah Doran. (Fifth generation of Moses Trimble and Jane Belcher.) Born on August 23, 1854 in Vermilion County, Illinois and died on April 3, 1939 in Oakwood, Vermilion County, Illinois. Married Ella.

The children of Charles and Ella Trimble:

C167—Lee Trimble. Born in August 1880 in Illinois.

C168—Luta Trimble. Born in November 1882 in Illinois

C169—Effa Trimble. Born in February 1884 in Illinois.

C170—Vana Trimble. Born in February 1886 in Illinois.

C171—Claud Trimble. Born in May 1892 in Illinois.

C172—Clair Trimble. Born in November 1892 in Illinois.

+ **C173—Sylvia Nell Trimble.** Born on August 21, 1895 in Oakwood, Illinois and died on December 16, 1986 Danville, Illinois. Married a Mr. Finley.

C69—Christopher Columbus Trimble. Son of William Jackson Trimble and Elizabeth Rector. (Fifth generation of Moses Trimble and Jane Belcher.) Born on August 10, 1842 and died on June 17, 1929. Married Elizabeth

Rector on December 17, 1839 in Grayson County, Virginia.

Columbus Trimble: Private, Company C, 8th Calvary. Enlisted April 27, 1862. AWOL for 85 days October 31, 1864.

The children of Christopher Columbus Trimble and Elizabeth Rector:

C174—Wells Trimble. Born about 1867.

+ **C175—Fidella "Dell" Trimble.** Born in 1868 in Virginia and died on August 7, 1936. Married William Preston "Bud" Kenny. He was born on August 1868.

C176—Mary Elizabeth Trimble. Born on February 21, 1869 in Oldtown, Virginia and died on February 4, 1870. She was less than a year old.

C177—Cora Jane Lee Trimble. Born about 1870.

C178—William Ambrose Trimble. Born on 1871 in Virginia and died in 1958 in Kingsport, Sullivan County, Tennessee.

+ **C179—Margaret Josephine "Josie" Trimble.** Born on March 11, 1874 in Virginia and died on May 1, 1951. Married Richard Duphy Bartlett in 1893 in Virginia.

C180—Sarah Emma Trimble. Born on December 12, 1875 in Carroll, Virginia.

C181—Sena Ann Trimble. Born on March 22, 1878 in Grayson, Virginia and died on April 4, 1932 in Coeburn, Virginia.

C182—Charles "Bud" Trimble. Born on September 26, 1880 and died on July 25, 1961.

C183—Alverta Trimble. Born on February 21, 1883 in Virginia and died on April 2, 1903.

C184—Alice Laura Trimble. Born on July 15, 1885 in Carroll, Virginia and died on July 1, 1964.

C185—James E. Chappell "Jimmy" Trimble. Born in August 1888 in Virginia.

C186—Bessie Alma Trimble. Born on September 4, 1893 and died on October 1, 1893. She was less than a month old.

C70—Susan Jane Trimble. Daughter of William Jackson Trimble and Elizabeth Rector. (Fifth generation of Moses Trimble and Jane Belcher.) Born on December 1, 1844 in Grayson County, Virginia and died on July 13, 1929 in Grayson County, Virginia. Married Reverend James M. Mooney on July 21, 1870 in Alleghany County, North Carolina.

The children of James M. Mooney and Susan Jane Trimble:

+ **C187—George W. Mooney.** Born in 1872 in Grayson, Virginia. Married to Margie Galyean on March 26, 1892.

C188—Jasper L. Mooney. Born on April 30, 1873 in Grayson County, Virginia and died on September 14, 1898 in Jacksonville, Florida.

C189—Clara E. Mooney. Born on June 12, 1875 in Grayson, Virginia and died on April 12, 1880 in Grayson, Virginia.

C190—Elbert Mooney. Born on July 10, 1876 in Grayson County, Virginia and died on August 187? in Grayson County, Virginia.

+ **C191—Sarah Annie Mooney.** Born on July 1, 1877 in Grayson, Virginia and died on April 11, 1915 in Grayson, Virginia. Married Jessie Aron Crissman on January 16, 1916.

C72—Evaline Trimble. Daughter of William Jackson Trimble and Elizabeth Rector. (Fifth generation of Moses Trimble and Jane Belcher.) Born on July 5, 1850 and died on January 17, 1903 in Grayson, Virginia. Married Logan Roberts. Logan was born on December 27, 1838 in North Carolina and died on January 21, 1923 in Carroll County, Virginia. He was son of Thompson Roberts and Saraphina Currin. Thompson was born in 1810 in Surry, North Carolina and died in Galax, Virginia. Saraphina was born about 1813 in Galax, Virginia and died on February 3, 1890 in Galax, Virginia.

Enlisted as a Private on April 27, 1862 at the age of 23 in Company C, 8th Cavalry Regiment Virginia.

The children of Logan Roberts and Evaline Trimble:

C192—Thomas Roberts. Born in 1874 in Virginia.

C193—Lola Bell Roberts. Born in 1877 in Virginia and died on December 22, 1950 in Galax, Carroll County, Virginia.

+ **C194—Sidney Roberts.** Born on February 19, 1887 in Virginia and died in January 1963 in Galax, Carroll County, Virginia. Married Ollie Mae Williams on January 28, 1914 in Edmonds, North Carolina.

C77—Eli Franklin Kain. Son of William Kain and Nancy Franklin Trimble. (Fifth generation of Moses Trimble and Jane Belcher.) Born on November 1855 in Virginia and died on February 21, 1923 in Virginia. Married to Matilda Nations on October 12, 1876 in Surry County, North Carolina.

The children of Eli Franklin Kain and Matilda Nations:

C195—Mellie Elvier Kain. Born in 1877 and died 1878.

C196—Joseph Cornelius "Neally" Kain. Born in 1880.

C197—Annice Ester Kain. Born on May 15, 1881 in Virginia and died on November 20, 1958 in Grayson County, Virginia. Married Garnett Reed Largin on December 23, 1914.

C198—Martin Tolliver Kain. Born in 1884 and died in 1964.

C199—Sarah Emer Kain. Born in 1895 and died in 1896.

Trimble Families of America

C82–Oscar Bobbitt Trimble. Son of John Bobbitt Trimble and Adelaide Owens. (Fifth generation of Moses Trimble and Jane Belcher.) Born on August 19, 1859 in Indiana and died on May 30, 1934. Married to Ida Mary Butler born on June 1860 in Indiana and died after 1930.

The children of Oscar Bobbitt Trimble and Ida Mary Butler:
> **C200–Clada A. Trimble.** Born in August 1882 in Decatur, Indiana.
> **C201–Ethel Beatrice Trimble.** Born in April 1885 in Decatur, Indiana. Married Christian A. Steen Born about 1875 in Denmark.

C113–Sarah Elizabeth Tigert. Daughter of James Tigert and Emelia Hendrick. (Fifth generation of Moses Trimble and Jane Belcher.) Born about 1842 in Warren County, Kentucky and died on December 30, 1922 in Douglas County, Missouri and is buried in the Fannon Cemetery. Several places have her birth date in 1852, but she is list in the 1850 census as age 8. Married John Wesley Kennedy. John was born on February 12, 1838 in Morgan County, Indiana and died on September 23, 1900 in Douglas County, Missouri.

The children of John Wesley Kennedy and Sarah Elizabeth Tigert:
> **C202–Stella Adaline Kennedy.** Born on August 6, 1883 in Douglas County, Missouri and died on June 7, 1960 in Douglas County, Missouri. Married Charles Monroe Spurlock on November 16, 1904 in Douglas County, Missouri.

C116–Joseph H. Tigert. Son of James Tigert and Emelia Hendrick. (Fifth generation of Moses Trimble and Jane Belcher.) Born on February 26, 1851 in Warren County, Kentucky and died on July 13, 1911 in Warren County, Kentucky.

The children of Joseph H. Tigert:
> **C203–Eva A. Tigert.** Born in October 1875 in Kentucky.
> **C204–James Blaine Tigert.** Born on April 16, 1884 in Warren County, Kentucky and died in April 1963 in Illinois. Married Millie Hood on December 19, 1906.
> **C205–Hugh Talmage Tigert.** Born on August 6, 1886 in Kentucky and died on September 25, 1939.
> **C206–Samuel G. Tigert.** Born on June 18, 1892 in Bowling Green, Kentucky and died in May 1966 in Indianapolis, Marion County, Indiana.

C139–John Henry Belcher. Son of John Wesley Belcher and Sarah Victoria Suddarth. (Sixth generation of Moses Trimble and Jane Belcher.) Born on April 6, 1871 in Indiana and died on March 17, 1938 in South Haven, Van

C – Moses Trimble

Buren, Michigan. Married Emily S. Highfill on June 22, 1892 in Taswell, Crawford County, Indiana. She was born on December 28, 1868 in Indiana and died on February 11, 1956 in Hartford, Van Buren County, Michigan.

The children of John Henry Belcher and Emily S. Suddarth:

+ **C207—Ora Lotha Belcher.** Born on May 8, 1894 in Taswell, Crawford County, Indiana and died on July 8, 1983 in Hesperia, Oceana County, Michigan. Married Samuel Robert Graham on February 19, 1910 at. St Joseph, Michigan.

C208—Myrtle E. Belcher. Born in May 1898 in Indiana.

C209—Hazel Belcher. Born in February 1900 in Indiana and died in July 1981 in Clinton, Vermillion County, Indiana.

C210—Ola Mae Belcher. Born on January 23, 1902 in Illinois and died on August 22, 1988 in Tampa, Hillsborough County, Florida.

C211—Ottis Belcher. Born on May 25, 1905 in Illinois and died on September 17, 1976 in Dearborn, Wayne County, Michigan.

C212—Elsie Marie Belcher. Born on October 12, 1907 in Taswell, Crawford County, Indiana and died on September 6, 1983 in Southfield, Oakland County, Michigan.

C160—James J. Trimble. Son of Volney Thorton Trimble and Anna L. Snipes. (Sixth generation of Moses Trimble and Jane Belcher.) Born in December 1877 in Indiana and died in July 1974 in Roberts, Ford County, Illinois. Married Mabel Hahn. Born about 1885 in Illinois.

The children of James Trimble and Mabel Hahn:

+ **C213—Harold Trimble.** Born about 1908 in Illinois and died in 1996. Married Thelma ——.

C214—Claude Clarence Trimble. Born in 1910 in Illinois and died in 1932.

C215—Cecil James Trimble. Born on January 28, 1913 in Illinois and died December 4, 2001 in Illinois. Married Ruth Dixon on August 21, 1937. Ruth was born on March 20, 1913 in Ford County, Illinois and died February 13, 2002 in De Kalb, De Kalb County, Illinois.

C216—Dale Trimble. Born about 1922 in Illinois and died in 1998.

C217—Mary Trimble. Born about 1924 in Illinois.

C173—Sylvia Nell Trimble. Daughter of Charles and Ella Trimble. (Sixth generation of Moses Trimble and Jane Belcher. Born on August 21, 1895 in Oakwood, Illinois and died December 16, 1986 Danville, Illinois. Married a Mr. Finley.

The child of —— Finley and Sylvia Trimble:

+ **C218—Helen Luella Finley.** Born on September 7, 1928 in Oakwood, Illinois and died on June 4, 1999 in Urbana, Illinois.

C175—Fidella "Dell" Trimble. Daughter of Christopher Columbus Trimble and Elizabeth Rector. (Sixth generation of Moses Trimble and Jane Belcher.) Born in 1868 in Virginia and died on August 7, 1936. Married William Preston "Bud" Kenny. He was born in August 1868.

The children of William Preston Kenny and Fidella Trimble:

C219—Ider M. Kenny. Born in April 1894.

C220—Fred Kenny. Born on October 15, 1895 and died on June 14, 1955.

C221—Charles Kenny. Born in August 1897.

C222—Garnet Kenny. Born in July 1899.

C223—Elmer James Kenny. Born on October 13, 1910 and died on March 22, 1991.

C179—Margaret Josephine "Josie" Trimble. Son of Christopher Columbus Trimble and Elizabeth Rector. (Sixth generation of Moses Trimble and Jane Belcher.) Born on March 11, 1874 in Virginia and died on May 1, 1951. Married Richard Duphy Bartlett in 1893 in Virginia. Richard was born on March 27, 1872 in Virginia and died on June 24, 1962 in Grayson, Virginia.

The children of Richard Duphy Bartlett and Margaret Josephine "Josie" Trimble:

C224—Clayton C. Bartlett. Born in September 1893 in Virginia and died on June 27, 1927 in Galax, Virginia.

+ **C225—Thomas Lester Bartlett.** Born on November 8, 1895 in Sulphur Springs, Virginia and died on December 18, 1972 in Galax, Virginia. Married Genevia Ella Wright.

C226—Lula M. Bartlett. Born on November 1897 in Virginia and died on February 28, 1986 in Galax, Virginia.

C227—Eddie C. Bartlett. Born in 1902 in Virginia.

C228—Bessie Lee Bartlett. Born on August 27, 1903 and died on September 25, 1994 in Mount Airy, Surry, North Carolina.

C229—Ruth J. Bartlett. Born on October 3, 1905 in Old Town, Grayson, Virginia and died on June 18, 1989 in Akron, Summit, Ohio.

C230—Clarence William Bartlett. Born in 1909 in Sulphur Springs, Virginia and died on March 12, 1985.

C231—Dottie H. Bartlett. Born in 1911 in Virginia.

C232—Gracie Virginia Bartlett. Born on September 19, 1912 in Old Town, Grayson, Virginia and died on March 10, 2000 in Akron, Summit, Ohio.

C187—George W. Mooney. Son of James M. Mooney and Susan Jane Trimble. (Sixth generation of Moses Trimble and Jane Belcher.) Born in 1872 in Grayson, Virginia. Married to Margie Galyean on March 26, 1892 in Glade Creek, Alleghany County, North Carolina.

The children George W. Mooney and Margie Galyean:

C233—Virginia Blache Mooney. Born in April 1894 in Virginia.

C234—Jasper Lee Mooney. Born on March 11, 1896 in Virginia and died 1930 in Virginia.

C235—Maude R. Mooney. Born on October 1, 1898 in North Carolina and died May 1978 in Galax, Galax City, Virginia.

C236—Mabel J. Mooney. Born in June 1898 in Virginia.

C237—James Staley Mooney. Born on October 6, 1900 in Virginia and died on September 8, 1902 in Galax County, Virginia.

C191—Sarah Annie Mooney. Daughter of James M. Mooney and Susan Jane Trimble. (Sixth generation of Moses Trimble and Jane Belcher.) Born on July 1, 1877 in Grayson, Virginia and died on April 11, 1915 in Grayson, Virginia. Married Jessie Aron Crissman on January 16, 1916. Jessie was born on August 28, 1880 in Surry County, North Carolina and died on December 11, 1958 in Virginia.

The children of Jessie Aron Crissman and Sarah Annie Mooney:

C238—Clara Crissman. Born on February 15, 1902 in Virginia and died in February 1984 in Richmond, Richmond City, Virginia.

C239—Susan Callie Crissman. Born on August 9, 1903 in Virginia and died on July 24, 1989 in Winston-Salem, Forsyth County, North Carolina. Married Alonzo A. "Lonnie" Hall on March 18, 1923 in Galax, Virginia. Lonnie was born on August 7, 1901 in Virginia and died in July 1981 in Richmond, Virginia.

C240—Dessie Crissman. Born on February 9, 1907 in Virginia and died in 1962 in Grayson, Virginia. Married Viles James Triplett, Born on March 24, 1911 in North Carolina and died on April 18, 1991 in Galax, Virginia.

C194—Sidney Roberts. Son of Logan Roberts and Evaline Trimble. (Sixth generation of Moses Trimble and Jane Belcher.) Born on February 19, 1887 in Virginia and died in January 1963 in Galax, Carroll County, Virginia. Married Ollie Mae Williams on January 28, 1914 in Edmonds, North Carolina. Her parent were Miles Parden Williams and Elizabeth Clester Fletcher. Miles was born in August 1865 in Independence, Grayson County, Virginia and died on January 10, 1928. Elizabeth was born in 1868 in

Virginia and died in January 1943.

The children of Sidney Roberts and Ollie Mae Williams:

C241—James Gray Roberts. Born on February 16, 1915 in Galax, Virginia and died on December 31, 1979 in Montgomery, North Carolina.

C242—Annie Pauline Roberts. Born on October 10, 1916 in Virginia and died on February 11, 1981.

C243—Bishop Hale Roberts. Born on September 6, 1918 in Galax, Virginia and died on November 15, 1968.

C244—Helen Louise Roberts. Born on December 22, 1923 in Galax, Virginia and died in Galax, Virginia.

+ **C245—Herman June Roberts.** Born on September 7, 1924 in Caroll County, Virginia and died on April 2, 1977 in Charlottesville, Virginia. Married Addie Lee Altice on May 30, 1944.

C246—Raymond Fred Roberts. Born on April 7, 1932 Galax, Virginia and died on August 16, 1983 in Galax, Virginia.

C207—Ora Lotha Belcher. Son of John Henry Belcher and Emily S. Suddarth (Seventh generation of Moses Trimble and Jane Belcher.) Born on May 8, 1894 in Taswell, Crawford County, Indiana and died on July 8, 1983 in Hesperia, Oceana County, Michigan. Married Samuel Robert Graham on February 19, 1910 at. St Joseph, Michigan. Samuel's parents were James Graham and Mary Ann Hudson. They were married on December 5, 1877. James was born in May 1855 in Ontario, Canada and died in 1923 in South Haven, Van Buren County, Michigan. Mary Ann was born in April 1858 in Ontario, Canada and died on May 1, 1950 in South Haven, Van Buren County, Michigan.

The children Samuel Robert Graham and Ora Lotha Belcher:

C247—Infant Graham. Born in 1910 and died in 1911.

C248—Alice Mildred Graham. Born on October 4, 1911 in Marissa, St Clair County, Illinois and died on October 1, 2001 in Fremont, Newaygo County, Michigan. Married Clifford G. Plowman on April 4, 1928 in South Bend, St Joseph County, Indiana.

C249—Lotha Marie Graham. Born on April 19, 1913 in South Haven, Van Buren County, Michigan and died on April 19, 1977 in Springville, Utah Co., Utah.

C250—Roberta Margaret Graham. Born on August 26, 1914 in South Haven, Van Buren County, Michigan and died on July 18, 1992 in Fennville, Allegan, Michigan. Married Ernest William Weber

C251—Francis Mae Graham. Born on May 15, 1916 in South Haven, Van Buren County, Michigan and died on July 4, 1964 in Chicago, Cook County, Illinois. Married Nicholas Wurtz about 1931 in Van Buren County, Michigan.

C252—Myrtle Lorene Graham. Born on September 3, 1917 in South Haven, Van Buren County, Michigan and died on August 14, 1992 in Kaiser Foundation Hospital, Mantua, Portage County, Ohio. Married Charles Allen Guyette on May 10, 1937 in Detroit, Wayne County, Michigan.

C253—Laura Emma Graham. Born on December 13, 1921 in South Haven, Van Buren County, Michigan and died on June 5, 1981 in White Cloud, Newaygo County, Michigan. Married Abraham Annis Nader in Detroit, Michigan.

C254—Henrietta Helen Graham. Born on April 1, 1923 in South Haven, Van Buren County, Michigan and died on August 10, 2001 in New Port Richey, Pasco County, Florida.

C255—Robert Owen Graham. Born on May 16, 1924 in South Haven, Van Buren, Michigan and died on November 15, 1987 in Saint Paul, Ramscy, Minnesota.

C256—Richard James Graham. Born on May 4, 1932 in Michigan and died on January 10, 2008 in Fremont, Newaygo, Michigan. He was in United States Air Force during The Korean Conflict.

C213—Harold Trimble. Son of James Trimble and Mabel Hahn. (Seventh generation of Moses Trimble and Jane Belcher.) Born about 1908 in Illinois and died 1996. Married Thelma ———. Thelma was born about 1912.

The children of Harold and Thelma Trimble:
C257—Anita Trimble. Born about 1934 in Illinois.
C258—Darrel Trimble. Born about 1938 in Illinois.

C218—Helen Luella Finley. Daughter of ——— Finley and Sylvia Trimble. (Seventh generation of Moses Trimble and Jane Belchcr.) Born on September 7, 1928 in Oakwood, Illinois and died on June 4, 1999 in Urbana, Illinois.

The children of Helen Luella Finley:
C259—Linda Gaye Solomon. Born on July 27, 1949 in Urban, Illinois.

C225—Thomas Lester Bartlett. Son of Richard Duphy Bartlett and Margaret Josephine "Josie" Trimble. (Seventh generation of Moses Trimble and Jane Belcher.) Born on November 8, 1895 in Sulphur Springs, Virginia and died on December 18, 1972 in Galax, Virginia. Married Genevia Ella Wright, born on February 13, 1897 in Virginia and died on November 7, November 1984 in Galax, Virginia.

The child of Thomas Lester Bartlett and Genevia Ella Wright:

C260—Dan Isaac Bartlett. Born on February 16, 1919 in Virginia and died on February 28, 1970 in Burlington, Alamance, North Carolina. Dan married and had two children, but their names are unknown.

C245—Herman June Roberts. Son of Sidney Roberts and Ollie Mae Williams. (Seventh generation of Moses Trimble and Jane Belcher.) Born on September 7, 1924 in Caroll County, Virginia and died on April 2, 1977 in Charlottesville, Virginia. Herman enlisted in the military on March 19, 1943. Serving during World War II. Married Addie Lee Altice on May 30, 1944. She was born on August 12, 1924 in Roanoke, Virginia and died on November 14, 1984 in Charlottesville, Virginia.

Addie was the daughter of Willie Theortis Altice and Cora L. Argabright. Willie born on May 31, 1894 in Virginia and died on August 16, 1965 in Salem, Virginia. Cora born about 1894 in Virginia and died in November 1966 in Franklin, Virginia.

The children of Herman June Roberts and Addie Lee Altice:

+ **C261—Linda Carolyn Roberts.** Born on October 1, 1947 in Roanoke, Virginia and died on March 2, 1987 in Charlottesville, Virginia. Married Williard Howard Birckhead in Charlottesville, Virginia.

C261—Linda Carolyn Roberts. Daughter of Herman June Roberts and Addie Lee Altice. (Eighth generation of Moses Trimble and Jane Belcher.) Born on October 1, 1947 in Roanoke, Virginia and died on March 2, 1987 in Charlottesville, Virginia. Married Williard Howard Birckhead in Charlottesville, Virginia. Williard was born in Charlottesville, Virginia and died about 2005 in Charlottesville, Virginia.

The child of Williard Howard Birckhead and Linda Carolyn Roberts:
C262—Anne Walling Birckhead.

D - David Trimble

David Trimble was one of the original five brothers coming to America from Armagh County, Ireland. He died in Montgomery County, Kentucky, in 1799.

D1—David Trimble was the progenitor of a large portion of the Trimbles in America today, especially the Trimbles of the Midwest and western states. This being true due to David and his descendents ever migrating westward as new areas of this country were opened for settlement.

David's wife was a Houston. We can find no court records of his marriage, but there was an old letter written by his eldest daughter, Elizabeth, in which she said her mother was a Houston. Also, General Sam Houston studied law under James Trimble (A21), a great-nephew of David, from Nashville, Tennessee. General Houston described James as a "kinsman." The Houstons and Trimbles lived on neighboring plantations in Virginia, the birthplace of General Sam Houston.

Like his brother James, David was a surveyor and was appointed on May 18, 1773, as deputy surveyor of Augusta County, Virginia. He was a large landowner in the Valley of Virginia, both at the Forks-of-James, east of Lexington, Virginia, and on Middle River, this being his home plantation. Just after the Revolutionary War, when his sons migrated to Kentucky around the Montgomery County area, David made the move with them. At this time John, James, and Moses were already deceased, also David's wife. This probably accounted for his decision to move from his home in Virginia to the Kentucky area.

The will of David Trimble is recorded at the Bourbon County, Kentucky, Courthouse.

It appears that David and James were the closer of the Five Trimble Brothers as their names appear together frequently on documents recorded in the Virginia valley. This close tie could have been due to them having the same profession of surveying.

The children of David Trimble and —— Houston:

+ **D2—John Trimble.** Born in 1740 in Frostburg, Allegany County, Maryland and died in 1803 in Mt Savage, Allegany County, Maryland. Married Margaret Arnold in 1768.

+ **D3—James Trimble.** Born on August 2, 1747, in the Valley of Virginia and died on June 26, 1815. Married Jane Young on March 29, 1773.

+ **D4—Thomas Trimble.** Born in 1748 and died in 1830. Married Abigail

Gatliff in November 1785 in Greenbrier County, now West Virginia.

D5—Nancy Trimble. Born in 1749 in Augusta County, Virginia and died in 1773. Married a Mr. King in 1770. Mr. King was born 1747. No children.

+ **D6—Isaac Trimble.** Born in 1752 in Augusta County, Virginia and died in 1816 in Bourbon County, Kentucky. Married Mary 'Polly' Graham on June 14, 1787.

+ **D7—George Trimble.** Born on January 1, 1756, in Augusta County, Virginia and died on December 14, 1814, in Bourbon County, Kentucky. Married Jean Armstrong.

+ **D8—Mary 'Polly' Trimble.** Born in 1759 and died on September 15, 1846. Married John McKinney on September 8, 1785.

+ **D9—David Trimble.** Born in 1760 in Augusta County, Virginia and died in 1827 in Montgomery County, Kentucky. Married Lucy Lacy.

+ **D10—William Trimble.** Born in 1760 in Augusta County, Virginia and died on June 6, 1840, in Pulaski County, Kentucky. Married to Mary Fleming on April 19, 1787, by the Reverend John Alderson in Greenbrier County, now West Virginia. William was given his pension as a Revolutionary War soldier on December 2, 1835.

+ **D11—Elizabeth "Betsy" Trimble.** Born in 1769 and died in 1843 in Madison County, Ohio. Married Fergus Graham on March 13, 1787, in Augusta County, Virginia. Fergus was the son of Arthur Graham.[28]

D2—John Trimble. Son of David Trimble and —— Houston. Born in 1740 in Frostburg, Allegany County, Maryland and died in 1803 in Mount Savage, Allegany County, Maryland. Married Margaret Arnold in 1768. Margaret born in 1738 in Allegany County, Maryland and died in 1770 in Allegany County, Maryland. She was the daughter of John and Margaret Arnold.

The children of John Trimble and Margaret Arnold:

+ **D12—Charlotte Trimble.** Born on February 25, 1765, in Frostburg, Maryland and died on May 1, 1844, in Barton, Maryland. Married William Shaw.

+ **D13—John Trimble, Jr.** Born in 1767 in Allegany County, Maryland and died in 1823 in Allegany County, Maryland. Married Elizabeth Brown.

+ **D14—Margaret Trimble.** Born in 1770 and died on January 11, 1859, in

---

[28] This marriage record was originally published in "Chronicles of the Scotts-Irish Settlement in Virginia, 1745-1800. Extracted from the Original Court Records of Augusta County" by Lyman Chalkley.

D - David Trimble

> Allegany County, Maryland. Married John Combs in 1795 Allegany County, Maryland.

+ **D15—Abigail Trimble.** Born in 1771 in Frostburg, Allegany County, Maryland and died on February 26, 1793. Married Cudberth Combs.

+ **D16—Henry Trimble.** Born in 1772 in Frostburg, Allegany County, Maryland and died in 1825 in Allegany County, Maryland. Married three times.

+ **D17—Catherine Trimble.** Born on September 22, 1774, in Allegany County, Maryland and died on August 19, 1815, in Allegany County, Maryland. Married Kelita Potter on November 15, 1792, in Allegany County, Maryland.

+ **D18—Sophia Trimble.** Born in 1774 and died in 1860 in Washington County, Pennsylvania. Married Peter Crow on March 21, 1799, in Allegany County, Maryland.

D3—James Trimble. Son of David Trimble and —— Houston. Born on August 2, 1747, in the Valley of Virginia and died on June 26, 1815. He was baptized in 1747 by the Reverend James Craig on May 18, 1773. Married Jane Young on March 29, 1773. Jane was born in 1749. He was appointed as overseer of roads in Augusta County, Virginia and was the first elder in the Springfield Presbyterian Church, which is now in Bath County (formerly Montgomery County, Kentucky).

The children of James Trimble and Jane Young:

+ **D19—Hugh Trimble.** Born in 1770. Married twice.

+ **D20—David Trimble.** Born in 1774 in Augusta County, Virginia. Married Mary "Polly" Telfrow on August 19, 1802, in Old Springfield Presbyterian Church, Bath County, Kentucky.

D21—Nancy Trimble. Born in 1778 in Augusta County, Virginia and died on December 7, 1819, in Mt. Sterling, Montgomery, Kentucky. Married Samuel Young in 1801.

D22—Sally Trimble. Born in 1780. Married a Mr. Johnston.

D23—Jane Trimble. Born in 1782 in Henderson, Kentucky and died in 1860 in Warren County, Missouri. Married John Northcutt in 1811 in the Old Springfield Presbyterian Church in Bath County, Kentucky, by the Reverend Joseph P. Howe. Moved to Warren County, Missouri, in 1820.

D24—Thomas Trimble. Born in 1786. Married Jane Young.

D25—Betsy Trimble. Born in 1788. Married a Mr. Lacy.

+ **D26—John Trimble.** Born in 1793 and died in 1854 and married Margaret Turley, born in 1792, died in 1861. They moved to Callaway County,

Missouri.

D27—Robert Trimble. Born on September 20, 1793, in Mount Sterling, Kentucky and died on August 14, 1869, in Randolph County, Missouri. Married and had one child.

D4—Thomas Trimble. Son of David Trimble and —— Houston. Born in 1748 in Augusta County, Virginia and died in 1830 in Fleming County, Kentucky. Married Abigail Gatliff on November 5, 1785, in Greenbrier County, now West Virginia.[29] Abigail was born in 1757 in Virginia and died in 1822 in Fleming County, Kentucky. Thomas was a church member and deacon of his church.

The children of Thomas Trimble and Abigail Gatliff:

+ **D28—Mary Trimble.** Born in 1785 in Greenbrier, Virginia (now West Virginia) and died in 1828 in Madison, Virginia. Married Arthur McMullin on August 17, 1802, in Garrard, Kentucky.

D29—Alexander Trimble. Born in1790.

D30—John Trimble. Born in 1790.

D6—Isaac Trimble. Son of David Trimble and —— Houston. Born in 1752 in Augusta County, Virginia and died in 1816 in Bourbon County, Kentucky. Moved with his father to Kentucky. Although they did not make the move until 1792, they probably had taken up land on which they were paying taxes as early as 1791. Isaac married Mary 'Polly' Graham, a sister of Fergus Graham who had married Isaac's sister Elizabeth Trimble. Isaac and Mary were married in Rockbridge County, Virginia, on June 14, 1787.

The children of Isaac Trimble and Mary 'Polly' Graham:

D31—David Trimble. Named in his grandfather David Trimble's will. It reads, "I give and bequeath unto Isaac Trimble's son David my sorrel mare This will is recorded in Bourbon County, Kentucky...."

+ **D32—Polly Trimble.** She married Samuel Gossett.

+ **D33—Tabitha Elizabeth Trimble.** Born in 1792 in Kentucky and died on April 5, 1862, in Nicholas County, Kentucky. Married John Laughlin on January 3, 1818, in Nicholas, Kentucky.

D7—George Trimble. Son of David Trimble and —— Houston. Born on January 1, 1756, in Augusta County Virginia and died on December 14,

---

[29] Dodd, Jordan R., et al. *Early American Marriages: Virginia to 1850.* Bountiful, UT, USA: Precision Indexing Publishers.

D - David Trimble

1814, in Bourbon County, Kentucky. George was bequeathed the farm where his father lived in his father's will, dated in 1799, in Bourbon County, Kentucky.

In Augusta County, Virginia, about the time the Trimble family moved to Kentucky, George Trimble had married Jean Armstrong on October 4, 1792, daughter of William. Jean was born on October 25, 1763, in Augusta County, Virginia and died on August 26, 1839, in Orange County, Indiana.

George served as a private in the company of his brother Captain James Trimble of the Augusta County, Virginia Militia.[30]

After George's death, his family lived on a farm in Northeast Township. Orange County, Indiana. In the Trimble Cemetery located there are recorded these burials: Jane Armstrong Trimble, Thomas, Mary, Margaret, and George Trimble. Orange County, Indiana, Cemetery Records, Vol. III, page 251.

The children of George Trimble and Jean Armstrong:

D34—Mary Trimble. Born on July 30, 1793, died on March 25, 1852.

D35—Thomas Trimble. Born on October 23, 1794, died on September 11, 1877.

D36—Margaret Trimble. Born on November 11, 1798, died on January 13, 1881. Her will was probated in 1882 naming heirs Amanda Stratton, my brothers Thomas and George. Orange County, Indiana, Wills, Vol. 1, page 68.

+ **D37—Sarah Jane Trimble.** Born on August 1, 1802, in Bourbon County, Kentucky and died on March 25, 1865, in Sharon, Whiteside County, Illinois. Married Nathan Martin on March 20, 1829.

D38—George Trimble. Born on December 11, 1804, died on July 24, 1876.

D39—Elizabeth Trimble.

D8—Mary 'Polly' Trimble. Daughter of David Trimble and ——— Houston. Born in 1759 in Augusta County, Virginia and died on September 15, 1846, in Bourbon County, Kentucky. Married John McKinney on September 20, 1785, in Augusta County, Virginia. John was born in 1760 in Augusta County, Virginia and died on September 27, 1825, in Warren County, Missouri. She seems to be the first of David Trimble's children to settle in

---

[30] Sons of the American Revolution Membership Applications, 1889-1970. Louisville, Kentucky: National Society of the Sons of the American Revolution. Microfilm, 508 rolls.

Trimble Families of America

D - David Trimble

Kentucky. In 1783 John McKinney was the first teacher in the first school in what is now Lexington, Kentucky. He was a Revolutionary soldier, surveyor, Native American fighter, member of the Constitutional Convention in Kentucky, and an elder in the Green Creek Church near Clintonville, Kentucky. He was named "Wildcat" because of the following incident as described in *History of Kentucky*:

The following account of a fight between a wild-cat and a school master pictures the dangers, from other than Native Americans. In 1783, Lexington was only a cluster of cabins, one of which, near the spot where the courthouse now stands, was used as a schoolhouse. One morning in May, McKinney, the teacher was sitting alone at his desk, busily engaged in writing, when hearing a slight noise at the door, turned his head and beheld an enormous cat, with her forefoot upon the step of the door, her tail curling over her back, bristles erect and eyes glancing rapidly through the room, as if in search of prey.

McKinney's position at first completely concealed him but at a slight and involuntary motion of his chair, at the sight of this shaggy inhabitant of the forest, attracted puss' attention thus their eyes met. Seeing his danger, McKinney hastily arose and attempted to snatch a cylindrical rule from a table which stood within reach, but the cat was too quick for him.

Darting upon him with the proverbial activity of her tribe, she fastened upon his side with her teeth, and began to rend and tear with her claws like fury. McKinney's clothes were in an instant torn from his side and his flesh dreadfully mangled by the enraged animal, whose strength and ferocity filled him with astonishment. He in vain attempted to disengage her from his side. Her long, sharp teeth were fastened between his ribs, and his efforts served but to enrage her the more. Seeing his blood flow very copiously from the numerous wounds in his side, he became seriously alarmed and not knowing what else to do, threw himself upon the edge of the table, and pressed her against the sharp corner with the whole weight of his body.

The cat now began to utter the most angry and discordant cries and McKinney at the same time lifting his voice in concert, the two together sent forth notes so doleful as to alarm the whole town. Women, who are always the first in hearing or spreading news, were now the first to come to McKinney's assistance. The boldest of them rushed in and seeing McKinney bending over the table and writhing his body as if in great pain, she at first supposed that he was laboring under a severe fit of the colic but quickly perceiving the cat, now in the agonies of death, screamed out, "Why, good

163

heaven! Mr. McKinney, what is the matter?"

"I have caught a cat, madam," replied he gravely turning around, with sweat streaming from his face, under the mingled operation of fright, fatigue and agony. Most of the neighbors had now arrived and attempted to disengage the dead cat from her antagonist, but so firmly were her tusks locked between his ribs that this was a work of no small difficulty. Scarcely had it been affected when McKinney became sick and was compelled to go to bed. In a few days however, he had entirely recovered and so late as 1820 was alive and a resident of Bourbon County, Kentucky, where he has often been heard to affirm that he at any time had rather fight two Native Americans than one wildcat.

The children of John McKinney and Mary 'Polly' Trimble:

+ **D40—Polly McKinney.** Born in 1784 in Bourbon County, Kentucky and died on September 10, 1842, in Livonia, Washington County, Indiana. Married Alexander McPheeters, Jr.

+ **D41—Alexander McKinney.** Born in 1787 in Bourbon County, Kentucky and died in 1840 in Warren County, Missouri. Married Nancy Bryan on March 31, 1814, in St Charles County, Missouri.

D42—John C. W. McKinney. Born about 1787 in Bourbon County, Kentucky.

D43—Sally A. McKinney. Born about 1790 in Bourbon County, Kentucky.

D44—Elizabeth McKinney. Born about 1795 in Bourbon County, Kentucky.

D45—James Harvey McKinney. Born about 1795 in Bourbon County, Kentucky.

D46—Martha "Patsy" McKinney. Born about 1795 in Bourbon County, Kentucky.

+ **D47—Clarissa Harlow McKinney.** Born in 1796 in Bourbon County, Kentucky and died in 1885 in Missouri. Married John Montgomery.

D9—David Trimble. Son of David Trimble and —— Houston. Born in 1760 in Augusta County, Virginia and died in 1827 in Mount Sterling, Montgomery County, Kentucky. He married Lucy Lacy from Greenbrier County now West Virginia on August 28, 1781. [31] [32] Lucy was born on March 2, 1763, in Greenbrier County, now in, West Virginia and died in March 1781 in Kentucky. They lived for approximately ten years in Greenbrier County

---

[31] Virginia, Marriage Records, 1700-1850, Page 621.

[32] West Virginia, Marriage Index, 1785-1971.

before migrating in 1797 to Kentucky.

They settled in Jeffersonville, Kentucky. David Trimble and Lucy Lacy were married by the Reverend John Alderson in Greenbrier County now West Virginia. The original manuscript of Reverend Alderson's marriage register, in which this marriage is recorded, is at the University of Richmond.

David was the progenitor of an exceptionally large number of descendents of which the author (John Farley Trimble) was able to locate more complete material. This is not due to David being the author's (John Farley Trimble) ancestor, but due to the records of David's lineage being more complete.

The children of David Trimble and Lucy Lacy:

+ **D48—Mark Trimble.** Born in 1782 in Greenbrier County, now West Virginia. Died on August 2, 1861, in Johnson County, Kentucky. Married Nancy Schubert.

+ **D49—Elizabeth "Betsy" Trimble.** Born in 1784 in Augusta, Virginia and died at an early age in 1817 in Floyd County, Kentucky. Married Caleb Kash. Betsy was probably the youngest daughter of David. She was the first wife of Caleb Kash. They lived at Daysboro, Morgan County, Kentucky. According to records of J. G. Trimble, Sr., she had six daughters and no sons.

+ **D50—John Trimble.** Born on January 12, 1787, in what is now Monroe County, West Virginia and died on October 7, 1870, in Hazel Green, Wolfe County, Kentucky. He married Nancy ——

+ **D51—William Trimble.** Born on January 12, 1787, in what is now Monroe County, West Virginia and died on October 2, 1870, in Hazel Green, Wolfe County, Kentucky. He married Eleanor O'Hair on November 15, 1814. Eleanor was born on October 14, 1797, and died on May 24, 1855, in Hazel Green, Wolfe County, Kentucky.

D52—Louisa Trimble. Born in June 1792 in Monroe County, West Virginia and died in 1892. He had two sons and two daughters by his first wife. They were divorced in 1838. The two sons by this marriage went over the land route in 1849 to California. (In an old letter of J. G. Trimble in 1909 he states that he had not heard from these two boys since.) The two daughters of David Clark Trimble married brothers by the names of William and Thomas Botts. They moved to Jackson County, Missouri. William Botts was elected sheriff of that county in 1852-1855. David Clark Trimble married a second time and moved westward. A son and daughter were born from the second marriage.

D53—Nancy Trimble. Born in 1790 in Monroe County, West Virginia. Married

Trimble Families of America

William Carter.

+ **D54—David Clark Trimble.** Born in June 1792 in Monroe County, West Virginia and died in 1828. He had two sons and two daughters by his first wife. They were divorced in 1838. The two sons by this marriage went over the land route in 1849 to California. (In an old letter of J. G. Trimble in 1909 he states that he had not heard from these two boys since.) The two daughters of David Clark Trimble married brothers by the names of William and Thomas Botts. They moved to Jackson County, Missouri. William Botts was elected sheriff of that county in 1852-1855. David Clark Trimble married a second time and moved westward. A son and daughter were born from the second marriage.

+ **D55—Isaac Trimble.** Born in 1794 in Virginia (now Monroe County, West Virginia) and died on October 7, 1870, in Jeffersonville, Montgomery County, Kentucky. Married Mary Young in 1821.

D56—Jane Trimble. Born in 1796 in Monroe County, West Virginia. Married Jacob Weagle.

+ **D57—Lucinda Trimble.** Born in 1800 in Monroe County, West Virginia and died in 1854 in Montgomery County, Kentucky. Married John Wymore.

D58—Polly Trimble. Married John Stevens.

D10—William Trimble. Son of David Trimble and ——— Houston. Born in 1760 in Augusta County, Virginia. He died on June 6, 1840, in Pulaski County, Kentucky. Married to Mary Fleming on April 19, 1787, by the Reverend John Alderson in Greenbrier County, now West Virginia. Mary was born on April 14, 1772.

William was given his pension as a Revolutionary War soldier on December 2, 1835. He lived for a time in Greenbrier County then moved on to Bourbon County, Kentucky, around 1792. After a time, they moved to Harrison County, Tennessee, but lived their last days in Pulaski County near Somerset, Kentucky.

The children of William Trimble and Mary Fleming:

+ **D59—David Franklin Trimble.** Born on January 20, 1788 and died on December 18, 1856 in Pulaski County, Kentucky. Married Nancy Tarter on November 15, 1821.

D60—James Trimble. Born in 1790. Married Harriet Triplitt on February 6, 1824.

+ **D61—Elizabeth "Betsy" Raburn Trimble.** Born in 1792. Married a Mr. Raburn. Married Christian Logan Tarter on November 4, 1817 in

Pulaski County, Kentucky. [33] [34]

+ **D62—William Clark Trimble.** Born in 1794. Married Phebe Smith on August 11, 1813.

+ **D63—Mary "Polly" Trimble.** Born in 1795 in Kentucky and died after 1870 in Pulaski County, Kentucky. Married Thomas Drenin on September 4, 1817.

D64—John Trimble. Born about 1800 in Kentucky. Married Margaret Hatchett on May 27, 1817.

D65—Joyce Trimble. Born after 1800 in Harrison County, Kentucky.

D66—Letisha Trimble. Born in 1802.

D67—Elizabeth Trimble. Born in 1804.

D11—Elizabeth "Betsy" Trimble. Daughter of David Trimble and —— Houston. Born in 1769, died in 1843 in Madison County, Ohio. She married Fergus Graham on March 13, 1787, in Augusta County, Virginia. [35] He was born in 1767 in Rockbridge County, Virginia, and died in 1836.

In David Trimble's will of September 6, 1798, recorded in Bourbon County, Kentucky, Betsy Graham was willed her father's bed and pewter tankard, etc. Also, to Fergus Graham, David bequeathed six shillings.

From a biographical sketch in The History of Madison County, Ohio, published in 1883, Fergus and Elizabeth Graham moved from Kentucky in 1807 to Madison County where they lived for over sixty years. He was a minister in the Christian church and organized the Antioch Church in Madison County. He owned 500 acres of land.

The children of Fergus Graham and Elizabeth Trimble:

D68—James Graham.

D69—Washington Graham.

D70—Joseph Graham.

D71—Walker Graham.

D72—Jane Graham.

---

[33] Dodd, Jordan. Kentucky Marriages, 1802-1850 [database on-line]. Provo, UT, USA: Ancestry.com Operations Inc., 1997.

[34] US Census Year: 1850; Census Place: Division 2, Pulaski, Kentucky; Roll: M432_217; Page: 120A; Image: 371.

[35] Dodd, Jordan. Virginia, Marriages, 1660-1800 [database on-line]. Provo, UT, USA: Ancestry.com Operations Inc, 1997.

Trimble Families of America

D - David Trimble

D73—Margaret Graham.
D74—Malinda Graham.
D75—Eliza Graham.

The preceding children married and moved westward settling in Indiana and Illinois. The following children married but remained in Ohio:

+ **D76—John Graham.** Married Lydia Alkire and settled on Deer Creek, Madison County, Ohio. He lived to be eighty-three years of age and was a captain in the War of 1812. He was a blacksmith and farmer.

+ **D77—Polly Graham.** Married Isaac Alkire.

D12—Charlotte Trimble. Daughter of John Trimble and Margaret Arnold. (Third generation of David Trimble and —— Houston.) Born on February 25, 1765 in Frostburg, Maryland and died on May 1, 1844 in Barton, Maryland. Married William Shaw. He was born on January 3, 1756 in Barton-On-Umber, Lincolnshire, England. and died on June 1, 1813 in Barton, Maryland.

The children of William Shaw and Charlotte Trimble:

D78—George Shaw. Born on December 24, 1785 in Allegany County, Maryland and died in 1807 in Ohio. Married Ruth Hawkins. She was born in 1789.

D79—John Shaw. Born on August 16, 1787 in Cresaptown, Allegany County, Maryland and died on August 28, 1842 in Danville, Knox County, Ohio.

D80—Margaret Shaw. Born on October 25, 1789 in Cresaptown, Allegany County, Maryland and died on October 13, 1868 in Sarahsville, Noble County, Ohio. Married Arthur Morrison on June 10, 1814 in Allegany County, Maryland.

+ **D81—Henry Nainby Shaw.** Born on March 4, 1792 in Cresaptown, Allegany County, Maryland and died on April 16, 1862 in Evansville, Preston County, West Virginia. Married Sidney Thompson Shaw.

D82—William Shaw. Born on December 2, 1794 in Cresaptown, Allegany County, Maryland and died on May 2, 1867 in Lonaconing, Allegany, Maryland.

+ **D83—Joseph Shaw.** Born on May 23, 1797 in Barton, Allegany County, Maryland and died on April 2, 1886 in Beacon, Mahaska County, Iowa. Married Frances Adison Swanson on April 22, 1826 in Allegany County, Maryland.

D84—David Shaw. Born on December 9, 1799 in Allegany County, Maryland and died on July 7, 1800 in Allegany County, Maryland.

D85—Elizabeth Shaw. Born on June 13, 1801 in Allegany County, Maryland and died on April 17, 1870 in Allegany County, Maryland. Married Daniel Sease on March 22, 1821 in Allegany, Maryland.

D86—Catherine Shaw. Born on August 9, 1802 in Allegany County, Maryland and died on February 16, 1886 in Allegany County, Maryland. Married David Inskeep on October 30, 1825.

D13—John Trimble, Jr. Son of John Trimble and Margaret Arnold. (Third generation of David Trimble and ——— Houston.) Born in 1767 in Allegany County, Maryland and died on November 1, 1823 in Mount Savage, Allegany County, Maryland. Married Elizabeth Brown in 1785 in Allegany County, Maryland.

The children of John Trimble, Jr. and Elizabeth Brown:

D87—Enoch Trimble. Born in 1801.

D88—Henry Trimble. Born in 1802.

+ **D89—Samuel Trimble.** Born on February 16, 1804 in Mt Savage, Allegany County, Maryland and died on August 8, 1896 in Danville, Knox County, Ohio. Married Susannah Hammon on December 16, 1828 in Cumberland, Allegany, Maryland.

D90—Ester Trimble. Born in 1807.

D91—Elizabeth Trimble. Born in 1809.

D92—Margaret Trimble. Born in 1809.

+ **D93—Joseph A. Trimble.** Born in 1816 in Maryland and died in 1897 in Maryland. Married Mariah A. Evans.

+ **D94—Ann Trimble.** Born on March 3, 1823 in Mt Savage, Allegany County, Maryland and died on May 20, 1906 in Chicago, Cook County, Illinois. Married twice.

D14—Margaret Trimble. Daughter of John Trimble and Margaret Arnold. (Third generation of David Trimble and ——— Houston.) Born in 1770 and died on January 11, 1859 in Allegany County, Maryland. Married John Combs in 1795 Allegany County, Maryland. John was born about 1760 and died on July 1, 1854 in Allegheny County, Maryland. His parents were John Combs born about 1741 in Virginia and Nancy Harding.

The child of John Combs and Margaret Trimble:

D95—Abagail Combs. Born in 1795 in Maryland and died in 1850 in Maryland.

+ **D96—Mary Margaret Combs.** Born about 1803 in Allegany County, Maryland and died before 1837 in Frostburg, Allegany County, Maryland. Married Josiah Porter.

D97—Anna Martha Combs.

+ **D98—Elisha Combs.** Married Elizabeth Neff.

D99—Sophie Combs.

D100—William Combs.

D15—Abigail Trimble. Daughter of John Trimble and Margaret Arnold. (Third generation of David Trimble and —— Houston.) Born in 1771 in Frostburg, Allegany County, Maryland and died on February 26, 1793. Married Cudberth Combs. Cudberth was born in 1770 and died in 1800. Cudberth is the son of Johnathon Combs.

The children of Cudberth Combs and Abigail Trimble:

D101—Mary Combs. Born in 1790.

+ **D102—Hanna Combs.** Born on May 30, 1798 in Preston, West Virginia and died on February 22, 1844 in Aurora, Preston County, West Virginia. Married John Samuel Porter on October 3, 1815 in Allegany, Maryland.

D103—Martha Patsy Combs. Born in 1798 in Maryland. Married John Easter on December 6, 1824 in Allegany County, Maryland.

D104—Catherine Combs. Born in 1800 in Maryland.

D105—Margaret Combs. Born in 1800 in Maryland.

D106—William Combs. Born in 1804 in Maryland and died on February 11, 1858 in Washington County, Pennsylvania.

D16—Henry Trimble. Son of John Trimble and Margaret Arnold. (Third generation of David Trimble and —— Houston.) Born in 1772 in Frostburg, Allegany County, Maryland and died in 1825 in Allegany County, Maryland. Married Margaret Critchfield on October 23, 1794 in Allegany County, Maryland.

The child of Henry Trimble and Margaret Critchfield:

+ **D107—Noah Trimble.** Born about 1808 in Wellersburg, Pennsylvania and died on August 27, 1892 in Cumberland, Maryland. Married Kate Workman.

D17—Catherine Trimble. Daughter of John Trimble and Margaret Arnold. (Third generation of David Trimble and —— Houston.) Born on September 22, 1774 in Allegany County, Maryland and died on August 19, 1815 in Allegany County, Maryland. Married Kelita Potter on November 15, 1792 in Allegany, Maryland. He was born on June 22, 1770 in New Providence, Union County, New Jersey and died on April 6, 1856 in Allegany County, Maryland.

The child of Kelita Potter and Catherine Trimble:

D108—Margaret Potter. Born on October 30, 1793 in Allegany County, Maryland and died on April 1, 1858.

D109—Sarah Potter. Born on June 7, 1795 in Allegany County, Maryland and died on July 20, 1862 in Allegany County, Maryland.

D110—David Potter. Born on June 7, 1795 in Allegany County, Maryland and died on February 20, 1846 in Preston County, West Virginia.

D111—Charlotte Potter. Born on June 11, 1797 in Allegany County, Maryland.

D112—Rebecca Potter. Born in 1797 in Maryland and died in Richland, Illinois.

D113—Vashti Potter. Born on June 8, 1801 in Allegany County, Maryland and died on September 16, 1870 in Gilmer County, West Virginia. Married Moses Ayers. He was born on February 17, 1798 in Allegany County, Maryland and died on February 19, 1866 in Fairfield, Lenawee County, Michigan.

D114—Catherine Potter. Born on March 21, 1803 in Georges Creek, Allegany County, Maryland and died on July 31, 1843 in Allegany County, Maryland.

D115—Kelita Potter, Jr. Born on March 4, 1806 in Allegany County, Maryland and died in Monroe, Perry County, Ohio.

D116—George H. Potter. Born in 1806 in Maryland.

D117—John Potter. Born in 1809.

D118—William Potter. Born on August 14, 1812 in Allegany County, Maryland and died in 1858.

D18—Sophia Trimble. Daughter of John Trimble and Margaret Arnold. (Third generation of David Trimble and —— Houston.) Born in 1774 and died in 1860 in Washington County, Pennsylvania. Married Peter Crow on March 21, 1799 in Allegany County, Maryland.

The children of Peter Crow and Sophia Trimble:

D119—Margaret Crow. Died in 1865 in Iowa. Married George Gilmer.

D120—Phillip A. Crow. Born in 1810 in Pennsylvania and died in 1836. Married Maria Best.

D121—William Crow. Born in 1823 in Pennsylvania. Married Margaret Chaney in 1845.

D19—Hugh Trimble. Son of James Trimble and Jane Young. (Third generation of David Trimble and —— Houston.) Born in 1770. Hugh married two times. First to Ellen Caldwell in 1802 in the Old Springfield in the Presbyterian Church in Bath County, Kentucky, by the Reverend Joseph P. Howe and second to Nancy Northcutt in 1811.

D - David Trimble

The children of Hugh Trimble and Ellen Caldwell:

+ **D122—James Baird Trimble.** Born on December 8, 1803, at Mount Sterling, Kentucky and died on March 6, 1881, at Trimble Station, Crawford County, Illinois. He married two times.

+ **D123—Polly Ann Trimble.** Married a Mr. Leach.

The children of Hugh Trimble and Nancy Northcutt:

D124—Elkana Trimble.

D125—Elder Trimble.

D20—David Trimble. Son of James Trimble and Jane Young. (Third generation of David Trimble and ——— Houston.) Born in 1775 in Virginia. Married Mary "Polly" Telfrow on August 19, 1802 in Old Springfield Presbyterian Church, Bath County, Kentucky by Joseph P. Howe. David was willed his father's home place.

The children of David Trimble and Mary "Polly" Trimble:

D126—Alexander Trimble.

D127—Emmeline Trimble.

D128—Jane Trimble.

D129—Sally Ann Trimble.

D130—Thomas Trimble.

+ **D131—Permelia Meloan Trimble.** Born on December 24, 1803 in Montgomery County, Kentucky and died on September 22, 1845 in Calloway, Kentucky. Married Wesley Daniel McCarty.

D26—John Trimble. Son of James Trimble and Jane Young. (Third generation of David Trimble and ——— Houston.) Born in 1793 in Kentucky, died in 1854 in Callaway County, Missouri. On September 9, 1819, he married Margaret Turley in Montgomery County, Kentucky. Margaret was born on April 3, 1792, and died on February 22, 1861, in Callaway County.

The children of John Trimble and Margaret Turley:

D132—James Trimble. Drowned as a child.

D133—William H. Trimble. Living in Audrain County, Missouri, in 1884 and died in 1889. He married Martha J. Hughes, born in 1823 and died in 1876.

D134—Thomas J. Trimble. Living in Callaway County, Missouri, in 1884.

D135—Benjamin F. Trimble. Died in California in 1849.

D136—John Trimble, Jr. Born in 1827 in Missouri.

D137—Samuel A. Trimble. Born on March 12, 1830 and died in 1909.

D138—Sarah Jane Trimble. Born in 1833 and married John P. Truitt.

Trimble Families of America

D28—Mary Trimble. Daughter of Thomas Trimble and Abigail Gatliff. (Third generation of David Trimble and —— Houston.) Born in 1785 in Greenbrier, Virginia (now West Virginia) and died in 1828 in Madison, Virginia. Married Arthur McMullin on August 17, 1802 in Garrard, Kentucky. Arthur was born in 1782 in Greenbrier County, Virginia and died in 1866 in Washington County, Kentucky.

The children of Arthur McMullin and Mary Trimble:

D139—Alexander McMullin. Born in 1805 in Madison County, Kentucky and died in 1840.

D140—Abigail McMullin. Born in 1812 in Madison County, Kentucky and died 1880 in Washington County, Kentucky.

D141—Nancy McMullin. Born in 1812 in Madison County, Kentucky.

+ **D142—James McMullin.** Born in December 1820 in Madison County, Kentucky and died on March 3, 1920 in Washington County, Kentucky. Married Lucinda Burns on August 7, 1842 in Washington County, Kentucky.

D143—Thomas McMullin. Born in 1822 in Madison, Madison County, Virginia and died in 1848 in Washington County, Kentucky.

D144—Drury McMullin. Born on April 4, 1825 in Paint Lick Creek, Madison County, Kentucky and died on June 24, 1904 in Waldron, Platte County, Missouri.

D32—Polly Trimble. Daughter of Isaac Trimble and Mary 'Polly' Graham. (Third generation of David Trimble and —— Houston.) She married Samuel Gossett. In the *Register of the Kentucky State Historical Society, Vol. 40,* page 149, appears the genealogy of the Gossett family:

Samuel Gossett first married Polly Trimble (before 1816), daughter of Isaac Trimble, son of David Trimble of Bourbon County, Kentucky: (See Bourbon County Deeds) Samuel Gossett and wife Polly of Montgomery County, Kentucky deed Polly Trimble and "whereon Polly Trimble now lives," being their interest in Isaac Trimble's land on October 11, 1816. Samuel Gossett married a second and third time.

The children of Samuel Gossett and Polly Trimble:

+ **D145—David Matthias Gossett.** Born on June 1, 1823 in Kentucky and died on November 13, 1895 in Austin, Cass County, Missouri. Married Mary Calistine Phillips on January 11, 1863 in Kansas City, Jackson County, Missouri.

D146—Isaac T. Gossett.

Trimble Families of America

D147—Jacob Gossett.

D33—Tabitha Elizabeth Trimble. Daughter of Isaac Trimble and Mary 'Polly' Graham. (Third generation of David Trimble and —— Houston.) Born in 1792 in Kentucky and died on April 5, 1862 in Nicholas County, Kentucky. Married John Laughlin on January 3, 1818 in Nicholas, Kentucky. John was born in 1786 in Virginia and died on July 24, 1868 in Nicholas County, Kentucky.

The children of John Laughlin and Tabitha Elizabeth Trimble:
  D148—Patsey Laughlin. Born in April 1822 in Bourbon, Kentucky and died on December 13, 1903 in Fleming, Kentucky. Married Montgomery Moore.
  D149—William F. Laughlin. Born in 1824 in Kentucky and died in 1880 in Kentucky.
  D150—John Laughlin. Born on December 15, 1825 in Kentucky, and died on December 20, 1919 in Kansas City, Jackson, Missouri.
  + **D151—Robert Luckie Laughlin.** Born on January 7, 1830 in Blue Lick Spring, Bourbon County, Kentucky and died on October 24, 1914 in Franklin County, Kansas. Married Rebecca Francis Githens in 1850.
  D152—James Laughlin. Born in 1831 in Bourbon County, Kentucky and died in 1910 in Nicholas County, Kentucky.
  D153—Isaac Price Laughlin. Born on September 19, 1833 in Bourbon County, Kentucky and died on January 12, 1908 in N Middletown, Bourbon County, Kentucky.
  D154—Elizabeth Laughlin. Born in 1835 in Nicholas County, Kentucky and died in 1934 in Nicholas County, Kentucky. Married Roland O. Thomas.
  D155—Eli Laughlin. Born on January 31, 1840 in Bourbon County, Kentucky and died on October 31, 1882 in Nicholas County, Kentucky. Married Millie B. Mann.

D37—Sarah Jane Trimble. Daughter of George Trimble and Jean Armstrong. (Third generation of David Trimble and —— Houston.) Born on August 1, 1802 in Bourbon County, Kentucky and died on March 25, 1865 in Sharon, Whiteside County, Illinois. Married Nathan Martin on March 20, 1829. Orange County, Indiana, Marriages, Vol. 5, page 97.

The children of Nathan Martin and Sarah Jane Trimble:
  + **D156—George Trimble Martin.** Born on February 4, 1830 and died on July 1, 1874.
  D157—John Stephen Martin. Born on August 26, 1831 and died on March 22, 1915.

174

D158—Enoch Mason Martin. Born on July 5, 1833 and died in May 1915.

D159—Sarah Jane Elizabeth Martin. Born on November 24, 1834 and died on June 1, 1853.

D160—Achsah Ann Martin. Born on November 16, 1836.

D161—Nathan Morrison Martin. Born on May 23, 1838 and died 1913.

D162—James Allen Martin. Born on January 10, 1840 and died on August 11, 1892.

D163—Amazetta Zenobia Martin. Born on February 6, 1842 and died on January 15, 1862.

D164—Mary Catherine Martin. Born on April 23, 1844.

D165—Henryetta Clay Martin. Born on April 13, 1846 and died on January 10, 1866.

D40—Polly McKinney. Daughter of John McKinney and Mary 'Polly' Trimble. (Third generation of David Trimble and —— Houston.) Born in 1784 in Bourbon County, Kentucky and died on September 10, 1842 in Livonia, Washington County, Indiana. Married Alexander McPheeters, Jr. Alexander was born in 1782 in Augusta County, Virginia and died on June 19, 1825 in Washington County, Indiana.

The children of Alexander McPheeters, Jr. and Polly McKinney:

D166—Jane McPheeters. Born on January 10, 1807 and died on March 7, 1847 in Livonia, Washington County, Indiana.

D167—John M. McPheeters. Born on September 8, 1808 in Kentucky and died on May 26, 1864 in Washington, Indiana.

D168—James H. McPheeters. Born on April 2, 1818.

D169—Mary Ann McPheeters. Born on April 4, 1820 and died December 15, 1834.

D170—William C. McPheeters. Born on January 5, 1821 in Jessamine County, Kentucky and died on April 17, 1885 in Vigo, Indiana.

D41—Alexander McKinney. Son of John McKinney and Mary 'Polly' Trimble. (Third generation of David Trimble and —— Houston.) Born in 1787 in Bourbon County, Kentucky and died in 1840 in Warren County, Missouri. Married Nancy Bryan on March 31, 1814 in St Charles County, Missouri. Nancy was born in 1797 in Kentucky and died in 1889 in Warren County, Missouri.

The children of Alexander McKinney and Nancy Bryan:

D171—Levina B. McKinney. Born in 1813 in St Charles County, Missouri.

D172—Jonathan McKinney. Born in 1815 in St Charles County, Missouri.

D - David Trimble

D173—John Campbell McKinney. Born on August 28, 1816 in St Charles County, Missouri and died on May 28, 1875 in Columbia, Missouri.

+ **D174—Mary Jane McKinney.** Born on July 13, 1818 in Montgomery County, Missouri and died on March 29, 1887 in Mexico, Missouri. Married James Callaway on July 19, 1838 in Warren County, Missouri.

D175—Harvey G. McKinney. Born in 1826 in Montgomery County, Missouri.

D176—Zerelda McKinney. Born in 1828 in Montgomery County, Missouri.

D177—Alexander W. McKinney. Born in 1830 in Montgomery County, Missouri.

D178—Martha L. McKinney. Born in 1832 in Montgomery County, Missouri.

D47—Clarissa Harlow McKinney. Daughter of John McKinney and Mary 'Polly' Trimble. (Third generation of David Trimble and —— Houston.) Born in 1796 in Bourbon County, Kentucky and died in 1885 in Missouri. Married John Montgomery. John was born in 1778 in Pennsylvania and died after 1850 in Orleans, Orange County, Indiana.

The children of John Montgomery and Clarissa Harlow McKinney:

D179—William H. Montgomery. Born on February 18, 1815 in Kentucky and died on August 26, 1902 in Orleans, Indiana.

D180—Mary Montgomery. Born about 1817 in Indiana and died before 1900.

D181—Martha Montgomery. Born about 1819 in Indiana.

D182—Emma Montgomery. Born about 1821 in Indiana and died about 1880.

D183—John Alexander Montgomery. Born in 1824 in Kentucky and died in 1877 in Indiana. Married Amanda N. Somerville on August 7, 1850 in Decatur County, Indiana. Amanda was born on February 23, 1833 in Indiana and died on January 4, 1915 in Brazil, Clay County, Indiana.

D184—Elizabeth Montgomery. Born on May 30, 1827 in Fayette County, Kentucky and died after 1850 in Illinois.

D185—James H. Montgomery. Born on 1828 in Indiana and died in 1850.

D186—Clarissa H. Montgomery. Born in 1829 in Indiana. Married Adam Alexander on January 22, 1851 in Decatur County, Indiana. Adam was born about 1825 in Indiana.

D187—Sarah T. Montgomery. Born in 1834 in Indiana. Married Abner Parke Bowlby on January 22, 1851 in Decatur County, Indiana. Abner was born on September 28, 1823 in New York and died in 1891 in Litchfield, Montgomery County, Illinois.

D188—Andrew Jackson Montgomery. Born in 1835 in Indiana.

D48—Mark Trimble. Son of David Trimble and Lucy Lacy. (Third generation

Trimble Families of America

of David Trimble and ——— Houston.) Born in 1782 in Greenbrier County, now West Virginia and died on August 2, 1861, in Johnson County, Kentucky. He fought in the war of 1812. Where he married Nancy Ellen Schubert. Nancy was born in 1793 in Greenbrier County, Virginia and died after 1870 in Barnett's Creek, Johnson County, Kentucky. Her parents were Dutch immigrants. She had a Dutch bible that she read.

Most of Mark Trimble's descendents remained on Barnett's Creek in Johnson County, Kentucky. There are numerous Trimbles living there today. In contrast, many of the early Trimble families migrated westward.

Labor Day of 1971, my wife and I (John Farley and Loretta Trimble) attended a Trimble reunion at Ashland, Kentucky. There were approximately sixty families in attendance. We have never met any finer people than these. Although we had not met these Trimble folks before we soon became "cousins" and truly friends. Food! There was an array of delicious and tasty dishes and one had to go for seconds.

The update author (Stanley Barry Trimble) remembers them twice visiting our reunion in Ashland, Kentucky. My father was president of this reunion 10 to 15 years. On the first trip they stayed in a motel. Dad asked where they stayed so on the second of the visits, they stayed at our house, the night before the reunion. I (Stanley Barry Trimble) gave up my bedroom for them to stay in, this happened often with out-of-town guests.

We wish to give credit and grateful appreciation to Betty Jo Burchett of Eastwood, Kentucky, Diana Trimble of Paris, Kentucky, and Dallas Trimble of Huntington, West Virginia, for their assistance on records of the Johnson County Trimbles.

We researched a Johnson County, Kentucky, history but found it to be incorrect in the assertion that the progenitor of these Johnson County Trimble families was William instead of Mark.

The children of Mark Trimble and Nancy Schubert:

+ **D189—David Trimble.** Born in 1819 in Kentucky and died in 1915 in Menifee, Kentucky. Married twice. First wife's name is not known. Married second time a Conley.

 D190—Lewis Trimble. Born in 1822 in Kentucky and died in September 1870 in Menifee, Kentucky.

+ **D191—James M. Trimble.** Born on January 1, 1825 in Barnett's Creek, Johnson County, Kentucky and died on November 11, 1891 in Barnett's Creek, Johnson County, Kentucky. He married two times. Served in the Confederacy during the Civil War.

D - David Trimble

+ **D192—Susannah Trimble.** Born on January 24, 1830 in Morgan County, Kentucky and died on April 12, 1863 in Johnson County, Kentucky. Married Dr. Nathaniel Picklesimer.

+ **D193—William "Bill Dodger" Trimble.** Born on October 28, 1836 in Morgan County, Kentucky and died on November 22, 1912 in Johnson County, Kentucky. Married Clarinda Ellen Picklesimer.

+ **D194—Nancy Jane Polly Trimble.** Born on June 2, 1844 in Johnson County, Kentucky. Married John Jasper Wheeler about 1861. John was born on November 9, 1837 in Johnson County, Kentucky and died on December 9, 1915 in Johnson County, Kentucky

D49—Elizabeth "Betsy" Trimble. Daughter of David Trimble and Lucy Lacy. (Third generation of David Trimble and ——— Houston.) Betsy was probably the youngest daughter of David. She was the first wife of Caleb Kash. They lived at Daysboro, Morgan County, Kentucky. Betsy died at an early age. Per records of J. G. Trimble, Sr., she had six daughters and no sons.

D50—John Trimble. Son of David Trimble and Lucy Lacy. (Third generation of David Trimble and ——— Houston.) Born in 1794 in Virginia (now Monroe County, West Virginia), and later moved to Montgomery County, Kentucky. He married Nancy ———.

The children of John and Nancy Trimble:
D195—William Trimble. Born in 1825.
D196—Sarah Trimble. Born in 1827.
D197—John Washington Trimble. Born in 1831.
D198—Angeline Trimble. Born in 1834.
D199—Lucinda Trimble. Born in 1835.
+ **D200—Richard Menifee Trimble.** Born on August 12, 1837, died on February 21, 1909. Married Armilda Hines Glover.

D51—William Trimble. Son of David Trimble and Lucy Lacy. (Third generation of David Trimble and ——— Houston.) Born in 1787 in Monroe County, West Virginia. Died in 1870 in Kentucky. He married Eleanor O'Hair on November 15, 1814. She was born on October 14, 1797, in Kentucky and died in 1855. In 1815, William and Eleanor began housekeeping in a log cabin on a large tract of land which he had previously bought for five cents an acre. They are buried at Hazel Green, Kentucky, and a large monument marks their graves.

William Trimble was a bugle boy in the War of 1812 and was an eyewitness to the killing of Native Americas Chief Tecumseh. As a young man he began buying lands in Morgan County, Kentucky, and built the town of Hazel Green, Kentucky. This tract of land was originally called Trimble's Store. William laid out the streets, sold lots, and later changed the name to Hazel Green. This log structure, which was the store, located on the corner of Main and State streets, now is the site of a restaurant.

He established several industries such as tanneries, lumber mills, and a spinning and weaving works. Thus, he became one of Kentucky's more affluent citizens. Although he had a large family of twelve children, one was willed at his father's death, nine farms. He is the progenitor of another outstanding line of the Trimble family. William built a vast trade of furs and cattle trading, and he was a dealer in lands and slaves. By the time, his village of twenty-seven lots became an established town in 1849, he had amassed a great fortune.

William Trimble was not a churchman, but he donated the land on which to build two churches at Hazel Green one for the white congregation and one for the black.

To each of his children at their marriage he gave a hand-woven colored coverlid made by slaves in his spinning and weaving house. Some of these coverlids are still in existence and are prized heirlooms.

The ravages of the Civil War, which spread over this little town, destroyed some of the dreams of William Trimble's building.

Being a large slave owner, William Trimble was a Southern sympathizer. This fact caused confrontation with Federal troops on occasions when they would go through this mountainous area. On one of these occasions William's son Asbury Trimble was bushwhacked while overseeing his father's tannery. Asbury's wife, who was expecting a child at the time, named the child *South* in defiance of the Union forces. This South Trimble later became a noted member of the U.S. Congress and is buried in Arlington National Cemetery.

The children of William Trimble and Eleanor O'Hair:

+ **D201—Evaline Trimble.** Born on January 14, 1816, died on February 20, 1889. Married James Felix McGuire.

+ **D202—Caroline Trimble.** Born on October 5, 1817, at Hazel Green, Kentucky, died on September 1, 1898. Married Stephen Swango.

+ **D203—William Preston Trimble.** Born on October 6, 1818, died on March 15, 1905. Married Sarah Kash on February 2, 1843.

+ **D204—David Shelton "Doc" Trimble.** Born on June 23, 1821 and died on July 24, 1907. He is buried at Hazel Green, Kentucky. He married two

Trimble Families of America

times.

+ **D205—James Greenville Trimble.** Born on June 15, 1823, died on June 22, 1919.

+ **D206—Stephen Asbury Trimble.** Born on December 3, 1825 died on October 15, 1864. Married Elizabeth South on July 7, 1863.

+ **D207—Emily Jane Trimble.** Born on January 4, 1828 and died on December 12, 1897. She married two times.

D208—Rose Ann Trimble. Born on January 3, 1830 and died on March 27, 1863. Married Edward A. Hensley and they lived near Maytown, Kentucky. They had three sons, but we do not have their names but do know they left Kentucky and went to New Mexico, Missouri, and Nebraska. Mr. Hensley spent the last years of his life in blindness.

+ **D209—Louisa Jane Trimble.** Born on October 16, 1831 and died in February 1922. Married two times.

+ **D210—Mary Elizabeth Trimble.** Born on November 3, 1833, died on May 10, 1903. Married James Turner.

D211—Nelson Harvey Trimble. Born on December 4, 1836 and died at the age of seventeen while attending school at Owingsville, Kentucky. He is buried at Hazel Green, Kentucky.

D212—Malissa Trimble. Born on January 20, 1839 and died on January 27, 1839. Malissa died in infancy.

D213—Jay Franklin Trimble. Born on December 29, 1840 and died on October 12, 1930. Married Lillian Shelton of Summersville, Tennessee. Jay was a well-educated man and amassed a large fortune through his real estate business in Nashville. It is not known if there were children from this marriage. In his will, Jay left $1,000 to the Hazel Green Cemetery Association and $7,000 for the buying of monuments for his beloved family of Hazel Green, Kentucky. It was his desire that an especially nice stone be placed at his mother's and father's graves.

D54—David Clark Trimble. Son of David Trimble and Lucy Lacy. (Third generation of David Trimble and ——— Houston.) Born in June 1792 in Monroe County, West Virginia and died in 1892. He had two sons and two daughters by his first wife. They were divorced in 1838. The two sons by this marriage went over the land route in 1849 to California. (In an old letter of J. G. Trimble in 1909 he states that he had not heard from these two boys since.) The two daughters of David Clark Trimble married brothers by the names of William and Thomas Botts. They moved to Jackson County, Missouri. William Botts was elected sheriff of that county in 1852-1855.

David Clark Trimble married a second time and moved westward. A son and daughter were born from the second marriage.

D55–Isaac Trimble. Son of David Trimble and Lucy Lacy. (Third generation of David Trimble and —— Houston.) Born in 1794 in Monroe County, Virginia (now West Virginia). Married Mary Young in 1821. Mary was later drowned in the Red River Flood in Kentucky. Isaac had a farm and lived near Jeffersonville, Montgomery County, Kentucky. He was in the lumber business and was prosperous both in farming and lumber.

The children of Isaac Trimble and Mary Young:

+ **D214–James Harvey Trimble.** Born on February 9, 1821, in Montgomery County, Kentucky, and died on February 9, 1910, near Camargo, Kentucky. Married Harriet Brush. He was deputy sheriff two terms: 1864-1868.

+ **D215–David Franklin "Doc" Trimble.** Born on October 14, 1824, at Montgomery County, Kentucky and died on September 16, 1865 (ambushed near Tick Town), Jeffersonville, Kentucky.

D216–Ann Trimble. Married Socrates Kincaid, a lawyer and planter living near Lexington, Kentucky. We have no further information on this family except a grandson of Socrates and Ann Trimble Kincaid named Garvice Kincaid is one of Kentucky's most wealthy men. He was born in 1912 and married Nell Wilson. His offices are based in Lexington, Kentucky. According to a tabloid on Mr. Kincaid, published by the *Courier Journal* of Louisville, Kentucky, March 24, 1968, his holdings include: thirteen banks, four of them in Florida, the Kentucky Central Life Insurance Company, television and radio stations, etc. He is a philanthropist with much attention on the needs of youth and the disabled.

D217–Martha Trimble. Married William Lamb. According to Campbell County, Kentucky, summons of July 18, 1867, the guardianship of young George Trimble, son of Doc and Narcissus Trimble, Martha's nephew, was given to her husband William Lamb. (We believe they went westward but have found no information concerning this group. The author (John Farley Trimble) researched the preceding brief records.)

D218–Evelyn Trimble. Married Mid Jameson. According to Estill County, Kentucky, summons of July 20, 1867, guardianship of young Marion Trimble, son of Doc and Narcissus Trimble, and Evelyn's nephew, was given to her husband Mid Jameson.

D219–Fannie Trimble. Married a Mr. Murphy.

D - David Trimble

D57—Lucinda Trimble. Daughter of David Trimble and Lucy Lacy. (Third generation of David Trimble and —— Houston.) Born in 1800 in Monroe County, West Virginia and died 1854 in Montgomery, Kentucky. Married John Wymore.

D59—David Franklin Trimble. Son of William Trimble and Mary Fleming. (Third generation of David Trimble and —— Houston.) Born on January 20, 1788 and died 1856.[36] Married Nancy Tarter on November 15, 1821. Nancy was born in 1798.

The children of David Franklin Trimble and Nancy Tarter:
D220—Elizabeth Trimble
D221—James Franklin Trimble
D222—Jane Trimble
D223—John Trimble
D224—Sarelda Trimble
D225—Thomas Crittenden Trimble
D226—Wesley Trimble
+ **D227—Cyrenius Wait Trimble.** Born on February 23, 1834 in Pulaski County, Kentucky and died on June 6, 1908. Married Melissa Davis on October 18, 1853 in Pulaski County, Kentucky.

D61—Elizabeth "Betsy" Raburn Trimble. Daughter of William Trimble and Mary Fleming. (Third generation of David Trimble and —— Houston.) Born in 1792 in Greenbrier County, Virginia and died on November 11, 1817 in Russell, Kentucky. Married Christian Logan Tarter on November 4, 1817 in Pulaski County, Kentucky.

The children of Christian Logan Tarter and Elizabeth "Betsy" Raburn Trimble:
D228—Polly Jane Tarter. Born in 1793 in Virginia and died in 1855 in Pulaski County, Kentucky.
D229—Christian Logan Tarter, Jr. Born in 1803 and died in 1870.
D230—Squire T. Tarter. Born in April 1819 in Pulaski County, Kentucky and died in 1906 in McBeath Cemetery, Russell, Kentucky.
D231—Reader W. Tarter. Born on January 18, 1821 in Pulaski County,

---

[36] Kentucky. Kentucky Birth, Marriage and Death Records - Microfilm (1852-1910). Microfilm rolls #994027-994058. Kentucky Department for Libraries and Archives, Frankfort, Kentucky.

Kentucky and died on December 19, 1872 in Russell, Kentucky.

D232—Enoch Lee Tarter. Born on September 9, 1822 in Pulaski County, Kentucky and died on April 25, 1891 in Pulaski County, Kentucky.

D233—Wesley Monroe Tarter. Born in 1824 and died in 1844.

D234—James A. Tarter. Born in 1825 in Pulaski County, Kentucky and died on December 14, 1866 in Russell, Kentucky.

D235—Cyrenius W. Tarter. Born in 1827 in Pulaski County, Kentucky and died in 1876 in Russell, Kentucky.

D62—William Clark Trimble. Son of William Trimble and Mary Fleming. (Third generation of David Trimble and ——— Houston.) *The History of Edgar County, Illinois*, says William C. Trimble arrived in 1826. He settled in Ross Township near the Prairie Township line. Edgar County was organized in 1823. It is said they lived on the border of civilization near the salt mines. He lived in Edgar County for twenty-seven years moving to Dallas County, Texas, where he died about 1878. He served in May's company in the Black Hawk Campaign in Illinois. While in Illinois, Phebe, his wife, must have died for we find he married on November 2, 1835, Bethenia Hayworth.

William Clark Trimble was born in 1794. He married Phebe Smith on August 11, 1813, in Fleming County, Kentucky. He was in the War of 1812, in Captain W. Bott's company, Second Regiment, Kentucky Mounted Volunteer Militia. He appears on the company payroll August 27-November 3, 1813.

On April 5, 1813, William Trimble, Jr., deeded to William Trimble, Sr., thirty-two acres on Wilson Run, lying and being in Fleming County, Kentucky.[37]

On October 8, 1824, Phebe Trimble and William Clark Trimble deeded to James Trimble two tracts containing one hundred five acres for the sum of $1,000; thirty-two acres were conveyed by William C., Jr., to William Trimble, Sr. That is about the time that Phebe and William Clark Trimble left Fleming County, Kentucky, and moved to Edgar County, Illinois.

The children of William Clark Trimble and Phebe Smith:

+ D236—Walter Ulyssess Trimble. Born in 1819 and died in 1874. Married

---

[37] Deed Book E, page 324. July 27, 1813, William Trimble, Sr., deeded to William Trimble, Jr., fifty-five acres on Fleming Creek, Deed Book G, page 82.

Elizabeth Fidelia Bacon on August 21, 1844.

D237—Green Clark Trimble. Born in 1822 in Kentucky and died in 1896 in Fair Play, Missouri. Married Sally Rodgers on May 1, 1833, in Edgar County, Illinois.

+ **D238—Thomas Dudley Trimble.** Born in 1815 and died on February 17, 1899. Married Eunice Rodgers on December 5, 1835, in Edgar County, Illinois.

D239—Nelson S. Trimble. Married Lydia J. ——.

D240—Allen Trimble. Married Sarah Jane Hayworth on November 9, 1841.

D241—William A. Trimble. Born in 1823. Married Mary A. —— about 1848. He was a Confederate soldier from Texas.

+ **D242—Andrew Jackson Trimble.** Born in Illinois and died in September of 1892 in Monmouth, Iowa. Married Louisa Hanson.

D243—Mary Ann Trimble. Married Solomon Hayworth on April 28, 1838, in Edgar County, Illinois.

D63—Mary "Polly" Trimble. Daughter of William Trimble and Mary Fleming. (Third generation of David Trimble and —— Houston.) Born in 1795 in Kentucky and died after 1870 in Pulaski County, Kentucky. Married Thomas Caughron on November 8, 1814 in Pulaski County, Kentucky. Thomas was born in 1790 in Virginia and died in 1870 in Nancy, Pulaski County, Kentucky.

They children of Thomas Caughron and Mary "Polly" Trimble:

+ **D244—Elizabeth F. Caughron.** Born in 1820 in Pulaski County, Kentucky and died in 1861 in Pulaski County, Kentucky. Married Benjamin J. Floyd on August 16, 1842 in Pulaski County, Kentucky.

D245—Peter Caughron. Born in 1820 in Pulaski County, Kentucky and died in 1842 in Pulaski County, Kentucky. Married Mary Barker.

D246—Blatchely Caughron. Born in 1823 in Pulaski County, Kentucky. Married Elizabeth E. Gossett.

D247—Nancy Caughron. Born in 1829 in Pulaski County, Kentucky. Married Franklin P. Jones.

D76—John Graham. Son of Fergus Graham and Elizabeth Trimble. (Fourth generation of David Trimble and —— Houston.) Lived to be eighty-three years of age Married Lydia Alkire and settled on Deer Creek, Madison County, Ohio. He was a captain in the War of 1812.

The children of John Graham and Lydia Alkire:

D248—Harrison Graham.

D249—Betsy Graham.

D250—Caroline Graham.

D251—Fergus Graham.

+ D252—Robert Graham. Married Anna Davidson.

D253—John Graham.

D254—Milton Graham.

D255—Emeline Graham.

D256—Margaret Graham.

D257—Maria Graham.

D258—Mary Graham. Died in infancy.

D77—Polly Graham. Daughter of Fergus Graham and Elizabeth Trimble. (Fourth generation of David Trimble and ——— Houston.) Married Isaac Alkire.

The children of Isaac Alkire and Polly Graham:

D259—Betsy Alkire.

D260—Fergus Alkire.

D261—Jackson Alkire.

D262—Cynthia Ann Alkire.

D263—Lucinda Alkire.

D264—Harrison Alkire.

D265—George Alkire.

D266—Martha Alkire.

D81—Henry Nainby Shaw. Son of William Shaw and Charlotte Trimble. (Fourth generation of David Trimble and ——— Houston.) Born on March 4, 1792 in Cresaptown, Allegany County, Maryland and died on April 16, 1862 in Evansville, Preston County, West Virginia. Married Sidney Thompson Shaw.[38]

The children of Henry Nainby Shaw and Sidney Thompson Shaw:

D267—Jane Shaw. Died on June 15, 1844.[39]

D268—Joseph Shaw. Born on October 4, 1818 and died on January 29, 1860. Married Highly Duckworth Shaw. She was born on September 6, 1814 and

---

[38] Find A Grave. Find A Grave. http://www.findagrave.com/cgi-bin/fg.cgi: accessed 4 February 2013. Find A Grave Memorial# 34647130.

[39] Find A Grave. Find A Grave. http://www.findagrave.com/cgi-bin/fg.cgi: accessed 4 February 2013. Find A Grave Memorial# 73087526.

D - David Trimble

died on April 1, 1900. [40]

D269—Louisa Shaw. Born on April 26, 1821 in Garrett County, Maryland and died on November 12, 1903. Married Jacob Humberston. [41]

D270—John Shaw. Born on December 12. 1822 in Allegany County, Maryland and died in March 1905 in Maryland. Married Nancy Catharine Michael on August 9, 1828 in Maryland. She was born on August 9, 1828 in Maryland and died on November 9, 1907. [42]

D271—William Shaw. Born on October 7, 1829 and died on January 27, 1915. [43]

D272—Martha Shaw. Born on May 31, 1831 in Barton Allegany County, Maryland and died on September 24, 1895 in Greene County, Ohio.

D273—Mary C. Shaw. Born on May 30, 1833 in Maryland and died on July 6, 1870 in Garrett County, Maryland. Married Andrew Jackson Michael on April 6, 1854. He was born on February 26, 1830 in Bloomington, Garrett County, Maryland and died on August 19, 1915 in Allegany County, Maryland.

D274—Sarah A. Shaw. Born on April 17, 1834 in Allegany County, Maryland and died on November 14, 1885 in Lebo, Coffey County, Kansas. Married B. F. Swindler on September 29, 1857 at Evansville, West Virginia. B. F. Swindler was born on January 28, 1830 and died on June 23, 1895.

D275—Highley Shaw. Born on March 30, 1835 in Allegany County, Maryland and died on October 5, 1905. Married Ezra Koontz in 1854. Ezra was born on February 15, 1831 in Maryland and died on July 14, 1908.

D276—Sidney Shaw. Born on March 16, 1837 and died on February 23, 1917. Married Isaac Walter. Isaac was born on February 28, 1833 and died on January 10, 1903.

D83—Joseph Shaw. Son of William Shaw and Charlotte Trimble. (Fourth

---

[40] Find A Grave. Find A Grave. http://www.findagrave.com/cgi-bin/fg.cgi: accessed 4 February 2013. Find A Grave Memorial# 32211842.

[41] Find A Grave. Find A Grave. http://www.findagrave.com/cgi-bin/fg.cgi: accessed 4 February 2013. Find A Grave Memorial# 102336598.

[42] Find A Grave. Find A Grave. http://www.findagrave.com/cgi-bin/fg.cgi: accessed 4 February 2013. Find A Grave Memorial# 92903896.

[43] Find A Grave. Find A Grave. http://www.findagrave.com/cgi-bin/fg.cgi: accessed 4 February 2013. Find A Grave Memorial# 33351050.

generation of David Trimble and —— Houston.) Born on May 23, 1797 in Barton, Allegany County, Maryland and died on April 2, 1886 in Beacon, Mahaska County, Iowa. Married Frances Adison Swanson on April 22, 1826 in Allegany County, Maryland. She was born in 1806 in Ireland and died on February 7, 1876.

The children of Joseph Shaw and Frances Swanson:

D277—Samuel Shaw. Born on January 10, 1832. Married Elizabeth H. Shroyer. She was born in 1837 and died in 1922.

D89—Samuel Trimble. Son of John Trimble, Jr. and Elizabeth Brown. (Fourth generation of David Trimble and —— Houston.) Born on February 16, 1804 in Mt Savage, Allegany County, Maryland and died on August 8, 1896 in Danville, Knox County, Ohio. Married Susannah Hammon on December 16, 1828 in Cumberland, Allegany County, Maryland.

Susannah was born on March 7, 1813 in Millwood, Knox County, Ohio and died on January 6, 1892 in Danville, Knox County, Ohio.

The children of Samuel Trimble and Susannah Hammon:

+ **D278—Mary Ann Trimble.** Born on April 22, 1830 in Pennsylvania and died on November 7, 1897 in Creston, Union County, Iowa. Married Robert Giffen Robeson.

+ **D279—John Trimble.** Born on December 28, 1831 in Alleghany County, Maryland and died on November 1, 1887. Married Catherine Lybarger.

D280—Elizabeth A. Trimble. Born on April 22, 1833 in Alleghany County, Maryland.

+ **D281—Enoch Trimble.** Born on September 18, 1836 in Millwood, Knox County, Ohio and died on May 29, 1904 in Danville, Knox County, Ohio. Married Esther Virginia Hettie Condit on August 20, 1865.

+ **D282—Henry H. Trimble.** Born on April 21, 1839 in Union Township, Knox County, Ohio and died on April 16, 1917 in Indianola, Warren County, Iowa. Married Sarah Jane McClure on October 25, 1866 in Clinton County, Indiana.

D283—Solomon Trimble. Born on February 27, 1841 in Millwood, Knox County, Ohio and died on January 18, 1887 in Butler, Knox County, Ohio

+ **D284—Eliza Lanett Trimble.** Born on April 22, 1842 in Millwood, Guernsey County, Ohio and died on June 26, 1927 in Danville, Knox County, Ohio. Married Henry W. Bonnett.

D285—Maria Florence Trimble. Born on March 25, 1849 in Millwood, Knox County, Ohio and died in 1936 in Morgan County, Ohio

D286—Josephine Trimble. Born on October 25, 1853 in Ohio and died in 1936.

D93—Joseph A. Trimble. Son of John Trimble, Jr. and Elizabeth Brown. (Fourth generation of David Trimble and —— Houston.) Born in 1816 in Maryland and died in 1897 in Maryland. Married Mariah A. Evans. Mariah was born in December 1823 in England and died in 1906 in Maryland.

The children of Joseph A. Trimble and Mariah A. Evans:

D287—Matilda Trimble. Born about 1847 in Maryland.

D288—John Trimble. Born about 1848.

D289—Winfield Trimble. Born about 1849.

D290—George Thomas Trimble. Born in August 1852 in Maryland and died in 1932 in Mount Savage, Allegany County, Maryland.

D291—Franklin Trimble. Born about 1855.

D292—Joseph H. Trimble. Born about 1860 in Maryland.

D293—Nellie M. Trimble. Born in June 1861 in Maryland.

D294—Walter Trimble. Born about 1863.

D295—Maud M. Trimble. Born in May 1870 in Maryland.

D94—Ann Trimble. Daughter of John Trimble, Jr. and Elizabeth Brown. (Fourth generation of David Trimble and —— Houston.) Born on March 3, 1823 in Mt Savage, Allegany County, Maryland and died on May 20, 1906 in Chicago, Cook County, Illinois. Ann married twice.

Married first, to Dr. Robert B. Gillespie on October 21, 1841 in Mt Savage, Allegany County, Maryland. Robert was born in 1817 in Pennsylvania and died on April 3, 1853 in Moundsville, Marshall County, West Virginia.

Married second, to Andrew V. Shurts. She was his second wife. Andrew was born on August 30, 1815 in Elizabeth, Union County, New Jersey. He was expert blacksmith. They had no children.

The children of Robert B. Gillespie and Ann Trimble:

+ **D296—Mary Elizabeth Gillespie.** Born on February 25, 1844 in Moundsville, Marshall County, West Virginia and died on October 23, 1893 in Clearfield, Taylor County, Iowa. Married Henry Kent Calkins.

D297—Janette Estelle Gillespie. Born about 1849.

D96—Mary Margaret Combs. Daughter of John Combs and Margaret Trimble. (Fourth generation of David Trimble and —— Houston.) Born about 1803 in Allegany County, Maryland and died before 1837 in Frostburg, Allegany County, Maryland. Married Josiah Porter on August 3, 1822 in Frostburg, Allegany County, Maryland. He was the son of Gabriel McKenzie Porter and

Rebecca Frost married on May 10, 1997 in Frostburg, Allegany County, Maryland. Gabriel was born on September 17, 1776 in Carrolton, Baltimore County, Maryland and died on April 20, 1842 in Tyrone Township, Fayette County, Pennsylvania. Rebecca was born about in 1780 in Frostburg, Allegany County, Maryland and died about 1837 in Fayette County, Pennsylvania. After Mary died Josiah married Sarah Porter and had twelve children more than the nine, he had with Mary.

The children of Josiah Porter and Mary Combs:

D298—John Wesley Porter. Born about 1823 in Maryland and died about 1883. Married Margaret Sease on June 16, 1845 in Allegany County, Maryland.

+ **D299—Rebecca Porter.** Born on October 1, 1824 in Eckhart, Allegany County, Maryland and died on March 28, 1900 in Eckhart, Allegany County, Maryland. Married John Samuel Porter on March 6, 1851 in Allegany County, Maryland.

D300—Sophia Porter. Born about 1825 in Maryland. Married John Anderson on May 16, 1844 in Allegany County, Maryland.

+ **D301—Margaret Emily Porter.** Born on September 22, 1827 in Allegany County, Maryland and died on May 15, 1910 in Allegany County, Maryland. Married John Ford on January 29, 1849 in Allegany County, Maryland.

D302—Gabriel Porter. Born about 1830.

D303—Elisha Porter. Born about 1832.

D304—Eleanor Ellen Porter. Born about 1833 in Maryland and died on January 31, 1915 in Eckhart Mines, Allegany County, Maryland. Married William Parker on November 11, 1850 in Allegany County, Maryland. William was born about 1825 in Maryland and died in October 1909.

D305—Nancy Porter. Born before 1836.

D306—Helen Porter. Born before 1837.

D307—Matilda Porter. Born about 1854 in Maryland.

D308—William Porter. Born about 1862 in Maryland.

D98—Elisha Combs. Son of John Combs and Margaret Trimble. (Fourth generation of David Trimble and ——— Houston.) Married Elizabeth Neff.

The child of Elisha Combs and Elizabeth Neff:

+ **D309—Francis Asbury Combs.** Born on February 17, 1837 in Maryland and died on February 19, 1878 in Union District, Monongalia County, West Virginia. Married Hannah J. Thomas on November 20, 1856 in

Trimble Families of America

Monongalia, West Virginia.

D102—Hanna Combs. Daughter of Cudberth Combs and Abigail Trimble (Fourth generation of David Trimble and ―― Houston.) Born on May 30, 1798 in Preston, West Virginia and died February 22, 1844 in Aurora, Preston County, West Virginia. Married John Potter on October 3, 1815 in Allegany, Maryland. John was born on September 1, 1790 in Frostburg, Allegany, Maryland and died on February 17, 1862 in Preston County, West Virginia.

The children of John Potter and Hanna Comb:

- **D310—Elizabeth Porter.** Born on August 22, 1817 in Frostburg, Allegany County, Maryland and died on February 12, 1897 Brownsville, Fayette County, Pennsylvania.

- **D311—William Thomas Porter.** Born on June 4, 1820 in Frostburg, Allegany County, Maryland and died on March 4, 1858 in Tucker County, West Virginia.

- +**D312—Samuel John Porter.** Born on July 16, 1822 in Frostburg, Allegany, Maryland and died on September 30, 1895 in Ogden Township, Lenawec County, Michigan. Married Elnora Rudolph on December 11, 1845 in Blissfield, Lenawee County, Michigan.

- **D313—Cudberth Porter.** Born in 1824 in Frostburg, Allegany, Maryland and died in1830 in Frostburg, Allegany, Maryland. He was about 6 years old.

- **D314—Levi Porter.** Born in 1827 in Frostburg, Allegany, Maryland and died in 1830 in Frostburg, Allegany, Maryland. He was about 3 years old.

- **D315—John Meyers Lawrence Porter.** Born on November 6, 1830 in Claryville, Allegany, Maryland and died in 1901 in Ogden, Lenawee County, Michigan.

- **D316—Mariah Porter.** Born on January 10, 1833 in Frostburg, Allegany, Maryland and died on February 12, 1921 in Elgon, West Virginia. Married Stephen Harsh on October 9, 1921 in Elgon, Preston County, West Virginia.

- **D317—Aden Clary Porter.** Born on February 23, 1835 in Frostburg Allegany County, Maryland and died on April 11, 1915 in Blissfield, Lenawee County, Michigan. Married Verlinda Wotring on December 7, 1858 in Tucker, West Virginia.

- **D318—Martha Ellen Porter.** Born on August 7, 1837 in Frostburg, Allegany County, Maryland and died on January 28, 1879 in Ogden, Lenawee, Michigan. Married John Peter Heckert on December 30, 1858 in West Virginia

D107—Noah Trimble. Son of Henry Trimble and Margaret Critchfield. (Fourth generation of David Trimble and —— Houston.) Born about 1808 in Wellersburg, Pennsylvania and died on August 27, 1892 in Cumberland, Maryland. Married three times. First, he married Catherine "Kate" Workman on April 14, 1846. She was born on November 14, 1810 on the Workman Farm, Zilman, Allegany County, Maryland. Second, he married to Deborah Kimmins on November 26, 1846. Third, he married Esther McCon on August 17, 1849.

The children of Noah Trimble and Kate Workman:

D319—Adam Trimble.

D320—Delia Trimble. Born in 1866 in Allegany County, Maryland. And died on September 9, 1892 in Cumberland, Allegany County, Maryland.

The child of Noah Trimble and Deborah Kimmins:

D321—Samuel Trimble. Born on June 28, 1848.

The children of Noah Trimble and Esther McCon:

D322—Thomas J. M. Trimble. Born in 1851.

D323—James A. Trimble. Born in 1852.

D324—Mary E. Trimble. Born in 1854.

D325—Harriet R. Trimble. Born in 1859.

D326—Cordelia M. Trimble. Born on March 20, 1861.

D122—James Baird Trimble. Son of Hugh Trimble and Ellen Caldwell. (Fourth generation of David Trimble and —— Houston.) Born on December 8, 1803, at Mount Sterling, Kentucky and died on March 6, 1881, at Trimble Station, Crawford County, Illinois. He married two times. Married first to Louisa Markley in 1832 at Crawford County, Illinois. Married second to Mary Ann Howie Dunlap.

James Baird settled in Crawford County in 1827. He had previously driven cattle to Chicago and liked the appearance of this area in Illinois and the following spring came on a visit to see his Uncle James Caldwell. (This was the year of the Big Snow, probably 1826.) He married Louisa Markley in 1832. She was from Hutsonville, Illinois. *The History of Crawford County* names him as one of the three first judges of the county. He had 900 acres of land when he died. His home is now called Trimble, Illinois. James Baird and Louisa are buried in Oak Grove Cemetery, northwest of Palestine, Illinois.

The children of James Trimble and Louisa Markley:

D327—Adaline Trimble. Born in 1833 and died in 1893. She married William Canby Steele whose parents came from Philadelphia in the 1800s and settled

D - David Trimble

in Crawford County, Illinois. They had previously lived at Terre Haute, Indiana.

D328—Ellen Jane Trimble. Married Dr. J. M. Barlow and had four children.

D329—Davidson Clark Trimble. He died at McKendree College in 1857.

D330—Ann Trimble. Married Dr. William H. Rubottom.

D331—Sarah Emily Trimble. Married Thomas Ruddell.

The children of James Baird Trimble and Mary Ann Howie Dunlap:

D332—Eliza Evaline Trimble. She did not marry.

D333—John Dunlap Trimble. He married Mary Thompson.

D334—Mary Good Trimble. She married Lewis E. Gordon.

D335—Everette Caldwell Trimble. He married Ida Gordon.

D336—Lenora Trimble. She married W. H. McKee.

D337—Martha Trimble. She was a medical doctor and married Dr. W. C. Pearce.

D123—Polly Ann Trimble. Daughter of Hugh Trimble and Ellen Caldwell. (Fourth generation of David Trimble and —— Houston.) She married a Mr. Leach.

The children of Mr. Leach and Polly Ann Trimble:

D338—Wilbur Leach.

D339—Marion Leach.

D131—Permelia Meloan Trimble. Daughter of David Trimble and Mary "Polly" Trimble. (Fourth generation of David Trimble and —— Houston.) Born on December 24, 1803 in Montgomery County, Kentucky and died on September 22, 1845 in Calloway, Kentucky. Married Wesley Daniel McCarty on February 17, 1825 in Montgomery County, Kentucky. He was born on April 20, 1805 in Virginia and died on July 27, 1847 in Murray, Calloway, Kentucky.

The children of Wesley Daniel McCarty and Permelia Trimble:

+ **D340—George William McCarty.** Born on December 18, 1825 in Montgomery County, Kentucky and died on July 13, 1894 in Le Roy, Coffey County, Kansas. Married twice.

+ **D341—Sally Ann McCarty.** Born on October 25, 1827 in Montgomery County, Kentucky. Married William W. Marberry.

+ **D342—John Alexander McCarty.** Born on June 5, 1829 in Montgomery County, Kentucky and died on January 18, 1902. Married to Susanna Nichols.

+ **D343—Mary Winifred McCarty.** Born on October 28, 1831 in Calloway

County, Kentucky. Married George W. Minnick.

+ **D344—Frances Emeline McCarty.** Born on December 8, 1833 in Calloway County, Kentucky. Married Andrew Grubaugh.

  D345—Susan Serena McCarty. Born on August 14, 1836 in Calloway County, Kentucky. Married Wallace W. Plymell.

+ **D346—James Henry McCarty.** Born on April 28, 1838 in Calloway County, Kentucky and died on September 3, 1890 in Edgar County, Illinois. Married Susanah J. Beavers.

  D347—Margrett Jane McCarty. Born on May 9, 1840 in Calloway County, Kentucky and died on November 20, 1843 in Calloway County, Kentucky.

  D348—Daniel Johnson McCarty. Born on March 25, 1843 in Calloway County, Kentucky.

  D349—Permelia Caroline McCarty. Born on May 20, 1845 in Calloway County, Kentucky and died on February 22, 1918. Married Henry C. Turner.

D142—James McMullin. Son of Arthur McMullin and Mary Trimble. (Fourth generation of David Trimble and —— Houston.) Born in December 1820 in Madison County, Kentucky and died on March 3, 1920 in Washington County, Kentucky. Married Lucinda Burns on August 7, 1842 in Washington County, Kentucky. Lucinda was born in 1823 in Washington County, Kentucky and died in October 1893 in Washington County, Kentucky.

The children of James McMullin and Lucinda Burns:

+ **D350—Mary Catherine McMullin.** Born on August 17, 1843 in Washington County, Kentucky and died on June 10, 1888 in Mercer County, Kentucky. Married James Thomas Black on November 15, 1860 in Washington County, Kentucky.

  D351—Melissa McMullin. Born on December 10, 1847 in Washington County, Kentucky and died on December 5, 1934 in Washington County, Kentucky.

  D352—unknown McMullin. Born in 1848 in Washington County, Kentucky and died August 11, 1855 in Washington County, Kentucky.

  D353—Clifton T McMullin. Born on January 8, 1857 in Washington County, Kentucky and died on May 7, 1920 in Washington County, Kentucky.

D145—David Matthias Gossett. Son of Samuel Gossett and Polly Trimble. (Fourth generation of David Trimble and —— Houston.) Born on June 1, 1823 in Kentucky and died on November 13, 1895 in Austin, Cass County, Missouri. Married Mary Calistine Phillips on January 11, 1863 in Kansas City, Jackson County, Missouri. She was born in July 1842 and died in May 1913. Mary was the daughter of John T. Phillips and Mary Hauser. John was

D - David Trimble

born on December 7, 1798 in North Carolina and died on September 30, 1874 in Austin, Cass County, Missouri. Mary was born about 1799 in Stokes, North Carolina and died about 1843 in Surry, North Carolina.

The children of Matthias Dudley Gossett and Mary Calistine Phillips:

D354—Elnora Gossett. Born on March 11, 1865 in Paola, Miami County, Kansas and died on December 29, 1938 in Rupert, Minidoka County, Idaho. Married William A. Goodman on September 22, 1891 in Austin, Cass County, Missouri.

D355—Minnie Gossett. Born on March 8, 1867 in Paola, Miami County, Kansas and died June 10, 1950 in Los Angeles, Los Angeles County, California. Married James Pringle on June 29, 1887 in Austin, Cass County, Missouri.

D356—Mary Donna Gossett. Born in December 1869 in Cass County, Missouri. Married John H. Hutton.

D151—Robert Luckie Laughlin. Son of John Laughlin and Tabitha Elizabeth Trimble. (Fourth generation of David Trimble and —— Houston.) Born on January 7, 1830 in Blue Lick Spring, Bourbon County, Kentucky and died on October 24, 1914 in Franklin County, Kansas. Married Francis Githens in 1850. She was born on February 20, 1831 in Bourbon County, Kentucky and died March 7, 1913 in Franklin, Kansas.

The children of Robert Luckie Laughlin and Rebecca Francis Githens:

+ **D357—John Breckenridge Laughlin.** Born on March 23, 1855 in Kentucky. Married Annie Morton in 1879.

D358—Elisa Laughlin. Born about 1858 in Kentucky.

+ **D359—Robert Luckie Laughlin.** Born on July 19, 1859 in Covington, Kentucky and died on May 19, 1943 in Kansas City, Missouri. Married Flora Lee Walker on November 15, 1882.

D360—Eli Laughlin. Born about 1863 in Kentucky.

D361—Richard Laughlin. Born about 1866 in Kentucky.

D362—William Laughlin. Born about 1868 in Kentucky.

D363—Sterling Laughlin. Born about 1870 in Kentucky.

D364—Steve Laughlin. Born in July 1871 in Kentucky.

D156—George Trimble Martin. Son of Nathan Martin and Sarah Jane Trimble. (Fourth generation of David Trimble and —— Houston.) Born on February 4, 1830 in Indiana and died on July 1, 1874 in Sharon, Whiteside County, Illinois. Married Margaret Jane Ferguson on April 11, 1850 in Washington County, Indiana. Margaret was born in 1829 in Washington, Indiana and died on March 28, 1900 in White County, Illinois. She is the daughter of Jesse Ferguson and Sally Scott. Jesse was born in 1783 in Virginia and died in 1845 in Northeast Township, Orange County, Indiana. Sally was born about 1785 in Virginia and died on June 11, 1842 in Livonia, Washington, Indiana.

The children of George Trimble Martin and Margaret Jane Ferguson:

D365—Nathan Walter Martin. Born on June 25, 1851 in Washington County, Indiana and died on November 13, 1912 in Washington, Daviess County, Indiana.

D366—unnamed daughter Martin. Born on 1852 in Washington County, Indiana.

D367—Sarah Dove Martin. Born on January 26, 1854 in Washington County, Indiana and died on February 8, 1879 in Portside, Whiteside County, Illinois.

D368—John Ferguson Martin. Born on September 10, 1855 in Washington County, Indiana and died in 1920.

D369—Emma Jessie Margaret Martin. Born on May 9, 1858 in Springhill, Whiteside, Illinois and died on May 20, 1920 in Deland, Volusia County, Florida.

D370—George William Martin. Born on September 26, 1860 in Washington County, Indiana and died on January 8, 1939 in Erie Village, Whiteside County, Illinois.

D371—Amazetta Jane Martin. Born on April 17, 1862 in Whiteside County, Illinois and died Iowa.

D174—Mary Jane McKinney. Son of Alexander McKinney and Nancy Bryan. (Fourth generation of David Trimble and ——— Houston.) Born on July 13, 1818 in Montgomery County, Missouri and died on March 29, 1887 in Mexico, Missouri. Married James Callaway on July 19, 1838 in Warren County, Missouri. James was born on April 24, 1816 in St Charles County, Missouri and died on July 11, 1889 in Warren County, Missouri.

The children of James Callaway and Mary Jane McKinney:

D372—John A. Callaway. Born on August 20, 1839 in Missouri and died on May 23, 1861 in Marthasville, Warren County, Missouri.

D373—James Marion Callaway. Born on October 1841 in Warren County, Missouri and died on December 6, 1841 in Warren County, Missouri.

D374—Julia A. Callaway. Born in 1844 in Missouri and died 1882.

D375—Verlena G. Callaway. Born on March 12, 1846 in Warren County, Missouri and died on April 14, 1891.

D - David Trimble

D376—Redmond Callaway. Born in 1849 in Missouri and died 1867 in Mexico, Audrain County, Missouri.

D377—Bascom Callaway. Born in in April 1853 and died on September 3, 1853.

D189—David Trimble. Son of Mark Trimble and Nancy Schubert. (Fourth generation of David Trimble and —— Houston.) David was born on May 1, 1819 in Johnson County, Kentucky and died on March 4, 1914 in Morgan County, Kentucky. [44] He married two times.

Married first, to Mary Jane McGuire in early 1840. Born on January 27, 1820 in Kentucky and died before 1855 in Kentucky.

Married second, to Sarah Conley on July 15, 1855 in Morgan County, Kentucky.

The original information on David Trimble's family furnished by James Trimble of Ashland, Kentucky. During the update information was found for the name of both wives and a more complete list of children. [45, 46, 47]

The children of David Trimble and Mary Jean McGuire:

D378—John Trimble. Born in 1840 in Kentucky.

D379—Nancy Jane Trimble. Born on November 19, 1847 in Morgan County, Kentucky and died on December 6, 1936 in Scioto County, Ohio. Married Edmund Keeton, Jr.

D380—Angeline Trimble. Born about 1849 in Morgan County, Kentucky.

The children of David Trimble and Sarah Conley:

D381—Mary Elizabeth Trimble. Born about 1857. Married a Mr. Adkins and had two children.

D382—Martha Ann Trimble. Born about 1858. Married a Mr. Adkins and had two children.

---

[44] Kentucky. Kentucky Birth, Marriage and Death Records – Microfilm (1852-1910). Microfilm rolls #994027-994058. Kentucky Department for Libraries and Archives, Frankfort, Kentucky.

[45] US Census Year: 1850; Census Place: Morgan, Kentucky; Roll: M432_214; Page: 87A; Image: 177.

[46] US Census Year: 1860; Census Place: District 1, Morgan, Kentucky; Roll: M653_388; Page: 472; Image: 476; Family History Library Film: 803388

[47] US Census Year: 1870; Census Place: West Liberty, Morgan, Kentucky; Roll: M593_490; Page: 328A; Image: 23; Family History Library Film: 545989.

D383—Sarah Trimble. Married a Mr. Conley and had five children.

D384—William Wallace Trimble. (Twin.) Born about 1860. Married and had three children.

D385—Bruce Trimble. (Twin.) Born about 1860. Married and they had two children.

D386—David Nelson Trimble. Born about 1862. Married and had four children.

+ **D387—Marion Grant Trimble.** Born about 1869. Married and had seven children.

D388—Emma Trimble. Married a Mr. Robbins and had seven children.

D191—James M. Trimble. Son of Mark Trimble and Nancy Schubert. (Fourth generation of David Trimble and —— Houston.) Born on January 1, 1825 in Barnett's Creek, Johnson County, Kentucky and died on November 11, 1891 in Barnett's Creek, Johnson County, Kentucky. He married two times.

'.Married first to Susan Tackett.

Married second Sarah Howes Baldwin. Sarah was born on March 19, 1829 and died on July 4, 1922.

He served in the Confederate Army during the Civil War, in the First Battalion, Kentucky Mounted Rifles as a Private.

The children of James Trimble and Susan Tackett:

D389—Nancy Trimble. Born about 1843.

+ **D390—John G. Trimble.** Born on March 22, 1844 and died on June 27, 1931. He married two times.

+ **D391—William Mark Trimble.** Born on February 16, 1851 in Barnett's Creek, Johnson County, Kentucky and died on March 7, 1911 in Redbush, Johnson County, Kentucky. Married Cynthia Essie "Cinda" Reed.

+ **D392—Jane Trimble.** Born in 1884 and married Jasper Wheeler.

+ **D393—Susanah Trimble.** Married Taylor Ramey in 1898.

The children of James Trimble and Sarah Howes Baldwin:

+ **D394—Millie Trimble.** Married James B. Lemaster.

+ **D395—Alice Trimble.** Married two times.

+ **D396—Minerva Trimble.** Married a Mr. Lemaster.

+ **D397—Lou Trimble.** Married John Picklesimer.

+ **D398—Ulysses Grant Trimble.** Born on May 13, 1869 in Barnett's Creek, Johnson County, Kentucky and died on February 14, 1944 in Johnson County, Kentucky. Married Patience Williams in 1890.

D192—Susannah Trimble. Daughter of Mark Trimble and Nancy Schubert. (Fourth generation of David Trimble and —— Houston.) Born on January 24, 1930 in Morgan County, Kentucky and died on April 12, 1863 in Johnson County, Kentucky. Married Dr. Nathaniel Picklesimer on October 19, 1847 in Morgan County, Kentucky. Nathaniel was born on August 18, 1827 in Floyd County, Kentucky and died on March 8, 1904 in Johnson County, Kentucky. Susannah' parents Mark and Nancy Trimble lived with them their last years.

> The children of Dr. Nathaniel Picklesimer and Susannah Trimble:
>
> **D399—Cecilia Emily Picklesimer.** Born on January 9, 1850 in Johnson County, Kentucky and died on September 25, 1870 in Johnson County, Kentucky.
>
> **D400—Nancy Elizabeth Picklesimer.** Born on July 14, 1852 in Johnson County, Kentucky and died in 1887.
>
> **D401—John Milton Picklesimer.** Born on August 22, 1854 in Johnson County, Kentucky and died on December 16, 1929 in Yeager, Pike County, Kentucky.
>
> **D402—Mary Susannah Picklesimer.** Born on December 27, 1856 in Johnson County, Kentucky and died on April 5, 1863.
>
> **D403—Martha Jane Picklesimer.** Born on February 2, 1859 Barnett's Creek, Johnson County, Kentucky and died on April 22, 1923 in Johnson Creek, Kentucky.
>
> **D404—Samuel Nathan Picklesimer.** Born on February 7, 1861 in Barnett's Creek, Johnson County, Kentucky and died on May 21, 1909 in Johnson County, Kentucky.
>
> **D405—Sarah E. Picklesimer.** Born on November 19, 1862 in Pickle Fork, Johnson County, Kentucky and died on November 9, 1953 in Johnson County, Kentucky.

D193—William "Bill Dodger" Trimble. Son of Mark Trimble and Nancy Schubert. (Fourth generation of David Trimble and —— Houston.) William was born on October 28, 1836 in Morgan County, Kentucky and died on November 22, 1912 in Johnson County, Kentucky. Married Clarinda Ellen Picklesimer on March 19, 1853 in Johnson County, Kentucky. Clarinda was born on January 1, 1837 in Floyd County, Kentucky. She is the daughter of John Picklesimer and Mary Ann "Polly" Tackett. John and Polly were married on October 19, 1826 in Floyd County, Kentucky. John was born in 1807 in Gallia County, Ohio and died on February 2, 1860 in Johnson County, Kentucky. Polly was born in 1806 in North Carolina and died in 1862 in Johnson County, Kentucky.

His grandson Palmer Trimble said that Bill Dodger was horse trader. During the civil war he sold horses to the Union Army. He had several black men that worked with him, one was named Sam Moneyhunt. On one his sales trips he came across a Confederate troop. They asked him what he was doing. He replied that he had horses that a general in the Confederacy was going to buy (he knew the general by name). They took him to the general and sold him the horses then went on his way. Another grandson Swanie Lee Trimble remembers Sam Moneyhunt still living on Barnett's Creek in Johnson County, Kentucky.

The children of William "Bill Dodger" Trimble and Clarinda Ellen Picklesimer:

+ **D406—John Mark Trimble.** Born on January 7, 1854. Married Clarinda Spradlin.

D407—Mary A. Trimble. Born about 1857.

+ **D408—David Nathaniel Trimble.** Born about 1859. Married Nan Vanhoose.

+ **D409—William Henry Trimble.** Born on November 23, 1863, died September 13, 1941. Married Sally Vanhoose.

D410—Martha Jane Trimble. Born on February 1863 in Johnson County, Kentucky and died 1928.

+ **D411—Greenville Trimble.** Born on August 6, 1866 in Johnson County, Kentucky and died on January 13, 1949 in Johnson County, Kentucky. Married Sadie Ealey.

+ **D412—Joseph Harman Trimble.** Born on October 30, 1871 and died in 1928, married Florence Ida Caudill on October 27, 1894.

+ **D413—Laura Mae "Dolly" Trimble.** Born on April 15, 1876 in Johnson County, Kentucky and died in 1953. Married twice, first to Joe Trimble, second John E. Ratliff.

+ **D414—Lydia Trimble.** Born in November 1873 in Johnson County, Kentucky and died on December 28, 1943 in Magoffin County, Kentucky. Married William Pickle.

+ **D415—Jane Trimble.** Married Daniel Harmon.

D194—Nancy Jane Polly Trimble. Daughter of Mark Trimble and Nancy Schubert. (Fourth generation of David Trimble and —— Houston.) Born on June 2, 1844 in Johnson County, Kentucky. Married John Jasper Wheeler about 1861. John was born on November 9, 1837 in Johnson County, Kentucky and died on December 9, 1915 in Johnson County, Kentucky. John is the son of John Wheeler and Anna Romey. John enlisted on

November 19, 1861 in Louisa, Kentucky into the Kentucky 14th Infantry of Union Army during the Civil War.[48]

The children of John Jasper Wheeler and Nancy Jane Polly Trimble:

D416—Sarah A. Wheeler. Born about 1862 in Kentucky.

D417—Edgar Wheeler. Born about 1866 in Kentucky.

D418—John B. Wheeler. Born about 1867 in Kentucky.

D419—James T. Wheeler. Born about 1869 in Kentucky.

D420—Mary M. Wheeler. Born about 1872 in Kentucky.

D421—Elizabeth Wheeler. Born about 1874 in Kentucky.

D422—Toby Wheeler. Born about 1880 in Kentucky.

D200—Richard Menifee Trimble. Son of John and Nancy Trimble. (Fourth generation of David Trimble and —— Houston.) Born on August 12, 1837, died on February 21, 1909, in Montgomery County, Kentucky. Married Armilda Hines Glover, born on January 18, 1835 and died on February 15, 1912. Richard Menifee Trimble served in the Confederate Army under General Buell. He was a veterinarian and farmer. They had two sons and a daughter, Kate, who died in her teens.

The children of Richard Menifee Trimble and Armilda Hines Glover:

+ **D423—John Crittenden Trimble.** Born on June 19, 1862 and died on January 1, 1930. Married twice.

+ **D424—Joe Trimble.** Married Rose Wills.

D425—Kate Trimble. Died in her teens.

D201—Evaline Trimble. Daughter of William Trimble and Eleanor O'Hair. (Fourth generation of David Trimble and —— Houston.) Born on January 14, 1816, died on February 20, 1889. Married James Felix McGuire. They lived at Saint Helens in Lee County, Kentucky. In her later years she became feeble and needed the use of a walking cane, yet as she would approach her church, she would hide the cane.

The children of James Felix McGuire and Evaline Trimble:

D426—Green McGuire. A Confederate soldier killed in battle.

D427—Simpson McGuire. He died of injuries received in the Civil War.

D428—Felix McGuire. Born on August 13, 1840 in Hazel Green, Kentucky and died July 19, 1911. Married Martha Payne Dixon of Maysville, Kentucky. He

---

[48] General Index to Pension Files, 1861-1934. Washington, D.C.: National Archives and Records Administration. T288, 546 rolls.

fought with John Hunt Morgan in the Civil War.

D429—Fletcher McGuire.

D430—Bascom McGuire.

D431—Brutus McGuire.

D432—Cassisus McGuire.

D433—Caroline McGuire.

D434—Ellen McGuire.

D435—Lou McGuire.

D202—Caroline Trimble. Daughter of William Trimble and Eleanor O'Hair. (Fourth generation of David Trimble and —— Houston.) Born on October 5, 1817, at Hazel Green, Kentucky, died on September 1, 1898. Married Stephen Swango on March 5, 1840 at Hazel Green where they remained their lifetimes.

The children of Stephen Swango and Caroline Trimble:

D436—Evaline Swango.

D437—Emily Jane Swango.

D438—Green Berry Swango.

D439—Zarilda Swango.

D440—Rose Ellen Swango.

D441—Elizabeth Swango.

D442—Alice Swango.

D443—Clara Swango.

D444—William Swango.

D203—William Preston Trimble. Son of William Trimble and Eleanor O'Hair. (Fourth generation of David Trimble and —— Houston.) Born on October 6, 1818, died on March 15, 1905. Married Sarah Kash on February 2, 1843 in Morgan County, Kentucky. Sarah was born on December 11, 1821 in Kentucky and died September 16, 1895. Her parents were Caleb Cash and Perthena Wilson. Caleb was born on October 10, 1773 in Greenbrier, Augusta, West Virginia. Perthena was born in 1802 in Kentucky and died after 1860. They first lived on Lacy Creek, later moving to Hazel Green. He inherited nine farms, from his father, William Trimble. Just before the Civil War he bought a little four-year-old colored girl who continued to live with the Trimbles after the war. They called her Ann. She has a daughter Kate who lives near Mount Sterling, Kentucky.

The children of William Preston Trimble and Sarah Kash:

+ D445—Angeline Trimble. Born on March 3, 1844 and died on February

D - David Trimble

20, 1918. Married Stephen Porter James.

+ **D446—Seaborn Trimble.** Born on November 24, 1848, died on January 21, 1916. Married Emma Wilson.

+ **D447—Josephine Trimble.** Born on May 1846. Married James Calvin Swango.

D448—Mary Ellen Trimble. She was killed at the age of fifty-seven in a home accident.

D449—Rose Trimble. Never married.

+ **D450—Frances Trimble.** Married Taylor Whaley.

+ **D451—Harlan Trimble.** Born on January 28, 1860 and died in 1942. Married Nannie James.

D204—David Shelton "Doc" Trimble. Son of William Trimble and Eleanor O'Hair. (Fourth generation of David Trimble and —— Houston.) Born on June 23, 1821 and died on July 24, 1907. He is buried at Hazel Green, Kentucky. He married two times: first, to Mariah Swango of Stillwater, Kentucky, on March 8, 1842, and second, to Thirza Matilda Catron on March 19, 1862. She was from Grayson County, Virginia, born on December 8, 1843, and died on February 9, 1931. David enjoyed hunting and was a woodsman. He was a large landowner, probably inherited from his father, William Trimble. When David Shelton married the second time to Thirza Catron, he moved to Menifee County, Kentucky, where he owned 1,000 acres of rich land covered with virgin timber. He had eighteen children and it is said that he never saw all of them together at one time.

The children of David Shelton "Doc" Trimble and Mariah Swango:

D452—Robert Letcher Trimble. Born on November 30, 1842 and died on April 24, 1909 married Mary Ellen Honn of Illinois.

D453—Mary Ellen Trimble. Born on November 21, 1844 and died on January 29, 1846.

D454—William Taylor Trimble. Born on December 22, 1846.

D455—Kelsey Howard Trimble. Born on October 7, 1849, died on October 27, 1850.

D456—Henry Howard Trimble. Born in 1852 and died in 1941. He lived in Missouri for several years.

D457—James Jesse Trimble. Born on September 5, 1854 and died on February 21, 1879, in Missouri.

D458—Daniel Boone Trimble. Born on January 11, 1857. He settled in Middletown, Ohio.

D459—Rose Maria Trimble. Born on December 14, 1858 and died on April

18, 1938. Married Abraham Hybarger from Paris, Illinois.

The children of David Trimble and Thirza Catron:

D460—Mary Blanche Trimble. Born on November 30, 1863, at Hazel Green, Kentucky and died on February 11, 1948. Married John Bercaw on March 18, 1888, at Paris, Illinois.

D461—Franklin Powell Trimble. Born in 1867 and died in 1946. Married Eliza Bush in 1894.

D462—Eliza Ellen Trimble. Born in 1870 and died in 1883 at the age of thirteen.

D463—Charles Nesbitt Trimble. Born in 1872 and died in 1946. He was born in Kentucky and moved to California.

+ **D464—Nancy Elizabeth Trimble.** Born on March 27, 1874, married Alfonso Frey on May 1, 1895, at Paris, Illinois.

D465—Thomas Turner Trimble. Born in 1876 and died in 1973. Married Lillian Henderson.

D466—Robert Riddle Trimble. Born on January 1, 1879. Married Pearl Martin in 1908 and they lived in California.

D467—David Crockett Trimble. Born on May 23, 1881. Married Lula Kilgore and they lived at the home place at Trimble Bend in Kentucky.

D468—Bruce Marian Trimble. Born on December 23, 1883 and died in 1933. Married Nettie Bowen. He is buried near Slade, Kentucky.

D469—Emma Jane Kash Trimble. Born on December 6, 1865 and died on February 8, 1906. Married Jesse Swango and lived in Wolfe County, Kentucky.

D205—James Greenville Trimble. Son of William Trimble and Eleanor O'Hair. (Fourth generation of David Trimble and ——— Houston.) Born on June 15, 1823 and died on June 22, 1919. Due to a scarcity of schools in this area, J. G. Trimble had only one or two months of schooling per year. Yet, due to his determination, he accumulated enough knowledge to be a learned man.

As a boy he hauled, in a wagon, goods for his father's store from Maysville, Kentucky. He married Nancy Mize from Estill County, Kentucky, on April 27, 1846.

In 1847 his two-story log house in Hazel Green, Kentucky, was ready for occupancy. Like his father, William, James Greenville Trimble liked to barter a bit. He brought goods in by wagons and traded them for honey, furs, and ginseng roots. He had vast lands, stock, and dealt in slaves. His four house slaves were named Julie Ann, Hannah, Jane, and Julia.

Trimble Families of America

J. G. Trimble was a staunch Democrat and a Southern sympathizer. During the Civil War, his store was burned by Union soldiers. In 1876 he sold his mountain business and settled in a colonial brick house on East Main Street in Mount Sterling, Kentucky. Luxuries exceeded necessities in this house and several Negro servants added a genial Southern atmosphere to the house and grounds.

He became president of the Mount Sterling State Bank, a position he held for many years. J. G. Trimble died on June 22, 1919, at the age of ninety-six. He is buried beside his wife in the Machpelah Cemetery at Mount Sterling.

The author (John Farley Trimble) has copies of several letters written by J. G. Trimble, one of which relates his falling down an elevator shaft at a hotel in Louisville, Kentucky. This resulted in his needing the aid of a walking cane for the remainder of his life.

Another letter tells that he never knew a Trimble to drink alcoholic spirits except himself which he did nightly, taking a spoonful for his stomach's sake.

The children of James Greenville Trimble and Nancy Mize:

+ D470—**Mary Clark Trimble.** Born on April 21, 1847 in Hazel Green, Kentucky and died on July 27, 1931. Married James Greenwade in Kentucky.

D471—**Rowena Belle Trimble.** Born in Hazel Green, Kentucky. Married Jesse Taylor Day.

+ D472—**Nelson Harvey Trimble.** Born on November 19, 1852 in Hazel Green, Kentucky and died in June 1937. Married two times.

+ D473—**Robert Mize Trimble.** Born on May 3, 1855 in Hazel Green, Kentucky. Married Isa White.

D474—**Ella O'Hair Trimble.** Born on August 22, 1857 and died on October 2, 1931. She was a well-educated and cultured woman. At the death of her mother, Nancy Mize Trimble, Ella became the efficient hostess at the J. Greenville Trimble home.

+ D475—**Bruce Walker Trimble.** Born on August 31, 1860 in Hazel Green, Kentucky and died in 1932. Married Cora Cassidy.

+ D476—**Fannie Lee Trimble.** Born on March 10, 1863 in Hazel Green, Kentucky and died on December 17, 1916. Married Thomas Jones.

+ D477—**James Greenville Trimble, Jr.** Born on August 16, 1870 in Hazel Green, Kentucky. He was unmarried.

D478—**Nancy Mize Trimble.** Born on February 12, 1866 in Hazel Green, Kentucky and died on January 6, 1946. She died in Lexington, Kentucky. Married William Holly.

Trimble Families of America

D206—Stephen Asbury Trimble. Son of William Trimble and Eleanor O'Hair. (Fourth generation of David Trimble and —— Houston.) Born on December 3, 1825, died on October 15, 1864. Married Elizabeth South on July 7, 1863. They had waited for thirteen years to marry because Elizabeth had promised her mother as she was dying that she would not marry until her youngest sister was grown.

On April 13, 1864, their son, South Trimble, was born. Soon afterward the Union soldiers came looking for Asbury. The captain asked what the baby's name was. Elizabeth held her baby and said, "His name is South just like my five brothers and every man in the Southern Army." A very brave woman.

The year after their marriage Asbury, a strong Confederate sympathizer, was hurrying to put some Negroes to work at the tannery at Hazel Green. He was shot and killed in ambush. Prior to this time Asbury had served as sheriff of the county.

Elizabeth South Trimble was born on September 30, 1830 and died on March 16, 1900. She lived to see her son, South, become a Democratic member of the Kentucky Legislature.

The only child of Stephen Trimble and Elizabeth South:

+ **D479—South Trimble.** Born on April 13, 1864 and died on November 23, 1946.

D207—Emily Jane Trimble. Daughter of William Trimble and Eleanor O'Hair. (Fourth generation of David Trimble and —— Houston.) Born on January 4, 1828 and died on December 12, 1897. She married two times: First to Reverend McKinley Cockrell, and second, to a Mr. Lacy. The Reverend Mr. Cockrell and Emily Jane were married on July 27, 1847. He was a minister of the Christian church and a co-laborer at Hazel Green, Kentucky, with Reverend Joseph Nickell. The Reverend Mr. Cockrell was from Breathitt County, Kentucky. He died at the age of twenty-eight. He was born on January 16, 1827 and died on January 22, 1855.

Later, she married a Mr. Lacy. This marriage was not successful. She resumed her name of Cockrell and lived at the William Trimble house at Hazel Green. Aunt Emily helped weave the first carpet for the Hazel Green Christian Church. She died at the home of her daughter, Mrs. W. O. Mize.

The children of Reverend McKinley Cockrell and Emily Jane Trimble:

+ **D480—Lou Ellen Cockrell.** Born on June 15, 1848 and died on May 26, 1926. Married William O. Mize.

Trimble Families of America

D - David Trimble

+ D481—Mary Belle Cockrell. Born on February 17, 1850 and died June 24, 1927. Married Drew S. Godsey who was born in 1848 and died in 1907. He was from Hazard, Kentucky.

D209—Louisa Jane Trimble. Daughter of William Trimble and Eleanor O'Hair. (Fourth generation of David Trimble and —— Houston.) Born on October 16, 1831 and died in February 1922. She is buried by her first husband at Hazel Green, Kentucky. Louisa Jane married two times. Married first to Preston Wilson. He was born on July 10, 1823 and died on January 1, 1862. Married second to John Wilson.

The children of Preston Wilson and Louisa Jane Trimble:

D482—Henry Wilson. Born in 1849 in Wolf County, Kentucky.

D483—Asberry Wilson. Born on May 15, 1851 in Wolf County, Kentucky and died on January 24, 1913 in Scotia, Greeley County, Nebraska.

D484—James Howard Wilson. Born in 1853 in Wolf County, Kentucky and died in 1900. Married Mary Conroy and lived in Missouri.

D485—Elvin Wilson. Born on September 15, 1855 in Morgan County, Kentucky and died in Oklahoma.

D486—Rose Ellen Wilson. Born on June 12, 1857 in Morgan County, Kentucky and died on July 26, 1945 in Independence, Jackson, Missouri.

D487—Elizabeth Ann Wilson. Born on March 23, 1859 in Morgan County, Kentucky and died on August 26, 1938 in Montgomery County, Kentucky.

The child of John Wilson and Louisa Jane Trimble:

D488—Harlan P. Wilson. Born in February 1870 in Morgan County, Kentucky.

D210—Mary Elizabeth Trimble. Daughter of William Trimble and Eleanor O'Hair. (Fourth generation of David Trimble and —— Houston.) Born on November 3, 1833, died on May 10, 1903. She is buried at Mount Sterling, Kentucky. Married James Turner on April 27, 1856. He was a wealthy landowner with many slaves. They lived on a farm between Hazel Green and West Liberty, Kentucky. After the Civil War, they moved to Covington, Kentucky, and James Turner became a wholesale clothier in Cincinnati, Ohio. He died in 1875 and is buried at Mount Sterling.

About 1889 Mary Elizabeth Turner went to Paris, Illinois. and spent her remaining years with her daughter Mrs. Belle Miller.

They had three children that died in infancy. The children of James and Mary Elizabeth Trimble Turner:

D489—Mary Belle Turner. She married her third cousin, Will Miller, a merchant in Paris, Illinois. She was a talented concert pianist, a very cultured and widely traveled lady, yet quite superstitious. While opening a gift one day, she screamed in fright for it was "peafowl feathers" and to her this meant bad luck. Within a short time, she did receive a telegram telling of the death of her brother, Harlan.

D490—Harlan Turner. He owned and operated the Mount Sterling Hotel. After separating from his wife, Gertrude, he purchased a Missouri ranch. He had one son, John, who settled in the West.

D491—Clarence Turner. Born on December 26, 1871 and died on July 12, 1950. He owned a jewelry store in Paris, Illinois, and a farm in Missouri. Married Josephine LaGrange, and they had one daughter named Josephine. She graduated from Ward-Belmont College in Nashville, Tennessee. Married Rolla Ralston, who operates an automobile agency in Albany, Oregon. They have three sons: William, John Reid, and Robert Turner Ralston.

D214—James Harvey Trimble. Son of Isaac Trimble and Mary Young. (Fourth generation of David Trimble and ——— Houston.) Born on February 9, 1821, in Montgomery County, Kentucky, and died on February 9, 1910, near Camargo, Kentucky. He is buried in the Trimble Cemetery near Mount Sterling, Kentucky. James Harvey married Harriet Brush, born on July 11, 1825, and died on July 2, 1886. She was from Montgomery County. James Harvey was a prominent citizen of Montgomery County being the deputy sheriff for two terms in the 1860s. He was a large landowner and businessman.

The children of James Harvey Trimble and Harriet Brush:

+ **D492—Frank M. Trimble.** Born on February 4, 1843, in Montgomery County, Kentucky. He died in Butler, Missouri. Married Sally Redmond.

D493—Mary E. Trimble. Born on August 28, 1844 and died on December 20, 1921 at Camargo, Kentucky. Married Amos Turley of Montgomery County, Kentucky.

D494—James Taylor Trimble. Born on June 13, 1846 and died on August 19, 1851 in Jeffersonville, Kentucky.

+ **D495—Cortez Trimble.** Born on August 28, 1848 and died on January 22, 1922. Married Lizzie Cundiff.

+ **D496—Josiah Anderson Trimble.** Born on August 5, 1850 and died on December 21, 1923. Married Betty Pendleton.

D497—John T. Trimble. Born on December 29, 1852 and died on April 4, 1921 in Camargo, Kentucky. Married Clay Parsons.

D - David Trimble

+ **D498—James Harvey Trimble, Jr.** Born on March 19, 1855, and died after 1937. Married Eunice Macy

+ **D499—Perry Trimble.** Born on December 19, 1857 and died before 1937. Married Amanda Yocum.

  D500—Christopher Columbus Trimble. Born on February 11, 1859 and died on July 21, 1937 in Camargo, Kentucky. Married Leila Orear.

+ **D501—Algin Trimble.** Born on February 23, 1861 and died on July 29, 1935. Married Emma Johnson

+ **D502—Harriet Newell Trimble.** Born on August 11, 1865. Married Elijah Clay Williams.

D215—David Franklin "Doc" Trimble. Son of Isaac Trimble and Mary Young. (Fourth generation of David Trimble and —— Houston.) Born on October 14, 1824, at Montgomery County, Kentucky and died on September 16, 1865 (ambushed near Tick Town), Jeffersonville, Kentucky. He married Narcissus Jane Fox in 1825. (David Franklin is the author's grandfather.) Narcissus died on December 4, 1908, at seventy-eight years of age of a heart attack. Doc, as David Franklin Trimble was more commonly known, was deputy sheriff of Montgomery County, Kentucky, from 1860 to 1861. His brother, James Harvey Trimble, was deputy sheriff two terms: 1864-1868.

Doc Trimble was a Union sympathizer during the Civil War. Kentucky was highly divided and a neutral state. It was overrun several times by both the Northern and Southern troops. Doc's eldest son John told the author (John Farley Trimble) years ago that he could remember the Southern troops coming to their door looking for his father. Doc kept his horse saddled at the rear of the house for escape into the woods as the Southern troops would approach.

According to the court depositions of his death, friends who were with him at the time of ambush say he planned to leave for Missouri the next day to buy lands for the relocation of his family as he had already sold most of his lands in Kentucky. It is ironical to note that his family were Union sympathizers while his Uncle William Trimble's family of Hazel Green, Kentucky, were avid Southern sympathizers. This lends truth to the statement that brother turned from brother and wounds were never healed from this terrible war. This shows what turmoil was caused by the Civil War in the border states; families were divided in allegiances; friends became enemies.

The events following Doc's assassination thus affecting his family were tragic. His wife, Narcissus Jane Fox Trimble, married a young Confederate soldier from Virginia named T. Samuel H. Jones, whom this author (John Farley Trimble) can remember. Jones was several years her junior. Jane sold her dower rights and taking her two-year-old child (the author's (John Farley Trimble) father) Frank, and her ten-year-old son Leander, left Kentucky in 1867 and moved to Nicholas County, West Virginia. She bought land at Nettie, Nicholas County, West Virginia. The other children, the oldest of whom was eighteen, and the youngest four, headed westward in a covered wagon. They never saw or heard from their mother again. The oldest son, John, who was sixteen at the time of his father's death, settled near Crawfordsville, Indiana. He became a prosperous farmer. This John, in some way, contacted the two brothers who stayed with his mother. (The author (John Farley Trimble) visited at his farm in the early 1930s.) John was under the impression that T. Samuel H. Jones bushwhacked his father, Doc. (The author (John Farley Trimble) has heard this rumor in his family, also.) However, one event discourages this idea. Doc's brother, James Harvey, was the bondsman for the marriage of Narcissus and T. Samuel H. Jones. James Harvey Trimble also bought the dower rights from Narcissus.

The children of David Franklin "Doc" Trimble and Narcissus Jane Fox that headed westward:

+ **D503—John Harrison Trimble.** Born on October 18, 1849 and died on May 6, 1932. Settled near Crawfordsville, Indiana. Married Charity Caster

+ **D504—Emily Trimble.** Born on July 29, 1849 and died on June 4, 1926. Married William Knox and settled in Nebraska.

D505—Sarah Trimble. Married a Mr. Stamper and settled in the state of Washington.

D506—George Trimble. He went westward.

D507—Mary Trimble. Married a Mr. Chisolm.

D508—Marion Trimble. He settled in Missouri. He was four years of age when his father died.

The children of David Trimble and Narcissus Fox that came into West Virginia with their mother, Narcissus Jane Fox Trimble and T. S. H. Jones:

+ **D509—Leander Trimble.** Born on June 24, 1857 and died on August 14, 1941. Married Margaret Whitman

+ **D510—Joseph Franklin (Frank) Trimble.**

D511—Salina Trimble. Died in infancy and is buried in the Trimble Cemetery where her father, Doc, is buried at Jeffersonville, Kentucky.

Trimble Families of America

D - David Trimble

D227—Cyrenius Wait Trimble. Son of Isaac Trimble and Mary Young. (Fourth generation of David Trimble and —— Houston.) Born on February 23, 1834 in Pulaski County, Kentucky and died on June 6, 1908. Married Melissa Davis on October 18, 1853 in Pulaski County, Kentucky. He was in the Nineteenth Infantry Kentucky, enlisted in 1862.

The children of Cyrenius Wait Trimble and Melissa Davis:

D512—Columa Trimble. Born on February 11, 1858 in Pulaski County, Kentucky and died on July 12, 1944 in Pulaski County, Kentucky. Married Perry Jasper Daulton in 1879.

D513—Naoma Trimble. Born on February 26, 1860 in Kentucky and died on June 2, 1898 in Kentucky. Married Samuel F. Tarter on April 8, 1883 in Pulaski County, Kentucky.

D514—Lemiel Trimble. Born on November 8, 1865 in Kentucky and died on December 3, 1937 in Clinton, Illinois. Married Lee Ann Light on April 11, 1889.

D515—Cynthia A. Trimble. Born about 1868 in Kentucky and died after 1880.

+ **D516—Sarah Jane Trimble.** Born on March 1870 in Kentucky and died on October 23, 1947 in Jackson, Minnesota. Married John L. Carney on November 3, 1892 in Pulaski County, Kentucky.

D517—Bula Trimble. Born on November 25, 1871 in Kentucky on August 16, 1891 in Kentucky. Never married.

D518—Sy Florumsy Trimble. Born on January 20, 1874 in Pulaski County, Kentucky and died on January 18, 1945 in Pulaski County, Kentucky. Married Polly Jane Vanhoosier.

D519—Blanch W. Trimble. Born on April 15, 1876 in Pulaski County, Kentucky and died 1957 in Pulaski County, Kentucky. Married Brent Tarter on October 6, 1898 in Pulaski County, Kentucky.

D520—Teberia Trimble. Born on June 1877 in Pulaski County, Kentucky and died on January 30, 1878 in Pulaski County, Kentucky as an infant.

D521—Nancy "Nannie" E. Trimble. Born on December 18, 1878 in Pulaski County, Kentucky and died in December 1971 in Paris, Bourbon County, Kentucky. Married James T. Dodson on September 27, 1900 in Scott County, Tennessee.

D236—Walter Ulyssess Trimble. Son of William Clark Trimble and Phebe Smith. (Fourth generation of David Trimble and —— Houston.) Born on October 4, 1819 in Flemming County, Kentucky and died on November 4, 1873 in Iowa.

Married first to Cynthia Wimple on May 1, 1833.

210

Married second to Elizabeth Fidelia Bacon on August 21, 1844 in Edgar County, Illinois. Elizabeth born about 1823 - 1826 and died on November 27, 1915 in Pierce City, Missouri.

The children of Walter Ulyssess Trimble and Elizabeth Fidelia Bacon:

D522—Abigail Cinthia Trimble. Born on August 20, 1845 in Edgar County, Illinois and died in January 1846 in Edgar County, Illinois.

D523—William Clark Trimble. Born on March 10, 1847, in Illinois and died on November 27, 1918, at Durant, Oklahoma.

D524—Andrew Jackson Trimble. Born in Illinois in 1848 and died in 1934 at Pierce City, Missouri.

D525—Francis Marion Trimble. Born in Iowa in 1851. Married Alice V. Kegley.

D526—Luther D. Trimble. Born in Iowa in 1855 and married Anna ———.

D527—Albert Milton Trimble. Born in Iowa in 1857.

D528—Emma M. Trimble. Born in Iowa in 1860 and married C. E. Foster. She died in Bonham, Texas.

+ **D529—Walter Ulysses Trimble.** Born on August 8, 1867 in Iowa and died in Durant, Oklahoma on February 12, 1912. He married Lina (Mary Adeline) Cobb on January 19, 1898.

D238—Thomas Dudley Trimble. Son of William Clark Trimble and Phebe Smith. (Fourth generation of David Trimble and ——— Houston.) Born on 1815 and died on February 17, 1899. Married Eunice Rodgers on December 5, 1835, in Edgar County, Illinois.

The children of Thomas Dudley Trimble and Eunice Rodgers:

D530—Elizabeth Trimble. Born on June 22, 1842 in Edgar, Illinois.

D242—Andrew Jackson Trimble. Son of William Clark Trimble and Phebe Smith. (Fourth generation of David Trimble and ——— Houston.) Born in Illinois and died in September of 1892 in Monmouth, Iowa. Married Louisa Hanson.

The children of Andrew Jackson Trimble and Louisa Hanson:

D531—Allen S. Trimble. Born in Monmouth, Iowa.

D532—Alva J. Trimble. Lived at Eureka Springs, Arkansas.

D244—Elizabeth F. Caughron. Daughter of Thomas Caughron and Mary "Polly" Trimble. (Fourth generation of David Trimble and ——— Houston.) Born in 1820 in Pulaski County, Kentucky and died in 1861 in Pulaski County, Kentucky. Married Benjamin Julian Floyd on August 16, 1842 in Pulaski County,

D - David Trimble

Kentucky. Benjamin was born on 1826 in Pulaski County, Kentucky and died on January 11, 1862 in Pulaski County, Kentucky.

Benjamin was the son of Rev. Matthew Floyd and Lucinda Shipley. They were married on July 18, 1822 in Wayne County, Kentucky. Rev. Matthew Floyd was born in 1778 in South Carolina and died in 1864 in Pulaski County, Kentucky. Lucinda Shipley was born in 1801 in Tennessee and died in 1884 in Pulaski County, Kentucky.

The children of Benjamin Julian Floyd and Elizabeth F. Caughron:

+ **D533—Elizabeth Lee Floyd.** Born on October 7, 1843 in Mill Springs, Pulaski County, Kentucky and died on April 5, 1909 in Centralia, Lewis County, Washington. Married Edward Robert Taylor on May 20, 1866 in Somerset, Pulaski County, Kentucky.

D534—Hardin Franklin Floyd. Born on 1844 in Pulaski County, Kentucky and died in 1914 in Daytona, Montgomery County, Ohio. Married twice. Married first to Welthy about 1869. Married second to Seralda Jane Leigh on June 24, 1874. Hardin enlisted as a private in Company F, 1st Regiment Kentucky Calvary Union on July 25, 1863 and was discharged in 1865.

D535—Matthew Floyd. Born in 1847 in Pulaski, Kentucky and died on March 31, 1864 in Richmond, Virginia. Married Ophelia Thompson on December 22, 1878.

D536—Thomas Floyd. Born on January 12, 1845 and died in 1864.

D537—Amanda Jane Floyd. Born on March 11, 1852 in Pulaski, Kentucky. Married Reuben P Floyd.

D538—Raney M. Floyd. Born on March 27, 1856 in Pulaski, Kentucky and died on March 16, 1917 in Lincoln, Kentucky. Married Lucinda Jane Trimble on January 11, 1874 in Pulaski County, Kentucky.

D539—William Walker Floyd. Born in 1857 and died in 1879.

D540—John L. Floyd. Born on July 5, 1861 in Pulaski County, Kentucky and died in 1908 in Lakeland, Jefferson County, Kentucky. Married Nancy Elizabeth Madden on September 21, 1882 in Pulaski County, Kentucky.

D252—Robert Graham. Son of John Graham and Lydia Alkire. (Fourth generation of David Trimble and —— Houston.) Married Anna Davidson.

The child of Robert Graham and Anna Davidson:

D541—Margaret Graham.

D542—Emily Graham.

D543—Margaret Graham. (2nd)

D544—Robert V. Graham.

D545—**William H. Graham.**

D546—**Taylor Graham.**

D278—Mary Ann Trimble. Daughter of Samuel Trimble and Susannah Hammon. (Fifth generation of David Trimble and —— Houston.) Born on April 22, 1830 in Virginia and died on November 7, 1897 in Creston, Union County, Iowa. Married Robert Giffen Robeson on May 29, 1849 in Millwood, Knox County, Ohio. Robert was born on May 28, 1828 in Millwood, Knox County, Ohio and died on September 18, 1891 in Creston, Union, Iowa

The children of Robert Giffen Robeson and Mary Ann Trimble:

+ **D547—Sarah Samantha Robeson.** Born in April 1850 in Ohio and died on March 7, 1931 in Marshalltown, Marshall County, Iowa. Married Evan D. Bryant.

+ **D548—Camilla Stuart Robeson.** Born on September 18, 1851 in Akron, Summit County, Ohio and died on February 25, 1935 in Carthage, Hancock County, Illinois. Married James A. Ogilvie.

D549—John Winfield Robeson. Born on April 14, 1853 in Ohio. Married Sophia E. Wallace. She was born in 1858.

D550—Susanna Anna Robeson. Born on February 25, 1856 in Knox County, Ohio and died on April 7, 1932 in Wilmington, Will County, Illinois. Married William Benjamin McDowell.

D551—Albert Delano Robeson. Born on March 4, 1858 in Ohio and died on February 25, 1940.

D552—Lovie Jane Robeson. Born on February 1861 in Ohio and died in 1933 in Indianola, Red Willow County, Nebraska. Married George Jackson Hewitt.

D553—Enoch Robeson. Born about 1861 in Iowa.

D554—Laura Robeson. Born about 1866 in Iowa.

D555—Moses A. Robeson. Born about 1869 in Iowa. Married Lily A. McCasslin.

D279—John Trimble. Son of Samuel Trimble and Susannah Hammon. (Fifth generation of David Trimble and —— Houston.) Born on December 28, 1831 in Alleghany County, Maryland and died on November 1, 1887. Married Catherine Lybarger.

Catherine was born in 1828 in Brown, Knox County, Ohio and died on April 25, 1901.

The children of John Trimble and Catherine Lybarger:

D - David Trimble

+ **D556—Clifford C. Trimble.** Born on October 1857 in Ohio and died in 1929. Married Alice E. Dalton.

D557—Elmer E. Trimble. Born in 1861 in Ohio. Married Mary E. ——.

D558—Columbus Delano Trimble. Born in July 1865 in Knox County, Ohio and died on January 20, 1946 in Grandview Heights, Franklin County, Ohio. Married Rosella M. Trimble in 1891 in Ohio.

D281—Enoch Trimble. Son of Samuel Trimble and Susannah Hammon. (Fifth generation of David Trimble and —— Houston.) Born on September 18, 1836 in Millwood, Knox County, Ohio and died on May 29, 1904 in Danville, Knox County, Ohio. Married Esther Virginia Hettie Condit on August 20, 1865 in Warren County, Iowa.[49]

Ester was born on August 23, 1841 in Indiana and died on January 6, 1915 in Iowa. She is the daughter of Daniel Mahlon Condit and Sarah M. Martindale. Daniel was born on May 9, 1819 in Orange, Essex, New Jersey and died on September 14, 1874 in Warren, Iowa. Sarah was born on May 1, 1820 in Gallia County, Ohio and died on January 7, 1899 in Indianola, Warren County, Iowa

The children of Enoch Trimble and Esther Virginia Hettie Condit:

+ **D559—Ross Malen Trimble.** Born on August 7, 1866 in Warren County, Iowa and died after 1880. Married Inez Marcella Thompson.

+ **D560—Grant Samuel Trimble.** Born in May 1867 in Liberty, Warren County, Iowa and died on May 11, 1925 in Toppenish, Yakima County, Washington. Married Laura Victoria Sturman on March 20, 1887.

D561—John Howard Trimble. Born in February 1870 in Iowa and died on November 30, 1932 in Devils Lake, Ramsey County, North Dakota. Married India F. Sandy in 1892.

D562—Nan Minnie Trimble. Born on March 16, 1872 in Liberty, Warren County, Iowa and died on August 1, 1892 in Brown County, Ohio.

D563—Alvin Trimble. Born on April 24, 1874 in Liberty, Warren County, Iowa and died on July 11, 1874 in Liberty, Warren, Iowa. He was only a few months old.

D564—Doctor Scott C. Trimble. Born on August 1877 in Liberty, Warren County, Iowa and died in April 1945 in Emporia, Lyon County, Kansas.

---

[49] US Census Year: 1880; Census Place: Liberty, Warren, Iowa; Roll: 368; Family History Film: 1254368; Page: 456C; Enumeration District: 236; Image: 0533.

Married Sarah Matilla Walker on March 24, 1952.

D565—Enoch Trimble. Born on December 1, 1879 in Liberty, Warren County, Iowa and died on August 23, 1950 in Washington. Married Eliza Virginia Livesay on February 7, 1901 in Liberty, Warren County, Iowa.

D282—Henry H. Trimble. Son of Samuel Trimble and Susannah Hammon. (Fifth generation of David Trimble and —— Houston.) Born on April 21, 1839 in Union Township, Knox County, Ohio and died April 16, 1917 in Indianola, Warren County, Iowa. Married Sarah Jane McClure on October 25, 1866 in Clinton County, Indiana.

The children of Henry H. Trimble and Married Sarah Jane McClure:

D566—William D. Trimble. Born in July 1866 in Iowa and died in December 1949 in New York.

D567—Charles M. Trimble. Born on September 1869 in Iowa and died on October 12, 1941 in Indianola, Warren County, Iowa

D568—Carrie Ruth Trimble. Born on November 6, 1873 in Iowa and died on March 12, 1964 in City of Industry, Los Angeles County, California.

D569—Hosea Albert Trimble. Born on October 22, 1881 in Warren County, Iowa and died in December 1978 in Martensdale, Warren County, Iowa

D284—Eliza Lanett Trimble. Daughter of Samuel Trimble and Susannah Hammon. (Fifth generation of David Trimble and —— Houston.) Born on April 22, 1842 in Millwood, Guernsey County, Ohio and died on June 26, 1927 in Danville, Knox County, Ohio. Married Henry W. Bonnett in Knox County, Ohio. Henry was born on October 30, 1844 in Ohio and died September 17, 1907 in Danville, Ohio.

The children of Henry W. Bonnett and Eliza Lanett Trimble:

+ D570—Everett Earl Bonnett. Born on September 10, 1882 in Union Township, Knox County, Ohio and died on July 7, 1956 in Akron, Summit County, Ohio. Married Agnes A. Beum on January 29, 1905.

D571—Anthony Bonnett. Born in 1806 in Nova Scotia, Canada.

D572—Sarah Elizabeth Bonnett. Born on May 10, 1867 in Wood County, West Virginia and died on February 17, 1947 in Parkersburg, West Virginia.

D573—Charles Dudley Bonnett. Born on February 17, 1873 in Pipesville, Knox, Ohio and died on October 2, 1957 in Portage, Ohio.

D574—Everard Earl Bonnett. Born on September 10, 1882 in Union Township, Knox County, Ohio and died on July 7, 1956 in Akron, Summit County, Ohio. Married Agnes A. Beum on January 29, 1905.

D296—Mary Elizabeth Gillespie. Daughter of Robert B. Gillespie and Ann

Trimble Families of America

Trimble. (Fifth generation of David Trimble and —— Houston.) Born on February 25, 1844 in Moundsville, Marshall County, West Virginia and died on October 23, 1893 in Clearfield, Taylor County, Iowa. Married Henry Kent Calkins on March 22, 1864 in Henry, Marshall County, Illinois. Henry was born on December 22, 1835 in Burlington, Bradford County, Pennsylvania and died on November 22, 1919 in Clearfield, Taylor County, Iowa.

The children of Henry Kent Calkins and Mary Elizabeth Gillespie:

D575—Estella Anna Calkins. Born on August 7, 1865 in Wythe, Hancock County, Illinois and died on March 24, 1959 in Los Angeles, Los Angeles County, California.

D576—Laura Zilphia Calkins. Born on March 14, 1868 in Wythe, Hancock County, Iowa and died on January 10, 1958 in Henry, Marshall County, Illinois.

D577—Addie B. Calkins. Born on August 17, 1870 in Wythe, Hancock County, Illinois and died on September 18, 1887 in Taylor, Iowa.

+ **D578—Mary C. Calkins.** Born on September 14, 1873 in Wythe, Hancock County, Illinois and died on January 25, 1959 in Clearfield, Taylor County, Iowa. Married Howard Leonard Knox.

D579—Hattie Gillespie Calkins. Born on January 10, 1876 in Wythe, Hancock County, Illinois and died on September 22, 1965 in Clearfield, Taylor, Iowa. Married Elbert Patterson Knox.

D580—Leonard Boyd Calkins. Born on August 10, 1878 in Clearfield, Taylor County, Iowa and died on November 9, 1960 in Billings, Yellowstone County, Montana.

D581—Henry Orlando Calkins. Born on April 18, 1881 in Wythe, Hancock County, Illinois and died on October 31, 1962 in Clearfield, Taylor County, Montana.

D582—Archie Everett Calkins. Born on August 20, 1883 in Ringgold, Iowa and died on December 14, 1963 in Clearfield, Taylor County, Iowa.

D583—Dollie C. Calkins. Born on March 13, 1888 in Taylor, Iowa and died on September 15, 1961 in Jefferson City, Jefferson County, Montana.

D584—Dora Calkins. Born on March 13, 1888 in Taylor, Iowa and died on August 20, 1904 in Glenwood, Mills County, Iowa.

D299—Rebecca Porter. Daughter of Josiah Porter and Mary Combs. (Fifth generation of David Trimble and —— Houston.) Born on October 1, 1824 in Eckhart, Allegany County, Maryland and died on March 28, 1900 in Eckhart, Allegany County, Maryland. Married John Samuel Porter on March

6, 1851 in Allegany County, Maryland.

John was born on January 27, 1828 in Eckhart, Allegany County, Maryland and died on November 9, 1882 in Eckhart, Allegany County, Maryland. He was the son of Michael G. Porter and Elizabeth Devore. Michael was born on April 12, 1792 in Midland, Allegany County, Maryland and died on February 15, 1877 in Frostburg, Allegany, Maryland. Elizabeth was born about 1793 in Midland, Allegany County, Maryland and died about 1851 in Eckhart, Allegany County, Maryland.

The children of John Samuel Porter and Rebecca Porter:

+ **D585—William Ward Porter.** Born on January 15, 1852 in Maryland and died on August 11, 1874 in Allegany County, Maryland. Married Mary R. Rase in about 1885.

+ **D586—Josiah J. Porter.** Born on October 1855 in Maryland and died on January 2, 1900 in Allegany County, Maryland. Married Elizabeth Rase before 1880.

+ **D587—Michael R. Porter.** Born on March 19, 1856 in Eckhart, Allegany County, Maryland and died on November 4, 1928 in Eckhart, Allegany County, Maryland. Married Mary Elizabeth Engle in about 1881.

+ **D588—John Wesley Porter.** Born on October 1863 in Maryland and died about 1947. Married Rosa Anna Trescher in about 1896.

D589—Margaret E. Porter. Born in March 1866 in Allegany County, Maryland and died on April 5, 1943 in Eckhart Mines, Allegany County, Maryland. Married Philip Rephann on September 21, 1884. Philip was born on March 30, 1856 in Allegany County, Maryland and died on April 17, 1936 in Eckhart Mines, Allegany County, Maryland.

D301—Margaret Emily Porter. Daughter of Josiah Porter and Mary Combs. (Fifth generation of David Trimble and ——— Houston.) Born on September 22, 1827 in Eckhart, Allegany County, Maryland and died on May 15, 1910 in Eckhart, Allegany County, Maryland. Married John Ford on January 29, 1849 in Allegany County, Maryland.

John was born on February 1, 1826 in Scotland and died on May 3, 1886 in Allegany County, Maryland

The children of John Ford and Margaret Emily Porter:

D590—John T. Ford. Born on July 7, 1850 in Allegany County, Maryland and died on August 19, 1864 in Allegany County, Maryland at the age of fourteen.

D591—Ellen R. Ford. Born on April 18, 1860 in Allegany County, Maryland

D - David Trimble

and died on November 30, 1869 in Allegany County, Maryland at the age of nine.

D592—Martin L. Ford. Born on August 2, 1863 in Allegany County, Maryland and died on August 28, 1863 in Allegany County, Maryland at less than a month old.

D309—Francis Asbury Combs. Daughter of Elisha Combs and Elizabeth Neff. (Fifth generation of David Trimble and ——— Houston.) Born on February 17, 1837 in Maryland and died on February 19, 1878 in Union District, Monongalia County, West Virginia. Married Hannah J. Thomas on November4 20, 1856 in Monongalia, West Virginia. She was born on July 21, 1839 in Evansville, Preston, Virginia and died on July 21, 1928 in Morgantown, Monongalia, West Virginia.

The children of Francis Asbury Combs and Hannah J. Thomas:

D593—Clide Combs.

+ **D594—Wilbur Layton Combs.** Born on October 20, 1857 in Morgantown, Monongalia, West Virginia and died on October 11, 1924. Married Virginia C. "Jennie" Smell.

+ **D595—Charles William Combs.** Born on January 14, 1860 in Morgantown, Monongalia, West Virginia and died on April 11, 1948 in Morgantown, Monongalia, West Virginia. Married Emma Louise Parfitt on September 19, 1880.

D596—Isobel Combs. Born on May 23, 1870 in Maryland, and died on November 18, 1890 in Morgantown, Monongalia, West Virginia.

D312—Samuel John Porter. Son of John Potter and Hanna Comb. (Fifth generation of David Trimble and ——— Houston.) Born on July 16, 1822 in Frostburg, Allegany, Maryland and died on September 30, 1895 in Ogden Township, Lenawee County, Michigan. Married Elnora Eliza Rudolph on December 11, 1845 in Blissfield, Lenawee County, Michigan. Elnora was born on September 14, 1828 in Aurora, West Virginia and died on April 17, 1909 in Ogden, Lenawee County, Michigan.

The children of Samuel John Porter and Elnora Eliza Rudolph:

D597—John Wesley Porter. Born in 1846 and died in 1880.

D598—Mary Elizabeth Porter. Born on March 6, 1848 in Preston County, West Virginia and died on June 8, 1885.

D599—William Laurence Porter. Born in March 1850 in Preston County, West Virginia and died in April 1926 in British Columbia, Canada.

D600—Benjamin L. Porter. Born in 1852 and died in 1855.

Trimble Families of America

D601—James Albert Porter. Born in 1854 in Preston County, Virginia and died on December 25, 1885 in Blissfield, Lenawee, Michigan.

D602—Marion Aden Porter. Born on May 14, 1856 in Preston County, Virginia and died on March 4, 1929 in Northville, Oakland, Michigan.

D603—Sarah Lucinda Porter. Born on October 10, 1858 in Preston County, West Virginia and died on March 28, 1910 in Denver, Adams County, Colorado.

D604—Lydia Saloma Porter. Born about 1860 in Virginia and died on December 10, 1922 in Blissfield, Lenawee County, Michigan.

D605—Edward Benson Porter. Born on April 1862 in Preston County, Virginia and died on February 25, 1931 in Waterville, Douglas, Washington.

D606—Oliver Daniel Porter. Born on April 1, 1864 in Preston County, West Virginia and died on June 25, 1944 in Ogden, Lenawee County, Michigan.

D607—Ellsworth Washington Porter. Born on May 19, 1866 in Ann Arbor, Washtenaw County, Michigan and died on February 26, 1943 in Boise, Ada County, Idaho.

D608—Roswell Howard Porter. Born on June 10, 1868 in Lenawee County, Michigan and died on November 23, 1949.

D340—George William McCarty. Son of Wesley Daniel McCarty and Permelia Trimble. (Fifth generation of David Trimble and —— Houston.) Born on December 18, 1825 in Montgomery County, Kentucky and died on July 13, 1894 in Le Roy, Coffey County, Kansas. Married twice. Married first, to Mary Ann Minnick on August 9, 1849 in Crawford County, Illinois. She was born on February 28, 1830 in Rockingham, Virginia and died on July 15, 1854 in Crawford County, Illinois.

Married second, Elisabeth Ann Weston on March 25, 1855 in Olney, Richland County, Illinois. She was born on October 12, 1832 in Franklin County, Indiana and died on August 3, 1894 in LeRoy, Coffey County, Kansas.

The child of George McCarty and Mary Ann Minnick:

D609—Mary Jane McCarty. Born on July 10, 1850 in Illinois and died on July 27, 1930 in Terre Haute, Vigo, Indiana. Married Thomas R. Burr.

The children of George McCarty and Elisabeth Ann Weston:

D610—Permelia Caroline McCarty. Born on February 23, 1856 in Olney, Richland County, Illinois and died on May 7, 1927 in Crescent, Logan County, Oklahoma. Married James Little McCammon.

D611—Margaret Ann McCarty. Born on July 10, 1858 in Olney, Richland

County, Illinois and died on November 2, 1915 in Ft. Leavenworth, Leavenworth County, Kansas. Married James Thomas McCorkell.

D612—James Daniel McCarty. Born on August 8, 1860 in Illinois and died on December 20, 1940 in Topeka, Shawnee County, Kansas. Married Anna Lucy Dibble.

D613—George David McCarty. Born on December 18, 1862 in Olney, Richland County, Illinois and died on August 25, 1863 in Olney, Richland County, Illinois.

D614—William Alexander McCarty. Born on July 4, 1864 in Olney, Richland County, Illinois and died on April 30, 1904 in Parsons, Labette County, Kansas. Married Lillian May Harris.

D615—Dora L. McCarty. Born on November 13, 1866 in Olney, Richland County, Illinois and died on November 6, 1949 in Caney, Montgomery County, Kansas.

D616—Laura Elizabeth McCarty. Born on March 6, 1869 in LeRoy, Coffey County, Kansas and died on March 4, 1943 in LeRoy, Coffey County, Kansas. Marriage Christopher Columbus Seyffer.

D617—Susan Serena McCarty. Born on August 16, 1872 in LeRoy, Coffey County, Kansas and died 1958.

D618—Clara Bertha McCarty. Born on April 21, 1874 in LeRoy, Coffey County, Kansas and died on September 22, 1955 in Sylvia, Reno County, Kansas. Married John Daniel Sullivan.

D619—Joseph Lee McCarty. Born on February 9, 1878 in LeRoy, Coffey County, Kansas and died on August 17, 1954 in Colorado Springs, Colorado. Married Myrtle L. Dunn.

D341—Sally Ann McCarty. Daughter of Wesley Daniel McCarty and Permelia Trimble. (Fifth generation of David Trimble and —— Houston.) Born on October 25, 1827 in Montgomery County, Kentucky. Married William W. Marberry on November 7, 1848 in Crawford County, Illinois.

The children of William Marberry and Sally Ann McCarty:

D620—Marion F. Marberry. Born in June 1850 in Crawford County, Illinois.

D621—Mary F. Marberry. Born in June 1850 in Crawford County, Illinois.

D342—John Alexander McCarty. Son of Wesley Daniel McCarty and Permelia Trimble. (Fifth generation of David Trimble and —— Houston.) Born on June 5, 1829 in Montgomery County, Kentucky and died on January 18, 1902. Married to Susanna Nichols on December 14, 1854 in Crawford, Illinois. She was born on August 22, 1837 in Illinois and died on June 4,

1887.

The children of John Alexander McCarty and Susanna Nichols:

D622—Merrill W. McCarty. Born on September 29, 1857 and died on January 29, 1858.

D623—Ida A. McCarty. Born on September 14, 1859 and died on June 6, 1888. Married John Wilson Cawood.

D624—Mary Elizabeth McCarty. Born on July 17, 1861.

D625—Francis M. McCarty. Born on September 25, 1864.

D626—Frances J. McCarty. Born on June 30, 1868.

D627—Findley N. McCarty. Born on October 19, 1870 and died on January 17, 1872.

D628—Willie A. McCarty. Born on November 7, 1872 and died on February 11, 1873.

D629—Charlie A. McCarty. Born on August 6, 1874.

D630—John E. McCarty. Born on August 17, 1877.

D343—Mary Winifred McCarty. Daughter of Wesley Daniel McCarty and Permelia Trimble. (Fifth generation of David Trimble and ——— Houston.) Born on October 28, 1831 in Calloway County, Kentucky. Married George W. Minnick on February 7, 1850 in Crawford County, Illinois. He was born in 1827 in Virginia and died in 1885.

The children of George W. Minnick and Mary Winifred McCarty:

D631—Ida Minnick.

D632—Jane Minnick.

D633—Jim Minnick.

D634—John Minnick.

D635—Lola Minnick.

D636—Mary Minnick.

D637—Permelia Minnick.

D638—Rose Minnick.

D639—Tom Minnick.

D640—William Minnick.

D344—Frances Emeline McCarty. Daughter of Wesley Daniel McCarty and Permelia Trimble. (Fifth generation of David Trimble and ——— Houston.) Born on December 8, 1833 in Calloway County, Kentucky. Married Andrew Grubaugh on December 4, 1856 in Crawford County, Illinois. He was born in 1833 in Ohio.

The children of Andrew Grubaugh and Frances Emeline McCarty:

D641—Anna Grubaugh.

D642—Charlie Grubaugh.

D643—Emma Grubaugh.

D644—Evertt Grubaugh.

D645—Fred Grubaugh.

D646—Nona Grubaugh.

D647—Orval Grubaugh.

D648—Wess Grubaugh.

D649—Ella Grubaugh.

D650—Douglas Grubaugh.

D346—James Henry McCarty. Son of Wesley Daniel McCarty and Permelia Trimble. (Fifth generation of David Trimble and —— Houston.) Born on April 28, 1838 in Calloway County, Kentucky and died on September 3, 1890 in Edgar County, Illinois. Married Susanah J. Beavers.

The children of James Henry McCarty and Susanah J. Beavers:

D651—Oliver Madison McCarty. Born on April 14, 1867 in Richland County, Illinois and died on July 19, 1914 in Parke County, Indiana. Married Annette Smith.

D652—Daniel Frederick McCarty. Born on June 28, 1869 in Richland County, Illinois.

D653—John William McCarty. Born on October 8, 1874 and died 1943 in Kansas.

D654—Iola Alice McCarty. Born on July 12, 1878 in Richland County, Illinois. Married Mr. Dodson.

D655—Bertie Ralph McCarty. Born on September 13, 1880 in Richland County, Illinois and died on October 11, 1905 in Parke County, Indiana.

D656—Cora Elizabeth McCarty. Born on August 12, 1883 in Richland County, Illinois and died on August 6, 1945 in Vermillion County, Indiana.

D657—Charles Edward McCarty. Born on July 16, 1886 in Richland County, Illinois and died on June 6, 1943 in Parke County, Indiana.

D350—Mary Catherine McMullin. Daughter of James McMullin and Lucinda Burns. (Fifth generation of David Trimble and —— Houston.) Born on August 17, 1843 in Washington County, Kentucky and died on June 10, 1888 in Mercer County, Kentucky. Married James Thomas Black on November 15, 1860 in Washington County, Kentucky. James was born on May 6, 1839 in Mercer County, Kentucky and died on February 26, 1921 in Mercer County, Kentucky.

The children of James Thomas Black and Mary Catherine McMullin:

D658—Margaret Ellen Black. Born on December 1, 1861 in Mercer County, Kentucky and died on July 18, 1924.

D659—John S. Black. Born about 1863 in Kentucky and died on September 9, 1939 in Texas, Washington County, Kentucky.

D660—Eliza Jane Black. Born on March 3, 1865 in Washington County, Kentucky and died on July 27, 1909 in Mercer County, Kentucky.

D661—Talitha M. Black. Born on July 16, 1866 in Mercer County, Kentucky and died on July 1, 1941.

D662—Mary Belle Black. Born on November 6, 1867 in Mercer County, Kentucky and died on November 21, 1938 in Milwaukee, Milwaukee County, Wisconsin.

D663—Robert Lee Black. Born on April 6, 1869 in Kentucky and died on March 31, 1933 in Louisville, Jefferson County, Kentucky.

D664—Benjamin Perry Black. Born on May 13, 1871 in Mercer County, Kentucky and died on October 26, 1957.

D665—Clifton Thomas Black. Born on October 8, 1872 in Mercer County, Kentucky and died on November 2, 1939 in Harrodsburg, Mercer County, Kentucky.

D666—William Keller Black. Born on December 26, 1873 in Mercer County, Kentucky and died on July 27, 1956 in Macomb, McDonough County, Illinois.

D667—Addison Kemper Black. Born on February 9, 1876 in Mercer County, Kentucky and died on October 29, 1945 in Harrodsburg, Mercer County, Kentucky.

D668—Addie K. Black. Born about 1876 in Kentucky.

D669—Lucinda Black. Born on June 16, 1877 in Mercer County, Kentucky and died on October 10, 1911 in Rose Hill, Mercer County, Kentucky.

+ **D670—Teresa A. Black.** Born on December 7, 1878 in Mercer County, Kentucky and died on December 12, 1911 in Mercer County, Kentucky. Married Charles Powell in 1896.

D671—Budia Black. Born on February 26, 1880 in Mercer County, Kentucky and died on April 13, 1881 in Mercer County, Kentucky.

D672—Marshall Black. Born 1880 in Kentucky.

D673—James Daniel "JD" Black. Born on September 26, 1881 in Mercer County, Kentucky and died on November 14, 1974.

D674—Leigh Black. Born on March 1, 1887.

D675—Ruah Frances Black. Born on July 20, 1887 in Mercer County, Kentucky and died on November 29, 1969 in Mercer County, Kentucky.

D676—Infant Black. Born and died on June 10, 1888 in Washington County, Kentucky.

D357—John Breckenridge Laughlin. Son of Robert Luckie Laughlin and Rebecca Francis Githens. (Fifth generation of David Trimble and —— Houston.) Born on March 23, 1855 in Kentucky. Married Annie Morton in 1879. She was born in 1862 in Cass, Missouri and died in 1951.

The child of John Breckenridge Laughlin and Annie Morton:

D677—Clora Lee Laughlin. Born about 1879 in Missouri.

D678—Clara Lee Laughlin. Born on January 7, 1880.

D679—Pearl L. Laughlin. Born in January 1880 in Missouri.

D680—Richard Forrest Laughlin. Born on October 16, 1881 in Missouri.

D681—George W. Laughlin. Born on August 14, 1883 in Missouri.

D682—Dora Laughlin. Born on October 20, 1884 in Missouri.

D683—Cora Lee Laughlin. Born in 1885.

D684—Jesse Ward Laughlin. Born on September 2, 1887.

D685—Mamie Lou Laughlin. Born on March 19, 1892 in Kansas and died on July 7, 1972 in Parsons, Labette County, Kansas.

D686—Alta May Laughlin. Born on January 29, 1895 in Kansas.

D687—Grover C. Laughlin. Born on March 17, 1897 in Kansas.

D688—Elmer R. Laughlin. Born on November 20, 1897 in Kansas.

D689—Eleanor Louise Laughlin. Born on October 29, 1900 in Kansas.

D690—John E. Laughlin. Born on May 6, 1904 in Kansas.

D359—Robert Luckie Laughlin. Son of Robert Luckie Laughlin and Rebecca Francis Githens. (Fifth generation of David Trimble and —— Houston.) Born on July 19, 1859 in Covington, Kentucky and died on May 19, 1943 in Kansas City, Missouri. Married Flora Lee Walker on November 15, 1882. Flora was born on April 27, 1861 in West Port, Jackson County, Missouri and died on January 1, 1926 in Lenexa, Kansas.

The children of Robert Luckie Laughlin and Flora Lee Walker:

+ D691—Harry Arthur Laughlin. Born on August 22, 1883 in Kansas and died on January 23, 1962 in Orange County, California. Married Marie E.

+ D692—Letha Lee Laughlin. Born on August 17, 1890 in Johnson County, Kansas and died on February 20, 1974 in Mcpherson, Mcpherson County, Kansas. Married Henry Shaw Cooper on January 19, 1910 in Lenexa, Johnson County, Kansas.

D387—Marion Grant Trimble. Son of David Trimble and Sarah Conley. (Fifth generation of David Trimble and —— Houston.) Born about 1869. Married and had seven children.

The children of Marion Grant Trimble:

D693—Bertha Trimble. Married a Mr. Lewis and has seven children.

D694—Lula Trimble. Married a Mr. Fannin and has five children.

+ **D695—James Trimble.** Born on March 15, 1902. Married and has one child.

D696—Elizabeth Trimble. Married a Mr. Holbrook and has seven children.

D697—Jennie Trimble. Married a Mr. Davis and has five children.

D698—Sherman Trimble. Married and has four children.

D699—Claude Trimble. Married and has three children.

D390—John G. Trimble. Son of James Trimble and Susan Tackett. (Fifth generation of David Trimble and —— Houston.) Born on March 22, 1844 and died on June 27, 1931. He married two times. Married first to Matilda Vanhoose. She was born in 1846 and died on January 27, 1913. Married second to Serena Reed Colvin.

The children of John G. Trimble and Matilda Vanhoose:

+ **D700—Clark Trimble.** Married twice.

+ **D701—Carl Trimble.** Born on March 11, 1870, died November 29, 1919.

+ **D702—William "Willie" Trimble.** Born on August 27, 1865 in Johnson County, Kentucky and died on November 28, 1937 in Barnett's Creek, Johnson County, Kentucky. Married Sola Gertrude Conley.

+ **D703—Paris Grant Trimble.** Born in 1872 and died in 1944.

+ **D704—Henry Elmer Trimble.** Born in 1878 and died in 1912.

+ **D705—Shelby "Shell" Trimble.** Born in 1880 and died in 1951.

+ **D706—Laura Trimble.** Born in 1876 and died in 1960.

D707—Flora Trimble. Died in infancy.

D391—William Mark Trimble. Son of James Trimble and Susan Tackett. (Fifth generation of David Trimble and —— Houston.) Born on February 16, 1851 in Barnett's Creek, Johnson County, Kentucky and died on March 7, 1911 in Redbush, Johnson County, Kentucky. He married Cynthia Essie Reed and lived in Johnson County, Kentucky. Cinda was born on January 16, 1847 in Barnett's Creek, Johnson County, Kentucky and died on May 15, 1932 in Morgan County, Kentucky.

The children of William Mark Trimble and Cynthia Essie "Cinda" Reed:

+ **D708—Charlie Trimble.** Born in 1874. Married Amanda Williams.

D - David Trimble

+ **D709—Lando Trimble.** Born in October 1877. Married Malissa Williams.
+ **D710—Julia Trimble.** Born in 1861. Married Manassa Stapleton.
+ **D711—Sarah Trimble.** Born in 1889, married Dock Salyers.
+ **D712—Albert Trimble.** Born in 1873, married Naoma Tackett.
  D713—Jane Trimble. Born in 1884, married William H. Lemaster.
+ **D714—John Elliott Trimble.** Born in 1888, married Selona Williams.
  D715—James Trimble. Born in 1886, married Myrtle Frazier.
  D716—Chester Trimble. Died at three months of age.

D392—Jane Trimble. Daughter of James Trimble and Susan Tackett. (Fifth generation of David Trimble and —— Houston.) Born in 1884 and married Jasper Wheeler.

Their children of Jasper Wheeler and Jane Trimble.
D717—Tobe Wheeler. Married first Jane McKenzie and second Susie Castle.
D718—John Wheeler. Married Cynthia Bailey.
D719—Elizabeth Wheeler.
D720—Mollie Wheeler. Married James P. Butler.

D393—Susanah Trimble. Daughter of James Trimble and Susan Tackett. (Fifth generation of David Trimble and —— Houston.) Married Taylor Ramey.

The child of Taylor Ramey and Susan Trimble:
+ **D721—Sherman Trimble Ramey.** Married Sherlie Williams.

D394—Millie Trimble. Daughter of James Trimble and Sarah Howes Baldwin. (Fifth generation of David Trimble and —— Houston.) Married James B. Lemaster.

The children of James Lemaster and Millie Trimble:
D722—Ollie Lemaster. Married Britton Spadlin.
D723—Lela Lemaster. Married Ollie Cooper.
D724—Octava Lemaster. Married Ray Pelphrey.
D725—Leona Lemaster. Married Anthony Dills.
D726—Eunice Lemaster.
D727—Buel Lemaster. Married Ruie Vanhoose.

D395—Alice Trimble. Daughter of James Trimble and Sarah Howes Baldwin. (Fifth generation of David Trimble and —— Houston.) Married two times: first, to Joel Deboard, and second, to David Fairchild.

The children of Joel Deboard and Alice Trimble:
D728—James Deboard. Married Civiliar Nickel.
D729—Lela Deboard. Married James Fugate.

The children of David Fairchild and Alice Trimble:

D730—Paris Fairchild. Married Nora Blair.

D731—Lillie Fairchild. Married Emerson Picklesimer.

D396—Minerva Trimble. Daughter of James Trimble and Sarah Howes Baldwin. (Fifth generation of David Trimble and —— Houston.) Married a Mr. Lemaster.

The children of Mr. LeMaster and Minerva Trimble:

D732—Flora Lemaster.

+ **D733—Alfred Lemaster.** Married two times. Married first to Jensie Caudill. Married second to Audrey Kelsey.

+ **D734—Clara Lemaster.** Married Paris Stapleton.

+ **D735—Rosa Lemaster.** Born in 1897. Married Daniel Boone Trimble (D767).

+ **D736—Mattie Lemaster.** Married John Davis. They had three daughters.

D737—John Walter Lemaster. Died in the army.

D738—Elexious Howes Lemaster.

D397—Lou Trimble. Daughter of James Trimble and Sarah Howes Baldwin. (Fifth generation of David Trimble and —— Houston.) Married John Picklesimer.

The children of John Picklesimer and Lou Trimble:

D739—Mintie Picklesimer. Married Alex Blair.

+ **D740—Ralph Picklesimer.** Married Virgie Blair.

+ **D741—Elzie Picklesimer.** Married Letta Reed.

+ **D742—Smith Picklesimer.** Married Chole Reed.

D743—Kelly Picklesimer. Married Bethel Rice.

+ **D744—James Picklesimer.** Married Bertha Blair.

+ **D745—Frank Pierce Picklesimer.** Married Ora Conley. They had one son.

+ **D746—Josie Picklesimer.** Married David Williams.

D747—Verna Picklesimer. Married a Mr. Salyer.

D398—Ulysses Grant Trimble. Son of James Trimble and Sarah Howes Baldwin. (Fifth generation of David Trimble and —— Houston.) Born on May 13, 1869 in Barnett's Creek, Johnson County, Kentucky and died on February 14, 1944 in Johnson County, Kentucky. Married Patience Williams. Several members of this family seemed to have died from the pandemic flu of 1919: Malta and Frank.

The children of Ulysses Grant Trimble and Patience Williams:

+ **D748—Stella Josephine Trimble.** Born on August 9, 1890 on Barnett's Creek, Johnson County, Kentucky and died on February 21, 1968 Paintsville, Johnson County, Kentucky. Married Milt LeMaster on March 25, 1926.

D749—Malta Mae Trimble. Born on December 17, 1893 in Kentucky and died on January 29, 1919. Married James Hackworth.

+ **D750—James Arthur Trimble.** Born on July 27, 1896 in Johnson County, Kentucky and died on March 26, 1969. Married Pearl Rice.

D751—Francis D. "Frank" Trimble. Born on May 4, 1898 in Johnson County, Kentucky and died on February 1, 1919 in Johnson County, Kentucky.

D752—Earl Trimble. Born on December 11, 1899 in Johnson County, Kentucky and died in 1899 in Floyd County, Kentucky.

D753—Vergie Trimble. Born on April 7, 1904 in Kentucky and died on August 29, 1973 in Salyersville, Magoffin County, Kentucky. Married Orville Hackworth.

D754—Luther Grant Trimble. Born on July 15, 1906 in Ivyton, Magoffin County, Kentucky and died on November 22, 1972 in Cabell County, West Virginia. Married Nora Tackett.

D755—Ruby Trimble. Born on August 6, 1912 in Trimble Gap, Johnson County, Kentucky and died on December 22, 1991 in Ashland, Boyd County, Kentucky. Married Emerson Caudill.

+ **D756—Clarence Benjamin Trimble.** Born on August 5, 1932 in Magoffin County, Kentucky and died on April 30, 1976 in Magoffin County, Kentucky.

D406—John Mark Trimble. Son of William "Bill Dodger" Trimble and Clarinda Ellen Picklesimer. (Fifth generation of David Trimble and ——— Houston.) Born on January 7, 1854, died on November 5, 1925. He married Clarinda Francis Spradlin on August 25, 1876 in Johnson County, Kentucky. She was born on April 8, 1860 in Denver, Johnson County, Kentucky and died on May 25, 1941 in Johnson County, Kentucky. John Mark was in the general merchandise business on Barnett's Creek, Johnson County, Kentucky, for forty years.

The children of John Mark Trimble and Clarinda Francis Spradlin:

D757—Mantford Trimble. Born and died in 1877.

+ **D758—Bertha Trimble.** Born on August 17, 1878 in Johnson County, Kentucky and died on March 22, 1908. Married Crate Davis.

+ **D759—Della Trimble.** Born on February 29, 1880 in Johnson County, Kentucky Married Leonard Caudill.

Trimble Families of America

+ **D760—Lindzey Trimble.** Born on April 18, 1881 in Johnson County, Kentucky and died on July 13, 1912 in Barnett's Creek, Johnson County, Kentucky. Married Flora Home.

D761—Elzie Trimble. Born on November 7, 1882 in Johnson County, Kentucky and died on September 4, 1942 in Johnson County, Kentucky. Married Ona Craft.

D762—Dennis Trimble. Born on September 17, 1884 and died on March 4, 1885.

+ **D763—Elmer S. Trimble.** Born on January 23, 1886 in Johnson County, Kentucky and died on January 27, 1972 in Gallipolis, Gallia County, Ohio. Married Tera Barnett.

+ **D764—Mahala Trimble.** Born on February 12, 1888 in Barnett's Creek, Johnson County, Kentucky and died on April 8, 1978 in Barnett's Creek, Johnson County, Kentucky. Married Byrd Preston.

+ **D765—Bruce C. Trimble.** Born on November 24, 1889 in Johnson County, Kentucky and died on July 19, 1963 in Huntington, Cabell County, West Virginia Born in 1889, died 1963. Married Norsie E. Reed on December 25, 1919. She was born in 1899 in Kentucky.

D766—Rutha Trimble. Born on November 1890 in Kentucky.

+ **D767—Daniel Boone Trimble.** Born on September 15, 1892 and died on March 10, 1963. He married Rosa LeMaster (D735). See her genealogy under No. D735.

+ **D768—Harry B. Trimble.** Born on March 24, 1893 in Johnson County, Kentucky, and died on January 14, 1978 in Pike County, Kentucky. Married Bessie Adams.

+ **D769—Shella Trimble.** Born on March 15, 1895 in Johnson County, Kentucky and died on December 24, 1987 in Franklin, Franklin County, Ohio. Married Sebastian Coldiron.

D770—Wince Trimble. Born in September 1896 in Kentucky and died on May 31, 1973 in Hagerhill, Johnson County, Kentucky Married two times: first, to Gypsie ——, and second, to Hannah Jean Ward. Wince was a member of the Fiscal Court of Johnson County, Kentucky. He was active for the improvement of the roads in the county and in later years was sheriff of Johnson County.

+ **D771—Quince Trimble.** Born on July 7, 1899 in Johnson County, Kentucky and died on March 4, 1970 in Columbus, Franklin County, Ohio. Married Lessie Lemaster.

D772—Clara Trimble. Born on October 3, 1902 in Johnson County, Kentucky

Trimble Families of America

and died on May 18, 1997 in Bexley, Franklin County, Ohio.

D408—David Nathaniel Trimble. Son of William "Bill Dodger" Trimble and Clarinda Ellen Picklesimer. (Fifth generation of David Trimble and ——— Houston.) Born on August 31, 1859 in Johnson County, Kentucky and died on March 24, 1940 in Johnson County, Kentucky. Married Nan Vanhoose.

The children of David Nathaniel Trimble and Nan Vanhoose:
   D773—Benton Trimble.
   D774—Cyrus Trimble. Married Bessie Salyer.
   D775—Tom Trimble. Married a Mollie Blair.
   D776—Stella Trimble. Never married.
   D777—Dora Trimble. Married Harry Mahan.
   D778—Zelda Trimble. Married Albert Picklesimer.

D409—William Henry Trimble. Son of William "Bill Dodger" Trimble and Clarinda Ellen Picklesimer. (Fifth generation of David Trimble and ——— Houston.) Born on November 23, 1863 and died on September 13, 1941. He married Sally Vanhoose, daughter of William Vanhoose. Sally was born on March 4, 1860 and died on April 6, 1932.

The children of William Trimble and Sally VanHoose:
 + **D779—Boe Trimble.** Born in 1886, married Zura Caudill.
 + **D780—Floyd Trimble.** Married Fona Ritchie.
 + **D781—James V. Trimble.** Married Mayme Goble.
 + **D782—Pierce Trimble.** Married Lena Caudill.
 + **D783—Newt Trimble.** Married Ethel Rice, first, and second, to Mary West.
 + **D784—Therman Trimble.** Married Mildred Caudill.
   D785—Laura Trimble. Never married.
 + **D786—Sada Trimble.** Married George Eally.

D411—Greenville Trimble. Son of William "Bill Dodger" Trimble and Clarinda Ellen Picklesimer. (Fifth generation of David Trimble and ——— Houston.) Born on August 6, 1866 in Johnson County, Kentucky and died on January 13, 1949 in Johnson County, Kentucky. Married Sadie Ealey.

The children of Greenville Trimble and Sadie Ealey:
 + **D787—Beulah G. Trimble.** Born on October 20, 1893 in Johnson County, Kentucky and died on December 29, 1927 in Magoffin County, Kentucky. Married Solon Prater.
   D788—Buell G. Trimble. Born on December 14, 1895 in Kentucky and died

on September 16, 1970 in Bellefontaine, Logan, Ohio. Married Reba Salyers.

D789—Hazel Trimble. Born on June 7, 1899 in Johnson County, Kentucky and died on January 28, 1994 in Johnson County, Kentucky. Never married but had a son Garth Trimble.

D790—Archie Trimble. Born on July 30, 1902 in Barnett's Creek, Johnson County, Kentucky and died on February 23, 1979 in Springfield, Clark County, Ohio. Married a Miss Williams.

D791—Ollie Trimble. Born on June 16, 1903 and died on February 12, 1997 in Louisa, Lawrence County, Kentucky. Married Jess Tackett.

D792—Ray Trimble. Born about 1908 in Kentucky and died on July 31, 1927 in Johnson County, Kentucky.

D793—Gracie Trimble. Married John Picklesimer.

D794—Vergie Trimble. Married a Samuel P. Blair.

D412—Joseph Harman Trimble. Son of William "Bill Dodger" Trimble and Clarinda Ellen Picklesimer. (Fifth generation of David Trimble and —— Houston.) Born on October 30, 1871 on Barnett's Creek, Johnson County Kentucky and died on November 3, 1928 on Barnett's Creek, Johnson County Kentucky. He married Florence Ida Caudill on March 2, 1876 on Pickle Fork, Johnson County Kentucky. She was born on October 26, 1877 at Barnett's Creek, Johnson County, Kentucky, and died on April 26, 1930. She was the daughter of Abraham Caudill and Jane Spradlin of Barnett's Creek, Kentucky.[50][51]

The children of Joseph Harman Trimble and Florence Ida Caudill:

+ **D795—Conroy Trimble.** Born on November 28, 1895 in Johnson County, Kentucky and died in August 1971 in Johnson County, Kentucky. He married Doshia Ann Blair.

+ **D796—McCoy Trimble.** Born on January 17, 1898 in Johnson County, Kentucky and died on December 28, 1989 in Fort Myers, Lee County, Florida. Married Ethel Fraley.

+ **D797—Palmer Trimble.** Born on August 9, 1901 in Johnson County,

---

[50] US Census:1910; Census Place: District 3, Johnson, Kentucky; Roll: T624_480; Page: 5B; Enumeration District:0071; FHL microfilm: 1374493

[51] US Census: 1920; Census Place: Barnett's Creek, Johnson, Kentucky; Roll: T625_583; Page: 2A; Enumeration District: 37; Image: 228

Kentucky and died on October 29, 1987 in Gallipolis, Gallia County, Ohio. Married Nola E. Webb on December 15, 1935.

+ **D798—Lelia Jane Trimble.** Born on October 3, 1906 in Johnson County, Kentucky and died on May 11, 1999 at Cabell Huntington Hospital, Huntington, West Virginia. Married, Flem Arrowood on November 27, 1924 in Paintsville, Johnson County, Kentucky.

+ **D799—William Wallace Trimble.** Born on November 21, 1908 in Johnson County, Kentucky, and died on May 28, 1965 in Boyd County, Kentucky. Married Rhena Mae Rice on June 22, 1932.

+ **D800—Clemince (Clemmons) "Pete" Trimble.** Born on September 11, 1911 in Johnson County, Kentucky and died on November 20, 1968 in Huntington, Cabell County, West Virginia. Married Mildred Preston on June 22, 1932.

+ **D801—Swanie Lee Trimble.** Born on February 10, 1914 at Barnett's Creek Johnson County, Kentucky and died on September 22, 1991 at Cabell County, West Virginia. Married Rhoda Tomblin on April 8, 1939.

+ **D802—Lola Marie Trimble.** Born on January 13, 1917 at Barnett's Creek, Johnson County, Kentucky and died on August 22, 2000 at South Point, Ohio. Married Floyd William Damron, first, and second, to Guy Puckett.

+ **D803—Lillian Margueritte Trimble.** Born on March 20, 1922 in Johnson County, Kentucky and died on May 1, 2009 at Emogene Dolin Jones Hospice House, Huntington, Cabell County, West Virginia. Married Thomas Ray Dick on August 25, 1956. Tom was born on May 28, 1937.

D413—Laura Mae "Dolly" Trimble. Daughter of William "Bill Dodger" Trimble and Clarinda Ellen Picklesimer. (Fifth generation of David Trimble and ——— Houston.) Born on April 15, 1876 in Johnson County, Kentucky and died in 1953 and buried in April 1853 in Ratliff Family Cemetery, Johnson County, Kentucky. Married twice, first to Joseph Joe Trimble. Joseph Born about 1875 in Johnson County, Kentucky and died after 1900. Married second John Elliott Ratliff. John Born on April 30, 1885 in Paintsville, Johnson County, Kentucky and died on April 4, 1954 in Johnson County, Kentucky.

The children of Joseph Trimble and Laura Mae "Dolly" Trimble:

+ **D804—Patrick H. Trimble.** Born on December 16, 1896 in Johnson County, Kentucky and died on May 20, 1951 in Johnson, Kentucky. Married a Julia Cane in 1917.

The children of John E. Ratliff and Dollie Trimble:

+ **D805—Farmer Ratliff.** Born on April 18, 1903 in Johnson County, Kentucky and died on May 23, 1963 in Johnson County, Kentucky. Married twice.

  D806—Fannie Ratliff. Born in 1904 in Johnson County, Kentucky and died in 1919 in Johnson County, Kentucky as a teenager.

+ **D807—Freddie Ratliff.** Born on June 28, 1908, in Johnson County, Kentucky and died on January 15, 1986 in Johnson County, Kentucky. Married Vena McKenzie. Great granddaughter Denise married Mark Castle.

+ **D808—Gordon Ratliff.** Born on April 6, 1911 in Barnett's Creek, Johnson County, Kentucky and died on February 6, 1991 in Jackson, Jackson County, Michigan. Married Bessie Spradlin.

+ **D809—Gladia Ratliff.** Born on July 31, 1913 in Johnson County, Kentucky and died on December 11, 1988 in Floyd County, Kentucky.

+ **D810—Sadie Ratliff.** Born on March 22, 1918 in Johnson County, Kentucky and died on June 29, 1984 in Floyd County, Kentucky. Married Earl Douglas Lemaster. [52]

+ **D811—Clara Ratliff.** Born on 1923 in Paintsville, Johnson County, Kentucky and on December 1, 1993 Paintsville, Johnson County, Kentucky. Married Hoy Preston. Hoy was born on February 14, 1918 in Johnson County, Kentucky and died on June 3, 1999 in Kentucky.

D414—Lydia Trimble. Daughter of William "Bill Dodger" Trimble and Clarinda Ellen Picklesimer. (Fifth generation of David Trimble and ——— Houston.) Born in November 1873 in Johnson County, Kentucky and died on December 28, 1943 in Magoffin County, Kentucky. Married William Pickle.

  The children of William Pickle and Lydia Trimble:
  D812—Irvin Pickle.
  D813—Marvin Pickle. Married a Picklesimer.
  D814—Rex Pickle.

D415—Jane Trimble. Daughter of William "Bill Dodger" Trimble and Clarinda Ellen Picklesimer. (Fifth generation of David Trimble and ——— Houston.) Married Daniel Harmon.

---

[52] Year: 1940; Census Place: Johnson, Kentucky; Roll: T627_1322; Page: 25A; Enumeration District: 58-2

Trimble Families of America

D - David Trimble

The children of Daniel Harmon and Jane Trimble:

D815—William G. Harmon. Married a Delphia Blair.

D816—Charles Harmon.

D817—Ida Harmon. Married James Culbertson.

D818—Elizabeth Harmon.

D423—John Crittenden Trimble. Son of Richard Menifee Trimble and Armilda Hines Glover. (Fifth generation of David Trimble and —— Houston.) Born on June 19, 1862 and died on January 1, 1930. John married two times: first, to Elizabeth Foley, and second, to Harriet Ryan.

John Crittenden Trimble lived the greater part of his life in Montgomery County, Kentucky, where his children were born and reared. He was a well-known farmer and livestock dealer, interested in civic affairs and the church. He served as magistrate for sixteen years which at that time consisted of welfare commissioner, justice of the peace, etc. He was, at one time a candidate for state representative to the Kentucky Legislature from the Ninetieth District.

We quote from Mrs. W. H. Yeary, Sr. (Georgia Trimble), "We feel we have been blessed in having such wonderful parents, who were devout in giving their children spiritual guidance and set a good example for good citizenship, and all have established Christian homes."

We are gratefully indebted to Mrs. W. H. Yeary, Box 75 Harrodsburg, Kentucky 40330, for the information of the John Crittenden Trimble family genealogy. The time and excellent way she prepared the material for us is greatly appreciated.

Died on January 1, 1929. Married Harriet Ryan, born on May 11, 1868, and died on May 21, 1935. They were married on February 15, 1888. John Crittenden was a farmer and lived in Lexington, Kentucky, having formerly lived at Mount Sterling, Kentucky.

The children of John Crittenden Trimble and Harriet Ryan:

+ **D819—Stanley Trimble.** Born on June 20, 1890 and died on August 11, 1971. Married Mattie Crockett, born on October 17, 1890.

+ **D820—J. Smith Trimble.** Born on January 10, 1892. Married Myrtle Hamilton.

+ **D821—Ella Lee Trimble.** Born on February 1, 1894. Married J. Edward Toy.

+ **D822—May Edward Trimble.** Born on September 28, 1895. Married Raymond W. Johnson.

+ **D823—Margaret Trimble.** Born on June 13, 1897. Married George Draper Hill.

+ **D824—Georgia Trimble.** Born on December 11, 1899. Married William Houston Yeary.

  D825—Mary Lockridge Trimble. Born on January 30, 1902 and died on January 30, 1904 as a toddler.

+ **D826—Nelson H. Trimble.** Born on March 20, 1904. Married Minnie Belle Fortune.

+ **D827—Catherine Ryan Trimble.** Born on April 19, 1906. Married Rollie B. Carroll.

+ **D828—Florence Rae Trimble.** Born on January 17, 1909. Married Burgin Howard Masters.

+ **D829—Paul Crittenden Trimble.** Born on November 20, 1911. Married Elizabeth Laudeman.

D424—Joe Trimble. Son of Richard Menifee Trimble and Armilda Hines Glover. (Fifth generation of David Trimble and —— Houston.) Married Rose Wills.

  The child of Joe Trimble and Rose Wills:

+ **D830—Lee Trimble.** All of these are deceased.

D445—Angeline Trimble. Daughter of William Preston Trimble and Sarah Kash. (Fifth generation of David Trimble and —— Houston.) Born on March 3, 1844, died on February 20, 1918. Married Stephen Porter James on June 29, 1865. Her husband was killed by a piano which turned over on him in the wagon while he was taking it over bad roads from the station at Torrent, Kentucky, to the Hazel Green Academy.

  The children of Stephen Porter James and Angeline Trimble:

D831—Asberry Scott James.
D832—James Foy James.
D833—Mallie James.
D834—Virginia James.
D835—Shelly Preston James.
D836—Sheffie Porter James.
D837—Howard James.
D838—Eliza James.
D839—Etta James.

D446—Seaborn Trimble. Son of William Preston Trimble and Sarah Kash. (Fifth generation of David Trimble and —— Houston.) Born on November 24, 1848, died on January 21, 1916. Married Emma Wilson on February 8, 1871.

Trimble Families of America

The children of Seaborn Trimble and Emma Wilson:

D840—Sarilda Alice Trimble. Born on January 6, 1872. Married James P. Lacy and had one daughter: Clemma Belle Lacy.

+ **D841—Clarence Trimble.** Born on October 17, 1874. Married Emma Green on January 18, 1900. They had nine children.

D842—Jordon Green Trimble. Born on January 23, 1872 and died on December 20, 1930.

+ **D843—Rose Trimble.** Born on December 26, 1879. Married J. R. Brooks on September 6, 1918. They settled on Lacy Creek on one of the Trimble farms.

+ **D844—James Calvin Trimble.** Born on December 1, 1882 and died on December 25, 1931. Married Lela Day.

D447—Josephine Trimble. Daughter of William Preston Trimble and Sarah Kash. (Fifth generation of David Trimble and ——— Houston.) Born on May 1846. Married James Calvin Swango in 1870 in Morgan County, Kentucky. James was born on October 10, 1843 and die on March 14, 1893 in Wolf County, Kentucky. They lived at Hazel Green, Kentucky.

The children of James Swango and Josephine Trimble:

D845—Ida Carry Swango. Born about 1872 in Kentucky.

+ **D846—Ava Ellen Swango.** Born in October 1879 in Wolf County, Kentucky. Married a Mr. Fallon.

D847—Ora Dale Swango. Born in August 1884 in Wolf County, Kentucky.

D848—Herbert Trimble "Erb" Swango. Born in February 1888 in Wolf County, Kentucky.

D450—Frances Trimble. Daughter of William Preston Trimble and Sarah Kash. (Fifth generation of David Trimble and ——— Houston.) Married Taylor Whaley of Cynthiana, Kentucky, in 1884

The child of Taylor Whaley and Frances Trimble:

D849—Charles Whaley.

D451—Harlan Trimble. Son of William Preston Trimble and Sarah Kash. (Fifth generation of David Trimble and ——— Houston.) Born on January 28, 1860 and died in 1942. Married Nannie James on April 14, 1888. They lived in Wolfe County, Kentucky, on a Trimble farm. He became known in his later years as "Uncle Harlan" and was well known in the Kentucky area for his mountain stories. He was quite a fiddle player and loved to play setback, a card game, and was a fox hunter. He was a horseback mail carrier.

Trimble Families of America

The child of Harlan Trimble and Nannie James:
D850—Roxie Edith Trimble. She died in childhood.

D464—Nancy Elizabeth Trimble. Daughter of David Shelton "Doc" Trimble and Thirza Matilda Catron. (Fifth generation of David Trimble and ——— Houston.) Born on March 27, 1874, and married Alfonso Frey on May 1, 1895, at Paris, Illinois.

The children of Alfonso Frey and Nancy Elizabeth Trimble:
+ **D851—Leo Frey.** Married Dorothy Williams and is a wholesale grocer in Paris, Illinois.

D852—Marie Frey. She had special training in music and served as a church organist for thirty years. The author and his wife were guests in the Frey home at Paris and were delighted as Miss Marie Frey sat at her grand piano and rendered exquisite music of the classics. Marie is much interested in flowers and the appearance of her lawn. She had just taken her renewal test for her driver's license as required by the state of Illinois for senior citizens. She was happy to have completed the test satisfactorily. A most gracious lady. She never married.

D853—Ruth Frey. A former teacher and historian. Ruth attended Transylvania College. A lady of rare talent. Much of our information in this book is through the excellent research of Ruth Frey. She is an accurate, detailed researcher and has spent many years compiling information of her ancestry. We are gratefully indebted to Miss Frey for her contributions toward this book. Ruth Frey and her sister Marie still live in the family home at 407 Marshall Street, Paris, Illinois 61944.

D854—Raymond Frey. Married Virginia McKnight and lives in Chicago, Illinois. He has two sons: James, who graduated from Harvard cum laude, and Michael, who also attended Harvard.

D470—Mary Clark Trimble. Daughter of James Greenville Trimble and Nancy Mize. (Fifth generation of David Trimble and ——— Houston.) Born on April 21, 1847 and died July 27, 1931. Married James Greenwade in Kentucky. In 1888 they moved to Hunnewell, Kansas.

The six children of James Greenwade and Mary Clark Trimble:
D855—Charlie Greenwade.
D856—Robert Greenwade.
D857—Clarence Greenwade.
D858—Nannie Belle Greenwade. Married a Mr. Hiatt.
D859—Ella Lee Greenwade. Married a Mr. Cady.

Trimble Families of America

D860—Cora Bruce Greenwade. Married a Mr. Geislin. They still own the wheat farm which J. G. Trimble gave to their mother Mary Clark Trimble Greenwade.

D472—Nelson Harvey Trimble. Son of James Greenville Trimble and Nancy Mize. (Fifth generation of David Trimble and —— Houston.) Born on November 19, 1852 and died in June 1937. Married two times: first, to Elizabeth Howe of Mount Sterling, Kentucky, and second, to Minnie Butler Threkeld of Shelbyville, Kentucky, on December 5, 1880. He owned real estate in Mount Sterling and was a wholesale grocer for many years. In his later years Nelson built the Trimble Theatre in Mount Sterling.

They had no children of their own but had two adopted daughters:

D861—Marguerite Trimble. Married Paul Hooven.

D862—Julia Morris Trimble. Married Alfred Gates of Indianapolis, Indiana. Julia and her husband now live in Saint Louis, Missouri.

D473—Robert Mize Trimble. Son of James Greenville Trimble and Nancy Mize. (Fifth generation of David Trimble and —— Houston.) Born on May 3, 1855. Married Isa White. Their home on West Main Street in Mount Sterling, Kentucky, was beautifully decorated and elegantly furnished. He was a very wealthy man, owning stock in several Kentucky firms. For several years he was director of the Louisville Gas and Electric Company.

The children of Robert Mize Trimble and Isa White:

D863—John White Trimble. Graduated from the University of Virginia. He operated a large farm in Montgomery County, Kentucky. He married Emma Reed and after his death she moved to Lexington, Kentucky.

D864—Mary Ray Trimble. She married an Englishman, Thurmond Lee, and they live in New York City where Mr. Lee is associated with the Dry Rock Bank.

D865—Robert Mize Trimble, Jr. He attended Center College in Kentucky and became a successful businessman in Florida. He was a philanthropist and listed many charitable organizations in his will.

D475—Bruce Walker Trimble. Son of James Greenville Trimble and Nancy Mize. (Fifth generation of David Trimble and —— Houston.) Born on August 31, 1860 and died in 1932. Married Cora Cassidy, the daughter of Judge Cassidy of Mount Sterling, Kentucky, in 1887. After graduating from college, Bruce became a minister of the Christian church. After serving a pastorate in California, Bruce returned to Mount Sterling and became the editor and co-owner of the Mount Sterling *Advocate* newspaper. Throughout the years of his life, he served as guest minister in many churches. They were liberal contributors to educational institutions so their money could be used for the education of deserving youths.

D476—Fannie Lee Trimble. Daughter of James Greenville Trimble and Nancy Mize. (Fifth generation of David Trimble and ——— Houston.) Born on March 10, 1863 and died on December 17, 1916. Married Thomas Jones of Clark County, Kentucky, on September 24, 1884. Her husband was the great-great-grandson of Thomas and Priscilla Jones who came to Boonesboro, Kentucky, with Daniel Boone. She died in Florida where Mr. Jones was owner of a wholesale coffee and spice business.

The children of Thomas Jones and Fannie Lee Trimble:
D866—Raymond Jones.
D867—Nelson Jones.
D868—Mary Jones.
D869—Bruce Jones.
D870—Kelly Jones.

D477—James Greenville Trimble, Jr. Son of James Greenville Trimble and Nancy Mize. (Fifth generation of David Trimble and ——— Houston.) Born on August 16, 1870 in Hazel Green, Kentucky. He was unmarried. He graduated from Transylvania College and the University of Virginia. In 1941 he sold his father's home at Mount Sterling. The author (John Farley Trimble) has talked to several people in Mount Sterling who remember J. Greenville, Jr. Several interesting stories have been told concerning him. One, for several years he had been engaged in courting a Mount Sterling woman, to whom he willed $100,000 at his death. On this, I (John Farley Trimble) do not have documented proof. The author (John Farley Trimble) has several copies of letters written by James Greenville, Jr., giving people lineage information on his family.

D479—South Trimble. Son of Stephen Trimble and Elizabeth South. (Fifth generation of David Trimble and ——— Houston.) Born on April 13, 1864, at Hazel Green, Kentucky, and died on November 23, 1946. He married Carrie Belle Allen, born on June 1, 1867, at Houston, Texas. When South was six, his widowed mother, Elizabeth, purchased a bluegrass farm, Bells Grove, near the Forks of Elkhorn, Kentucky. This was where he grew up and attended Franklin County Public Schools, also the Excelsior Institute in Frankfort, Kentucky, and a Louisville business college.

South was a Democratic member of the Kentucky Legislature and Speaker

Trimble Families of America

of the House in 1900. He helped steer Kentucky through the difficult period following the assassination of Governor Goebel. To celebrate his eightieth and eighty-second birthdays the House of Representatives gave him oral tributes. We quote Mr. Ludlow of Indiana who on April 13, 1944, said, "South Trimble, the beloved clerk of the House is 80 years old today. His friends are legion. He has been in many a sharp political fight, but has always managed to emerge without scars of heart burnings, either his own or the other fellow, for he is a kind, understanding soul, who binds men to him with hoops of steel..."

During the tributes on his eightieth birthday Mr. McCormick of Massachusetts said that credit should also be given his mother who contributed so much to the molding of his character. Also, his wife who for fifty-nine years had been a great credit to South's progress.

South Trimble was a typical Kentucky gentleman. He loved tradition and history, the manners, customs, and institutions of his native state.

Each Saint Patrick's Day, South would wear a green necktie in tribute to his Irish ancestors.

The children of South Trimble and Carrie Belle Allen:

D871—James Frank Trimble. Died in 1945 at the age of forty-nine. He married Mildred Hamie and lived in Kansas City, Missouri, where he was associated with Morris and Company and Armour and Company.

+ **D872—Maria Trimble.** Married Carlos Fish. She was a widow early and served as postmaster in Frankfort, Kentucky, for eighteen years.

D873—Stephen Asbury Trimble. Died at the age of six.

+ **D874—Margaret Allen Trimble.** Married David Lynn, an architect at the Capitol in Washington, D.C. Their children: David, South Trimble, Margaret, and Acheson.

+ **D875—South Trimble, Jr.** Married Elaine Lazaro, a daughter of a Louisiana congressman. South is an attorney-at-law in Washington, D.C.

+ **D876—Frances Marie Trimble.** Married A. C. Wallace, a banker. They live in Chevy Chase, Maryland.

D480—Lou Ellen Cockrell. Daughter of Reverend McKinley Cockrell and Emily Jane Trimble. (Fifth generation of David Trimble and ——— Houston.) Born on June 15, 1848 and died on May 26, 1926. Married William O. Mize.

The child of William O. Mize and Lou Ellen Cockrell:

+ **D877—Carl Mize.** Married Carrie Rose.

Trimble Families of America

D481—Mary Belle Cockrell. Daughter of Reverend McKinley Cockrell and Emily Jane Trimble. (Fifth generation of David Trimble and ——— Houston.) Born on February 17, 1850 and died on June 24, 1927. Married Drew S. Godsey who was born in 1848 and died in 1907. He was from Hazard, Kentucky.

The child of Drew S. Godsey and Mary Belle Cockrell:

D878—Henry Godsey. Born on September 11, 1868 and died on September 22, 1908. Henry married Bertie Snail of Danville, Kentucky. He was a lawyer and served as clerk of the house in Washington, D.C. In 1912 Mary Bell Godsey married William Mulhollon of Missouri, a barber.

D492—Frank M. Trimble. Son of James Harvey Trimble and Harriet Brush. (Fifth generation of David Trimble and ——— Houston.) Born on February 4, 1843, in Montgomery County, Kentucky. He died in Butler, Missouri. Married Sally Redmond. Frank was married other times. We do not know the other wives' names.

The children of Frank M. Trimble and Sally Redmond:

D879—Jesse Trimble. Married Minnie Frezel. They had two daughters: Prudence and Hortense. Jesse was a druggist and died at Long Beach, California.

D880—Molly Trimble. Married a Mr. Miller and had one son: Newell Miller.

D495—Cortez Trimble. Son of James Harvey Trimble and Harriet Brush. (Fifth generation of David Trimble and ——— Houston.) Born on August 28, 1848, and died on January 22, 1922, in Morgan County, Kentucky. He married Lizzie Cundiff.

The children of Cortez Trimble and Lizzie Cundiff:

D881—Mary Trimble.
D882—Joe Trimble.
D883—Perry Trimble.
D884—Andrew Trimble.

D496—Josiah Anderson Trimble. Son of James Harvey Trimble and Harriet Brush. (Fifth generation of David Trimble and ——— Houston.) Born on August 5, 1850, and died on December 21, 1923, at Camargo, Kentucky. On December 13, 1871, he married Betty Pendleton. She was born on April 12, 1851 and died June 23, 1929. They are buried at Machpelah Cemetery at Mount Sterling, Kentucky. Josiah was a farmer and merchant.

The children of Josiah Anderson Trimble and Betty Pendleton:

Trimble Families of America

+ **D885—Thomas Franklin Trimble.** Born on February 4, 1873 and died on November 20, 1934. On October 16, 1896, he married Nancy Dolly Sewell.

+ **D886—Mary Beulah Trimble.** Born on January 3, 1875 and died on November 22, 1880, at the age of five years.

D887—Sallie Newell Trimble. Born on October 25, 1877 and died in October 1951 at Lexington, Kentucky. She married three times. Married first to Allie Faulk on December 22, 1921. Married second to Andrew Couch. Married third to Samuel Deal.

+ **D888—Lillian Trimble.** Born in 1879, married Dr. D. H. Bush.

+ **D889—Jesse Pendleton Trimble.** Born in 1887 and died in 1964.

D498—James Harvey Trimble, Jr. Son of James Harvey Trimble and Harriet Brush. (Fifth generation of David Trimble and —— Houston.) Born on March 19, 1855, and died after 1937 at Nashua, Iowa. He married Eunice Macy of Iowa. He lived at Clear Lake, Iowa, where he farmed.

The children of James Harvey Trimble and Eunice Macy:

D890—Molly Trimble. Married Charles Woolford.

D891—Harvey Everett Trimble. A minister of the Disciples of Christ church.

D892—Matthew Trimble.

D499—Perry Trimble. Son of James Harvey Trimble and Harriet Brush. (Fifth generation of David Trimble and —— Houston.) Born on December 19, 1857, and died before 1937 at Winchester, Kentucky. Married Amanda Yocum. Perry was a farmer, and they are buried at Myers Graveyard, Montgomery County, Kentucky.

The children of Perry Trimble and Amanda Yocum:

D893—Harriet Trimble. She married a Mr. Dixon and lived in Chicago, Illinois.

D894—Prudence Trimble. Married Clem —— and lived at Winchester, Kentucky.

D895—Prewitt Trimble. He was lost on a hunting trip in the West.

D501—Algin Trimble. Son of James Harvey Trimble and Harriet Brush. (Fifth generation of David Trimble and —— Houston.) Born on February 23, 1861, at Mount Sterling, Kentucky. He is buried in Antioch Cemetery, Montgomery County, Kentucky. Algin died on July 29, 1935. He married Emma Johnson of Johnson Station, Kentucky. Algin Trimble was a merchant.

The children of Algin Trimble and Emma Johnson:

+ **D896—Mary Beulah Trimble.** Born on March 29, 1888 in Mount Sterling, Kentucky and died on February 6, 1968. Married Virgil Donahue

+ **D897—Harriett Newell Trimble.** Born on May 8, 1900 at Johnson Station, Kentucky married Sydney A. Ensor.

+ **D898—Josephine T. Trimble.** Born in 1903, married E. C. Collins.

Other children of Algin Trimble:

D899—John Clay Trimble.

D900—Johnson Trimble.

D901—Ethel Trimble. Married a Beckham.

D502—Harriet Newell Trimble. Daughter of James Harvey Trimble and Harriet Brush. (Fifth generation of David Trimble and —— Houston.) Born on August 11, 1865. Married Elijah Clay Williams of Camargo. She is buried at the Williams Branch Cemetery, Johnson County, Kentucky. They lived at the Williams Branch farm.

The children of Elijah Clay Williams and Harriet Newell Trimble:

+ **D902—Bessie Williams.** Born on August 22, 1888. Married Manuel Salyer.

+ **D903—Dora Clay Williams.** Born in 1889 and died in 1960.

+ **D904—Blanche Newell Williams.** Born in 1891, married Floyd Ballard Halsey.

D503—John Harrison Trimble. Son of David Franklin "Doc" Trimble and Narcissus Jane Fox. (Fifth generation of David Trimble and —— Houston.) Born on October 18, 1849, and died on May 6, 1932, at Crawfordsville, Indiana. He married Charity Caster on March 1, 1876, and lived at Darlington, Indiana. He was a prosperous farmer. (The author was at his home in 1931.)

The children of John Harrison Trimble and Charity Caster:

D905—George E. Trimble. Born on March 1, 1877 and died on January 5, 1887 at almost ten years old.

+ **D906—Mary Elizabeth Trimble.** Born on July 22, 1879, married Zenophon Hopkins.

+ **D907—Roy Caster Trimble.** Born in 1882 and married Mary Potts.

+ **D908—John Sherman Trimble.** Born in 1884, married Mary Mulligan.

D504—Emily Trimble. Daughter of David Franklin "Doc" Trimble and Narcissus Jane Fox. (Fifth generation of David Trimble and —— Houston.) Born on July 29, 1849 and died on June 4, 1926. She married William E.

Trimble Families of America

Knox on May 30, 1867. He was a Union soldier. They moved to Nebraska, where they homesteaded 150 acres, which she still owned at her death in 1926. They lived in Riverdale, Nebraska.

The children of William E. Knox and Emily Trimble:

D909—Oscar Knox. He was state senator in Nebraska and had six children.

D910—Frank Knox.

D911—Homer Knox. Married and had six children.

D912—George Knox. Married and had two children.

D913—Abby Mae Knox. Born in 1878, died at the age of thirteen.

We are gratefully indebted to Betty Pope of Elwood, Nebraska, for the information concerning her grandmother Emily Knox. Betty and her brother were the last to be born on the old home place. Oscar and Ella Knox are buried at Kearney Cemetery, Nebraska. George Knox is buried at Banners Ferry, Idaho. W. E. Knox, Emily, Abby Mae, and Franklin Knox are all buried on the same lot in the Riverdale Cemetery. Homer and Lottie Knox are buried in the Riverdale Cemetery.

D509—Leander Trimble. Son of David Franklin "Doc" Trimble and Narcissus Jane Fox. (Fifth generation of David Trimble and ——— Houston.) Known as "Lee," he was about ten years of age when he left Kentucky with his mother and settled in Nicholas County, West Virginia. Lee was born at Mount Sterling, Kentucky, on June 24, 1857. He married Margaret Whitman on October 5, 1879. She was fourteen years of age. Margaret was born in 1865 and died in 1940. Lee died on August 14, 1941, in Nicholas County on the Trimble farm at Nettie, West Virginia. He was a prosperous farmer.

The children of Leander Trimble and Margaret Whitman:

+**D914—William Trimble.** Born on June 13, 1880, died on August 9, 1955. Married twice.

D915—Elizabeth Trimble. Known as "Aunt Lizzie." She never married.

+**D916—Worth Trimble.** Born in 1885. Worth married two times.

+**D917—Lola Ann Trimble.** Born in 1889. Married Rush Groves.

+**D918—Okey Ulysses "Les" Trimble.** Born in 1891.

+**D919—Bessie Lee Trimble.** Born in 1894. Married Volley Andrew Bailes.

+**D920—Edward A. Trimble.** Born on March 27, 1897. Married Pearl Groves. Edward worked for a while in the author's half-brother's barbershop at Richwood, West Virginia. He worked for Ray Trimble. Edward was a large man in stature and very handsome.

+**D921—Allen S. Trimble.** Born on August 27, 1900. Married Grace

Griffey.

D510–Joseph Franklin (Frank) Trimble. Son of David Franklin "Doc" Trimble and Narcissus Jane Fox. (Fifth generation of David Trimble and —— Houston.) Born on September 13, 1865, at Mount Sterling, Kentucky, and died on July 4, 1950, at Richwood, West Virginia. Frank married two times. Married first to Barbara Lucy Wright on March 20, 1888, by the Reverend P. H. Thomlinson at Nettie, West Virginia. Married second to Arabella Collins on January 18, 1912, at the home of her father, J. W. Collins of Beaver, West Virginia, Nicholas County. They were married by the Reverend Shelly McMillion, a lifetime friend of Frank Trimble.

Frank was a farmer and merchant most of his life. It was him and his personality traits that caused his son, the author, to become interested in the research of the Trimble family history. Frank was two years old when his mother Narcissus and T. S. H. Jones began the migration from Kentucky to Nicholas County. The two most predominant traits I noticed in my father were: his courage and his integrity, more so than I had seen in any other man. His word was his bond. He was extremely hard working, industrious man even though an education at that time in the backwoods of West Virginia was limited above reading, writing, and arithmetic. There was no high school within fifty miles of his home.

For some reason Narcissus chose not to inform her sons Leander and Frank of their name Trimble. They thought they were Joneses until they went to pick up some mail at the post office and opened a letter to their mother from Kentucky calling them Trimble.

The relationship of Frank Trimble to his fellowman was another trait that made him outstanding. To Frank there was no one inferior or superior to him. He never felt superior to his fellowman, yet at the same time he would never feel inferior. Everyone was treated alike whether he be rich or poor. Frank sought to be and was fair with everyone.

In the mercantile business he lost thousands of dollars in bad debts. He never sued a man in his life because to him the Bible taught against it.

One of the author's greatest regrets is that his father never lived to learn of the distinguished line of ancestors from which he descended, the majority of whom possess some of the same family traits as his own. In other words, whatever principles with which God endowed them are not for sale.

My father's peculiarities made him an interesting man. Frank never sought the services of a doctor until just before his death. He did his own doctoring. As he was bitten several times while berry picking by rattler and copperhead

D - David Trimble

snakes (so prevalent in the mountainous regions), he always carried a pocketknife and a bottle of turpentine for such times. He would cut the bite area and pour the turpentine into the cut and resume berry picking. When a tooth needed to be extracted, Frank used a pair of wire pliers to do the job. If a tooth rubbed the gum, he would take a file and level it down.

He had several horses on the farm. He was an able blacksmith and made and shod his own horses.

Bees were a hobby with Frank. He never wore protection from them. His theory was they knew if you were afraid and would only sting those who were.

Frank had a natural understanding of animals and their ways. He was often called upon by neighboring farmers when an animal became ill.

When electricity first came to the mountainous region where Frank lived, the current was not always available. It is said that he would moisten his finger and put it in the socket to see if the current was on.

He was against believe in card playing as he felt it to be evil. Yet he was a domino player. He read the Bible regularly. His rules were unorthodox. He always appeared clean shaven. His attire was always dress pants, dress shirt and tie, suspenders, belt, and hat. His shoes were never the work type. He was a man of medium stature.

You could hear him softly humming or whistling to himself. Frank was quiet and everyone was his friend. He was a true pioneer making his living from the soil.

The children of Frank Trimble and Barbara Lucy Wright:

D922—Felix Trimble. Born around 1890, he died in 1906 of diphtheria. He is buried in the Trimble Cemetery at Nettie, West Virginia.

+ **D923—Ray Trimble.** Born on December 23, 1893, died in 1960. Married twice.

D924—Arthur Trimble. Born around 1896, died in childhood of a heart condition.

+ **D925—Marion Everette Trimble.** Born in 1900, died in March 1967.

The children of Frank Trimble and Arabella Collins:

+ **D926—John Farley Trimble.** Born on April 17, 1913 in Beaver, Nicholas County, West Virginia and died on October 15, 1982 in Summersville, Nicholas County, West Virginia. Married two times:

+ **D927—James Walter Trimble.** Born in 1928. Married Winojean Erwin. Arabella Collins Trimble. Second wife of Frank Trimble was born on September 11, 1893, at Birch River, West Virginia. She is the daughter of the late John Wiley Collins and Dicia Mullens Collins. Her father

Trimble Families of America

was born in Kentucky and was a Union soldier in the Civil War. He migrated to Nicholas County, West Virginia, after the war. Arabella was his youngest child. She was eighteen years old when she and my father were married. She married in her later life Alexander Garten, who died in 1970.

Arabella stills lives in her home at Muddlety, West Virginia, near Summersville, and at the age of eighty is alert and quite active in her church the Muddlety Baptist. Here she is every time a service is held. She also goes to revivals and gospel songfests at neighboring towns. It is said you will find Mrs. Garten at any revival within thirty or forty miles of her home. In her rural community she is a religious inspiration calling new Christians her "spiritual children." She has an uncanny memory of old folk ballads. She still sings with a clear voice and does so almost constantly. Arabella is a woman of careful dress. She has beautiful long silver-gray hair which crowns her stature.

It would be rare to go to Mrs. Garten's and not find guests. The neighbors and church folk come regularly, and one might say, often. She says no one comes to her house but Christians because anyone else would not be interested in the Bible talks and praises of God. For a lady of her advanced years, she has been blessed with a multitude of friends. Mrs. Garten is an excellent mountain cook, and all enjoy her pan-fried corn bread and pickled beans.

As there was quite an age difference between Arabella and Frank Trimble, she always called him "Mr. Trimble" and had a high respect and deep love for him.

D516—Sarah Jane Trimble. Daughter of Cyrenius Wait Trimble and Melissa Davis. (Fifth generation of David Trimble and —— Houston.) Born in March 1870 in Kentucky and died on October 23, 1947 in Jackson, Minnesota. Married John L. Carney on November 3, 1892 in Pulaski County, Kentucky. John was born on April 8, 1870 in Ulster County, New York and died in 1895 in Pulaski County, Kentucky.

The children of John L. Carney and Sarah Jane Trimble:
  D928—Arval Carney. Born on July 1, 1893 in Kentucky and died on September 18, 1959 in Cottonwood County, Minnesota. Married Mable E. Morton.
+ **D929—John Andrew Carney.** Born on March 7, 1895 in Pulaski County, Kentucky and died on March 16, 1964 in Cottonwood County, Minnesota. Married Lena Jessie Pratt.

D - David Trimble

D529—Walter Ulysses Trimble. Son of Walter Ulyssess Trimble and Elizabeth Fidelia Bacon. (Fifth generation of David Trimble and —— Houston.) Born on August 8, 1867 in Iowa and died on February 12, 1912, at Durant, Oklahoma. Married Lina (Mary Adeline) Cobb on January 19, 1898, in West Plains, Missouri. They moved to Bonham, Texas, in 1899. He was a band conductor and a photographer.

The child of Walter Ulysses Trimble and Mary Cobb:

+ **D930—Emma Mae Trimble.** Born on July 31, 1900, in Bonham, Texas. Married Henry Bryan Metcalf of Durant, Oklahoma on July 10, 1920. Bryan Metcalf died on January 3, 1965, at Durant.

D533—Elizabeth Lee Floyd. Daughter of Benjamin Julian Floyd and Elizabeth F. Caughron. (Fifth generation of David Trimble and —— Houston.) Born on October 7, 1843 in Mill Springs, Pulaski County, Kentucky and died on April 5, 1909 in Centralia, Lewis County, Washington. Married Edward Robert Taylor on May 20, 1866 in Somerset, Pulaski County, Kentucky.

Edward was born on October 18, 1847 in Natural Springs, Carrol County, Virginia and died on December 22, 1918 in Centralia, Lewis County, Washington. He was the son of Hiram Ashley Taylor and Martha Jane Hilton. Hiram was born on July 7, 1818 in Natural Bridge, Rockbridge County, Virginia and died on June 7, 1911 in Mill Springs, Pulaski County, Kentucky. Martha was born on May 12, 1825 in Wheeling, Marshall County, West Virginia and died on April 6, 1908 in Mill Springs, Pulaski County, Kentucky.

The children of Edward Robert Taylor and Elizabeth Lee Floyd:

+ **D931—Mary Jane Taylor.** Born on April 13, 1867 in Pulaski County, Kentucky and died on January 6, 1906 in Sumner, Garfield County, Oklahoma. Married twice.

+ **D932—James William Taylor.** Born on December 10, 1868 in Overton, Tennessee and died on November 6, 1948 in Dayton, Oregon. Married Laverna Carolina Dee Kerr on April 8, 1895 in Whitewright, Texas.

+ **D933—John Franklin Taylor.** Born on February 26, 1871 in Pulaski County, Kentucky and died on April 10, 1937 in Centralia, Lewis County, Washington.[53] Married Emma Etta Allen on November 22, 1900 in Perry, Oklahoma.

---

[53] Washington, Death Certificates, 1907-1960. Salt Lake City, Utah: FamilySearch, 2013.

D934—Rainey LaFayette Taylor. Born on September 9, 1872 in Pulaski County, Kentucky and died on March 20, 1944 in Centralia, Lewis County, Washington.

D935—Martha Elizabeth Taylor. Born on December 30, 1873 in Pulaski County, Kentucky and died on August 10, 1954 in Payton, Saskatchewan.

D936—Moses Edward Taylor. Born on July 10, 1875 in Pulaski County, Kentucky and died on March 31, 1956 in Vancouver, Clark County, Washington.

D937—Joseph Green Taylor. Born on March 28, 1877 in Pulaski County, Kentucky and died 1877.

D938—Walter Newton Taylor. Born on September 3, 1879 and died in 1970 in Ohio.

D547—Sarah Samantha Robeson. Daughter of Robert Giffen Robeson and Mary Ann Trimble. (Sixth generation of David Trimble and —— Houston.) Born on April 1850 in Ohio and died on March 7, 1931 in Marshalltown, Marshall County, Iowa. Married Evan D. Bryant on February 23, 1869 in Indianola, Warren, Iowa.

Evan was born on October 28, 1833 in Franklin, Hendricks County, Indiana and died on September 22, 1905 in Warren County, Iowa.

The children of Evan D. Bryant and Sarah Samantha Robeson:

D939—Nancy Ella Bryant. Born on January 1870 in Iowa. Married Thomas Graham Davis.

D940—Charles E. Bryant. Born in 1872 in Iowa.

D941—Silas Robert Bryant. Born on November 1, 1873 in Warren, Iowa and died in 1930 in North Dakota. Married Susie Grizzella Braucht

D942—Mary Belle Bryant. Born on December 21, 1876 in White Oak Township, Warren County, Iowa and died before 1907. Married William Egbert Labertew.

D943—Evan Davis Bryant. Born in October 1880 in White, Oceania County, Iowa and died in 1958. Married Minnie O'Fear.

D944—Nellie M. Bryant. Born in October 1880 in Iowa.

D548—Camilla Stuart Robeson. Daughter of Robert Giffen Robeson and Mary Ann Trimble. (Sixth generation of David Trimble and —— Houston.) Born on September 18, 1851 in Akron, Summit County, Ohio and died on February 25, 1935 in Carthage, Hancock County, Illinois. Married James A. Ogilvie on December 14, 1871 in Indianola, Warren County, Iowa.

James was born on December 1844 in Ohio and died on January 9, 1915

Trimble Families of America

in Carthage, Hancock County, Illinois.

The children of James A. Ogilvie and Camilla Stuart Robeson:

D945—Nellie May Ogilvie. Born and died in 1873.

+ **D946—Edward James Ogilvie.** Born on April 29, 1875 in Carthage, Hancock County, Illinois and died on January 25, 1940 in Carthage, Hancock County, Illinois. Married Mary Grace Wright.

D947—Minnie Dell Ogilvie. Born on November 1877 in Carthage, Hancock County, Illinois and died in 1964 in Carthage, Hancock County, Illinois. Married Jesse Warren Willey.

D948—Chester Roy Ogilvie. Born on January 3, 1879 in Carthage, Hancock County, Illinois and died on August 4, 1965 in Cass County, Illinois. Married Lucy Viola Mills.

D949—Frank Robinson Ogilvie. Born on December 18, 1882 in Carthage, Hancock County, Illinois and died on April 18, 1922 in Carthage, Hancock County, Illinois. Married Jennie ——.

D950—Earl D. Ogilvie. Born on May 14, 1885 in Carthage, Hancock County, Illinois and died on June 18, 1937 in Long Beach, Los Angeles County, California. Married Kathryn ——.

D951—Beulah Forest Ogilvie. Born on January 24, 1890 in Carthage, Hancock County, Illinois and died on August 19, 1988 in Carthage, Hancock County, Illinois. Married Charles Gaylord Boston.

D556—Clifford C. Trimble. Son of John Trimble and Catherine Lybarger (Sixth generation of David Trimble and —— Houston.) Born on October 1857 in Ohio and died in 1929. Married Alice E. Dalton. She was born in June 1860 in Illinois and died in 1937.

The children of Clifford C. Trimble and Alice E. Dalton:

D952—James Trimble. Born on July 1884 in Iowa, he lived in Omaha, Douglas County, Nebraska in 1920 so he died after 1920. Married Della J. ——.

+ **D953—Worley Clifford Trimble.** Born on July 1885 in Iowa and died in 1949. Married Iva Pearl Sly

D954—Fred H. Trimble. Born on March 15, 1892 in Iowa and died on September 18, 1989 in La Junta, Otero, Colorado. Married Pearl C. Trimble.

D559—Ross Malen Trimble. Son of Enoch Trimble and Esther Virginia Hettie Condit. (Sixth generation of David Trimble and —— Houston.) Born on

August 7, 1866 in Liberty Warren County, Iowa and died on August 22, 1948 in Westhope, Bottineau, North Dakota. Married Inez M. in 1888.[54]

The children of Ross Malen Trimble and Inez M.:

D955—Elmer Allen Trimble. Born on February 2, 1890 in Liberty Center, Warren County, Iowa.

D956—Delbert Trimble. Born on April 4, 1892 in Liberty Center, Warren County, Iowa.

D957—Ruby Ruth Trimble. Born on February 18, 1894 in Iowa.

D958—Vier Trimble. Born on October 1896 in Iowa.

D959—Marie Trimble. Born about 1902 in Iowa.

D960—Hattie Trimble. Born on May 2, 1905 in Westhope, Bott County, North Dakota.

D961—Hettie Trimble. Born about 1906 in North Dakota.

D560—Grant Samuel Trimble. Son of Enoch Trimble and Esther Virginia Hettie Condit. (Sixth generation of David Trimble and —— Houston.) Born on May 1867 in Liberty, Warren County, Iowa and died on May 11, 1925 in Toppenish, Yakima County, Washington. Married Laura Victoria Sturman on March 20, 1887. She was born in 1868 in Iowa.

The children of Grant Samuel Trimble and Laura Victoria Sturman:

D962—Donald Enoch Trimble. Born on January 8, 1891 in Liberty Center, Warren County, Iowa and died on September 13, 1973 in Toppenish, Yakima County, Washington.

D963—Leota M. Trimble. Born on August 6, 1893 in Iowa and died on December 5, 1977 in Toppenish, Yakima, Washington.

D964—Clarence G. Trimble. Born on October 6, 1895 in New Virginia, Warren County, Iowa and died on June 9, 1946 in Walla Walla, Walla Walla County, Washington.

D965—Fay Helen Trimble. Born in 1899 in Iowa.

D966—Felix T. Trimble. Born in 1901 in North Dakota.

D967—Arthur J. Trimble. Born in 1904 in North Dakota.

D968—Carol U. Trimble. Born on June 3, 1909 in North Dakota and died on October 16, 1984 in Toppenish, Yakima County, Washington.

D570—Everard Earl Bonnett. Son of Henry W. Bonnett and Eliza Lanett

---

[54] US Census Year: 1910; Census Place: Richburg, Bottineau, North Dakota; Roll: T624_1139; Page: 8A; Enumeration District: 0013; FHL microfilm: 1375152

D - David Trimble

Trimble. (Sixth generation of David Trimble and —— Houston.) Born on September 10, 1882 in Union Township, Knox County, Ohio and died on July 7, 1956 in Akron, Summit County, Ohio. Married Agnes A. Beum on January 29, 1905. Agnes was born on February 22, 1882 in Danville, Knox County, Ohio and died on April 30, 1928 in Columbus, Franklin County, Ohio. [55] [56]

The children of Everard Earl Bonnett and Agnes A. Beum:

D969—Clarence B. Bonnett. Born on December 18, 1905 in Ohio and died on February 29, 1984 in Ashley, Delaware County, Ohio.

D970—Charles Henry Bonnett. Born on December 18, 1905 in Ohio and died on December 15, 1976 in Whitehouse, Lucas County, Ohio.

+ **D971—Margaret Louise Bonnett.** Born on November 5, 1910 in Danville, Knox, Ohio and died on October 27, 2001 in Ashley, Delaware County, Ohio. Married George Cecil Ireland in 1928.

D972—Leroy Pete Bonnett. Born on September 11, 1912 in Ohio and died on December 4, 2001 in Roanoke, Virginia. Married Velma Pauline Garey.

D973—Frances Irene Bonnett. Born on November 12, 1919 in Ohio and died on February 5, 1999 in Lakewood, Jefferson County, Colorado. Married Ronald Wilber Fehr.

D578—Mary C. Calkins. Daughter of Henry Kent Calkins and Mary Elizabeth Gillespie. (Sixth generation of David Trimble and —— Houston.) Born on September 14, 1873 in Wythe, Hancock County, Illinois and died on January 25, 1959 in Clearfield, Taylor County, Iowa. Married Howard Leonard Knox. Howard was born on September 25, 1873 in Iowa and died on September 10, 1962 in Lenox, Taylor, Iowa.

The children of Howard Leonard Knox and Mary C. Calkins:

D974—Evelyn E. Knox. Born about 1904 in Taylor, Iowa and died after 1959.

D975—Winifred Knox. Born on September 25, 1909 in Grant, Taylor County, Iowa and died on November 1, 1993 in Clearfield, Taylor County, Iowa.

D585—William Ward Porter. Son of John Samuel Porter and Rebecca Porter. (Sixth generation of David Trimble and —— Houston.) Born on January 15,

---

[55] US Census Year: 1910; Census Place: Akron Ward 4, Summit, Ohio; Roll: T624_1233; Page: 9A; Enumeration District:0144; FHL microfilm: 1375246.

[56] US Census Year: 1920; Census Place: Berlin, Delaware, Ohio; Roll: T625_1377; Page: 3A; Enumeration District: 54; Image: 48.

1852 in Maryland and died on August 11, 1874 in Allegany County, Maryland. Married Mary R. Rase about 1885. Mary was born in October 1866 in Maryland and died about 1921 in Allegany County, Maryland.

The children of William Ward Porter and Mary Rase:

D976—Leota A. Porter. Born on January 1888 in Maryland. Married Albert L. Engle on January 5, 1920. Albert was born about 1883 in Maryland.

D977—Adella W. Porter. Born in May 1897 in Maryland.

D586—Josiah J. Porter. Son of John Samuel Porter and Rebecca Porter. (Sixth generation of David Trimble and —— Houston.) Born in October 1855 in Maryland and died on January 2, 1900 in Allegany County, Maryland. Married Elizabeth Rase before 1880. Elizabeth was born in April 1858 in Maryland and died about 1930 in Allegany County, Maryland.

The children of Josiah J. Porter and Elizabeth Rase:

D978—Cecelia E. Porter. Born on April 1880 in Maryland and died about 1960 in Allegany County, Maryland. Married Walter Engle on June 19, 1900. Walter was born about 1878 and died about 1940.

D979—Sophia P. Porter. Born on April 15, 1883 in Maryland and died on May 6, 1976 in, Allegany, Maryland. Married Herbert Griffith in June 1905. Herbert was born about 1881 in Maryland.

D980—Louis Gilbert Porter. Born on November 1, 1890 in Eckhart Mines, Allegany County, Maryland and died about 1935 in Allegany County, Maryland. Married Gladys R. Sleeman on February 2, 1920. Gladys was born on April 7, 1893 and died September 1982.

D587—Michael R. Porter. Son of John Samuel Porter and Rebecca Porter. (Sixth generation of David Trimble and —— Houston.) Born on March 19, 1856 in Eckhart, Allegany County, Maryland and died on November 4, 1928 in Eckhart, Allegany County, Maryland. Married Mary Elizabeth Engle in about 1881.

Mary was born about 1858 in Allegany County, Maryland and died about 1907 in Allegany County, Maryland.

The children of Michael R. Porter and Mary Elizabeth Engle:

+ D981—Laura Margaret Miranda Porter. Born on September 1881 in Eckhart, Allegany County, Maryland and died about 1965 in Eckhart, Allegany County, Maryland. Married George R. Ryan on June 20, 1900.

D982—Genieva Elizabeth Porter. Born on August 12, 1891 in Eckhart, Allegany County, Maryland and died January 23, 1930 in Eckhart, Allegany County, Maryland. Married twice William Steven Delaney.

Trimble Families of America

D588—John Wesley Porter. Son of John Samuel Porter and Rebecca Porter. (Sixth generation of David Trimble and —— Houston.) Born on October 1863 in Maryland and died about 1947. Married Rosa Anna Trescher in about 1896. Rosa was born on February 1871 in Maryland and died about 1932.

The children of John Wesley Porter and Rosa Anna Trescher:

D983—Bertie Elizabeth Porter. Born on November 2, 1896 in Maryland and died in December 1974. Married Trubadour Lewis in March 1920. Trubadour was born on September 14, 1896 in Maryland and died in February 1968.

D984—John Marshall Porter. Born on September 13, 1898 in Maryland and died on April 22, 1988. Married M. Elizabeth Jeffries in March 1920. She was born in April 1920.

D985—Lillian Pearl Porter. Born on April 1903 in Maryland.

D594—Wilbur Layton Combs. Son of Francis Asbury Combs and Hannah J. Thomas. (Sixth generation of David Trimble and —— Houston.) Born on October 20, 1857 in Morgantown, Monongalia, West Virginia and died on October 11, 1924. Married Virginia C. "Jennie" Smell. She was born on June 6, 1855 in Deacin Creek, Monongalia, West Virginia and died on December 22, 1941 in Monongalia County, West Virginia.

The children of Wilbur Combs and Jennie Smell:

D986—Edith Ellwood Combs. Born on June 4, 1890 in Monongalia, West Virginia.

D987—Wayne Francis Combs. Born on October 20, 1892 in Morgantown, Monongalia County, West Virginia and died on April 9, 1949 in Morgantown, Monongalia County, West Virginia.

D595—Charles William Combs. Son of Francis Asbury Combs and Hannah J. Thomas. (Sixth generation of David Trimble and —— Houston.) Born on January 14, 1860 in Morgantown, Monongalia County, West Virginia and died on April 11, 1948 in Morgantown, Monongalia County, West Virginia. Married Emma Louise Parfitt on September 19, 1880. She was born on January 16, 1860 in West Virginia.

The children of Charles Combs and Emma Parfitt:

D988—John Ralph Combs. Born on August 11, 1881 in Morgantown, Monongalia County, West Virginia and died in January 1975 in Morgantown, Monongalia County, West Virginia.

D989—Clyde Francis Combs. Born on August 5, 1884 in West Virginia and died in February 1967 in Morgantown, Monongalia, West Virginia.

D670—Teresa A. Black. Son of James Thomas Black and Mary Catherine McMullin. (Sixth generation of David Trimble and —— Houston.) Born on December 7, 1878 in Mercer County, Kentucky and died on December 12, 1911 in Mercer County, Kentucky. Married Charles Powell in 1896. Charles was born on November 14, 1874 in Mercer County Kentucky and died on July 18, 1948 in Mercer County, Kentucky.

The children of Charles Powell and Teresa Black:

D990—Julius Kemper Powell. Born on March 17, 1899 in Kentucky and died on December 29, 1980 in Harrodsburg, Mercer County, Kentucky.

+ **D991—Eula Dee Powell.** Born on January 2, 1909 in Jenkinsville, Kentucky and died on July 1, 2002 in Greenwood, Clark County, Wisconsin. Married Earnest Harlow.

D691—Harry Arthur Laughlin. Son of Robert Luckie Laughlin and Flora Lee Walker. (Sixth generation of David Trimble and —— Houston.) Born on August 22, 1883 in Kansas and died on January 23, 1962 in Orange County, California. Married Marie E. born about 1887 in Kansas and died on January 18, 1958.

The children of Harry Arthur Laughlin and Marie E.:

D992—Leetta M. Laughlin. Born about 1909 in Kansas and died on November 13, 2000 in Portland, Clackamas County, Oregon.

D993—Margaret Louise Laughlin. Born on December 21, 1910 in Lenexa, Johnson County, Kansas, and died on November 30, 1983 in Los Angeles County, California.

D994—Helen Roberta Laughlin. Born on July 25, 1912 in Olathe, Johnson County, Kansas and died in 1985 in Topeka, Shawnee County, Kansas.

D995—Roberta Laughlin. Born about 1913.

D996—Betty Marie Laughlin. Born on September 28, 1922 in Olathe, Johnson County, Kansas and died on July 2, 1982 in Buena Park, Orange County, California.

D692—Letha Lee Laughlin. Daughter of Robert Luckie Laughlin and Flora Lee Walker. (Sixth generation of David Trimble and —— Houston.) Born on August 17, 1890 in Johnson County, Kansas and died on February 20, 1974 in Mcpherson, Mcpherson County, Kansas. Married Henry Shaw Cooper on January 19, 1910 in Lenexa, Johnson County, Kansas. Henry was born in January 1888 in Green County Missouri and died on April 1, 1970 in Forsyth, Taney County, Missouri.

Trimble Families of America

The children of Henry Shaw Cooper and Letha Lee Laughlin:

+ **D997—Thelma Pauline Cooper.** Born on November 16, 1912 in Kansas and died on September 19, 1981 in Dexter, Penobscot County, Maine. She married twice.

D695—James Trimble. Son of Marion Grant Trimble. (Sixth generation of David Trimble and —— Houston.) Born on March 15, 1902. Lives in Ashland, Boyd County, Kentucky, and retired from the Armco Steel Corporation where he was superintendent of power, electric, steam and water, and air. He is an electrical engineer, registered in Kentucky. He attended Berea College and Kentucky State, a member of the Methodist church, a worker in the Scouts, member of the Masons, 33-degree Scottish Rite Mason.

D700—Clark Trimble. Son of John G. Trimble and Matilda VanHoose. (Sixth generation of David Trimble and —— Houston.) Clark married two times: first, to Dell Rice, and second, to Allie Pelphrey.

The children of Clark Trimble and Dell Rice:

D998—Lula Trimble. Married Sherman LeMasters. They had one child who died when it was born and at which time Lula died also.

The children of Clark Trimble and Allie Pelphrey:

D999—Drucey Trimble. Deceased, no children.

D1000—John Trimble. Married and has no children, lives in Middletown, Ohio.

+ **D1001—Sula Trimble.** Married to William Ivey. Their address: 3304 Arch Wood, Cleveland, Ohio.

D1002—Shelton Trimble. Married and has no children.

D1003—Clarence Trimble. Never married and is deceased.

D1004—Pearl Trimble. Married a Mr. Waldo of Cleveland, Ohio. She had a son, Jack. He was adopted by her brother Clarence (D1003), who with the help of his mother Allie Trimble reared Jack.

D701—Carl Trimble. Son of John G. Trimble and Matilda VanHoose. (Sixth generation of David Trimble and —— Houston.) Born on March 11, 1870 and died on November 29, 1919. He married Laura Picklesimer, who was born on November 17, 1874, and died on July 27, 1961. This family lived at Mount Sterling, Kentucky, and had nine children. Mrs. Trimble later lived and died in Indianapolis, Indiana. She was buried there. Mr. Trimble is buried in the family cemetery on Pickle Fork at Barnett's Creek, Kentucky.

The children of Carl Trimble and Laura Picklesimer:

+ **D1005—Iva Trimble.** Born in 1892, married Ernest Hall.

+ **D1006—Ova Trimble**. Born in 1893, married Arthur Welch.

D1007—Mae Trimble. Born on April 12, 1898. Married John Hall, who was born on June 2, 1885, and died on March 13, 1952. They had no children. Her address is Route 3, Box 172, Fairland, Indiana.

D1008—John Trimble. Born on January 6, 1900. Married Minnie McCoy, who was born on October 12, 1909. They had no children. Their address: Route 2, Mount Sterling, Kentucky.

D1009—Carroll Trimble. Born on December 8, 1906. Married Bertha Centers. Their address: 6241 South Arlington Avenue, Indianapolis, Indiana.

D1010—Grace Trimble. Born on February 25, 1909 and died on December 7, 1969. Married Sheldon Pattison, born on November 4, 1907. He is a Methodist minister. Their address: 231 Redwood Lane, Decatur, Illinois.

+ **D1011—Rucker Jim Trimble**. Born in 1911 and married Iva Centers.

+ **D1012—Paris Nelson Trimble**. Born in 1913 and married Olive Davis Sparks.

+ **D1013—Sterling Sidney Trimble**. Born in 1916 and married Alice Parker.

D702—William "Willie" Trimble. Son of John G. Trimble and Matilda VanHoose. (Sixth generation of David Trimble and ——— Houston.) Born on August 27, 1865 in Johnson County, Kentucky and died on November 28, 1937 in Barnett's Creek, Johnson County, Kentucky. Married Sola Conley, who was born on December 1968 in Johnson County, Kentucky and died on May 23, 1961 in Barnett's Creek, Johnson County, Kentucky.

The children of William Trimble and Sola Conley:

D1014—Paris Trimble. Married Lucinda Fannin and had two sons: Bill and Chester, Married Ann Daniels.

+ **D1015—Myrtle Trimble**. Married two times: first, to Everett Reed, and second, to George Hall. The Halls live at 1011 Renick Court, Baltimore, Maryland.

+ **D1016—James Trimble**. He married two times: first, to a Caudill, and second, to Ruth Murphy.

+ **D1017—Gillie Trimble**. Married Sam Kennard.

+ **D1018—Goldie Trimble**. Married Henry Brown.

+ **D1019—Theodore (Ted) Trimble**. Born on October 14, 1904 in Johnson County, Kentucky and died on December 28, 1935 in Johnson County, Kentucky. He married Lula Picklesimer.

+ **D1020—John Trimble**. Born on September 7, 1906 and married Maymie Home.

+ **D1021—Florence Allen Trimble**. Married Martin Blair.

Trimble Families of America

D - David Trimble

D703—Paris Grant Trimble. Son of John G. Trimble and Matilda VanHoose. (Sixth generation of David Trimble and —— Houston.) Born on November 2, 1872 and died on March 27, 1944. Married Dora Picklesimer, born on September 10, 1897, and died sometime between 1904 and 1909. The following is part of an article which appeared in the *Baptist Tidings*, after Paris's death. "From the very earliest dawn, the sires of this good man have been God fearing people and through their humbleness and earnestness of spirit have been known the county wide by all the people. He like his sires from early youth feared and loved God and in his 17th year gave his heart to God and was baptized into the Baptist faith taking his membership with the Old Barnett's Creek Church.

"Within this and adjoining counties, Paris has been known and recognized by all to be one among the most outstanding citizens. He was particularly known for his earnestness of truth and honesty toward his fellow man. Paris was blessed with wonderful health, all his life until just a few years before his death, when he discovered that he was suffering from Bright's disease."

Paris Grant Trimble married two times: first, to Dora Picklesimer, and second, to Nancy B. Gullett Craft in September 1909. Nancy died on November 5, 1947.

The children of Paris Grant Trimble and Dora Picklesimer:
+ **D1022—June Trimble.** Born on June 9, 1898, married Everett Gullett.
 D1023—Gladys Trimble. Died in infancy.
+ **D1024—Elva Trimble.** Died in 1959.
+ **D1025—Robert Eldon (Bob) Trimble.** Married Anna Picklesimer.

The child of Paris Trimble and Nancy Craft:
+ **D1026—Jewell Trimble.** Born in 1914 and married Ora Green.

D704—Henry Elmer Trimble. Son of John G. Trimble and Matilda VanHoose. (Sixth generation of David Trimble and —— Houston.) Born on February 26, 1878 and died on September 11, 1912. Married Martha Auxier on January 5, 1901. She was born on August 2, 1879 and died on July 30, 1957. They lived at Barnett's Creek, Kentucky, and at Volga, Kentucky, while Mr. Trimble lived. After his death, Martha Trimble lived in Paintsville, Kentucky, and married W. H. Vaughan. He died in the 1920s. Martha was a teacher in the Johnson County Schools. Later the children knew her as Mrs. Vaughan when she retired from teaching. She later worked as secretary for her son in the county judge's office. They are buried in the family cemetery at Barnett's Creek, Kentucky.

The children of Henry Elmer Trimble and Martha Auxier:

+ **D1027—Rexford Raymond Trimble.** Born in 1902.

  D1028—Celesta Pearl Trimble. Born on August 10, 1903 and died on February 1, 1904 as an infant.

+ **D1029—Victoria Auxier Trimble.** Born in 1907. Married Delmas Preston.

  D1030—John Sanford Trimble. Born on August 5, 1910 and died on January 21, 1911.

D705—Shelby "Shell" Trimble. Son of John G. Trimble and Matilda VanHoose. (Sixth generation of David Trimble and ——— Houston.) Born on August 12, 1880 and died on February 10, 1951. Married Cora Webb on December 25, 1901. She was born on February 14, 1884 and died on September 19, 1969.

The children of Shelby Trimble and Cora Webb:

+ **D1031—Susie Trimble.** Born on October 18, 1902 and died on January 10, 1947. Married Dennie Blair.

+ **D1032—Fanny Trimble.** Born on August 10, 1904 in Kentucky and died on December 3, 1965 in Johnson County, Kentucky.

+ **D1033—John Powell Trimble.** Born on March 19, 1906 and died on September 15, 1968. Married Irene Sheppard. John was a dealer in livestock.

+ **D1034—Dixie Trimble.** Born on June 22, 1908. Married Bert Estep.

+ **D1035—Matilda Trimble.** (twin) Born on November 5, 1912 and died on July 17, 1959. Married Fred Preston.

  D1036—Marinda Trimble. (twin) Born on November 5, 1912. Married Millard Overly and had no children. They live at Dayton, Ohio.

+ **D1037—Laura Trimble.** Born on September 17, 1914, and died on October 2, 1995 in Magoffin County, Kentucky. Married Irvin Cantrell.

D706—Laura Trimble. Daughter of John G. Trimble and Matilda VanHoose. (Sixth generation of David Trimble and ——— Houston.) Born on March 28, 1876 and died on March 28, 1960. Married John Paris (Deal) Pelphrey, born on January 3, 1872, and died on January 28, 1919.

The child of John Paris Pelphrey and Laura Trimble:

+ **D1038—Frank Pelphrey.** Born in 1897.

D708—Charlie Trimble. Son of William Mark Trimble and Cynthia Essie "Cinda" Reed. (Sixth generation of David Trimble and ——— Houston.) Born in 1874. Married Amanda Williams.

D - David Trimble

The children of Charlie Trimble and Amanda Williams:

D1039—Solan Trimble. Married Mayme Burchett.

D1040—Bruce Trimble. Married Vesta Cantrell.

D1041—Wannie Trimble. Married Dixon. They had two children.

D1042—Connil Trimble.

D709—Lando Trimble. Son of William Mark Trimble and Cynthia Essie "Cinda" Reed. (Sixth generation of David Trimble and —— Houston.) Born in October 1877. Married Malissa Williams.

The son of Lando Trimble and Malissa Williams:

D1043—Ray Trimble.

D710—Julia Trimble. Daughter of William Mark Trimble and Cynthia Essie "Cinda" Reed. (Sixth generation of David Trimble and —— Houston.) Born in July 1861 and married Manassa Stapleton.

The five children of Manassa Stapleton and Julia Trimble:

+ **D1044—Gracie Stapleton.** Married Ossie Cantrell.

D1045—Versa Stapleton. Married McKenzie.

D1046—William Stapleton. Married Tera Davis. They had twins.

D1047—Betty Lou Stapleton.

D1048—Hagar Stapleton. Married a Miss Stapleton, the daughter of Link Stapleton.

D711—Sarah Trimble. Daughter of William Mark Trimble and Cynthia Essie "Cinda" Reed. (Sixth generation of David Trimble and —— Houston.) Born in May 1889. Married Dock Salyers

The children of Dock Salyers and Sarah Trimble:

D1049—Mayme Lou Salyers.

D1050—William Salyers.

D1051—Bruce Salyers.

D712—Albert Trimble. Son of William Mark Trimble and Cynthia Essie "Cinda" Reed. (Sixth generation of David Trimble and —— Houston.) Born on February 28, 1873, and married Naoma Tackett. She was born in 1878 and died 1965.

The children of Albert Trimble and Naoma Tackett:

+ **D1052—Grant Trimble.** Born on June 28, 1896. Married Zellia Sturgill.

+ **D1053—Frank Trimble.** Born on November 10, 1898. Married Hester Lemaster.

+ **D1054—Malta May Trimble.** Born on March 9, 1906. Married Henry

Ward.

D1055—**Alkie Lee Trimble.** Born on December 8, 1908. Married John Castle. John was born on November 1, 1905 in Flatgap, Johnson County, Kentucky and died on December 12, 1989 in Johnson County, Kentucky. They had eighteen children, but we do not have their names.

D1056—**John G. Trimble.** Born on March 8, 1914. Married Kitty Turner and had thirteen children but we do not have their names.

+ D1057—**Fred Trimble.** Born on May 9, 1918. Married Evalee King.

+ D1058—**James Albert Trimble.** Born on October 9, 1926. Married Pearl Picklesimer.

+ D1059—**Beulah G. Trimble.** Born on July 4, 1922. Married Euel Baldwin.

D1060—**Markie Trimble.** Born on January 7, 1916.

D1061—**Daniel Harry Trimble.** Born on November 25, 1924 and died in 1987. Married Gracie Burchett. She was born in 1934 and died 1998.

D714—**John Elliott Trimble.** Son of William Mark Trimble and Cynthia Essie "Cinda" Reed. (Sixth generation of David Trimble and —— Houston.) Born on June 16, 1888, at Barnett's Creek, Kentucky and died on April 7, 1954 and is buried in the Day Cemetery at Lenox, Kentucky. He married Selona Williams on February 2, 1901. She was born on July 3, 1885, in Red Bush, Johnson County, Kentucky and died in 1966. He was a farmer and owned a farm in Lenox, Kentucky.

The children of John Elliot Trimble and Selona Williams:

D1062—**Granville W. Trimble.** Born on October 22, 1901 in Lenox, Morgan County, Kentucky and died on April 4, 1993 in North Baltimore, Wood County, Ohio. Married Katie Conley and they had ten children.

D1063—**Mary Trimble.** Born in 1909. Married Ira Ison and they live at Cow Branch, Kentucky. They had five children.

D1064—**Albert Trimble.** Born on November 4, 1913. Married Moselle Caskey and they have five children. They live at Lenox, Kentucky, on the old home farm.

+ D1065—**Clara Trimble.** Born on November 11, 1906. Married Audie Atkins and had eleven children. Both Clara and Audie are deceased.

D1066—**Martha Trimble.** Born on March 4, 1911. Died at fifteen years of age of tuberculosis.

D1067—**Stella Trimble.** Born in 1918. Died of pneumonia at age one and a half years.

D1068—**Verna Trimble.** Born on June 4, 1916. Married Jim Henry Doolin and they have four children. They live at Dehart, Kentucky.

Trimble Families of America

D - David Trimble

+ **D1069—Ora Trimble.** Born on February 2, 1902 and died on November 16, 1964. Married Edna Lewis on October 20, 1920, at Lucille, Kentucky.

D1070—John Elliott Trimble, Jr. Born on April 17, 1922. Died of measles complications at an early age.

D721—Sherman Trimble Ramey. Son of Taylor Ramey and Susan Trimble. (Sixth generation of David Trimble and —— Houston.) Married Sherlie Williams.

The children of Sherman Trimble Ramey and Sherlie Williams:
D1071—James H. Ramey. Married Beecher Roberts Williams.
+ **D1072—Manie Ramey.** Married Vint Davis.
D1073—Birdie Ramey. Married Hervie Stombaugh.
+ **D1074—Doris Ramey.** Married Maxie Stapleton.
D1075—Joe Marion Ramey. Married a Robinson.
D1076—James Ramey. Married Mary Fyffe.
D1077—Keith Ramey. Married a Persinger.

D733—Alfred Lemaster. Son of Mr. LeMaster and Minerva Trimble. (Sixth generation of David Trimble and —— Houston.) Alfred LeMaster married two times. Married first to Jensie Caudill. Married second to Audrey Kelsey. There were no children in the second marriage.

The children of Alfred LeMaster and Jensie Caudill:
D1078—Avaneil Lemaster.
D1079—Alfretta Lemaster. Married a Mr. Witten.
D1080—Kitty Belle Lemaster. Married a Mr. Reed.
D1081—John William Lemaster.
D1082—Charles Weldon Lemaster.
D1083—Howard Wendell Lemaster.

D734—Clara Lemaster. Daughter of Mr. LeMaster and Minerva Trimble. (Sixth generation of David Trimble and —— Houston.) Married Paris Stapleton of Flat Gap, Kentucky.

The children of Paris Stapleton and Clara LeMaster:
D1084—Joe Stapleton. Married Pauline Salyer.
D1085—Fred Stapleton. Married June Pelphrey.
D1086—Flora Pauline Stapleton.

D735—Rosa Lemaster. Daughter of Mr. LeMaster and Minerva Trimble. (Sixth generation of David Trimble and —— Houston.) Married Daniel Boone

262

Trimble (D767). Rosa was born on June 21, 1897 and died in 1945.

The list of their children will appear under D767—Daniel Boone Trimble.

D736—Mattie Lemaster. Daughter of Mr. LeMaster and Minerva Trimble. (Sixth generation of David Trimble and ——— Houston.) Married John Davis.

The children of John Davis and Mattie LeMaster:

D1087—Helen Davis. Married a Picklesimer.

D1088—Herma Lee Davis. Married a Ward.

D1089—Ella Frances Davis.

D740—Ralph Picklesimer. Son of John Picklesimer and Lou Trimble. (Sixth generation of David Trimble and ——— Houston.) Married Virgie Blair.

The children of Ralph Picklesimer and Virgie Blair:

D1090—Mae Picklesimer. Married a Mr. Preston.

D1091—Wayne Picklesimer.

D1092—Robert Picklesimer. He is a minister.

D1093—Ralph Picklesimer, Jr.

D1094—Carrie Marie Picklesimer.

D1095—Eva Lee Picklesimer. Lives in California.

D1096—Jack Picklesimer.

D741—Elzie Picklesimer. Son of John Picklesimer and Lou Trimble. (Sixth generation of David Trimble and ——— Houston.) Married Letta Reed.

The children of Elzie Picklesimer and Letta Reed:

Twins that died.

D1097—Nadine Picklesimer. Married Wayne Blanton of Staffordsville, Kentucky, and they have a daughter Sandra Kay.

D1098—Elbert Franklin Picklesimer.

D1099—Oneida Picklesimer. Married a McKenzie.

D1100—Glenn Picklesimer.

D742—Smith Picklesimer. Son of John Picklesimer and Lou Trimble. (Sixth generation of David Trimble and ——— Houston.) Married Chole Reed.

The children of Smith Picklesimer and Chole Reed:

D1101—Emerold Picklesimer. Married Ray Salyer.

D1102—Martin Picklesimer. Married Mabel Tackett.

D1103—Victoria Picklesimer. Married Elmer Williams.

D1104—Leroy Picklesimer. Married Pauline Rudd.

D1105—Maxine Picklesimer. Married Earl Oliver.

Trimble Families of America

D - David Trimble

D744—James Picklesimer. Son of John Picklesimer and Lou Trimble. (Sixth generation of David Trimble and —— Houston.) Married Bertha Blair.

The children of James Picklesimer and Bertha Blair:
D1106—Pearl Picklesimer. Married James Albert Trimble.
D1107—Faye Picklesimer. Married a Ratliff.
D1108—Leo Picklesimer. Married a Davis.

D745—Frank Pierce Picklesimer. Son of John Picklesimer and Lou Trimble. (Sixth generation of David Trimble and —— Houston.) Born on November 13, 1898 in Johnson County, Kentucky and died on October 10, 1979 Staffordsville, Johnson County, Kentucky. Married Ora Mae Conley on September 26, 1919 in Johnson County, Kentucky. Ora Mae Conley was born on June 3, 1901 in Johnson County, Kentucky and died on June 30, 1983 in Bowie, Prince Georges, Maryland. [57]

The children of Frank Pierce Picklesimer and Ora Mae Conley:
D1109—Willard Douglas Picklesimer. Born on February 22, 1922 in Paintsville, Johnson County, Kentucky and died on March 25, 2013 in Westway, El Paso County, Texas. Married Mary Mann on February 27, 1940 in Floyd County, Kentucky.
D1110—Jean Claire Picklesimer. Born on February 19, 1926 in Johnson County, Kentucky and died on December 22, 1926 in Johnson County, Kentucky.

D746—Josie Picklesimer. Daughter of John Picklesimer and Lou Trimble. (Sixth generation of David Trimble and —— Houston.) Married David Williams.

The children of David William and Jose Picklesimer:
D1111—Juanita Picklesimer. Died at age six.
D1112—Keith Picklesimer.
D1113—Jack Picklesimer.

D748—Stella Josephine Trimble. Daughter of Ulysses Grant Trimble and Patience Williams. (Sixth generation of David Trimble and —— Houston.) Born on August 9, 1890 on Barnett's Creek, Johnson County, Kentucky and died on February 21, 1968 Paintsville, Johnson County, Kentucky. Married

---

[57] Year: 1900; Census Place: Magisterial District 3, Johnson, Kentucky; Page: 3; Enumeration District: 0040; FHL microfilm: 1240534

Frances Milt Lemaster. Francis Milt LeMaster was born on April 18, 1890 in Johnson County, Kentucky and died February 3, 1973 in Tipp City, Miami County, Ohio.

The children of Francis Milt LeMaster and Stella Josephine Trimble:

D1114—John Grant Lemaster. Born on June 2, 1927 in Barnett's Creek, Johnson County, Kentucky and died on June 13, 1927 in Barnett's Creek, Johnson County, Kentucky at two weeks old.

D1115—Robert Milton Lemaster. Born on January 15, 1930 in Barnett's Creek, Johnson County, Kentucky and died on March 20, 2007 in Tipp City, Miami County, Ohio. Married Betty Jane Reynolds. She was born on December 19, 1929 in Barnett's Creek, Johnson County, Kentucky and died on November 15, 2013 in Tipp City, Miami County, Ohio.

D750—James Arthur Trimble. Son of Ulysses Grant Trimble and Patience Williams. (Sixth generation of David Trimble and —— Houston.) Born on July 27, 1896 in Johnson County, Kentucky and died on March 26, 1969. Married Pearl Rice on September 20, 1918 in Kentucky. Pearle was born on January 1, 1887 in Johnson County, Kentucky and died on October 15, 1958 in Columbus, Franklin County, Ohio.

The children of James Arthur Trimble and Pearle Rice:

D1116—Chester Arthur Trimble. Born on June 4, 1920 in Pike County, Kentucky and died on February 24, 1972 in Ohio. Married Florence ——. They were divorced on July 10, 1968 in Lawrence County, Ohio.

D1117—Arnold Clyde Trimble. Born on June 4, 1920 in Ivyton, Magoffin County, Kentucky and died on February 24, 1972 in Ohio. Married Myrtle Margaret Taylor. She was born on November 17, 1927 in Archer City, Texas and died on June 5, 2011 in Lexington, Fayette County, Kentucky.

D756—Clarence Benjamin Trimble. Son of Ulysses Grant Trimble and Patience Williams. (Sixth generation of David Trimble and —— Houston.) Born on August 5, 1932 in Magoffin County, Kentucky and died on April 30, 1976 in Magoffin County, Kentucky. Married Kathy Marshall.

D758—Bertha Trimble. Daughter of John Mark Trimble and Clarinda Francis Spradlin. (Sixth generation of David Trimble and ——— Houston.) Born on August 17, 1878 in Johnson County, Kentucky and died on March 22, 1908. Married Crate Davis.

The one son of Crate Davis and Bertha Trimble:

D1118—Burgess Davis. Married Margie Cantrell.

D - David Trimble

D759—Della Trimble. Daughter of John Mark Trimble and Clarinda Francis Spradlin. (Sixth generation of David Trimble and —— Houston.) Born on February 29, 1880 in Johnson County, Kentucky Married Leonard Caudill in 1896 in Johnson County, Kentucky. He was born on August 3, 1876 in Barnett's Creek, Johnson County, Kentucky.

The child of Leonard Caudill and Della Trimble:
D1119—Villetta Caudill. Born in 1896.

D760—Lindzey Trimble. Son of John Mark Trimble and Clarinda Francis Spradlin. (Sixth generation of David Trimble and —— Houston.) Born on April 18, 1881 in Johnson County, Kentucky and died on July 13, 1912 in Barnett's Creek, Johnson County, Kentucky. Married Flora Home.

The children of Lindzey Trimble and Flora Home:
D1120—Wayne Trimble.
D1121—Faye Trimble. Married Warren Salyers.
D1122—Anna Mae Trimble.

D763—Elmer S. Trimble. Son of John Mark Trimble and Clarinda Francis Spradlin. (Sixth generation of David Trimble and —— Houston.) Born on January 23, 1886 in Johnson County, Kentucky and died on January 27, 1972 in Gallipolis, Gallia County, Ohio. Married Tera Barnett.

The child of Elmer S. Trimble and Tera Barnett:
D1123—Sammie Trimble.

D764—Mahala Trimble. Daughter of John Mark Trimble and Clarinda Francis Spradlin. (Sixth generation of David Trimble and —— Houston.) Born on February 12, 1888 in Barnett's Creek, Johnson County, Kentucky and died on April 8, 1978 in Barnett's Creek, Johnson County, Kentucky. Married Byrd Preston.

The children Byrd Preston and Mahala Trimble:
D1124—Gracie Preston.
D1125—Valerie Preston. Married a Mr. Thompson.
D1126—Irene Preston.
D1127—Bonnie Ruby Preston.
D1128—Byrd Oliver Preston. Married Walta Lee Daniel.

D765—Bruce C. Trimble. Son of John Mark Trimble and Clarinda Francis Spradlin. (Sixth generation of David Trimble and —— Houston.) Born on November 24, 1889 and died on July 19, 1963. Married Norsie E. Reed on December 25, 1919. Norsie was born on April 10, 1898.

The children of Bruce Trimble and Norsie Reed:

+ **D1129—Davis Reed Trimble.** Born on May 24, 1921.

+ **D1130—Granville Trimble.** Born on August 20, 1922. Married Billie Marie Allen of Richmond, Kentucky.

+ **D1131—Georgene Trimble.** Born on January 27, 1924. Married Charles McKenzie of Barnett's Creek, Kentucky.

+ **D1132—John Mark Trimble.** Born on January 10, 1927. Married Janet Louise Marsh on June 12, 1927.

  D1133—Paul Wade Trimble. Born on June 30, 1928. Married Anna Lee Haines of Paintsville, Kentucky. They have no children.

  D1134—Lorene Trimble. Born on July 11, 1930. Married Ted Carney. Lived at 910 D. Hampshire Drive, Louisville, Kentucky 40207.

D767—Daniel Boone Trimble. Son of John Mark Trimble and Clarinda Francis Spradlin. (Sixth generation of David Trimble and —— Houston.) Born on September 5, 1892 and died in 1963. Married Rosa LeMaster (D735) in 1924. Rosa was born on June 21, 1897 and died in 1945. Boone was sheriff of Johnson County, Kentucky from 1950 to 1954.

The children of Daniel Boone Trimble and Rosa LeMaster:

+ **D1135—Emogene Trimble.** Born on January 21, 1925. Married Carl Benson.

  D1136—Lucille Trimble. Born on May 20, 1926. She is deceased.

+ **D1137—Loretta Trimble.** Born on October 14, 1927. Married James Eldon Reed, born on August 20, 1924. They lived at 1744 Academy Place, Dayton, Ohio.

+ **D1138—William Lindsey Trimble.** Born on May 23, 1929. Married Beulah Frances McKenzie.

+ **D1139—Byron Douglas Trimble.** Born on May 27, 1931 and died December 29, 2018 in Beavercreek, Ohio. Married Geneva Dawson on April 27, 1956.

+ **D1140—Betty Rose Trimble.** Born on October 23, 1932. Married Arnold Reed, born on September 13, 1930, of Flat Gap, Kentucky.

+ **D1141—Daniel Boone Trimble, Jr.** Born in 1935.

  D1142—Dorothy Evelyn Trimble. Born on October 23, 1937. She is deceased.

D768—Harry B. Trimble. Son of John Mark Trimble and Clarinda Francis Spradlin. (Sixth generation of David Trimble and —— Houston.) Born on March 24, 1893 in Johnson County, Kentucky, and died on January 14, 1978 in Pike County, Kentucky. Married Bessie Adams.

Trimble Families of America

The children of Harry B. Trimble and Bessie Adams:

D1143—Bud Trimble. Born on February 9, 1925 in Oil Springs, Johnson County, Kentucky and died on March 18, 1992 in Pikeville, Pike County, Kentucky.

D1144—Donald Trimble. Born on January 7, 1928 in Barnett's Creek, Johnson County, Kentucky and died on January 26, 1997 in Hagerhill, Johnson County, Kentucky.

D1145—Mabel Trimble. Born on July 12, 1920 in Barnett's Creek, Johnson County, Kentucky and died on August 10, 2007 in Paducah, McCracken County, Kentucky. Married Lenis Herbert Valentine.

D1146—Mary Ruth Trimble. Born on August 17, 1923 in Barnett's Creek, Johnson County, Kentucky and died on July 1, 2016 in Pikeville, Pike County, Kentucky.

D769—Shella Trimble. Daughter of John Mark Trimble and Clarinda Francis Spradlin. (Sixth generation of David Trimble and —— Houston.) Born on March 15, 1895 in Johnson County, Kentucky and died on December 24, 1987 in Franklin, Franklin County, Ohio. Married Sebastian Coldiron.

The two children of Sebastian Coldiron and Shella Trimble:

D1147—Marjorie Coldiron.
D1148—Mark Coldiron.

D771—Quince Trimble. Son of John Mark Trimble and Clarinda Francis Spradlin. (Sixth generation of David Trimble and —— Houston.) Born on July 7, 1899 in Johnson County, Kentucky and died on March 4, 1970 in Columbus, Franklin County, Ohio. Married Lessie Lemaster.

The children Quince Trimble and Lessie LeMaster:

D1149—Clarence Trimble.
D1150—Walter Ray Trimble.
D1151—David Trimble.
D1152—Alfred Trimble.
D1153—Mary Frances Trimble.
D1154—Reva Trimble.
D1155—Robert Bruce Trimble.

D779—Boe Trimble. Son of William Trimble and Sally VanHoose. (Sixth generation of David Trimble and —— Houston.) Born on September 21, 1886 and died on June 29, 1959. Married Zuria Caudill, born on February 6, 1889.

The children of Boe Trimble and Zuria Caudill:

+ **D1156—Ulis Trimble.** Born on January 12, 1908. Married Iva Hackworth.

+ **D1157—Vensil A. Trimble.** Born on September 29, 1914. Married Gladys Ingraham.

+ **D1158—Avanell Trimble.**

   D1159—Sarah Louisa Trimble. Born on December 20, 1931. She lives at 2051 Tamarack, Lexington, Kentucky.

D780—Floyd Trimble. Son of William Trimble and Sally VanHoose. (Sixth generation of David Trimble and —— Houston.) Married on Fona Ritchie. This family lives at Chillicothe, Ohio.

   The children of Floyd Trimble and Fona Ritchie:

   D1160—Raymond Trimble.

   D1161—Ellis Trimble.

   D1162—Hagar Trimble.

   D1163—Geneive Trimble.

   D1164—Ruby Trimble.

   D1165—Francis Trimble.

D781—James V. Trimble. Son of William Trimble and Sally VanHoose. (Sixth generation of David Trimble and —— Houston.) Married Mayme Goble.

   The children of James V. Trimble and Mayme Goble:

+ **D1166—Elnora Trimble.** Married Byrd Rondall Ison, a Baptist minister of Midway, Kentucky.

+ **D1167—Anna Jean Trimble.** Married Franklin C. Cunningham of Austin, Texas.

+ **D1168—James William Trimble.** Married Joyce Hall. They live at Pikesville, Kentucky.

D782—Pierce Trimble. Son of William Trimble and Sally VanHoose. (Sixth generation of David Trimble and —— Houston.) Married Lena Caudill.

   The children of Pierce Trimble and Lena Caudill:

   D1169—Billie Jack Trimble. deceased.

   D1170—Bruedia Trimble. Married Howard Nutt.

D783—Newt Trimble. Son of William Trimble and Sally VanHoose. (Sixth generation of David Trimble and —— Houston.) Newt married two times: first, to Ethel Rice, and second, to Mary West.

   The children of Newt Trimble and Ethel Rice:

   D1171—Leon Trimble. Married Joan Wheeler.

D - David Trimble

D1172—Nevia Trimble.

D1173—Donald Bert Trimble. Married Ernestine Trimble.

The children of Newt Trimble and Mary West:

D1174—Joyce Trimble. Married Billy Ross.

D1175—Jean Trimble. Married John Ball.

D1176—Carol Trimble.

D784—Therman Trimble. Son of William Trimble and Sally VanHoose. (Sixth generation of David Trimble and —— Houston.) Married Mildred Caudill.

The children of Therman Trimble and Mildred Caudill:

D1177—Oral C. Trimble. Killed in World War II in U.S. Navy.

D1178—Ronald C. Trimble.

D1179—Carroll Trimble.

D1180—Howard Trimble.

D1181—Gene Trimble.

D1182—Alvin Trimble.

D786—Sada Trimble. Daughter of William Trimble and Sally VanHoose. (Sixth generation of David Trimble and —— Houston.) Married George Eally.

The children of George Eally and Sada Trimble:

+ **D1183—Ruth Eally.** Married Clyde Williams of Oil Springs, Kentucky.

+ **D1184—Ruie Eally.** Married Bob Reed.

D1185—Marshall Eally. Married Gladys McFaddin.

D1186—Orville Eally. Married Mary Fannin.

D1187—Arnold Eally.

D1188—Chat Eally. Married a Branham.

D1189—Betty Eally. Married Billy Robinson.

D787—Buell G. Trimble. Son of Green Trimble and Sadie Ealey. (Sixth generation of David Trimble and —— Houston.) Born in 1896 and died on September 16, 1970. Married on Reba Salyers the daughter of Addison Salyers.

The children of Buell Trimble and Reba Salyers:

D1190—Audrey Trimble. Married Joseph Webber of Columbus, Ohio.

D1191—Barbara Trimble. Married James Nichols of Columbus, Ohio.

D1192—Willis Trimble. Lives in San Jose, California.

D1193—Roger Trimble. Lives in San Diego, California.

D1194—Glenn Trimble. Lives in Worthington, Ohio.

D1195—Patrick Trimble. Lives in West Liberty, Ohio.

D795—Conroy Trimble. Son of Joseph Harman Trimble and Florence Ida Caudill. (Sixth generation of David Trimble and —— Houston.) Born on November 28, 1895 in Johnson County, Kentucky and died on August 7, 1971 in Johnson County, Kentucky. Married Doshia Ann Blair on October 21, 1916 in Johnson County, Kentucky. Doshia was born on September 11, 1897 in Johnson County, Kentucky and died on September 18, 1972 in Johnson County, Kentucky. She was daughter of Alamander Blair and Artelia Blair who were married on November 27, 1896. They were married for almost 68 years.[58]

Conroy would say, "He had six children and six granddaughters, and none had a sister." Each child only had one daughter. He was a construction foreman building homes in Paintsville, Kentucky during the 1920's. His boss asked him why he had not bought one of the houses they were building. So, he bought the next one when it was finished. When the stock market crashed in 1929, he owned one house which he was renting and was buying a second. After the market crashed. He sold both houses and moved back to the house his father built on Barnett's Creek in Johnson County, Kentucky. His father Joseph Harmon Trimble had died just a year before the Stock Market Crash. They lived with his mother for a few years until she died. They survived and even prospered during the Great Depression. The raised most of their own food. Vegetable gardens on several fields, a couple of other fields that were mostly hill side was used to raise feed corn for the livestock and the chickens which supplied fresh eggs.

Their last child Leroy caught Scarlett Fever as an infant. It affected his hearing and was deaf. Despite being the middle of the great Depression. Leroy was sent to a deaf school in Danville, Kentucky.

The children of Conroy Trimble and Doshia Ann Blair:

+ **D1196—Kermit Hanson Trimble.** Born on July 24, 1917 in Johnson County, Kentucky and died on June 9, 1996 at Paintsville, Johnson County, Kentucky. Married Margie Caudill on April 25, 1936. She is the daughter of Luther Caudill.

+ **D1197—Chloe Belle Trimble.** Born on September 27, 1918 in Johnson County, Kentucky and died on July 9, 1999 in Johnson County, Kentucky. Married William Allen "Bill" Caudill on June 4, 1938.

---

[58] US Census: 1930; Census Place: District 1, Johnson, Kentucky; Roll: 761; Page: 12B; Enumeration District: 0004; Image: 126.0; FHL microfilm: 2340496

D - David Trimble

+ **D1198—Kenneth Archer Trimble.** Born on December 12, 1921 in Johnson County, Kentucky and died on February 21, 2002 in Johnson County, Kentucky. Married Mary P. Biggs on March 14, 1942.

+ **D1199—Kathleen Trimble.** Born on September 8, 1924 in Johnson County, Kentucky. Married Theodore "Tom" Colvin on November 16, 1946.

+ **D1200—Clifford Eldon Trimble.** Born on September 3, 1926 in Johnson County, Kentucky and died on July 20, 1995 in Ashland, Boyd County, Kentucky Married Doris Deloris Price on January 28, 1950.

+ **D1201—Leroy Trimble.** Born on August 14, 1928 in Johnson County, Kentucky and died on August 1, 1972 in Hamilton, Butler County, Ohio. Married Paula Earlene Matthews on January 26, 1950. Paula was born on January 19, 1927 in Glasgow, Kentucky and died on April 8, 2007 in La Grange, Kentucky.

D796—McCoy Trimble. Son of Joseph Harman Trimble and Florence Ida Caudill. (Sixth generation of David Trimble and —— Houston.) Born on January 17, 1898, and married Ethel Fraley on July 11, 1924.

The children of McCoy Trimble and Ethel Fraley:

+ **D1202—Genevieve B. Trimble.** Married Ben Becker.

+ **D1203—Mary M. Trimble.** Married Warren K. Halstead.

+ **D1204—Sheila F. Trimble.** Married twice.

D797—Palmer Trimble. Son of Joseph Harman Trimble and Florence Ida Caudill. (Sixth generation of David Trimble and —— Houston.) Born on August 9, 1901 in Johnson County, Kentucky and died on October 29, 1987 in Gallipolis, Gallia County, Ohio. Married Nola Elizabeth Webb on December 15, 1935. Nola was born on May 23, 1918 and died on March 27, 2002.[59][60][61] Palmer enlisted in the Army on November 3, 1919 and was discharged on November 2, 1920. He enlisted the second time on December 5, 1920 and was discharged December 4, 1923. He enlisted the third time on

---

[59] Death Certificate No. 020506, Gallia County, Ohio.

[60] 1930 US Federal Census, Magisterial District 3, Johnson County, Kentucky, Supervisor's District Number 8, Enumeration District Number 58-7, Sheet Number 9B.

[61] 1910 US Federal Census, Johnson County, Kentucky, Johnson County, Kentucky, Supervisor's District Number 10, Enumeration District Number 71, Sheet Number 5B.

May 23, 1928 and was discharged January 29, 1930.[62]

The children of Palmer Trimble and Nola Webb:

+ **D1205—Arma Lea Trimble.** Born on November 10, 1938. Married Kenneth Wayne Robinson.

+ **D1206—Ronald Eugene Trimble.** Born on May 27, 1941. Married Jane M. Hartlieb.

+ **D1207—Donna Jean Trimble.** Born on February 24, 1950. Married Robert O. Schmoll, Jr. on February 15, 1974.

D798—Lelia Jane Trimble. Daughter of Joseph Harman Trimble and Florence Ida Caudill. (Sixth generation of David Trimble and ——— Houston.) Born on October 3, 1906 at Barnett's Creek, Johnson County, Kentucky and died on May 11, 1999 at Cabell Huntington Hospital, Huntington, West Virginia. Married Flem Arrowood on November 27, 1924 in Paintsville, Johnson County, Kentucky. Flem was born on February 24, 1906 at Pigeon Roost, Greasy Creek, Johnson County, Kentucky.

The children of Flem Arrowood and Lelia Trimble:

+ **D1208—Jeanetta Arrowood.** Born on October 12, 1925 on Barnett's Creek, Johnson County, Kentucky. Married Arthur Browning.

+ **D1209—Carmel Ray Arrowood.** Born on February 22, 1928. Married Lova Kitchens.

+ **D1210—Lovella F. Arrowood.** Born on April 16, 1930. Married Harold Fry.

+ **D1211—Larry G. Arrowood.** Born on September 21, 1935. Married Lillian Smith.

D799—William Wallace Trimble. Son of Joseph Harman Trimble and Florence Ida Caudill. (Sixth generation of David Trimble and ——— Houston.) Born on November 21, 1908 in Johnson County, Kentucky, and died on May 28, 1965 in Boyd County, Kentucky. Married Rhena Mae Rice on June 22, 1932. Rhena Mae was born on November 29, 1914 at Barnett's Creek, Johnson County, Kentucky and died on March 12, 1999 at King's Daughters' Medical Center, Ashland, Boyd County, Kentucky.

The children of William Wallace Trimble and Rhena Mae Rice:

---

[62] U.S., Department of Veterans Affairs BIRLS Death File, 1850-2010[database on-line]. Provo, UT, USA: Ancestry.com Operations, Inc., 2011.

D - David Trimble

+**D1212—Reece Kenyon Trimble.** Born on January 4, 1934 at Johnson County, Kentucky. Married twice.

+**D1213—William Francis "Bill" Trimble.** Born on July 25, 1936 at Pilgrim, Kentucky and died on December 26, 1997 in Ashland, Boyd County, Kentucky. Married Martha Anderson.

D1214—Reona Mae Trimble. Born on July 22, 1939. Never married.

D800—Clemince (Clemmons) "Pete" Trimble. Son of Joseph Harman Trimble and Florence Ida Caudill. (Sixth generation of David Trimble and —— Houston.) Born on September 11, 1911 in Johnson County, Kentucky and died on November 20, 1968 in Huntington, Cabell County, West Virginia. Married Mildred Preston on June 22, 1932. Mildred was born on February 18, 1913 at Johnson County, Kentucky and died on July 19, 2000 at St. Mary's Hospital, Huntington, Cabell County, West Virginia.

The child of Clemince "Pete" Trimble and Mildred Preston:

+**D1215—Joe Langley Trimble.** Born on March 1, 1936 in Johnson County, Kentucky and died on November 11, 1980 in Huntington, West Virginia. Married Nancy M. Trogton.

D801—Swanie Lee Trimble. Son of Joseph Harman Trimble and Florence Ida Caudill. (Sixth generation of David Trimble and —— Houston.) Born on February 10, 1914 in Barnett's Creek, Johnson County, Kentucky and died on September 22, 1991 in Huntington, Cabell County, West Virginia. Married Rhoda Tomblin on April 8, 1939. Rhoda was born on October 9, 1921 in McComas, Wayne County, West Virginia and died on August 17, 1999 in Huntington, Cabell County, West Virginia. She was the daughter of John Tomlin and Cassie Maynard.

The children of Swanie Lee Trimble and Rhoda Tomblin:

+**D1216—Dallas Leon Trimble.** Born December 27, 1939 in Huntington, West Virginia. Married Loretta F. Sharp.

+**D1217—Mary Elizabeth Trimble.** Born on August 20, 1942 in Huntington, Cabell County, West Virginia. Married Rayburn Jack Perry.

D802—Lola Marie Trimble. Daughter of Joseph Harman Trimble and Florence Ida Caudill. (Sixth generation of David Trimble and —— Houston.) Born on January 13, 1917 at Barnett's Creek, Johnson County, Kentucky and died on August 22, 2000 at South Point, Ohio. Married Floyd William Damron on January 25, 1938. He was born on May 1, 1912 in Dunlow, Wayne County, West Virginia and died on January 8, 1948 in Knott County, Kentucky,
Married the second time to Guy Stewart Puckett but they had no children.

The children of Floyd William Damron and Lola Marie Trimble:

+ **D1218—James Wayne "Buckshot" Damron.** Born on September 5, 1938. Married Mary L. Black.

+ **D1219—Ida Lou Damron.** Born on February 26, 1940. Married Dennis Lee Bowen on June 17, 1960.

D1220—Floyd W. Damron, Jr.

+ **D1221—Phyllis J. Damron.** Married William R. Bocook.

+ **D1222—Virginia Gale Damron.** Born on May 15, 1944 in Huntington, West Virginia and died on April 24, 2020 in Coal Grove, Ohio. Married Michael F. Fizer.

D803—Lillian Margueritte Trimble. Daughter of Joseph Harman Trimble and Florence Ida Caudill. (Sixth generation of David Trimble and —— Houston.) Born on March 20, 1922 in Johnson County, Kentucky and died on May 1, 2009 at Emogene Dolin Jones Hospice House, Huntington, Cabell County, West Virginia. Married Thomas Ray Dick on August 25, 1956. Tom was born on May 28, 1937 and died June 15, 2021.

The children of Tom Dick and Lillian Trimble:

+ **D1223—Larry Ray Dick.** Born on December 31, 1957. Married Gloria Angela Sandon.

+ **D1224—Gary Lee Dick.** Born on May 28, 1959. Married Pamala Sue Dickerson.

D804—Patrick H. Trimble. Son of Joseph Trimble and Laura Mae "Dolly" Trimble. (Sixth generation of David Trimble and —— Houston.) Born on December 16, 1896 in Johnson County, Kentucky and died on May 20, 1951 in Johnson, Kentucky. Married a Julia Cane in 1917.

The children of Patrick H. Trimble and Julia Cane:

+ **D1225—Johnnie Patrick Trimble.** Born on October 18, 1918 in Johnson County, Kentucky and died on July 10, 1987 in Columbus, Franklin County, Ohio. Married twice.

+ **D1226—Claude Trimble.** Born on January 2, 1921 in Wheelwright, Floyd County, Kentucky and died on August 15, 1982 in Columbus, Franklin, Ohio. He enlisted in the army infantry on December 19, 1940 at Fort Thomas Newport, Kentucky. He was single at the time. He was discharged on November 4, 1945.[63] Married Mary Anne O'Neil. She

---

[63] Electronic Army Serial Number Merged File, 1938-1946 [Archival Database]; ARC:

Trimble Families of America

was born in 1923.

D1227—Mable Trimble. Born on February 22, 1923 in Floyd County, Kentucky and died on June 11, 2003 at Residence in Columbus, Franklin County, Ohio. Married Amos Wright.

D1228—Margarett "Margie" Trimble. Born on November 17, 1924 in Floyd County, Kentucky and died on June 27, 1980 in Mount Carmel Medical Center, Columbus, Franklin County, Ohio.

D1229—Clyde Trimble. Born in 1928 in Kentucky and died in 1930 in Kentucky at two years of age.

D805—Farmer Ratliff. Son of John E. Ratliff and Laura Mae "Dolly" Trimble. (Sixth generation of David Trimble and —— Houston.) Born on April 18, 1903 in Johnson County, Kentucky and died on May 23, 1963 in Johnson County, Kentucky. Married twice. Married Lavada Spradlin on July 17, 1922 in Paintsville, Johnson County, Kentucky. Married Martha Ann Spradlin on October 19, 1925 at the home of Roy Estep, Johnson County, Kentucky.

The children of Farmer Ratliff and Lavada Spradlin:

D1230—John D. Ratliff. Born on March 11, 1925 in Johnson County, Kentucky.

The children of Farmer Ratliff and Martha Ann Spradlin:

D1231—Marvin E. Ratliff. Born on April 21, 1927 in Johnson County, Kentucky and died on August 24, 1988 in Johnson, Kentucky.

D1232—Jack Ratliff. Born on October 10, 1929 in Johnson County, Kentucky and died on February 24, 1983 in Oklahoma.

D1233—Burnam Henry Ratliff. Born on August 18, 1933 in Johnson County, Kentucky and died on August 22, 1964 in home of his mother on Barnett's Creek, Johnson County, Kentucky.

D807—Freddie Ratliff. Son of John E. Ratliff and Laura Mae "Dolly" Trimble. (Sixth generation of David Trimble and —— Houston.) Born on June 28, 1908 in Johnson County, Kentucky and died on January 15, 1986 in Johnson County, Kentucky. Married Pina McKenzie. She was born in 1911 and died in 1993. She was the daughter Frank McKenzie and Servilla Kimbler. Frank and Servilla were married in 1898. Frank McKenzie was born on July 1874.

1263923. World War II Army Enlistment Records; Records of the National Archives and Records Administration, Record Group 64; National Archives at College Park. College Park, Maryland, U.S.A.

Servilla Kimbler was born about 1885. Great granddaughter Denise married Mark Castle.

The children of Freddie Ratliff and Pina McKenzie:

D1234—John F. Ratliff. Born on October 14, 1928 in Johnson County, Kentucky and died January 2, 1995.

D1235—Betty Carol Ratliff. Born on October 16, 1940 in Johnson County, Kentucky and died February 2002.

D1236—Doris Ratliff. Married Donald Haney.

D1237—Faith Ratliff.

D1238—unnamed Ratliff.

D1239—unnamed Ratliff.

D1240—Mary Ratliff.

D1241—Ernest Ratliff.

D808—Gordon Ratliff. Son of John E. Ratliff and Laura Mae "Dolly" Trimble. (Sixth generation of David Trimble and —— Houston.) Born on April 6, 1911 in Barnett's Creek, Johnson County, Kentucky and died on February 6, 1991 in Jackson, Jackson County, Michigan. Married Bessie Spradlin. Bessie was born on March 5, 1916 in Johnson County, Kentucky.

The children of Gordon Ratliff and Bessie Spradlin:

D1242—Gilbert Ratliff. Born on May 10, 1935 and died on April 5, 2005 in Tampa, Hillsborough County, Florida.

D1243—Dolly Ratliff. Born on February 6, 1947 in Johnson County, Kentucky.

D1244—Tavie Ratliff.

D1245—Dewey Ratliff.

D1246—Vada Ratliff.

D1247—Wilbur Ratliff.

D809—Gladia Ratliff. Daughter of John E. Ratliff and Laura Mae "Dolly" Trimble. (Sixth generation of David Trimble and —— Houston.) Born on July 31, 1913 in Johnson County, Kentucky and died on December 11, 1988 in Paintsville, Johnson County, Kentucky. Married Delmar Fraley on March 15, 1930.

The children of Delmar Fraley and Gladia Ratliff:

D1248—Charles Edward Fraley. Born on April 1, 1933 in Johnson County, Kentucky and died on February 8, 1981 in Columbus, Franklin County, Ohio.

D1249—Bill Fraley. Born on April 18, 1936 in Johnson County, Kentucky and died April 12, 2001 in Henderson, Henderson County, Kentucky.

D1250—David D. Fraley. Born on February 7, 1949 in Johnson County, Kentucky and died on June 29, 1990 in Columbus, Franklin County, Ohio. They five boys and four girls no names are known.

D810—Sadie Ratliff. Daughter of John E. Ratliff and Laura Mae "Dolly" Trimble. (Sixth generation of David Trimble and —— Houston.) Born on March 22, 1918 in Johnson County, Kentucky and died on June 29, 1984 in Floyd County, Kentucky. Married Earl Douglas Lemaster. He was born on October 16, 1914 in Ohio and died on July 28, 1964 in Franklin County, Ohio.

The children of Earl Douglas Lemaster and Sadie Ratliff:
D1251—Carenna Lemaster. Born about 1935 in Kentucky.
D1252—Earl Douglas Lemaster, Jr. Born about 1937 in Kentucky.
D1253—Ernest Gene Lemaster. Born about 1940 in Kentucky.

D811—Clara Ratliff. Daughter of John E. Ratliff and Laura Mae "Dolly" Trimble. (Sixth generation of David Trimble and —— Houston.) Born in 1923 in Paintsville, Johnson County, Kentucky and died on December 1, 1993 Paintsville, Johnson County, Kentucky. Married Hoy Preston. Hoy was born on February 14, 1918 in Kentucky and died on June 3, 1999 in Kentucky. Hoy enlisted during World War II on January 26, 1943.[64]

The children of Hoy Preston and Clara Ratliff:
D1254—Joseph Preston.
D1255—Unnamed Preston.

D819—Stanley Trimble. Son of John Crittenden Trimble and Harriet Ryan. (Sixth generation of David Trimble and ——— Houston.) Born on June 20, 1890 and died on August 11, 1971. Married Mattie Crockett, born on October 17, 1890. H. Stanley was a retired building superintendent at Lexington, Kentucky.

The children of Stanley Trimble and Mattie Crockett:
+ **D1256—John Thomas Trimble.** Born on November 8, 1912 and died on March 11, 1959 Married Geneva Arnold. Married Geneva Arnold.
+ **D1257—William Bush Trimble.** Born in 1914.

---

[64] Electronic Army Serial Number Merged File, 1938-1946 [Archival Database]; ARC: 1263923. World War II Army Enlistment Records; Records of the National Archives and Records Administration, Record Group 64; National Archives at College Park. College Park, Maryland, U.S.A.

+ **D1258—Elizabeth Trimble.** Born on October 13, 1917. Married Stanley Rogers.

+ **D1259—Sudie Mae Trimble.** Born on July 5, 1919. Married Joel Moore.

+ **D1260—Emmett Ryan Trimble.** Born in 1923.

+ **D1261—Frances Allene Trimble.** Born on October 7, 1931. Married George Sallee.

D820—J. Smith Trimble. Son of John Crittenden Trimble and Harriet Ryan. (Sixth generation of David Trimble and —— Houston.) Born on January 10, 1892. Married Myrtle Hamilton, born on March 30, 1900. J. Smith is a retired C.P.A. in Terre Haute, Indiana. He is a World War I veteran.

The children of J. Smith Trimble and Myrtle Hamilton:

+ **D1262—Audrey Jane Trimble.** Born on July 26, 1923. Married Richard Van Allen.

D821—Ella Lee Trimble. Daughter of John Crittenden Trimble and Harriet Ryan. (Sixth generation of David Trimble and —— Houston.) Born on February 1, 1894. Married J. Edward Toy, who died on May 9, 1955. He was a farmer at Mount Sterling, Kentucky.

The children of J. Edward Toy and Ella Lee Trimble:

+ **D1263—J. Edward Toy, Jr.** Born on December 15, 1916. Married Beulah Myers. He was in World War II from November 1943 to June 1946.

+ **D1264—John Crittenden Toy.** Born on August 14, 1918. Married Gertrude Fletcher. John was in World War II from in June 1941 to May 1945 and was at Schofield Barrack when Pearl Harbor was Bombed.

D822—May Edward Trimble. Daughter of John Crittenden Trimble and Harriet Ryan. (Sixth generation of David Trimble and —— Houston.) Born on September 28, 1895. Married Raymond W. Johnson, who died in April 1947. They lived in Wayne, Michigan.

The children of Raymond W. Johnson and May Edward Trimble:

+ **D1265—Nelson Johnson.** Born on March 10, 1916 and died on April 13, 1969. Married Gretchen ——.

+ **D1266—Merle Johnson.** Born on August 27, 1918. Married Ruth.

+ **D1267—Hamet Jane Johnson.** Born on May 11, 1922. Married Woody King.

+ **D1268—Cordelia Ann Johnson.** Born on November 18, 1924. Married Fred DuValle.

+ **D1269—Lou Johnson.** Born on January 24, 1929. Married Arthur Cole.

Trimble Families of America

D823—Margaret Trimble. Daughter of John Crittenden Trimble and Harriet Ryan. (Sixth generation of David Trimble and —— Houston.) Born on June 13, 1897. Married George Draper Hill, born on July 6, 1900, and died on June 22, 1953. He was a farmer and they lived at Versailles, Kentucky.

The children of George Draper Hill and Margaret Trimble:

+ **D1270—Robert Draper Hill.** Born on January 12, 1920. Married Lorraine Wright of Connecticut. He is a stockbroker in New York and a veteran of World War II.

+ **D1271—Marcella Haggard Hill.** Born on October 13, 1923. Married William Howard Chapman, a salesman and farmer at Versailles, Kentucky.

+ **D1272—Wilbur Marks Hill.** Born on July 3, 1927. Married Wanda Baker. He is a farmer at Versailles, Kentucky, and a veteran of World War II.

D824—Georgia Trimble. Daughter of John Crittenden Trimble and Harriet Ryan. (Sixth generation of David Trimble and —— Houston.) Born on December 11, 1899. Married William Houston Yeary, a retired businessman of Harrodsburg, Kentucky. He was born on July 3, 1899.

The children of William Houston Yeary and Georgia Trimble:

+ **D1273—Georgia Doris Yeary.** Born on February 17, 1926. Married a Mr. Rice and lives in Texas.

+ **D1274—William Houston Yeary, Jr.** Born on December 25, 1932. Married Loretta Ann Phelps of Burgin, Kentucky. He is a veteran of the Korean Conflict, enlisting in the U.S. Air Force in 1951, serving until 1955.

D826—Nelson H. Trimble. Son of John Crittenden Trimble and Harriet Ryan. (Sixth generation of David Trimble and —— Houston.) Born on March 20, 1904. Married Minnie Belle Fortune, Born on April 1, 1915. Nelson is a retired businessman of Mount Sterling, Kentucky.

The children Nelson H. Trimble and Minnie Belle Fortune:

+ **D1275—Patricia Joyce Trimble.** Born on March 4, 1933. Married Frank Alien Carroll, whose career is with the United States Air Force. They live in California.

D1276—Maybelle Trimble. Born on April 29, 1935. Married a Mr. Tabone and their daughter, Lisa Annette Tabone, born on November 4, 1963.

D1277—Joe Morris Trimble. Born on September 28, 1940. He is a veteran of four years in the U.S. Air Force and was stationed in the Far East.

D827—Catherine Ryan Trimble. Daughter of John Crittenden Trimble and Harriet Ryan. (Sixth generation of David Trimble and ——— Houston.) Born on April 19, 1906. Married Rollie B. Carroll, born on December 16, 1905. He is a retired businessman of Lexington, Kentucky.

The children of Rollie B. Carroll and Catherine Ryan Trimble:

+ **D1278—Anne Ryan Carroll.** Born on February 26, 1929. Married Orville Thomas Reynolds, born in 1926.

+ **D1279—Gene Paul Carroll.** Born on November 20, 1932. Married Lois Ann Peyton. He is a veteran of the U.S. Air Force, 1951-1955. He was in the European theater and Korean Conflict.

+ **D1280—Rollie B. Carroll, Jr.** Born on November 5, 1937. Married Jane Elliot Darnall.

D1281—Wayne King Carroll. Born on October 7, 1939 and died August 30, 1959.

D1282—David Alan Carroll. Born on October 17, 1951. Married Robin Lynn Hamilton.

D828—Florence Rae Trimble. Daughter of John Crittenden Trimble and Harriet Ryan. (Sixth generation of David Trimble and ——— Houston.) Born on January 17, 1909. Married Burgin Howard Masters, born in 1907. They live in Lexington, Kentucky.

The children of Burgin Howard Masters and Florence Rae Trimble:

+ **D1283—Barbara Howard Masters.** Born on February 16, 1932. Married Herbert Clyde Riggs.

+ **D1284—Nancy Clay Masters.** Born on October 30, 1934. Married James Lewis Baldwin.

+ **D1285—Virginia Rae Masters.** Born on July 5, 1941. Married Harvey Thomas Farris.

D829—Paul Crittenden Trimble. Son of John Crittenden Trimble and Harriet Ryan. (Sixth generation of David Trimble and ——— Houston.) Born on November 20, 1911. Married Elizabeth Laudeman. Paul is a retired salesman. They live in Lexington, Kentucky. He is a veteran of World War II.

The children of Paul Crittenden Trimble and Elizabeth Laudeman:

+ **D1286—Gary Lee Trimble.** Born on September 13, 1932. A veteran of the Korean Conflict, he was in the U.S. Air Force from 1951 to 1955.

+ **D1287—Robert Crittenden Trimble.** Born on January 16, 1935. Married Anne Crane.

Trimble Families of America

+**D1288—Janice Dale Trimble.** Born on April 26, 1938. Married Robert Duff.

D830—Lee Trimble. Son of Joe Trimble and Rose Wills. (Sixth generation of David Trimble and —— Houston.)

The children of Lee Trimble:

D1289—Robert Joseph Trimble. Deceased.

D1290—daughter Trimble. Living with her mother in Mount Sterling, Kentucky.

D841—Clarence Trimble. Son of Seaborn Trimble and Emma Wilson. (Sixth generation of David Trimble and —— Houston.) Born on October 17, 1874. Married Emma Green on January 18, 1900. They lived on a tract of the William Trimble farm.

The children of Clarence Trimble and Emma Green:

+**D1291—Emma Golden Trimble.** Born on May 13, 1901. Married Jim Goin and they lived at Irvine, Kentucky.

D1292—Beulah Fern Trimble. Born on September 14, 1902. Married J. B. Hughes on November 26, 1932 and lived in Florida.

+**D1293—Mazie Trimble.** Born on February 6, 1906. Married Everette Nickell in 1923.

+**D1294—Robert Bruce Trimble.** Born on January 25, 1909. He was the only son of Clarence and Emma Trimble. Married Helen Davenport of Linn, Ohio, on December 18, 1948.

D1295—Mattie Alice Trimble. Born on July 30, 1911 and died July 7, 1926.

+**D1296—Ruth Esther Trimble.** Born on April 4, 1915. Married Carl Thomas Gillen and lives in Cincinnati, Ohio.

+**D1297—Ruby Christine Trimble.** Born on November 18, 1916. Married Harold Deatherage on May 31, 1941. They live at Earlington, Kentucky.

+**D1298—Marie Trimble.** Born on January 30, 1922. Married Charles Brown on December 1, 1942. They live in Louisville, Kentucky.

D1299—Maxine Trimble. Born on January 9, 1923. She lives in Cincinnati, Ohio.

D843—Rose Trimble. Daughter of Seaborn Trimble and Emma Wilson. (Sixth generation of David Trimble and —— Houston.) Born on December 26, 1879. Married J. R. Brooks on September 6, 1918. They settled on Lacy Creek on one of the Trimble farms.

The children of J. R. Brooks and Rose Trimble:

D1300—India Alice Brooks.
D1301—Robert Campbell Brooks.

D844—James Calvin Trimble. Son of Seaborn Trimble and Emma Wilson. (Sixth generation of David Trimble and —— Houston.) Born on December 1, 1882 and died on December 25, 1931. Married Lela Day. Lela died on January 1, 1932, a week after James died.

The children of James Calvin Trimble and Lela Day:

D1302—Toney Trimble. He lives in Middletown, Ohio.
D1303—James Ralph Trimble. Born on September 1, 1929. Married Gertrude Cockerham at Campton, Kentucky. They have one son: James Clarence Trimble.
D1304—Eunice Trimble. Born on September 8, 1931. Married Austine Oldfield on November 5, 1948. They live in Middletown, Ohio, and have a son, James Bernard.

D846—Ava Ellen Swango. Daughter of James Swango and Josephine Trimble (Sixth generation of David Trimble and —— Houston.) Born on October 1879 in Wolf County, Kentucky. Married a Mr. Fallon who was born about 1879.

The children of Mr. Fallon and Ava Swango:

D1305—Josephine Fallon. Born about 1909 in Texas.

D851—Leo Frey. Son of Alfonso Frey and Nancy Elizabeth Trimble. (Sixth generation of David Trimble and —— Houston.) Married Dorothy Williams and is a wholesale grocer in Paris, Illinois.

The children of Leo Frey and Dorothy Williams:

D1306—Robert Allen Frey.
D1307—Elizabeth Frey.
D1308—Leo Shelton Frey.

D872—Maria Trimble. Daughter of South Trimble and Carrie Belle Allen. (Sixth generation of David Trimble and —— Houston.) Married Carlos Fish. She was a widow early and served as postmaster in Frankfort, Kentucky, for eighteen years.

The children of Carlos Fish and Maria Trimble:

D1309—Carlos Fish. He was a doctor in Louisville, Kentucky.
D1310—unnamed son Fish. He was a lawyer in New Orleans, Louisiana.
D1311—Helen Fish. Died in 1954.
D1312—Carrie Belle Fish. Married C. T. Eddie of Lexington, Kentucky.

D874—Margaret Allen Trimble. Daughter of South Trimble and Carrie Belle Allen. (Sixth generation of David Trimble and —— Houston.) Married David Lynn, an architect at the Capitol in Washington, D.C.

The children of David Lynn and Margaret Allen Trimble:
D1313—David Lynn.
D1314—South Trimble Lynn.
D1315—Margaret Lynn.
D1316—Acheson Lynn.

D875—South Trimble, Jr. Son of South Trimble and Carrie Belle Allen. (Sixth generation of David Trimble and —— Houston.) Married Elaine Lazaro, a daughter of a Louisiana congressman. South is an attorney-at-law in Washington, D.C.

The children of South Trimble, Jr. and Elaine Lazaro:
D1317—Elaine Trimble.
D1318—South Trimble, III.
D1319—Mary Trimble.
D1320—Stephen Asbury Trimble.
D1321—James Trimble.

D876—Frances Marie Trimble. Daughter of South Trimble and Carrie Belle Allen. (Sixth generation of David Trimble and —— Houston.) Married A. C. Wallace, a banker.

The children of A. C. Wallace and Frances Marie Trimble:
D1322—John Wallace. Born in Chevy Chase, Maryland.
D1323—Mary Wallace. Born in Chevy Chase, Maryland.
D1324—Carrie Belle Wallace. Born in Chevy Chase, Maryland.

D877—Carl Mize. Son of William O. Mize and Lou Ellen Cockrell. (Sixth generation of David Trimble and —— Houston.) Married Carrie Rose.

The children of Carl Mize and Carrie Rose:
D1325—Miriam Elizabeth Mize.
D1326—Oldham Mize.

D885—Thomas Franklin Trimble. Son of Josiah Anderson Trimble and Betty Pendleton. (Sixth generation of David Trimble and —— Houston.) Born on February 4, 1873 and died November 20, 1934. He is buried at Winchester, Kentucky. On October 16, 1896, he married Nancy Dolly Sewell, born on January 16, 1880. Thomas was a wholesale grocer and attended the Disciples of Christ church.

The children of Thomas Franklin Trimble and Nancy Dolly Sewell:

D1327—Mona Marsden Trimble. Born on July 13, 1897, and died October 16, 1966, at Winchester, Kentucky.

+ **D1328—Martha Newell Trimble.** Born on December 2, 1899.

D1329—Elizabeth Trimble. Born on September 4, 1905, at Mount Sterling, Kentucky.

D1330—Joseph Sewell Trimble. Born on July 19, 1908, in Clark County, Kentucky, and died June 12, 1920.

+ **D1331—Nancye Bush Trimble.** Born in 1915.

D886—Mary Beulah Trimble. Daughter of Josiah Anderson Trimble and Betty Pendleton. (Sixth generation of David Trimble and ——— Houston.) Born on January 3, 1875 and died on November 22, 1880, at the age of five years.

D888—Lillian Trimble. Daughter of Josiah Anderson Trimble and Betty Pendleton. (Sixth generation of David Trimble and ——— Houston.) Born on December 31, 1879. Married Dr. David H. Bush on June 14, 1903. They were married at Newport, Kentucky. Her husband, Dr. Bush, was a medical doctor at Mount Sterling, Kentucky, and died on November 7, 1958.

The three children of Dr David H. Bush and Lillian Trimble:

D1332—Lucille Bush. Born on July 26, 1904. She never married. Lucille is a well-educated, learned, and genteel lady who oversaw the music department at a private academy in Massachusetts.

+ **D1333—Joe Milbert Bush.** Born on December 17, 1905. On December 18, 1937, he married Martha Frances Bogie. Joe is a physician still practicing at Mount Sterling, Kentucky. He lives at the beautiful old home place on the outskirts of Mount Sterling.

+ **D1334—Bessie Mae Bush.** Born on March 27,1909. Lillian Bush, still living in 1971, furnished the author the information on her line of the Trimble family as he visited in her home at Mount Sterling. Mrs. Bush and the author are cousins. It is remarkable that at the advanced age of ninety-two Mrs. Bush remains a vivacious, alert, and genteel lady. She still ran her various farms and several rental buildings in Mount Sterling from her wheelchair with the use of the telephone.

D889—Jesse Pendleton Trimble. Son of Josiah Anderson Trimble and Betty Pendleton. (Sixth generation of David Trimble and ——— Houston.) Born on April 19, 1887 and died January 14, 1964. Married Anna Mae McCourt on February 3, 1894. He was a certified public accountant at Louisville, Kentucky. Jesse is buried at Winchester Cemetery.

Trimble Families of America

The children of Jesse Pendleton Trimble and Anna Mae McCourt:

D1335—James Joseph Trimble. Born on November 17, 1919. Married Mary Jo Gonyer on April 14, 1945, at San Antonio, Texas. They now live in Orlando, Florida. They have a son, Thomas Trimble.

D1336—John Pendleton Trimble. Born on March 29, 1924. Married Doris Mae Stauble of Louisville, Kentucky, on October 7, 1961.

D896—Mary Beulah Trimble. Daughter of Algin Trimble and Emma Johnson. (Sixth generation of David Trimble and —— Houston.) Born on March 29, 1888 in Mount Sterling, Kentucky and died on February 6, 1968. She is buried at Machpelah Cemetery in Mount Sterling. Married Virgil Donahue of Ironton, Ohio, on December 5, 1904.

The children of Virgil Donahue and Mary Beulah Trimble:

+ **D1337—Eula Mae Donahue.** Born on December 5, 1905. Married Verna Lee Hayes.

+ **D1338—Bertha Ray Donahue.** Born in 1909. Married John R. Tipton on March 25, 1930.

D897—Harriett Newell Trimble. Daughter of Algin Trimble and Emma Johnson. (Sixth generation of David Trimble and —— Houston.) Born on May 8, 1900 at Johnson Station, Kentucky. Married Sydney A. Ensor on May 1, 1917.

The children of Sydney A. Ensor and Harriett Newell Trimble:

D1339—Emma Elizabeth Ensor. Born on November 7, 1918. Married Reuben McLain.

D1340—Pauline Grace Ensor. Born on December 27, 1919. Married Herschel Moore.

D1341—Elnora Ensor. Born on May 27, 1922. Married Ernest Profitt.

D1342—Roberta Arle Ensor. Born on October 14, 1924. She married two times: first, to Calvin Norris, and second, to Bill Hicks.

D1343—Sydney A. Ensor, Jr. Born on April 12, 1927. Married Juanita Henry.

D1344—Adali Earl Ensor. Born on April 15, 1931. Married Peggy at Cincinnati, Ohio.

D1345—Donald Ray Ensor. Born on September 17, 1933. Married Ann Otis.

D1346—Harold Clay Ensor. Born on September 17, 1933. Married Evelyn Greenwade.

D898—Josephine T. Trimble. Daughter of Algin Trimble and Emma Johnson. (Sixth generation of David Trimble and —— Houston.) Born on March 2, 1903. Married Ellis Clay Collins on April 27, 1921, at Mount Sterling,

Kentucky. Josephine was a saleslady and lived in Dayton, Ohio. Ellis died on January 20, 1952.

The children of Ellis Clay Collins and Josephine T. Trimble:

D1347—Herman Cecil Collins. Born on May 27, 1922, died January 29, 1942.

D1348—Thelma Katherine Collins. Born on March 16, 1925. Married John D. Manning on August 22, 1952. They have one child.

D1349—Evelyn Grace Collins. Born on August 3, 1927. Married Paul Eubanks on December 18, 1948.

D1350—Paul Allen Collins. Born on June 20, 1932. Married Elizabeth Skidmore on July 18, 1956. They have one child.

D1351—Edna Ruth Collins. Born on September 18, 1934. Married Kenneth Blauvelt on May 25, 1957. They have four children.

D902—Bessie Williams. Daughter of Elijah Clay Williams and Harriet Newell Trimble. (Sixth generation of David Trimble and —— Houston.) Born on August 22, 1888. Married Manuel Salyer on November 31, 1910, at Volga, Kentucky.

The children of Manuel Salyer and Bessie Williams:

D1352—John M. Salyer. Born on October 25, 1911. Married Nancy Kennedy of Denver, Colorado.

D1353—C. Woodrow Salyer. Born on December 31, 1913, and died on November 8, 1930, at Louisa, Kentucky.

D1354—Hetty M. Salyer. Born on November 12, 1917. Married a Mr. Gregory on September 4, 1936. He is from New York.

D1355—Paul M. Salyer. Born on July 12, 1922. Married Betty Hinkle of Franklin, Tennessee.

D903—Dora Clay Williams. Daughter of Elijah Clay Williams and Harriet Newell Trimble. (Sixth generation of David Trimble and —— Houston.) Born on November 25, 1889 and died on August 22, 1960. She is buried at Machpelah Cemetery, Mount Sterling, Kentucky. Married Ballard Floyd Stafford on January 6, 1910.

The children of Ballard Floyd Stafford and Dora Clay Williams:

D1356—Neva Clay Stafford. Born on September 22, 1910. Married J. R. Lykins on April 14, 1934.

D1357—Mary Edith Stafford. Born on April 20, 1913. Married O. M. Patrick on June 25, 1937.

D1358—Blanche Stafford. Born on December 5, 1914. Married Charles L. Smith of Michigan on May 17, 1947.

D1359—Robert Trimble Stafford. Born on March 20, 1917, died July 28, 1967. Married Myrtle Gullett on January 4, 1937.

D1360—Mergie Elizabeth Stafford. Born on January 16, 1918. Married Forest Kirkpatrick on October 28, 1939.

D1361—Mable Marie Stafford. Born on June 17, 1922. Married Frank LaVielle.

D1362—Ballar Floyd Stafford, Jr. Born on February 10, 1928. Married Joyce Martin on December 29, 1961.

D904—Blanche Newell Williams. Daughter of Elijah Clay Williams and Harriet Newell Trimble. (Sixth generation of David Trimble and —— Houston.) Born on April 17, 1891. Married Floyd Ballard Halsey on January 6, 1910.

The children of Floyd Ballard Halsey and Blanche Newell Williams:

D1363—Jesse Letcher Halsey. Born on January 4, 1911, and died on February 28, 1964, at Decatur, Illinois. Married Evelyn Lucille Walls on April 15, 1932.

D1364—Floyd Russell Halsey. Born on August 30, 1912. Married Anna Faulker of Maryland in April 1944.

D1365—Lucille Halsey. Born on April 15, 1915. Married Barnell E. Roberts on March 10, 1934.

D1366—Raymond E. Halsey. Born on July 23, 1922, and died on May 23, 1943, at Corpus Christi, Texas.

D1367—Eddie Carroll Halsey. Born on December 3, 1930. Married Wanda Lee Carroll of Indiana on March 16, 1949.

D906—Mary Elizabeth Trimble. Daughter of John Harrison Trimble and Charity Caster. (Sixth generation of David Trimble and —— Houston.) Born on July 22, 1879 and died on February 24, 1966. Married Zenophon Hopkins.

The children of Zenophon Hopkins and Mary Elizabeth Trimble:

D1368—Dorothy Frances Hopkins. (Adopted.) Born on June 19, 1911 and died on January 29, 1946.

D1369—Wilne Louise Hopkins. Born on April 28, 1915. Died in infancy.

+**D1370—John Isaac Hopkins.** Born on December 15, 1918. Married Lucille Quig, and lives at Mace, Indiana. He is a carpenter by trade.

D907—Roy Caster Trimble. Son of John Harrison Trimble and Charity Caster. (Sixth generation of David Trimble and —— Houston.) Born on July 7, 1882. Married Mary Potts on December 22, 1905. He was in the wholesale nursery business and is now in a Crawfordsville nursing home where the author visited him in 1970.

The children of Roy Caster Trimble and Mary Potts:

+ **D1371—Raymond Edward Trimble.** Born on October 19, 1906. Married Grace Abbey of England.

+ **D1372—Hazel Marie Trimble.** Born in 1908.

+ **D1373—Owen Leroy Trimble.** Born on June 11, 1912. Married Margaret Brown and they live at New Market, Indiana.

+ **D1374—Helen May Trimble.** Born on December 16, 1915. Married Wendell Simpson on May 15, 1937. They live at New Market, Indiana.

 D1375—Byron Eugene Trimble. Born on October 19, 1926. He died at birth.

D908—John Sherman Trimble. Son of John Harrison Trimble and Charity Caster. (Sixth generation of David Trimble and —— Houston.) Born in 1884 and died in 1929. Married Mary Mulligan.

The children of John Sherman Trimble and Mary Mulligan:

+ **D1376—Robert Trimble.** Born on October 19, 1916. Married Martha Shannon on May 21, 1949.

 D1377—Stanley Trimble. Born on September 28, 1918. Married Lela Hester. Stanley is a farmer. They live near Linnsburg, Indiana. They have no children.

D914—William Trimble. Son of Leander Trimble and Margaret Whitman. (Sixth generation of David Trimble and —— Houston.) Born on June 13, 1880 and died on August 9, 1955. William married two times: first, to Runa Groves, and second, to Cleo Groves.

The children of William Trimble and Cleo Groves:

 D1378—Dessie Trimble. Married a Mr. Neff.

+ **D1379—Thelma Trimble.** Married a Mr. Skaggs.

 D1380—Bonnie Trimble. Married a Mr. Spencer.

D916—Worth Trimble. Son of Leander Trimble and Margaret Whitman. (Sixth generation of David Trimble and —— Houston.) Born on December 8, 1885. Worth married two times: first, to Gertrude Vance, and second, to Bessie Bays. Worth, whom the author knew well, lived in Richwood, West Virginia, and was a prosperous businessman. In later years, Worth and his family moved to Coral Gables, Florida. His two living children also moved to Florida. Worth and Gertrude Vance married on April 11, 1906, and she died April 8, 1950. He married Bessie Bays in his later years, they had no children. Bessie died in 1969.

The children of Worth Trimble and Gertrude Vance:

Trimble Families of America

D1381—**Helen Trimble.** Married a Mr. Smith of Richwood, West Virginia. They owned a dry-cleaning plant. Helen died during the birth of her first child. Helen was an exceptionally beautiful lady.

+ D1382—**Vance Trimble.** Married Gwen O'Dell. He now lives in Florida.

+ D1383—**Jean Trimble.** Married Warren Sefton of Richwood, West Virginia.

D1384—**Gerald Vance Trimble.** Born on 1912 and died in Charleston, West Virginia. No children.

D917—**Lola Ann Trimble.** Daughter of Leander Trimble and Margaret Whitman. (Sixth generation of David Trimble and —— Houston.) Born on December 28, 1889 and died on April 8, 1950. Married Rush Hereford Groves of Nettie, West Virginia, on April 11, 1906.

The children of Rush Hereford Groves and Lola Ann Trimble:

+ D1385—**Russie Gay Groves.** Married two times: first, to Delbert Groves, and second, to William Rader.

D1386—**Eskel Fay Groves.** Married Laura Cartwright.

D1387—**Alma Irene Groves.** Married W. W. Taylor.

D918—**Okey Ulysses "Les" Trimble.** Son of Leander Trimble and Margaret Whitman. (Sixth generation of David Trimble and —— Houston.) Born on October 10, 1891 and died on November 26, 1960. Married Lela V. Brown.

The children of Okey Ulysses "Les" Trimble and Lela V. Brown:

D1388—**Fred Okey Trimble.** Married Penny Gore.

D1389—**Oran Ralph Trimble.** Married Harriet Hanna.

D1390—**Ovid Leroy Trimble.** Married Sarah Kellam.

D1391—**Agnes Marie Trimble.** Married Jack W. Smith.

D919—**Bessie Lee Trimble.** Daughter of Leander Trimble and Margaret Whitman. (Sixth generation of David Trimble and —— Houston.) Born on September 13, 1894. Married Volley Andrew Bailes on June 15, 1913. Volley died on June 15, 1954. The author can remember Aunt Bessie visiting in his home when he was a child.

The children of Volley Andrew Bailes and Bessie Lee Trimble:

+ D1392—**Gladys Virginia Bailes.** Married two times: first, to Lewis M. Power, and second, to Charles Fisher.

+ D1393—**Okey Lester Bailes.** Born on March 14, 1918. Married Leona Mary Malouse on October 15, 1943. Okey is an enthusiastic genealogist. He has devoted much of his life to the research and study of family history. His relentless interest and contribution of material to this author is greatly appreciated. Okey has two years of college and armed force duty of five years in World War II and two years in the Korean Conflict. Okey lives at 1808 E. 7th Street, Parkersburg, West Virginia 26101.

D1394—Audrey Grace Bailes. Married John T. Allen.

D920—Edward A. Trimble. Son of Leander Trimble and Margaret Whitman. (Sixth generation of David Trimble and ——— Houston.) Born on March 27, 1897. Married Pearl Groves. Edward worked for a while in the author's half-brother's barbershop at Richwood, West Virginia. He worked for Ray Trimble. Edward was a large man in stature and very handsome.

The child of Edward A. Trimble and Pearl Groves:
D1395—Margaret Trimble.

D921—Allen S. Trimble. Son of Leander Trimble and Margaret Whitman. (Sixth generation of David Trimble and ——— Houston.) Born on August 27, 1900. Married Grace Griffey.

The children of Allen S. Trimble and Grace Griffey:
D1396—Charles Lee Trimble. Died on June 20, 1947. Married Helen Brooks.
D1397—Helen Trimble.
D1398—Mildred Trimble.
D1399—Evelyn Trimble.

D923—Ray Trimble. Son of Frank Trimble and Barbara Lucy Wright. (Sixth generation of David Trimble and ——— Houston.) Born on December 23, 1893 and died in 1960. Ray married two times: first, on August 12, 1918, to Lou Marsh from Walkersville, West Virginia, and second, to Dorothy Gibson of Richwood, West Virginia.

The children of Ray Trimble and Lou Marsh:
+ **D1400—Gailord Washington Trimble.** Born on September 13, 1920, at Tioga, West Virginia. Married Mondene McClung of Nallen, West Virginia, where they now live. They were married on December 14, 1945. They have a son, Donald Wayne Trimble.
D1401—Mary Venell Trimble. Born on April 24, 1923. She never married. Mary has managed, for several years, a motel at Craigsville, West Virginia.
D1402—John Ray Trimble. Born on February 11, 1925. Married Eneberg McMillion on January 25, 1951. He has two children (stepchildren): Rickey and Sharon. This family lives at Richwood, West Virginia.

D - David Trimble

+ D1403—Betty Jean Trimble. Born on January 22, 1929. Married Clyde Perkins on May 4, 1952.

D925—Marion Everette Trimble. Son of Frank Trimble and Barbara Lucy Wright. (Sixth generation of David Trimble and —— Houston.) Born in 1900 and died in March 1967. Married Belle George in 1927. Everette lived all his life in Nicholas County, West Virginia, He was the author's half-brother. In describing my brother's attributes, the one word "Goodness" would seem to best suffice.

The children of Everette Trimble and Belle George:

+ D1404—Arthur Lee Trimble. Born in August 1933 at Birch River, West Virginia. Married Elizabeth Dyer of Hookersville, West Virginia. They live in Kent, Ohio.

D1405—Marion Everette Trimble, Jr. Born on March 22, 1937, at Craigsville, West Virginia. Married Catherine Woods.

D926—John Farley Trimble. Son of Frank Trimble and Arabella Collins. (Sixth generation of David Trimble and —— Houston.) Born on April 17, 1913 in Beaver, Nicholas County, West Virginia and died on October 15, 1982 in Summersville, Nicholas County, West Virginia. Married two times: first, on August 17, 1935, to Vernice Copeland, born on March 26, 1908, and second, to Annetta Cooper Wentz, born on March 9, 1937. They were married October 10, 1970, in Indiana. Vernice Copeland Trimble, first wife of J. F. Trimble, was a woman of high moral and religious principles. She was an educated woman and had a profound influence on the rearing of their two sons in the instilling of these moral values. The author wishes to give acknowledgment of her help in the early years of research for the book.

John Farley Trimble graduated from Webster Springs High School in 1931 and attended Fairmont State College in Fairmont, West Virginia. For a brief time, he taught school but found his interests too varied for the confinement of the classroom. He has been successful in various fields of selling. John has been director of sales for several land companies with his offices based in New York, Chicago, Columbus, Ohio, and Washington, D.C. For several years he was in business for himself, principally automobile dealerships. For the past several years, when the "genealogy bug" bit and he began research for the book, all other business took a secondary role. When the book is completed, John Farley plans to retire in his native home of Nicholas County, West Virginia. His home is in Summersville, West Virginia. John Farley married the second time to Annetta Cooper Wentz,

Born on March 9, 1937, whom he had known since she was a child. She is the daughter of the Reverend and Mrs. L. B. Cooper of Summersville. John Farley and Annetta had a child who died prematurely, however, she has a son by a former marriage, Eugene Earl Wentz II, born on June 24, 1957. Annetta attended West Virginia Institute of Technology, Montgomery, West Virginia, and Alderson-Broaddus College, Philippi, West Virginia, and taught school in Pittsburgh, Pennsylvania, and in West Virginia. The research and compiling of a genealogy requires so much patience that without the aid and persistence of my wife, Annetta Trimble, this book might never have been published.

The children of John Farley Trimble and Vernice Copeland:

+ **D1406—Maurice Copeland Trimble.** Born on July 12, 1936. Married Mary Ursula

+ **D1407—Michael Anthony Trimble.** Born on February 16, 1942, at Richwood, West Virginia. Married on March 24, 1967, at Crab Orchard, West Virginia, to Loretta Lively.

D927—James Walter Trimble. Son of Frank Trimble and Arabella Collins. (Sixth generation of David Trimble and ——— Houston.) Born on February 28, 1928, at Richwood, West Virginia. Married Winojean Erwin on April 22, 1948, at Radford, Virginia. Jean was born on January 19, 1932. James and his family live at Meadowlark Drive, Portage, Indiana. He is a supervisor at a firebrick making plant in Gary, Indiana, and Winojean is head bookkeeper for Bosak Car Agency of Gary. Both are devout Christians in the Portage Baptist Church and believe that all we have has come from God and should be returned to Him and His work. The James Trimble home bustles with discipline, activity, respect for one another, and deep love and concern for mankind. During mealtime prayer one can hear the heartwarming petition to God for those in need. These valuable teachings of James and Jean Trimble have greatly affected their two lovely daughters, Judith Estelle and Shelley Lynn. Judith has been on the Bible Quiz Team of the Youth for Christ at her church and Shelley is a children's choir pianist and director at the church. The strongest characteristic that the author sees in his brother James Walter is that which he saw in his father, his integrity.

The children of James Walter Trimble and Winojean Erwin:

D1408—Judith Estelle Trimble. Born in May 1950. Judy graduated from the University of Indiana in May 1972 with honors. She has a B.S. in business administration. She is employed by the Bosak Motor Company of Gary,

Indiana, as head of the leasing department.

D1409—Shelley Lynn Trimble. Born on January 5, 1956. Shelley is a student at Portage High School, Portage, Indiana, where she is a member of the high school band.

D929—John Andrew Carney. Son of John L. Carney and Sarah Jane Trimble. (Sixth generation of David Trimble and —— Houston.) Born on March 7, 1895 in Pulaski County, Kentucky and died on March 16, 1964 in Cottonwood County, Minnesota. Married Lena Jessie Pratt. She was born on June 22, 1896 in Minnesota and died on March 7, 1987 in Jackson County, Minnesota.

The children of John Andrew Carney and Lena Jessie Pratt:

D1410—John F. Carney. Born about 1918 in Cottonwood County, Minnesota and died June 8, 1987 in Eufaula, Barbour County, Alabama. Married Magdalene Clara Olson on September 22, 1940.

D1411—Ruth E. Carney. Born about 1920 in Cottonwood County, Minnesota.

D930—Emma Mae Trimble. Daughter of Walter Ulysses Trimble and Mary Cobb. (Sixth generation of David Trimble and —— Houston.) Born on July 31, 1900, in Bonham, Texas and died on January 3, 1965, at Durant. Married Henry Bryan Metcalf

Their children of Henry Bryan Metcalf and Emma Mae Trimble:

+**D1412—Emma Jean Metcalf.** Born on March 16, 1921, at Durant, Oklahoma. Married Raymond R. Sirkle on September 22, 1939, at Oklahoma City.

+**D1413—Mary Katherine Metcalf.** Born on September 27, 1923, at Durant, Oklahoma. Married O. A. Benovsky on September 4, 1948, in Dallas, Texas.

D931—Mary Jane Taylor. Daughter of Edward Robert Taylor and Elizabeth Lee Floyd. (Sixth generation of David Trimble and —— Houston.) Born on April 13, 1867 in Pulaski County, Kentucky and died on January 6, 1906 in Sumner, Garfield County, Oklahoma. Married twice. Married first to John Crittendon Lee on October 9, 1883 1861 in Pulaski County, Kentucky. He was born on November 27, 1861 in Pulaski County, Kentucky and died on November 9, 1892 in Burnsides, Pulaski County, Kentucky.

Married second to Robert D. Davis about in 1895 in Perry, Oklahoma Territory. Robert was born on August 22, 1855 in Somerset, Pulaski County, Kentucky and died on March 21, 1920 in Sumner, Noble County, Oklahoma. They raised Robert's children from a previous marriage: Halick,

Baxter, Alice, Walter, Liss, and George.

The children of John Crittendon Lee and Mary Jane Taylor:

D1414–Martha Belle Lee. Born on January 10, 1886 in Burnside, Pulaski County, Kentucky and died on November 26, 1981 in Chickasha, Grady County, Oklahoma.

D1415–Mary Margaret Lee. Born on February 5, 1888 in Kentucky and died on November 9, 1980 in Nebraska.

D1416–Eva Carolina Lee. Born on August 1890 in Kentucky and died on October 12, 1950.

D1417–Johnny Lee. Born in 1891 in Kentucky and died in 1891 as an infant.

The children of Robert D. Davis and Mary Jane Taylor:

D1418–Gertrude Opal Davis. Born on March 5, 1896 in Noble County, Oklahoma and died on August 16, 1981 in Concord, Contra Costa County, Oklahoma.

D1419–Gustie Davis. Born on March 1897 in Oklahoma.

D1420–Edna Ola Davis. Born on February 4, 1898 in Noble County, Oklahoma and died in November 1983 in Clear Lake, Lake County, California.

D1421–Norman Ophas Davis. Born on March 7, 1901 in Noble County, Oklahoma and died January 12, 1991 in Alameda County, California.

D1422–Robert D. Davis. Born on January 23, 1903 in Noble County, Oklahoma and died on January 25, 1903 in Sumner, Noble County, Oklahoma.

D932–James William Taylor. Daughter of Edward Robert Taylor and Elizabeth Lee Floyd. (Sixth generation of David Trimble and —— Houston.) Born on December 10, 1868 in Overton, Tennessee and died on November 6, 1948 in Dayton, Oregon. Married Laverna Carolina Dee Kerr on April 8, 1895 in Whitewright, Texas. Laverna was born on January 15, 1874 in Putnam, Tennessee and died September 20, 1964 in Oregon.

The children of James William Taylor and Laverna Carolina Dee Kerr:

D1423–Mallie Ruth Taylor. Born on January 29, 1897 in Whitewright, Texas and died on July 3, 1967 in Multnomah, Portland, Oregon. Married Newton Otis Miller.

D1424–Grace Ila Taylor. Born on August 10, 1901 in Pawnee, Oklahoma, and died on November 18, 1958 in Wheatland, Marion, Oregon. Married Worth Oscar Wiley.

D1425–Robert Henry Taylor. Born on March 12, 1904 in Bonham, Fannin

County, Texas and died in March 1977 in Oregon.

D1426—Allie Mae Taylor. Born about 1908 in Texas.

D1427—Willetta Maxine Taylor. Born on July 29, 1912 in Whiteson, Oregon and died July 12, 1956 in Dallas, Collin County, Texas.

D933—John Franklin Taylor. Daughter of Edward Robert Taylor and Elizabeth Lee Floyd. (Sixth generation of David Trimble and —— Houston.) Born on February 26, 1871 in Pulaski County, Kentucky and died April 10, 1937 in Centralia, Lewis County, Washington.[65] Married Emma Etta Allen on November 22, 1900 in Perry, Oklahoma. Emma was born on November 2, 1878 in Manhattan, Riley County, Kansas and died on August 8, 1977 in Centralia, Lewis County, Washington.

The children of John Franklin Taylor and Emma Etta Allen:

D1428—Dow Mitchel Taylor. Born on September 12, 1901 in Perry, Oklahoma Territory and died in February 1974 in Springfield, Lane County, Oregon.

D1429—Maynard F. Taylor. Born about 1903 in Okmulgee, Oklahoma and died on June 12, 1930 in Centralia, Lewis County, Washington. Married Edna Marie Shepherd in 1926.

D1430—Leland Taylor. Born in 1905 in Okmulgee, Native Americans Territory, Oklahoma and died in 1905 in Okmulgee, Native Americans Territory, Oklahoma as an infant.

D1431—Edith Julia Taylor. Born on December 22, 1906 in Chehalis, Lewis County, Washington and died on July 24, 1977 in Centralia, Lewis County, Washington. Married I. L. Linscott in 1924.

D1432—Orville Taylor. Born on November 7, 1911 in Centralia, Lewis County, Washington and died in December 1971 in Centralia, Lewis County, Washington. Married Henrietta M. Walker in 1932

D1433—Clyde Asahel Taylor. Born about 1912.

D946—Edward James Ogilvie. Son of James A. Ogilvie and Camilla Stuart Robeson. (Seventh generation of David Trimble and —— Houston.) Born on April 29, 1875 in Carthage, Hancock County, Illinois and died on January 25, 1940 in Carthage, Hancock County, Illinois. Married Mary Grace Wright.

Mary was born on February 8, 1875 in Carthage, Hancock County, Illinois and died in December 1964.

---

[65] Washington, Death Certificates, 1907-1960. Salt Lake City, Utah: FamilySearch, 2013.

The children of Edward James Ogilvie and Mary Grace Wright:

+ **D1434—Ralph Wright Ogilvie.** Born on December 23, 1893 in Hancock, Illinois and died on May 11, 1961. Married Jessie E. Thompson.

D1435—Dorothy Margaret Ogilvie. Born on November 5, 1917 in Illinois and died on January 29, 2007 in Harrisonville, Cass County, Missouri. Married Donald Francis Ellis on September 14, 1946 in Kansas City, Jackson County, Missouri. Donald was born on August 22, 1924 in Trenton, Grundy County, Missouri and died on November 3, 2004 in Harrisonville, Cass County, Missouri.

D1436—Ethel Dell Ogilvie. Born on January 25, 1896 in Carthage, Hancock County, Illinois and died in April 1985 in Harrisonville, Cass County, Missouri. She owned a Beauty Parlor.

D1437—Charles Ogilvie. Born on November 21, 1899 in Illinois and died on September 27, 1981 in Harrisonville, Cass County, Missouri. Married Gertrude Cecelia Flynn.

D953—Worley Clifford Trimble. Son of Clifford C. Trimble and Alice E. Dalton. (Seventh generation of David Trimble and —— Houston.) Born in July 1885 in Iowa and died in 1949. Married Iva Pearl Sly, she was born in 1886 in Nebraska and died in 1970 in Chilliwack, Nebraska.

The children of Worley Clifford Trimble and Iva Pearl Sly:

D1438—Ruth Leona Trimble. Born on August 5, 1905 in Nebraska and died on September 30, 1988 in Chilliwack, British Columbia.

D971—Margaret Louise Bonnett. Daughter of Everard Earl Bonnett and Agnes A. Beum. (Seventh generation of David Trimble and —— Houston.) Born on November 5, 1910 in Danville, Knox County, Ohio and died on October 27, 2001 in Ashley, Delaware County, Ohio. Married George Cecil Ireland in 1928. George was born on June 19, 1892 in East Tawas, Iosco County, Michigan and died on December 9, 1962 in Morrow, Morrow County, Ohio.

The children of George Cecil Ireland and Margaret Louise Bonnette:

D1439—George E. Ireland. Born on September 4, 1929 in Delaware County, Ohio and died on April 29, 1986 in Tampa, Hillsborough County, Florida.

D1440—Donald E. Ireland. Born on July 29, 1931 in Marengo, Morrow County, Ohio and died on February 10, 2001 in Van Wert, Van Wert County, Ohio

D1441—Richard Thomas Ireland. Born on October 16, 1932 in Marengo County, Ohio and died on January 20, 1992.

D1442—Dr. Robert Lawrence Ireland. Born on February 1, 1936 in Marion

Trimble Families of America

County, Ohio and died on October 12, 2004 in Tucson, Pima County, Arizona.[66]

D981—Laura Margaret Miranda Porter. Daughter of Michael R. Porter and Mary Elizabeth Engle. (Seventh generation of David Trimble and ——— Houston.) Born in September 1881 in Eckhart, Allegany County, Maryland and died about 1965 in Eckhart, Allegany County, Maryland. Married George R. Ryan on June 20, 1900. George was born about 1881 in West Virginia.

The children of George R. Ryan and Laura Margaret Miranda Porter:

> **D1443—Myrtle G. Ryan.** Born on June 5, 1904 in Eckhart Mines, Allegany County, Maryland and died on December 19, 2001 in Frostburg, Allegany County, Maryland. Married Charles E. Porter before 1928. Charles was born on April 21, 1902 in Maryland and died on August 30, 1963.

> **D1444—Robert Ryan.** Born on January 26, 1907 in Maryland and died May 1969.

> **D1445—Viva Ryan.** Born about 1911 in Maryland and died on December 19, 2001.

> **D1446—Russell W. Ryan.** Born on October 15, 1917 in Maryland and died October 23, 1990.

D991—Eula Dee Powell. Daughter of Charles Powell and Teresa Black. (Seventh generation of David Trimble and ——— Houston.) Born on January 2, 1909 in Jenkinsville, Washington County Kentucky and died on July 1, 2002 in Greenwood, Clark County, Wisconsin. Married twice.

Married Earnest Harlow. He was born on June 19, 1904 in Willisburg, Kentucky and died on February 25, 1931 in DeKalb, DeKalb County, Illinois.

The children of Earnest Harlow and Eula Dee Powel:

> **+ D1447—John B. "Buddy" Harlow.** Born on May 31, 1927 and died April 10, 2008 in Menomonee Falls, Waukesha County, Wisconsin. Married unnamed.

D997—Thelma Pauline Cooper. Daughter of Henry Shaw Cooper and Letha Lee Laughlin. (Seventh generation of David Trimble and ——— Houston.) Born on November 16, 1912 in Kansas and died on September 19, 1981 in

---

[66] Ohio Birth Records. Columbus, Ohio: Ohio Vital Records Office.

Dexter, Penobscot County, Maine. She married twice. Married Russell Francis Forbes. He was born on September 18, 1910 in Marshallville, Illinois and died on November 23, 1995 in Wichita, Sedgwick County, Kansas. Married Albion Keeler Smith about October 1951. Al was born on March 23, 1901 in Westerly, Rhode Island and died on August 9, 1981 in Dexter, Penobscot County, Maine.

The children of Russell Francis Forbes and Thelma Pauline Cooper:

D1448—Rose Mary Forbes. Born on October 17, 1929 in Kansas and died on November 20, 2002 in Wichita, Kansas.

D1449—Betty Ruth Forbes.

D1450—William Forbes. Born on January 27, 1932 in Wichita, Kansas and died on August 20, 1992 in Wichita, Kansas.

D1451—Charlotte Carole Forbes. Born on November 29, 1933 in Wichita, Kansas and died on February 22, 2007 in Jackson, Jackson County, Michigan.

D1452—Clifford Melvin Forbes. Born on June 29, 1935 in Kansas and died on September 30, 2003 in Seymore, Jackson County, Indiana.

D1453—Thdone P. Forbes.

D1001—Sula Trimble. Daughter of Clark Trimble and Allie Pelphrey. (Seventh generation of David Trimble and ——— Houston.) Married to William E. Ivey. The lived at 3304 Arch Wood, Cleveland, Ohio.

The child of William E. Ivey and Sula Trimble:

D1454—Mary Esther Ivey. Married and has a son.

D1005—Iva Trimble. Daughter of Carl Trimble and Laura Picklesimer. (Seventh generation of David Trimble and ——— Houston.) Born on May 14, 1892, and married Ernest Hall, born on November 5, 1892. They live at 1025 North Emerson Avenue, Indianapolis, Indiana 46219.

The children of Ernest Hall and Iva Trimble:

+ D1455—Henry Carl Hall. Born on March 25, 1919. He married Martha Elson on November 28, 1946. Henry was a Baptist minister. His address was Box 138, Gladwin, Michigan.

D1456—Alois Hall. Born on March 2, 1920 and died on March 31, 1923 as a small child.

D1006—Ova Trimble. Daughter of Carl Trimble and Laura Picklesimer. (Seventh generation of David Trimble and ——— Houston.) Born on November 3, 1893. Married Arthur Welch, born on August 4, 1894, and

Trimble Families of America

died on August 31, 1965. They lived at 124 S. Willow Avenue, Sugar Creek, Missouri.

The children of Arthur Welch and Ova Trimble:

+ **D1457—James Carl Welch.** Born on January 12, 1920. Married Delcie Webb and they live at 14705 E. 39th Street, Independence, Missouri.

+ **D1458—Arthur Welch, Jr.** Born on February 27, 1925. Married Mary Ann ———. They live in Kearney, Missouri.

+ **D1459—Betty Welch.** Born on March 7, 1930. Married Gregg Tindall. They live at 2607 Scott, Independence, Missouri.

+ **D1460—Bobby Clay Welch.** Born on August 14, 1933. Married Ellen Duncan. Bobby is a lawyer in Sugar Creek, Missouri.

D1011—Rucker Jim Trimble. Son of Carl Trimble and Laura Picklesimer. (Seventh generation of David Trimble and ——— Houston.) Born on April 22, 1911. Married Iva Centers, born on August 23, 1914. They were married on April 15, 1933, and live at Route 2, Mount Sterling, Kentucky.

The children of Rucker Jim Trimble and Iva Centers:

+ **D1461—Janet Trimble.** Born on July 28, 1935, and married Eugene Spencer. They live on Route 2, Mount Sterling, Kentucky.

+ **D1462—Ewell Lee Trimble.** Born on November 28, 1936. Married Effa D. Hutison.

+ **D1463—DeLaura Jean Trimble.** Born on March 17, 1938. Married James Stiltner and they live at Frenchburg, Kentucky.

D1464—Charley Wayne Trimble. Born on August 30, 1939. He is not married.

D1012—Paris Nelson Trimble. Son of Carl Trimble and Laura Picklesimer. (Seventh generation of David Trimble and ——— Houston.) Born on December 5, 1913. Married Olive Davis Sparks and they live at Route 6, Box 241, Bloomington, Indiana.

The children of Paris Nelson Trimble and Olive Davis Sparks:

D1465—Dianna Trimble. Married Joe Stanger. They live at Bloomington, Indiana.

D1466—Phillip Ray Trimble. He lives on River Avenue, Indianapolis, Indiana.

D1467—Linda Trimble. Married Ellis George. They live at Road 46, Bloomington, Indiana.

D1468—Larry Dale Trimble. Deceased.

D1013—Sterling Sidney Trimble. Son of Carl Trimble and Laura Picklesimer. (Seventh generation of David Trimble and ——— Houston.) Born on

November 18, 1916. Sterling married two times. Married first to Alice Parker. They were divorced. Married second to Barbara Davis.

The children of Sterling Sidney Trimble and Alice Parker:

+ **D1469—Ronald Kent Trimble.** Married Jean Quillan.

+ **D1470—Michael Carl Trimble.** Married Sherlyn —— They live at Route 3, Spencer, Indiana.

+ **D1471—David Lee Trimble.** Married Sharon ——. They have a stock sales company at Cloverdale, Indiana.

D1472—Gary Trimble. He lives at Bloomington, Indiana.

D1473—Bradley Trimble. He lives at Bloomington, Indiana.

+ **D1474—Saundra Gay Trimble.** Married Melvin Lady and they live at Route 7, Bloomington, Indiana.

The child of Sterling Sidney Trimble and Barbara Davis Trimble:

D1475—Sterling Sidney Trimble, Jr.

D1015—Myrtle Trimble. Daughter of William Trimble and Sola Conley. (Seventh generation of David Trimble and ——— Houston.) Married two times: first, to Everett Reed, and second, to George Hall. The Halls live at 1011 Renick Court, Baltimore, Maryland.

The children of Everett Reed and Myrtle Trimble:

D1476—Bill Reed.

D1477—Doug Reed.

The children of George Hall and Myrtle Trimble:

D1478—George Emeral Hall.

D1479—Jack Hall.

D1480—Betty Lou Hall.

D1481—Morgan Hall.

D1016—James Trimble. Son of William Trimble and Sola Conley. (Seventh generation of David Trimble and ——— Houston.) He married two times: first, to a Caudill, and second, to Ruth Murphy.

The children of James Trimble and Ruth Murphy:

D1482—Carl Trimble.

D1483—Elizabeth Trimble.

D1484—Betty Jo Trimble.

D1485—Maxine Trimble.

D1486—Donald Trimble.

D1017—Gillie Trimble. Son of William Trimble and Sola Conley. (Seventh

Trimble Families of America

D - David Trimble

generation of David Trimble and —— Houston.) Married Sam Kennard

The children of Sam Kennard and Gillie Trimble:

D1487—Clarence Kennard.

D1488—Edward Kennard. Married Ruth DeBore.

D1018—Goldie Trimble. Daughter of William Trimble and Sola Conley. (Seventh generation of David Trimble and —— Houston.) Married Henry Brown

The children of Henry Brown and Goldie Trimble:

D1489—Jewell Trimble Brown.

D1490—Bill Trimble Brown.

D1019—Theodore (Ted) Trimble. Son of William Trimble and Sola Conley. (Seventh generation of David Trimble and —— Houston.) Born on October 14, 1904 in Johnson County, Kentucky and died on December 28, 1935 in Johnson County, Kentucky. He married Lula Picklesimer.

The children of Theodore Trimble and Lula Picklesimer:

D1491—Theodore Rosevelt Trimble, Jr. Born on May 1929 in Van Lear, Johnson County, Kentucky and died September 1930 in Johnson County, Kentucky at the age of 14 months.

D1492—Flora Gertrude Trimble.

+ **D1493—Robert Paul Trimble.** Born on 1933 and died 1991. married Joann Peck.

D1494—Gladys Lillian Trimble. Born on February 20, 1935 in Paintsville, Johnson County, Kentucky and died December 5, 1997 in Paintsville, Johnson County, Kentucky.

D1020—John Trimble. Son of William Trimble and Sola Conley. (Seventh generation of David Trimble and —— Houston.) Born on September 7, 1906. Married Maymie Home, born on August 15, 1907. They lived at Staffordsville, Kentucky.

The children of John Trimble and Maymie Home:

+ **D1495—Pauline Trimble.** Born on November 13, 1929. Married William E. (Jack) Tackett, born on November 3, 1922.

+ **D1496—Billie Jean Trimble.** Born on February 7, 1931 Married Donald E. Huston.

D1497—John Mark Trimble, Jr. Born on June 20, 1934, and died in January 1935.

+ **D1498—Markus Ray Trimble.** Born on December 16, 1939. Married

Glenna Williams.

D1021—Florence Allen Trimble. Daughter of William Trimble and Sola Conley. (Seventh generation of David Trimble and —— Houston.) Married Martin Blair.

The children of Martin Blair and Florence Allen Trimble, we do not have the names of all of them:

D1499—Charles Blair.

D1500—Agnes Blair.

D1501—Goldie Blair.

D1502—Betty Blair. Married Hershell Conley.

D1022—June Trimble. Daughter of Paris Grant Trimble and Dora Picklesimer. (Seventh generation of David Trimble and —— Houston.) Born on June 9, 1898. Married Everett Gullett on September 5, 1914. They live in Delaware.

The children of Everett Gullett and June Trimble:

+ **D1503—Opal Gullett.** Born on September 6, 1915. Married Francis Martin in 1933.

D1504—Dora Gullett. Married in 1946 to Wilson Reynolds. No children.

+ **D1505—Paris Ezekiel Gullett.** Married Jean Ruggles.

+ **D1506—Agnes Gullett.** Married twice.

D1507—Robert Taylor Gullett. Deceased.

D1508—Helen Gullett. Died in infancy.

D1509—Sherman Lee Gullett. Died in infancy.

+ **D1510—Lillian Gullett.** Married Jim Meade in 1956.

+ **D1511—Eldon Gullett.** Married in 1954 to Loretta Vaughters.

D1024—Elva Trimble. Daughter of Paris Grant Trimble and Dora Picklesimer. (Seventh generation of David Trimble and —— Houston.) Married two times: first, to Frank Bayes in 1916, and second, to Jeffrey Bruce Roberts in 1929.

The child of Frank Bayes and Elva Trimble:

D1512—Karl Bayes. Born on October 15, 1917. Died in infancy.

The child of Jeffrey Bruce Roberts and Elva Roberts:

+ **D1513—Jeffrey Bruce Roberts, Jr.** Born on October 15, 1930. Married Yolonda —— of Tucson, Arizona.

D1025—Robert Eldon "Bob" Trimble. Son of Paris Grant Trimble and Dora Picklesimer. (Seventh generation of David Trimble and —— Houston.) Married Anna Picklesimer in December 1922.

Trimble Families of America

The children of Robert Eldon "Bob" Trimble and Anna Picklesimer:

+ **D1514—Frances Trimble.** Born on July 23, 1924. Married Virgil Tague of 127 Noble, La Porte, Indiana.

+ **D1515—Charles G. Trimble.** Born on February 13, 1926. Married Marsha ——.

+ **D1516—Ruby Carroll Trimble.** Born on July 17, 1933. Married Ollis Pigman.

D1026—Jewell Trimble. Daughter of Paris Grant Trimble and Nancy Craft Trimble. (Seventh generation of David Trimble and —— Houston.) Born on March 26, 1914. Married on February 9, 1937, to Ora Green, He was born on March 1, 1911, of Ashland, Kentucky.

Jewell raised two stepchildren and one foster daughter.

+ **D1517—Bobby Green.** Born on March 22, 1929. Married Edsel Rice.

+ **D1518—James E. Green.** Born on September 5, 1931. Married Phyllis Fulks in 1954.

+ **D1519—Delena Jewell Baldwin.** Born on June 30, 1949. Married Larry Blanton in 1968.

D1027—Rexford Raymond Trimble. Son of Henry Elmer Trimble and Martha Auxier. (Seventh generation of David Trimble and —— Houston.) Born on January 18, 1902 and died on March 18, 1959. Married on February 21, 1922, to Bertha Mae Blanton, born in 1899. They lived at Volga, Kentucky.

The children of Rexford Raymond Trimble and Bertha Mae Blanton:

+ **D1520—Anna Martha Trimble.** Born on December 10, 1922. Married on December 23, 1942, to Oval D. Williams, born in 1921. They live at 6049 Whitman Road, Columbus, Ohio.

D1521—Victoria Avanell Trimble. Born on January 16, 1924. Married Carl William Allen on November 2, 1947. He was born in 1922. They live at 5104 Fey Court, Louisville, Kentucky. Their daughter, Carla Louise Allen, was born on July 13, 1963, and died the same day.

D1522—Rexford Raymond Trimble, Jr. Born on August 14, 1925, and died on October 17, 1926 as a toddler.

+ **D1523—Betty Jo Trimble.** Born on July 21, 1932. Married Henry Edward Burchett on June 1, 1952. He was born on March 3, 1933. They were divorced in 1965. Betty Jo lives at 16206 Pamela Jo Avenue, Eastwood, Kentucky. (We are gratefully indebted to Betty Jo for much hard work and research in the information she has given us for this genealogy.)

+ **D1524—John Henry Trimble.** Born on June 21, 1934 in Volga, Kentucky and died on June 8, 2009 in Ashland, Boyd County, Kentucky. Married Vella Ruth Ferguson on February 27, 1960. She was born in 1933 and died on June 17, 2009. John and Vella buried in Rose Hill Cemetery in Ashland, Boyd County, Kentucky. They lived at 3314 Pine Haven Drive, Ashland, Boyd County, Kentucky.

D1029—Victoria Auxier Trimble. Daughter of Henry Elmer Trimble and Martha Auxier. (Seventh generation of David Trimble and —— Houston.) Born on January 17, 1907 and died on July 17, 1970. Married Delmas Preston. Delmas died on March 16, 1954.

The children of Delmas Preston and Victoria Auxier Trimble:

D1525—Martha Belle Preston. Born on September 4, 1930. Married Charles K. Franklin on September 6, 1952. They live at 324 S. Ashburton Road, Columbus, Ohio. No children.

+ **D1526—Delmas Jay Preston, Jr.** Born on May 4, 1936. Married Nieda Lee Vickers in December 1959. They live at 718 Middletown Avenue, Westwood, Ohio.

D1527—William Cyrus Preston. Born on February 11, 1947. Married Carolyn June Well on August 23, 1968.

D1528—Malinda Ann Preston. Born on January 11, 1952. She is attending Eastern State College in Richmond, Kentucky.

D1031—Susie Trimble. Daughter of Shelby Trimble and Cora Webb. (Seventh generation of David Trimble and —— Houston.) Born on October 18, 1902 and died on January 10, 1947. Married Dennie Blair

The children of Dennie Blair and Susie Trimble:

D1529—John Shell Blair.
D1530—Clara May Blair.
D1531—June Marie Blair.
D1532—Euell Gordon Blair.
D1533—Hattie Katherine Blair.
D1534—Dorothy Sue Blair.
D1535—Carol Blair.

D1032—Fanny Trimble. Daughter of Shelby Trimble and Cora Webb. (Seventh generation of David Trimble and —— Houston.) Born on August 10, 1904 in Kentucky and died on December 3, 1965 in Johnson County, Kentucky. She married Charlie H. Colvin on June 19, 1965 in Johnson County, Kentucky. Charles was born on July 14, 1895 in Kentucky and died on October 13, 1980 in Paintsville, Johnson County, Kentucky. He is the son of

D - David Trimble

Henry J. Colvin and Celia Jane Picklesimer. Henry was born on June 22, 1865 in Johnson County, Kentucky and died on January 2, 1929 in Johnson County, Kentucky. Celia was born on June 24, 1865 in Barnett's Creek, Johnson County, Kentucky and died on March 23, 1959 in Barnett's Creek, Johnson County, Kentucky.

The children of Charlie H. Colvin and Fanny Trimble:

D1536—Gerald Colvin. Born on August 23, 1928 in Johnson County, Kentucky and died on July 30, 2000 in Johnson County, Kentucky

+ **D1537—Vivian Ruth Colvin.** Married Robert Preston of Wittensville, Kentucky.

+ **D1538—Lillian Jo Ann Colvin.** Married Bill Meadows.

D1033—John Powell Trimble. Son of Shelby Trimble and Cora Webb. (Seventh generation of David Trimble and —— Houston.) Born on March 19, 1906 and died on September 15, 1968. Married Irene Sheppard. John was a dealer in livestock.

Their children of John Powell Trimble and Irene Sheppard:

D1539—Shelby C. Trimble. Lived Route 3, Maysville, Kentucky.

D1540—Cora Katherine Trimble.

D1541—John Powell Trimble, Jr.

D1034—Dixie Trimble. Daughter of Shelby Trimble and Cora Webb. (Seventh generation of David Trimble and —— Houston.) Born on June 22, 1908. Married Bert Estep.

The children of Bert Estep and Dixie Trimble:

D1542—William Jack Estep. Married Joan Curtiss. They have a daughter, Linda Ann.

D1543—Sally Estep. Married Bill Smith. Their children: Mary Sue, Sherri Lynn, and Sharen Kay.

D1544—Trilby Estep. Married Paul Roger Daniel. Their children: Roy Douglas, Rita Deloris, Darlene, and Tammy Lynn.

D1545—Phillip Roger Estep.

D1546—James Arie Estep.

D1547—Brenda Estep. Married Larry Blanton. They have a daughter, Misty Carol.

D1548—Emma Kristine Estep. Married.

D1035—Matilda Trimble. (twin) Daughter of Shelby Trimble and Cora Webb. (Seventh generation of David Trimble and —— Houston.) Born on

Trimble Families of America

November 5, 1912 and died on July 17, 1959. Married Fred Preston.

The children of Fred Preston and Matilda Trimble:

D1549—**Virginia Elaine Preston.** Married Cecil Preston

D1550—**Nellie Preston.**

D1551—**John Fred Preston.**

D1037—**Laura Trimble.** Daughter of Shelby Trimble and Cora Webb. (Seventh generation of David Trimble and —— Houston.) Born on September 17, 1914, and died on October 2, 1995 in Magoffin County, Kentucky. Married Irvin Cantrell.

The children of Irvin Cantrell and Laura Trimble:

D1552—**Robert George Cantrell.**

+ D1553—**Ethel Janet Cantrell.** Married Sam Burke. They lived in Dayton, Ohio.

D1038—**Frank Pelphrey.** Son of John Paris Pelphrey and Laura Trimble. (Seventh generation of David Trimble and —— Houston.) Born on March 2, 1897 and died on December 14, 1962. Married Merzie Vanhoose, born in 1902 and died in 1957.

The children of Frank Pelphrey and Merzie Vanhoose:

+ D1554—**Earl Pelphrey.** Born on February 14, 1924. Married Pauline Phelps, born 1925.

+ D1555—**Olga Pelphrey.** Born on April 25, 1925, and married Don H. Mohler, born 1922.

D1556—**David Paris Pelphrey.** Born on September 29, 1927. Married Betty McKenzie.

+ D1557—**Lowell Pelphrey.** Born on June 1, 1929. Married Betty Ruth Williams, born 1931.

+ D1558—**Billie Lee Pelphrey.** Born on December 11, 1932. Married Jessie Lee Hall.

+ D1559—**Christine Pelphrey.** Born on July 3, 1931. Married James H. Wright, born in 1933. They live at Red Bush, Kentucky.

D1560—**Maxine Pelphrey.** Born on July 3, 1931. Married Wayne Blair and they live at Barnett's Creek, Kentucky. No children.

+ D1561—**Bennie Pelphrey.** Born on April 8, 1937. Married Janet Keaton.

D1044—**Gracie Stapleton.** Daughter of Manassa Stapleton and Julia Trimble. (Seventh generation of David Trimble and —— Houston.) Married Ossie Cantrell.

Trimble Families of America

D - David Trimble

The children of Ossie Cantrell and Gracie Stapleton:

D1562—Edith Cantrell. Married Oran Estep.

D1563—Wayne Cantrell.

D1564—Bond Cantrell.

D1052—Grant Trimble. Son of Albert Trimble and Naoma Tackett. (Seventh generation of David Trimble and ———— Houston.) Born on June 28, 1896. Married Zellia Sturgill.

The children of Grant Trimble and Zellia Sturgill:

D1565—David Trimble.

D1566—June Trimble.

D1567—Christine Trimble.

D1053—Frank Trimble. Son of Albert Trimble and Naoma Tackett. (Seventh generation of David Trimble and ———— Houston.) Born on November 10, 1898. Married Hester Lemaster.

The daughter Frank Trimble and Hester Lemaster:

D1568—Helen Trimble.

D1054—Malta May Trimble. Daughter of Albert Trimble and Naoma Tackett. (Seventh generation of David Trimble and ———— Houston.) Born on March 9, 1906. Married Henry Ward.

The children of Henry Ward and Malta May Trimble:

D1569—Betty Joe Ward.

D1570—Mary Louise Ward.

D1571—Henry Paul Ward.

D1572—Imogene Ward.

D1057—Fred Trimble. Son of Albert Trimble and Naoma Tackett. (Seventh generation of David Trimble and ———— Houston.) Born on May 9, 1918. Married Evalee King.

The children of Fred Trimble and Evalee King:

D1573—Martha Lou Trimble.

D1574—Philip Ray Trimble.

D1575—Eunice Roena Trimble.

D1576—Dixie Lee Trimble.

D1058—James Albert Trimble. Son of Albert Trimble and Naoma Tackett. (Seventh generation of David Trimble and ———— Houston.) Born on October 9, 1926. Married Pearl Picklesimer.

The children of James Albert Trimble and Pearl Picklesimer:

D1577—Annetta Trimble.

D1578—Ruby Jewel Trimble.

D1579—Donald Trimble.

D1580—Jerry Trimble.

D1059—Beulah G. Trimble. Daughter of Albert Trimble and Naoma Tackett. (Seventh generation of David Trimble and —— Houston.) Born on July 4, 1922. Married Euel Baldwin.

The son of Euel Baldwin and Beulah G. Trimble:

D1581—Daniel Harry Baldwin. Married Grade Burchett and had six children.

D1065—Clara Trimble. Daughter of John Elliot Trimble and Selona Williams. (Seventh generation of David Trimble and —— Houston.) Born on November 11, 1906. Married Audie Atkins and had eleven children. Both Clara and Audie are deceased.

The children of Audie Atkins and Clara Trimble:

D1582—Ernie Adkins. Married Minnie Bell Ison.

D1583—Bernice Adkins. Married Arthur Johnson.

D1584—Mary Adkins. Married Robert Wallen

D1585—Lizzie Adkins. Married Lee Riggsby.

D1586—Clifford Adkins. Married Maxine Johnson.

D1587—Lina Adkins. Died at 3 years old.

D1588—Everett Adkins. Married Mae Allen

D1589—Martha Adkins. Married Elmer Wolfenbarger.

D1590—Julie Adkins. Married Woodrow Johnson.

D1591—John Adkins. Married Linda Helton.

D1592—Curtis Adkins. Married Faye Birchwell.

D1593—Ira Adkins. Married Jan Lewis.

D1594—Imogene Adkins. Married Bobby McGuire.

D1069—Ora Trimble. Son of John Elliot Trimble and Selona Williams. (Seventh generation of David Trimble and —— Houston.) Born on February 2, 1902 at Relief, Johnson County, Kentucky and died on November 16, 1964. He married Edna Lewis on October 20, 1920, at Lucille, near Middle Fork Sandy in Elliott County, Kentucky. Edna was born on February 9, 1902 at Lucille, near Middle Fork Sandy in Elliott County, Kentucky.

Their children of Ora Trimble and Edna Lewis:

+ D1595—Eulah Trimble. Born on March 8, 1922 in Lenox, Kentucky. She

D - David Trimble

was married twice. We do not know who she married the first time. She married Charles Hughes and lives in Marion, Ohio.

+ **D1596—Dolly Trimble.** Born on November 20, 1924, at Open Fort Sandy in Elliott County, Kentucky. She married Robert Chester Vicker, Jr.

+ **D1597—James Robert Trimble.** Born on December 20, 1926, at Lenox, Kentucky. He married Ann Elizabeth May. Robert Trimble died in a truck accident on February 7, 1968. (We are gratefully indebted to Miss Diana Lynn Trimble of 118 Nineteenth Street, Paris, Kentucky 40361, for the vast amount of information given us concerning her Trimble line.)

  D1598—David Trimble. Died at birth.

+ **D1599—Ray Trimble.** Born on March 9, 1930, at Lenox, Kentucky. He married Lou Barker.

+ **D1600—Lawrence Trimble.** Born on May 25, 1932, at Lenox, Kentucky. Married Thelma Jean Adkins.

+ **D1601—Albert Trimble.** Born on September 16, 1934, at Lick Branch in Morgan County, Kentucky. Married Mildred Smith.

+ **D1602—Charles Trimble.** Born on March 5, 1939, at Mordica in Morgan County, Kentucky. Married Lorene Ison.

+ **D1603—Donald Trimble.** (Twin.) Born on October 20, 1942, at Mordica in Morgan County, Kentucky and 2015. Married Wilma Cantrell.

+ **D1604—Ronald Trimble.** (Twin.) Born on October 20, 1942. He married Peggy Sue Stacy.

D1072—Manie Ramey. Daughter of Sherman Trimble Ramey and Sherlie Williams. (Seventh generation of David Trimble and —— Houston.) Married Vint Davis.

The children of Vint Davis and Manie Ramey:

D1605—James W. Davis.

D1606—Clarence E. Davis. Married Hester Jenkins.

D1074—Doris Ramey. Daughter of Sherman Trimble Ramey and Sherlie Williams. (Seventh generation of David Trimble and —— Houston.) Married Maxie Stapleton.

The children of Maxie Stapleton and Doris Ramey:

D1607—Charles Stapleton.

D1608—Doris Stapleton.

D1129—Davis Reed Trimble. Son of Bruce Trimble and Norsie Reed. (Seventh generation of David Trimble and —— Houston.) Born on May 24, 1921.

Married Mary Elizabeth Fairchild.

The children of Davis Reed Trimble and Mary Elizabeth Fairchild:

+ **D1609—Virginia Bruce Trimble.** Married Leroy Pelphrey. Their children: Sheila, Bruce, and Susan.

+ **D1610—Davis Reed Trimble, Jr.**

+ **D1611—Jackie Dean Trimble.**

+ **D1612—Janie Trimble.**

+ **D1613—Robert Paul Trimble.**

+ **D1614—Debra Trimble.** Married to Berry Jo Ward.

D1130—Granville Trimble. Son of Bruce Trimble and Norsie Reed. (Seventh generation of David Trimble and ——— Houston.) Born on August 20, 1922. Married Billie Marie Allen of Richmond, Kentucky.

The children of Granville Trimble and Billie Marie Allen:

D1615—Allen C. Trimble.

D1616—Tony Trimble.

D1617—Arminta Trimble.

D1618—Morton Bruce Trimble.

D1131—Georgene Trimble. Daughter of Bruce Trimble and Norsie Reed. (Seventh generation of David Trimble and ——— Houston.) Born on January 27, 1924. Married Charles McKenzie of Barnett's Creek, Kentucky.

The children of Charles McKenzie and Georgene Trimble:

D1619—Jeanna Frances McKenzie.

D1620—Lora Ellen McKenzie.

D1621—Melinda McKenzie.

D1622—Mary Anna McKenzie.

D1623—Elaine McKenzie.

+ **D1624—Charles Michael McKenzie.** Married Joan Blanton.

D1132—John Mark Trimble. Son of Bruce Trimble and Norsie Reed. (Seventh generation of David Trimble and ——— Houston.) Born on January 10, 1927. Married Janet Louise Marsh on June 12, 1927. They lived on Church Street, Paintsville, Kentucky.

Their children of John Mark Trimble and Janet Louise Marsh:

D1625—Marky Trimble.

D1626—Anne Wade Trimble.

D1627—David Trimble.

D1628—Phillip Trimble.

D - David Trimble

D1135—Emogene Trimble. Daughter of Daniel Boone Trimble and Rosa Lemaster. (Seventh generation of David Trimble and —— Houston.) Born on January 21, 1925. Married Carl Benson, born in 1926. They live at Spring Valley, Ohio.

Their children of Carl Benson and Emogene Trimble:
D1629—Mary Jean Benson. Born in 1947.
D1630—David Carl Benson. Born in 1946.
D1631—Deborah Rose Benson. Born in 1951.
D1632—Sharon Gale Benson. Born in 1954.
D1633—John Mark Benson. Born in 1956.

D1137—Loretta Trimble. Daughter of Daniel Boone Trimble and Rosa Lemaster. (Seventh generation of David Trimble and —— Houston.) Born on October 14, 1927. Married James Eldon Reed. H was born on August 20, 1924. They lived at 1744 Academy Place, Dayton, Ohio.

The son of James Eldon Reed and Loretta Trimble:
D1634—Jimmy Eldon Reed. Born on September 25, 1950.

D1138—William Lindsey Trimble. Son of Daniel Boone Trimble and Rosa Lemaster. (Seventh generation of David Trimble and —— Houston.) Born on May 23, 1929. Married Beulah Frances McKenzie. They live at Barnett's Creek, Kentucky.

The children of William Linsey Trimble and Beulah Frances McKenzie:
D1635—Douglas Trimble. Born in 1953.
D1636—Harry Daniel Trimble. Born in 1955.
D1637—David Randall Trimble. Born in 1956.
D1638—Steven Trimble. Born in 1959.

D1139—Byron Douglas Trimble. Son of Daniel Boone Trimble and Rosa Lemaster. (Seventh generation of David Trimble and —— Houston.) Born on May 27, 1931 and died December 29, 2018 in Beavercreek, Ohio. Married Geneva Dawson on April 27, 1956. They were married 63 years. She was born in 1936. They live in Dayton, Ohio. He graduated from Oil Springs High School and attained an Associate degree in accounting. He served in the United States Air Force, stationed at Yokota Air Force Base in Japan. He has the following grandchildren Timothy, Ben, Byron, Blake, Chris, Donovan, and Dillion and four great grandchildren Emma Kate, Everly, Caitlyn, and Elliot.

The children of Byron Douglas Trimble and Geneva Dawson:

D1639—William Keith Trimble. Born in 1959. Married Karen.

D1640—Michael Douglas Trimble. Born in 1960. Married Terry.

D1641—Kevin Earl Trimble. Born in 1969 and is deceased.

D1642—Donald Trimble. Married Stephanie.

D1140—Betty Rose Trimble. Daughter of Daniel Boone Trimble and Rosa Lemaster. (Seventh generation of David Trimble and ——— Houston.) Born on October 23, 1932. Married Arnold Reed, born on September 13, 1930, of Flat Gap, Kentucky.

The son of Arnold Reed and Betty Rose Trimble:

D1643—Jeffrey Arnold Reed. Born on April 12, 1968.

D1141—Daniel Boone Trimble, Jr. Son of Daniel Boone Trimble and Rosa Lemaster. (Seventh generation of David Trimble and ——— Houston.) Born on July 6, 1935. Married Mary Louise Wooten, Born in 1942. They live at Louisville, Kentucky.

The children of Daniel Boone Trimble, Jr. and Mary Louise Wooten:

D1644—Danna Louise Trimble. Born in 1968.

D1645—Dannele Lynn Trimble. Born in 1970.

D1156—Ulis Trimble. Son of Boe Trimble and Zuria Caudill. (Seventh generation of David Trimble and ——— Houston.) Born on January 12, 1908. Married Iva Hackworth.

The children of Ulis Trimble and Iva Hackworth:

D1646—John Martin Trimble. Born on March 3, 1938. Married Maudie Williams. They have a daughter, Katrina, Born on December 31, 1969.

D1647—Charlotte Ann Trimble. Born on September 24, 1939. Married Gilbert Byerman.

+ **D1648—Mary Lou Trimble.** Born on May 24, 1942. Married Donald Johnson.

D1649—Steven Paul Trimble. Born on May 6, 1956.

D1157—Vensil A. Trimble. Son of Boe Trimble and Zuria Caudill. (Seventh generation of David Trimble and ——— Houston.) Born on September 29, 1914 in Johnson County, Kentucky and died on December 23, 1988 in Middletown, Butler County, Ohio. Married Gladys Ingraham. Vensil was a vocational agricultural teacher in 1940.

The children of Vensil Trimble and Gladys Ingraham:

D1650—Elouise Trimble. Born on November 28, 1940.

D1651—Betty Jewell Trimble. Born on April 10, 1945. Vensil Trimble married

D - David Trimble

the second time to Helen Cox. They have a daughter:

D1652—Vickie Lynn Trimble. Born on May 1956.

D1158—Avanell Trimble. Daughter of Boe Trimble and Zuria Caudill. (Seventh generation of David Trimble and —— Houston.) Born on September 21, 1916. Married John Dills, Jr., born on 1914 and died in 1948. Avanell lives in Lexington, Kentucky.

The child of John Dills, Jr. and Avanell Trimble:

+ **D1653—Judith Nell Dills.** Married the Reverend Thomas A. Smith, pastor of Palmyra, Indiana, Baptist Church.

D1166—Elnora Trimble. Daughter of James V. Trimble and Mayme Goble. (Seventh generation of David Trimble and —— Houston.) Married Byrd Rondall Ison, a Baptist minister of Midway, Kentucky.

The children of Byrd Rondall Ison and Elnora Trimble:

D1654—Marcia Jean Ison. Married Malcolm Endicott.

D1655—Melanie Carol Ison.

D1656—Elizabeth Annelson Ison.

D1167—Anna Jean Trimble. Daughter of James V. Trimble and Mayme Goble. (Seventh generation of David Trimble and —— Houston.) Married Franklin C. Cunningham of Austin, Texas.

The children of Franklin C. Cunningham and Anna Jean Trimble:

D1657—Frank Alan Cunningham. Married Connie Florence.

D1658—James Gregory Cunningham.

D1168—James William Trimble. Son of James V. Trimble and Mayme Goble. (Seventh generation of David Trimble and —— Houston.) Married Joyce Hall. They live at Pikesville, Kentucky.

The children of James William Trimble and Joyce Hall:

D1659—Terry Neil Trimble.

D1660—Joan Trimble.

D1661—Jimmie Trimble.

D1662—Todd Trimble.

D1183—Ruth Eally. Daughter of George Eally and Sada Trimble (Seventh generation of David Trimble and —— Houston.) Married Clyde Williams of Oil Springs, Kentucky.

The children of Clyde Williams and Ruth Eally:

D1663—Cecil Martin Williams. Married Jacqueline Dean Hakefield on June 6,

1953, and they live in England.

D1664—George Rondell Williams.

D1184—Ruie Eally. Daughter of George Eally and Sada Trimble (Seventh generation of David Trimble and —— Houston.) Married Bob Reed.

The children of Bob Reed and Ruie Eally:

D1665—Billie Jean Reed.

+ **D1666—Bobby Joe Reed.** Married Laura Alice Meade.

D1667—Wilma Dean Reed.

D1668—Janice Reed.

D1196—Kermit Hanson Trimble. Son of Conroy Trimble and Doshia Ann Blair. (Seventh generation of David Trimble and —— Houston.) Born on July 24, 1917 in Johnson County, Kentucky and died on June 9, 1996 in Paintsville, Johnson County, Kentucky. Married Margie Caudill of Johnson County, Kentucky on April 25, 1936. Margie was born on June 9, 1918 in Johnson County, Kentucky and died on May 5, 2009 in Johnson County, Kentucky. She was the daughter of Wallace Luther Caudill and Lillie Spradlin married on June 24, 1917. Wallace was born on February 23, 1893 in Johnson County, Kentucky and died January 8, 1960. Lillie was born on May 16, 1889 in Johnson County, Kentucky and died on December 2, 1955.

Kermit was a rigger for drilling in oil fields. He was with a crew that struck poisonous gas and could not work at drilling afterwards.

Their children of Kermit Hanson Trimble and Margie Caudill:

+ **D1669—Sue Lovanna Trimble.** Born on May 9, 1938. Married Alex Allen McCarty.

+ **D1670—Donald Eugene Trimble.** Born on December 23, 1939. Married Beatrice Carolyn Salyer.

D1671—Wilma Dean Trimble. Born on August 6, 1942. She died at birth.

+ **D1672—Darrell Conard Trimble.** Born on March 9, 1947. Married Linda Fern Blevins.

+ **D1673—David Carroll Trimble.** Born on August 23, 1949. Married Mina Lou Smith.

+ **D1674—Larry Allen Trimble.** (Twin.) Born on July 10, 1953. Married Deborah Marlene Salyer.

+ **D1675—Gary Steven Trimble.** (Twin.) Born on July 10, 1953. Married Marsha Yvonne Castle.

D1197—Chloe Belle Trimble. Daughter of Conroy Trimble and Doshia Ann Blair. (Seventh generation of David Trimble and —— Houston.) Born on

Trimble Families of America

D - David Trimble

September 27, 1918 in Johnson County, Kentucky and died on July 9, 1999 in Johnson County, Kentucky. Married John William Allen "Bill" Caudill on June 4, 1938. Bill was born on August 10, 1914 in Johnson County and died on May 4, 1968 in Johnson County, Kentucky. Bill was the son of Menifee Caudill and Emma Collins. Menifee was born in February 1883 and died in 1959. Emma was born in 1886 and died in 1963.

Bill enlisted in the army May 18, 1944 serving during World War II and was discharged in 1945. He was wounded in the invasion of Germany. [67]

He developed Leukemia and would travel to Washington DC every month to receive experimental treatment at National Institute of Health in Bethesda Maryland. He would often stay overnight at Clifford Trimble's house in Ashland, Kentucky before catching a morning flight to DC for treatment.

Bill attended Morehead State University in Morehead, Kentucky. He was a schoolteacher and principal at schools in eastern Kentucky and southern Ohio. Chloe worked in the cafeteria at schools in Johnson County, Kentucky.

After Bill died Chloe married Buel Blanton

Chloe was good seamstress. She made great quilts.

Their children of John William Allen "Bill" Caudill and Chloe Belle Trimble:

+ **D1676—Eldon Caroll Caudill.** Born on July 24, 1939 and died on July 4, 2002 at Oil Springs, Johnson County, Kentucky. Married Carole Conley.

+ **D1677—Phillip Hager Caudill.** Born on January 20, 1944 and died September 3, 2021 in Paintsville, Kentucky. Married Mary Linda Blair.

+ **D1678—Linda Lou Caudill.** Born on December 29, 1946. Married Charles Eldon Blair.

D1198—Kenneth Archer Trimble. Son of Conroy Trimble and Doshia Ann Blair. (Seventh generation of David Trimble and —— Houston.) Born on December 12, 1921 in Johnson County, Kentucky and died on February 21, 2002 in Johnson County, Kentucky. Married Mary Biggs on March 14, 1942. Mary was born on January 30, 1923 in Olive Hill, Carter County, Kentucky

---

[67] Electronic Army Serial Number Merged File, 1938-1946 [Archival Database]; ARC: 1263923. World War II Army Enlistment Records; Records of the National Archives and Records Administration, Record Group 64; National Archives at College Park. College Park, Maryland, U.S.A.

and died in October 2012 in Paintsville, Johnson County, Kentucky. Mary is the daughter of Joseph Biggs and Cornelia Evans. Mary carried four children to term, but only one survived being born. The ones that did not survive weighed between 13 and 15 pounds. Now days with better procedures the three that died could be saved.

Ken was minister or preacher with the United Baptist. His younger brother, my father Clifford Eldon Trimble was also a preacher with the United Baptist. They were the two that looked most alike. They were often confused for each other when visiting churches.

Ken owned and ran a dairy farm in Johnson County, Kentucky before moving to Columbus, Ohio where he was a construction supervisor building homes for many years.

As a teen Ken was kicked in the cheek by a mule. It broke his cheek bone. During World War II, he tried to volunteer but they refused to let him join because he would have trouble with a gas mask fitting.

The children of Kenneth Archer Trimble and Mary Biggs:

D1679—Roger Trimble. Born and died on February 7, 1943.

+ **D1680—Helen Kaye Trimble.** Born on August 21, 1944. Married Russell Castle.

D1681—Rodney Trimble. Born and died on September 14, 1946.

D1682—Nelia Ann Trimble. Born and died on August 24, 1947.

D1199—Kathleen Trimble. Daughter of Conroy Trimble and Doshia Ann Blair. (Seventh generation of David Trimble and —— Houston.) Born on September 8, 1924 in Johnson County, Kentucky and died. Married Theodore "Tom" Colvin on November 16, 1946. Tom born on November 23, 1920 in Van Lear, Johnson County, Kentucky and died on June 10, 2011 at Paul B. Hall Medical Center, Paintsville, Johnson County, Kentucky. Tom was the son of Morris Colvin and Erie Arms who were married on May 15, 1918. Morris was born in September 1894 and died on July 23, 1964. Erie was born in July 1897 and died on October 2, 1966 and is buried Denver Hill Cemetery, Denver, Johnson County, Kentucky

Tom had damage to the lens of eyes and had problems seeing.

The children of Theodore "Tom" Colvin and Kathleen Trimble:

+ **D1683—Joe Kenneth Colvin.** Born on October 3, 1947. Married Judi Blanton.

+ **D1684—Jerry Morris Colvin.** Born on November 27, 1949. Married Sharon Blair.

+ **D1685—Glenda Theo Colvin.** Born on August 9, 1954. Married Alvin Lee Blair.

+ **D1686—Jedford "Jake" Gay Colvin.** Born on December 19, 1961 and died December 24, 2021. Married Wilma Bailey.

D1200—Clifford Eldon Trimble. Son of Conroy Trimble and Doshia Ann Blair. (Seventh generation of David Trimble and —— Houston.) Born on September 3, 1926 in Johnson County, Kentucky and died on July 20, 1995 in Ashland, Boyd County, Kentucky. Married Doris Deloris Price on January 28, 1950. Doris was born on January 22, 1932 in Johnson County, Kentucky and died on May 2, 2001 in Ashland, Boyd County, Kentucky. Doris was the daughter of Joe Cephus Price and Josephine May.

Joe Cephus Price was born on September 7, 1910 in Johnson County, Kentucky and died on September 2, 1963 in Mansfield, Richland County, Ohio. Josephine May was born on June 3, 1914 in Johnson County, Kentucky and died on September 15, 1985 in Paintsville, Johnson County, Kentucky. Joe and Josephine were married on May 7, 1931 in Paintsville, Johnson County, Kentucky.

Clifford served in the US Army. He enlisted on May 25, 1945 and was discharged in 1946. He was drafted while still in high school, he took his physical in Huntington, West Virginia. He was told to go finish high school and would start basic training after he graduated. In the spring after graduation, he traveled to Texas on a new train for basic training. When he arrived, there were too many recruits for that session with those that had been caught AWOL. So, the army started at the top of the list and when they had enough, everyone else was on KP. The cooks knew that they were on KP because of class size so they ate well. After 13 weeks they started a new class. So, he served basic training twice. While he was in basic training Japan surrendered on August 15, 1945, ending the war. He got to go home for Thanksgiving before deployment. He took a train back to Kentucky. It was on old train with no heat, and he about froze.

He was stationed as a guard at a prison for US soldiers in the state of New York. He had to carry a 45 pistol, after he was there a few weeks an order was issued that guards had to be over 21 to carry a pistol, so he was assigned as a driver but had never drove. He went to the motor pool a sergeant showed him the gears on a jeep then he drove to the end of the tarmac and back. The sergeant signed off on his driver's license. He was to transport the other guards to and from the towers. He had a bunch of guards piled in the jeep and he started around the prison. He came to a big mud hole, so he

318

whipped the wheel to one side to go around it then whipped the wheel back. The guards he was transporting were piled in the back of the jeep. One guard said, "Trimble, if you're goin' to drive like that, I want a walk."

Dad was a minister in the United Baptist Church. United Baptist churches has no musical instruments. They do not use prepared sermons. Ministers are not paid. A church does not have a full-time minister, they have an elected Moderator and an Assistant Moderator, and they may not be members of the church where they served. Clifford was Assistant Moderator at several churches. Clifford preformed over one hundred marriages. He and his brother Kenneth married most of my cousins. My brother and I were taper lighters so much that we did not need to rehearse.

Clifford worked for Armco Steel in the Hot Strip Department in Ashland, Boyd County, Kentucky starting 1955. I started working at Armco Steel in 1973 and had transferred to the Hot Strip Department. The day after Christmas 1978, He was helping get the mill ready to start rolling, when a computer turned on the table rolls, he was standing on. He went between two rolls a space of five and three eighths inch. Although he never returned to work, those that worked at the plant with him called him the miracle man. Dad spent over 80 days in the hospital. He lived another 17 years.

The area where he went through the roll was clean because I had cleaned it out working evening shift the night before. After I had washed all the scale from that area my boss came by and said I was on the wrong side. But I believe I cleaned the correct side.

Dad bought a farm and subdivided it. He did not want to be vain and name it after himself. Mom wanted it named Trimble Terrace. The real estate agent just wanted to sell lots, so he suggested Dorcliff Heights for Doris and Clifford. There are some strange tales as to how it got its name. Dad later said he wished he listened to mom.

Mom and Dad had three children and all three were born in a different county.

The children of Clifford Eldon Trimble and Doris Deloris Price:

+ **D1687—Stanley Barry Trimble.** Born on September 2, 1954 in Johnson County, Kentucky. Married five times.

+ **D1688—Stewart Lee Trimble.** Born on October 9, 1956 in Greenup County, Kentucky. Married Loretta Jean Gullett.

+ **D1689—Melanie DeAlice Trimble.** Born on March 29, 1969, Boyd County, Kentucky. Married Jeffery Carlton Bingham.

D1201—Leroy Trimble. Son of Conroy Trimble and Doshia Ann Blair.

Trimble Families of America

(Seventh generation of David Trimble and —— Houston.) Born on August 14, 1928 in Johnson County, Kentucky and died on August 1, 1972 in Hamilton, Ohio. After a day spent riding a bicycle, he came home and started feeling bad. He had a heart attack. Married Paula Earlene Matthews on January 26, 1950. Paula was born on January 19, 1927 in Glasgow, Kentucky and died on April 8, 2007 in Louisville, Kentucky. Daughter of Ballard Matthews and Earle Mathews. Ballard was born on July 30, 1895 and died on September 17, 1978. Earle was born on October 3, 1904 and died on November 20, 2000.

Leroy had Scarlet Fever when he was infant and was deaf. Even during the Great Depression, a way was found for him to attend a deaf school in Danville, Kentucky. He ran track for the deaf school, the first in a running family. Leroy and his next oldest brother Clifford were the closest in age so during summer vacation they spent lots of time together. Clifford learned how to speak with his hand by talking to his brother as they roamed the hills around their home. Leroy worked as a typesetter for Cincinnati Enquirer.

Their children of Leroy Trimble and Paula Earlene Matthews:

+ **D1690—Peggy Ann Trimble.** Born on May 29, 1952. Married Dennis Baker.

+ **D1691—Randall Allen Trimble.** Born on April 12, 1956 in Mount Sterling, Kentucky. Married Terri Hill.

D1202—Genevieve B. Trimble. Daughter of McCoy Trimble and Ethel Fraley. (Seventh generation of David Trimble and —— Houston.) Married Ben Becker.

The children of Ben Becker and Genevieve B. Trimble:
D1692—Cheryl A. Becker.
D1693—Deborah J. Becker.
D1694—Beverly L. Becker.
D1695—Linda S. Becker.
D1696—Stephen T. Becker.

D1203—Mary M. Trimble. Daughter of McCoy Trimble and Ethel Fraley. (Seventh generation of David Trimble and —— Houston.) Married Warren K. Halstead.

The children of Warren K. Halstead and Mary M. Trimble:
D1697—Tersa Lynn Halstead.
D1698—Warren J. Halstead.
D1699—Valerie L. Halstead.

D1204—Sheila F. Trimble. Daughter of McCoy Trimble and Ethel Fraley. (Seventh generation of David Trimble and ——— Houston.) Married first to John R. Gallion.

Married second to Joel D. Alger.

The children of John R. Gallion and Sheila F. Trimble:

D1700—John R. Gallion.

D1701—David M. Gallion.

The children of Joel D. Alger and Sheila F. Trimble:

D1702—Alexander K. Alger.

D1703—Desiree L. Alger.

D1205—Arma Lea Trimble. Daughter of Palmer Trimble and Nola Webb. (Seventh generation of David Trimble and ——— Houston.) Born on November 10, 1938. Married Kenneth Wayne Robinson on August 9, 1958. Kenneth was born January 9. Wayne was the son of Kenneth Williard Robinson and Ruth Elizabeth Bender.

The children of Kenneth Wayne Robinson and Arma Lea Trimble:

+ **D1704—Mitchell Eric Robinson.** Born on September 2, 1959. Married Chris Haukaus on April 3, 1999.

+ **D1705—Michelle Elizabeth Robinson.** Born on April 30, 1661.

D1706—Mark Elton Robinson. Born on September 10, 1963. Married Waetraud Gisla Christian Paech on September 12, 1987.

D1206—Ronald Eugene. Trimble. Son of Palmer Trimble and Nola Webb. (Seventh generation of David Trimble and ——— Houston.) Born on May 27, 1941 Lovely, Martin County, Kentucky and died on May 28, 2011 in Gallipolis, Gallia County, Ohio. Married Jane M. Hartlieb on April 5, 1964. Jane was born on October 25, 1944 in Sawyer North Dakota. The story goes that Ronald was so handsome because he was born in the county between Lovely and Beauty Kentucky. Ronald Trimble and Jane Hartlieb divorced on April 26, 1978. Ronald remarried Linda Sue Bays on May 4, 1978. Ronald and Sue divorced and remarried and divorced again.

The children of Ronald Eugene Trimble and Jane Hartlieb:

+ **D1707—Lillian Elise Trimble.** Born on May 1, 1965 in Gallipolis, Ohio. Married Charles Elbert Masters Jr.

D1708—Ronald Joseph Trimble. Born on April 21, 1966 in Gallipolis Ohio. Lives in Washington D.C. Married to Michael Glenn Ives on June 6, 2010. Thanks to Joe for the information on the family of Palmer Trimble.

+ **D1709—Belinda Sue Trimble.** Married Dale Eugene McCarty on July 15,

D - David Trimble

1995.

D1207—Donna Jean Trimble. Daughter of Palmer Trimble and Nola Webb. (Seventh generation of David Trimble and —— Houston.) Born on February 24, 1950. Married Robert O. Schmoll, Jr. on February 15, 1974.

The children of Robert O. Schmoll, Jr. and Donna Jean Trimble:
D1710—Lauren Schmoll.

D1208—Jeanetta Arrowood. Daughter of Flem Arrowood and Lelia Trimble. (Seventh generation of David Trimble and —— Houston.) Born on October 12, 1925 on Barnett's Creek, Johnson County, Kentucky. Married Arthur Browning born on December 31, 1924.

The children of Arthur Browning and Jeanetta Arrowood:
+ **D1711—Arthetta Browning.** Married Gary J. Taylor and they have a son, Michael J. Taylor.
D1712—Daniel Todd Browning. Born on July 11, 1949 and died April 3, 2010 at Hospice by the Sea, Hollywood, Broward County, Florida.
D1713—John Richard "Ric" Browning. Born on December 14, 1958.

D1209—Carmel Ray Arrowood. Son of Flem Arrowood and Lelia Trimble. (Seventh generation of David Trimble and —— Houston.) Born on February 22, 1928. Married Lova Kitchens.

The children of Carmel Ray Arrowood and Lova Kitchens:
D1714—Vickie Arrowood.
D1715—Elaine Arrowood.
D1716—Kim Arrowood.
D1717—Yvonne Arrowood. Married David A. Gritt.

D1210—Lovella F. Arrowood. Daughter of Flem Arrowood and Lelia Trimble. (Seventh generation of David Trimble and —— Houston.) Married Harold Fry.

The children of Harold Fry and Lovella F. Arrowood:
D1718—David Fry.
D1719—Tom Fry.
D1720—Nancy Fry.
D1721—Bill Fry.
D1722—Teresa Fry. Married Roger Stephens.

D1211—Larry G. Arrowood. Son of Flem Arrowood and Lelia Trimble. (Seventh generation of David Trimble and —— Houston.) Born on

September 21, 1935. Married Lillian Smith. Enlisted in the Air force on March 19, 1954 in Ashland, Kentucky. He took basic training in Sampson Air Force Base, New York. He was discharged from active duty in October 1957 at Maxwell Air Force base in Alabama. "President Eisenhower cut back on the Armed Forces at that time and every one that would be discharged in the next 6 months had a choice to get out early, so I took it."

The children of Larry G. Arrowood and Lillian Smith:

D1723—Rebecca K. Arrowood.

D1724—Larry L. Arrowood.

D1725—Rodney V. Arrowood.

D1212—Reece Kenyon Trimble. Son of William Wallace Trimble and Rhena Mae Rice. (Seventh generation of David Trimble and —— Houston.) Born on January 4, 1934 at Johnson County, Kentucky and died on September 19, 2009 at Our Lady of Bellefonte Hospital, Russell, Greenup County, Kentucky.

Married first to Katy Lee. Her last name is unknown.

Married second to Linda Lou Ferrell. She was born on February 11, 1953.

The children of Reece Kenyon Trimble and Linda Lou Ferrell:

D1726—Brian Scott Trimble. Born on July 5, 1977 in Ashland, Kentucky.

D1727—Andrea Dawn Trimble. Born on April 28, 1986 in Ashland, Kentucky.

D1213—William Francis "Bill" Trimble. Son of William Wallace Trimble and Rhena Mae Rice. (Seventh generation of David Trimble and —— Houston.) Born on July 25, 1936 at Pilgrim, Kentucky and died on December 26, 1997 at King's Daughters' Medical Center, Ashland, Boyd County, Kentucky. Married Martha Anderson.

The children of William Francis "Bill" Trimble and Martha Anderson:

D1728—Rhena Trimble.

D1729—Anna Trimble.

D1215—Joe Langley Trimble. Son of Clemince "Pete" Trimble and Mildred Preston. (Seventh generation of David Trimble and —— Houston.) Born on March 1, 1936 in Meally, Kentucky and died on November 11, 1980 in Huntington, Cabell County, West Virginia. Married Nancy May Trogton, born on July 20, 1943 in Wayne, West Virginia. Joe was a barber in Huntington, West Virginia.

The children of Joe Langley Trimble and Nancy May Trogton:

D1730—Stephanie Ann Trimble. Born on August 17, 1963 in Huntington,

D - David Trimble

Cabell County, West Virginia.

+ **D1731—Shelby Jean Trimble.** Born on June 25, 1965 in Huntington, Cabell County, West Virginia. Married John Martin Cole.

D1732—Samuel Trimble. Born on December 8, 1975 in Huntington, Cabell County, West Virginia.

D1216—Dallas L. Trimble. Son of Swanie Lee Trimble and Rhoda Tomblin. (Seventh generation of David Trimble and —— Houston.) Born December 27, 1939 in Huntington, West Virginia. Married Loretta Fay Sharp on March 29, 1960. Loretta was born on August 24, 1944 at Huntington, Cabell County, West Virginia and died on October 20, 1995 at Ohio University Hospital, Columbus, Ohio. She had Leukemia.

Married second to Betty Ann (Osburn) Adkins on April 4, 1997. Betty Ann was born September 28, 1943. Her first husband was Marshall Adkins. He was born February 15, 1946 and died February 15, 1994.

For 20 years or more Dallas and Loretta were the Secretary and Treasurer for the Trimble Reunion that was held at Armco in Ashland, Kentucky. They were responsible for getting the gifts or prizes of the Oldest Man, the Oldest Woman and the Youngest Child. The Youngest Child prize was always a silver cup engraved with Trimble Reunion Youngest Child and the year. They also mailed invitations to remind everyone of the reunion. This was a lot of hard work maintaining address and mailing invitations. They were also the historians for the reunion. Many thanks for all the work over the years. We give our thanks to Dallas for the information on the genealogy of the Joseph Harman Trimble family.

Dallas worked at Armco Steel in Ashland, Kentucky in the Coating Department.

The child of Dallas Trimble and Loretta Sharp:

+ **D1733—Michael Leon Trimble.** Born on November 13, 1961 on Huntington, West Virginia. Married twice.

D1217—Mary Elizabeth Trimble. Daughter of Swanie Lee Trimble and Rhoda Tomblin. (Seventh generation of David Trimble and —— Houston.) Born on August 20, 1942 in Huntington, Cabell County, West Virginia. Married Rayburn Jack Perry on November 28, 1959 in Lavalette, West Virginia. He was born on February 12, 1940 in Wayne County, West Virginia.

Their children of Rayburn Jack Perry and Mary Elizabeth Trimble:

+ **D1734—Sharon Denise Perry.** Born on August 31, 1961 in Huntington, West Virginia. Married Twice.

+ **D1735—Sarah Denell Perry.** Born on August 22, 1963 in Cabell Huntington Hospital in Huntington West Virginia. Married Steve Myrtle in August 2002 in Corpus Christi, Texas.

+ **D1736—Sandra Denice Perry.** Born on December 12, 1964 in Huntington, West Virginia. Married Mr. Fry. They divorced.

D1218—James Wayne "Buckshot" Damron. Son of Floyd William Damron and Lola Marie Trimble. (Seventh generation of David Trimble and —— Houston.) Born on September 5, 1938. Married Mary L. Black.

The children of James Wayne "Buckshot" Damron and Mary L. Black:

D1737—Floyd Damron.

+ **D1738—Lloyd Damron.** Married Tammy.

D1739—James William Damron II. Born on September 2, 1941 in Dunlow, Wayne County, West Virginia and died on October 9, 1941 in Dunlow, Wayne County, West Virginia at one month old.

D1219—Ida Lou Damron. Daughter of Floyd William Damron and Lola Marie Trimble. (Seventh generation of David Trimble and —— Houston.) Born on February 26, 1940. Married Dennis Lee Bowen on June 17, 1960. Dennis was born on March 3, 1939 and died on March 14, 2010.

The children of Dennis Lee Bowen and Ida Lou Damron:

D1740—Denise Carol Bowen. Born on May 31, 1961 in Huntington, West Virginia. Married first to Neil Edwin Stowasser on January 30, 1982. They divorced in 2001.

Married second to James David Smith on August 23, 2003. He was born on September 24, 1960. They divorced in March 2011.

+ **D1741—Deborah Gayle Bowen.** Born on February 9, 1964 in Guthrie Hospital, Huntington, West Virginia. Married Terry Lee Bower on July 19, 1986 at Sybene Missionary Baptist Church, Chesapeake, Ohio.

D1221—Phyllis J. Damron. Daughter of Floyd William Damron and Lola Marie Trimble (Seventh generation of David Trimble and —— Houston.) Married William R. Bocook.

The children of William R. Bocook and Phyllis J. Damron:

D1742—Billy R. Bocook.

+ **D1743—Gregory Scott Bocook.** Born on August 12, 1964 in Huntington, West Virginia. Married Angela Marcum. Born on September 23, 1963.

D1744—David L. Bocook.

D1222—Virginia Gale Damron. Daughter of Floyd William Damron and Lola

D - David Trimble

Marie Trimble. (Seventh generation of David Trimble and —— Houston.) Born on May 15, 1944 in Huntington, West Virginia and died April 24, 2020 in Coal Grove, Ohio. Married Michael F. Fizer on February 1, 1962. Mike was born on April 17, 1943 in Ashland, Kentucky and died January 15, 2016 in Coal Grove, Ohio. He worked for Armco Steel in Ashland, Kentucky in the Coating Department. They were a member of 39th Street Baptist Church in Ashland, Kentucky. Mike was the son of Shirley W. Fizer and Vivian Louise.

The children of Michael F. Fizer and Virginia Gale Damron:

D1745—Michael Dale Fizer. Born on June 20, 1963 in Huntington, West Virginia. Married Roxan Drown on February 3, 1985. She was born on September 23, 1963 in Ironton, Ohio.

D1746—Kimberly Deeann Fizer. Married Donnie Hughes from Fairlawn, West Virginia.

D1223—Larry Ray Dick. Son of Tom Dick and Lillian Trimble (Seventh generation of David Trimble and —— Houston.) Born on December 31, 1957. Married Gloria Angela Sandon on October 25, 1980. Gloria was born on February 28, 1957.

The children of Larry Ray Dick and Gloria Angela Sandon:

+ **D1747—Daniel Ray Dick.** Born on November 30, 1981 in Venice, Italy.

D1748—Lauren Nicole Dick. Born on January 30, 1989 in Venice, Italy.

D1224—Gary Lee Dick. Son of Tom Dick and Lillian Trimble (Seventh generation of David Trimble and —— Houston.) Born on May 28, 1959. Married Pamala Sue Dickerson. She was born on November 26, 1958.

The children of Gary Lee Dick and Pamela Dickerson:

+ **D1749—John William Dick.** Born on January 19, 1979.

D1225—Johnnie Patrick Trimble. Son of Patrick H. Trimble and Julia Cane. (Seventh generation of David Trimble and —— Houston.) Born on October 18, 1918 in Johnson County, Kentucky and died on July 10, 1987 in Columbus, Franklin County, Ohio. Married twice. Married first, Virginia Dare Nelson. She was born on August 29, 1925 in Lincoln, West Virginia and died May 1992 in Kentucky.

Married second Irene May Stump. She was born on November 14, 1924 in Athens, Ohio and died on November 23, 1997 in Columbus, Franklin County, Ohio.

The children of Johnnie Patrick Trimble and Virginia Dare Nelson:

+ **D1750–Johnnie Trimble, Jr.** Born on March 28, 1938 in Paintsville, Kentucky and died July 24, 2022 in Varina, Virginia. Married first to Elodie Bratton on May 1, 1962 from Tacoma Washington in Tacoma Washington and married second to Jean Hogue Trimble on June 19, 1982. He was known on the radio as DJ Big John Trimble. He has been on the cover of People Magazine and is well known within the country music area.

The children of Johnnie Trimble:

D1751–James Harold Trimble. Born on January 18, 1943 in Paintsville, Johnson County, Kentucky and died on March 9, 1994 in Burlington County, New Jersey.

The children of Johnnie Trimble and Irene May Stump:

D1752–Evelyn Ann Trimble. Born on May 3, 1947 in Columbus, Franklin County, Ohio and died on January 14, 2013 in Columbus, Franklin County, Ohio.

D1226–Claude Trimble. Son of Patrick H. Trimble and Julia Cane. (Seventh generation of David Trimble and —— Houston.) Born on January 2, 1921 in Wheelwright, Floyd County, Kentucky and died on August 15, 1982 in Columbus, Franklin County, Ohio. Married Mary Anne O'Neil. He enlisted in the army infantry on December 19, 1940 at Fort Thomas Newport, Kentucky. He was single at the time. He was discharged on November 4, 1945.[68] He married Maryann in 1942. She was born in 1923.

The child of Claude Trimble and Mary Anne O'Neil:

D1753–Claude P. Trimble. Born on August 7, 1943 in Jefferson County, Kentucky and died June 30, 1982.

D1256–John Thomas Trimble. Son of Stanley Trimble and Mattie Crockett. (Seventh generation of David Trimble and —— Houston.) Born on November 8, 1912 and died on March 11, 1959. Married Geneva Arnold. John Thomas was a veteran of World War II.

The children of John Thomas Trimble and Geneva Arnold:

D1754–John Thomas Trimble, Jr.

---

[68] Electronic Army Serial Number Merged File, 1938-1946 [Archival Database]; ARC: 1263923. World War II Army Enlistment Records; Records of the National Archives and Records Administration, Record Group 64; National Archives at College Park. College Park, Maryland, U.S.A.

D - David Trimble

D1755—Frank Eldon Trimble. He is deceased.

D1756—Mary Jo Trimble.

D1257—William Bush Trimble. Son of Stanley Trimble and Mattie Crockett. (Seventh generation of David Trimble and —— Houston.) Born on April 18, 1914 and died on April 3, 1967. Married Elizabeth Reynolds.

The children William Bush Trimble and Elizabeth Reynolds:

D1757—Marvin Lee Trimble. A veteran of the U.S. Navy.

D1758—Emma Jean Trimble. Married a Mr. Stevens.

D1258—Elizabeth Trimble. Daughter of Stanley Trimble and Mattie Crockett. (Seventh generation of David Trimble and —— Houston.) Born on October 13, 1917. Married Stanley Rogers.

The children of Stanley Rogers and Elizabeth Trimble:

D1759—Gilbert Ray Rogers.

D1760—Mary Margaret Rogers.

D1761—Demoss Rogers.

D1762—Bonnie R. Ritchie Rogers.

D1763—Robert Joseph Rogers.

D1764—Billy Rogers. He was a veteran of the U.S. Army.

D1259—Sudie Mae Trimble. Daughter of Stanley Trimble and Mattie Crockett. (Seventh generation of David Trimble and —— Houston.) Born on July 5, 1919. Married Joel Moore.

The daughter of Joel Moore and Sudie Mae Trimble:

D1765—Marilyn Joyce Moore.

D1260—Emmett Ryan Trimble. Son of Stanley Trimble and Mattie Crockett. (Seventh generation of David Trimble and —— Houston.) Born on July 24, 1923 and died December 21, 1962. Married Geneva Romans. Emmett was a veteran of the U.S. Army.

The child of Emmett Ryan Trimble and Geneva Romans:

D1766—Sandra Dee Trimble. Married a Mr. Martin.

D1261—Frances Allene Trimble. Daughter of Stanley Trimble and Mattie Crockett. (Seventh generation of David Trimble and —— Houston.) Born on October 7, 1931. Married George Sallee.

The children of George Sallee and Frances Allene Trimble:

D1767—Larry Allen Sallee.

D1768—George Douglas Sallee. Born on August 21, 1954.

D1769—Thomas Lynn Sallee. Born on July 4, 1960.

D1262—Audrey Jane Trimble. Daughter of J. Smith Trimble and Myrtle Hamilton. (Seventh generation of David Trimble and —— Houston.) Born on July 26, 1923. Married Richard Van Allen.

The children of Richard Van Allen and Audrey Jane Trimble:
D1770—Abbie Lou Allen. Born in 1949.
D1771—Kristie Lee Allen. Born in 1951.
D1772—Susan Jane Allen. Born in 1954.
D1773—Zahni Dee Allen. Born in 1957.

D1263—J. Edward Toy, Jr. Son of J. Edward Toy and Ella Lee Trimble. (Seventh generation of David Trimble and —— Houston.) Born on December 15, 1916. Married Beulah Myers. He was in World War II from November 1943 to June 1946.

The children of J. Edward Toy, Jr. and Beulah Myers:
D1774—Edwina Gail Toy. Born in 1942. Married a Mr. Niemeyer.
D1775—Linda Sue Toy. Born in 1946. Married a Mr. McGuire.
D1776—Kathy Marie Toy. Born in 1952.

D1264—John Crittenden Toy. Son of J. Edward Toy and Ella Lee Trimble. (Seventh generation of David Trimble and —— Houston.) Born on August 14, 1918. Married Gertrude Fletcher. John was in World War II from June 1941 to May 1945 and was at Schofield Barrack when Pearl Harbor was bombed.

The children of John Crittenden Toy and Gertrude Fletcher John:
D1777—Pamela Jane Toy. Born in 1947. Married a Mr. Ishmael.
D1778—Sandra Lee Toy. Born in 1954.

D1265—Nelson Johnson. Son of Raymond W. Johnson and May Edward Trimble. (Seventh generation of David Trimble and —— Houston.) Born on March 10, 1916 and died on April 13, 1969. Married Gretchen ——.

The children of Nelson and Gretchen Johnson:
D1779—Kenneth Johnson.
D1780—Jill Johnson.

D1266—Merle Johnson. Son of Raymond W. Johnson and May Edward Trimble. (Seventh generation of David Trimble and —— Houston.) Born on August 27, 1918. Married Ruth.

The children of Merle and Ruth Johnson:

D - David Trimble

    D1781—Kimberly Johnson.
    D1782—Joyce May Johnson.
    D1783—Amy Lynn Johnson.
    D1784—Mary Ann Johnson.

D1267—Hamet Jane Johnson. Daughter of Raymond W. Johnson and May Edward Trimble. (Seventh generation of David Trimble and —— Houston.) Born on May 11, 1922. Married Woody King.

    The children of Woody King and Hamet Jane Johnson:
    D1785—Maria Jo King.
    D1786—Woody Lynn King.
    D1787—James King.
    D1788—Robert Eugene King.
    D1789—Lou Anne King.

D1268—Cordelia Ann Johnson. Daughter of Raymond W. Johnson and May Edward Trimble. (Seventh generation of David Trimble and —— Houston.) Born on November 18, 1924. Married Fred DuValle.

    The child of Fred DuValle and Cordelia Ann Johnson:
    D1790—Lance Edward DuValle. Born on October 5, 1961.

D1269—Bertie Lou Johnson. Daughter of Raymond W. Johnson and May Edward Trimble. (Seventh generation of David Trimble and —— Houston.) Born on January 24, 1929. Married Arthur Cole.

    The children of Arthur Cole and Bertie Lou Johnson:
    D1791—Christine Diane Cole.
    D1792—Susan Catherine Cole.
    D1793—Arthur Raymond Cole.
    D1794—two children Cole. They died January 31, 1958. (twins).

D1270—Robert Draper Hill. Son of George Draper Hill and Margaret Trimble. (Seventh generation of David Trimble and —— Houston.) Born on January 12, 1920. Married Lorraine Wright of Connecticut. He is a stockbroker in New York and a veteran of World War II.

    The children of Robert Draper Hill and Lorraine Wright:
    D1795—Robert Draper Hill, Jr. Born on December 29, 1954
    D1796—Melissa Wright Hill. Born on December 4, 1956.
    D1797—Elizabeth Porter Hill. Born on May 8, 1959.

D1271—Marcella Haggard Hill. Daughter of George Draper Hill and Margaret

Trimble. (Seventh generation of David Trimble and —— Houston.) Born on October 13, 1923. Married William Howard Chapman, a salesman and farmer at Versailles, Kentucky.

The children of William Howard Chapman and Marcella Haggard Hill:

D1798—William Spurgeon Chapman. Born in 1954.

D1799—Margaret Louise Hope Chapman. Born in 1958.

D1800—Holly Dodge Chapman. Born in 1958.

D1801—Howard Townsend Chapman. Born in 1970.

D1272—Wilbur Marks Hill. Son of George Draper Hill and Margaret Trimble. (Seventh generation of David Trimble and —— Houston.) Born on July 3, 1927. Married Wanda Baker. He is a farmer at Versailles, Kentucky, and a veteran of World War II.

The children of Wilbur Marks Hill and Wanda Baker:

D1802—George Weldon Hill. Born on July 5, 1957 and died at birth.

D1803—Lea Anne Hill. Born on July 30, 1959.

D1804—Wilbur Marks Hill, Jr. Born in 1961.

D1805—John Crittenden Hill. Born in 1962.

D1273—Georgia Doris Yeary. Daughter of William Houston Yeary and Georgia Trimble. (Seventh generation of David Trimble and —— Houston.) Born on February 17, 1926. Married a Mr. Rice and lives in Texas.

The children of Mr. Rice and Georgia Doris Yeary:

D1806—John Parks Rice. Born on January 21, 1947.

D1807—Jacquelyn Schwein Rice. Born on January 23, 1947.

D1274—William Houston Yeary, Jr. Son of William Houston Yeary and Georgia Trimble. (Seventh generation of David Trimble and —— Houston.) Born on December 25, 1932. Married Loretta Ann Phelps of Burgin, Kentucky. He is a veteran of the Korean Conflict, enlisting in the U.S. Air Force in 1951, serving until 1955.

The children of William Houston Yeary, Jr and Loretta Ann Phelps:

D1808—William Yeary, III. Born on April 28, 1953.

D1809—Timothy Scott Yeary. Born on March 13, 1956.

D1810—Kevin Emerson Yeary. Born on April 24, 1959.

D1811—Gina Lee Yeary. Born on July 28, 1971.

D1275—Patricia Joyce Trimble. Daughter of Nelson H. Trimble and Minnie Belle Fortune. (Seventh generation of David Trimble and —— Houston.) Born on March 4, 1933. Married Frank Alien Carroll, whose career is with

Trimble Families of America

the United States Air Force. They live in California.

The children of Frank Alien Carroll and Patricia Joyce Trimble:
D1812—Gerald Alien Carroll. Born on July 19, 1954.
D1813—Jeffrey Bryan Carroll. Born on October 22, 1955.
D1814—Cynthia Gail Carroll. Born on August 14, 1957.
D1815—Scott Emerson Carroll. Born in February 1960.
D1816—Marilee Carroll. Born on December 15, 1961.

D1278—Anne Ryan Carroll. Daughter of Rollie B. Carroll and Catherine Ryan Trimble (Seventh generation of David Trimble and —— Houston.) Born on February 26, 1929. Married Orville Thomas Reynolds. He was born in 1926.

The children of Orville Thomas Reynolds and Anne Ryan Carroll:
D1817—Eric Thomas Reynolds.
D1818—Gregory Ryan Reynolds. Born in 1952.
D1819—Dale Coleman Reynolds. Born in 1955.
D1820—Leslie Orville Reynolds. Born in 1961.
D1821—Todd Carroll Reynolds. Born in 1963.

D1279—Gene Paul Carroll. Son of Rollie B. Carroll and Catherine Ryan Trimble. (Seventh generation of David Trimble and —— Houston.) Born on November 20, 1932. Married Lois Ann Peyton. He is a veteran of the U.S. Air Force, 1951 to 1955. He was in the European theater and Korean Conflict.

The children Gene Paul Carroll of Lois Ann Peyton:
D1822—Valeria Ann Carroll. Born in 1960.
D1823—Paula Gene Carroll. Born in 1962.
D1824—Susan Desiree Carroll. Born in 1963.

D1280—Rollie B. Carroll, Jr. Son of Rollie B. Carroll and Catherine Ryan Trimble. (Seventh generation of David Trimble and —— Houston.) Born on November 5, 1937. Married Jane Elliot Darnall.

The child of Rollie B. Carroll, Jr. and Jane Elliot Darnall:
D1825—Helena Faith Carroll. Born on May 20, 1961.

D1283—Barbara Howard Masters. Daughter of Burgin Howard Masters and Florence Rae Trimble. (Seventh generation of David Trimble and —— Houston.) Born on February 16, 1932. Married Herbert Clyde Riggs.

The children of Herbert Clyde Riggs and Barbara Howard Masters:
D1826—Burgin Radford Riggs. Born in 1954.
D1827—Mira Ann Riggs. Born in 1957 and is deceased.

D1828—Barrett Wesley Riggs. Born in 1959.

D1829—Delia Rae Riggs. Born in 1964.

D1284—Nancy Clay Masters. Daughter of Burgin Howard Masters and Florence Rae Trimble. (Seventh generation of David Trimble and ——— Houston.) Born on October 30, 1934. Married James Lewis Baldwin.

The children of James Lewis Baldwin and Nancy Clay Masters:

D1830—James Lee Baldwin. Born in 1960.

D1831—Gregory Lewis Baldwin. Born in 1965.

D1832—Laura Jane Baldwin. Born in 1969.

D1285—Virginia Rae Masters. Daughter of Burgin Howard Masters and Florence Rae Trimble. (Seventh generation of David Trimble and ——— Houston.) Born on July 5, 1941. Married Harvey Thomas Farris.

The children of Harvey Thomas Farris and Virginia Rae Masters:

D1833—Michael Thomas Farris. Born in 1965.

D1834—Susan Rae Farris. Born in 1968.

D1286—Gary Lee Trimble. Son of Paul Crittenden Trimble and Elizabeth Laudeman. (Seventh generation of David Trimble and ——— Houston.) Born on September 13, 1932. A veteran of the Korean Conflict, he was in the U.S. Air Force from 1951 to 1955.

The children of Gary Lee Trimble:

D1835—Stephen Paul Trimble. Born in 1963.

D1836—Stacy Elizabeth Trimble. Born in 1967.

D1287—Robert Crittenden Trimble. Son of Paul Crittenden Trimble and Elizabeth Laudeman. (Seventh generation of David Trimble and ——— Houston.) Born on January 16, 1935. Married Anne Crane.

The children of Robert Crittenden Trimble and Anne Crane:

D1837—Robert Crittenden Trimble, Jr. Born in 1957.

D1838—Mark Crane Trimble. Born in 1959.

D1839—Amy Marie Trimble. Born in 1972.

D1288—Janice Dale Trimble. Daughter of Paul Crittenden Trimble and Elizabeth Laudeman. (Seventh generation of David Trimble and ——— Houston.) Born on April 26, 1938. Married Robert Duff.

The children of Robert Duff and Janice Dale Trimble:

D1840—Carla Christina Trimble. Born in 1954.

D1841—Kenneth Clark Trimble. Born in 1961.

Trimble Families of America

D - David Trimble

D1291—Emma Golden Trimble. Daughter of Clarence Trimble and Emma Green. (Seventh generation of David Trimble and —— Houston.) Born on May 13, 1901. Married Jim Goin and they lived at Irvine, Kentucky.

The children of Jim Goin and Emma Golden Trimble:
D1842—Howard Goin.
D1843—Virginia Goin.
D1844—James Goin.
D1845—Eddie Roy Goin.

D1293—Mazie Trimble. Daughter of Clarence Trimble and Emma Green. (Seventh generation of David Trimble and —— Houston.) Born on February 6, 1906. Married Everette Nickell in 1923.

The children of Everette Nickell and Mazie Trimble:
D1846—Everette Nickell.
D1847—Margie Nickell.

D1294—Robert Bruce Trimble. Son of Clarence Trimble and Emma Green. (Seventh generation of David Trimble and —— Houston.) Born on January 25, 1909. He was the only son of Clarence and Emma Trimble. Married Helen Davenport of Linn, Ohio, on December 18, 1948.

The daughter of Robert Bruce Trimble and Helen Davenport
D1848—Donna Sue Trimble. Born on April 19, 1956.

D1296—Ruth Esther Trimble. Daughter of Clarence Trimble and Emma Green. (Seventh generation of David Trimble and —— Houston.) Born on April 4, 1915. Married Carl Thomas Gillen and lives in Cincinnati, Ohio.

The son of Carl Thomas Gillen and Ruth Esther Trimble:
D1849—Carl Thomas Gillen.

D1297—Ruby Christine Trimble. Daughter of Clarence Trimble and Emma Green. (Seventh generation of David Trimble and —— Houston.) Born on November 18, 1916. Married Harold Deatherage on May 31, 1941. They live at Earlington, Kentucky.

The children of Harold Deatherage and Ruby Christine Trimble:
D1850—Carol Ann Deatherage.
D1851—Harold Bruce Deatherage.

D1298—Marie Trimble. Daughter of Clarence Trimble and Emma Green. (Seventh generation of David Trimble and —— Houston.) Born on January 30, 1922. Married Charles Brown on December 1, 1942. They live in

334

Louisville, Kentucky.

The children of Charles Brown and Marie Trimble:

D1852—Sandra Jean Brown.

D1853—Charles Edward Brown.

D1854—Janet Marie Brown.

D1328—Martha Newell Trimble. Daughter of Thomas Franklin Trimble and Nancy Dolly Sewell. (Seventh generation of David Trimble and —— Houston.) Born on December 2, 1899. Married William Ellsworth Davis of Winchester, Kentucky on July 13, 1927. William was born on December 30, 1896 in Milton, Oregon. Martha was a teacher and missionary of the Disciples of Christ church.

The children of William Ellsworth Davis and Martha Newell Trimble:

+ **D1855—William Ellsworth Davis, Jr.** Born on August 13, 1929, at Wema in the Belgian Congo. He married Charlotte McIntyre of Atlanta, Georgia on April 5, 1953. William is an engineer.

+ **D1856—Thomas Austin Davis.** Born on May 31, 1934, at Lotumbe in the Belgian Congo. Married Patricia Ann Denham of Woodkirk, England, on March 31, 1959. Thomas is a college professor.

D1331—Nancye Bush Trimble. Daughter of Thomas Franklin Trimble and Nancy Dolly Sewell. (Seventh generation of David Trimble and —— Houston.) Born on September 3, 1915, at Winchester, Kentucky. She married two times: first, to Jasper David Hodson, and second, to Thomas N. Pettus.

The children of Jasper David Hodson and Nancye Trimble:

D1857—Mona Elizabeth Hodson. Born on July 20, 1943, at Louisville, Kentucky, and married Jay Allen Kilgore on April 1, 1966, at Denver, Colorado. They have a child, Kalyn Janene, born on December 28, 1966.

The children of Thomas N. Petus and Nancye Trimble:

+ **D1858—David Jasper Hodson Pettus.** Born on May 22, 1942, at Louisville, Kentucky. Married Linda Joyce Robertson at Houston, Texas.

D1859—Joseph Trimble Hodson Pettus. Born in August 1947 at Louisville, Kentucky. Married Judith Carol Neuno on August 27, 1969, at Littleton, Colorado.

D1860—James Alfred Pettus. Born on October 3, 1950.

D1333—Joe Milbert Bush. Son of Dr David Hardman Bush and Lillian Trimble. (Seventh generation of David Trimble and —— Houston.) Born on

Trimble Families of America

December 17, 1905., Married Martha Frances Bogie on December 18, 1937. Joe is a physician still practicing at Mount Sterling, Kentucky. He lives at the beautiful old home place on the outskirts of Mount Sterling.

The children of Joe Milbert Bush and Martha Frances Bogie:

D1861—David Hardman Bush II. Born on January 15, 1948 in Mount Sterling, Kentucky.

D1862—Robert Herriott Bush. Born on June 13, 1952.

D1334—Bessie Mae Bush. Daughter of Dr. David H. Bush and Lillian Trimble. (Seventh generation of David Trimble and —— Houston.) Born on March 27, 1909 and died on November 30, 1965. She was married on June 16, 1934, to Garrard Riley, Jr.

The children of Garrard Riley, Jr. and Bessie Mae Bush:

D1863—Walter Garrard Riley, III. Died at birth.

+ **D1864—Betty Lou Riley.** Born on August 28, 1940, at Mount Sterling, Kentucky. Married Henry Franklin McGuire on June 2, 1963.

+ **D1865—Joe David Riley.** Born on November 29, 1946, at Mount Sterling, Kentucky. Married Paula Dodd on September 15, 1966.

D1337—Eula Mae Donahue. Daughter of Virgil Donahue and Mary Beulah Trimble. (Seventh generation of David Trimble and —— Houston.) Born on December 5, 1905. Married Verna Lee Hayes on March 29, 1923.

The children of Verna Lee Hayes and Eula Mae Donahue:

D1866—Helen Clay Hayes. Born on December 31, 1923. Married Owen P. Cooper on July 14, 1956.

D1867—Woodford Thomas Hayes. Born on February 10, 1926 and died on March 28, 1927.

D1868—Marvin Edward Hayes. Born on September 26, 1928. Married Zahoma Dyer of Jeffersonville, Indiana, on September 3, 1955.

D1869—Harold Lee Hayes. Born on May 2, 1933. Married Ruth Bowles on May 10, 1956.

D1870—Mary Ray Hayes. Born on September 16, 1935. Married Donald Montgomery on October 28, 1961.

D1871—Judith Ann Hayes. Born on November 10, 1940. Married Charles Newkirk on January 25, 1959.

D1872—Carol Marie Hayes. Born on June 11, 1943. Married Howard Webb, Jr., on November 25, 1966.

D1338—Bertha Ray Donahue. Daughter of Virgil Donahue and Mary Beulah

Trimble. (Seventh generation of David Trimble and —— Houston.) Born on July 22, 1909. Married John R. Tipton on March 25, 1930.

The children of John R. Tipton and Bertha Ray Donahue:

D1873—Tamara Ann Tipton. Born on July 11, 1942. Married Julian D. Williams, Jr., on November 27, 1968.

D1874—Virginia Barsha Tipton. Born on August 7, 1947. Married Meredith Reynolds on November 26, 1966.

D1370—John Isaac Hopkins. Son of Zenophon Hopkins and Mary Elizabeth Trimble (Seventh generation of David Trimble and —— Houston.) Born on December 15, 1918. Married Lucille Quig, and lives at Mace, Indiana. He was a carpenter by trade.

The children of John Isaac Hopkins and Lucille Quig:

D1875—Susan Irene Hopkins. Born on February 2, 1943. Married Charles Elliott and they have a son William Franklin Elliott.

+ **D1876—Marietta Maxine Hopkins.** Born on September 2, 1944. She married Paul Hines.

D1371—Raymond Edward Trimble. Son of Roy Caster Trimble and Mary Potts. (Seventh generation of David Trimble and —— Houston.) Born on October 19, 1906. Married Grace Abbey of England. He is now retired, and Grace is head housekeeper at the Holiday Inn at Crawfordsville, Indiana.

The children of Raymond Edward Trimble and Grace Abbey:

+ **D1877—Betty Jane Trimble.** Born on June 13, 1928. Married Charles Hutchison. Betty is bookkeeper at Elston Indiana Bank and Charles is a farmer. They live at Parkersburg, Indiana.

+ **D1878—Raymond Edward Trimble, Jr.** Born on July 10, 1948. Married Barbara Dvorak. He is an artist. They live at East Greenville, Pennsylvania.

D1372—Hazel Marie Trimble. Daughter of Roy Caster Trimble and Mary Potts. (Seventh generation of David and —— Houston Trimble.) Born on November 18, 1908. Married Otis James Bayless on December 31, 1934. They live at Alamo, Indiana. Otis is a book repairman at the R. R. Donnelly Printing Company.

The children of Otis James Bayless and Hazel Marie Trimble:

+ **D1879—Jerry Dean Bayless.** Born on June 21, 1939. Married Joann Quisenberry on September 7, 1958. Jerry works at the R. R. Donnelly Printing Company, and they live near Crawfordsville, Indiana.

+ **D1880—Larry Joe Bayless.** Born on June 21, 1939. Married Doris Ball on September 1, 1961. Larry works for Indiana Bell Telephone Company. They live at Brownsburg, Indiana. Larry is working towards a degree in business administration.

+ **D1881—James Bayless.** Born on May 20, 1944. Married Susan Campbell and they live near Brownsburg, Indiana. Both are graduates of Indiana State University. He is computer manager for Indiana Bell Telephone Company in Indianapolis, Indiana.

D1373—Owen Leroy Trimble. Son of Roy Caster Trimble and Mary Potts. (Seventh generation of David and —— Houston Trimble.) Born on June 11, 1912. Married Margaret Brown and they live at New Market, Indiana.

The children of Owen Leroy Trimble and Margaret Brown:

D1882—Paul Eugene. Born on April 24, 1956.

D1883—Beth Ann Trimble. Born on May 8, 1963.

D1374—Helen May Trimble. Daughter of Roy Caster Trimble and Mary Potts. (Seventh generation of David and —— Houston Trimble.) Born on December 16, 1915. Married Wendell Simpson on May 15, 1937. They live at New Market, Indiana.

The child of Wendell Simpson and Helen May Trimble:

+ **D1884—Michael Kent Simpson.** Born on November 5, 1943. Married Jo Ann Stout on October 21, 1967. They live in Columbus, Indiana.

D1376—Robert Trimble. Son of John Sherman Trimble and Mary Mulligan. (Seventh generation of David and —— Houston Trimble.) Born on October 19, 1916. Married Martha Shannon on May 21, 1949.

The children of Robert Trimble and Martha Shannon:

D1885—Cheryl Ann Trimble. Born on July 13, 1951.

D1886—Pamela Kay Trimble. Born on March 2, 1956.

D1379—Thelma Trimble. Daughter of William Trimble and Cleo Groves. (Seventh generation of David and —— Houston Trimble.) Married a Mr. Skaggs.

The children of Mr. Skaggs and Thelma Trimble:

D1887—Betty Skaggs.

D1888—Thomas Skaggs.

D1889—Donald Skaggs.

D1890—Nelson Skaggs.

D1891—James Skaggs.

D1892–Alice Skaggs.

D1893–Gene Skaggs.

D1382–Vance Trimble. Son of Worth Trimble and Gertrude Vance. (Seventh generation of David and —— Houston Trimble.) Married Gwen O'Dell. He now lives in Florida.

The children of Vance Trimble and Gwen O'Dell:

D1894–Vance Trimble.

D1895–Barbara Trimble.

D1383–Jean Trimble. Daughter of Worth Trimble and Gertrude Vance. (Seventh generation of David and —— Houston Trimble.) Married Warren Sefton of Richwood, West Virginia.

The son of Warren Sefton and Jean Trimble:

D1896–Thomas Sefton.

D1385–Russie Gay Groves. Daughter of Rush Hereford Groves and Lola Ann Trimble. (Seventh generation of David and —— Houston Trimble.) Married two times: first, to Delbert Groves, and second, to William Rader.

The children of Delbert Groves and Russie Gay Groves:

D1897–Nina Ellen Groves.

D1898–Leo Ray Groves.

The children of William Rader and Russie Gay Groves:

D1899–William Alton Rader.

D1900–Kenneth Hereford Rader.

D1392–Gladys Virginia Bailes. Daughter of Volley Andrew Bailes and Bessie Lee Trimble. (Seventh generation of David and —— Houston Trimble.) Married two times: first, to Lewis M. Power, and second, to Charles Fisher.

The children of Lewis M. Power and Gladys Virginia Bailes:

D1901–Linn Lee Power.

D1902–Elizabeth Ann Power.

The children of Charles Fisher and Gladys Virginia Bailes:

D1903–Sandra Leigh Fisher.

D1904–Charles E. Fisher.

D1393–Okey Lester Bailes. Son of Volley Andrew Bailes and Bessie Lee Trimble. (Seventh generation of David and —— Houston Trimble.) Born on March 14, 1918. Married Leona Mary Malouse on October 15, 1943. Okey is an enthusiastic genealogist. He has devoted much of his life to the research and study of family history. His relentless interest and contribution of material to this author is greatly appreciated. Okey has two years of college and armed force duty of five years in World War II and two years in the Korean Conflict. Okey lives at 1808 E. 7th Street, Parkersburg, West Virginia 26101.

The children of Okey Lester Bailes and Leona Mary Malouse:

D1905—Susan Lee Bailes. Born on May 23, 1946, Married John D. Slonager IV on July 3, 1965.

+ D1906—Robert Joseph Bailes. Born on April 19, 1948. Married Susan Nicholas on June 22, 1968

D1907—Diana Rosemary Bailes. Born on September 16, 1953.

D1400—Gailord Washington Trimble. Son of Ray Trimble and Lou Marsh. (Seventh generation of David Trimble and —— Houston.) Born on September 13, 1920, at Tioga, West Virginia. Married Rose Mondene McClung of Nallen, where they now live.

The son of Gailord Washington Trimble and Rose Mondene McGlung:

D1908—Donald Wayne Trimble. Born on October 22, 1947. Married Barbara Green of Lookout, West Virginia. Wayne Trimble is employed by the National Bank of Commerce in Charleston, West Virginia, where he is operations officer in the bank's credit department. Wayne graduated from Nuttall High School in Lookout and attended West Virginia State College at Institute, West Virginia. Wayne and Barbara Trimble are the parents of Michael Wayne Trimble, born on October 8, 1970. They live at Dunbar, West Virginia.

D1403—Betty Jean Trimble. Daughter of Ray Trimble and Lou Marsh. (Seventh generation of David Trimble and —— Houston.) Born on January 22, 1929. Married Clyde Perkins on May 4, 1952.

The children of Clyde Perkins and Betty Jean Trimble:

D1909—Janet Kay Perkins. Born on May 21, 1955. They live at Cowen, West Virginia.

D1910—Larry Ray Perkins. Born on October 19, 1956. They live at Cowen, West Virginia.

D1911—Jeffrey Clyde Perkins. Born on March 22, 1958. They live at Cowen, West Virginia.

D1912—Debra Jean Perkins. Born on August 1, 1961. They live at Cowen, West Virginia.

D1404—Arthur Lee Trimble Son of Everette Trimble and Belle George. (Seventh generation of David Trimble and ——— Houston.) Born in August 1933 at Birch River, West Virginia. Married Elizabeth Dyer of Hookersville, West Virginia. They live in Kent, Ohio.

The children of Arthur Lee Trimble and Elizabeth Dyer:
D1913—Arthur Lee Trimble, Jr. Born in 1960.
D1914—James Earl Trimble. Born in 1964.

D1406—Maurice Copeland Trimble. Son of John Farley Trimble and Vernice Copeland. (Seventh generation of David Trimble and ——— Houston.) Born on July 12, 1936, at Richwood, West Virginia. Married Mary Ursula Watson of Manotick, Canada. Mary was born on September 25, 1933 and is the daughter of Harry and Anna Watson of Manotick. Maurice and Mary were married on May 17, 1958, in Canada. She is a graduate registered nurse and Maurice owns his own business in Valparaiso, Indiana, where they now live. At the time of the writing of this book (first edition), this family is on a several weeks tour of the British Isles.

The children of Maurice Copeland Trimble and Mary Ursula Watson:
D1915—Mark Trimble. Born on April 30, 1959 in Canada.
D1916—Rhonda Trimble. Born on October 31, 1961 in Canada.
D1917—Timothy Trimble. Born on November 24, 1962 in Canada.
D1918—James Trimble. Born on November 24, 1962 in Canada.

D1407—Michael Anthony Trimble. Son of John Farley Trimble and Vernice Copeland. (Seventh generation of David Trimble and ——— Houston.) Born on February 16, 1942, at Richwood, West Virginia. Married on March 24, 1967, at Crab Orchard, West Virginia, to Loretta Lively, daughter of Carnie and Judah Irene Lively. She was born on September 24, 1932 in Weirwood, West Virginia, Michael graduated on June 8, 1969, from the School of Business at Valparaiso University in Indiana with magna cum laude honors. He is associated with Peat, Marwick and Mitchell and Company in Roanoke, Virginia, as a certified public accountant.

The children of Michael Anthony Trimble and Loretta Lively:
+ D1919—John Michael Trimble. Born on June 15, 1968.
+ D1920—Paul Anthony Trimble. Born on January 18, 1972. Married to Rebecca Mattson Trimble.

D1412—Emma Jean Metcalf. Daughter of Henry Bryan Metcalf and Emma Mae Trimble. (Seventh generation of David Trimble and ——— Houston.) Born on

Trimble Families of America

March 16, 1921, at Durant, Oklahoma. Married Raymond R. Sirkle on September 22, 1939, at Oklahoma City.

The children of Raymond R. Sirkle and Emma Jean Metcalf:

+ **D1921—Sharon Katherine Sirkle.** Born on February 5, 1941 in Durant, Oklahoma. Married Stanley Knight.

+ **D1922—Raymond Bryan Sirkle.** Born on May 19, 1948 in Prestonsburg, Kentucky. Married Sharyn ——.

D1413—Mary Katherine Metcalf. Daughter of Henry Bryan Metcalf and Emma Mae Trimble. (Seventh generation of David Trimble and —— Houston.) Born on September 27, 1923, at Durant, Oklahoma. Married O. A. Benovsky on September 4, 1948, in Dallas, Texas.

The children of O. A. Benovsky and Mary Katherine Metcalf:

D1923—Nancy Ann Benovsky. Born on March 19, 1954, at Dallas, Texas.

D1924—Linda Katherine Benovsky. Born on November 26, 1957.

D1434—Ralph Wright Ogilvie. Son of Edward James Ogilvie and Mary Grace Wright. (Eighth generation of David Trimble and —— Houston.) Born on December 23, 1893 in Hancock, Illinois and died on May 11, 1961. Married Jessie E. Thompson on December 24, 1914 in Quincy, Adams County, Illinois. Jessie was born on April 23, 1895 in Pilot Grove, Hancock County, Illinois and died on December 25, 1981 in Harrisonville, Cass County, Missouri.

The child of Ralph Wright Ogilvie and Jessie E. Thompson:

D1925—Dorothy Margaret Ogilvie. Born on November 5, 1917 in Illinois and died on January 29, 2007 in Harrisonville, Cass County, Missouri. Married Donald Francis Ellis on September 14, 1946 Kansas City, Jackson County, Missouri. Donald was born on August 22, 1924 in Trenton, Grundy County, Missouri and died on November 3, 2004 in Harrisonville, Cass County, Missouri.

D1447–John B. "Buddy" Harlow. Son of Earnest Harlow and Eula Dee Powel. (Eighth generation of David Trimble and —— Houston.) Born on May 31, 1927 and died on April 10, 2008 in Menomonee Falls, Waukesha County, Wisconsin. Married unnamed.

The child of John B "Buddy" Harlow:

D1926—Thomas Jay Harlow. Born in 1949.

D1455–Henry Carl Hall. Son of Ernest Hall and Ivan Trimble. (Eighth generation of David Trimble and —— Houston.) Born on March. 25, 1919.

He married Martha Elson on November 28, 1946. Henry was a Baptist Minister. His lived in Gladwin, Michigan.

The children of Henry Carl Hall and Martha Elson:

D1927—James H. Hall.

D1928—John D. Hall.

D1457—James Carl Welch. Son of Arthur Welch and Ova Trimble (Eighth generation of David Trimble and —— Houston.) Born on January 12, 1920. Married Delcie Webb and they live at 14705 E. 39th Street, Independence, Missouri.

The children of James Carl Welsh and Delcie Webb:

D1929—Terry Welch.

D1930—Sherre Welch.

D1458—Arthur Welch, Jr. Son of Arthur Welch and Ova Trimble (Eighth generation of David Trimble and —— Houston.) Born on February 27, 1925. Married Mary Ann ——. They live in Kearney, Missouri.

The children of Arthur Welch, Jr. and Mary Ann ——:

D1931—Ronald Welch. He is with the U.S. Navy

D1932—Pamela Welch.

D1933—Claudia Welch.

D1934—Paula Welch.

D1935—Cindy Welch.

D1936—Laura Jo Welch.

D1459—Betty Welch. Daughter of Arthur Welch and Ova Trimble (Eighth generation of David Trimble and —— Houston.) Born on March 7, 1930. Married Gregg Tindall. They live at 2607 Scott, Independence, Missouri.

The children of Gregg Tindall and Betty Welch:

D1937—Debra Tindall.

D1938—Kristy Tindall.

D1939—Larry Gregg Tindall.

D1460—Bobby Clay Welch. Son of Arthur Welch and Ova Trimble (Eighth generation of David Trimble and —— Houston.) Born on August 14, 1933. Married Ellen Duncan. Bobby is a lawyer in Sugar Creek, Missouri.

The children of Bobby Clay Welch and Ellen Duncan:

D1940—Denise Welch.

D1941—Andra Welch.

Trimble Families of America

D1461—Janet Trimble. Daughter of Rucker Jim Trimble and Iva Centers. (Eighth generation of David Trimble and —— Houston.) Born on July 28, 1935, and married Eugene Spencer. They live on Route 2, Mount Sterling, Kentucky.

The children of Eugene Spencer and Janet Trimble:
D1942—John Tracy Spencer. Born on January 14, 1954.
D1943—Janella Spencer. Born on June 14, 1956.
D1944—Marquelaha Spencer. Born on November 1, 1957.
D1945—Joyce Ann Spencer. Born on July 1, 1960.

D1462—Ewell Lee Trimble. Son of Rucker Jim Trimble and Iva Centers. (Eighth generation of David Trimble and —— Houston.) Born on November 28, 1936. Married Effa D. Hutison.

The son of Ewell Lee Trimble and Effa D. Hutison:
D1946—Rickey Lee Trimble. Born on December 4, 1960.

D1463—DeLaura Jean Trimble. Daughter of Rucker Jim Trimble and Iva Centers. (Eighth generation of David Trimble and —— Houston.) Born on March 17, 1938. Married James Stiltmer. They live in Frenchburg, Kentucky.

The children of James Stiltmer and DeLaura Jean Trimble:
D1947—Wesley Lee Stiltmer. Born on February 19, 1959.
D1948—Jimmy Wayne Stiltmer. Born on October 2, 1963.

D1469—Ronald Kent Trimble. Son of Sterling Sidney Trimble and Alice Parker. (Eighth generation of David Trimble and —— Houston.) Married Jean Quillan.

The children of Ronald Kent Trimble and Jean Quillan:
D1949—Geneva Trimble.
D1950—Thelma Trimble.
D1951—Kenneth Trimble.
D1952—Keith Trimble.
D1953—Nathaniel Trimble.

D1470—Michael Carl Trimble. Son of Sterling Sidney Trimble and Alice Parker. (Eighth generation of David Trimble and —— Houston.) Married Sherlyn ——. They live at Route 3, Spencer, Indiana.

The children of Michael Carl Trimble and Sherlyn ——:
D1954—Sidney Trimble.
D1955—Michael Carl Trimble, Jr.
D1956—LoAnn Trimble.

D1957—Phillip N. Trimble.

D1958—David B. Trimble.

D1471—David Lee Trimble. Son of Sterling Sidney Trimble and Alice Parker. (Eighth generation of David Trimble and —— Houston.) Married Sharon ————. They have a stock sales company in Cloverdale, Indiana.

The children of David Lee Trimble and Sharon ——:

D1959—Randy Trimble.

D1960—Ricky Trimble.

D1474—Saundra Gay Trimble. Daughter of Sterling Sidney Trimble and Alice Parker. (Eighth generation of David Trimble and —— Houston.) Married Melvin Lady and they live at Route 7, Bloomington, Indiana.

The children of Melvin Lady and Saundra Gay Trimble:

D1961—Clint E. Lady.

D1962—Brent Lady.

D1493—Robert Paul Trimble. Son of Theodore Trimble and Lula Picklesimer. (Eighth generation of David Trimble and —— Houston.) Born in 1933 in Barnett's Creek, Johnson County, Kentucky and died in 1991 in Paintsville, Johnson County, Kentucky. Married Joann Peck. She was born on October 18, 1934 and August 13, 2022 at Paintsville ARH, Paintsville, Kentucky. She was the daughter of Walter Jay Pack and Marie Rice.

The children of Robert Paul Trimble and Jo Ann Peck:

+ **D1963—David Paul "Odie" Trimble.** Born on May 19, 1951 in Johnson County, Kentucky and died on December 12, 2018 in Pikeville, Kentucky.

+ **D1964—Judy Ann Trimble.** She was a runner on the Paintsville High School Track Team, going to the state meet.

D1965—Brenda Sue Trimble.

D1966—Shirley Sue Trimble.

D1495—Pauline Trimble. Daughter of John Trimble and Maymie Home. (Eighth generation of David Trimble and —— Houston.) Born on November 13, 1929. Married William E. "Jack" Tackett, born on November 3, 1922.

The children of William E. "Jack" Tackett and Pauline Trimble:

D1967—Elizabeth Ann Tackett. Born on June 8, 1950, Married Larry M. Butcher. He was born in 1950.

D1968—Brenda Kay Tackett. Born on August 16, 1952.

D - David Trimble

D1969—Pamela Sue Tackett. Born on November 25, 1954.
D1970—Billy Francis Tackett. Born on October 30, 1956.
D1971—Robbyn Lynn Tackett. Born on July 25, 1960.

D1496—Billie Jean Trimble. Daughter of John Trimble and Maymie Home. (Eighth generation of David Trimble and —— Houston.) Born on February 7, 1931 Married Donald E. Huston.

The children of Donald Huston and Billie Jean Trimble:
D1972—Mitchel Lynn Huston. Born on April 10, 1951.
D1973—Mark Huston. Born on January 31, 1960.

D1498—Markus Ray Trimble. Son of John Trimble and Maymie Home. (Eighth generation of David Trimble and —— Houston.) Born on December 16, 1939. Married Glenna Williams.

The children of Markus Ray Trimble and Glenna Williams:
D1974—John Walter. Born on June 18, 1960.
D1975—Leslie Ray Trimble. Born on August 30, 1966.

D1503—Opal Gullett. Daughter of Everett Gullett and June Trimble. (Eighth generation of David Trimble and —— Houston.) Born on September 6, 1915. Married Francis Martin in 1933.

The children of Francis Martin and Opal Gullett:
+ **D1976—David Martin.** Married Gretchen Ames.
+ **D1977—James Robert Martin.** Married Rose Marie Hanks.
+ **D1978—Lucille Martin.** Married Robert Bischoff.

D1505—Paris Ezekiel Gullett. Daughter of Everett Gullett and June Trimble. (Eighth generation of David Trimble and —— Houston.) Married Jean Ruggles.

The children of Paris Ezekiel Gullett and Jean Ruggles:
D1979—Dorinda Gullett.
D1980—Linda Gullett. Married James Layne in 1968.
D1981—Robert Paris Gullett.
D1982—James Mark Gullett.

D1506—Agnes Gullett. Daughter of Everett Gullett and June Trimble. (Eighth generation of David Trimble and —— Houston.) Married twice. Married first to Carl Lundy. Married second to William Kapp.

The daughter of Carl Lundy and Agnes Gullett:
D1983—Carolyn Gullett Lundy.

The children of William Kapp and Agnes Gullett:

D1984—Barbara Kapp.

D1985—Patricia Kapp.

D1510—Lillian Gullett. Daughter of Everett Gullett and June Trimble. (Eighth generation of David Trimble and —— Houston.) Married Jim Meade in 1956. Lillian married the second time to Atue Shah in 1966.

The children of Jim Meade and Lillian Gullett:

D1986—Julia Meade.

D1987—Melori Lou Meade.

D1511—Eldon Gullett. Son of Everett Gullett and June Trimble. (Eighth generation of David Trimble and —— Houston.) Married in 1954 to Loretta Vaughters.

The children of Eldon Gullett and Loretta Vaughters:

D1988—Melanie Gullett.

D1989—Wade Gullett.

D1990—Darrell Gullett.

D1991—Brian Gullett.

D1513— Jeffrey Bruce Roberts, Jr. Son of Frank Bayes and Elva Trimble. (Eighth generation of David Trimble and —— Houston.) Born on October 15, 1930. Married Yolonda —— of Tucson, Arizona.

Their children Bruce Roberts, Jr. and Yolonda ——:

D1992—Mark Roberts.

D1993—Dave Roberts.

D1994—Bruce Roberts, III.

D1995—Maria Roberts.

D1996—Elva Grace Roberts.

D1514—Frances Trimble. Daughter of Robert Eldon "Bob" Trimble and Anna Picklesimer. (Eighth generation of David Trimble and —— Houston.) Born on July 23, 1924. Married Virgil Tague of 127 Noble, La Porte, Indiana.

The children of Virgil Tague and Frances Trimble:

D1997—Keith Tague.

D1998—Kristi Tague.

D1515—Charles G. Trimble. Son of Robert Eldon "Bob" Trimble and Anna Picklesimer. (Eighth generation of David Trimble and —— Houston.) Born on February 13, 1926. Married Marsha ——.

Trimble Families of America

The children of Charles G. Trimble and Marsha ——:

D1999—Charles Trimble, Jr.
D2000—Sonjia Trimble.
D2001—Robert Trimble.

D1516—Ruby Carroll Trimble. Daughter of Robert Eldon "Bob" Trimble and Anna Picklesimer. (Eighth generation of David Trimble and —— Houston.) Born on July 17, 1933. Married Ollis Pigman.

The child of Ollis Pigman and Ruby Carroll Trimble:

D2002—Carolyn Trimble.

D1517—Bobby Green. Daughter of Ora Green and stepdaughter of Jewel Trimble. (Eighth generation of David Trimble and —— Houston.) Born on March 22, 1929. Married Edsel Rice.

The children of Edsel Rice and Bobby Green:

D2003—Kathy Rice. Married Roger Abbott. Their daughter Dana born in 1952.

D1518—James E. Green. Son of Ora Green and stepdaughter of Jewel Trimble. (Eighth generation of David Trimble and —— Houston.) Born on September 5, 1931. Married Phyllis Fulks in 1954.

The children of James E. Green and Phyllis Fulks:

D2004—James Gregory Green.
D2005—Terri Ann Green.
D2006—Todd Dean Green.

D1519—Delena Jewell Baldwin. The foster daughter of Ora Green and Jewel Trimble. (Eighth generation of David Trimble and —— Houston.) Born on June 30, 1949. Married Larry Blanton in 1968.

The daughter of Larry Blanton and Delena Jewel Baldwin:

D2007—Vicki Shauna Blanton. Born on April 9, 1970.

D1520—Anna Martha Trimble. Daughter of Rexford Raymond Trimble and Bertha Mae Blanton. (Eighth generation of David Trimble and —— Houston.) Born on December 10, 1922. Married on December 23, 1942, to Oval D. Williams, born in 1921. They live at 6049 Whitman Road, Columbus, Ohio.

The children of Oval D. Williams and Anna Martha Trimble:

D2008—John Dennis Williams. Born on August 18, 1950. He attends Miami of Ohio University.
D2009—Lynn Edward Williams. Born on January 9, 1954.

D1523—Betty Jo Trimble. Daughter of Rexford Raymond Trimble and Bertha Mae Blanton. (Eighth generation of David Trimble and ——— Houston.) Born on July 21, 1932. Married Henry Edward Burchett on June 1, 1952. He was born on March 3, 1933. They were divorced in 1965. Betty Jo lives at 16206 Pamela Jo Avenue, Eastwood, Kentucky. (We are gratefully indebted to Betty Jo for much hard work and research in the information she has given us for this genealogy.)

Their children of Edward Burchett and Betty Jo Trimble:

D2010—Vicky Jo Burchett. Born on January 19, 1958.

D2011—David Edward Burchett. Born on December 28, 1962.

D1524—John Henry Trimble. Son of Rexford Raymond Trimble and Bertha Mae Blanton. (Eighth generation of David Trimble and ——— Houston.) Born on June 21, 1934 and died on June 8, 2009. Married Vella Ruth Ferguson on February 27, 1960. She was born on September 23, 1933 and died on June 17, 2009. John and Vella buried in Rose Hill Cemetery in Ashland, Boyd County, Kentucky. They lived at 3314 Pine Haven Drive, Ashland, Boyd County, Kentucky.

The children of John Henry Trimble and Vella Ruth Ferguson:

D2012—Jacqueline Denise Trimble. Born on April 16, 1961.

+ **D2013—Rexford Lee Trimble.** Born on January 2, 1966. Married on Mary Katherine Worthington on August 17, 1991. She was born on August 29, 1970.

D1526—Delmas Jay Preston, Jr. Son of Delmas Preston and Victoria Auxier Trimble. (Eighth generation of David Trimble and ——— Houston.) Born on May 4, 1936. Married Nieda Lee Vickers in December 1959. They live at 718 Middletown Avenue, Westwood, Ohio.

The children of Delmas Jay Preston, Jr. and Nieda Lee Vickers:

D2014—Delmas J. Preston. Born on September 8, 1961.

D2015—Charles Jackson Preston. Born on November 16, 1962.

D2016—Jonathan Lee Preston. Born on July 14, 1964.

D1537—Vivian Ruth Colvin. Daughter of Charlie H. Colvin and Fanny Trimble. (Eighth generation of David Trimble and ——— Houston.) Married Robert Preston of Wittensville, Kentucky.

The children of Robert Preston and Vivian Ruth Colvin:

D2017—Michael Preston.

D2018—Charles Virgil Preston.

D1538—Lillian Jo Ann Colvin. Daughter of Charlie H. Colvin and Fanny Trimble. (Eighth generation of David Trimble and —— Houston.) Married Bill Meadows.

    The children of Bill Meadows and Lillian Jo Ann Colvin:

D2019—Gregory Meadows.

D2020—Larry Meadows.

D2021—Kristie Renae Meadows.

D1553—Ethel Janet Cantrell. Daughter of Irvin Cantrell and Laura Trimble. (Eighth generation of David Trimble and —— Houston.) Married Sam Burke They lived in Dayton, Ohio.

    The children of Sam Burke and Ethel Janet Cantrell:

D2022—Edna Marie Burke.

D2023—James Leroy Burke.

D2024—Keith Eugene Burke.

D2025—Sam Burke, Jr.

D2026—Mary Elizabeth Burke.

D1554—Earl Pelphrey. Son of Frank Pelphrey and Merzie Vanhoose. (Eighth generation of David Trimble and —— Houston.) Born on February 14, 1924. Married Pauline Phelps, born in 1925.

    The children of Earl Pelphrey and Pauline Phelps:

D2027—George Pelphrey. Born in 1946.

D2028—Billy Ray Pelphrey. Born in 1947.

D2029—Paulette Pelphrey. Born in 1949.

D2030—Leon Pelphrey. Born in 1951.

D2031—Erma Pelphrey. Born in 1954.

D2032—Murzie Pelphrey. Born in 1956.

D2033—Samuel Pelphrey. Born in 1958.

D2034—Ova Pelphrey. Born in 1963.

D2035—Denise Pelphrey. Born in 1965.

D1555—Olga Pelphrey. Daughter of Frank Pelphrey and Merzie Vanhoose. (Eighth generation of David Trimble and —— Houston.) Born on April 25, 1925, and married Don H. Mohler. He was born in 1922.

    The children of Don H. Mohler and Olga Pelphrey:

D2036—Linda Mohler. Born in 1950.

D2037—Donald R. Mohler. Born in 1953.

D1557—Lowell Pelphrey. Son of Frank Pelphrey and Merzie Vanhoose. (Eighth generation of David Trimble and —— Houston.) Born on June 1, 1929. Married Betty Ruth Williams, born in 1931.

Their children of Lowell Pelphrey and Betty Ruth Williams:

D2038—Debra L. Pelphrey. Born in 1957.

D2039—Eric Scott Pelphrey. Born in 1960.

D2040—Michael Lowell Pelphrey. Born in 1963.

D1558—Billie Lee Pelphrey. Daughter of Frank Pelphrey and Merzie Vanhoose. (Eighth generation of David Trimble and —— Houston.) Born on December 11, 1932. Married Jessie Lee Hall.

The children of Billie Lee Pelphrey and Jessie Lee Hall:

D2041—Merisa Jo Pelphrey. Born in 1953.

D2042—Randy Allen Pelphrey. Born in 1954.

D2043—Jerry Lee Pelphrey. Born in 1956.

D2044—Brenda E. Pelphrey. Born in1962.

D1559—Christine Pelphrey. Daughter of Frank Pelphrey and Merzie Vanhoose. (Eighth generation of David Trimble and —— Houston.) Born on July 3, 1931. Married James H. Wright, born in1933. They live at Red Bush, Kentucky.

The children of James H. Wright and Christine Pelphrey:

D2045—Teresa Ann Wright. Born in 1960.

D2046—James Douglas Wright. Born in 1963.

D1561—Bennie Pelphrey. Son of Frank Pelphrey and Merzie Vanhoose. (Eighth generation of David Trimble and —— Houston.) Born on April 8, 1937. Married Janet Keaton.

The children of Bennie Pelphrey and Janet Keaton:

D2047—Jeffery Scott Pelphrey. Born in 1959.

D2048—Bennie Eugene Pelphrey. Born in 1960.

D2049—Tammy Marie Pelphrey. Born in 1961.

D1595—Eulah Trimble. Daughter of Ora Trimble and Edna Lewis. (Eighth generation of David Trimble and —— Houston.) Born on March 8, 1922, at Lenox, Kentucky. She married Charles Hughes and lives in Marion, Ohio. Eulah has two children by a previous marriage:

The children of Charles Hughes and Eulah Trimble

D2050—Wanda Rae Watts. Married to Ronald Hughes.

D2051—William Foster Watts.

Trimble Families of America

D1596—Dolly Trimble. Daughter of Ora Trimble and Edna Lewis. (Eighth generation of David Trimble and —— Houston.) Born on November 20, 1924, at Open Fort Sandy in Elliott County, Kentucky. She married Robert Chester Vicker, Jr. This family lives in Phoenix, Arizona.

The children of Robert Chester Vicker, Jr. and Dolly Trimble:
D2052—Kenneth Chester Vicker.
D2053—James Thomas Vicker.
D2054—Richard Ray Vicker.

D1597—James Robert Trimble. Son of Ora Trimble and Edna Lewis. (Eighth generation of David Trimble and —— Houston.) Born on December 20, 1926 at Lenox, Kentucky and died in a truck accident on February 7, 1968. He married Ann Elizabeth May. (We are gratefully indebted to Miss Diana Lynn Trimble of 118 Nineteenth Street, Paris, Kentucky 40361, for the vast amount of information given us concerning her Trimble line.)

The three daughters of James Robert Trimble and Ann Elizabeth May:
D2055—Diana Lynn Trimble.
D2056—Janice Marie Trimble.
D2057—Patsy Delores Trimble.

D1599—Ray Trimble. Son of Ora Trimble and Edna Lewis. (Eighth generation of David Trimble and —— Houston.) Born on March 9, 1930, at Lenox, Kentucky. He married Lou Barker.

The children of Ray Trimble and Lou Baker:
D2058—Linda Sue Trimble.
D2059—Danny Ray Trimble.
D2060—Phillip Trimble.
D2061—Timothy Trimble.
D2062—Vicky Lynn Trimble.

D1600—Lawrence Trimble. Son of Ora Trimble and Edna Lewis. (Eighth generation of David Trimble and —— Houston.) Born on May 25, 1932, at Lenox, Kentucky. Married Thelma Jean Adkins.

The children of Lawrence Trimble and Thelma Jean Adkins:
D2063—Deborah Gayle Trimble.
D2064—Gary Wayne Trimble.
D2065—Gilbert Lynn Trimble.
D2066—Lawrence Anthony Trimble.
D2067—Charlotte Ann Trimble.

Trimble Families of America

D1601—Albert Trimble. Son of Ora Trimble and Edna Lewis. (Eighth generation of David Trimble and —— Houston.) Born on September 16, 1934, at Lick Branch in Morgan County, Kentucky. Married Mildred Smith. They lived in Paris, Kentucky.

The children of Albert Trimble and Mildred Smith:

D2068—Dana Trimble.
D2069—David Trimble.

D1602—Charles Trimble. Son of Ora Trimble and Edna Lewis. (Eighth generation of David Trimble and —— Houston.) Born on March 5, 1939 in Mordica, Morgan County, Kentucky. Married Lorene Iso. He is the only Trimble son who now (1975) lives in Morgan County, Kentucky.

The sons of Charles Trimble and Lorene Iso:

D2070—Charles Martin Trimble.
D2071—Robert Glenn Trimble.

D1603—Donald Trimble. (Twin.) Son of Ora Trimble and Edna Lewis. (Eighth generation of David Trimble and —— Houston.) Born on October 20, 1942, at Mordica in Morgan County, Kentucky and died in 2015. Married Wilma Cantrell. They lived in New Carlisle, Ohio.

The son of Donald Trimble and Wilma Cantrell:

D2072—Donald Stephen Trimble. Born on July 20, 1964 in Xenia, Ohio and died March 11, 2019 in Fairborn, Ohio.

D1604—Ronald Trimble. (Twin.) Son of Ora Trimble and Edna Lewis. (Eighth generation of David Trimble and —— Houston.) Born on October 20, 1942 died 2019. He married Peggy Sue Stacy. They lived in Lexington, Kentucky. He served in the Army from1963 to 1966 in Munich, Germany.

The sons of Ronald Trimble and Peggy Sue Stacy:

+ **D2073—Ronald Scott Trimble.** Born on March 20, 1966 in West Liberty, Kentucky. Married Cathline Birchwell in Lexington, Fayette County, Kentucky.

D2074—John Anthony Trimble. Born on April 13, 1967 in Bourbon County, Kentucky. Married Fedda Goldforth on October 30, 1988 in Lexington, Fayette County Kentucky.

+**D2075—Gregory Allen Trimble.** Born on December 21, 1971 in Lexington, Fayette County, Kentucky. Married Cherl Mcintosh.

D1609—Virginia Bruce Trimble. Married Leroy Pelphrey. Their children: Sheila Pelphrey, Bruce Pelphrey, and Susan Pelphrey.

Trimble Families of America

D1610—Davis Reed Trimble, Jr. Born December 5, 1946 in Paintsville, Johnson County, Kentucky and died on September 26, 2005 from Non-Small Lung Cancer in Van Lear, Johnson County, Kentucky. Married Brenda Kay Manns in 1983. Divorced She is from Breathitt County Kentucky and is the daughter of Ted Manns and Nora Clemons of Breathitt.

The child of Davis Reed Trimble, Jr. and Brenda Kay Manns:

D2076—Amy Elizabeth Trimble. Born March 29, 1984 at Central Baptist Hospital in Lexington, Kentucky. Married Thomas Dean Yates of Allen, Kentucky on June 16, 2011. He is the son of William Thomas Yates and Donna Gail Elliott. Divorced in May 2018.

D1611—Jackie Dean Trimble. Has one son: Jay Patrick Trimble. Jay has a son named Johnathan Gage Trimble.

D1612— Charolette Jane "Janie" Trimble. Died January 13, 2015 from cancer. Married Ellis Marvin Howard.

They have three children:

D2077—Jeffery Allen Howard. The children Alexander Reed Howard, Allen Michael Howard, Sean Thomas Howard and Shelby Ann Howard. His son Sean was murdered in Lexington Kentucky on August 5, 2017.

D2078—Stephanie Elaine Howard. Married Chip Phelps They are divorced now. The children: Kaden Hope Phelps and Jimmy Trey Phelps.

D2079—Jamie Scott Howard. Married Donna Castle Howard. They are divorced now. The children: Payton Chance Howard, Rileigh Nicole Howard and Kenan Howard

D1613—Robert Paul Trimble. Married Gale Branham.

The children of Robert Paul Trimble and Gale Branham

D2080—Holly Rochelle Married to Kent Preece and they have two children, Madison Bailey Preece and Kenton Ryley Preece.

D2081—Todd Matthew Trimble. Married to Jessie Victoria McFaddin. They have two children, Tyler Davis Trimble and Lauren Brooke Trimble.

D1614—Debra Trimble. Married to Berry Jo Ward.

D1624—Charles Michael McKenzie. Son of Charles McKenzie and Georgene Trimble. (Eighth generation of David Trimble and ——— Houston.) Married Joan Blanton.

The son of Charles Michael McKenzie and Joan Blanton.

D2082—Tony McKenzie.

Trimble Families of America

D1648—Mary Lou Trimble. Daughter of Ulis Trimble and Iva Hackworth. (Eighth generation of David Trimble and —— Houston.) Born on May 24, 1942. Married Donald Johnson.

The children of Donald Johnson and Mary Lou Trimble:
D2083—Debra Johnson. Born in 1965.
D2084—Timothy Johnson. Born on September 21, 1967.

D1653—Judith Nell Dills. Son of John Dills, Jr. and Avanell Trimble. (Eighth generation of David Trimble and —— Houston.) Married the Reverend Thomas A. Smith, pastor of Palmyra, Indiana, Baptist Church.

The children of Reverend Thomas Smith and Judith Nell Dills:
D2085—John David Smith. Born in 1963.
D2086—Mark Andrew Smith. Born in 1965.

D1666—Bobby Joe Reed. Son of Bob Reed and Ruie Eally. (Eighth generation of David Trimble and —— Houston.) Married Laura Alice Meade.

The children of Bobby Joe Reed and Laura Alice Meade:
D2087—Alice Marie Reed.
D2088—Ranny Martin Reed.
D2089—Danny Dean Reed.
D2090—Bobby David Reed.
D2091—Arnold William Reed.

D1669—Sue Lovanna Trimble. Daughter of Kermit Hanson Trimble and Margie Caudill. (Eighth generation of David Trimble and —— Houston.) Born on May 9, 1938 in Johnson County, Kentucky. Married Alex Allen McCarty of Johnson County, Kentucky on July 12, 1957 ceremony by Lonzie Reed. Alex was born on January 6, 1936 in Barnett's Creek, Johnson County, Kentucky and died on October 29, 1979 in Dallas, Texas. He was the son of Raymond Allen McCarty and Elizabeth Ann Preston who were married on June 24, 1917. Raymond was born on February 15, 1915 and died on November 4, 2010 in Mesquite, Texas. Elizabeth was born on July 22, 1920 in Johnson County, Kentucky and died on November 4, 2010 in Mesquite, Texas.

Alex was in the Air Force. He was stationed at Wright Patterson Air Force Base, Greenland, and Saudi Arabia.

The children of Alex Allen McCarty and Sue Lovanna Trimble:
D2092—Debra Ann McCarty. Born on April 22, 1958 and died April 23, 1958. She only lived one day.

Trimble Families of America

D - David Trimble

+ **D2093—Dianne Kaye McCarty.** Born on March 27, 1959 in Paintsville, Johnson County, Kentucky and died November 4, 2004 in Lexington, Fayette County, Kentucky. Married Jimmy Darrell Ward.

D2094—Christopher Allen McCarty. Born on October 9, 1960 in Paintsville, Johnson County, Kentucky. Married Lisa Collette Hannahs on June 30, 2006 in Covington, Kenton County, Kentucky. Lisa was born on December 13, 1958, daughter of Gallahue Hannahs and Zena Jackson.

+ **D2095—Bryan Bandy McCarty.** Born on May 12, 1962 in Kings Daughters Hospital, Ashland, Boyd County, Kentucky. Married Gina Lea Smith on January 13, 1982 in Hamilton Butler County, Ohio.

+ **D2096—Kevin Eugene McCarty.** Born on April 3, 1964 in Springfield, Ohio. Married Lisa Spradlin.

D1670—Donald Eugene Trimble. Son of Kermit Hanson Trimble and Margie Caudill. (Eighth generation of David Trimble and —— Houston.) Born on December 23, 1939 in Barnett's Creek, Johnson County, Kentucky. Married Beatrice Carolyn Salyer of Ashland, Boyd County, Kentucky on July 23, 1960 at the home of her parents. Carolyn was born on March 21, 1940. Her Parents were Sanford Hendrix "Sanky" Salyer and Dollie G. McCarty. Sanky was born on October 29, 1918 in Johnson County, Kentucky and died on May 3, 1998. Dollie was born on August 20, 1921 in Johnson County, Kentucky and died February 2, 2007 King's Daughters Medical Center, Ashland, Boyd County, Kentucky.

Donald worked for Armco Steel in Ashland, Kentucky. He started worked in the Coating Department but later transferred to the Rigger Shop where he worked until he retired. Donald was a Captain on Westwood Fire Department from 1970 to 1998.

The children of Donald Trimble and Carolyn Salyer:

+ **D2097—Donetta Carol Trimble.** Born on May 20, 1961 in Ashland, Boyd County, Kentucky. Married Dirk Nicholson Nall on December 7, 1981.

D2098—Duane Keith Trimble. Born on September 16, 1963 in Ashland, Boyd County, Kentucky. Never Married. He is a Captain on the Ashland Fire Department in Ashland, Kentucky.

D2099—Scott Edwin Trimble. Born on March 28, 1971 in Ashland, Boyd County, Kentucky. Never Married.

D1672—Darrell Conard Trimble. Son of Kermit Hanson Trimble and Margie Caudill. (Eighth generation of David Trimble and —— Houston.) Born on March 9, 1947 at Barnett's Creek, Johnson County, Kentucky.

Darrell was Sergeant E5 in the US Army stationed in Germany. He enlisted on September 20, 1966 and discharged on September 1, 1968.

He retired from CSX Railroad. Married Linda F. Blevins on February 14, 1969 in the home of his uncle Clifford Trimble in Boyd County, Kentucky, who also performed the ceremony. Linda was born on March 30, 1947 in Ashland, Boyd County, Kentucky. Linda's parents were Morton Blevins and Rhoda McDowell. Morton born on January 9 and died in 1966. Rhoda was born on October 28, 1907 in Elliott County, Kentucky and died on September 27, 1986 in King's Daughters' Medical Center, Ashland, Boyd County, Kentucky.

The children of Darrell Conard Trimble and Linda F. Blevins:

+ **D2100—Marcelli Fern Trimble.** Born on September 10, 1970. Married Steven Gauze on August 7, 1999 in Lovely, Martin County, Kentucky.

+ **D2101—Brett Douglas Trimble.** Born on April 27, 1974. Married to Recie Darnell Reynolds.

+ **D2102—Amy Lynett Trimble.** Born on November 22, 1975. Married Gary Lemaster.

D1673—David Carroll Trimble. Son of Kermit Hanson Trimble and Margie Caudill. (Eighth generation of David Trimble and —— Houston.) Born on August 23, 1949 at Barnett's Creek, Johnson County, Kentucky.

David was a Specialist 4th Class Medical Specialist in the US Army serving at Fort Rucker, Alabama. He enlisted May 12, 1969 and was discharged May 11, 1971.

Married Mina Lou Smith of Rush, Boyd County, Kentucky on November 1, 1974 in the home of his uncle Clifford Trimble in Boyd County, Kentucky. Clifford performed the ceremony. Mina was born on June 22, 1953 in Ashland, Boyd County, Kentucky. They live at Rush, Boyd County, Kentucky. Mina is the daughter of Harry Smith and Francis Lorene Hall. Harry was born on April 7, 1921 in Floyd County, Kentucky and died April 15, 1983 Boyd County, Kentucky. Francis was born on February 16, 1926 in Four Mile Creek, Boyd County, Kentucky. Harry and Francis married February 11, 1946 in Catlettsburg, Boyd County, Kentucky.

David was saved on January 25, 1979 and baptized at Little Martha United Baptist Church in Ashland, Boyd County, Kentucky. He is a minister at Oak Springs United Baptist Church in Ashland, Boyd County, Kentucky.

David worked for Armco Steel in Ashland, Kentucky. He worked in the Metallurgical Department until he retired.

Trimble Families of America

D - David Trimble

The children of David Carroll Trimble and Mina Lou Smith:

+ **D2103—Cynthia Dawn Trimble.** Born on August 17, 1975. Married David Shane Marushi.

+ **D2104—Kelly DeAnn Trimble.** Born on June 13, 1979. Married Michael Woodson Workman Jr.

D1674—Larry Allen Trimble. (Twin.) Son of Kermit Hanson Trimble and Margie Caudill. (Eighth generation of David Trimble and —— Houston.) Born on July 10, 1953 on Barnett's Creek, Johnson County, Kentucky. Married Deborah Marlene Salyers on April 28, 1978 at the home of Debbie's parents in Oil Springs, Johnson County, Kentucky. The ceremony performed by his uncle Kenneth Trimble. She was the daughter of Joe Edward Salyers and Elizabeth Jane Kelsey. Joe was born on September 6, 1933 and died on October 25, 2007 at Ashland, Boyd County, Kentucky. Elizabeth was born on December 9, 1934. Joe and Elizabeth married on November 13, 1953.

Larry was in the Air Force stationed Thailand and South Carolina. He served from 1971 to 1974.

He was employed by CSX railroad, working the station in Paintsville, Kentucky. When C&O consolidated its traffic control to Jacksonville, Florida, he was transferred to Jacksonville, Florida.

The children of Larry Allen Trimble and Deborah Marlene Salyers:

+ **D2105—April Nicole Trimble.** Born on December 30, 1978. Married Jarret Vincent.

+ **D2106—Tara Autumn Trimble.** Born on October 13, 1982. Married David Robert Cornish.

D2107—Marlana Dawn Amber Trimble. Born on February 22, 1985.

D1675—Gary Steven Trimble. (Twin.) Son of Kermit Hanson Trimble and Margie Caudill. (Eighth generation of David Trimble and —— Houston.) Born on July 10, 1953 in Johnson County, Kentucky. Married Marsha Yvonne Castle of Ashland, Boyd County, Kentucky on August 26, 1972, ceremony performed by his uncle Clifford Trimble. Marsha was born on December 18, 1954. Marsha is the daughter of Carl Castle and Mary Jean Salyers. Carl was born on December 14, 1933 and died June 21, 2011. Mary was born on August 28, 1938 and died on March 2, 2004. Gary and Marsha are divorced in 1985. Married Pamalene Lemasters on September 30, 1989.

Gary lives on Barnett's Creek, Johnson County, Kentucky. He works for CSX Railroad.

The children of Gary Steven Trimble and Marsha Yvonne Castle:

+ **D2108—Dale Edward Trimble.** Born on October 6, 1974. Married Rosettia Gay Caudill.

+ **D2109—Hayley Miranda Trimble.** Born on January 30, 1978. Married Charles Mason Woodruff.

D1676—Eldon Caroll Caudill. Son of John William Allen "Bill" Caudill and Chloe Belle Trimble. (Eighth generation of David Trimble and ——— Houston.) Born on July 24, 1939 and died July 4, 2002 at Oil Springs, Johnson County, Kentucky. Married Carole Dean Conley on June 10, 1961 in Johnson County, Kentucky at her parent's house. The ceremony by his uncle Kenneth Trimble. Carole is the daughter of Kermit Martin Conley Sr. and Pauline Caudill. Kermit Conley was born on December 27, 1906 and died on September 15, 1981. Pauline was born on March 10, 1913 and died June 7, 2012.

Eldon was chief of volunteer Oil Springs Fire Department for several years. Eldon worked for C&O railroad in Paintsville, Johnson County, Kentucky.

The children of Eldon Caroll Caudill and Carole Dean Conley:

+ **D2110—Eldon Leo Caudill.** Born on April 29, 1962. Married Vicki Lynn Adkins.

+ **D2111—Joyce Lynn Caudill.** Born on May 9, 1963. Married Larry Meadows.

+ **D2112—Belinda Carole Caudill.** Born on May 23, 1966. Married Joseph Scott Blanton.

D1677—Phillip Hager Caudill. Son of John William Allen "Bill" Caudill and Chloe Belle Trimble. (Eighth generation of David Trimble and ——— Houston.) Born on January 20, 1944 and died September 3, 2021 in Paintsville, Kentucky. Married Mary Linda Blair on December 16, 1967 at Beechwall Church, Johnson County ceremony by his uncle Kenneth Trimble, Kentucky. Linda was born on March 29, 1949 at Asa Creek, Johnson County, Kentucky.

Phillip served in the US Army as a Specialist 5th Class. He was stationed as a driver. He enlisted June 25, 1965 and was discharged June 15, 1967. He was a fire fighter at Oil Springs Fire Department, serving a Chief part of the time.

Linda is the daughter of Dexter Blair and Bessie Mae Hitchcock. Dexter was born on April 12, 1908 in Johnson County, Kentucky and died on

D - David Trimble

December 19, 1980 in Leander, Johnson County, Kentucky. Bessie was born on June 10, 1912 in Johnson County, Kentucky and died on October 19, 1990 Oil Springs, Johnson County, Kentucky.

The children of Phillip Hager Caudill and Linda Blair:

+ **D2113—Christina Lynn Caudill.** Born on April 20, 1968 in St. Joseph Hospital, Lexington, Fayette County, Kentucky. Married Lonnie Franklin Lemaster on August 25, 1990.

+ **D2114—William Dexter Caudill.** Born on April 8, 1971 in Paintsville, Johnson County, Kentucky. Married Mary Linda Blair on May 8, 1993.

D1678—Linda Lou Caudill. Daughter of John William Allen "Bill" Caudill and Chloe Belle Trimble. (Eighth generation of David Trimble and ——— Houston.) Born on December 29, 1946. Married Charles Eldon Blair on June 19, 1965 at Denver, Johnson County Kentucky, ceremony performed by her uncle Kenneth Trimble. Charles was born on December 7, 1943. Charles is the son of Turrell Wilton Blair and Iva Joy Blair. Turrell was born on July 29, 1914 and died on July 10, 1992 at Johnson County, Kentucky. Iva was born on January 3, 1920 and died on February 17, 1986.

Charles was volunteer member of Oil Spring Fire Department. He was a carpenter.

The children of Charles Eldon Blair and Linda Lou Caudill:

+ **D2115—Kathy Jo Blair.** Born on June 9, 1966 in Paintsville, Johnson County, Kentucky. Married Jimmy Music.

+ **D2116—Teresa Ann Blair.** Born on April 11, 1970. Married James Larry Blanton.

+ **D2117—Charlena Blair.** Born on February 23, 1975. Married Daren Glen Gamble.

D1680—Helen Kaye Trimble. Daughter of Kenneth Archer Trimble and Mary Biggs. (Eighth generation of David Trimble and ——— Houston.) Born on August 21, 1944 Paintsville. Married Russell Castle on December 22, 1962 at Paintsville United Baptist Church, Paintsville, Johnson County, Kentucky ceremony by her dad. They live at River, Johnson County, Kentucky. Russell is the son of Willard Castle and Hazel Murray. Hazel was born on February 6, 1920 in Johnson County, Kentucky and died on August 23, 2010 at Lowmansville, Johnson County, Kentucky.

Russell worked in coal preparation for 27 years.

The children of Russell Castle and Helen Kaye Trimble:

+ **D2118—Michael Gayle Castle.** Born on October 7, 1963. Married Dottie

N. Meade.

+ **D2119—Paul Keith Castle.** Born on September 24, 1965. Married Lora Lynn Rucker.

+ **D2120—Mark Kenneth Castle.** Born on January 8, 1969. Married Rowena Denise Simpson.

+ **D2121—Anna Maria Castle.** Born on May 30, 1973. Married Timothy Dean Slone.

D1683—Joe Kenneth Colvin. Son of Theodore "Tom" Colvin and Kathleen Trimble. (Eighth generation of David Trimble and ——— Houston.) Born on October 3, 1947. Married Judi Blanton on July 12, 1970. Judy is the daughter of Hurbert Blanton Jr. and Carol Jean May. Hurbert was born on March 15, 1924 and died on March 28, 1986.

The children of Joe Kenneth Colvin and Judi Blanton:

D2122—Marsha Jo Colvin. Born on April 5, 1971. Never married.

D1684—Jerry Morris Colvin. Son of Theodore "Tom" Colvin and Kathleen Trimble. (Eighth generation of David Trimble and ——— Houston.) Born on November 27, 1949. Married Sharon Blair on June 11, 1971 at Home of Sharon's parents: Turrell & Ivy Joy Blair in Johnson County, Kentucky, ceremony performed by his uncle Clifford Trimble. Sharon was born on December 10, 1952. Sharon is the daughter of Turrell Wilton Blair and Iva Joy Blair. Turrell was born on July 29, 1914 and died on July 10, 1992 in Paul B. Hall Hospital, Paintsville, Johnson County, Kentucky. Iva was born on January 3, 1920 and died on February 17, 1986.

The children of Jerry Morris Colvin and Sharon Blair:

+ **D2123—Crystal Sharon Colvin.** Born on November 23, 1972. Married James Edward Workman.

+ **D2124—Jerry Edward "Jay" Colvin.** Born on July 22, 1974. Married Tonjua Kaye DeLong.

D1685—Glenda Theo Colvin. Daughter of Theodore "Tom" Colvin and Kathleen Trimble. (Eighth generation of David Trimble and ——— Houston.) Born on August 9, 1954 in Johnson County, Kentucky. Married Alvin Lee Blair on June 7, 1975 at Beechwall United Baptist Church, Leander, Johnson County, Kentucky, ceremony performed by her uncle Kenneth Trimble. Alvin was born on June 25, 1952 in Johnson County, Kentucky. Alvin is that son of Kelly Herbert Blair and Bessie Mae Ratliff. Kelly was born on April 12, 1917 and died November 22, 1983. Bessie was born on June 10, 1912 and died on October 19, 1990.

D - David Trimble

The children of Alvin Blair and Glenda Theo Colvin:

D2125–Jason Thomas Blair. Born on September 20, 1977. Never married.

+ **D2126–Andrea Lee Blair.** Born on February 16, 1980. She has two children.

D1686–Jedford Gay "Jake" Colvin. Son of Theodore "Tom" Colvin and Kathleen Trimble. (Eighth generation of David Trimble and —— Houston.) Born on December 19, 1961 and died December 24, 2021. Married three first to Debra Leigh Music then second to Norma Jean "Bookie" Fairchild on October 23, 1967 then third to Wilma Bailey.

The child of Jedford Gay "Jake "Colvin and Debra Music:

D2127–Morgan Paige Colvin. Born on September 26, 1983. Married Jonathan Shaw. They have a daughter Isily Grace Shaw born on September 2, 2009.

The child of Jedford Gay "Jake" Colvin and Bookie Fairchild:

D2128–Jake Ryan Colvin. Born on May 1, 1991.

D1687–Stanley Barry Trimble. Son of Clifford Eldon Trimble and Doris Deloris Price. (Eighth generation of David Trimble and —— Houston.) Born on September 2, 1954 in the old Paintsville Hospital, Paintsville, Johnson County, Kentucky.

Married first to Cheri Lynn Barker on January 28, 1975 at Rose Hill Church, Ashland, Boyd County, Kentucky. This was also the 25th anniversary of Stanley's parents Clifford and Doris Trimble. Cheri was born on October 15, 1955 in Ashland, Boyd County, Kentucky and died on September 9, 1979 in a single car accident in Sardinina, Ohio. She is buried Rosehill Cemetery, Ashland, Boyd County, Kentucky. Cheri was the daughter of Charles Keaton "Chuck" Barker and Denise Loranie Ashley. Chuck and Loranie married 1954. Chuck was born on September 7, 1933 in Pike County, Ohio and died on July 3, 1977 in Highland County, Ohio. Loranie was born on April 13, 1935 and died on August 11, 1994 in Ashland, Boyd County, Kentucky.

Married second to Sandra J. Reffitt on November 22, 1980 Boyd County, Kentucky and divorced later that year.

Married third to Louella Ann Coffee on July 2, 1982 in Boyd County, Kentucky and divorced in 1986.

Married fourth to Joyce Alberta Miner on February 22, 1991 in Catlettsburg, Boyd County, Kentucky. Joyce was born on December 15, 1950 in Kingwood, West Virginia. Joyce was the daughter of Nelson Miner and Mildred.

Stanley worked for Armco Steel in Ashland, Kentucky for 19 years. Laid off when most of the plant was shut down in 1992. He went back to school receiving a Bachelor of Business Administration in Management Information Systems. With three thousand people out of work from the steel plant and looking for work, He looked for work where he liked the weather. He found work as a computer programmer with the state of Florida in Tallahassee, Florida. He worked for eight different departments.

Joyce died on October 20, 2008 from Ovarian Cancer in Crawfordville, Wakulla County, Florida. She was buried in the Trimble Cemetery on US 460 in Johnson County, Kentucky.

Stanley met Theresa Lynn Crosby Jones on Match.com. Theresa was living Walterboro, Colleton County, South Carolina. Married on February 14, 2009 in Walterboro, Colleton County, South Carolina. Theresa is the daughter of Launie Crosby and Sarah Turner. Launie was born on September 25, 1917 in Colleton County, South Carolina and died on May 25, 1999 in Colleton County, South Carolina. Sarah was born on October 16, 1927 in Pelham, Georgia and died on September 23, 2010 in Colleton County, South Carolina.

Stanley retired on February 1, 2010 and moved to Walterboro, Colleton County, South Carolina.

Stanley has always been interested in his ancestry, so he contacted John Farley Trimble's son Michael, who gave Stanley permission to update and reprint the book.

Stanley was a volunteer member of Summit Ironville Volunteer Fire Department for 15 years.

The children of Stanley Barry Trimble and Cheri Lynn Barker:

+ **D2129—Shellie Denise Trimble.** Born on August 27, 1975. Married David Scott Clark on June 1, 1996 in Ashland, Boyd County, Kentucky.

D2130—Houston Ashley Trimble. Born on January 25, 1977. He has three last names. Houston from —— Houston, Ashley from his great grandfather on his mother's side, Robert Ashley. Robert had no sons and five daughters.

D1688—Stewart Lee Trimble. Son of Clifford Eldon Trimble and Doris Deloris Price. (Eighth generation of David Trimble and —— Houston.) Born on October 9, 1956 at Bellefonte, Greenup County, Kentucky. Married Loretta Jean Gullett on June 13, 1975. Loretta was born on September 13, 1957 in Boyd County, Kentucky.

Stewart was a volunteer member of Russell Fire Department after moving to Summit, Kentucky, he came an Assistant Chief of Summit Ironville

Volunteer Fire Department. Stewart lives in Summit, Boyd County, Kentucky. He worked for C&O on repair track, repairing railroad cars in Russell, Greenup County, Kentucky. He retired from C&O railroad and the fire department in 2018.

The children of Stewart Lee Trimble and Loretta Jean Gullet:

+ **D2131—Joshua Bradley "Brad" Trimble.** Born on February 1, 1978 Married first Leslie Ann White. Married second April Sunshine Grant.

+ **D2132—Jeremy Blake Trimble.** Born on December 12, 1980 Married Heather Kay Shanks.

+ **D2133—Amanda Courtney Trimble.** Born on January 7, 1983 Married Mason Neil Miller.

+ **D2134—Nickolas Adam Trimble.** Born on January 5, 1985 Married Susan Eastridge on July 22, 2011.

D1689—Melanie DeAlice Trimble. Daughter of Clifford Eldon Trimble and Doris Deloris Price. (Eighth generation of David Trimble and ——— Houston.) Born on March 29, 1969 in Ashland, Boyd County. In junior high school Melanie played basketball, near the end of basketball session all junior high basketball players meet at the high school for a two-mile run. Near the end all the girls were back there and over here was a girl who had run for years and in middle of between both was Melanie who was running her first race. Mel ran track, cross county and played basketball in high school. She ran in the state cross country meet five different years and five different years in track in the 1600 and 3200. Melanie ran track and cross country for Anderson University in Indiana. Melanie is a teacher in Indiana. She has also been a coach for both the cross-country and track teams. This is where Melanie met Jeff her future husband, he ran for the men's track and cross county. Melanie and Jeff are members of our running family.

Married Jeffery Carlton Bingham on May 20, 1989 in Boyd County, Kentucky. Jeff was born on January 1, 1966 in Homestead, Dade County, Florida. Jeffery is the son of Joseph Carlton Bingham and Mary Elizabeth Gardner. They were married on November 29, 1956 in Bunker Hill, Indiana. Joseph was born on August 19, 1933 in Louisville, Kentucky. Mary was born on September 7, 1937 in Peru, Indiana and died on March 27, 2014 in Peru, Indiana.

Jeffery enlisted in the Marines in October 1989 as a Second Lieutenant to learn to fly. He attended flight school in Pensacola, Florida. He was assigned to fly CH-46 helicopter. He was stationed in North Carolina and Okinawa, Japan. He was discharged in June 2000. After leaving the marines Jeffery started flying for NetJets. Jeffery has run in many marathon races and several triathlons.

The children of Jeffery Bingham and Melanie Trimble:

+ **D2135—Jacob Carlton Bingham.** Born on May 4, 1993. Married Destynne Moore.

D2136—Joshua Clifford Bingham. Born on January 5, 1998.

D2137—Sarah Elizabeth Bingham. Born on September 5, 2000.

D1690—Peggy Ann Trimble. Daughter of Leroy Trimble and Paula Earlene Matthews (Eighth generation of David Trimble and ——— Houston.) Born on May 29, 1952 in Mt. Sterling, Kentucky. Married Dennis Baker on July 30, 1977. Dennis was born on September 13, 1957. They live in Louisville, Kentucky.

The children of Dennis Baker and Peggy Ann Trimble:

+ **D2138—Ryan Afton Baker.** Born on June 10, 1980. Married Kirsti Linda Pfeffer.

+ **D2139—Mathew Scott Baker.** Born on October 24, 1981. Never married.

D2140—Lauren Ashley Baker. Born on September 19, 1985. Never married.

D1691—Randall Allen Trimble. Son of Leroy Trimble and Paula Earlene Matthews (Eighth generation of David Trimble and ——— Houston.) Born on April 12, 1956 in Mount Sterling, Kentucky. Married Terri Hill on January 30, 1982. Terri was born on December 27, 1957. Randy is a great beautician and owns his own beauty shop in Paintsville, Johnson County, Kentucky.

The children of Randy Allen Trimble and Terri Hill:

+ **D2141—Krystle Michelle Trimble.** Born on May 29, 1985. Married Mr. Wells on August 24, 2013 in the Smoky Mountains, Tennessee. They live in Johnson County, Kentucky.

D2142—Morgan Brittney Trimble. Born on September 5, 1988.

D1704—Mitchell Eric Robinson. Son of Kenneth Wayne Robinson and Arma Lea Trimble. (Eighth generation of David Trimble and ——— Houston.) Born on September 2, 1959. Married Patsy Fillinger. Patsy was born on January 9, 1965. Mitch and Patsy divorced. Mitch married Chris Haukaus on April 3, 1999.

The children of Mitchell Eric Robinson and Patsy Fillinger:

D2143—Christopher Andrew Robinson. Born on July 18, 1985.

D2144—Jeremy Allen Robinson. Born on November 10, 1986.

D1705—Michelle Elizabeth Robinson. Daughter of Kenneth Wayne Robinson

D - David Trimble

and Arma Lea Trimble. (Eighth generation of David Trimble and —— Houston.) Born on April 30, 1661. Married to Bernard Innis Raysor III on February 4, 1991. Bernard was born on December 26, 1962.

The child of Michelle Elizabeth Robinson and Bernard Raysor:
D2145—Shelbi Lea Raysor. Born on March 1, 1993.

D1707—Lillian Elise Trimble. Daughter of Ronald Eugene Trimble and Jane Hartlieb. (Eighth generation of David Trimble and —— Houston.) Born on May 1, 1965 in Gallipolis, Ohio. Married Charles Elbert Masters Junior on December 31, 1992. Charles Elbert Masters was born on July 7, 1959.

The child of Lillian Elise Trimble:
D2146—Mathew Shawn Trimble. Born on March 1, 1993.

The children of Charles Masters and Lillian Trimble:
D2147—Charlene Renee Masters. Born on September 30, 1993.
D2148—Dalton Ronald Masters. Born on August 12, 1995.
D2149—Coalton Palmer Masters. Born on February 4, 1997.

D1709—Belinda Sue Trimble. Daughter of Ronald Eugene Trimble and Jane Hartlieb. (Eighth generation of David Trimble and —— Houston.) She had a daughter by Ron Evans Jr. Married Dale Eugene McCarty on July 15, 1995.

The child of Ron Evans, Jr. and Belinda Sue Trimble:
+**D2150—Kristen Nicole McCarty.** Born on September 2, 1995 as Kristen Nicole Evans, later she was adopted by Dale. Married John Cody New.

The child of Dale Eugene McCarty and Belinda Trimble:
D2151—Nathan Charles McCarty. Born on June 16, 1997.

Belinda divorced Dale McCarty. Belinda married Brian Brown. Brian agreed to allow his oldest son to be carry the Surname of Trimble.

The children of Brian Brown and Belinda Sue Trimble:
D2152—Jacob Charles Brown. Born on December 27, 2000.
D2153—Savannah Elise Brown. Born on September 24, 2002.
D2154—Allison Paige Brown. Born on March 15, 2004.

D1711—Arthetta Browning. Daughter of Arthur Browning and Jeanetta Arrowood. (Eighth generation of David Trimble and —— Houston.) Married Gary J. Taylor.

The child of Gary J. Taylor and Arthetta Browning:
+**D2155—Michael J. Taylor.** Born on November 27, 1967 in Huntington, West Virginia.

D1731—Shelby Jean Trimble. Son of Joe Langley Trimble and Nancy May Trogton. (Eighth generation of David Trimble and —— Houston.) Born on June 25, 1965 in Huntington, Cabell County, West Virginia. Married John Martin Cole on March 7, 1987 in Huntington, Cabell County, West Virginia.

The children of John Martin Cole and Shelby Jean Trimble:

D2156—Megan Elizabeth Cole. Born on December 6, 1992 Clinton Township, Macomb County, Michigan.

D2157—Travis Jennings Cole. Born on March 31, 1995 Clinton Township, Macomb County, Michigan.

D1733—Michael Leon Trimble. Son of Dallas Trimble and Loretta Sharp. (Eighth generation of David Trimble and —— Houston.) Born on November 18, 1961 in Huntington, West Virginia. Married first to Lori Wolford to July 1, 1988.

Married second to Lisa Maynard on December 4, 1993. She was born on June 11, 1968.

The children of Michael Leon Trimble and Lori Wolford:

+ **D2158—Candace Nicole Trimble.** Born on September 11, 1989. Married Richard Pendrey.

D2159—Steven Tyler Trimble. Born on April 12, 1991.

The child of Michael Leon Trimble and Lisa Maynard:

D2160—Whitney Hope Trimble. Born on June 9, 1995. Married Nathan Blankenship on October 19, 2019.

D1734—Sharon Denise Perry. Daughter of Rayburn Jack Perry and Mary Elizabeth Trimble. (Eighth generation of David Trimble and —— Houston.) Born August 31, 1961. Married first to Laken Orville Tawney in 1981.

Married second to Samuel Scott Fry on November 1, 2004 in Catlettsburg, Kentucky.

The child of Laken Orville Tawney and Sharon Denise Perry:

+ **D2161—Elizabeth Ann Tawney.** Born on March 27, 1982 in Huntington, West Virginia. Married Charles Jason Gilkerson.

D1735—Sarah Denell Perry. Daughter of Rayburn Jack Perry and Mary Elizabeth Trimble. (Eighth generation of David Trimble and —— Houston.) Born on August 22, 1963 in Cabell Huntington Hospital in Huntington West Virginia. Married Steve Myrtle in August 2002 in Corpus Christi, Texas.

The children of Steve Myrtle and Sarah Denell Perry:

D2162—Amanda Rae Myrtle. Born on March 4, 1985 in Huntington West

Virginia.

D2163—Jessica Renee McCann. Born on March 16, 1987 in Huntington West Virginia.

D1736—Sandra Demice Perry. Daughter of Rayburn Jack Perry and Mary Elizabeth Trimble. (Eighth generation of David Trimble and —— Houston.) Born on December 12, 1964 in Huntington, West Virginia. Married Terry Craig in 1998. They divorced in 2007.

The children of Terry Craig and Sandra Dee Perry:

+ **D2164—Rachel Craig.** Born on October 4, 1993 in Hamilton, Ohio. Married Kyle Slone on August 4, 2012.

D2165—Christina Craig. Born on November 28, 1994 in Hamilton, Ohio.

D2166—Angela Craig. Born on October 27, 1997 in Anderson, Ohio.

D1738—Lloyd Damron. Son of James Wayne "Buckshot" Damron and Mary L. Black. (Eighth generation of David Trimble and —— Houston.) Married Tammy.

The child of Lloyd and Tammy Damron:

D2167—Jacob Damron.

D1741—Deborah Gayle Bowen. Daughter of Dennis Lee Bowen and Ida Lou Damron (Eighth generation of David Trimble and —— Houston.) Born on February 9, 1964 in Guthrie Hospital, Huntington, West Virginia. Married Terry Lee Bower on July 19, 1986 at Sybene Missionary Baptist Church, Chesapeake, Ohio. Terry was born on July 22, 1963 in Westmoreland Hospital, Greensburg, Pennsylvania. Terry's parents are James Alan Bower Sr. and Gertrude Jean Lynn. They were married June 28, 1952 Jeans was born on September 28. James was born on December 5, 1929. Samantha Gayle Bower born on December 15, 1989.

The child of Terry Lee Bower and Deborah Gayle Bowen:

D2168—Gayle Bower. Born on December 15, 1989.

D1743—Gregory Scott Bocook. Son of William R. Bocook and Phyllis J. Damron. (Eighth generation of David Trimble and —— Houston.) Born on August 12, 1964 in Huntington, West Virginia. Married Angela Marcum. Born on September 23, 1963.

The children of Gregory Scott Bocook and Angela Marcum:

D2169—Amanda Alcfair Bocook. Born on July 30, 1987 in Ironton, Ohio.

D2170—Ariel A'shap Bocook. Born on November 4, 1991 in Ashland, Kentucky.

Trimble Families of America

D1747—Daniel Ray Dick. Son of Larry Ray Dick and Gloria A. Sandon. (Eighth generation of David Trimble and —— Houston.) Born on November 30, 1981 in Venice, Italy. Married Jamie ——

The child of Daniel Ray and Jamie Dick:

D2171—Makayla Dick. Born on January 29, 2004.

D1749—John William Dick. Son of Gary Lee Dick and Pamela Dickerson. (Eighth generation of David Trimble and —— Houston.) Born on January 19, 1979.

Married second to Deanna Dyer.

The child of John William Dick:

D2172—Casper Aiden Dick. Born on May 13, 1999.

The child of John William Dick and Deanna Dyer:

D2173—Bridgett Erin Dick. Born on June 2, 2008.

D1750—Johnnie Trimble, Jr. Son of Johnnie Patrick Trimble and Virginia Dare Nelson. (Eighth generation of David Trimble and —— Houston.) Born on March 28, 1938 in Paintsville, Kentucky and died July 24, 2022 in Varina, Virginia. Married first to Elodie Bratton on May 1, 1962 from Tacoma Washington in Tacoma Washington and married second to Jean Hogue Trimble on June 19, 1982. He was known on the radio as DJ Big John Trimble. He has been on the cover of People Magazine and is well known within the country music area.

Christmas 1954, John is asked by Mrs. Alice Montgomery, his high school speech and drama teacher, to do one of the voices for a Christmas play that was broadcast live on the local radio station in John's hometown, Paintsville, Kentucky.

In the spring of 1955 Mrs. Montgomery ask John if he would be interested in doing a one hour after school teen program with Mary Ford, another student of the class. the program featured school news and the popular music of the day.

Until then John had only dreamed of being on the radio while playing records on his grandmother's Victoria and talking into a can.

The morning after graduation John moved to Charleston, West Virginia to work for WTIP radio and broadcast live six nights a week from the original Shoney's drive inn restaurant where he played original rock n' roll music and chatted with listeners, who stopped by the studio. from there John moved back to Kentucky to work for WDOC in Prestonsburg. after two years John went into the U.S. army.

Trimble Families of America

D - David Trimble

After basic training at Ft. Knox, Kentucky. John was assigned to the little theatre at Fort Lewis were worked as a M.C. and comic of several types of live shows at service clubs and many off post venues such as prisons, hospitals etc. John also was the drill master of the most famous drill and show team in the world. the 8th. infantry "bullets". he and his fellow performers, Clyde croft from mule shoe, Texas and Thomas Walker of Baltimore, Maryland won first place at the Fort Lewis entertainment contest. first place at the sixth army entertainment contest in San Francisco, California and later third place in the army (worldwide) contest held at Fort Lee, Virginia. after his service years John returned to radio at KLO radio in Little Rock, Arkansas. a year later John joined his first full time country station, KBBA in Benton a suburb of little rock as the new program manager. two years later John was offered a job at the first all country music F.M. station in the world, WVHI in Evansville, Indiana. while there, John owned and announced a live music show named the country castle show music program broadcast each Friday night from a local hotel.

One year later John was offered a job as music director and afternoon show host on KMO radio, the "country giant" in the Tacoma / Seattle market. John opened a booking agency and brought many of the top recording artist to perform in the northwest. John later started an all-night show directed toward truckers.

Next John was offered a job with KGA in Spokane, Washington. KGA was a 50,000-watt station and was heard from the great divide to the Pacific Ocean and from the Mexican border to north Alaska. after a year he was offered a job broadcasting live six nights a week from Kelly's truck stop on i-20 over 50,000-watt KWKH in Shreveport, LA. after three years. Walt Williams, program director of WRVA, another 50.000-watt station covering 38 states and eastern Canada from Richmond, Virginia walked into the studio one night and offered John a job broadcasting six nights a week from the Hugh Jarrell truck stop in Doswell 23 miles north of Richmond. this job lasted 18 years. John then moved to full time country music station WXGI in Richmond as a show host and program director. today John broadcasts from his back-yard studio in Varina, Virginia on WCLM radio in Richmond and on bigjohntrimble.com 24 / 7 worldwide.

The children of Johnnie Trimble, Jr. and Elodie Bratton:

+ **D2174—Johnnie Trimble III PhD.** Born on October 7, 1963. Married three times.

+ **D2175—Bradley Alan Trimble.** Born on October 17, 1964. Married Gwyn

Meadows in Tacoma, Washington in 1984.

D2176—Patrick Carl Trimble. Born on November 23, 1969. Married Tammy Wieland Dunn on July 20, 2021 in Destin, Florida on the beach.

D1855—William Ellsworth Davis, Jr. Son of William Ellsworth Davis and Martha Newell Trimble. (Eighth generation of David Trimble and ——— Houston.) Born on August 13, 1929, at Wema in the Belgian Congo. He married Charlotte McIntyre of Atlanta, Georgia, on April 5, 1953. William is an engineer.

The children of William Ellsworth Davis, Jr. and Charlotte McIntyre:

D2177—William Ellsworth Davis III. Born on March 29, 1954, at Paris, Kentucky.

D2178—Jon Henderson Davis. Born on September 12, 1956, at Hamilton, Ohio.

D2178—Deborah Newell Davis. Born on January 14, 1958.

D1856—Thomas Austin Davis. Son of William Ellsworth and Martha Newell Trimble. (Eighth generation of David Trimble and ——— Houston.) Davis Born on May 31, 1934, at Lotumbe in the Belgian Congo. Married Patricia Ann Denham of Woodkirk, England, on March 31, 1959. Thomas is a college professor.

The children of Thomas Austin Davis and Patricia Ann Denham:

D2180—Thomas Austin Davis.

D2181—Patricia Ann Davis.

D1858—David Jasper Hodson Pettus. Born on May 22, 1942, at Louisville, Kentucky. Married Linda Joyce Robertson at Houston, Texas.

The child of David Jasper Hodson Pettus and Linda Joyce Robertson:

D2182—Amy Ruth Pettus. Born in 1967.

D1864—Betty Lou Riley. Daughter of Garrard Riley, Jr. and Bessie Mae Bush. (Eighth generation of David Trimble and ——— Houston.) Born on August 28, 1940, at Mount Sterling, Kentucky. Married Henry Franklin McGuire on June 2, 1963.

The children of Henry Franklin McGuire and Betty Lou Riley:

D2183—David Garrard McGuire. Born on April 23, 1965.

D2184—Franklin Riley McGuire. Born on October 26, 1967, at North Vernon, Indiana.

D2185—Patrick Lee McGuire. Born on July 13, 1969 in North Vernon, Indiana.

D1865—Joe David Riley. Son of Garrard Riley, Jr. and Bessie Mae Bush. (Eighth generation of David Trimble and —— Houston.) Born on November 29, 1946, at Mount Sterling, Kentucky. Married Paula Dodd on September 15, 1966.

The children of Joe David Riley and Paula Dodd:
D2186—Joe David Riley, Jr. Born on May 15, 1967.

D1876—Marietta Maxine Hopkins. Son of John Isaac Hopkins and Lucille Quig. (Eighth generation of David Trimble and —— Houston.) Born on September 2, 1944. She married Paul Hines.

The children of Paul Hines and Marietta Maxine Hopkins:
D2187—Brian Scott Hines. Born on August 2, 1966.
D2188—Dawn Rene Hines. Born on May 15, 1968.

D1877—Betty Jane Trimble. Daughter of Raymond Edward Trimble and Grace Abbey. (Eighth generation of David Trimble and —— Houston.) Born on June 13, 1928. Married Charles Hutchison. Betty is bookkeeper at Elston Indiana Bank and Charles is a farmer. They live at Parkersburg, Indiana.

The children of Charles Hutchison and Betty Jane Trimble:
D2189—Randy Hutchison. Born on September 29, 1955.
D2190—Kathy Hutchison. Born on November 9, 1958.

D1878—Raymond Edward Trimble, Jr. Son of Raymond Edward Trimble and Grace Abbey. (Eighth generation of David Trimble and —— Houston.) Born on July 10, 1948. Married Barbara Dvorak. He is an artist. They live at East Greenville, Pennsylvania.

The children Raymond Edward Trimble, Jr. and Barbara Dvorak:
D2191—Melissa Cyne Trimble. Born on June 7, 1968.
D2192—Kimberley Sue Trimble. Born on January 13, 1970.

D1879—Jerry Dean Bayless. Son of Otis James Bayless and Hazel Marie Trimble (Eighth generation of David Trimble and —— Houston.) Born on June 21, 1939. Married Joann Quisenberry on September 7, 1958. Jerry works at the R. R. Donnelly Printing Company, and they live near Crawfordsville, Indiana.

The children of Jerry Dean Bayless and Joann Quisenberry:
D2193—Gregory Bayless. Born on February 12, 1961.
D2194—Brenda Ann Bayless. Born on October 4, 1963.

D1880—Larry Joe Bayless. Son of Otis James Bayless and Hazel Marie Trimble

Trimble Families of America

(Eighth generation of David Trimble and —— Houston.) Born on June 21, 1939. Married Doris Ball on September 1, 1961. Larry works for Indiana Bell Telephone Company. They live at Brownsburg, Indiana. Larry is working towards a degree in business administration.

The children of Larry Joe Bayless and Doris Ball:
D2195—Diana Bayless. Born on December 8, 1963.
D2196—David Joe Bayless. Born on May 7, 1965.

D1881—James Bayless. Son of Otis James Bayless and Hazel Marie Trimble (Eighth generation of David Trimble and —— Houston.) Born on May 20, 1944. Married Susan Campbell and they live near Brownsburg, Indiana. Both are graduates of Indiana State University. He is computer manager for Indiana Bell Telephone Company in Indianapolis, Indiana.

The children of James Bayless and Susan Campbell:
D2197—Kevin Scott Bayless. Born on June 17, 1966.
D2198—Susan Michelle Bayless. Born on April 5, 1969.

D1884—Michael Kent Simpson. Son of Wendell Simpson and Helen May Trimble (Eighth generation of David Trimble and —— Houston.) Born on November 5, 1943. Married Jo Ann Stout on October 21, 1967. They live in Columbus, Indiana,

The son of Michael Kent Simpson and Jo Ann Stout:
D2199—Ross Allen Simpson. Born on December 5, 1969.

D1906—Robert Joseph Bailes. Son of Okey Lester Bailes and Leona Mary Malouse. (Eighth generation of David Trimble and —— Houston.) Born on April 19, 1948. Married Susan Nicholas on June 22, 1968

The son of Robert Joseph Bailes and Susan Nicholas:
D2200—Jason Robert Bailes. Born on November 18, 1969.

D1919—John Michael Trimble. Son of Michael Anthony Trimble and Loretta Lively. (Eighth generation of David Trimble and —— Houston.) Born on June 15, 1968. Married Trish James. Born on April 14, 1970 in Columbia, South Carolina. They live in Adrian, Michigan.

The children of John Michael Trimble and Trish James:
D2201—Abigail Grace Trimble. Born on November 20, 1998 in Greenville, South Carolina.
D2202—Madeline Elizabeth Trimble. Born on May 23, 2001 in Dallas, Texas.

D1920—Paul Anthony Trimble. Son of Michael Anthony Trimble and Loretta

Lively. (Eighth generation of David Trimble and —— Houston.) Born on January 18, 1972. Married to Rebecca Mattson. Born on March 19, 1975 in Parma, Ohio.

The children of Paul Anthony Trimble and Rebecca Mattson:
D2203—Laken Alexandra Trimble. Born on August 2, 2001.
D2204—Paul William Trimble. Born on November 28, 2005.
D2205—Ava Juliet Trimble. Born on July 23, 2007.

D1921—Sharon Katherine Sirkle. Daughter of Raymond R. Sirkle and Emma Jean Metcalf. (Eighth generation of David Trimble and —— Houston.) Born on February 5, 1941 in Durant, Oklahoma. Married Stanley Knight

The children of Stanley Knight and Sharon Katherine Sirkle:
D2206—Paul Bryan Sirkle.
D2207—David Sirkle.

D1922—Raymond Bryan Sirkle. Son of Raymond R. Sirkle and Emma Jean Metcalf. (Eighth generation of David Trimble and —— Houston.) Born on May 19, 1948 in Prestonsburg, Kentucky. Married Sharyn ——.

The children of Raymond Bryan Sirkle and Sharyn ——:
D2208—Tiffany Jean Sirkle. Born on December 7, 1967, at Lexington, Kentucky.
D2209—Joey Sirkle. Born in September 1970.

D1963—David Paul "Odie" Trimble. Son of Robert Paul Trimble and Jo Ann Peck. (Ninth generation of David Trimble and —— Houston.) Born on May 18, 1951 in Johnson County, Kentucky and died on December 12, 2018 in Pikeville, Kentucky.
Married first to Elizabeth Ann Juniper of Point Pleasant, West Virginia.
Married second to Rose Jean Music of Nippa, Kentucky.
Married third to Ethel Carlene Boggs of Warsaw Indiana.

The children of Dave Paul "Odie" Trimble and Elizabeth Ann Juniper:
+ D2210—Jodi Rae Ann Trimble. Born on July 3, 1995 in Kentucky. Married Walter Boggs on May 10, 2015.
D2211—Victoria Sue Ann Trimble. Born on July 3, 1998.

The child of Dave Paul "Odie" Trimble and Rose Jean Music:
D2212—Sherri Rose Trimble. Born in 1972.
D2213—Adrienne Glen Neely Trimble.

The child of Dave Paul "Odie" Trimble and Ethel Carlene Boggs:
D2214—Amber Leigh Ann Trimble.

D1964–Judy Trimble. Daughter of Robert Paul Trimble and Jo Ann Peck. (Ninth generation of David Trimble and —— Houston.) She was a runner on the Paintsville High School Track Team, going to the state meet.

The children of Judy Trimble:

D2215–Jason Williams.

D2216–Jeremy Skeens.

+ **D2217–Denieka Skeens.** Born on August 7, 1990 in Paintsville, Johnson County, Kentucky.

D1976–David Martin. Son of Francis Martin and Opal Gullett. (Ninth generation of David Trimble and —— Houston.) Married Gretchen Ames.

The children of David Martin and Gretchen Ames:

D2218–Laura Martin.

D2219–Kraig Martin.

D1977–James Robert Martin. Son of Francis Martin and Opal Gullett. (Ninth generation of David Trimble and —— Houston.) Married Rose Marie Hanks.

The children of James Robert and Rose Marie Hanks:

D2220–Dean Martin.

D2221–Gary Martin.

D2222–Kenneth Edward Martin.

D1978–Lucille Martin. Daughter of Francis Martin and Opal Gullett. (Ninth generation of David Trimble and —— Houston.) Married Robert Bischoff.

The son of Lucille Martin. and Robert Bischoff.

D2223–Robert John Martin.

D2013–Rexford Lee Trimble. Son of John Henry Trimble and Vella Ruth Ferguson. (Ninth generation of David Trimble and —— Houston.) Born on January 2, 1966. Married Mary Katherine Worthington on August 17, 1991. She was born on August 29, 1970.

The children of Rexford Lee Trimble and Mary Worthington:

D2224–Haley Brooke Trimble. Born on December 21, 1997.

D2225–Peyton Jon Trimble. Born on August 9, 2008.

D2073–Ronald Scott Trimble. Son of Ronald Trimble and Peggy Sue Stacy. (Ninth generation of David Trimble and —— Houston. Born on March 20, 1966 in West Liberty, Kentucky. Married Cathline Birchwell in Lexington, Fayette County, Kentucky.

Trimble Families of America

D - David Trimble

The children of Ronald Scott and Trimble and Cathline Birchwell:

D2226—Cassidy Ann Trimble. Born on December 21, 1988 in Lexington, Fayette County, Kentucky.

D2227—Kelsey Michelle Trimble. Born in 1990 in Lexington, Fayette County, Kentucky.

D2228—Travis Wayne Trimble. Born in Lexington, Fayette County, Kentucky.

D2075—Gregory Allen Trimble. Son of Ronald Trimble and Peggy Sue Stacy. (Ninth generation of David Trimble and —— Houston.) Born on December 21, 1971 in Lexington, Fayette County, Kentucky. Married Cherl Mcintosh.

The children of Gregory Allen Trimble and Cherl Mcintosh:

D2229—Tessa Lynn Trimble. Born in 1988 in Lexington, Fayette County, Kentucky.

D2230—Alexa Susanne Trimble. Born in 1989 in Lexington, Fayette County, Kentucky.

D2231—Gregory Allen Trimble, II. Born in Lexington, Fayette County, Kentucky and died 2019 during Army boot camp in Fort Sill, Oklahoma.

D2232—Joshua Remmington Trimble. Born in Lexington, Fayette County, Kentucky.

D2233—Jeremiah Archer Trimble. Born in Lexington, Fayette County, Kentucky.

D2234—Tracy Diane Trimble. Born in Lexington, Fayette County, Kentucky.

D2093—Dianne Kaye McCarty. Daughter of Alex Allen McCarty and Sue Lovanna Trimble. (Ninth generation of David Trimble and —— Houston.) Born on March 27, 1959 in Paintsville, Johnson County, Kentucky. and died November 4, 2004 in Lexington, Fayette County, Kentucky. Married Jimmy Darrell Ward.

The children of Jimmy Darrell Ward and Dianne Kaye McCarty:

+ **D2235—Andrea Suzanne Ward.** Born on September 16, 1979. Married Jason T. Kestner.

+ **D2236—Brandon Alexander Ward.** (Twin) Born on June 17, 1981 in King's Daughters Hospital, Ashland, Boyd County, Kentucky. Married Keri Anne Russell.

D2237—Nicole Gracestine Ward. (Twin) Born on June 17, 1981, in King's Daughters Hospital, Ashland, Boyd County, Kentucky.

Married first to Shannon Kimelton on August 5, 2000 and divorced 2002.

Married the second time to Joshua Dean Scaggs. Joshua died on

October 19, 2011 in Ashland, Boyd County, Kentucky. The funeral was on October 24, 2011 and was buried in Ashland, Boyd County, Kentucky. No children.

+ **D2238—Alicia Renee' Ward.** Born on November 22, 1982. Married Joe "Joey" Smith III.

D2095—Bryan Bandy McCarty. Son of Alex Allen McCarty and Sue Lovanna Trimble. (Ninth generation of David Trimble and —— Houston.) Born on May 12, 1962 in King's Daughters' Hospital, Ashland, Boyd County, Kentucky. Married Gina Lea Smith on January 13, 1982 in Hamilton Butler County, Ohio. Bryan and Gina were married by the Juvenile Judge in his chambers, since Gina was 15 years old at the time. She is the daughter of James D. Smith and Eveline "Evy" Williams. James was born on July 5, 1936. Evy was born on December 20, 1938.

The children of Bryan Bandy McCarty and Gina Lea Smith:

+ **D2239—Mistia Lynn McCarty.** Born on February 12, 1981. Married Ryan Alexander Estep.

D2240—Brianna Bandi McCarty. Born on August 24, 1993 in Columbus, Franklin County, Kentucky.

D2096—Kevin Eugene McCarty. Son of Alex Allen McCarty and Sue Lovanna Trimble. (Ninth generation of David Trimble and —— Houston.) Born on April 3, 1964 in Springfield, Ohio. Married Lisa Spradlin on March 5, 1985 at the home of Clifford Eldon Trimble in Ashland, Boyd County, Kentucky. Clifford performed the marriage.

The children of Kevin McCarty and Lisa Spradlin:

+ **D2241—Brittany LeAnne McCarty.** Born on October 4, 1986 in Dallas Texas. Married Charles Worden on November 22, 2006 in Columbus, Ohio.

D2242—Kristen Paige McCarty. Born on April 14, 1994 and died April 14, 1994.

D2243—Taylor Paige McCarty. Born on June 3, 1995 in Columbus, Ohio.

D2244—Hannah Rose McCarty. Born on December 26, 1996 in Columbus, Ohio.

D2097—Donetta Carol Trimble. Daughter of Donald Trimble and Carolyn Salyer. (Ninth generation of David Trimble and —— Houston.) Born on May 20, 1961 in King's Daughters Hospital, Ashland, Boyd County, Kentucky. Married twice. Married first Dirk Nicholson Nall on December 7, 1981. Married second Mark Brown on May 1, 2004.

Trimble Families of America

D - David Trimble

The children of Dirk Nicholson Nall and Donetta Carol Trimble:

+ **D2245—Myranda Dawn Nall.** Born on September 4, 1982. Married Justin Ted Boyd.

+ **D2246—Afton Cheri Nall.** Born on May 14, 1984. Married Adam Seth Carroll.

D2247—Zachary Austin Nall. Born on May 6, 1985. Married Aliza Dettmer. Zachary currently serving in the Air Force, stationed at Lakenheath Air Force Base in United Kingdom. His tour is 2012 through 2016.

D2100—Marcelli Fern Trimble. Daughter of Darrell Conard Trimble and Linda F. Blevins. (Ninth generation of David Trimble and ——— Houston.) Born on September 10, 1970 in Ashland, Boyd County, Kentucky. Married twice. Married first to Brett Alan Huff on October 12, 1991 and divorced in 2009.

Married second to Steven Gauze on August 7, 1999 in Lovely, Martin County, Kentucky.

The children of Steven Gauze and Marcelli Fern Trimble:

D2248—Joshua Steven Gauze. Born on August 7, 2002 at Huntington, West Virginia.

D2249—Kaitlyn Aleksandra Gauze. Born on March 23, 2004 at Huntington, West Virginia.

D2101—Brett Douglas Trimble. Son of Darrell Conard Trimble and Linda Barns. (Ninth generation of David Trimble and ——— Houston.) Born on April 27, 1974. Married to Recie Darnell Reynolds in Van Lear Freewill Baptist Church, Van Lear, Johnson County, Kentucky. Recie was born on August 10, 1976, the daughter of Earl and Lena Reynolds.

The children of Brett Douglas Trimble and Recie Darnell Reynolds:

D2250—Austin Douglas Hanson Trimble. Born on December 11, 1995 at Johnson County, Kentucky.

D2251—Danna Marie Trimble. Born on April 1, 1997 at Mary Chiles Hospital, Mount Sterling, Kentucky.

D2252—Holli Renee Trimble. Born on December 6, 1998 at Mary Chiles Hospital, Mount Sterling, Kentucky.

D2102—Amy Lynett Trimble. Daughter of Darrell Conard Trimble and Linda F. Blevins. (Ninth generation of David Trimble and ——— Houston.) Born on November 22, 1975. Married twice. Married first to Bryan Scott Lafferty on February 14, 1998 and divorced September 2006. Bryan was born on April 15, 1969.

Married second Gary Lemaster on January 21, 2012. Gary is the son of

Larry Lemaster and Iva Hanna. Gary was born on May 27, 1971 at Findlay, Ohio.

D2103—Cynthia Dawn Trimble. Daughter of David Carroll Trimble and Nina Lou Smith. (Ninth generation of David Trimble and ——— Houston.) Born on August 17, 1975. Married David Shane Marushi on July 11, 1998 at Ironville Enterprise Baptist Church, Ashland, Boyd County, Kentucky.

Cindy was saved on July 28, 1991 at Oak Springs United Baptist Church, Ashland, Boyd County, Kentucky and baptized on August 11, 1991 Oak Springs.

The children of David Shane Marushi and Cynthia Dawn Trimble:
D2253—Camron David Marushi. Born on December 11, 2001.
D2254—Brady Hansen Marushi. Born on December 10, 2007 in King's Daughters Medical Center, Ashland, Boyd County, Kentucky.

D2104—Kelly DeAnn Trimble. Daughter of David Carroll Trimble and Nina Lou Smith. (Ninth generation of David Trimble and ——— Houston.) Born on June 13, 1979. Married Michael Woodson Workman Jr. on August 20, 2005 at Unity Baptist Church, 29th St., Ashland, Boyd County by Donald Young, Kentucky. Michael was born on June 16, 1978. Michael is the son of Michael Workman Sr. and Kathy ———.

The children of Michael Woodson Workman and Kelly Deann Trimble:
D2255—Greyson Michael Workman. Born on April 30, 2012.

D2105—April Nicole Trimble. Daughter of Larry Allen Trimble and Deborah Marlene Salyers. (Ninth generation of David Trimble and ——— Houston.) Born on December 30, 1978 at Highlands Regional Hospital, Prestonsburg, Floyd County, Kentucky. Married two times first to Robert Levi Nett on June 28, 2002 at Middleburg, Florida. Robert was born on July 2, 1980. Robert and April divorced in September 2006. Second marriage to Jarret Vincent on May 29, 2007 in Grand Cayman Islands. Jarret is the son of Ronald Vincent and Kathleen Eve Merindino. Ronald was born on February 2, 1948. Kathleen was born on October 6, 1949.

The children of Jarret Vincent and April Nicole Trimble:
D2256—Jackson Ross Vincent. Born on December 27, 2009 in Jacksonville, Florida.
D2257—Abby Kathleen Vincent. Born on November 9, 2012 in Jacksonville, Florida.

D2258—Amelia Jane Vincent. Born on December 24, 2014 in Cedar Rapids Iowa.

D2106—Tara Autumn Trimble. Daughter of Larry Allen Trimble and Deborah Marlene Salyers. (Ninth generation of David Trimble and —— Houston.) Born on October 13, 1982. Married David Robert Cornish on November 23, 2005.

The children of David Robert Cornish and Tara Autumn Trimble:
D2259—Taylor Kelsey Cornish. Born on August 1, 2003.
D2260—Tanner David Cornish. Born on August 13, 2009.

D2108—Dale Edward Trimble. Son of Gary Stevens Trimble and Marsha Yvonne Castle. (Ninth generation of David Trimble and —— Houston.) Born on October 6, 1974. Married twice. Married first to Sabrina Jean Porter on August 30, 1997 and divorced in 2000. Sabrina is the daughter of Terry Lynn Porter and Barbara Jean Tackett.

Married second to Rosettia Gay Caudill on November 16, 2001 at Riceville Freewill Baptist Church, Swamp Branch, Johnson County, Kentucky. She was born on August 21, 1976.

Married third to Deidra Monroe.

The child of Dale Edward Trimble and Deidra Monroe:
D2261—Lane Edward Trimble. Born on November 14, 2014.

D2109—Hayley Miranda Trimble. Daughter of Gary Stevens Trimble and Marsha Yvonne Castle. (Ninth generation of David Trimble and —— Houston.) Born on January 30, 1978. Married Charles Mason Woodruff on December 30, 2000 at First United Methodist Church, Frankfort, Kentucky. Charles was born on March 11, 1978.

The children of Charles Mason Woodruff and Hayley Miranda Trimble:
D2262—Isabelle Marie Woodruff. Born on May 8, 2005 in Lexington, Kentucky.
D2263—Charles Jackson Woodruff. Born on January 24, 2007 in Lexington, Kentucky.
D2264—Henry Mason Woodruff. Born on December 31, 2008.
D2265—William Pierce Gene Woodruff. Born on December 16, 2010.

D2110—Eldon Leo Caudill. Son of Eldon Caroll Caudill and Carole Dean Conley. (Ninth generation of David Trimble and —— Houston.) Born on April 29, 1962. Married Vicki Lynn Adkins on March 24, 1985.

The children of Eldon Leo Caudill and Vicki Lynn Adkins:

D2266—Whitney Dawn Caudill. Born on February 5, 1988.

D2267—Hannah Belle Caudill. Born on March 23, 1998.

D2111—Joyce Lynn Caudill. Daughter of Eldon Caroll Caudill and Carole Dean Conley. (Ninth generation of David Trimble and ——— Houston.) Born on May 9, 1963. Married Larry Meadows on March 15, 1986 in Tom's Creek Freewill Baptist Church, Nippa, Kentucky.

The children of Larry Meadows and Joyce Lynn Caudill:

+ **D2268—Zachary Mathew Meadows.** Born on December 12, 1987. Married Jessica Nicole Music on July 18, 2009. Jessica was born in 1987.

+ **D2269—Larissa Jo Meadows.** Born on January 16, 1991. Married Jordan Tyler Witten on October 11, 2014 in Johnson County, Kentucky.

D2112—Belinda Carole Caudill. Daughter of Eldon Caroll Caudill and Carole Dean Conley. (Ninth generation of David Trimble and ——— Houston.) Born on May 23, 1966. Married Joseph Scott Blanton on October 28, 1989 in Paintsville, Johnson County, Kentucky. He is the son David Blanton and Elizabeth ———.

The children of Joseph Blanton and Belinda Carole Caudill:

D2270—Joseph Scott Blanton II. Born on August 28, 1991.

D2271—David Hunter Blanton. Born on August 23, 1994.

D2272—Wynter Hope Blanton. Born on December 16, 2004.

D2113—Christina Lynn Caudill. Daughter of Phillip Hager Caudill and Linda Blair. (Ninth generation of David Trimble and ——— Houston.) Born on April 20, 1968 in St. Joseph Hospital, Lexington, Fayette County, Kentucky. Married Lonnie Franklin Lemaster.

The child of Lonnie Franklin Lemaster and Christina Lynn Caudill:

D2273—Montana LeAnna Lemaster. Born on October 19, 1994.

D2114—William Dexter Caudill. Son of Phillip Hager Caudill and Linda Blair. (Ninth generation of David Trimble and ——— Houston.) Born on April 8, 1971 in Paintsville, Johnson County, Kentucky. Married twice first to Karen Renee Lee on May 8, 1993 and the second time Married Mary Linda Blair.

The children of William Dexter Caudill and Karen Renee Lee:

D2274—Marcus Alan Caudill. Born on August 28, 2001 in Lexington, Kentucky.

D2275—Phillip Mathew Caudill. Born on August 14, 2006 in King's Daughters Medical Center, Ashland, Boyd County, Kentucky.

Trimble Families of America

D2115—Kathy Jo Blair. Daughter of Phillip Hager Caudill and Linda Blair. (Ninth generation of David Trimble and ——— Houston.) Born on June 9, 1966. Married Jimmy Music.

The children of Jimmy Music and Kathy Jo Blair:
D2276—Aaron Mykal Music. Born on December 7, 1996.
D2277—Andrew Christian Music. Born on June 7, 2000.

D2116—Teresa Ann Blair. Daughter of Phillip Hager Caudill and Linda Blair. (Ninth generation of David Trimble and ——— Houston.) Born on April 11, 1970. Married James Larry Blanton.

The children of James Larry Blanton and Teresa Ann Blair:
D2278—Charles Christopher Blanton. Born on November 23, 1989.
D2279—James Coby Blanton. Born on July 16, 1992.

D2117—Charlena Blair. Daughter of Charles Eldon Blair and Linda Lou Caudill. (Ninth generation of David Trimble and ——— Houston.) Born on February 23, 1975. Married Daren Glen Gamble.

The children of Daren Glen Gamble and Charlena Blair:
D2280—Daren Blake Gamble. Born on April 30, 1999.
D2281—Chloie Elizabeth Gamble. Born on July 9, 2002.
D2282—Claire Alise Gamble. Born on February 16, 2004.

D2118—Michael Gayle Castle. Son of Russell Castle and Helen Kaye Trimble. (Ninth generation of David Trimble and ——— Houston.) Born on October 7, 1963 Columbus, Ohio. Married Dottie N. Meade. Dottie born on August 16, 1964. She is the daughter of Cecil Meade and Marsha Castle.

The children of Michael Gayle Castle and Dottie N. Meade:
+ **D2283—Jerrod Michael Castle.** Born on January 1, 1983. Married Dottie N. Meade on May 31, 2002.
+ **D2284—Mikka Jade Castle.** Born on June 18, 1986. Married Nathaniel Dean Slone.

D2119—Paul Keith Castle. Son of Russell Castle and Helen Kaye Trimble. (Ninth generation of David Trimble and ——— Houston.) Born on September 24, 1965. Married Lora Lynn Rucker.

The children of Paul Keith Castle and Lora Lynn Rucker:
D2285—Brooklynn Allise Castle. Born on October 3, 1991.
D2286—Lakin Deshae Castle. Born on December 19, 1992.
D2287—Riley Alexis Castle. Born on December 17, 2000.
D2288—Dalton Russell Castle. Born on June 12, 2002.

D2120—Mark Kenneth Castle. Son of Russell Castle and Helen Kaye Trimble. (Ninth generation of David Trimble and ——— Houston.) Born on January 8, 1969. Married Rowena Denise Simpson on November 3, 1990 at Rockhouse Freewill Baptist Church, Johnson County, Kentucky. Rowena is the daughter of Roy R. Simpson and Donna Ratliff. Mark is a physical therapist at the Paul B. Hall Hospital, Paintsville, Johnson County, Kentucky.

The children of Mark Kenneth Castle and Rowena Denise Simpson:
D2289—Tanner Royce Castle. Born on January 11, 2004.

D2121—Anna Maria Castle. Daughter of Russell Castle and Helen Kaye Trimble. (Ninth generation of David Trimble and ——— Houston.) Born on May 30, 1973. Married Timothy Dean Slone on June 3, 1995 at Van Lear Freewill Baptist Church, Johnson County, Kentucky. Timothy is the son of Reverend Hubert Slone and Linda ———.

The children of Timothy Dean Slone and Anna Maria Castle:
D2290—Isaac David Slone. Born on June 27, 2001.
D2291—Sarah Kaye Slone. Born on November 21, 2002.
D2292—Jacob William Slone. Born on June 18, 2004.
D2293—Micaiah Grace Slone. Born on July 6, 2005.

D2123—Crystal Sharon Colvin. Son of Jerry Morris Colvin and Sharon Blair. (Ninth generation of David Trimble and ——— Houston.) Born on November 23, 1972. Married James Edward Workman on December 16, 1995 at Van Lear Freewill Baptist Church, Johnson County, Kentucky. James is the son of Charles E. Workman and Caroline ———.

The children of James Edward Workman and Crystal Sharon Colvin:
D2294—Emily Grace Workman. Born on May 5, 1999.
D2295—Kyle Edward Workman. Born on August 30, 2002.

D2124—Jerry Edward "Jay" Colvin. Son of Jerry Morris Colvin and Sharon Blair. (Ninth generation of David Trimble and ——— Houston.) Born on July 22, 1974. Married Tonjua Kaye DeLong on September 3, 1994. Tonjua is the daughter of Michael DeLong and Mary ———.

The children of Jerry Edward "Jay" Colvin and Tonjua Kaye DeLong:
D2296—Jacab Michael Colvin. Born on March 23, 1999.
D2297—Jonathan Case Colvin. Born on November 12, 2004.

D2126—Andrea Lee Blair. Daughter of Alvin Blair and Glenda Theo Colvin. (Ninth generation of David Trimble and ——— Houston.) Born on February 16, 1980.

D - David Trimble

The children of Andrea Lee Blair:

D2298—Madison Brook Blair. Born on August 8, 2000.

D2299—Ethan Michael Blair. Born on August 16, 2001.

D2129—Shellie Denise Trimble. Daughter of Stanley Barry Trimble and Cheri Lynn Barker. (Ninth generation of David Trimble and —— Houston.) Born on August 27, 1975. Married David Scott Clark on June 1, 1996 in Ashland, Boyd County, Kentucky. While her father was going to Marshall University as a returning student, she was going to Morehead State University. During Christmas break she stayed with her father in his apartment in Huntington, West Virginia. Her school started a week after her father's. He was working at the bookstore during that extra week, making sure the students got the correct books off the shelves. He got Shellie to tag along, they always needed help. After just a few minutes she realized she could do it and the manager said they needed the help. She would earn a few dollars also. That is where she met her future husband David Scott Clark. He graduated the same year as her father. Shellie later graduated from Concord, West Virginia with a bachelor's degree in Early Childhood Education. She then went The University of West Virginia and earned a master's degree in Special Education.

Scott has run in many marathon races. We are a family of runners.

The children of David Scott Clark and Shellie Denise Trimble:

D2300—Joseph Scott Clark. Born on February 12, 1999. Joseph had perfect attendance all the way through public school. He was Valedictorian for his class. His SAT score was so high he was a National Merit Scholar. He could attend any college on a free ride. He went to the University of Kentucky on a Paterson scholarship. He graduated with a Bachelor of Science in Computer Engineering with highest honors, Summa Cum Laude. He did his last years online because of Covid. His advisor told him if he wanted to get his PhD, that he would see that he got room, board, tuition, books a stipend, but he would have to go to the University of Tennessee at Knoxville, because his advisor had a new job there. His mother told him just one thing, she was not wearing orange.

D2301—Melanie "Melly" Denise Clark. Born on January 14, 2002. Melly also, had perfect attendance all the way through public school. She graduated with highest honors. She had to take her last few months of high school classes online because of Covid. She qualified for a Yeager Scholarship at Marshall University. Which pays for everything. She will graduate from the same school as her father and her grandfather. Third generation.

D2302—Christopher David Lee. He is a foster child. Born on September 9, 1999. Shellie fostered Chris during high school. He attended youth group at church with Scott and Shellie. During Chris's senior year his mother died and he has stayed with Shellie and Scott. Christopher started baking cupcakes, some of the best cupcakes. He also started cooking. He is good at it. So, he enrolled in culinary school. He just graduated in the top of his class. He is working for one of the best restaurants in Charleston, West Virginia. He is black but he is still family.

D2131—Joshua Bradley "Brad" Trimble. Son of Stewart Lee Trimble and Loretta Jean Gullet. (Ninth generation of David Trimble and ——— Houston.) Born on February 1, 1978. Married first Leslie Ann White. They divorced.

Married second to April Sunshine Grant on January 12, 2008. She is the daughter of Thomas David Grant and Patricia Elizabeth Greear. They were married on May 30, 1976. Thomas was born on October 8, 1956 in Cabell County, West Virginia. Patricia was born on December 20, 1957 in Campton, Kentucky. Brad and Sunshine own and run a Giovanni's Pizza Restaurant in Ashland.

The children of Joshua Bradley "Brad" Trimble and Leslie Ann White:

D2303—Baylee Sue Trimble. Born on September 21, 2002 in Ashland, Boyd County, Kentucky.

The children of Joshua Bradley "Brad" Trimble and April Sunshine Grant:

D2304—Thomas Daniel Trimble. Born on September 1, 2008 in Huntington, Cabell County, West Virginia.

D2305—Sophia Ruth Trimble. Born on April 4, 2011 in Huntington, Cabell County, West Virginia.

Brad raised Sunshine's daughter by Robert Vankueren:

D2306—Jewelia Rose Vankueren. Born on March 5, 2003 in Huntington, Cabell County, West Virginia.

D2132—Jeremy Blake Trimble. Son of Stewart Lee Trimble and Loretta Jean Gullet. (Ninth generation of David Trimble and ——— Houston.) Born on December 12, 1980 Married Heather Kay Shanks. Born on February 5, 1980 at Ashland, Boyd County, Kentucky. She is the daughter of Frank Shanks and Teresa Reibold. Frank was born on August 8, 1958 in Ashland, Boyd County, Kentucky. Teresa was born on August 9, 1958 in Ashland, Boyd County, Kentucky.

The children of Jeremy Blake Trimble and Heather Kay Shanks:

    D2307—Christian Ray Trimble. Born on April 6, 2002.

    D2308—Mason Storm Trimble. Born on November 8, 2002

    D2309—Blake Ryan Trimble. Born on July 25, 2003.

    D2310—Trevor Austin Trimble. Born on July 21, 2006.

    D2311—Izzabella Grace Trimble. Born on April 11, 2010.

    D2312—Gabryella Jane Lee Trimble. Born on May 20, 2012

D2133—Amanda Courtney Trimble. Daughter of Stewart Lee Trimble and Loretta Jean Gullet. (Ninth generation of David Trimble and —— Houston.) Born on January 7, 1983 Married Mason Neil Miller on May 25, 2002 in Boyd County, Kentucky.

    The children of Mason Neil Miller and Amanda Courtney Trimble:

    D2313—Kati Doreen Miller. (twin born premature) Born on August 17, 2004 in Boyd County Kentucky.

    D2314—Karlee Jean Miller. (twin born premature) Born on August 17, 2004 in Boyd County Kentucky.

    D2315—Addison Nickole Miller. Born on February 27, 2007 in Boyd County Kentucky.

    D2316—Ella Maci Miller. Born on July 24, 2017 in Boyd County, Kentucky.

D2134—Nickolas Adam Trimble. Son of Stewart Lee Trimble and Loretta Jean Gullet. (Ninth generation of David Trimble and —— Houston.) Born on January 5, 1985. Married Susan Eastridge on July 22, 2011. She was born on August 26, 1985 at Campbellsville, Kentucky. She is the daughter of Gregory Dale Eastridge and Janet Rae Thompson. They were married October 5, 1979. Gregory was born on January 3, 1960 in Campbellsville, Taylor County, Kentucky. Janet was born on May 15, 1962 in Campbellsville, Taylor County, Kentucky. Nick was a Marine, he enlisted on January 26, 2003. He was discharged on January 21, 2007. He was deployed to Iraq for seven months.

    The children of Nickolas Adam Trimble and Susan Eastridge:

    D2317—Zoey Abigail Trimble. Born on July 12, 2012 in Boyd County, Kentucky.

    D2318—Sadie Jane Trimble. Born on September 19, 2014 in Boyd County, Kentucky.

    D2319—Layne Alexander Trimble. Born on April 17, 2019 in Boyd County, Kentucky.

D2135—Jacob Carlton Bingham. Son of Jeffery Carlton Bingham and Melanie DeAlice Trimble. (Ninth generation of David Trimble and —— Houston.)

Born on May 4, 1993. Married Destynne Moore. Enlisted in the Marines.

The children of Jacob Carlton Bingham and Destynne Moore:

D2320—Jacob Carlton Bingham II. Born on December 12, 2017 at Camp Lejeune, North Carolina.

D2321—Madison Renee Bingham. Born on March 9, 2020 at Camp Lejeune, North Carolina.

D2322—Theodore Bazooka Bingham. Born on December 26, 2021.

D2138—Ryan Afton Baker. Son of Dennis Baker and Peggy Ann Trimble. (Ninth generation of David Trimble and —— Houston.) Born on June 10, 1980. Married Kirsti Linda Pfeffer on August 10, 2002 in Louisville, Kentucky. Kirsti was born on February 14, 1980.

The child of Ryan Afton Baker and Kirsti Linda Pfeffer:

D2323—Olivia Kate Baker. Born on March 4, 2008.

D2139—Mathew Scott Baker. Son of Dennis Baker and Peggy Ann Trimble. (Ninth generation of David Trimble and —— Houston.) Born on October 24, 1981. Never married.

D2324—Blaire Everson Baker. Born on December 21, 2019.

D2141—Krystle Michelle Trimble. Daughter of Randy Allen Trimble and Terri Hill. (Ninth generation of David Trimble and —— Houston.) Born on May 29, 1985. Married Taylor Wells on August 24, 2013 in the Smoky Mountains, Tennessee. He is the son of Jeff and Donna Wells.

The children of Taylor Wells and Krystle Michelle Trimble:

D2325—Kinley Grace Wells. Born on May 27, 2014 in Lexington, Kentucky.

D2150—Kristen Nicole McCarty. Daughter of Ron Evans, Jr. and Belinda Trimble. (Ninth generation of David Trimble and —— Houston.) Born on September 2, 1995. Dale adopted Kristen changing her name to Kristen Nicole McCarty. Married John Cody New on January 29, 2013 in Mason County, West Virginia.

The children of John Cody New and Kristen Nicole McCarty:

D2326—Hailey Lyricakiss New. Born on October 6, 2011 in Gallipolis, Ohio.

D2327—Emily Renee New. Born on August 29, 2014 in Pasadena Texas.

D2155—Michael J. Taylor. Son of Gary J. Taylor and Arthetta Browning. (Ninth generation of David Trimble and —— Houston.) Born on November 27, 1967 in Huntington, West Virginia. Married Jeanette Sue Artis.

The children of Michael J. Taylor and Jeanette Sue Artis:

Trimble Families of America

D2328—Abigal Grace Taylor. Born on October 24, 2011.

D2158—Candace Nicole Trimble. Daughter of Michael L. Trimble and Lori Wolford. (Ninth generation of David Trimble and ——— Houston.) Born on September 11, 1989. Married Richard Pendrey.

The child of Richard Pendrey and Candance Nicole Trimble:
D2329—Mathew Pendrey. (Stepson) Born on October 24, 2011.

D2161—Elizabeth Ann Tawney. Daughter of Laken Orville Tawney and Sharon Denise Perry. (Ninth generation of David Trimble and ——— Houston.) Born on March 27, 1982 in Huntington, West Virginia. Married Charles Jason Gilkerson on October 26, 2002 in Huntington, West Virginia.

They are raising Charles' children from a previous marriage.
D2330—Bailey Andrew Gilkerson. Born on July 16, 1996 in Columbus, Ohio.
D2331—Elijah Jordon Gilkerson. Born on April 18, 1998 in Columbus, Ohio.
D2332—Jacob Jayce Edward Gilkerson. Born on September 13, 1999 in Mobile, Alabama.

The child of Charles Jason Gilkerson and Sharon Denise Perry:
D2333—Jocelyn Nicole Gilkerson. Born on April 18, 2009 in Huntington, West Virginia.

D2164—Rachel Craig. Daughter of Terry Craig and Sandra D. Perry. (Ninth generation of David Trimble and ——— Houston.) Born on October 4, 1992 in Hamilton Ohio. Married Kyle Slone on August 4, 2012.

They are raising his son from a previous marriage.
D2334—Hayden Sloan. Born on August 23, 2009.

D2174—Johnnie Trimble III PhD. Son of Johnnie Trimble, Jr. and Elodie Bratton. (Ninth generation of David Trimble and ——— Houston.) Born on October 7, 1963. Married three times. First, he married Angela Bunger. Second, he married to Susan Wright. Third, he married to Nichole M. Cloughly. He went to Liberty University A.A. in Religion, and a B.S. in Psychology. Then he went to Virginia Commonwealth University for his Masters in sports leadership with a concentration on sports psychology. Then Kennedy University for PhD in sports psychology. Johnnie is a psychologist and lives in Richmond, Virginia.

The child of Johnnie Trimble, III PhD. and Angela Bunger:
D2335—Shannon Renee' Trimble. Born on January 26, 1985 in Richmond, Virginia. Married Robert Luman. They live in Anchorage Alaska.

The child of Johnnie Trimble, III PhD. and Susan Wright:

D2336—Caitlin Berkley Trimble. Born on January 28, 1993 in Richmond, Virginia. She is at James Madison University.

D2175—Bradley Alan Trimble. Son of Johnnie Trimble, Jr. and Elodie Bratton. (Ninth generation of David Trimble and ——— Houston.) Born on October 17, 1964 in Tacoma, Washington. Married Gwyn Meadows in 1984 in Tacoma, Washington.

Brad enlisted in the Reserve National Guard of Virginia in July 1983 to July 1986 He was on Active Duty in Fort Lewis Washington from 1986 to 1989 as a Corporal.

D2337—Andrew Alan Trimble. Born on September 11, 1985 in Fort Lewis, Washington.

D2338—Christopher Kenneth Trimble. Born on April 17, 1988 Richmond, Virginia.

D2210—Jodi Rae Ann Trimble. Daughter of Dave Paul "Odie" Trimble and Elizabeth Ann Juniper. (Ninth generation of David Trimble and ——— Houston.) Born on July 3, 1995. in Kentucky. Married Walter Boggs on May 10, 2015 in Johnson County, Kentucky.

The children of Walter Boggs and Jodi Rae Ann Trimble:

D2339—Linkin Dean Boggs. Born on November 28, 2017 in Johnson Co., Ky

D2340—Odie David Boggs. Born on May 12, 2020 in Johnson County, Kentucky.

D2341—Kimberly Elizabeth Boggs. Born on March 25, 2022 in Johnson County, Kentucky.

D2217—Denieka Skeens. Daughter of Judy Trimble. (Ninth generation of David Trimble and ——— Houston.) Born on August 7, 1990 in Paintsville, Johnson County, Kentucky.

The child of Danieka Skeens:

D2342—Davin Joseph.

D2235—Andrea Suzanne Ward. Daughter of Jimmy Darrell Ward and Dianne Kaye McCarty. (Tenth generation of David Trimble and ——— Houston.) Born on September 16, 1979. Married twice. First married Jason T. Kestner. Second married Nicholas Hale on April 10, 1999.

The child of Jason T. Kestner and Andrea Suzanne Ward:

D2343—Izabella Dianne Kestner. Born on October 25, 2006.

D2236—Brandon Alexander Ward. (Twin) Son of Jimmy Darrell Ward and

Dianne Kaye McCarty. (Tenth generation of David Trimble and —— Houston.) Born on June 17, 1981. Brandon married twice. First to Tonya Campbell on September 23, 2000. She was born on September 22, 1983, divorced in 2003. Second, married Keri Anne Russell.

The child of Brandon Alexander Ward and Keri Anne Russell:

D2344—Kailey Brooke Ward. Born on November 9, 2003 in King's Daughters Hospital, Ashland, Boyd County, Kentucky.

D2238—Alicia Renee' Ward. Daughter of Jimmy Darrell Ward and Dianne Kaye McCarty. (Tenth generation of David Trimble and —— Houston.) Born on November 22, 1982. Married Joe "Joey" Smith III on August 14, 2004 in East Kermit Church of God, East Kermit, West Virginia. He was the son of Joe Smith II and Shirley ——.

The children of Joe "Joey" Smith III and Alicia Renee' Ward:

D2345—Joseph Austin Smith. Born on May 23, 2006 at Cabell Hospital, Huntington, Cabell County, West Virginia.

D2346—Kaleb Parker Smith. Born on August 27, 2010.

D2239—Mistia Lynn McCarty. Daughter of Bryan Bandy McCarty and Gina Lea Smith. (Tenth generation of David Trimble and —— Houston.) Born on February 12, 1981 in Hamilton Butler County, Ohio. Married Ryan Alexander Estep on September 4, 2009. Ryan was born on December 11, 1990. They divorced in 2011.

The children of Mistia McCarty:

D2347—Alexis Renee' Daughtery. Born on April 3, 2000 in King's Daughters Hospital, Ashland, Boyd County, Kentucky. She is the daughter of Ryan Daughtery.

D2348—Marie Lynn Brown. Born on April 25, 2003. She is the daughter of John Brown.

D2349—Nathan Bryan Barker. Born on November 6, 2007. He is the son of Brandon Baker.

D2241—Brittany LeAnne McCarty. Daughter of Kevin McCarty and Lisa Spradlin. (Tenth generation of David Trimble and —— Houston.) Born on October 4, 1986 in Dallas Texas. Married Charles Worden on November 22, 2006 in Columbus, Ohio.

The children of Charles Worden and Brittany LeAnne McCarty:

D2350—Jaycob Steven Worden. Born on July 8, 2010.

D2245—Myranda Dawn Nall. Daughter of Dirk Nicholson Nall and Donetta

Carol Trimble. (Tenth generation of David Trimble and —— Houston.) Born on September 4, 1982. Married Justin Ted Boyd on December 21, 2002 in Westwood Enterprise Baptist Church, Westwood, Boyd County, Kentucky. Justine is the son of Patty Nicely.

The children of Justin Ted Boyd and Myranda Dawn Nall:

D2351—Titus Donavan Boyd. Born on November 14, 2006.

D2352—Tatum Rae Ann Boyd. Born on December 28, 2009.

D2353—Abram Justin Boyd. Born on March 15, 2011.

D2354—Julius Boyd. Born on July 26, 2014.

D2246—Afton Cheri Nall. Daughter of Dirk Nicholson Nall and Donetta Carol Trimble. (Tenth generation of David Trimble and —— Houston.) Born on May 14, 1984. Married Adam Seth Carroll on July 15, 2006 in Afton's grandparents Donald and Carolyn Trimble's back yard Ashland, Boyd County, Kentucky.

The children of Adam Seth Carroll and Afton Cheri Nall:

D2355—Amalie Grace Carroll. Born on October 12, 2008.

D2356—Ayris Seth Carroll. Born on April 6, 2011.

D2268—Zachary Mathew Meadows. Son of Larry Meadows and Joyce Lynn Caudill. (Tenth generation of David Trimble and —— Houston.) Born on December 12, 1987. Married Jessica Nicole Music on July 18, 2009. Jessica was born in 1987.

The children of Zachary Mathew Meadows and Jessica Nicole Music:

D2357—Ellee Joann Meadows. Born on November 3, 2016 in Lexington, Kentucky.

D2269—Larissa Jo Meadows. Daughter of Larry Meadows and Joyce Lynn Caudill. (Tenth generation of David Trimble and —— Houston.) Born on January 16, 1991. Married Jordan Tyler Witten on October 11, 2014 in Johnson County, Kentucky.

The children of Jordan Tyler Witten and Larissa Jo Meadows:

D2358—Jaxson Matthew. Born on May 26, 2010 in Pikeville, Kentucky.

D2359—Hattie Ann Witten. Born on December 10, 2016 in Ashland, Kentucky.

D2360—Reid Tyler Witten. Born on February 14, 2021 in Ashland, Kentucky.

D2283—Jerrod Michael Castle. Son of Michael Gayle Castle and Dottie N. Meade. (Tenth generation of David Trimble and —— Houston.) Born on January 1, 1983. Married Dottie N. Meade.

D - David Trimble

The children of Jerrod Michael Castle and Dottie N. Meade:

D2361—Connor Michael Castle. Born on March 22, 2004 in King's Daughters Hospital, Ashland, Boyd County, Kentucky.

D2362—Kennadi Ann Castle. Born on January 27, 2007 in King's Daughters Hospital, Ashland, Boyd County, Kentucky.

D2284—Mikka Jade Castle. Daughter of Michael Gayle Castle and Dottie N. Meade. (Tenth generation of David Trimble and —— Houston.) Born on June 18, 1986. Married Nathaniel Dean Slone on July 2, 2011 at her parents' home. Mike and Dottie at River, Johnson County, Kentucky.

The children of Nathaniel Dean Slone and Mikka Jade Castle:

D2363—Wyatt Elmer Slone. Born on January 23, 2012.

E - Alexander Trimble

E1—Alexander Trimble was the youngest of the Five Trimble Brothers. He was in his early teens when his four older brothers migrated to the Valley of Virginia. Such a move would have been an interruption in Alexander's education from the established schools of Philadelphia, Pennsylvania, to the frontier area in Virginia. He was left in Philadelphia with a cousin, the Reverend Gilbert Tennent, pastor of the Second Presbyterian Church.

On June 20, 1754, Alexander Trimble married Eleanor Rogers of Abington, Pennsylvania. She was the sister of the Reverend John Rogers, moderator of the General Assembly in the United States.

The date of Alexander's death is unknown to us, but we do know it was prior to the year 1769, as we find a record on the church books telling of his widow, Eleanor Trimble, being baptized and her profession of faith into the church on the 5th of May 1769. He died a young man.

Alexander and Eleanor Trimble seem to have had several children, the eldest being James.

Alexander served under the Christopher Gist Company in 1756. He was thirty-five years of age then.

The son of Alexander Trimble and Eleanor Rogers:

+ E2—James Trimble.

E2—James Trimble. Son of Alexander Trimble and Eleanor Rogers. Born on July 19, 1755, at Philadelphia, Pennsylvania, and died on January 26, 1836. James was the eldest of several children, and we find, though young at the time of his father's death, he manifested all those qualities of mind and heart for which he was so justly noted throughout a long life devoted to the service of his country. "When but a mere boy he assisted his mother in the care of a store. One day a gentleman, Mr. Tilghman, secretary of the Land Office under the Proprietors, called and made some purchases. When young Trimble made out his bill, the gentleman was so much pleased with his writing and business style that he at once took measures to secure his services in his department. Mr. Hamilton states that he was apprenticed as a clerk in the Land Office about 1770, when he was fifteen years old."

The endorsement upon the archives of the Board of War and Council of Safety recently recovered, indicated that he was subordinate clerk in the State Council as early as 1775, and when Col. Timothy Matlack became the first secretary of the Commonwealth on March 6, 1777, James Trimble became deputy secretary, and so continued down to Thursday, January 14, 1837.

Pending some difficulties with the council regarding his accounts of his money trust, Colonel Matlack resigned his position as secretary, and on March 25, 1783, General John Armstrong, Jr., was appointed in his place. General Armstrong was elected a member of Congress in 1787, and on the 7th of November, Charles Biddle took his place. Mr. Biddle remained in office until January 19, 1791, when Alexander Dallas, Esq., was commissioned by Governor Mifflin as the first secretary under the Constitution of 1790, and on the 12th of March 1791, the very day the governor approved the act providing for a deputy secretary, Mr. Dallas appointed James Trimble to be the deputy secretary, and this appointment was approved by the governor.

His records were models of neatness, his papers elaborately endorsed, and filed with great care, so that in the days of tallow candles, he could enter his office at night, and without striking a light lay his hand on any paper he wished.

James Trimble was described as a man of slight stature, solemn suit of short black clothes, queue, long hose, buckle shoes, quick eye, brisk movements, and dignified address. When he died many felt that Harrisburg, Pennsylvania, had lost its last gentleman of the old school, for in the judgment of his contemporaries he was a faithful public servant, a man of unimpeachable integrity.

James Trimble helped pack and remove the state papers. at the time the British occupied Philadelphia, and again when the seat of government was moved to Lancaster in 1799, and from Lancaster to Harrisburg, in 1812. He was a member of the Second Presbyterian Church in Philadelphia.

James died on January 26, 1836, at the age of eighty-one years, having served his country faithfully for sixty-five of those years. His only fault was being on the wrong side of politics from the party then coming into office. Surely party spirit must have been at fever heat to remove such a public servant, without some sort of retired-list position for him. The mortification was too great for him to bear, for he died in just eleven days after his removal, of a broken heart. It is said that James would rather have paid his own salary than be moved from office, for he would not live a week afterwards; and this statement resulted in truth.

James Trimble married Clarissa Hastings, widow of John Hastings. Clarissa was the daughter of Betsy Ross, more well known for her flag making. Betsy Ross was married two times. Clarissa was by her first husband,

John Ross, who was an upholsterer, to which pursuit his widow added that of flag making. Betsy made flags for the government, an occupation which she and her family carried on for many years. Betty Ross (or Betsy) is said to have made the first American flag with stars and stripes. John and Elizabeth Claypoole lived in the little old house, still standing (No. 239 Arch Street), for three years after their marriage. He was Betty's second husband. Elizabeth Claypoole died on January 30, 1836. Clarissa H. Trimble died at Lancaster, Pennsylvania, on February 6, 1810.

Of their eleven children, only two survived their parents. They were James Trimble, who died in 1838, and Thomas R. Trimble, who died in 1868.

The children of James Trimble and Clarissa Hastings:

E3—Alexander Trimble. Born in March 1783 and died in 1784.

E4—Elizabeth Trimble. Born on October 13, 1784 and died young.

E5—Elinor Trimble. Born on July 5, 1786. She died on November 2, 1809, in Philadelphia. Elinor married William Boyd.

E6—Maria Trimble. Born on August 3, 1788 and died on September 12, 1790.

E7—James Trimble. Born on April 18, 1790 and died on June 22, 1838.

E8—Clarissa Sidney Trimble. Born on January 31, 1792 and died on June 21, 1832. Married Daniel Reigart.

E9—Mary Trimble. Born on January 20, 1794 and died on July 3, 1797.

E10—Eliza Trimble. Born on December 23, 1795 and died on June 14, 1797.

E11—Susannah Trimble. Born in November 1797 and died in 1798 at Germantown.

E12—Thomas Rogers Trimble. Born in August 1799 and died on September 8, 1868.

E13—William Claypoole Trimble. Born in January 1802.

"The Quaker"

F - Joseph 'The Quaker' Trimble

F1–Joseph "The Quaker" Trimble (we use Quaker to identify this Joseph Trimble). Born on July 10, 1720 in Antrim County, Ireland and died between February 9, 1784 and November 29, 1785.[69] Joseph was the son of John and Mary Trimble.

When about eighteen years of age Joseph took passage on a vessel to North America and presumably landed in Pennsylvania or Delaware since shortly thereafter, he engaged himself to serve a Reverend William Brown of, Chester County, Pennsylvania (now part of Cecil County, Maryland). He was employed by the Reverend Mr. Brown to drive a team of oxen which furnished power for the latter's mill. His term of service was completed in 1741, Joseph became Reverend Mr. Brown's partner in the operation of the mill and purchased a piece of property in the Village of Brick Meeting House, now Calvert Post Office. There he built himself a home and upon its completion invited his parents in Ireland to join him. This they reportedly set out to do, but the vessel was lost at sea. He was the son of William and Mary Trimble. William Trimble was born in 1690.

Joseph Trimble was married on January 31, 1744 or 1745 in Nottingham, Pennsylvania to Sarah Churchman,[70] the daughter of John Churchman, the emigrant, and the sister of John Churchman, a well-known Quaker minister. There were three children by this marriage. Sarah Churchman was born on May 17, 1716 in Pennsylvania and died on October 28, 1750.[71]

Joseph married for the second time to Ann Chandler on February 25, 1753. Born in 1721. She was the daughter of William Chandler of Linden Grove, Chester County, Pennsylvania.[72] He had six children by his marriage to

---

[69] The Trimble Family Descendants of Joseph Trimble of Pennsylvania and Maryland, by Patricia Law Hatcher, FASG, Newbury Street Press, Boston, Massachusetts, 2007, page 84.

[70] East Nottingham Monthly Meeting, 78(Swarthmore MR-B176).

[71] The family group, with birth dates for the children of John and Hannah Churchman, is recorded at New Garden Monthly Meeting, abstracted in Charlotte Meldrum and Martha Reamy, Early Church Records of Chester County, Pennsylvania, Volume 2 (Westminster, Md.: Family Line Publications, 1997), 2:115; See also Hatcher, "The English Origin of the Churchman Family," PGM 44)2006): 322-35

[72] Source number: 8931.482; Source type: Family group sheet, FGSE, listed as parents;

F - Joseph "The Quaker" Trimble

Ann Chandler. Ann was born on February 27, 1721. [73]

We have been unable to establish, through fact, the exact way in which this branch of the Trimbles was related to the Five Trimble Brothers. Yet we have read copies of old letters written by members of both families calling each other "cousin," such as the letter written on March 24, 1824, by David Trimble, grandson of Joseph "The Quaker," to Allen Trimble, grandson of John, one of the Five Trimble Brothers, ending with the following closing, "Giving my respects to all my relations, I am your friend, David Trimble." Also, in the memoirs of General Isaac Ridgeway Trimble, grandson of Joseph "The Quaker," we read of William C. Trimble, U.S. Senator of Ohio and grandson of John Trimble, one of the Five Trimble Brothers, as he made a trip to West Point Academy and admonished Isaac Ridgeway to study harder and raise his academic standings.

The children of Joseph Trimble and Sarah Churchman:

+ **F2—William Trimble**. Born on October 1, 1745 and died on May 30, 1819.

+ **F3—John Trimble**. Born on December 16, 1746. Died about 1809.

F4—Mary Trimble. Born on July 11, 1748.

The children of Joseph Trimble and Ann Chandler:

+ **F5—Joseph Trimble, Jr.** Born on October 29, 1754, and died on December 5, 1831.

+ **F6—Thomas Trimble**. Born on May 4, 1756 in East Nottingham, Chester County, Pennsylvania and died in 1806 in Westmoreland, Pennsylvania. Married Elizabeth Crow in 1777.

F7—Jacob Trimble. Born on February 27, 1758.

F8—Sarah Trimble. Born on May 23, 1760.

+ **F9—James Trimble**. Born on April 20, 1762 and died on December 5, 1831. Married three times.

F10—Elisha Trimble. Born on August 28, 1765. Died in 1848.

F2—William Trimble. Son of Joseph Trimble and Sarah Churchman. He was born on October 1, 1745 in Nottingham, Pennsylvania and died on May 30, 1819. William married Mary McMillian, daughter of James McMillian.

Number of Pages: 1

[73] Ancestry.com. U.S., Quaker Meeting Records, 1681-1935 [database on-line]. Provo, UT, USA: Ancestry.com Operations, Inc., 2014.

Trimble Families of America

F - Joseph "The Quaker" Trimble

William settled first in Berkeley County, now West Virginia. Here his first son, Robert, was born. Mary's brother, John McMillian, was employed along with Daniel Boone by the Transylvania Land Company. They had been hired to establish the Fort of Boonesboro and blaze trails so that the people who had bought land from Transylvania could settle thereon. Probably influenced by his brother-in-law, William Trimble purchased 1,000 acres on Howard Creek, near the fort. William and family joined a group of immigrants heading westward into Kentucky. The trip began in October 1779 and was completed with their arrival at Fort Boonesboro near Christmastime. William and Mary Trimble had a son, Robert, who was three years of age at the time of this migration.

Hostile Native Americans attacked the party in route to Kentucky but were repulsed by the immigrants. It was during this troublesome encounter that Mary Trimble gave birth to their first daughter, Margaret. She, being a most courageous pioneer woman, chose to continue the journey immediately rather than endanger the lives of others, they are being in fear of another Native Americans attack. One of William Trimble's young slaves was killed during this attack. John McMillian, Mary's brother, was shot by Native Americans on the trail. He asked to be propped up against a tree with his gun and a jug of water and for the party to proceed with its journey. Since it was not yet safe for the colonists to settle on their new lands, they would stay at night in Fort Boonesboro while using the daytime to clear their lands and build their homes. Actual settlement on their lands began around 1783-84. As there were no schools in this frontier area of Kentucky, James McMillian began the educational training of his daughter's children.

According to Judge John Trimble, son of William Trimble and Mary McMillian, in his autobiography, his Uncle Robert McMillian was a graduate of the "log college" in Washington, Pennsylvania. This school was later called Washington and Jefferson College. The establishment of this "log college" was due to the efforts of Robert's uncle, the Reverend John McMillian. When Robert McMillian returned to Kentucky, he, too, assisted in the educational instruction of William and Mary Trimble's children.

The children of William Trimble and Mary McMillian:

+ **F11—Robert Trimble.** Born in 1777 in Berkeley County, Virginia (now West Virginia). Married Nancy Timberlake. The twentieth justice of the U.S. Supreme Court.

 F12—Margaret Trimble. Born in 1779 on the trail from Berkeley County, Virginia (now West Virginia), to Boonesboro, Kentucky. Married Robert

Morrow.

+ **F13—Judge John Trimble.** Born on December 4, 1783. He married two times: first, to Catherine Wilson, and second, to Elizabeth D. Porter.

+ **F14—Judge James Trimble.** Born in 1784 in Kentucky. Married to Mary Lane.

F15—Jane Trimble. Born in 1785 and died in 1855. Married Robert M. Evans.

+ **F16—Mary 'Polly' Trimble.** Born in 1790 and died in 1866. Married in 1812 to Joel Pruitt.

F17—Elizabeth Trimble. Married James W. Jones. They had two sons, one of whom was Judge James Jones.

F3—John Trimble. Son of Joseph Trimble and Sarah Churchman. Born on December 16, 1746, at Nottingham Turnpike, Chester County, Pennsylvania and died about 1809 at Chillicothe, Ohio.

The present Maryland branch of the Trimble family is descended from John. On December 10, 1772, he married Katherine Wilson, the daughter of Samuel and Catherine Wilson. John and his wife moved to Frederick County, Virginia, in 1775. There were three children by this marriage. John married second Rachel Ridgeway.

The children of John Trimble and Katherine Wilson:

F18—Ann Trimble. Born on August 15, 1774 and died on June 16, 1849. She married Joshua Woodrow and settled in Hillsboro, Ohio. Ann's daughter married the eldest son of Governor Allen Trimble of Ohio.

F19—Samuel Trimble. Born on February 26, 1777. He died as a boy in a logging accident at his father's mill.

+ **F20—David Trimble.** Born on October 22, 1779 and died on October 26, 1842 at Argillite Furnace, Greenup County, Kentucky. David and his brother, John partnered with Richard Deering in 1816 to build and operate Argillite Furnace.

The children of John Trimble and Rachel Ridgeway:

F21—Sarah Churchman Trimble. Born in 1782 and married Pearson Starr on December 14, 1806.

F22—Charity Trimble. Born on July 29, 1790, married James McClintock on March 11, 1811.

F23—Catherine Trimble. Born in 1792 and married Isaiah Morris of Wilmington, Ohio.

The children of John Trimble and Rachel Ridgeway:

F24—John Trimble. Born in 1794 and married Elizabeth Ann Winn of

Winchester, Kentucky, on April 25, 1838, in Clark County, Kentucky. He was a clerk of the court in Greenup, Kentucky.

F25—William Trimble. Born on April 3, 1797 and married Livana Stewart. He became a territorial judge in Arkansas through President John Quincy Adams.

+ **F26—General Isaac Ridgeway Trimble.** Born on May 20, 1804, in Culpeper County, Virginia.

F6—Thomas Trimble. Son of Joseph Trimble and Ann Chandler. Born on May 4, 1756 in East Nottingham, Chester County, Pennsylvania and died 1806 in Westmoreland County, Pennsylvania. Married Elizabeth Crow in 1777. She was born about 1755 in Westmoreland County, Pennsylvania and died in 1827 in Westmoreland County, Pennsylvania.

The children of Thomas Trimble and Elizabeth Crow:

F27—Thomas Trimble. Born on January 7, 1785 in Westmoreland County, Pennsylvania, was living in Indiana County, Pennsylvania, in 1849. He died January 9, 1853. He married Sarah Matthews, on December 8, 1812. She was born on August 22, 1790 and died on June 6, 1875.

F28—Elizabeth Trimble. Born in 1775 in Westmoreland County, Pennsylvania and died on April 11, 1845.

F9—James Trimble. Son of Joseph Trimble and Ann Chandler. Born on April 20, 1762 and died on December 5, 1831. Married first to Sarah Job on March 20, 1788. She was born on March 11, 1760 and died on February 7, 1807.

Married second to Elizabeth Wilkinson on May 10, 1809. She was born in London Grove, Chester, Pennsylvania and died on October 4, 1820.

Married third to Elizabeth Giles Chandler on January 10, 1822.

The children of James Trimble and Sarah Job:

F29—Joseph Trimble. Born on March 7, 1789 and died on January 31, 1872.

F30—Job Trimble. Born on February 23, 1791 and died in 1866 in Illinois.

F31—Thomas Trimble. Born on May 5, 1793 and died in 1856 in Illinois.

F32—Ann Trimble. Born on February 20, 1795. Married Williams Phillips.

F33—Rees Trimble. Born on January 10, 1797.

F34—James Trimble. Born on February 23, 1799. Married Hannah Mendenhall.

F35—Reuben Trimble. Born on June 14, 1803 and died on July 1, 1803 as small infant.

F11—Robert Trimble. Son of William Trimble and Mary McMillian. (Third generation of Joseph Trimble and Sarah Churchman.) Born in 1777 in Berkeley County, Virginia (now West Virginia), and died on August 25, 1828, in Washington, D.C. Robert Trimble was one of the more prominent Trimbles in America. Had he not died at the early age of fifty-one during the height of his career he would have accomplished even more. Robert Trimble was a justice of the United States Supreme Court at the time of his death.

When a lad of three years of age, Robert and his family settled at Fort Boonesboro, Kentucky. His early education came from the instruction of his grandfather, James McMillian, and an uncle, Robert McMillian. At age eighteen, he entered Bourbon Academy at Cane Ridge, later Paris, Kentucky, but was forced to withdraw after a year because of an attack of bilious fever, a complaint of which he later died.

Robert taught a while in Bourbon County before entering Pisgah Academy in Woodford County, Kentucky. This school later united with Transylvania University. He was an exceedingly promising student and was taken into the law office of George Nicholas, Kentucky's first attorney general, until the latter's death on August 1, 1799.

Trimble next read law under Honorable James Brown, Kentucky's first secretary of state, whose offices were at Frankfort, Kentucky. In 1800, Robert was licensed to practice before the Court of Appeals of Kentucky and began practice at Paris, Kentucky.

In 1802, Robert Trimble was elected to the House of Representatives from Bourbon County. About this time the event of national concern was the conspiracy of Aaron Burr. Benjamin Sebastin, the judge of the court of appeals, was accused of being a collaborator with Burr, causing his resignation. Governor Christopher Greenup of Kentucky offered this $ 1,000-a-year post of judgeship to Robert Trimble, which he accepted. This decision was largely due to the insistence of the close friend of Robert, Judge Thomas Todd. If this friendship was not so strong Robert would probably have declined the position due to his lucrative Paris law practice. Judge Todd later became Kentucky's first Supreme Court justice, a position Robert Trimble later held.

President James Madison appointed Robert Trimble to the position of a federal judge in 1817. In this service, Trimble was spotlighted as being a Federalist. Robert Trimble believed strongly that federal laws were to have dominance over state laws to keep this nation strong. This theory of his caused great dissension among the large landowners in Kentucky and other states.

Trimble Families of America

In 1826 Justice Todd died. His oft expressed desire for Robert Trimble to succeed him coincided with that of President John Quincy Adams. Robert Trimble was a Jeffersonian in all his political views. The opposing political position being held by John Quincy Adams. It seems politically uncustomary therefore that Robert Trimble would be J. Q. Adams's only appointment to the Supreme Court. (The author's personal view of this: It was through the influence of Henry Clay that this appointment was made. Clay had been a lifelong friend of the Trimbles. During the national election J. Q. Adams's opponent was Andrew Jackson and neither received most electoral votes causing the election to be thrown into the House of Representatives to elect the president. Henry Clay, at the time, was Speaker of the House. Andrew Jackson was sure he would be elected because of his expected support from Clay. However, Clay surprised the nation by giving his support to John Quincy Adams. It stands to reason the tremendous influence Clay would therefore have with Adams.)

Robert Trimble was nominated as a justice of the Supreme Court on April 11, 1826 and was approved by Congress on May 9, 1826. This appointment was delayed over a month due to a fight in the Senate over Trimble's strong Federalist views. Upon taking his seat on the Supreme Court bench, Robert adopted the constitutional doctrines of Chief Justice John Marshall. The twentieth justice of the U.S. Supreme Court, Trimble proved to be a strong supporter of Chief Justice Marshall. However, his most famous opinion came in a case in which he opposed the chief justice in sustaining the power of the states to apply insolvency laws.

He served a little more than two years when he died on August 25, 1828, of the bilious fever. The author has seen several stories written of the talents of this man. However, we will repeat but one, that of a fellow justice story:

"Perhaps no man ever on the bench gained so much in so short a period of his judicial career. No man could bestow more thoroughness, more caution, more candor or more research upon any legal investigation than did he. He loved the Union with an unfaltering love and was ready to make any sacrifice for its perpetuity. He was patriot in the true sense."

His premature death cut off an exceptionally high talent. Although he did not live in the western part of Kentucky, a county was named for him. The history of this county is found in Et Cetera at the end of this book.

Allen Trimble's autobiography tells that Robert Trimble visited in James Trimble's home when Allen was just a boy. This shows the close contact between these two branches of Trimbles. William A. Trimble, the U.S.

Senator from Ohio and brother of Governor Allen Trimble, studied law under Robert Trimble.

Robert Trimble married Nancy Timberlake and they were the parents of a large family.

The children of Robert Trimble and Nancy Timberlake:

+ **F36—Henry Trimble.** Born in Bourbon County, Kentucky. Died in August 1858 in Atcheson County, Missouri. He studied law and medicine but practiced neither. Henry left Kentucky in 1856 and engaged in farming in Missouri. He married Nancy S. Wyatt of Nicholas County, Kentucky, on December 24, 1837. Of their children we know only of Robert W.

F37—Robert Trimble, Jr. Born in 1814 and died in 1831 at the age of seventeen years.

F38—William Trimble. Born in 1820 and died in 1839 at the age of nineteen years.

F39—James Clark Trimble. Died at the age of four years.

F40—Mary Jane Trimble. Married James C. Ford on June 10, 1830. He was a prominent and wealthy resident of Louisville, Kentucky.

F41—Caroline Trimble. Married Jefferson Scott.

F42—Juliet Trimble. Born in 1812 and died in 1833.

F43—Rebecca Trimble. Married Garret Davis.

F44—Nannie Trimble. Married Benjamin Shackelford in 1834.

F45—Eliza Trimble. Married Thomas Arnold.

F13—Judge John Trimble. Son of William and Mary McMillan Trimble. (Third generation of Joseph Trimble and Sarah Churchman.) Born on December 4, 1783. He married two times: first, to Catherine Wilson, and second, to Elizabeth D. Porter, born on July 2, 1804, and died on March 16, 1843.

At the age of nineteen he became private secretary to his brother-in-law Robert Evans, territorial governor of Indiana. After remaining in Vincennes, Indiana, for two years John returned to Paris, Kentucky, where he studied and practiced law. He was appointed circuit judge of the area and served in the Kentucky Legislature in 1826-33 and 1835. He was appointed to a federal judgeship by John Quincy Adams but refused because of ill health. His death occurred July 9, 1852, at Cynthiana, Kentucky, where he is buried. John was an able lawyer, and few could cope with him in arguing an abstract question of law depending on principle. He was a noble citizen as was his brother Judge Robert Trimble.

We have seen other children accredited to Judge John Trimble, but we have been able to document only one child:

+ **F46—William Wallace Trimble.** Born on December 31, 1821, at Cynthiana, Kentucky, and died on August 31, 1886. William married two times: first, to Eliza Jean Waller, and second, to Mary Barlow.

F14—Judge James Trimble. Son of William Trimble and Mary McMillian. (Third generation of Joseph Trimble and Sarah Churchman.) Born in 1784 in Kentucky and died in 1881 and is buried at Lytle, Texas. Married to Mary Lane. James was the third son of William and Mary Trimble. Judge James Trimble was born at Fort Boonesboro, Kentucky. He studied law in Kentucky and moved to Raymond, Mississippi, upon his appointment by John Quincy Adams as federal judge of that area.

The children of Judge James Trimble and Mary Lane:

+ **F47—Edwin B. Trimble.** Born on April 8, 1808. Married Dorothy Graham.

F48—James Trimble, Jr.

F49—Benjamin Trimble.

F50—William Trimble.

F51—Frederick Trimble.

F52—Andrew Trimble.

F16—Mary 'Polly' Trimble. Daughter of William Trimble and Mary McMillian. (Third generation of Joseph Trimble and Sarah Churchman.) Born in 1790 and died 1866. Married in 1812 to Joel Pruitt, born in 1787 and died in 1847. They set up Woodbourne Plantation in Howard County, Missouri. We know nothing more of this family except Mary Pruitt Mitchell of Independence, Missouri, was accepted into the Daughters of the American Revolution through her lineage of William Trimble.

The children of Joel Pruitt and Mary "Polly" Trimble:

F53—Maria Louisa Prewitt. Born on April 28, 1815 in Bourbon County, Kentucky and died on February 4, 1849 in St Louis, St Louis, Missouri. Married James Harrison on December 3, 1830 in Howard County, Missouri.

F54—Margaret Elizabeth Prewitt. Born on November 9, 1816 in Bourbon County, Kentucky and died on June 15, 1901 in Nevada, Vernon County, Missouri. Married George Washington Givens on February 12, 1834 1830 in Howard County, Missouri.

F55—Robert Trimble Prewitt. Born on August 1, 1818 in Bourbon County, Kentucky and died on September 16, 1873 in Fayette, Howard County, Missouri. Married Martha Ann Williams on February 13, 1844 in Howard

County, Missouri.

F56—Benjamin Mosby Prewitt. Born on December 17, 1819 in Boyle County, Kentucky and died in 1849 in California.

F57—Patrick Henry Prewitt. Born on July 18, 1820 in Bourbon County, Kentucky and died in 1841 in Howard County, Missouri.

F58—William Wallace Prewitt I. Born on May 16, 1822 in Paris, Bourbon County, Kentucky and died on October 8, 1910 in Vernon County, Missouri. Married Mary Jane Sample on June 3, 1845 in Fayette, Howard County, Missouri.

F59—Mary Jane Prewitt. Born on May 27, 1824 in Fayette, Howard County, Missouri and died on November16, 1897 in St. Louis, Missouri. Married William Nicholas Switzer before 1850.

F60—Joel Moss Prewitt II. Born on April 3, 1826 in Fayette, Howard County, Missouri and died in 1852 in Breckenridge, Caldwell, Missouri. Married Caroline Shaw on September 26, 1850 in St Francois, Missouri.

F61—Edgar Ward Prewitt. Born on February 10, 1828 in Kentucky and died in August 1866 in St Louis, Missouri. He enlisted in Union 40th Regiment, Missouri Infantry Company: K in 1863.

F62—James Moss Prewitt. Born on January 10, 1830 in Howard County, Missouri and died on November 3, 1898 in Kansas City, Jackson County, Missouri. Married Susan Abigail Nave on July 21, 1874 in Jackson County, Missouri. He enlisted in Union 11th Regiment, Missouri Cavalry Company as a Private.

F63—Paul Jones Prewitt. Born on January 10, 1830 in Howard County, Missouri and died on June 21, 1895 in Garland, Dallas County, Texas. Married Sarah Tomlinson "Sallie" Moss. He enlisted in the Missouri State Guard 7th Regiment 8th Division for the Confederacy.

F64—Theodore Frelinghuysen Prewitt I, M.D. Born on March 1, 1832 in Fayette, Howard County, Missouri and died on October 17, 1904 in St Louis, St Louis County, Missouri.

F65—Laura Cornelia Prewitt. Born on January 16, 1834 in Howard County, Missouri and died on June 28, 1859 in Utica, Livingston, Missouri.

F66—Nancy Prewitt. Born in 1835 in Kentucky and died in 1836 in Kentucky as a small child.

F20—David Trimble. Son of John Trimble and Katherine Wilson. (Third generation of Joseph Trimble and Sarah Churchman.) Born on October 22, 1779 and died on October 26, 1842 at Argillite Furnace, Greenup County, Kentucky. His will was probated on March 6, 1843. David never married.

In 1799 he graduated from William and Mary College and afterwards moved to Mount Sterling, Kentucky, at the age of twenty-one where he was the first lawyer to practice in this town. He served in the War of 1812, was elected as a Democratic representative to the Fifteenth and four succeeding Congresses (March 4, 1817-March 3, 1827).

Richard Deering moves to Kentucky about 1800. He found rich iron ore in Greenup County. In 1815, he built a small cupola to produce farm and kitchen implements. He had such success that he partnered with the Trimble brothers, David and John, in 1816 to build and operate Argillite Furnace. It started operations in 1818. This was the first furnace in the Hanging Rock Iron Region, which was noted for the quality of iron. Argillite Furnace was a cold blast, charcoal furnace powered by a under flow water wheel. The success they had with Argillite furnace they built Enterprise Furnace.

He was highly influential in early Kentucky politics as he was one of the first congressmen from that state. David fought in one of the last duels in the United States. An opponent challenging his seat in Congress, in his campaigning made statements which David considered as slanderous. Thereupon, David challenged this opponent to a duel. Due to a law in Kentucky prohibiting such an act of dueling, they went south into Tennessee. In the confrontation David's opponent was seriously wounded. Shortly afterwards David retired from politics and went into private enterprise, that of iron making.

David was a staunch friend and supporter of Henry Clay and an advocate of Clay's presidential aspirations. (The author John Farley Trimble has a copy of a letter from David Trimble to Governor Allen Trimble of Ohio in which he advised Governor Trimble, "If Ohio gives its support to Clay, he will then be a Presidential Candidate." In the years following this letter the Whig Party began to lose its national prominence and was ultimately replaced by the Republican Party.

F26—General Isaac Ridgeway Trimble. Son of John Trimble and Rachel Ridgeway. (Third generation of Joseph Trimble and Sarah Churchman.) Born on May 20, 1804, in Culpeper County, Virginia. Isaac, the youngest child of John Trimble and Rachel Ridgeway, adopted the middle name Ridgeway to distinguish himself from cousins also having the Christian name of Isaac. His father, who owned farmlands, a sawmill, and a "merchant mill" in Culpeper County, sold most of his real estate between 1796 and 1801. The balance, consisting of the two mills and seventy-two acres, was disposed of under the terms of an agreement signed on November 4, 1801. The sales were reportedly made necessary to make good on notes John Trimble had endorsed for a friend. Together with his wife Rachel and younger children (other members of his family had already moved West), John made the journey to Redstone, Fayette County, Pennsylvania, between February and April 1802 em route to Ohio. Because of Native American problems they were forced to remain in Redstone for four years. However, between May and July 1806 this family continued to Ross County, Ohio, where they settled in Kinnikkinnick, near Chillicothe. John Trimble and his wife Rachel died within a week of one another in 1809 from a prevailing fever, and young Isaac Trimble was placed in the charge of his elder sister, Mrs. Joshua Woodrow of Hillsboro, Ohio. When nine years of age, Isaac was taken to Chillicothe where he lived with another sister, Mrs. James McClintock. Two years later, in 1815, he was again moved, this time to Mount Sterling, Kentucky, where his half-brother David Trimble was practicing law.

In 1818 Isaac Ridge way Trimble secured, through his half-brother David, who was then a congressman, an appointment to the Military Academy at West Point, from which he graduated in 1822 in the top section of his class and received his commission as second lieutenant of artillery. Several years later he was transferred to the Corps of Engineers in which he remained until 1834 when he resigned from the army. Both as an officer and subsequent thereto he was associated as a civil engineer with the construction of a number of roads, canals, and railroads including the survey of a route from Washington, D.C., to New Orleans, the C&O Canal, the Northern Central Railroad linking Philadelphia, Wilmington, and Baltimore, a line between Baltimore and York, Pennsylvania, now part of the Pennsylvania Central System, and just prior to the Civil War, a railroad between Habana and Santiago de Cuba. In August 1834, Isaac Trimble was sent to England and France by several Boston railroad companies to consult with George Stephenson, the builder of the first steam locomotive, and to purchase rolling stock, and remained abroad until the following year.

The character and determination that characterized General Isaac Ridgeway Trimble throughout his life may have come to light when he, at age sixteen years, upon receiving his appointment to West Point, rode a horse from Mount Sterling, Kentucky, through a large portion of Native Americans country to New York State. He would ride at night and sleep some during the day in hiding from a possible Native Americans attack.

Although a Southerner in sympathy and Marylander by adoption (he took up residence in Baltimore shortly after leaving the army), Isaac Ridgeway

Trimble Families of America

F - Joseph "The Quaker" Trimble

Trimble was initially opposed to secession, believing that the differences between the states should be settled by peaceful means. However, an order for his arrest issued by the Federal authorities on April 19, 1861, because of his action in destroying, on the orders of the governor of Maryland and the mayor of Baltimore, several bridges on the railroad line to Wilmington, led him to offer his services to the Confederacy. He was appointed brigadier general, Confederate States of America, and subsequently was promoted to major general. Isaac Ridgeway Trimble's war record is mentioned in several books on the War Between the States and are available to the reader at any library. Following the war, Isaac lived in Baltimore with a country home, Ravenshurst, in Baltimore County. He died on January 10, 1888, and is buried in Greenmount Cemetery, Baltimore.

General Trimble married two times: first, to Maria Ferguson Presstman on July 4, 1831, the daughter of William Presstman of Baltimore and Ann Cattell Presstman of "The Oaks" plantation on the Ashley River, South Carolina. Following Maria's death in 1854, he married her sister Ann Calhoun Presstman, who died in 1879. There were no children by the second marriage but four by the first.

General Trimble was nearing sixty years of age at the beginning of the Civil War. In the war, officers of his rank were generally young men who had shortly before graduated from West Point, such as J. E. B. Stuart, the latter upon resigning from the Union Army and joining the Confederate forces were usually given much higher ranks. General Trimble appeared to be a favorite of Stonewall Jackson, as when Jackson was given a higher promotion, he had Trimble promoted also, under him, to assume the command of Jackson's former troops. General Trimble was wounded and during his recuperation period was taken out of actual combat, thus being given command of troops in the Shenandoah Valley.

On the eve of the Battle of Little Round Top (Pickett's Charge) General Trimble rejoined Lee at Gettysburg. Lee replaced another general with Isaac Trimble and he commanded one of the three divisions that were in Pickett's Charge. According to one version of later history, Pickett was not in this charge, the account said he was AWOL and was scheduled for court martial but that the trial was never held as Lee was on the defensive the remainder of the war and needed all his general officers as now, he had lost Stonewall Jackson, General Isaac R. Trimble, and later, J. E. B. Stuart. General Lee in his memoirs says that had he not lost so many of his best generals the outcome might have been different.

409

Trimble Families of America

During the charge at Gettysburg, General Trimble was again wounded resulting in the loss of a leg. He spent the next two years as a prisoner of war in a Union prison camp. Upon his release, now past sixty years of age, the "old warrior" single leggedly set out once more to join General Lee in Virginia. It was in Lynchburg, Virginia, that he received word of Lee's surrender. On September 22, 1862, Stonewall Jackson wrote the adjutant general: "I respectfully recommend that Brig. General I. R. Trimble be appointed to Major General. It is proper, in this connection, to state that I do not regard him as a good disciplinarian, but his success in battle has induced me to recommend his promotion. I will mention but one instance, though several might be named, in which he rendered distinguished service. After a day's march of over 30 miles, he ordered his command, consisting of two small Regiments, the 21st of Georgia and the 21st of North Carolina to charge the enemy's position at Manassas Junction. This charge resulted in the capture of several prisoners and 8 pieces of artillery. I regard that day's achievement as the most brilliant that has come under my observation during the present war."

In a copy of a letter, which the author has, from President Abraham Lincoln to Governor A. W. Bradford of Maryland, dated November 2, 1863, it tells of the stubbornness of I. R. Trimble. ". . for example, General Trimble, captured fighting us at Gettysburg, is, without recanting his treason, a legal voter, by the laws of Maryland. Even General Schenck's order admits him to vote, if he recants his treason upon oath." Lincoln was not in favor of Trimble voting without recanting the treason of joining the Confederacy.

The author quoted the above to show the complete dedication Isaac had to his cause. A characteristic which seems to be present in much of the Trimble lineage.

The children of General Isaac Ridgeway Trimble and Maria Ferguson Presstman:

+ **F67—David Churchman Trimble.** Married Sally Scott Lloyd.
+ **F68—William Presstman Trimble.** Married a Mrs. Gittings of Baltimore and died in 1912.

F36—Henry Trimble. Son of Robert Trimble and Nancy Timberlake. (Fourth generation of Joseph Trimble and Sarah Churchman.) Born in Bourbon County, Kentucky and died in August 1858 in Atcheson County, Missouri. He studied law and medicine but practiced neither. Henry left Kentucky in 1856 and engaged in farming in Missouri. He married Nancy S. Wyatt of Nicholas County, Kentucky, on December 24, 1837. Of their children we know only of Robert W.

The son of Henry Trimble and Nancy S. Wyatt:

F69—Robert W. Trimble. Born on July 24, 1841, in Nicholas County, Kentucky. He went westward and engaged in the freighting business. Robert married Martha Starnes in 1867. Their children: Henry, William, Irene, and Alma Trimble.

F46—William Wallace Trimble. Son of Judge John Trimble and Catherine Wilson. (Fourth generation of Joseph Trimble and Sarah Churchman.) Born on December 31, 1821, at Cynthiana, Kentucky, and died on August 31, 1886. William married two times: first, to Eliza Jean Waller, and second, to Mary Barlow. Mary was born in Scotland. William Wallace is buried at Cynthiana, Kentucky. He practiced law in Cynthiana for twenty years and was appointed county attorney for Harrison County, Kentucky, 1844-47. In 1873, his family moved to Covington, Kentucky. William Wallace was author of Trimble's Kentucky Digest which was used as a textbook in the University of Cincinnati Law School for many years. According to the *Biography Cyclopedia of the Commonwealth of Kentucky*, these descendants of William Trimble who settled in the Fort of Boonesboro, were probably the best educated men in Kentucky.

The children of William Wallace Trimble and Mary Barlow:

F70—Fannie Trimble. Born about 1854. Married George Fackler of New York City. She was a popular debutante in Washington, D.C., in 1870 and was presented to the Court of Saint James.

F71—Lawrence Trimble. Born about 1856. Died early in youth.

F72—Kate Trimble. Born about 1858. Married Edward J. Woolsey of New York City.

F73—Helen B. Trimble. Born about 1861. Married Arthur Highton of London, England.

+ **F74—William Pitt Trimble.** Born on February 2, 1863 in Cynthiana, Kentucky and died on March 19, 1943 in Seattle, King County, Washington. Married Cassandre (Cannie) Ford on November 10, 1897.

F75—Robert John Trimble. Born about 1870. He was educated at Harvard and Kenyon colleges.

F47—Edwin B. Trimble. Son of Judge James Trimble and Mary Lane. (Fourth generation of Joseph Trimble and Sarah Churchman.) Born on April 8, 1808, in Kentucky and died on July 11, 1869, of snakebite in Lytle, Texas. He married Dorothy Graham in 1828.

Trimble Families of America

The children of Edwin B. Trimble and Dorothy Graham:

F76—John Graham Trimble. Born in 1829 in Kentucky and died in 1921 in Texas. He married Eliza Griswald and they lived at Bandera, Texas. They have a daughter Medora, Married Dr. J. T. Bynum and they live at Hamlin, Texas. Medora has six children.

+ **F77—James Trimble.** Born in 1830 and died on February 14, 1862, at Prestonsburg, Kentucky. Married Mary Margaret Martin.

F78—Frederick Trimble. Drowned at twenty-eight years of age in the Red River in Texas. He never married but was engaged to a beautiful girl named Mary Owens.

F79—Thomas Graham Trimble. Born in 1847 and died in 1933 at Austin, Texas.

F80—Robert Trimble. Born in 1850 and was murdered in San Antonio, Texas, in 1877.

+ **F81—Josephine Trimble.** Born in 1842 and died in 1932 at San Antonio, Texas. Married Thomas McDaniel.

F82—Edwin Trimble, Jr. Died in 1862. He was killed in the Civil War. He was a colonel in the Fourteenth Cavalry of the Confederate Army.

+ **F83—Medora Trimble.** Born in 1850. Married Robert S. Ragsdale.

+ **F84—Alice Trimble.** Born in 1852 in Kentucky and died in 1930 in Lytle, Texas. She married William Lytle.

F85—Mary Trimble. Married a Mr. Carpenter and they live in New Orleans, Louisiana. They have a son, William.

F67—David Churchman Trimble. Son of General Isaac Ridgeway Trimble and Maria Ferguson Presstman. (Fourth generation of Joseph Trimble and Sarah Churchman.) David was a graduate of Harvard College in the class of 1854 and was elected its class marshal. He married Sally Scott Lloyd, the daughter of Edward Lloyd of "Wye House," Talbot County, Maryland. Because of poor health he did not take part in the Civil War and died before his father. Both he and his wife, who died in 1913, are buried in the Lloyd Family Cemetery at "Wye House."

The son of David Churchman Trimble and Sally Scott Lloyd:

+ **F86—Isaac Ridgeway Trimble II.** Born in 1861. Married Margaret Emily Jones.

F68—William Presstman Trimble. Married a Mrs. Gittings of Baltimore and died in 1912.

The daughter of William Presstman Trimble and Mrs. Gittings:

F87—Maria Trimble. Married a Mr. Dimpfel.

F74—William Pitt Trimble. Son of William Wallace and Mary Barlow Trimble. (Fifth generation of Joseph Trimble and Sarah Churchman.) Born on February 2, 1863 in Cynthiana, Kentucky and died March 19, 1943 in Seattle, King County, Washington. He married Cassandre "Cannie" Ford of Covington, Kentucky on November 10, 1897. Cannie was born on November 15, 1870 and died on December 7, 1929 drown when her car ran off Elliott Bay pier into the water. She was a member of the Colony Club and the National Society of Colonial Dames.

William Pitt attended the University of Cincinnati Law School in 1886, and Ecole Alsatienne, Paris. He practiced law in Kentucky but settled in Seattle, Washington, in 1894 where he was a prominent lawyer and businessman. He was one of the State of Washington's most wealthy men. Some of his activities: director of Washington Trust Company, Washington Securities Company, Seattle Lighting Company, chairman of Seattle Transit Company, vice-president of Seattle Planning Committee, Republican presidential elector in 1908. He was an Episcopalian. The clubs in which he held membership were quite numerous, a few are: University, College, Ranier, Engineers, Seattle Golf, Tacoma Golf and Country Club, Chevy Chase Country Club, and National Republican (N.Y.). His office was in the Dexter Horton Building.

(We have in our possession a tabloid in the Seattle Times of April 6, 1969, entitled, "William Pitt Trimble: THE BARON OF BLAKE" written by Bob Roberts.) William Pitt bought Blake Island, a land mass of 465 acres, off the coast of Seattle and as described in the tabloid, "The story of this piece of land is actually the story of a remarkable man who did remarkable things during a remarkable time in the history of Seattle."

To a substantial degree he made much of that history. Seattle was a city of 35,000 when, in 1890, William Pitt Trimble opened his law office in this city. He was a big man, tall and erect, and aristocratic in bearing and dress. For an aristocrat he was indeed. In real estate and its promotion, he was a genius. It made him a millionaire. He owned much of the choice commercial property in Seattle. He owned two miles of waterfront on Bainbridge Island, also the building now occupied by the J. C. Penney Company, and the entire block where the National Bank of Commerce now sits. He seemed to have the golden touch. William Pitt Trimble purchased a piece of land at the foot of Magnolia Bluff for $2,500 and later sold it for eleven times the original price. Another piece of land purchased for $15,000 was sold later by William Pitt for $127,000.

Blake Island was renamed Trimble Island which became one of the most beautiful estates in the country. William H. Taft, secretary of war, was a guest on the island. No firearms were discharged here because of the bird sanctuary. The mail boat stopped daily at the island. Mrs. Trimble's library held a matchless collection of Northwest history and Americana. Yet a series of events changed this idyll into a tragedy. Mrs. Trimble drowned when her car plunged off Elliott Bay pier into the water on December 7, 1929. William Pitt Trimble never went back to his island after his wife's death. He seemed to have gone into a state of mental depression, along with the economic depression, which found him property poor. William Pitt retired to a small house on Capitol Hill where he prepared his own meals and rode a streetcar to town. On March 29, 1943, he died in Seattle.

The beautiful estate changed into a plunderer's delight. It is now a state park.

The author has told this story in detail, not because William Pitt Trimble was a wealthy and prosperous man, but because his worldly possessions became meaningless after the death of the woman he loved. With her, it all had meaning, without her, nothing mattered. It is a beautiful love story.

The children William Pitt Trimble and Cassandre "Cannie" Ford:

F88—Francis Ford Trimble. Born on October 31, 1898 in Seattle, Washington and died after 1943. He graduated from Groton School, Groton, Massachusetts. He graduated from West Point U.S. Military Academy in New York in 1920. Served as a Lieutenant aide-de-camp to General Douglas MacArthur for 7 years in Philippines. He was a Colonel and lived in San Francisco when his father died in 1943.

F89—Mary Barlow Trimble. Born on May 17, 1900. Married L. E. Gowen.

F90—William Pitt Trimble, Jr. Born in 1902.

F91—Augusta Trimble. Born on April 2, 1904 and died after 1943.

+ **F92—Webb Ware Trimble.** Born on March 10, 1906 and died after 1943. He was a Captain at Fort Sills, Oklahoma.

F77—James Trimble. Son of Edwin B. Trimble and Dorothy Graham. (Fifth generation of Joseph Trimble and Sarah Churchman.) Born in 1830 and died on February 14, 1862, at Prestonsburg, Kentucky. He is buried in the May Cemetery. James married Mary Margaret Martin, daughter of the Honorable John Preston Martin, congressman from Kentucky.

The child of James Trimble and Mary Margaret Martin:

F93—James Trimble. Born on July 19, 1862. married two times: first, to Lizzie

Hatcher, and second, to Lizzie Firor.

F81—Josephine Trimble. Daughter of Edwin B. Trimble and Dorothy Graham. (Fifth generation of Joseph Trimble and Sarah Churchman.) Born in 1842 and died in 1932 at San Antonio, Texas. She married Thomas McDaniel.

The children of Thomas McDaniel and Josephine Trimble:

F94—Forrest McDaniel. Lives at Marquez, Texas, and has three children.

F95—Helen McDaniel. Married a Mr. Peel. She is postmaster at Jourdanton, Texas, and has three children.

F96—Laura McDaniel. Married Fred Carrington and lives at Marquez, Texas.

F97—John McDaniel.

F98—Alice McDaniel.

F99—Ruth McDaniel. She lives in San Antonio, Texas.

F83—Medora Trimble. Daughter of Edwin B. Trimble and Dorothy Graham. (Fifth generation of Joseph Trimble and Sarah Churchman.) Born in 1850 and died in 1900 at Stamford, Texas. Married Robert S. Ragsdale in 1872.

The children of Robert S. Ragsdale and Medora Trimble:

F100—Thomas Ragsdale. Married and lives in San Antonio, Texas. He has eight children.

F101—Margaret Ragsdale. Married J. H. Johnson and they live at Stamford, Texas. She has four children.

F102—Robert S. Ragsdale. Married and has four children. He is an attorney and lives at Burkburnett, Texas.

F103—Josephine Ragsdale. Married a Mr. Taupshaw, president of Stamford First National Bank.

F104—Lillith Ragsdale. She is unmarried and lives at Stamford, Texas.

F105—Sarah Alice Ragsdale. Married O. E. Casey of Galveston, Texas, and they have three children.

F84—Alice Trimble. Daughter of Edwin B. Trimble and Dorothy Graham. (Fifth generation of Joseph Trimble and Sarah Churchman.) Born in 1852 in Kentucky and died in 1930 in Lytle, Texas. She married William Lytle.

The children of William Lytle and Alice Trimble:

F106—William Lytle.

F107—Margaret Lytle. Married A. Baltherick and lives at Lytle, Texas.

F108—Edwin Lytle. She was married and lives at Dallas, Texas.

F109—Mabel Lytle. Married Dr. Carrington and they live in Marquez, Texas, and have four sons.

F110—Alice Lytle. Married A. G. Gridley, a cashier of the bank in Lytle, Texas, and they have five children.

F86—Isaac Ridgeway Trimble II. Son of David Churchman Trimble and Sally Scott Lloyd. (Fifth generation of Joseph Trimble and Sarah Churchman.) He spent his early youth at "Wye House" where he was born in 1861. "Wye Heights" was his mother's plantation on the Eastern Shore of Maryland. He died in Baltimore in February 1908.

Isaac attended a military academy at Winchester, Virginia, and subsequently Johns Hopkins University in Baltimore from which he graduated in 1882, and afterwards the Medical School of the University of Maryland also in Baltimore from which he received his M.D. degree.

In addition to serving as professor of surgery at that medical school, he became one of the two leading surgeons of Baltimore and principal surgical consultant to the B&O Railroad. He was also chief surgeon of the Fifth Regiment of the Maryland National Guard and accompanied it to Key West, Florida, during the Spanish-American War. While there a severe typhoid fever epidemic broke out among the troops and he was placed in charge of the hospital train which took them to a recuperation camp on Long Island, New York.

Dr. Trimble was likewise a foremost citizen of Maryland and when he died of septicemia when only forty-six years of age, his funeral was attended by hundreds and a memorial resolution voted by the Maryland Legislature was passed. He is buried at the Lloyd Cemetery at the "Wye House."

Dr. Isaac R. Trimble married Margaret Emily Jones in October 1898. She was born in 1866 and died in 1954. She was the daughter of Theodore and Johanna Catherine (Myers) Jones of New York City.

The children of Dr. Isaac Ridgeway Trimble, II and Margaret Emily Jones:

+ **F111—Margaret Lloyd Trimble.** Born on July 12, 1899 and died in January 1931. Married Harold de Ropp.

+ **F112—Isaac Ridgeway Trimble, Jr.** Born on December 28, 1901. married Frances Hartley-Smith.

+ **F113—David Churchman Trimble.** Born on September 6, 1902. Married Anne George Harvey.

+ **F114—Theodore Francis Trimble.** Born on February 28, 1904 and died in April 1940.

F115—Johanna Catherine Trimble. Born in 1906 and died in infancy.

+ **F116—William Cattell Trimble.** Born on May 2, 1907. Married Nancy

Trimble Families of America

Gordon Carroll.

F92—James Trimble. Son of James Trimble and Mary Margaret Martin. (Sixth generation of Joseph Trimble and Sarah Churchman.) Born on July 19, 1862, at Prestonsburg, Kentucky, and died August 6, 1939, at Washington, D.C., where he was a prosperous banker. James married two times: first, to Lizzie Hatcher on October 27, 1891, at Catlettsburg, Kentucky, and second, to Lizzie Firor, born on June 28, 1865, at Catlettsburg and died May 11, 1941, at Washington, D.C.

The children of James Trimble and Lizzie Hatcher:

F117—Andrew Trimble.

The children of James Trimble and Lizzie Firor:

+ **F118—Malcolm Firor Trimble.** Born on April 29, 1893. Married Mildred Ingraham.

+ **F119—James Trimble.** Married and died around September 1901.

F111—Margaret Lloyd Trimble. Daughter of Dr. Isaac Ridgeway Trimble and Margaret Emily Jones. (Sixth generation of Joseph Trimble and Sarah Churchman.) Born on July 12, 1899 and died in January 1931. Married Harold de Ropp, the son of Baron and Baroness Alfred de Ropp of New York and California on August 6, 1919.

The two children of Harold de Ropp and Margaret Lloyd Trimble:

F120—Margaret Elizabeth Ropp. Born in 1921. Married Paul F. duVivier February 4, 1944. They have two children.

F121—Alison Arden Ropp. Born in 1925 and married Dr. Lawrence H. Wharton, Jr., in 1947. They have three children.

F112—Isaac Ridgeway Trimble, Jr. Son of Dr. Isaac Ridgeway Trimble and Margaret Emily Jones. (Sixth generation of Joseph Trimble and Sarah Churchman.) Graduated from Princeton University in 1922 where he was vice-president of his class, and Johns Hopkins Medical School in 1926. Like his father, he has become one of the leading surgeons of Baltimore and is a member and past officer of several medical and surgical societies. He was also associate professor of surgery at Johns Hopkins and enjoys a national reputation in his field. He was commissioned lieutenant colonel in the U.S. Army Medical Corps in 1941 and subsequently promoted to colonel. His entire military service during World War II was in the Pacific area where he was appointed chief surgical consultant on the staff of General MacArthur.

Dr. Trimble married Frances Hartley-Smith, the daughter of Captain and

Mrs. Hartley-Smith of Sydney, Australia, in 1945.

The children of Isaac Ridgeway Trimble, Jr. and Frances Hartley-Smith:

F122—Isaac Ridgeway Trimble III. Born in 1947. Graduated from Princeton, A.B., in 1969 and Harvard Medical School.

F123—Elizabeth Hartley Trimble. Born in 1949. Attended Wellesley College in 1966.

F124—Edward Lloyd Trimble. Born in 1955.

F113—David Churchman Trimble. Son of Dr. Isaac Ridgeway Trimble and Margaret Emily Jones. (Sixth generation of Joseph Trimble and Sarah Churchman.) Graduated from Princeton University in 1924 and the Virginia Theological Seminary in 1929. He also attended the College of Preachers of the National Cathedral in Washington, D.C. He has had parishes in Maryland and Arizona. He was appointed canon of the Episcopal Cathedral in Phoenix, Arizona, and is presently rector of two churches in western Maryland. He married Anne George Harvey, the daughter of Joshua George and Bessie May (Norris) Harvey of Reisterstown, Maryland, on September 4, 1942.

Their children of David Churchman Trimble and Anne George Harvey:

F125—Joan Trimble. Born on October 18, 1945. Married John Bruns of California in 1966.

F126—David Churchman Trimble, Jr. Born on October 17, 1947, and graduated from the U.S. Naval Academy in 1969 and presently is an ensign in the U.S. Navy.

F127—Anne Dorsey Trimble. Born on December 21, 1949. Attended Scripps College, 1967.

F114—Theodore Francis Trimble. Son of Dr. Isaac Ridgeway Trimble, II and Margaret Emily Jones. (Sixth generation of Joseph Trimble and Sarah Churchman.) Graduated from Princeton University cum laude in 1927 and the University of Rochester Medical School in 1931. He was never married. At the time of his death in an automobile accident, he was practicing medicine as a neurosurgeon in Corpus Christi, Texas.

F116—William Cattell Trimble. Son of Dr. Isaac Ridgeway Trimble, II and Margaret Emily Jones. (Sixth generation of Joseph Trimble and Sarah Churchman.) Graduated from Princeton University cum laude in 1930 and the National War College in 1947. He was a United States Foreign Service officer from 1931 until his retirement in 1968. Biographic data concerning his service are contained in Who's Who in America. William married Nancy

Gordon Carroll, the daughter of Douglas Gordon and Amalie Louise (Hack) Carroll of "Oakdene," Brooklandville, Maryland, on April 2, 1934.

Their children of William Cattell Trimble and Nancy Gordon Carroll:

+ **F128—William Cattell Trimble, Jr.** Born on February 7, 1935, graduated from Princeton, A.B., in 1958, the University of Maryland Law School in 1964, ensign and subsequently lieutenant (j.g.), USNR, 1958-61. He married Barbara Symington, daughter of Stuart Symington, Jr., and Barbara Phipps Janney Symington of "Locust Hill," Glyndon, Maryland, on June 24, 1960.

+ **F129—Carroll Lloyd Trimble.** Born on October 25, 1938, married John Godfrey Lowell Cabot of Massachusetts in July 1960. She graduated from Bryn Mawr College, A.B., in 1960.

F130—Theodore Ridgeway Trimble. Born on May 12, 1945. Graduated from Randolph-Macon College, A.B., in 1968, U.S. Army in 1968, commissioned second lieutenant, infantry, June 1969 and assigned with U.S. forces in Korea in 1973.

F118—Malcolm Firor Trimble. Son of James Trimble and Lizzie Firor. (Seventh generation of Joseph Trimble and Sarah Churchman.) Born on April 29, 1893, at Catlettsburg, Kentucky, and died on February 12, 1935, at Tulsa, Oklahoma. Married on February 5, 1917, at Sapulpa, Oklahoma, to Mildred Ingraham, born on January 17, 1896, in Wapella, Illinois.

Their children of Malcolm Firor Trimble and Mildred Ingraham:

F131—Mary Margaret Trimble. Born on November 12, 1917, at Washington, D.C. She has been a civil servant for the last twenty-eight years. Mary Margaret is a librarian and employed by the Defense Department. She is unmarried.

+ **F132—Malcolm Trimble.** Born on August 5, 1923, at Muskogee, Oklahoma. He is a professional electrical engineer with Joe Poole, constructional engineer. Married on June 12, 1947, in California to Claudia Bergeron, born on December 13, 1921. They were divorced in 1956.

F119—James Trimble. Son of James Trimble and Lizzie Firor. (Seventh generation of Joseph Trimble and Sarah Churchman.) Married and died about September 1901.

The children of James Trimble:

F133—Gloria Trimble. She died at age six.

F134—James Trimble. He was killed on Iwo Jima at age of eighteen.

419

F128—William Cattell Trimble, Jr. Son of William Cattell Trimble and Nancy Gordon Carroll. (Seventh generation of Joseph Trimble and Sarah Churchman.) Born on February 7, 1935, graduated from Princeton, A.B., in 1958, the University of Maryland Law School in 1964, ensign and subsequently lieutenant (j.g.), USNR, 1958-61. He married Barbara Symington, daughter of Stuart Symington, Jr., and Barbara Phipps Janney Symington of "Locust Hill," Glyndon, Maryland, on June 24, 1960.

The children of William Cattell Trimble, Jr. and Barbara Symington:
F135—William Cattell Trimble, III. Born on January 9, 1962.
F136—Marjorie Mills Trimble. Born in January 1965.

F129—Carroll Lloyd Trimble. Daughter of William Cattell Trimble and Nancy Gordon Carroll. (Seventh generation of Joseph Trimble and Sarah Churchman.) Born on October 25, 1938, married John Godfrey Lowell Cabot of Massachusetts in July 1960. She graduated from Bryn Mawr College, A.B., in 1960.

The children of John Godfrey Lowell Cabot and Carroll Lloyd Trimble:
F137—John Ridgeway Cabot. Born on December 9, 1961.
F138—Andrew Lowell Cabot. Born on August 25, 1964.

F132—Malcolm Trimble. Son of Malcolm Firor Trimble and Mildred Ingraham. (Seventh generation of Joseph Trimble and Sarah Churchman.) Born on August 5, 1923, at Muskogee, Oklahoma. He is a professional electrical engineer with Joe Poole, constructional engineer. Married on June 12, 1947, in California to Claudia Bergeron, born on December 13, 1921. They were divorced in 1956.

The compiler is indebted to William Cattell Trimble, U.S. Ambassador Ret., for the information on the descendants of General Isaac Ridgeway Trimble. W. C. Trimble is one of the most distinguished of the Trimbles in America. The compiler did not elaborate on his career as it is published in several biographies, such as *Who's Who in America,* but he like myself is extremely interested in his family genealogy and was a great help to me in the early compilation of this book.

The children of Malcolm Trimble and Claudia Bergeron:
F139—Nancy Louise Trimble. Born on October 11, 1950 in Houston, Texas.
F140—Margaret Ann Trimble. Born on July 16, 1949 in Houston and married in January 1967 to Howard Wright Cook. They have one daughter Tammy Lynn, born on June 13, 1967, at Houston.

Four Pre-Revolution Immigrants 1730s

G - William Trimble "The Settler."
H - John Trimble "North Mountain."
I - Walter and Rosanna Trimble.
J - James and Grace Trimble "Plantationer."

This section traces the historical genealogy of four pre-Revolution immigrants that migrated to America from Ireland in the early 1730s. These four settlers came from County Tyrone and Antrim.

Accompanying each immigrant is an identifying description to distinguish him from other Johns, Jameses, Williams, and Walters who were in America then.

G - William 'The Settler' Trimble

G1—William Trimble, "The Settler," migrated to America from Ireland in 1730 with his wife and son John. William's family was one of the first to cross the Susquehanna and settle in Cumberland County near where now stands the town of Shippensburg, Pennsylvania. Records at Carlisle, Pennsylvania, show he was tax collector for then Lancaster County, now Cumberland County, in 1739. William died in 1749. His wife, Mary, died in 1766.

The children of William and Mary Trimble:

+ **G2—John Trimble.** Died in 1790. Married Sarah McDowell.

  G3—Janet B. Trimble. Born in 1732 and died in 1831 at Newburg, Pennsylvania. Married Thomas McClelland in 1763.

+ **G4—Susann Trimble.** Died in 1755. Married William Linn.

G2—John Trimble. Son of William and Mary Trimble. John married Sarah McDowell, daughter of John McDowell. They had four sons in the Revolutionary War, John, James, George, and William II. John Trimble was the first tax collector in Hopewell Township, Cumberland County, Pennsylvania. John had 150 acres in Hopewell Township and his daughter was the first white child born in Hopewell. The house in which she was born was built by friendly Native Americans and was only recently (1900) demolished. It was near the present site of Newburg, a village laid out in 1819 by Thomas Trimble, son of William II. John later bought a 207-acre farm, near Newburg, where his family moved. In 1776 he sold the farm to the Reverend Robert Cooper. John is buried at Hanna's Graveyard, Newburg, Pennsylvania.

The children of John Trimble and Sarah McDowell:

+ **G5—William Trimble II.** Born in 1736 in Newberry, Cumberland County, Kentucky. Married Jane Sterrett.

  G6—John Gervin Trimble.

  G7—Alexander Trimble.

  G8—James Trimble.

  G9—George Trimble.

  G10—Thomas Trimble.

  G11—Joseph Trimble.

  G12—Jean Trimble. Married Joseph Hillson.

  G13—Mary Trimble. Married William Steele of Derry.

  G14—Elizabeth Trimble. Married Joseph Robinson.

G15—Sarah Trimble.

G4—Susanna Trimble. Daughter of William and Mary Trimble. Married John Linn, Scotts-Irishman, who was a squatter on the Manor of Mange, Adams County, Pennsylvania. He was born in Ireland in 1722, was an officer in Middle Spring Church. In June 1755, he was in Philadelphia with his wagon and was pressed into service to haul supplies to General Braddock's Army and was at the noted defeat. He died on April 16, 1812 and was buried at Middle Spring. He and his father migrated from Ireland in 1732 and settled near Roxburg in Franklin County, Pennsylvania, in 1736, where he died at nearly one hundred years of age. His father fought on the side of the "Orange" at Boyne, on July 12, 1690. Susanna Trimble Linn was the ancestress of Mrs. Russell Sage, whose husband amassed a fortune as a partner of Jay Gould. They owned several railroads, Western Union, etc. His widow gave $16 million to charity. Susanna died at Shippensburg Fort in 1755 from exposure in great flight from Native Americans.

The children of John Linn and Susanna Trimble:

+ **G16—Reverend William Trimble Linn.** Born on February 27, 1752, in Lurgan Township, Franklin County, Pennsylvania, and died in 1808 in Albany, New York. William married three times.

G17—John Linn. Born on April 2, 1754. Married Ann Fleming.

G5—William Trimble II. Son of John Trimble and Sarah McDowell. (Third generation of William and Mary Trimble.) Born in 1736 at Newberry, Cumberland County, Kentucky and died in 1798. Married Jane Sterrett in 1767 by the Reverend Robert Cooper. She was born in 1743 and died in 1824. William served in the Revolutionary War as a private in the First Battalion from 1777 to 1779. William is buried at Middle Springs Lower Graveyard. He served as

When Jane, his widow, died she left a bequest to the Theological Seminary at Princeton, an endowment of a scholarship to students.

The children of William Trimble II and Jane Sterrett:

+ **G18—William Trimble III.** Born on December 12, 1771. Married Elizabeth McCormick.

G19—Susannah Trimble. Born on August 23, 1775 and died in May 1793. She was unmarried.

+ **G20—Jane Trimble.** Born on October 8, 1777 and died in October 1832. Married twice.

+ **G21—John Trimble.** Born on May 23, 1780. Married Rachel Hanna.

+ **G22—Thomas Trimble.** Born on July 16, 1782. Married two times: first, to Mary Woods, and second, to Sarah Urie.

+ **G23—James Trimble.** Born on August 30, 1784. Married Sarah Wylie.

G24—Margaret Trimble. Born on November 30, 1786 and died in August 1804. She died near Rushville, Ohio, and was never married.

+ **G25—Mary Polly Trimble.** Born on January 28, 1790. Married Joseph Donovan on October 31, 1816.

G26—Elizabeth "Betsy" Trimble. Born on January 28, 1790. Married on August 30, 1820, to James P. Beatty.

+ **G27—David Sterrett Trimble.** Born on October 14, 1792. Married Margaret Sterrett.

G28—Reverend Joseph Trimble. Born on December 4, 1795 near Shippensburg, Pennsylvania and died on August 11, 1824 in Madison, Indiana. He was unmarried. A graduate of Princeton Theological School, he was licensed October 8, 1823, by the Presbytery of Carlisle, Pennsylvania. Joseph was a missionary in Indiana in 1823-24 and graduated from Jefferson College in 1819, which is located at Canonsburg, Pennsylvania, later combined with Washington College to become Washington and Jefferson College located at Washington, Pennsylvania. Joseph joined the Middle Springs Church in Pennsylvania on October 13, 1816.

G16—Reverend William Trimble Linn. Son of John Linn and Susanna Trimble. (Third generation of William and Mary Trimble.) Born on February 27, 1752, in Lurgan Township, Franklin County, Pennsylvania, and died in 1808 in Albany, New York. William married three times. Married first to Rebecca Blair on January 10, 1774, she was the daughter of Reverend John Blair. Married second to Catherine Moore, the widow of Dr. Moore of New York. Married third to Helen Hanson.

William Trimble Linn divided honors at Princeton with Aaron Burr in English and oratory. After studying in the School of Robert Smith at Piqua under Dr. Duffield, he entered Princeton and graduated in 1792. He was ordained in the ministry at Philadelphia in 1775 and was appointed chaplain in the War of the Revolution, serving in the fifth and sixth battalions, on February 15, 1776. He accepted a call to the Big Spring Presbyterian Church, on April 9, 1777, and continued to 1784, performing faithfully his duties as a minister. He was then elected principal of Washington Academy, Maryland, but due to sickness in his family, had to resign.

He accepted a call to Elizabeth town, New Jersey, in 1786 and in 1787 he was called to be collegiate pastor of the Reformed Dutch Church in New York.

Trimble Families of America

He served until 1805. After entering upon his work here, he was chosen first chaplain to Congress in May 1789. In his position in New York, Dr. Linn rose to great eminence in the ministry and attained a reputation for talents and eloquence second to no other at that time in New York City. Owing to declining health he resigned in 1805 and moved to Albany, New York. There he engaged in supply to the church, preaching once each Sabbath for one year. In the meantime, he was chosen president of the college at Schenectady, New York, but was unable to accept owing to rapidly failing health.

William Trimble Linn studied theology with his pastor, Robert Cooper. Cooper was moderator of the synod of New York and Philadelphia, in May 1776, and it was common to see him in earnest conversation with the youngest member of the synod, William Linn.

William Trimble Linn was prominent in early American theology and education, sharing top honors at Princeton University with Aaron Burr in the field of oratory, he was an officer in the Revolution and was selected to give the eulogy of George Washington's death before the Society of the Cincinnati in New York City of which he was a member. This eulogy is in the Library at Mount Vernon, a copy of which the author has in his files. The Society of the Cincinnati was formed by officers of the Revolution. It was named for Cincinnatus, the Greek patriarch, who lived on his quiet farm but would go and lead the Greek soldiers when his country was in trouble. Cincinnati, Ohio, was named in honor of the society. The following are a few quotes from the eulogy given by William Trimble Linn:

". . God prepared his servant, and in time opened to him a vast scene, on which all his talents had their utmost exertion, and expanded in full display.

"When God in his adorable providence intends to accomplish some glorious work upon earth, he provides and prepares his instruments among the children of men.

"The name of WASHINGTON will be revered while the American empire endures; yea, until this globe itself be wrapt in the last fires, and the angel shall 'sear by him that liveth forever and ever, and that time shall be no longer.'

"The question will be agitated by posterity, whether he was the greater general or statesman? The controversy can be settled only by admitting that he was 'first in war, and first in peace.'"

The eulogy is forty-four pages in length and was delivered to the New York State Society of the Cincinnati on February 2, 1800.

G18—William Trimble III. Son of William Trimble II and Jane Sterrett.

Trimble Families of America

(Fourth generation of William and Mary Trimble.) Born on December 12, 1771, in Cumberland County, Pennsylvania. He died on July 25, 1829. William married Elizabeth McCormick in 1798. They were married by the Reverend Robert Cooper. She and William III are buried in the Old Tent Cemetery near Colfax, Ohio. William III was educated at Princeton University and Dickinson College at Carlisle, Pennsylvania. He was a surveyor and was employed to survey the Old Zanesville Road. He was a member of the legislature of Ohio as representative and senator for sixteen years and was a charter member of the First Presbyterian Church in Lancaster, Pennsylvania. William also served on the Ohio Library Board and was engaged in hauling provisions to the army in the Northwest. A staunch Whig, at one time he had a tannery and hotel in Pleasant Township. William and his wife Elizabeth settled on land in this township where he served as justice of the peace, which he was at his death. He performed his first marriage in 1801.

When Elizabeth McCormick was a young girl, she was captured by the Native Americans and taken to Canada. Her father, Adam McCormick, followed and paid for her return.

The children of William Trimble III and Elizabeth McCormick:

+ **G29—Jane Trimble.** Born on September 25, 1800 and died on December 17, 1881. Married Judge William McClung on December 23, 1824. Judge McClung was born in 1787 and died in 1876. Both are buried at Old Tent Cemetery near Colfax, Ohio. William McClung was a prominent citizen and was elected to the state legislature. He was a soldier in the War of 1812, a justice of the peace and member of the West Rushville Presbyterian Church.

+ **G30—William Sterrett Trimble.** Born on June 19, 1802. Married Ann Elizabeth Black.

+ **G31—James Trimble.** Born on March 30, 1804. Married Ann Elizabeth Crane.

G32—Isabelle Trimble. Born on October 24, 1806. Married Isaac Sadler. Their children: Elizabeth, Watson, and Alice Sadler.

G33—Eliza Trimble. Born on February 14, 1809. Married Robert Reese. Their children: Elizabeth, Benjamin, Robert, William, and Clara, Married Charles Fultz, their children: Yetta, born in 1881 and died in 1957. Yetta married George Gravett and they have a daughter, Mary Jane, born in 1909; and Littleton Fultz, who died young.

G34—John Trimble. Born on May 5, 1811 and died on October 14, 1840. He was unmarried.

+ **G35—Mary Polly Trimble.** Born on November 7, 1813 and died on March 18, 1862. Married on April 22, 1833, to Peter Lamb.

+ **G36—Thomas Trimble.** Born on January 16, 1816 and died on May 19, 1862. Married Samantha Jane Hooker on August 22, 1848.

+ **G37—Robert Trimble.** Born on May 10, 1819 and died on December 14, 1891. Married Maria D. Armstrong in 1852; she died on February 13, 1888. They lived in Urbana, Ohio, later moving to Nebraska. In 1873 they moved to Columbus, Ohio.

+ **G38—Lucinda D. Trimble.** Born om August 8, 1821. Married John McClelland, who was a merchant at Lancaster, Ohio. They moved to Lincoln, Nebraska.

G39—Joseph Trimble. Born on June 25, 1824 and died on September 28, 1826. He died in childhood.

G20—Jane Trimble. Daughter of William Trimble II and Jane Sterrett. (Fourth generation of William and Mary Trimble.) Born on October 8, 1777 and died in in October 1832. Married James Barr

The children of James Barr and Jane Trimble:

+ **G40—Joseph Barr.** Married Orpha ——.

G21—John Trimble. Son of William Trimble II and Jane Sterrett. (Fourth generation of William and Mary Trimble.) Born on May 23, 1780 and died on July 26, 1845. Married Rachel Hanna. John was a soldier in the War of 1812. He took an active part in everything that was for the promotion of good and the development and best interests of the pioneer and community of whom he was one. He was a justice of the peace and an elder in the Presbyterian church. Both John and Rachel are buried at Mount Vernon, Ohio.

The children of John Trimble and Rachel Hanna:

G41—William Sterrett Trimble. Born on 1808 and died on April 5, 1866. He was unmarried.

+ **G42—Samuel Hanna Trimble.** Born in 1804 and died on December 22, 1841. Married Jane —— on September 30, 1830.

+ **G43—John Trimble, Jr.** Born on September 20, 1806. John married three times.

G44—Nancy M. Trimble. Born in 1809 and died on June 3, 1865. She was unmarried.

G45—Thomas Trimble. Born in 1814 and died in 1832. He was unmarried.

+ **G46—James Scott Trimble.** Born in 1818. Married Margaret Shaw.

G22—Thomas Trimble. Son of William Trimble II and Jane Sterrett. (Fourth generation of William and Mary Trimble.) Born on July 16, 1782 and died on August 17, 1844. Thomas married two times: first, to Mary Woods, and second, to Sarah Urie in 1826. Thomas surveyed and laid out the town of Newburg, Pennsylvania, in 1819.

The children of Thomas Trimble and Mary Woods:

G47—William Trimble. Born on January 5, 1812 and died on September 19, 1815.

+ **G48—Samuel Woods Trimble.** Born on July 12, 1813. Married Mary Caldwell.

G49—Jonathan Edwards Trimble. Born on August 2, 1815 and died on February 19, 1820.

+ **G50—Susan Margaret Trimble.** Born on July 2, 1817. Married William S. Caldwell.

+ **G51—William Pitt Trimble.** Born on August 15, 1819. Married Pamela A. Gates.

The children of Thomas Trimble and Sarah Urie:

+ **G52—Frances Mary Trimble.** Born on May 9, 1828. Married William Wiley on September 16, 1847.

G53—Thomas Urie Trimble. Born on June 12, 1830 and died in October 1847. He is buried at Carlisle, Pennsylvania.

+ **G54—Sarah Ellen Trimble.** Born on September 14, 1834. Married Robert F. Gibson on May 5, 1851.

G55—Catharine Jane Trimble. Born on October 31, 1838. Married Justus Davis. Their children: Horace, Thomas, and Mary Davis.

G23—James Trimble. Son of William Trimble II and Jane Sterrett. (Fourth generation of William and Mary Trimble.) Born on August 30, 1784 and died November 18, 1845. Married Sarah Wylie on March 10, 1808. Sarah (Sally) was born in 1772 and died on February 6, 1850. Both are buried at Mount Vernon, Ohio.

The children of James Trimble and Sarah Wylie:

G56—Margaret Trimble. Born on April 15, 1809 and died on March 16, 1874. Married William M. Day.

G57—Jane Trimble.

+ **G58—Eliza Trimble.** Married Stephen Day.

G59—Newton Trimble. He was unmarried.

G60—Sarah Trimble. Born in 1815 and died on November 30, 1878. Married Lucien L. Benedict. They are buried at Mount Vernon, Ohio.

+ **G61—James W. Trimble.** Born on April 1, 1819 and died on June 22, 1861. He married Elizabeth Wright. Attended Oberlin College from 1839 to 1843. They are buried at Mount Vernon, Ohio.

G25—Mary Polly Trimble. Daughter of William Trimble II and Jane Sterrett. (Fourth generation of William and Mary Trimble.) Born on January 28, 1790. Married Joseph Donovan on October 31, 1816.

The children of Joseph Donovan and Mary Polly Trimble:

G62—Robert Donovan. Born in 1817 and married Eliza J. Shearer.

G63—William Donovan. Born in 1819 and married Rosannah Baker.

G64—John Carren Donovan. Born in 1822 and died in 1823.

G65—Joseph Donovan. Born in 1824 and married first, Sarah Douglas, and second, Widow Holt.

G66—Martha Donovan. Born in 1827 and married Benjamin Beall.

G67—Jane Elizabeth Donovan. Born in 1829 and married Stephen Douglas.

G68—Mary Polly Donovan. Born in 1832.

G27—David Sterrett Trimble. Son of William Trimble II and Jane Sterrett. (Fourth generation of William and Mary Trimble.) Born on October 14, 1792 and died on September 7, 1837. Married Margaret Sterrett, who was born in 1800 and died on April 9, 1851. They are buried at Mansfield, Ohio. They went to Ohio about in 1816 and lived near Mansfield where they acquired land.

The children of David Sterrett Trimble and Margaret Sterrett:

G69—William Sterrett Trimble. Born in 1815 and died on June 12, 1865. He never married. William is buried at Mansfield, Ohio. William and his maiden sister lived together. One day he took his rifle and went to hunt crows. No one will ever know the circumstances, but a few years later, a skeleton and rifle were found in a remote area. One leg bone showed a reunited fracture. They were led to believe it was him.

+ **G70—Sarah Jane Trimble.** Born in 1816. Married John Marshall.

+ **G71—Anna Mary Trimble.** Born in 1820. Married William Crum.

+ **G72—David Sterrett Trimble, Jr.** Born on February 4, 1822 and died on April 19, 1904. Married Hanna G. Campbell in 1854. David was a farmer in Mansfield, Ohio.

+ **G73—Thomas Woods Trimble.** Born in 1824 and died in September 1855. Married Margaret Craig.

+ **G74—James S. Trimble.** Born on February 2, 1826. Married Lucinda Ann Murphy.

+ **G75—Joseph B. Trimble.** Born in 1828. He lived at one time in Idaho.
    Married first to Annetta Condon.
    Married second to Elizabeth Demer.

G76—Elizabeth Trimble. Born in 1829. She never married.

+ **G78—Martha Ellen Trimble.** Born in 1830; married John Gibson. They lived at Vicksburg, Michigan. She sent a New Testament to Delia L. Trimble Brook on February 24, 1881.

+ **G79—Susan Trimble.** Born in 1832; married Moses Thompson and lived at Altoona, Pennsylvania.

G80—Rebecca G. Trimble. Born in 1834 and died on September 10, 1884. She never married.

+ **G81—John S. Trimble.** Born in 1837. Married Belle Spear of Shelby, Ohio.

G82—Ebenezer Trimble. Born in 1837. He never married. During the Civil War Ebenezer died in prison camp.

G29—Jane Trimble. Daughter of William Trimble III and Elizabeth McCormick. (Fourth generation of William and Mary Trimble.) Born on September 25, 1800 and died on December 17, 1881. Married Judge William McClung on December 23, 1824. Judge McClung was born in 1787 and died in 1876. Both are buried at Old Tent Cemetery near Colfax, Ohio. William McClung was a prominent citizen and was elected to the state legislature. He was a soldier in the War of 1812, a justice of the peace and member of the West Rushville Presbyterian Church.

The child of Judge William McClung and Jane Trimble:
G83—Martha McClung. Married a Mr. Cowan.

G30—William Sterrett Trimble. Son of William Trimble III and Elizabeth McCormick. (Fifth generation of William and Mary Trimble.) Born on June 19, 1802 and died on March 29, 1862. Married Ann Elizabeth Black on September 13, 1827, in Fairfield County, Ohio. Both are buried in the Old Cemetery, Rochester, Indiana.
Married second George Perchbacker and they have no children.

The children of William Sterrett Trimble and Ann Elizabeth Black:
G84—Mary Trimble. Born on September 19, 1828 on Michigan Road Rochester, Fulton County, Indiana and died on June 15, 1845. She is buried in the Old Cemetery, Rochester, Indiana.

Trimble Families of America

+ **G85—William Black Trimble.** Born in 1831 on Michigan Road Rochester, Fulton County, Indiana and died in 1919. Married Margaret Elder. William and his brother John went West during the Gold Rush of 1849 and experienced many exciting adventures in the five years they remained in California.

+ **G86—John Trimble.** Born in 1833 on Michigan Road Rochester, Fulton County, Indiana. Married Lydia King.

G87—Thomas Trimble. Born on December 30, 1836 on Michigan Road Rochester, Fulton County, Indiana and died on January 30, 1860. He was editor and proprietor of the first newspaper in Rochester, Indiana, The Sentinel, which has continued publication ever since. He is buried in the Old Cemetery, Rochester, Indiana.

G88—Elizabeth Trimble. Born in 1838 on Michigan Road Rochester, Fulton County, Indiana and died in 1863. She is buried in the Odd Fellows Cemetery, Rochester, Indiana.

G89—Martha Jane Trimble. Born on October 10, 1840 on Michigan Road Rochester, Fulton County, Indiana and died on February 13, 1916. Married two times, first Dr. A. L. Plank in 1873. He was born in 1827. Martha supervised their elegant home, according to the New Historical Atlas of Fulton County, Indiana, she did so "in true womanly manner." They had no children.

+ **G90—Lucinda Trimble.** Born on May 10, 1844 on Michigan Road Rochester, Fulton County, Indiana and died on January 2, 1909. Married William Newton Westfall on November 20, 1867. They are buried in the Odd Fellows Cemetery at Ellensburg, Washington.

G91—Isabelle Trimble. Born on December 21, 1846 on Michigan Road Rochester, Fulton County, Indiana and died on October 20, 1921. Married William Wood in 1846. They are buried at Rochester, Indiana.

G31—James Trimble. Son of William Trimble III and Elizabeth McCormick. (Fifth generation of William and Mary Trimble.), in Ohio and died on April 24, 1872. Married Ann Elizabeth Crane on November 24, 1829.

The children of James Trimble and Ann Elizabeth Crane:

+ **G92—Amanda Trimble.** Born on June 6, 1831. Married Reverend Dr. Mechlin.

G93—Mary Ann Trimble. Born on September 7, 1832. Died October 7, 1851, and is buried at Pleasant Hill Cemetery, Fairfield County, Ohio.

+ **G94—Ann Elizabeth Trimble.** Born on June 23, 1834. Married Reverend George W. Bushy on October 19, 1852.

G95—Olivia Trimble. Born on March 31, 1837 and died young.

G96—Lucy Ann Trimble. Born on February 19, 1839. Married a Reverend Mr. Weber.

G97—Caroline Trimble. Born on March 10, 1841. Married a Reverend Mr. Herring.

G98—Louise Trimble. Born in March 1843. Married Reuben Geiser.

G99—James Harvey Trimble. Born on February 5, 1845. Died young.

G100—Thomas Trimble. Born on December 17, 1846.

G101—Ashbury Clark Trimble. Born on September 30, 1849.

G102—Laura Adelaide Trimble. Born on July 14, 1851 and died on November 22, 1851. She is buried at Lancaster, Ohio.

+ **G103—George Washington Trimble.** Born on May 21, 1853. Married Elizabeth Geiser.

G35—Mary Polly Trimble. Daughter of William Trimble III and Elizabeth McCormick. (Fifth generation of William and Mary Trimble.) Born on November 7, 1813 and died on March 18, 1862. Married on April 22, 1833, to Peter Lamb.

The children of Peter Lamb and Mary Polly Trimble:

G104—William Isaac Lamb.

G105—Thomas Lamb.

G106—Amelia Lamb. Born in 1840 and died in 1926.

G107—Mary Elizabeth Lamb. Born in 1838 and died in 1901.

G108—John L. Lamb.

G109—James Lamb.

G110—Peter Lamb. He served in the Civil War.

G111—Sylvester Lamb. He was the Independent senator of Ohio from Lucas County for three years and a lawyer in Toledo, Ohio.

G36—Thomas Trimble. Son of William Trimble III and Elizabeth McCormick. (Fifth generation of William and Mary Trimble.) Born on January 16, 1816 and died on May 19, 1862. Married Samantha Jane Hooker on August 22, 1848.

The children of Thomas Trimble and Samantha Jane Hooker:

G112—Elizabeth Trimble. Born on April 7, 1858.

G113—Nannette Trimble. Born on September 13, 1865 and married Charles Peters.

G114—Jeane Trimble.

G115—Joseph Trimble. Born on August 12, 1849.

G116—Samantha Trimble. Born on June 29, 1852.

G117—William H. Trimble. Born on December 4, 1855.

G37—Robert Trimble. Son of William Trimble III and Elizabeth McCormick. (Fifth generation of William and Mary Trimble.) Born on May 10, 1819 and died on December 14, 1891. Married Maria D. Armstrong in 1852; she died on February 13, 1888. They lived in Urbana, Ohio, later moving to Nebraska. In 1873 they moved to Columbus, Ohio.

The children of Robert Trimble and Maria D. Armstrong:

G118—Oliver Trimble. Born on September 21, 1857, and married Genevieve —— ——, he was a druggist and later lived in Nebraska.

G119—Allen Trimble. She died in infancy.

G120—Robert Trimble. Born on September 21, 1826.

G38—Lucinda D. Trimble. Daughter of William Trimble III and Elizabeth McCormick. (Fifth generation of William and Mary Trimble.) Born on August 8, 1821. Married John McClelland, who was a merchant at Lancaster, Ohio. They moved to Lincoln, Nebraska.

The children of John McClelland and Lucinda D. Trimble:

G121—Catherine McClelland.

G122—John. McClelland.

G123—George. McClelland.

G40—Joseph Barr. Son of James Barr and Jane Trimble. (Fifth generation of William and Mary Trimble.) Married Orpha ———,

The children of Joseph Barr and Orpha ———:

G124—Nettie Barr.

G125—Hattie Barr.

G126—Polly Barr. Married a Mr. Devor.

G42—Samuel Hanna Trimble. Son of John Trimble and Rachel Hanna (Fifth generation of William and Mary Trimble.) Born in 1804 and died on December 22, 1841. Married Jane ——— on September 30, 1830,

The children of Samuel Hanna Trimble and Jane ———:

G127—Joseph P. Trimble.

G128—Louise Trimble.

G129—Edson Trimble.

G130—Amanda Trimble.

G43—John Trimble, Jr. Son of John Trimble and Rachel Hanna. (Fifth generation of William and Mary Trimble.) Born on September 20, 1806 and died on December 28, 1889. He was in the tannery business and afterwards dealt mostly with his farming until 1834 when he went to Mount Vernon, Ohio, where he did both carpentry work and farming. He was in chandlery (candle business) for seven years; they manufactured some one hundred tons of candles per year.

John married first on July 15, 1835 to Nancy G. Drake.

Married second to Eliza Day on March 15, 1841.

Married third, to Ruth H. Boyd on May 27, 1872. Ruth died of cancer on August 1, 1886.

The children of John Trimble and Nancy G. Drake:

G131—Asa Mahan Trimble. Born on September 30, 1836 and died on May 21, 1903. Asa was unmarried and a member of the Sixty-fifth Ohio Infantry in the War Between the States.

The children of John Trimble and Eliza Day:

G132—Emma Jane Trimble. Died on May 19, 1879. Married Harrison Stevens on June 25, 1878. She attended Oberlin College at Mount Vernon, Ohio, and at her death the minister said of her, "She was a sweet and lovely Christian."

G133—John Nevin Trimble. Born in 1847 and died in 1891. Never married.

G134—Elizabeth Ellen Trimble. Born in 1852 and died in 1916. Never married.

+ **G135—William Edgar Trimble.** Born in 1853. Married Lavanna Haigwood.

+ **G136—Anna Eliza Trimble.** Married Dr. R. W. Colville.

G46—James Scott Trimble. Son of John Trimble and Rachel Hanna. (Fifth generation of William and Mary Trimble.) Born in 1818 and died in 1889. Married Margaret Shaw. James is listed in the History of Morrow County, Ohio, as one of the leading businessmen of early Mount Gilead. He owned a dry goods store, bank, and a warehouse for grain. His home on Iberia Street was one of the finest in Mount Gilead, Ohio.

The children of James Scott Trimble and Margaret Shaw:

G137—Ella A. Trimble.

G138—Alice R. Trimble.

G139—Alexander G. Trimble.

G140—Nannie Trimble.

G48—Samuel Woods Trimble. Son of Thomas Trimble and Mary Woods. (Fifth generation of William and Mary Trimble.) Born on July 12, 1813 and died on May 10, 1854. Married Mary Caldwell. Samuel was an Abolitionist and was an active worker in its cause.

The children of Samuel Woods Trimble and Mary Caldwell:

G141—Thomas Heber Trimble. Born in 1841. Married Ella Dickey. He was a respected businessman in Mount Vernon, Ohio, and he served in the Civil War. They had a son, Joseph Dickey Trimble.

G142—Mary Woods Trimble. Born in 1848 and died in 1918. Married Thomas Hutson.

G143—Carrie Trimble. Born in 1851 and died in childhood.

G144—Anna Violette Trimble. Born in 1864 and died in childhood.

G50—Susan Margaret Trimble. Daughter of Thomas Trimble and Mary Woods (Fifth generation of William and Mary Trimble.) Born on July 2, 1817. Married William S. Caldwell.

The children of William S. Caldwell and Susan Margaret Trimble:

G145—Andrew Woods Caldwell.

G146—Mary Jane. Caldwell.

G147—Susan Scott Caldwell.

G148—James Sterrett Caldwell.

G149—George Washington Caldwell.

G150—Samuel H. Thomas Caldwell.

G151—Margaret Anna Caldwell.

G152—Rebecca Caldwell.

G51—William Pitt Trimble. Son of Thomas Trimble and Mary Woods. (Fifth generation of William and Mary Trimble.) Born on August 15, 1819 and died on July 8, 1875. Married Pamela A. Gates. William Pitt was a pioneer in the tomato canning industry and was in Wesleyville, Pennsylvania. He was deputy registrar and recorder for the probate of wills for Erie, Pennsylvania. Wesleyville was a station along the famous Underground Railroad and William Pitt was an active worker in this movement.

The children of William Pitt Trimble and Pamela A. Gates:

G153—Thomas Woods Trimble. Born on September 10, 1858 and died on June 28, 1875. He was unmarried.

+ **G154—William Scott Trimble.** Born on June 17, 1861. Married Albertina Brandenberg.

G155—Mary Edna Trimble.

G52—Frances Mary Trimble. Daughter of Thomas Trimble and Mary Woods.

Trimble Families of America

(Fifth generation of William and Mary Trimble.) Born on May 9, 1828. Married William Wiley on September 16, 1847.

The children of William Wiley and Frances Mary Trimble:
G156—Thomas Wiley.
G157—William Wiley.
G158—Eldora Wiley.
G159—Mary Wiley.

G54—Sarah Ellen Trimble. Daughter of Thomas Trimble and Mary Woods. (Fifth generation of William and Mary Trimble.) Born on September 14, 1834. Married Robert F. Gibson on May 5, 1851.

The children of Robert F. Gibson and Sarah Ellen Trimble:
G160—Harry Gibson.
G161—Frederick Gibson.
G162—May Gibson.
G163—Ella Gibson.

G58—Eliza Trimble. Daughter of James Trimble and Sarah Wylie. (Fifth generation of William and Mary Trimble.) Married Stephen Day

The child of Stephen Day and Eliz Trimble:
G164—Annis Day.

G61—James W. Trimble. Son of James Trimble and Sarah Wylie. (Fifth generation of William and Mary Trimble.) Born on April 1, 1819 and died on June 22, 1861. He married Elizabeth Wright. Attended Oberlin College from 1839 to 1843. They are buried at Mount Vernon, Ohio.

The children of James W. Trimble and Elizabeth Wright:
G165—Mary Etta Trimble. Married a Mr. Cummings.
G166—Margaret Trimble. Married Joseph B. Lindley.

G70—Sarah Jane Trimble. Daughter of David Sterrett Trimble and Margaret Sterrett. (Fifth generation of William and Mary Trimble.) Born in 1816. Married John Marshall.

The children of John Marshall and Sarah Jane Trimble:
G167—Elizabeth Marshall.
G168—Margaret Marshall.
G169—Harrison Marshall.

G71—Anna Mary Trimble. Daughter of David Sterrett Trimble and Margaret Sterrett. (Fifth generation of William and Mary Trimble.) Born in 1820.

Married William Crum.

The children of William Crum and Anna Mary Trimble:

G170—Jane Crumb. Married Frank Fritz.

G171—Clara Ellen Crumb. Married John Smith.

G172—James Crumb.

G173—John Crumb.

G174—William Crumb. Married Betty Vandebogart.

G72—David Sterrett Trimble, Jr. Son of David Sterrett Trimble and Margaret Sterrett. (Fifth generation of William and Mary Trimble.) Born on February 4, 1822 and died on April 19, 1904. Married Hanna G. Campbell in 1854. David was a farmer in Mansfield, Ohio.

The children of David Sterrett Trimble and Hanna G. Campbell:

G175—Mary M. Trimble. Died on May 29, 1934.

G176—Martha T. Trimble. Died in the middle 20s, she was never married and moved to Wooster, Ohio, in 1919. She died of cancer.

Neither Mary nor Martha Trimble married so they adopted a child, Marian Johnston, but returned her at twelve years of age.

G73—Thomas Woods Trimble. Son of David Sterrett Trimble and Margaret Sterrett. (Fifth generation of William and Mary Trimble.) Born in 1824 and died in September 1855. Married Margaret Craig.

The children of Thomas Woods Trimble and Margaret Craig:

G177—William Trimble.

+ **G178—Thomas Woods Trimble.** Married twice.

G74—James S. Trimble. Son of David Sterrett Trimble and Margaret Sterrett. (Fifth generation of William and Mary Trimble.) Born on February 2, 1826 and died on June 9, 1913. He married Lucinda Ann Murphy on October 7, 1847.

The children of James Trimble and Lucinda Ann Murphy:

G179—William Leander Trimble. Born on December 24, 1849 and died on August 24, 1855.

G180—David Frank Trimble. Born on December 8, 1852 and died on May 31, 1921. Married Maria Boals. He was a representative from the Eighth Legislative District of Whitman County, Washington. He lived in Palouse, Washington.

G181—John Marion Trimble. Born on March 29, 1855 and died February 21, 1909. Married Emma Brown.

+ **G182—Laura Ellen Trimble.** Born on January 18, 1858 and died on November 16, 1911. Married Frank Mabee.

+ **G183—Willard Lincoln Trimble.** Born on March 27, 1860. Married Sara Lou Lucinda McConnell

G184—Ellsworth Trimble. Born on September 20, 1862. and died on November 8, 1862.

+ **G185—Dr. Charles Elmore Trimble.** Born on November 15, 1863. Married two times: first, on February 22, 1888, to Miss Cora A. Condit, and second, to Emma Harris.

G186—James Trimble. Born on November 19, 1865 and died on October 16, 1866.

G187—Della Louise Trimble. Born on November 18, 1868 and died in 1940. She married William Scott Brook.

G75—Joseph B. Trimble. Son of David Sterrett Trimble and Margaret Sterrett. (Fifth generation of William and Mary Trimble.) Born in 1828 and married two times: first, to Annetta Condon, and second, to Elizabeth Demer. He lived at one time in Idaho.

The children of Joseph B. Trimble and Annetta Condon:

+ **G188—William Trimble.** Married Maybelle Hale.

G189—Ira Trimble. Never married.

G78—Martha Ellen Trimble. Daughter of David Sterrett Trimble and Margaret Sterrett. (Fifth generation of William and Mary Trimble.) Born in 1830; married John Gibson. They lived at Vicksburg, Michigan. She sent a New Testament to Delia L. Trimble Brook on February 24, 1881.

The children of John Gibson and Martha Ellen Trimble:

G190—James E. Gibson.

G191—Joseph Gibson. Married Bessie Metcalf.

G192—Alice Gibson.

G193—Frank Gibson. Married and had four children.

G194—William Gibson.

G195—Amos Gibson. Married Anna Gates.

G79—Susan Trimble. Daughter of David Sterrett Trimble and Margaret Sterrett. (Fifth generation of William and Mary Trimble.) Born in 1832; married Moses Thompson and lived at Altoona, Pennsylvania.

The children of Moses Thompson and Susan Trimble:

G196—William Thompson.

G197—Edwin Thompson.

G81—John S. Trimble. Son of David Sterrett Trimble and Margaret Sterrett. (Fifth generation of William and Mary Trimble.) Born in 1837. Married Belle Spear of Shelby, Ohio.

The children of John S. Trimble and Belle Spear:

+ **G198—Ulysses Trimble.** Married Marie Cumberworth.

G199—Blanche Trimble. Married a Mr. McMahon.

G200—Louise Trimble.

G85—William Black Trimble. Son of William Sterrett Trimble and Ann Elizabeth Black. (Sixth generation of William and Mary Trimble.) Born in 1831 on Michigan Road Rochester, Fulton County, Indiana and died in 1919. Married Margaret Elder. William and his brother John went West during the Gold Rush of 1849 and experienced many exciting adventures in the five years they remained in California.

The children of William Black Trimble and Margaret Elder. William:

G201—Francis Trimble. Born on September 9, 1862 and died on June 4, 1863.

+ **G202—Edward T. Trimble.** Born on June 14, 1864 and died in 1941 Married Charlotte Atkinson.

G86—John Trimble. Son of William Sterrett Trimble and Ann Elizabeth Black. (Sixth generation of William and Mary Trimble.) Born in 1833 and died in 1910. Married Lydia King in 1858. They are buried in the Odd Fellows Cemetery, Rochester, Indiana. John went West with his brother William Black Trimble (G84) during the Gold Rush.

The children of John Trimble and Lydia King:

+ **G203—Thomas Chalmer Trimble.** Born in 1859. Married Ida Martindale.

+ **G204—Laura Elizabeth Trimble.** Born on February 27, 1862. Married Walter Cummings.

G205—Clinton Trimble. Born in 1864 and died in 1937. He is buried in Odd Fellows Cemetery in Rochester, Indiana.

+ **G206—Martha Trimble.** Born in 1886. Married Charles Bash.

+ **G207—Eunice Trimble.** Born in 1869 and married in 1892 to Howard Reed. He was a farmer and raised full-blooded stock. Howard was educated at DePauw University and was a teacher. They spent four years in the West mining and prospected from British Columbia to Mexico.

G208—John Trimble. Died in infancy.

+ G209—Jay Trimble. Born in 1879. Married twice.

G90—Lucinda Trimble. Daughter of William Sterrett Trimble and Ann Elizabeth Black. (Sixth generation of William and Mary Trimble.) Born on May 10, 1844 and died on January 2, 1909. Married William Newton Westfall on November 20, 1867. They are buried in the Odd Fellows Cemetery at Ellensburg, Washington.

The children of William Newton Westfall and Lucinda Trimble:

G210—Deane Trimble Westfall. Born in 1868 and died in 1892.

+ G211—Isabelle Westfall. Born in 1873. Married Henry Morse.

G92—Amanda Trimble. Daughter of James Trimble and Ann Elizabeth Crane. (Sixth generation of William and Mary Trimble.) Born on June 6, 1831. Married Reverend Dr. Mechlin.

The children of Reverend Dr. Mechlin and Amanda Trimble:

G212—Susan Mechlin.

G213—Cyrus Mechlin.

G214—Alice Mechlin.

G215—Herbert Mechlin.

G216—Elizabeth Mechlin.

G94—Ann Elizabeth Trimble. Daughter of James Trimble and Ann Elizabeth Crane. (Sixth generation of William and Mary Trimble.) Born on June 23, 1834. Married Reverend George W. Bushy on October 19, 1852.

The children of Reverend George W. Bushy and Ann Elizabeth Trimble:

G217—Laura Bushy.

G218—Ida Bushy.

G219—Carrie Bushy.

G103—George Washington Trimble. Son of James Trimble and Ann Elizabeth Crane. (Sixth generation of William and Mary Trimble.) Born on May 21, 1853 and died on December 31, 1923. Married Elizabeth Geiser on June 15, 1877.

The children of George Washington Trimble and Elizabeth Geiser:

G220—Zella Evelyn Trimble. Born on April 24, 1880. Married James Dallow in 1905.

+ G221—Elmer George Trimble. Born on September 11, 1883. Married Harriet Pulford; and second married Patricia Vaughn.

+ G222—Charles M. Trimble. Born on August 11, 1885. Married Helen

Matt.

+ **G223—Helen Trimble.** Born on April 8, 1915. Married Carl Brown in 1940.

+ **G224—Dorothy Trimble.** Born on July 17, 1916. Married James Claar on June 5, 1937.

G135—William Edgar Trimble. Son of John Trimble and Eliza Day. (Sixth generation of William and Mary Trimble.) Born in 1853 and died in 1919. Married Lavanna Haigwood.

The children of William Trimble and Lavanna Haigwood:

G225—Anna May Trimble. Married Leary Bedell Johnston.

G226—Sarah Elizabeth Trimble.

G227—John William Trimble.

G228—Alberta Trimble.

G136—Anna Eliza Trimble. Daughter of John Trimble and Nancy G. Drake. (Sixth generation of William and Mary Trimble.) Married Dr. R. W. Colville.

The children of Dr. R. W. Colville of Anna Eliza Trimble:

G229—Helen Elizabeth Colville. Married Howard Sevits.

G230—Anna Ruth Colville. Married Walter Stewart and had one child, Marian Stewart.

G154—William Scott Trimble. Son of William Pitt Trimble and Pamela A. Gates. (Sixth generation of William and Mary Trimble.) Born on June 17, 1861 and died on April 12, 1914. Married Albertina Brandenberg of Switzerland.

The children of William Scott Trimble and Albertina Brandenberg:

+ **G231—Albertina Marie Trimble.** Born on August 14, 1894. Married Walter O. Anderson.

G232—William Clinton Trimble. Born on October 17, 1896 and died on April 18, 1898.

+ **G233—George Francis Trimble.** Born on March 22, 1898. Married Gladys Irene Klokow.

G178—Thomas Woods Trimble. Son of Thomas Woods Trimble and Margaret Craig (Sixth generation of William and Mary Trimble.) Married first to Lillian Ellis.

Married second to Elizabeth Martin.

The daughter of Thomas Woods Trimble and Lillian Ellis:

Trimble Families of America

G234—Ethel Trimble. Married Fred A. Klann.

G182—Laura Ellen Trimble. Daughter of James Trimble and Lucinda Ann Murphy (Sixth generation of William and Mary Trimble.) Born on January 18, 1858 and died on November 16, 1911. Married Frank Mabee.

The children of Frank Mabee and Laura Ellen Trimble:
Floyd Trimble and Chub Trimble. (twins). They died at birth.
G235—Vere Trimble. Born in 1887 and died in 1966. Married Lila Wiley.

G183—Willard Lincoln Trimble. Son of James S. Trimble and Lucinda Ann Murphy. (Sixth generation of William and Mary Trimble.) Born on March 27, 1860 and died on January 16, 1939. Married Sara Lou Lucinda McConnell on May 14, 1884. Both are buried at Ontario, Ohio.

The children of Willard Lincoln Trimble and Sara Lou Lucinda McConnell:
G236—Ethel May Trimble. Born on July 27, 1886 and died on November 11, 1918. Married Charles Sargel.
+ **G237—James Willard Trimble.** Born on March 26, 1888. Married Harriet Freese.
+ **G238—Lucinda Ann Trimble.** Born on February 13, 1890 and died on February 9, 1918. Married Harland Turner.
G239—Charles Clinton Trimble. Born on March 23, 1892. He was unmarried.
+ **G240—Martha Viola Trimble.** Born on February 9, 1894 and died on October 22, 1965. She married two times, first, to Edward Horning, and second, to Bert Crager.
G241—Bessie Blanche Trimble. Born on January 16, 1897. Married Gail Heichel.
G242—Lester Dale Trimble. Born on April 22, 1899. He married two times: first, to Eva Simon, and second, to Thelma Black. He has a daughter, Jean Marie, born in 1921, and married William Papes.
G243—Leland Earl Trimble. Born on April 20, 1900. He married twice. Married first to Helen Thornburg and they divorced. Married second to Georgianna Walters.
+ **G244—Lois Alfreida Trimble.** Born on September 27, 1903 in Mansfield, Ohio and died on March 29, 1968 in Lonoke, Lonoke County, Arkansas. She married two times: first, to Albert Hicks, and second, to Morris Franklin Cramner. They live at Anaheim, California.
+ **G245—Laura Ellen Trimble.** Born on September 19, 1906. Married Herbert Allen Scarbrough and they live at Fort Lauderdale, Florida.

Trimble Families of America

G - William "The Settler" Trimble

G185–Dr. Charles Elmore Trimble. Son of James S. Trimble and Lucinda Ann Murphy. (Sixth generation of William and Mary Trimble.) Born on November 15, 1863, on a farm in Richland County, Ohio. Dr. Trimble taught general practice at Starling Medical College, which is now the Medical Department of the University of Ohio at Columbus. The early education of Charles included the invigorating influences and discipline of the home farm life. Later he took a course in the Northwestern Ohio Normal University at Ada. His academic education was supplemented by his attending Western Reserve University at Cleveland. He was matriculated in Starling Medical College, Columbus, and graduated in 1890 with a degree of Doctor of Medicine. He was a Republican, Presbyterian, Mason, Thirty-second degree of the Scottish Rite in the Consistory at Columbus. He was actively affiliated with York Rite Organization and gained the title of noble in the Mystic Shrine and was a member of the Bucyrus Lodge, No. 156, Benevolent and Protective Order of Elks. Dr. Charles Trimble married two times: first, on February 22, 1888, to Miss Cora A. Condit, and second, to Emma Harris.

The children of Dr. Charles Elmore Trimble and Cora A. Condit:

+ **G246–Starling F. Trimble.** Born on May 6, 1893. Married Joanna Mincks.
+ **G247–Cecil Trimble.** Born on April 10, 1891 and died on May 20, 1969. She married William F. Miller.

G188–William Trimble. Son of Joseph B. Trimble and Annetta Condon. (Sixth generation of William and Mary Trimble.) Married Maybelle Hale.

The children of William Trimble and Maybelle Hale:

G248–Sterrett Hale.
G249–Elizabeth Hale.

G198–Ulysses Trimble. Son of John S. Trimble and Belle Spear (Sixth generation of William and Mary Trimble.) Married Marie Cumberworth.

The daughter of Ulysses Trimble and Marie Cumberworth:

G250–Mildred Trimble.

G202–Edward T. Trimble. Son of William Black Trimble and Margaret Elder. William. (Seventh generation of William and Mary Trimble.) Born on June 14, 1864 and died in 1941. Married Charlotte Atkinson.

The one son of Edward T. Trimble and Charlotte Atkinson:

G251–Carleton A. Trimble. Born on June 12, 1893.

G203–Thomas Chalmer Trimble. Son of John Trimble and Lydia King. (Seventh generation of William and Mary Trimble.) Born in 1859. Married

G - William "The Settler" Trimble

Ida Ethelen Martindale.

The children of Thomas Trimble and Ida Martindale:

+ G252—Clara Arabell Trimble. Born on April 22, 1882 in Richland Center, Indiana and died on November 17, 1974 in Plymouth, Indiana. Married Linton Quivey on November 4, 1899 in Rochester, Indiana.

G253—Chalmer Trimble.

G254—Martha Trimble.

G255—Ethel Trimble.

G256—Muriel Trimble.

G257—Marie Trimble.

G204—Laura Elizabeth Trimble. Daughter of John Trimble and Lydia King. (Seventh generation of William and Mary Trimble.) Born on February 27, 1862 and died on May 4, 1905. Married Walter Cummings in 1878.

The children Walter Cummings and Laura Elizabeth Trimble:

G258—Mae Cummings. Born in 1879, married Walter Thompson.

G259—Louise Cummings. Born in 1886. Married George Killen, and second, to Dr. E. Remington in 1952 at Augusta, Georgia.

Fellows Cemetery in Rochester, Indiana.

G206—Martha Trimble. Daughter of John Trimble and Lydia King. (Seventh generation of William and Mary Trimble.) Born in 1886. Married Charles Bash.

The children of Charles Bash and Martha Trimble:

G260—Clarence Bash.

G261—Ralph Bash.

G262—John Bash.

G207—Eunice Trimble. Son of John Trimble and Lydia King. (Seventh generation of William and Mary Trimble.) Born in 1869 and married in 1892 to Howard Reed. He was a farmer and raised full-blooded stock. Howard was educated at DePauw University and was a teacher. They spent four years in the West mining and prospected from British Columbia to Mexico.

The children of Howard Reed and Eunice Trimble:

G263—Robert Reed.

G264—Donald Reed.

G265—Joseph Reed. He was a medical doctor in Long Beach, California.

G209—Jay Trimble. Son of John Trimble and Lydia King. (Seventh generation of William and Mary Trimble.) Born in 1879. Married twice:

Married first to Nona Miller.

Married second to Alice.

The son of Jay Trimble:

G266—Clinton Trimble. He was a professor at UCLA in Los Angeles, California.

G211—Isabelle Westfall. Daughter of William Newton Westfall and Lucinda Trimble (Seventh generation of William and Mary Trimble.) Born in 1873, married Henry Morse.

The daughter of Henry Morse and Isabelle Westfall:

+ **G267—Jean Rice Morse.** Married William M. Silliphant, a doctor. Jean is a graduate of Smith College, Massachusetts. They have two children: Mary Ruth and Elizabeth.

G221—Elmer George Trimble. Son of George Washington Trimble and Elizabeth Geiser. (Seventh generation of William and Mary Trimble.) Born on September 11, 1883, and married in 1911 to Harriet Pulford; and second, Elmer married Patricia Vaughn.

The children of Elmer George Trimble and Harriet Pulford:

G268—George Elmer Trimble. Born on September 26, 1920, and married Patricia V. May.

G269—John Pulford Trimble. Born on July 7, 1922, and married Lila Klingensmith.

The children of Elmer George Trimble and Patricia Vaughn:

G270—Cheri Trimble. Born on July 21, 1946.

G271—George Trimble. Born on August 2, 1950.

G222—Charles M. Trimble. Son of George Washington Trimble and Elizabeth Geiser. (Seventh generation of William and Mary Trimble.) Born on August 11, 1885 and died on September 12, 1953. Married Helen Matt in 1904. He was a game warden, and they owned the Trimble Greenhouses and the Quality Flower Shop from 1924 to 1940.

The children of Charles Trimble and Helen Matt:

G272—Richard Trimble. Born on April 28, 1905. Unmarried.

+ **G273—Harriet Trimble.** Born on April 28, 1906, and married Dr. James Donovan.

G274—Isabelle Trimble. Died as infant.

+ **G275—George Trimble.** Born on May 3, 1913 and died in 1969. Married

Trimble Families of America

Ruth Davis.

G223—Helen Trimble. Born on April 8, 1915. Married Carl Brown in 1940.

The daughter of Carl Brown and Helen Trimble:
G276—Carol Jo Brown. Born on December 21, 1942.

G224—Dorothy Trimble. Daughter of George Washington Trimble and Elizabeth Geiser. (Seventh generation of William and Mary Trimble.) Born on July 17, 1916. Married James Claar on June 5, 1937.

The children of James Claar and Dorothy Trimble:
G277—Linda Claar. Born on August 13, 1940. Married Arthur Dignore.
G278—Cathy Ann Claar. Born on October 12, 1949. Married Larry Crawford.
G279—Anna May Claar. Married Leary Bedell Johnston.

The children of Leary Bedell Johnston and Anna May Trimble:
G280—Elizabeth Johnston.
G281—Anna Louise Johnston.
G282—May Johnston.

G231—Albertina Marie Trimble. Daughter of William Scott Trimble and Albertina Brandenberg (Seventh generation of William and Mary Trimble.) Born on August 14, 1894. Married Walter O. Anderson.

The children of Walter O. Anderson and Albertina Marie Trimble:
G283—Walter Clinton Anderson. Married Shirley Kathryn Zeitler.
G284—Julia Marie Anderson. Married Joseph Lyle Graham. He was vice-president of the Mellon Bank.

G233—George Francis Trimble. Son of William Scott Trimble and Albertina Brandenberg. (Seventh generation of William and Mary Trimble.) Born on March 22, 1898, and married Gladys Irene Klokow. George was born in Erie, Pennsylvania. They were married on July 2, 1923, in Cleveland, Ohio, by the Reverend Ellis E. Eklof of Bethel Baptist Church. Gladys was born on November 9, 1900, in Cleveland. George Francis graduated from embalmer's school and had an embalmer and undertaker license. Gladys graduated from business college. (The author and his wife enjoyed George Francis and Gladys Trimble's visit to our home when we lived in Granville, Ohio. We are gratefully indebted to this couple for the excellent material on their Trimble family line. A lovely and charming couple.)

The children of George Francis Trimble and Gladys Irene Klokow:
+G285—June Alberta Trimble. Born on July 25, 1924, in Cleveland. Married Louis William Wearsch on April 24, 1943, at Lorain, Ohio.

June attended Lorain Business College and Louis is a carpenter by trade.

+ **G286—Richard George Trimble.** Born on July 25, 1927 in Cleveland, Ohio. Married Naomi Ruth Peacock.

G287—William Pitt Trimble. Born on January 1, 1933, in Lorain, Ohio. He was the first New Year baby in 1933. Married Marian Alice Eddy on April 2, 1955, at Lyndhurst, Ohio. William attended Wittenberg University and was in the service in 1955. Later he graduated from Ohio State University in Columbus, Ohio, on December 16, 1960, with a B.S. degree in business administration. Marian graduated from Wittenberg in 1955.

+ **G288—James Francis Trimble.** Born on May 19, 1936. Married Sara Ann Bednarik on June 18, 1959.

+ **G289—Judith Ann Trimble.** Born on January 28, 1944. Married Richard Edward Mbiad on May 9, 1964. He was born in New York City. Judith graduated from Cleveland Academy for Professional Secretaries in June 1963. Richard graduated from Kent State University in December 1965.

G237—James Willard Trimble. Son of Willard Lincoln Trimble and Sara Lou Lucinda McConnell. (Seventh generation of William and Mary Trimble.) Born on March 26, 1888. Married Harriet Freese.

The children of Harriet Freese and James Willard Trimble:

G290—Winifred Alberta. Born in 1915. Married Richard Hayes.

G291—Gerald Willard. Born in 1929 and died in 1947.

G238—Lucinda Ann Trimble. Daughter of Willard Lincoln Trimble and Sara Lou Lucinda McConnell. (Seventh generation of William and Mary Trimble.) Born on February 13, 1890 and died on February 9, 1918. Married Harland Turner.

The children of Harold Turner and Lucinda Ann Trimble:

G292—Merle Everett.

G293—Stanley Elwood Turner.

G240—Martha Viola Trimble. Daughter of Willard Lincoln Trimble and Sara Lou Lucinda McConnell. (Seventh generation of William and Mary Trimble.) Born on February 9, 1894 and died on October 22, 1965. She married twice. Married first to Edward Horning. Married second to Bert Crager.

The children of Edward Horning and Martha Viola Trimble:

G294—Mary Estelle Horning.

G295—Esther Horning.

G241—Bessie Blanche Trimble. Daughter of Willard Lincoln Trimble and Sara Lou Lucinda McConnell. (Seventh generation of William and Mary Trimble.) Born on January 16, 1897. Married Gail Heichel.

The children of Gail Heichel and Bessie Blanche Trimble:
G296—Bertha May Heichel. Born in 1919. Married Walter Skinner.
G297—Mary Winona Heichel. Born in 1927. Married Earl Tyree.
G298—David Trimble Heichel. Born in 1921 and died in infancy.

G244—Lois Alfreida Trimble. Daughter of Willard Lincoln Trimble and Sara Lou Lucinda McConnell. (Seventh generation of William and Mary Trimble.) Born on September 27, 1903 in Mansfield, Ohio and died on March 29, 1968 in Lonoke, Lonoke County, Arkansas. She married twice. Married first to Albert Hicks. Married second to Morris Franklin Cramner. They live at Anaheim, California.

The children of Morris Franklin Cramner and Lois Alfreida Trimble:
G299—Laura Cramner. Born in 1925. Married James Leonard.
G300—John Albert Cramner. Born 1928. Married Betty Priest.
G301—Morris Cramner. Born in 1939.
G302—Paul Cramner. Born in 1941.

G245—Laura Ellen Trimble. Daughter of Willard Lincoln Trimble and Sara Lou Lucinda McConnell. (Seventh generation of William and Mary Trimble.) Born on September 19, 1906. Married Herbert Allen Scarbrough and they live at Fort Lauderdale, Florida.

The children Herbert Allen Scarbrough and Laura Ellen Trimble:
G303—Lois Scarbrough. Born in 1927. Married Asler D. Seymour.
G304—John Herbert Scarbrough. Born in 1931. Married Margaret Bowdew.

G246—Starling F. Trimble. Son of Dr. Charles Elmore Trimble and Cora A. Condit. (Seventh generation of William and Mary Trimble.) Born on May 6, 1893 and died on July 7, 1942. Married Joanna Mincks. He was born in Crestline, Ohio. Starling was postmaster and mayor of Crestline at the time of his death.

The children of Starling F. Trimble and Joanna Mincks:
+ **G305—John Starling Trimble.** Born on July 26, 1928. Married Nancy Ritzhaupt.
+ **G306—Mary Ann Trimble.** Born on December 29, 1926, at Crestline, Ohio. She married David Clearly and lives at Drexel Hill, Pennsylvania.

G247—Cecil Trimble. Son of Dr. Charles Elmore Trimble and Cora A. Condit (Seventh generation of William and Mary Trimble.) Born on April 10, 1891 and died on May 20, 1969. She married William F. Miller.

The children of William F. Miller and Cecil Trimble:

+ **G307—Dr. Charles Miller.** Born in 1917. Married Bernece Cowell. He was a veterinarian.

G308—Marjorie Ann Miller. Born in 1926. Married Paul J. Miller. She teaches in Willard, Ohio.

G252—Clara Arabell Trimble. Daughter of Thomas Trimble and Ida Martindale. (Eighth generation of William and Mary Trimble.) Born on April 22, 1882 in Richland Center, Indiana and died on November 17, 1974 in Plymouth, Indiana. Married Linton Quivey on November 4, 1899 in Rochester, Indiana. Linton was born on November 29, 1870 in Fulton County, Indiana and died on July 10, 1938. Linton was farmer. When the depression hit, he could no longer work the farm. It was difficult for an older man to find work. He struggled to send his daughter, Edna, through Ball State Teacher College in Muncie, Indiana. Clara was an employee of Schoonover Department Store in Argos, Indiana. She was a member of Argos United Methodist Church.

The children of Linton Quivey and Clara Arabell Trimble:

+ **G309—Mildred Ethelyn Quivey.** Born on July 1, 1902 in Green Township, Marshall County, Indiana and died on February 22, 1972 in Argos, Marshall County, Indiana. Married Leonard John Gibbons on February 1, 1922. Leonard was born on November 29, 1900 in Fulton, Indiana and died on July 10, 1987.

G310—Gertrude Quivey. Born on October 1, 1905 and died on February 14, 1910 as a small child.

G311—Irene Quivey. (twin) Born on June 17, 1910 in Green Township, Marshall County, Indiana and died on July 1, 1910 as an infant.

G312—L. Dean Quivey. (twin) Born on June 17, 1910 in Green Township, Marshall County, Indiana and died on January 3, 1911 as an infant.

+ **G313—Sarah Belle Quivey.** Born on April 5, 1912 in Green Township, Marshall County, Indiana and died on May 23, 1987 in Culver, Marshall County, Indiana. Married Maurice Reinhold in 1936 Maurice was born in 1896 and died in 1983.

G314—Russell L. Quivey. Born on March 10, 1914 in Green Township, Marshall County, Indiana and died on May 7, 1915 in Green Township,

Marshall County, Indiana as an infant.

+ **G315—Edna Bernice Quivey.** Born on September 3, 1917 in Green Township, Marshall County, Indiana and died November 30, 2003 in Indianapolis, Marion County, Indiana. Married Robert Carlson Staley on November 23, 1940.

G267—Jean Rice Morse. Daughter of Henry Morse and Lucinda Trimble (Seventh generation of William and Mary Trimble.) Married William M. Silliphant, a doctor. Jean is a graduate of Smith College, Massachusetts.

The two children of William M. Silliphant and Jean Rice:

G316—Mary Ruth Silliphant.

G317—Elizabeth Silliphant.

G273—Harriet Trimble. Daughter of Charles Trimble and Helen Matt. (Eighth generation of William and Mary Trimble.) Born on April 28, 1906. Married Dr. James Donovan.

The children of Dr. James Donovan and Harriet Trimble:

G318—James Donovan. Born in 1934.

G319—Barbara Donovan. Born in1940.

G275—George Trimble. Son of Charles Trimble and Helen Matt. (Eighth generation of William and Mary Trimble.) Born on May 3, 1913 and died in 1969. Married Ruth Davis.

The children George Trimble and Ruth Davis:

G320—Lawrence Trimble. Born in1940.

G321—Susanna Trimble. Born in 1941.

G322—Cheryl Trimble. Born in 1944.

G323—Molly Trimble. Born in 1946.

G285—June Alberta Trimble. Daughter of George Francis Trimble and Gladys Irene Klokow (Eighth generation of William and Mary Trimble.) Born on July 25, 1924, in Cleveland. Married Louis William Wearsch on April 24, 1943, at Lorain, Ohio. June attended Lorain Business College and Louis is a carpenter by trade.

The children of Louis William Wearsch and June Alberta Trimble:

G324—Linda Wearsch. Born on February 21, 1948.

G325—Thomas William Wearsch. Born on November 8, 1949.

G326—Pamela Ann Wearsch. Born on October 28, 1956.

G327—Louis William Wearsch, Jr. Born on July 30, 1959.

G286–Richard George Trimble. Son of George Francis Trimble and Gladys Irene Klokow. (Eighth generation of William and Mary Trimble.) Born on July 25, 1927 in Cleveland, Ohio. Married Naomi Ruth Peacock of Clifton, Texas, on October 2, 1954. He graduated from Fred Archer's School of Photography, Los Angeles, California. He served in the navy and the air force. Ruth is a registered nurse.

The children of Richard Trimble and Naomi Peacock:
G328–Michael Allan Trimble. Born on September 12, 1955.
G329–Scott Andrew Trimble. Born on August 25, 1957.
G330–Traci Lynn Trimble. Born on December 11, 1968.

G288–James Francis Trimble. Son of George Francis Trimble and Gladys Irene Klokow. (Eighth generation of William and Mary Trimble.) Born on May 19, 1936. Married Sara Ann Bednarik on June 18, 1959.

The children of James Francis Trimble and Sara Ann Bednarik:
G331–Jennifer Lynn Trimble. Born on October 25, 1966.
G332–James Francis Trimble, Jr., Born on February 11, 1969.

G289–Judith Ann Trimble. Daughter of George Francis Trimble and Gladys Irene Klokow. (Eighth generation of William and Mary Trimble.) Born on January 28, 1944. Married Richard Edward Mbiad on May 9, 1964. He was born in New York City. Judith graduated from Cleveland Academy for Professional Secretaries in June 1963. Richard graduated from Kent State University in December 1965.

The children of Richard Edward Mbiad and Judith Ann Trimble:
G333–Kimberlee Irene Mbiad. Born on July 1, 1966.
G334–Kellee Ann Mbiad. Born on April 23, 1968.

G305–John Starling Trimble. Son of Starling F. Trimble and Joanna Mincks. (Eighth generation of William and Mary Trimble.) Born on July 26, 1928, at Crestline, Ohio. He married Nancy Ritzhaupt. John Starling is associated with the National Bank of Cleveland. He graduated from Ohio University in 1954. (We are gratefully indebted to John Starling for the excellent genealogy of this Trimble lineage.)

The children of John Starling Trimble and Nancy Ritzhaupt:
G335–Jonathan Brook Trimble. Born on February 15, 1959, at Cleveland, Ohio.
G336–Drew Elizabeth Trimble. Born on January 1, 1962.

G306–Mary Ann Trimble. Daughter of Starling F. Trimble and Joanna Mincks.

Trimble Families of America

(Eighth generation of William and Mary Trimble.) Born on December 29, 1926, at Crestline, Ohio. She married David Clearly and lives at Drexel Hill, Pennsylvania.

The child of David Clearly and Mary Ann Trimble:

G337—Joanne Elizabeth Clearly. Born on January 10, 1962.

G307—Dr. Charles Miller. Son of William F. Miller and Cecil Trimble (Eighth generation of William and Mary Trimble.) Born in 1917. Married Bernece Cowell. He was a veterinarian.

The children of Dr. Charles Miller and Bernece Cowell:

G338—Elizabeth Miller. Born in 1952.

G339—Ross William Miller. Born in 1955.

G309—Mildred Ethelyn Quivey. Daughter of Linton Quivey and Clara Arabell Trimble (Ninth generation of William and Mary Trimble.) Born on July 1, 1902 in Green Township, Marshall County, Indiana and died on February 22, 1972 in Argos, Marshall County, Indiana. Married Leonard John Gibbons on February 1, 1922. Leonard was born on November 29, 1900 in Fulton, Indiana and died on July 10, 1987.

The children of Leonard John Gibbons and Mildred Ethelyn Quivey:

+ **G340—Harold "Gibby" Cecil Gibbons.** Born on February 4, 1923 in Indiana and died on December 7, 2008 in Rochester, Indiana. Married Marjory Evelen Waltz in 1946. Marjory was born in 1927 and died in 2014.
+ **G341—Katheryn "Katie" Marie Gibbons.** Born in 1924. Married Harold "Hattie" Eugene Hatten in 1944. Harold was born in 1918 and died in 2005.
+ **G342—Roy Chalmers Gibbons.** Born in 1926 and died in 2003. Married Nancy Suzanne Mow in 1948. Nancy was born in 1927.
+ **G343—Robert Linton Gibbons.** Born on November 14, 1926. Married Joyce Ellen Douglass in 1959. Joyce was born in 1937.
+ **G344—Frank Eugene "Gene" Gibbons.** Married Jeanette Sue Horn in 1957. Jeanette was born in 1937.

G313—Sarah Belle Quivey. Daughter of Linton Quivey and Clara Arabell Trimble (Ninth generation of William and Mary Trimble.) Born on April 5, 1912 in Green Township, Marshall County, Indiana and died on May 23, 1987 in Culver, Marshall County, Indiana. Married Maurice Reinhold in 1936 Maurice was born in 1896 and died in 1983.

The children of Maurice Reinhold and Sarah Belle Quivey:

+ **G345—Judith Ann Reinhold.** Born in 1937. Married Herbert Bunch in 1959.

Herbert was born in 1932.

G315—Edna Bernice Quivey. Daughter of Linton Quivey and Clara Arabell Trimble (Ninth generation of William and Mary Trimble.) Born on September 3, 1917 in Green Township, Marshall County, Indiana and died on November 30, 2003 in Indianapolis, Marion County, Indiana. Married Robert Carl Staley on November 23, 1940 in Rochester, Indiana. Robert was born on November 3, 1916 in Walnut Township, Marshall County, Indiana and died on May 14, 1999 in Indianapolis, Marion County, Indiana. Bob was the son of Frank Staley and Ethel Haines. They were married on June 16, 1906. Frank Staley was born on April 21, 1884 and died on June 18, 1941 in Chicago, Illinois. Ethel was born on November 21, 1881 in Argos, Indiana and died on September 9, 1970 in Argos, Indiana.

Edna Graduated from Ball State Normal School in Muncie, Indiana. She was a charter member of Alpha Sigma Alpha Sorority at Ball State. She taught elementary school teacher for 20 years retiring in 1975. She was a member of First United Methodist Church of South Bend, Indiana.

Bob was a World War II veteran. He landed in Liverpool on his birthday, on November 3, 1943. He was assigned to General Eisenhower's headquarters, where he was to serve as a jeep driver. Except for the nightly buzz bombs which flew overhead at 2 am and for one 100-pound bomb that landed in camp but failed to explode, things were calm. Even Ike was calm and talked freely with his men when he had the time. Bob even got invited to the wedding of Ike's aide. Bob's primary responsibility was to drive an orderly down to headquarters twice a day. In his leisure time he discovered the game of golf (but some of the fairways had big divots – where bombs had hit). He was later stationed in Frankfort, Germany.

The children of Robert Carl Staley and Edna Bernice Quivey:

+ **G346—Susan Beth Staley.** Born in 1946 in Plymouth, Indiana. Married John Warren Bloom in 1968. John was born in 1945.

+ **G347—Richard Carl Staley.** Born on March 6, 1943. Married twice.

G340—Harold "Gibby" Cecil Gibbons. Son of Leonard John Gibbons and Mildred Ethelyn Quivey (Tenth generation of William and Mary Trimble.) Born on February 4, 1923 in Indiana and died om December 7, 2008 in Rochester, Indiana. Married Marjory Evelen Waltz in 1946. Marjory was born in 1927 and died in 2014.

The children of Harold "Gibby" Cecil Gibbons and Marjory Evelen Waltz:

+ **G348—Harold Devon Gibbons.** Born in 1953. Married first to Deborah Reed. Married second to Chris Newell.

G349—Donald Linton Gibbons. Born in 1954, Married Walter Howard.

G341—Katheryn "Katie" Marie Gibbons. Daughter of Leonard John Gibbons and Mildred Ethelyn Quivey (Tenth generation of William and Mary Trimble.) Born in 1924. Married Harold "Hattie" Eugene Hatten in 1944. Harold was born in 1918 and died in 2005.

The children of Harold "Hattie" Eugene Hatten and Katheryn "Katie" Marie Gibbons:

G350—Barbara Ruth Hatten. Born in 1945. Married first to James J. MacQuire in 1970. Married Dana Howett in 1983.

+ **G351—Paul Arthur Hatten.** Born in 1949. Married first to Sue Ann Woods in 1970. Married second to Anita Clare Thiel in 1989. Anita was born in 1954.

G342—Roy Chalmers Gibbons. Son of Leonard John Gibbons and Mildred Ethelyn Quivey (Tenth generation of William and Mary Trimble.) Born in 1926 and died 2003. Married Nancy Suzanne Mow in 1948. Nancy was born in 1927.

The children of Roy Chalmers Gibbons and Nancy Suzanne Mow:

+ **G352—David Roy Gibbons.** Born in 1952. Married Rebecca Heiland in 1970.

+ **G353—Charles Michael Gibbons.** Born in 1953. Married Theresa Wilkinson in 1977 Theresa was born in 1958.

+ **G354—Timothy Lee Gibbons.** Born in 1955 and died in 2014. Married first to Bonnie Zehner in 1978. Married second to Caroline ——.

+ **G355—Susan Michele Gibbons.** Born 1959. Married Jeffrey Lee Miller in 1978.

G343—Robert Linton Gibbons. Son of Leonard John Gibbons and Mildred Ethelyn Quivey (Tenth generation of William and Mary Trimble.) Born on November 14, 1926 and died on December 17, 2014. Married Joyce Ellen Douglass in 1959. Joyce was born in 1937.

The children of Robert Linton Gibbons and Joyce Ellen Douglass:

+ **G356—Karen Sue Gibbons.** Born in 1960. Married Darrell Lee Carnean in 1980. Darrell was born 1960.

G357—John Robert Gibbons. Born in 1963. Married first to Cheryl Turner in 1990.

Married second to Susan Marie (Conner) Jones in 1998.

+ **G358—Brenda Kay Gibbons.** Born in 1963. Married first to Patrick Joseph Conner in 1988. Married second to Kevin Dale Case.

Married second to Kevin Dale Case in 2000. Kevin was born in 1962.

+ **G359—Linda Marie Gibbons.** Born in 1965. Married Scott Clayton Riley in 1992. Scott was born in 1965.

G344—Frank Eugene "Gene" Gibbons. Son of Leonard John Gibbons and Mildred Ethelyn Quivey (Tenth generation of William and Mary Trimble.) Married Jeanette Sue Horn in 1957. Jeanette was born in 1937.

The children of Frank Eugene "Gene" Gibbons and Jeanette Sue Horn:

+ **G360—Cindy Arlene Gibbons.** Born in 1960. Married James Robert Lilley in 1957. James was born in 1951.

G361—Charles Eugene Gibbons. Born in 1962. Married Jean Loraine (Greiner) Neureuther in 1966. Jean was born in 1933.

G362—Cathy Annette Gibbons. Born in 1963.

G345—Judith Ann Reinhold. Daughter of Maurice Reinhold and Sarah Belle Quivey. (Tenth generation of William and Mary Trimble.) Born in 1937. Married Herbert Bunch in 1959. Herbert was born in 1932.

The children of Herbert Bunch and Judith Ann Reinhold:

+ **G363—Lisa Ann Bunch.** Born in 1962. Married Terry Charles Richardson in 1983 Terry was born in 1954 and died in 2010. Married David Brening in 2004. David was born in 1953.

+ **G364—Allison Kay Bunch.** Born 1966. Married John David Gray Dixon in 1990. John was born in 1967.

+ **G365—Amy Elizabeth Bunch.** Born in 1971. Married David Lee Maddy in 1996. David was born in 1966.

G346—Susan Beth Staley. Daughter of Robert Carl Staley and Edna Bernice Quivey. (Tenth generation of William and Mary Trimble.) Born in 1946 in Plymouth, Indiana. Married John Warren Bloom in 1968. John was born in 1945.

The children of John Warren Bloom and Susan Beth Staley:

+ **G366—Kristi Ann Bloom.** Born on July 21, 1972 in West Lafayette, Indiana. Married Travis John Kuntz in 2004. Travis was born in1973.

+ **G367—Lori Beth Bloom.** Born on October 24, 1976 in Ames, Iowa. Married Christopher Ryan Wolf in 2002. Christopher was born in 1975.

G347—Richard Carl Staley. Son of Robert Carl Staley and Edna Bernice

Quivey. (Tenth generation of William and Mary Trimble.) Born on March 6, 1943. He graduated from South Bend College of Commerce. He served 5 years in the Navy and served in Vietnam. With his accounting background he served as payroll clerk. He married first to Frances Jo Varro in 1965 in South Bend, Indiana. He retired from the Central Intelligence Agency. Richard impersonates Santa Claus at Christmas.

Married second to Elaine M. Dobbins in 1985. Elaine was born in 1961. She lived in Baltimore, Maryland area. Elaine was a student of forestry at Wake Community College before graduating from Campbell University with a degree in entomology.

The children of Richard Carl Staley and Frances Jo Varro:

+ **G368—Sheila Staley.** Born in 1968. Married first to Dwayne Larue in 1988. Married second to Clint Dewispelaere in 1999. Married third to Gerald McLane.

G348—Harold Devon Gibbons. Son of Harold "Gibby" Cecil Gibbons and Marjory Evelen Waltz (Eleventh generation of William and Mary Trimble.) Born in 1953. Married first to Deborah Reed. Married second to Chris Newell.

The children of Harold Devon Gibbons and Deborah Reed:

G369—Austin James Gibbons. Born in 1980. Married Ashley.

G351—Paul Arthur Hatten. Son of Harold "Hattie" Eugene Hatten and Katheryn "Katie" Marie Gibbons. (Eleventh generation of William and Mary Trimble.) Born in 1949. Married first to Sue Ann Woods in 1970. Married second to Anita Clare Thiel in 1989. Anita was born in 1954.

The children of Paul Arthur Hatten and Sue Ann Woods:

G370—Chad David Hatten. Born in 1973. Married Rachel —— in 2003.
G371—Cara Elizabeth Hatten. Born in 1977.

The children of Paul Arthur Hatten and Anita Clare Thiel:

G372—Emma Katheryn Hatten. Born in 1991.

G352—David Roy Gibbons. Son of Roy Chalmers Gibbons and Nancy Suzanne Mow. (Eleventh generation of William and Mary Trimble.) Born in 1952. Married Rebecca Heiland in 1970.

The children of David Roy Gibbons and Rebecca Heiland:

+ **G373—Corey James Gibbons.** Born in 1972. Married Brenda.
+ **G374—Jessica Lee Gibbons.** Born in 1977. Married wife's name is unknown.
+ **G375—Jason David Gibbons.** Born in 1979. Married Nina Browning.

Trimble Families of America

G353—Charles Michael Gibbons. Son of Roy Chalmers Gibbons and Nancy Suzanne Mow. (Eleventh generation of William and Mary Trimble.) Born in 1953. Married Theresa Wilkinson in 1977 Theresa was born in 1958.

The children of Charles Michael Gibbons and Theresa Wilkinson:
G376—Heather Nichole Gibbons. Born in 1984.
G377—Charles Michael Gibbons. Born in 1987.

G354—Timothy Lee Gibbons. Son of Roy Chalmers Gibbons and Nancy Suzanne Mow. (Eleventh generation of William and Mary Trimble.) Born in 1955 and died in 2014. Married Bonnie Zehner in 1978. Married second to Caroline ———.

The children of Timothy Lee Gibbons and Bonnie Zehner:
G378—Candy Suzanne Gibbons. Born in 1979. Married Vincent Geiger.
+ **G379—Crystal Lynn Gibbons**. Born in 1980. Married Jason Jersey.

G355—Susan Michele Gibbons. Daughter of Roy Chalmers Gibbons and Nancy Suzanne Mow. (Eleventh generation of William and Mary Trimble.) Born in 1959. Married Jeffrey Lee Miller in 1978.

The children of Jeffrey Lee Miller and Susan Michele Gibbons:
G380—Bryn Miller. Born in 1981.
G381—Aspen Shae Miller. Born in1983.

G356—Karen Sue Gibbons. Daughter of Robert Linton Gibbons and Joyce Ellen Douglass. (Eleventh generation of William and Mary Trimble.) Born in 1960. Married Darrell Lee Carmean in 1980. Darrell was born in 1960.

The children of Darrell Lee Carmean and Karen Sue Gibbons:
G382—Erick Ryan Carmean.
G383—Gary Robert Carmean. Born in 1984.
G384—Daral Leann Carmean. Born in 1986.

G358—Brenda Kay Gibbons. Daughter of Robert Linton Gibbons and Joyce Ellen Douglass. (Eleventh generation of William and Mary Trimble.) Born in 1963. Married first to Patrick Joseph Conner in 1988. Married second to Kevin Dale Case.

The children of Patrick Joseph Conner and Brenda Kay Gibbons:
G385—Patrick Isaiah Conner. Born in 1989.
G386—Kathryn June Conner. Born in 1992.

G359—Linda Marie Gibbons. Daughter of Robert Linton Gibbons and Joyce Ellen Douglass. (Eleventh generation of William and Mary Trimble.) Born in 1965. Married Scott Clayton Riley in 1992. Scott was born in 1965.

The children of Scott Clayton Riley and Linda Marie Gibbons:

G387—Suzanne Irene Riley. Born in 1995.

G388—Sean Douglas Riley. Born in 1998.

G389—Patrick James Riley. Born in 2001.

G360—Cindy Arlene Gibbons. Daughter of Frank Eugene "Gene" Gibbons and Jeanette Sue Horn. (Eleventh generation of William and Mary Trimble.) Born in 1960. Married James Robert Lilley in 1957. James was born in 1951.

The children of James Robert Lilley and Cindy Arlene Gibbons:

G390—Chelsea Yvonne Lilley. Born in 1982. Married Jason Hagin.

G391—Patrick Marshall Lilley. Born in 1987.

G363—Lisa Ann Bunch. Daughter of Herbert Bunch and Judith Ann Reinhold. (Eleventh generation of William and Mary Trimble.) Born in 1962. Married Terry Charles Richardson in 1983 Terry was born in 1954 and died in 2010. Married David Brening in 2004. David was born in 1953.

The children of Terry Charles Richardson and Lisa Ann Bunch:

G392—Megan Elise Richardson. Born in 1992.

G393—Timothy Charles Richardson. Born in 1995. Married Jessica Katelyn Rushing in 2014.

G364—Allison Kay Bunch. Daughter of Herbert Bunch and Judith Ann Reinhold. (Eleventh generation of William and Mary Trimble.) Born in 1966. Married John David Gray Dixon in 1990. John was born in 1967.

The children of John David Dixon and Allison Kay Bunch:

G394—Matthew Thomas Dixon. Born in 1995.

G395—Alexander Mitchell Dixon. Born in 1999.

G365—Amy Elizabeth Bunch. Daughter of Herbert Bunch and Judith Ann Reinhold. (Eleventh generation of William and Mary Trimble.) Born in 1971. Married David Lee Maddy in 1996. David was born in 1966.

The children of David Lee Maddy and Amy Elizabeth Bunch.

G396—Sarah Elizabeth Maddy. Born in 2000.

G397—Samuel David Maddy. Born in 2003.

G366—Kristi Ann Bloom. Daughter of John Warren Bloom and Susan Beth Staley. (Eleventh generation of William and Mary Trimble.) Born on July 21, 1972 in West Lafayette, Indiana. Married Travis John Kuntz in 2004. Travis was born in 1973. She has a degree in Psychology from the University of

Arizona in Tucson and a master's degree from Northern Arizona University in Flagstaff. She is an associate provost at the University of Illinois.

The children of Travis John Kuntz and Kristi Ann Bloom:

G398—Connor John Kuntz. Born in 2006.

G399—Logan Owen Kuntz. Born in 2009.

G367—Lori Beth Bloom. Daughter of John Warren Bloom and Susan Beth Staley. (Eleventh generation of William and Mary Trimble.) Born on October 24, 1976 in Ames, Iowa. Married Christopher Ryan Wolf in August 2002. Christopher was born on May 3, 1975 in South Bend, Indiana. He is the son of Carl Alois Wolf and Barbara Jean Stiffler.

Lori received a Degree in History from Butler University in May 1999. She is working for the Championships Division of the National Collegiate Athletic Association in Indianapolis, Indiana.

Christopher received a dual major degree in Electrical Engineering and IT from Purdue University in Lafayette, Indiana.

The children of Christopher Ryan Wolf and Lori Beth Bloom:

G400—Audrey Elizabeth Wolf. Born on June 1, 2005 in Indianapolis, Indiana.

G401—Ryan Benjamin Wolf. (triplet) Born on May 22, 2009 in Indianapolis, Indiana.

G402—Jenna Christine Wolf. (triplet) Born on May 22, 2009 in Indianapolis, Indiana.

G403—Claire Lauren Wolf. (triplet) Born on May 22, 2009 in Indianapolis, Indiana.

G368—Sheila Staley. Daughter of Richard Carl Staley and Frances Jo Varro. (Eleventh generation of William and Mary Trimble.) Born in 1968.

Married first to Dwayne Larue in 1988. Married second to Clint Dewispelaere in 1999. Married third to Gerald McLane.

The children of Clint Dewispelaere and Sheila Staley:

G404—Zachary Alan Dewispelaere. Born in 2000.

G405—Riley Ann Dewispelaere. Born in 2003.

G373—Corey James Gibbons. Son of David Roy Gibbons and Rebecca Heiland (Twelfth generation of William and Mary Trimble.) Born in 1972. Married Brenda.

The child of Corey James and Brenda Gibbons:

G406—Brenna Michelle Gibbons. Born in 2000.

G374—Jessica Lee Gibbons. Daughter of David Roy Gibbons and Rebecca

Heiland (Twelfth generation of William and Mary Trimble.) Born in 1977. Married husband's name is unknown.

The children of Jessica Lee Gibbons:
G407—Rebecca Suzanne. Born in 1992.
G408—Brayton Allen Meyers. Born in 2000.

G375—Jason David Gibbons. Son of David Roy Gibbons and Rebecca Heiland (Twelfth generation of William and Mary Trimble.) Born in 1979. Married Nina Browning.

The children of Jason David Gibbons and Nina Browning:
G409—Nichole Leann Gibbons. Born in 1998.
G410—Narissa Ann Gibbons. Born in 2000.

G379—Crystal Lynn Gibbons. Daughter of Timothy Lee Gibbons and Bonnie Zehner (Twelfth generation of William and Mary Trimble.) Born in 1980. Married Jason Jersey.

The children of Jason Jersey and Crystal Lynn Gibbons:
G411—Gabrielle Lawren Gibbons. Born in 1999.

H - "North Mountain" John Trimble

H1—John Trimble referred to as the "North Mountain" John, settled in the North Mountain area, a few miles west of Staunton, Virginia, in Augusta County in 1733. He was probably a brother of James "The Plantationer" and Walter, Married Rosanna. He was also probably a first cousin of the Five Trimble Brothers as two of them, John and David, settled near "North Mountain" John.

Part of the land owned by "North Mountain" John, near Staunton in the mid-1700s, is still today farmed by a Trimble descendant. This is the longest period the compiler has ever known of a parcel of land remaining in one family. John died in 1790. His wife was Ann whom he married in Ireland.

The children of John and Ann Trimble:

H2—Margaret Trimble. Born prior to 1740 and married a Mr. McClenackan.

H3—Mary Trimble. Born prior to 1740 and married a Mr. Philson.

H4—Jean Trimble. Baptized on October 20, 1741, by Reverend John Craig of Augusta County, Virginia.

+ **H5—John Trimble, Jr.** He was baptized on March 9, 1744.

H6—James Trimble. Born on June 1, 1746 and died on October 10, 1774. He died in the Battle of Point Pleasant. This was the major action of Dunmore's War. The only war declared by a state, Virginia, against Shawnee and Mingo tribes.

H7—Walter Trimble. Married but had no children.

+ **H8—Robert Trimble.**

H9—Joseph Trimble. Died young sometime prior to 1789. Married Jean Finley in Virginia. They had one son, John Trimble, who was an orphan. This child is mentioned in his grandfather John Trimble's will.

H10—Elizabeth Trimble. Married James Elliot in 1771. We know nothing more of Elizabeth's family except that David Trimble, one of the Five Trimble Brothers, mentions children in his will.

H5—John Trimble, Jr. Son of John and Ann Trimble. He was baptized on March 9, 1744, and died on April 22, 1824, on his plantation near Swoope, Augusta County, Virginia. He is buried in Glebe Burial Grounds near Swoope.

The children of John Trimble, Jr.:

H11—William Trimble.

H12—Elijah Trimble.

461

H13—Joseph Trimble.

+ **H14—James Trimble.** Born in 1783 and married Eliza S. ——.

H15—Polly Trimble. Married William Young of Augusta County, Virginia, on November 14, 1809.

H16—Peggy Trimble. Married Thomas P. Smith in Augusta County, Virginia, on January 4, 1808.

H8—Robert Trimble. Son of John and Ann Trimble. He lived on a plantation in Augusta County, Virginia, adjoining his father's land. His will was written on October 29, 1789. We do not know who Robert married.

Robert Trimble had a son:

+ **H17—James B. Trimble.** Born in 1785. Married Margaret Peggy Wilson.

H14—James Trimble. Son of John Trimble, Jr. (Third generation of John and Ann Trimble.) Born in 1783 and married Eliza S.

The children of James Trimble and Eliza S. ——:

H18—Susan J. Trimble. Born in 1830.

H19—John D. Trimble. Born in 1833.

H20—Elizabeth M. Trimble. Born in 1835.

H21—James W. Trimble. Born in 1837.

H22—Joseph M. Trimble. Born in 1841.

H23—George W. Trimble. Born in 1846.

H17—James B. Trimble. Son of Robert Trimble. (Third generation of John and Ann Trimble.) Born in 1785 in Virginia and died in April 1862. Married Margaret Peggy Wilson in 1805 in Augusta County, Virginia. From a humble beginning through strength and perseverance he had accumulated a vast estate.

The children of James B. Trimble and Margaret Peggy Wilson:

H24—Mary Trimble. Married Ephraim Greeding.

+ **H25—John W. Trimble.** Born in 1808 and married Philicies ——.

+ **H26—William W. Trimble.** Born on December 26, 1810. He married two times: first, to Jane McDowell, and second, to Lizzie A. Gilkeson.

H27—Rebecca Trimble. Born in 1812 and married James Gilkeson.

H28—Jane Trimble. Married David McCutcheon.

H29—Elizabeth Trimble. Born in 1815 and married Peter Shickel.

H30—Margaret Trimble. Married Christian Bear.

+ **H31—Joseph B. Trimble.** Born in 1819 and died in 1909. Married Rachel A. Crawford.

H32–Nathaniel C. Trimble. Born in 1826.

+ **H33–James W. Trimble.** Born in 1817. Married Isabella ———.

H25–John W. Trimble. Son of James B. Trimble and Margaret Peggy Wilson. (Fourth generation of John and Ann Trimble.) Born in 1808 and married Philicies ———.

The children of John and Philicies Trimble:

H34–George B. Trimble. Born in 1829 in Virginia. Married Mary ——— and they lived in S. Fork Township, Monroe County, Missouri, in 1860. They lived on the same farm as George's uncle, James W. Trimble.

H35–Mary M. Trimble. Born in 1832. She was still living with her father in 1860.

H26–William W. Trimble. Son of James B. Trimble and Margaret Peggy Wilson. (Fourth generation of John and Ann Trimble.) Born on December 26, 1810. He was living in Callaway County, Missouri, in 1880. William W. attended Washington and Lee University and graduated in 1840 as valedictorian of his class. He then entered Princeton University and became a presbyterian minister. He married two times: first, to Jane McDowell, and second, to Lizzie A. Gilkeson.

The children of William W. Trimble and Jane McDowell:

H36–Mary V. Trimble. No further record.

H37–John McDowell Trimble.

The children of William W. Trimble and Lizzie A. Gilkeson:

H38–Mary Virginia Trimble. Married William Sterrett Trimble (H47).

H39–William Stuart Trimble.

H40–James Gilkeson Trimble.

H31–Joseph B. Trimble. Son of James B. Trimble and Margaret Peggy Wilson. (Fourth generation of John and Ann Trimble.) Born in 1819 at Augusta County, Virginia, and died in 1909. Married Rachel A. Crawford. Joseph B. was a farmer and miller.

The children of Joseph B. Trimble and Rachel A. Crawford:

H41–Alice Trimble. Born in 1847.

H42–Crawford McChesney Trimble. Born in 1849.

H43–Nannie W. Trimble. Born in 1851.

H44–James B. Trimble. Born in 1853.

H45–William Trimble. Born in 1855.

+ **H46–John E. Trimble.** Born in 1859. Married Fannie Thompson.

Trimble Families of America

H33—James W. Trimble. Son of James B. Trimble and Margaret Peggy Wilson. (Fourth generation of John and Ann Trimble.) Born in 1817 in Virginia and died in Monroe County, Missouri. He married Isabella ———. They migrated to Monroe County in the 1850's.

The children of James W. and Isabella Trimble:

+ **H47—William Sterrett Trimble.** Born in 1847 in Virginia. Married Mary Virginia Trimble (H38).

H48—Mary Trimble. Born in 1850 in Virginia.

H49—George S. Trimble. Born in 1853 in Virginia.

H50—John Trimble. Born in 1856.

H51—Joseph Trimble. Born in 1858 in Missouri.

H46—John E. Trimble. Son of Joseph B. Trimble and Rachel A. Crawford. (Fifth generation of John and Ann Trimble.) Born on March 12, 1859, in Virginia and died on February 14, 1941, in Augusta County, Virginia. He married Fannie Thompson.

The three sons of John E. Trimble and Fannie Thompson:

+ **H52—William Wallace Trimble.** Born on March 20, 1888. Married two times: first, to Sally Wayland, and second, to Genevieve Barksdale.

+ **H53—Joseph Marshall Trimble.** Married Nancy Crawford

H54—James Edwin Trimble. Born in 1896 and died in 1968. He never married.

H47—William Sterrett Trimble. Son of James W. and Isabella Trimble. (Fifth generation of John and Ann Trimble.) Born in 1847 in Virginia. Married Mary Virginia Trimble (H38). She was his cousin, the daughter of William W. Trimble (H26).

The child of William Sterrett Trimble and Mary Virginia Trimble:

+ **H55—Dr. Harry Evans Trimble.** Born on October 21, 1888. He married Agnes Malley.

H52—William Wallace Trimble. Son of John E. Trimble and Fannie Thompson. (Sixth generation of John and Ann Trimble.) Born on March 20, 1888, in Augusta County, Virginia. He died on April 14, 1965, in Augusta County. William W. married two times: first, to Sally Wayland, and second, to Genevieve Barksdale. He continued the operation of the family farm located about nine miles west of Staunton, Virginia. This was called Trimble's Mill Farm.

The children of William Wallace Trimble and Sally Wayland:

H56—Walter Haynes Trimble. Married Elizabeth Bare and they have two adopted children. He lives on Trimble's Mill Farm with his family.

Trimble Families of America

The children of William Wallace and Genevieve Barksdale Trimble:

H57—William Wallace Trimble, Jr. Born on April 19, 1923. Married Gallic Anthony and they have two sons.

H58—Giles Trimble. Born on April 19, 1923. Married Lucille Areheart. Giles is an engineer.

H53—Joseph Marshall Trimble. Son of John E. Trimble and Fannie Thompson. (Sixth generation of John and Ann Trimble.) He lived for a while as a farmer in Greene County, Alabama, from 1919 to 1926. Then moved to Hot Springs, Virginia, where he was employed as manager of the farms and dairy owned by the Homestead Hotel Company.

The children of Joseph Marshall Trimble and Nancy Crawford:

+ **H59—Elizabeth Trimble.** Born in 1917 and married Hubert Parrer.

+ **H60—John Marshall Trimble.** Born in 1922 and married Mary Sue Lowman.

+ **H61—Ellen Thompson Trimble.** Born in 1924 (twin) and married Robert E. Morton.

+ **H62—Robert Finley Trimble.** Born in 1924 (twin) and married Sara Concklin.

H55—Dr. Harry Evans Trimble. Son of William Sterrett Trimble and Mary Virginia Trimble. (Sixth generation of John and Ann Trimble.) Born on October 21, 1888. He married Agnes Malley on December 18, 1919. Dr. Trimble was a prominent government medical officer and is listed in *Who's Who in America.* He did extensive research on his Trimble family lineage.

The children of Dr. Harry Evans Trimble and Agnes Malley:

H63—William M. Trimble.

H64—Mary Ellen Trimble.

H65—John McD. Trimble.

H59—Elizabeth Trimble. Daughter of Joseph Marshall Trimble and Nancy Crawford. (Seventh generation of John and Ann Trimble.) Born in 1917 and married Hubert Parrer.

The children of Hubert Parrer and Elizabeth Trimble:

H66—Nancy Ellen Parrer.

H67—Harriet Parrer.

H60—John Marshall Trimble. Son of Joseph Marshall Trimble and Nancy Crawford. (Seventh generation of John and Ann Trimble.) Born in 1922 and married Mary Sue Lowman.

The children of John Marshall Trimble and Mary Sue Lowman:

H68—James Trimble.

H69—Marsha Trimble.

H70—Miller Trimble.

H61—Ellen Thompson Trimble. Daughter of Joseph Marshall Trimble and Nancy Crawford. (Seventh generation of John and Ann Trimble.) Born in 1924 (twin) and married Robert E. Morton.

The children of Robert E. Morton and Ellen Thompson Trimble:

H71—Robert Morton.

H72—Geri Morton.

H73—David Morton.

H62—Robert Finley Trimble. Son of Joseph Marshall Trimble and Nancy Crawford. (Seventh generation of John and Ann Trimble.) Born in 1924 (twin) and married Sara Concklin. They have two children. (We are deeply and gratefully indebted to Robert Finley for the data on his line of the Trimble family.) Brigadier General Robert F. Trimble was born in Boligee, Alabama on July 26, 1924. Robert entered the United States Military Academy at West Point, New York, in July 1942 and graduated in June 1945, with a B.S. degree and a commission in the Air Corps of the U.S. Army. Later during the years of 1949-51, he attended the University of Michigan and obtained an M.A. in business administration. As a pilot, Robert initially trained in B-25 and B-17 aircraft. However, changes in requirements resulted in his flying RF-51 and RB-26 photo reconnaissance aircraft in Europe, special air mission VC-47 aircraft in the States, and F-48 fighter Bomber aircraft in Korea. After rising to the level of "Command Pilot," his assignment to procurement duties resulted in the discontinuance of his regular flying duties.

He was appointed director of Procurement Policy of Headquarters, U.S. Air Force, and in December 1970 he was selected for promotion to the rank of brigadier general with promotion to become effective August 1971.

The children of Robert Finley Trimble and Sara Concklin:

H74—Sara Jean Trimble.

H75—Robert Lewis Trimble.

We wish to give Eugene E. Trimble credit for his extensive work on the Trimble families in Pre-Revolution Immigrant Section from which record we quote almost verbatim, and in some instances, we have been able to extend a few families. Also, the Kelly Trimble Papers, contained in the University of Virginia Library, have been a source of informative help in compiling Staunton, Virginia, Trimbles.

In Michael Woods Trimble's memoirs, now contained in the Library of Congress, he states that his grandfather was John Trimble, and his father was John Trimble. Eugene E. Trimble says Michael Woods Trimble was the son of John and grandson of Walter. After reading and re-reading Michael Woods Trimble's material and finding it to be beautifully written and documented, it is my assumption he knew his grandfather was John. This, as previously stated, contradicts the Eugene E. Trimble theory.

If Michael Woods Trimble's memoirs be correct, the John Trimble (H5) would not be the son of John, because the father of Michael Woods Trimble died in Tennessee. The John Trimble, Jr., (H5) would therefore be the son of David Trimble, one of the Five Trimble Brothers, of which the compiler has been unable to find any record of in our research, except that he signed the deeds with his father David when David was moving to Kentucky.

However, we shall, in our book, continue with the Eugene E. Trimble account of the John lineage. We added these closing paragraphs of these two opposing views if some interested genealogist in the future might desire to make a more extensive research and challenge both versions in hope of finding documented proof of the correct one.

I - Walter and Rosanna Trimble

I1—Walter Trimble Born in 1701 in either Scotland or Armagh County, Ireland and migrated from Ireland in the 1730's to America. Married Rosanna. She was born in 1701 in Washington County, Virginia and died on February 28, 1801 in Green County, Tennessee. Upon moving to Virginia, he bought land in the North Mountain area which he later sold to his son Robert when he moved to South Carolina. Walter lived but a short time in South Carolina when he moved to east Tennessee. He died in 1791 in Washington County, Tennessee.

Walter, John, and James "The Plantationer" were in all probability brothers. His descendants mostly migrated westward, as his brother James's descendants settled in Georgia. Walter's sons served in the Revolutionary War.

The children of Walter and Rosanna Trimble:

+ **I2—Robert Trimble.** Born in 1739 in Augusta County, Virginia and died 1815 in Arkansas. Married Hannah Moffitt in 1764 in Augusta County, Virginia.

I3—Margaret Trimble. Born on August 27, 1740 and died on September 13, 1801. She married Michael Woods and lived in Washington County, Tennessee.

+ **I4—John Trimble.** Married Susanna Woods.

I5—William Trimble. He was baptized on April 30, 1747.

I2—Robert Trimble. Son of Walter and Rosanna Trimble. Born in 1739 in Augusta County, Virginia and died in 1815 in Arkansas. He was living in Russell County, Virginia, in 1771 and was a captain in the American Revolution. Robert married Hannah Moffitt in 1764 in Augusta County, Virginia, a stepdaughter of John of the Five Trimble Brothers. Hannah was born in 1742 in Augusta County, Virginia. He migrated to Kentucky in the company of settlers around in 1784 led by James Trimble, son of John. After game became scarce in Bourbon County, Kentucky, Robert migrated to the new lands of western Kentucky, for he was a great hunter and Native American fighter.

The children of Robert Trimble and Hannah Moffitt:

I6—Joseph Trimble. Born in 1772.

+ **I7—James Trimble.** Born in 1774 in August County, Virginia and died April 6, 1820 in Batesville, Arkansas. Married Elizabeth Stewart.

I8—George Trimble. Born in 1776.

I9—William Trimble. The only record of William that we have is from the autobiography of Governor Allen Trimble, Ohio. William was accused of being an accessory to his younger brother Robert Trimble, Jr., in the shooting of a sheriff. (See Robert Trimble, Jr., No. I10.) From this incident William served a term in prison.

I10—Robert Trimble, Jr. Our record of Robert Trimble, Jr., comes from "the autobiography of Governor Allen Trimble of Ohio". Robert, when a young man, went to the territory of now Texas. He engaged in the enterprise of catching wild horses, taming them, driving them into Kentucky and selling them below market value. This venture was quite a topic of conversation within the county, now Livingston" County. The sheriff made the remark he thought Robert had stolen these horses. Upon hearing of this statement Robert, Jr., said he would see the sheriff and he would either apologize or "I'll kill him." The following day Robert armed himself with a brace of pistols. William, his brother, followed trying to dissuade Robert, but to no avail. They rode within ten feet of the sheriff's door. He came to his door with a rifle taking aim at Robert Trimble, but Robert shot the sheriff through the heart, and he died. This occurrence created great excitement throughout the county. The sheriff had been respectfully connected with and supposedly a relative of Isaac Shelby, then governor of Kentucky. Robert made his escape although a reward of $500 was offered by Governor Shelby. William Trimble was tried as an accessory and sentenced to prison. Robert Trimble, in his escape to Texas, changed his name and fought under Andrew Jackson against the British in the War of 1812.

I11—John Trimble. Born in 1765 in Augusta County, Virginia and died in 1830 in Izard, Arkansas.

I4—John Trimble. Son of Walter and Rosanna Trimble. He was baptized in 1774 by the Reverend Mr. Craig in Augusta County, Virginia. John died in Jefferson County, Mississippi, in 1822. On February 18, 1768, he married Susanna Woods.

The children of John Trimble and Susanna Woods:

+I12—Archibald Trimble. Born on December 19, 1768. Archibald married three times. Married first to Mary Glass. Married second to Nancy Shines. Married third to Margaret H. Reese.

I13—Robert Trimble. Married Mary Gibson in 1800 and they lived in Mississippi.

I14—John Trimble.

I15—Walter Trimble.

I16—Rosanna Trimble. Married Thomas Richie.

I17—Isabell Trimble. Married Archibald Lackey.

I18—Mary Trimble. Married William Lackey.

+**I19—Michael Woods Trimble.** Born on January 13, 1788 and died after 1860. He married Catherine Sharp.

I7—James Trimble. Son of Robert Trimble and Hannah Moffitt. (Third generation of Walter and Rosanna Trimble.) Born in 1774 in August County, Virginia and died 1841 in Batesville, Arkansas. Moved to Kentucky and then to Arkansas. He married Elizabeth Wallace Stewart in 1806 in Clinton, Van Buren County, Arkansas. She was born in 1789 in Culpepper, Virginia and died in 1836 in Batesville, Arkansas. James was a surveyor and was prominent in both Kentucky and Arkansas in his profession.

The children of James Trimble and Elizabeth Stewart:

+**I20—Walker Wallace Trimble.** Born on March 22, 1808 in Livingston County, Kentucky and died on October 9, 1840 in Van Buren Co, Arkansas. Married Elizabeth Ann Garner on April 21, 1836.

+**I21—Moffett Edrington Trimble.** Born on April 25, 1809 in Livingston County, Kentucky and died in 1855 in Independence County, Arkansas. Married Mary Evelyn Garner.

I22—Harriet Trimble. Born on December 4, 1812 in Livingston County, Kentucky and died on January 1, 1894 in McHue, Independence County, Arkansas. Married Thomas S. Carter on May 23, 1833 in Independence Co, Arkansas.

+**I23—Jackson Stewart Trimble.** Born on March 28, 1815 in Livingston County, Kentucky and died on January 1, 1897 in Sulphur Rock, Independence County, Arkansas. Married Catherine P. Hamilton.

I24—Milton Trimble. Born in 1816 in Kentucky and died 1859. He married Mary ——.

I25—John Wesley Trimble. Born about 1819 in Kentucky and died December 1849 in Independence County, Arkansas.

I26—Mary Ann Trimble. Born about 1821 in Kentucky and died in 1858 in Independence County, Arkansas.

I27—Harvey Stewart Trimble. Born about 1823 in Kentucky and died in April 1848 in Victoria, Victoria County, Texas

+**I28—James Trimble.** Born in March 1827 in Arkansas and died Caldwell County, Texas. He married Sarah Margaret Wood on October 4, 1848.

I29—Lucinda Elizabeth Trimble. Born about 1828 and died 1853.

I12—Archibald Trimble. Son of John Trimble and Susanna Woods. (Third generation of Walter and Rosanna Trimble.) Born on December 19, 1768, and died on August 16, 1826, at Mooresville, Alabama. Archibald married three times: first, to Mary Glass; second, to Nancy Shines; and third, to Margaret H. Reese.

The children of Archibald Trimble and Mary Glass:

I30—**Robert C. Trimble.** Died in Fairview, Texas, about 1880.

The children of Archibald Trimble and Nancy Shines:

+ I31—**James Harvey Trimble.** Born on August 3, 1808. Married two times: first, to Sarah Ann Pope, second, to Ann Stratton Harris.

I32—**Joseph A. Trimble.** He was a physician in Russellville, Alabama.

I33—**Elizabeth Trimble.** She married Thomas S. Jones of Russellville, Alabama.

The child of Archibald Trimble and Margaret H. Reese:

+ I34—**Green W. Trimble.** Born on May 22, 1822. Married two times: First, to Ella Barksdale, second to Rebecca Thomas.

I19—**Michael Woods Trimble.** Son of John Trimble and Susanna Woods. (Third generation of Walter and Rosanna Trimble.) Born on January 13, 1788, on the headwaters of French River in east Tennessee and died after 1860 in Jefferson County, Mississippi. In 1832 he married Catherine Sharp of Adams County. Michael and John Trimble, his father, were members of the Mechlenburg Convention.

The children of Michael Woods Trimble and Catherine Sharp:

I35—**John Pickens Trimble.** (Twin.) Born on December 3, 1834 and died in 1862.

I36—**William Albert Trimble.** (Twin.) Born on December 3, 1834 and died on March 11, 1909.

I37—**Adderson Trimble.** Died before the Civil War.

I38—**Catherine Amanda Trimble.** Born on November 26, 1836.

I39—**Esther Ann Trimble.** Born on August 12, 1840, in Jefferson County, Mississippi, and died on June 24, 1925, in the same county. She married Albert Rudolph Cordes on June 23, 1870. He was born in Hamburg, Germany, in 1836.

I20—**Walker Wallace Trimble.** Son of James Trimble and Elizabeth Stewart. (Fourth generation of Walter and Rosanna Trimble.) Born on March 22, 1808 in Livingston County, Kentucky and died on October 9, 1840 in Van Buren Co, Arkansas. Married Elizabeth Ann Garner on April 21, 1836 in Clinton, Van Buren County, Arkansas.

The children of Walker Wallace Trimble and Elizabeth Garner:

I40—Sarah Elizabeth Trimble. Born in 1837 in Van Buren County, Arkansas and died August 21, 1837.

I41—James Conway Trimble. Born on December 4, 1838 in Conway, Arkansas and died on May 12, 1912 in Corsicana, Navarro County, Texas.

I21—Moffett Edrington Trimble. Son of James Trimble and Elizabeth Stewart. (Fourth generation of Walter and Rosanna Trimble) Born on April 25, 1809 in Livingston County, Kentucky and died in 1855 in Independence County, Arkansas. Married Mary Evelyn Garner. Mary was born in 1819 in Lincoln, Tennessee and died on April 15, 1978 in Texas.

The children of Moffett Edrington Trimble and Mary Evelyn Garner:

+ I42—Samuel Walker Trimble. Born on August 20, 1838 in San Antonio, Bexar, Texas and died on February 21, 1915 in Del Rio, Texas. Married Harriet Merrit Fannie Spear.

I43—Harriet Trimble. Born in 1846.

I44—Leroy Williams Trimble. Born in 1848 in Washington, Texas and died on March 8, 1926 in Austin, Williamson County, Texas.

I45—Margaret Trimble. Born in June 1850.

I46—Edward J. Trimble. Born on December 22, 1852 in San Antonio, Bexar County, Texas and died on April 23, 1921 in Tampo, Mexico.

I23—Jackson Stewart Trimble. Son of James Trimble and Elizabeth Stewart. (Fourth generation of Walter and Rosanna Trimble) Born on March 28, 1815, in Kentucky and died on January 1, 1897 in Sulpher Rock, Independence County, Arkansas. In 1889 he was living at Sulphur Rock, Arkansas. Jackson served from 1850 to 1864 in the house and senate of the state of Arkansas. He was a Southern sympathizer, a Jeffersonian Democrat. He married Catherine P. Hamilton and they had a daughter. Jackson was active in the fight for education and temperance. He has been described thusly that his life was gentle and the elements so mixed in him that nature might stand up and say to all the world, "This is a Man."

The child of Jackson Stewart Trimble and Catherine P. Hamilton:

I47—Elvira Trimble. She married Joseph Wright.

I28—James Trimble. Son of James Trimble and Elizabeth Stewart. (Fourth generation of Walter and Rosanna Trimble.) Born in March 1827 in Arkansas and died Caldwell County, Texas. He married Sarah Margaret Wood on October 4, 1848. Sarah was born in May 1832 in Arkansas.

The children of James Trimble and Sarah Margaret Wood:

148—Harriet Ann Trimble. Born on September 5, 1849 in Arkansas and died on December 29, 1915 in Caldwell County, Texas.

149—Harvey S. Trimble. Born on September 1850, in Independence County, Texas. Married to Mahala A. Bogard on November 14, 1877 in Caldwell County, Texas.

131—James Harvey Trimble. Son of Archibald Trimble and Nancy Shines. (Fourth generation of Walter and Rosanna Trimble.) Born on August 3, 1808, in Knox County, Tennessee. James Harvey married two times: first, to Sarah Ann Pope on November 18, 1835, in Tuscumbia, Alabama; second, to Ann Stratton Harris, on May 20, 1858, in Franklin County, Alabama.

The children of James Harvey Trimble and Sarah Ann Pope:

150—Laura E. Trimble. Born on November 19, 1836, in Alabama. She died on July 28, 1890, in Clarksdale, Mississippi.

151—Charles Shines Trimble. Born on January 6, 1838, in Tuscumbia, Alabama.

152—Jessie Trimble. Born on August 7, 1841, in Alabama and married Thomas B. Glenn in November 1864.

153—James Harvey Trimble. Born on September 6, 1849.

The children of James Harvey and Ann Stratton Harris Trimble:

154—Sarah Ann Trimble. Born in 1859 in Franklin County, Alabama.

155—John Walter Trimble. Born on May 5, 1863, in Franklin County, Alabama.

134—Green W. Trimble, Dr. Son of Archibald Trimble and Margaret H. Reese. (Fourth generation of Walter and Rosanna Trimble.) Born on May 22, 1822, in Alabama. He was living in Grenada, Mississippi, in 1896. Green W. married two times: First, to Ella Barksdale in 1842 in Alabama. She died in 1846. Second, he married Rebecca Thomas in 1854. Dr. Green Trimble was a prominent medical doctor and president of the State Medical Association of Alabama.

The child of Dr. Green W. Trimble and Ella Barksdale:

156—Joseph H. Trimble. Died in 1875. We have no further information.

The children of Dr. Green W. Trimble and Rebecca Thomas:

157—Mary Trimble. Married Curtis H. Guy.

158—Charles Trimble.

142—Samuel Walker Trimble. Son of Moffett Edrington Trimble and Mary Evelyn Garner (Fifth generation of Walter and Rosanna Trimble.) Born on

Trimble Families of America

August 20, 1838 in San Antonio, Bexar, Texas and died on February 21, 1915 in Del Rio, Texas. Married Harriet Merrit Fannie Spear on December 1, 1875 in Atascosa, Texas. Samuel was a private in Company E Texas Calvary of Confederate States during the Civil War.

The children of Samuel Walker Trimble and Harriet Merrit Fannie Spears:

I59—May Trimble. Born on September 2, 1876 in Pleasanton, Atascosa, Texas and died on July 13, 1928 in Caldwell, Texas.

+ **I60—Wesley Walker Trimble.** Born in 1878 in San Antonio, Bexar County, Texas and died on July 26, 1944 in Lehi, Maricopa County, Arizona. Married Rosa May Edwards on December 26, 1906 in Texas.

I61—Pauline Maggie Trimble. Born in January 1879.

I62—Ira L. Trimble. Born in 1882 in Texas and died on August 19, 1911 in Bexar, Texas.

I63—Adaline Wallace 'Addie' Trimble. Born in December 1883 in Texas and died on November 29, 1940 in Val Verde, Texas.

I64—Dee Trimble. Born in February 1885 in Texas.

I65—Frances Trimble. Born in September 1888 in Texas and died in 1978 and died in Kerrville, Kerr County, Texas

I60—Wesley Walker Trimble. Son of Samuel Walker Trimble and Harriet Fannie Spears. (Sixth generation of Walter and Rosanna Trimble.) Born in 1878 in San Antonio, Bexar County, Texas and died on July 26, 1944 in Lehi, Maricopa County, Arizona. Married Rosa May Edwards on December 26, 1906 in Texas. She was born on May 3, 1883 and died on October 30, 1961 Phoenix, Arizona.

The children of Wesley Walker Trimble and Rosa May Edwards:

+ **I66—Ira Walker Trimble.** Born on October 3, 1908 in San Antonio, Texas and died on February 8, 1979 in Phoenix, Arizona. Married Margaret Juanita Rogers. She was born on February 16, 1918 in Bay City, Arkansas and died on January 12, 1998 in Phoenix, Arizona.

I67—Sadie Trimble. Born in 1910 in Texas.

I68—Jeffie Elizabeth Trimble. Born in 1911 in Bexar County, Texas and died in Bexar County, Texas.

I69—Julia Francis Trimble. Born in 1913 in Bexar County, Texas and died in Bexar County, Texas.

I70—David Oliver Trimble. Born in 1916 in San Antonio, Bexar County, Texas and died in Arizona. Married Virginia Mae "Ginny" Manning. She was born on July 29, 1914 in Oklahoma and died November 24, 2002.

> **171—Garner Trimble.** Born in 1916 in San Antonio, Bexar, Texas and died in 1917 in San Antonio, Bexar, Texas.

> **172—Jack Trimble.** Born on December 13, 1921 in Tempe, Maricopa County, Arizona and died on October 10, 1949 in Tempe, Maricopa County, Arizona.

166—Ira Walker Trimble. Son of Wesley Walker Trimble and Rosa May Edwards. (Seventh generation of Walter and Rosanna Trimble.) Born on October 3, 1908 in San Antonio, Texas and died on February 8, 1979 in Phoenix, Arizona. Married Margaret Juanita Rogers in 1935. She was born on February 16, 1918 in Bay City, Arkansas and died on January 12, 1998 in Phoenix, Arizona.

The children of Ira Walker Trimble and Margaret Juanita Rogers:

173—Died in infancy

174—Charlie Trimble.

175—Marshall Trimble. He is the Official Arizona Historian.

176—Dan Trimble.

J - James 'Plantationer' and Grace Trimble

J1—James Trimble "Plantationer" was born in 1712 in Armagh, Ireland and died in South Carolina in 1767. He married a woman, probably in Ireland, known only as Grace.

In 1742 James purchased 402 acres in the Valley of Virginia on Moffitts Creek. James, in 1754, sold his land and migrated with Grace to South Carolina. Here he settled neighboring Patrick Calhoun, father of John C. Calhoun, the noted Statesman. Most of the Georgia Trimbles are descendants of James and Grace.

The children of James and Grace Trimble:

+**J2—Joseph Trimble.** Born before 1744. Married two times: first, to Elizabeth ——, and second, to Martha Bowles.

+**J3—James Trimble.** Married Esther ——.

+**J4—Moses Trimble.** Born in Virginia about 1754 and died in 1828 in Newton County, Georgia. Married to Catherine Lewis.

+**J5—John Trimble.** Born in 1755. Married Charity Redwine.

J6—Robert Trimble. We find no further record of this Robert.

J2—Joseph Trimble. Son of James and Grace Trimble. Born before 1744 and died in 1808 in Greene County, Georgia. He married two times: first, to Elizabeth Crawford, and second, to Martha Bowles at Petersburg, Georgia.

The children of Joseph Trimble and Elizabeth Crawford:

+**J7—James Trimble.** Born on December 4, 1770. We do not know the name of the first wife; second, he married Margaret Gillispie.

J8—Elizabeth Trimble. She married a Calhoun and moved to Mississippi.

+**J9—John Trimble.** Born in 1773. Married Mary Ann Harris.

+**J10—Moses Trimble.** Born on January 12, 1777. He married two times: first, to Rebecca Harris, and second, to Jane Simons.

J11—Joseph Trimble. Born in South Carolina in 1779 and died in 1857 in Rutherford County, Tennessee. Married Nancy ——. He was a planter and had numerous slaves. In his will he directed that his slaves select their own masters and be sold to these men at two-thirds of their actual value. An old Negro slave woman named Suckey was not to be sold but was to be given a life maintenance from his estate.

J12—Jane Trimble. Married Thomas Coleman in 1805.

+**J13—William Trimble.** Born before 1791. Married Harriet Welborn.

+**J14—Robert Trimble.** Born prior to 1781. Married Ruth Thrasher.

J15—Isaac Trimble. He was killed at age seventeen in a hunting accident.

The children of Joseph Trimble and Martha Bowles:

J16—Charles Trimble. Born after 1799; was living in 1867 in Rutherford County, Tennessee.

J17—Martha Trimble. Born in 1805 and died in 1878.

J3—James Trimble. Son of James and Grace Trimble. He married Esther ———.

The children of James and Esther Trimble:

J18—James Trimble. Died unmarried on March 27, 1797.

J19—Joseph Trimble.

J20—Esther Trimble. Married Robert Smith.

J21—Sarah Trimble. Married a Mr. Shannon and lived in Abbeville County, South Carolina.

J22—John Trimble. Married Jane ———. They had nine children. John's family seems to have adapted the name Turnbull. Several of his children settled in Florida.

J4—Moses Trimble. Son of James and Grace Trimble. Born in Virginia about 1754. Moses moved with his father James to South Carolina and later settled in Wilkes County, Georgia. He died in 1828 in Newton County, Georgia. Married about 1788 to Catherine Lewis. Moses served in the American Revolution as a Lieutenant from which service he received several grants of land in Georgia.

The children of Moses Trimble and Catherine Lewis:

+J23—James L. Trimble. Born on December 18, 1789. Married Martha Bishop.

+J24—John Haddon Trimble. Born about 1792. Married Elizabeth Evans.

+J25—Philip Lewis Trimble. Born in 1794.

J26—Sarah Trimble. Born in 1796.

J27—Esther Trimble. Born in 1799.

+J28—Moses Trimble. Born in 1801. Married Mary Lovvorn.

+J29—Elisha Trimble. Born in 1803. Married Elizabeth Johnson.

J5—John Trimble. Son of James and Grace Trimble. Born in 1755 and died about 1835. He was a Revolutionary War soldier of South Carolina and Georgia. Married Charity Redwine and his family lived in Wilkes County, Georgia.

The children of John Trimble and Charity Redwine:

+J30—James Trimble. Married two times.

J - James and Grace Trimble

J31—Moses Trimble.

+**J32—Joseph Trimble.** Born in 1778. Married Nancy ——.

J33—William Trimble.

J34—Nancy Trimble. Married in 1828 to Jacob Redwine.

J35—Lucy Trimble. Married December 3, 1818, to Samuel Sewell.

J36—Arminda Trimble. Married on January 25, 1829, to William Hathcock.

J37—Elizabeth Trimble. Married on January 28, 1817, to John W. Lowrey.

J7—James Trimble. Son of Joseph Trimble and Elizabeth Crawford. (Third generation of James and Grace Trimble.) Born on December 4, 1770, in South Carolina. He died on February 22, 1812, in Livingston County, Kentucky. James married two times. We do not know the name of the first wife; second, he married Margaret Gillispie in 1802.

The children of James Trimble and his first wife:

J38—Elizabeth Trimble.

J39—Jane Trimble. Born in 1799.

The children of James Trimble and Margaret Gillispie:

J40—Catherine C. Trimble. Born on October 3, 1803 and died on March 12, 1850.

J41—Matthew Trimble. Born on August 15, 1805 and died in infancy.

J42—Fanny Trimble. Born on October 3, 1807 and died in childhood.

J43—Joseph Trimble. Born on August 11, 1809 and died in infancy.

+**J44—Isaac Trimble.** Born on December 4, 1810. Married three times.

J9—John Trimble. Son of Joseph Trimble and Elizabeth Crawford. (Third generation of James and Grace Trimble.) Born in 1773 and died on April 18, 1850, in Troup County, Georgia. Married Mary Ann Harris.

The children of John Trimble and Mary Ann Harris:

+**J45—Joseph Trimble.** Born in Morgan County, Georgia, in 1810 and died in 1864 in Troup County, Georgia. Married in 1835 to Sarah Horton.

J46—Winnie Trimble.

+**J47—Moses Trimble.** Born in 1817 and died in 1895. Married two times.

J48—Rebecca Trimble. Married John Black.

J49—Caroline Trimble. Died in Chambers County, Alabama; she married David Moon.

J50—Sarah Trimble. Married two times: first, to Barnie Pace, and second, to a Mr. House and they lived in Texas.

J10—Moses Trimble. Son of Joseph Trimble and Elizabeth Crawford. (Third generation of James and Grace Trimble.) Born in 1771 or 1780 in South Carolina. He died on August 14, 1843 in Tallapoosa County, Alabama. Born on January 12, 1777 in Abbeville, South Carolina and died on March 12, 1855 in Dadeville, Tallapoosa, Alabama. He married two times: first, to Rebecca Harris, and second, to Jane Simons. In 1840 Moses was listed in that census as owning thirteen slaves.

The children of Moses Trimble and Rebecca Harris:

+**J51—James Trimble.** Born on October 29, 1805. Married Clarissa Bigelow.

J52—William Trimble. He was a merchant in Wetumpka, Alabama. He died leaving no family.

+**J53—Benjamin Trimble.** Born about 1810. Married two times.

J54—John Trimble. He lived at Wetumpka, Alabama.

J55—Nancy Trimble. Married Noel Pace and moved to Dallas, Texas.

J13—William Trimble. Son of Joseph Trimble and Elizabeth Crawford. (Third generation of James and Grace Trimble.) Born before 1791 and died in 1825. Married Harriet Welborn in 1818. In 1825 William was riding over his plantation directing the work of his slaves when a thunderstorm arose. He sought shelter under a tree which was struck by the lightning thus killing him.

The children of William Trimble and Harriet Welborn:

+**J56—Augustus Crawford Trimble.** Born on December 11, 1818. Married two times.

J57—Melissa Trimble. Married Dr. Elijah George.

J58—Louisa A. Trimble. Married Dr. Elijah George after the death of her sister Melissa.

J14—Robert Trimble. Son of Joseph Trimble and Elizabeth Crawford. (Third generation of James and Grace Trimble.) Born prior to 1781. He was living in Morgan County, Georgia, in 1830. Married Ruth Thrasher.

The children of Robert Trimble and Ruth Thrasher:

J59—John B. Trimble. Born in 1809.

J60—Robert W. Trimble. Born in 1812.

J61—Albert G. Trimble. Born in 1815.

J62—Elizabeth L. Trimble. Born in 1817.

J63—Joseph M. Trimble. Born in 1818.

J64—Susan C. Trimble. Born in 1824.

J65—Amanda M. Trimble. Born in 1826.

J23—James L. Trimble. Son of Moses Trimble and Catherine Lewis. (Third generation of James and Grace Trimble.) Born on December 18, 1789, and died on February 24, 1860, in Newton County, Georgia. Married Martha Bishop on March 1, 1832.

The children of James L. Trimble and Martha Bishop:

J66—Melissa Trimble. Born in 1833.

J67—Virginia Trimble. Born in 1835.

J68—Jane Trimble. Born in 1838.

J69—William Trimble. Born in 1841.

J70—John Trimble. Born in 1843.

J71—George Trimble. Born in 1845 and died in the Civil War.

J72—Mary Trimble. Born in 1847.

J73—Martha Trimble. Born in 1849.

J24—John Haddon Trimble. Son of Moses Trimble and Catherine Lewis. (Third generation of James and Grace Trimble.) Born about 1792 and died in 1829 in Newton County, Georgia. Married Elizabeth Evans on July 9, 1816.

The children of John Haddon Trimble and Elizabeth Evans:

J74—Martha Trimble. Born in 1817 and married John Lovvorn on June 19, 1836.

J75—Catherine A. Trimble. Born in 1819.

+**J76—A. Sidney Trimble.** Born in 1820. He married Margaret L. Crews.

+**J77—Milton Conyers Trimble.** Born on October 28, 1823 or 1827. Married two times: first, to Sarah Ann Lovvorn, and second, to Susan Copeland.

+**J78—Elisha Newton Trimble.** Born in 1825 and married Martha Chambers.

J25—Philip Lewis Trimble. Son of Moses Trimble and Catherine Lewis. (Third generation of James and Grace Trimble.) Born in 1794 and died on October 15, 1867. He moved to Cherokee County, Texas, about 1840.

The children of Philip Lewis Trimble:

+**J79—John Lewis Trimble.** Born in 1815. Married Jane Martin Garner.

+**J80—James M. Trimble.** Born in 1818. Married Nancy Roark.

J81—Nancy Trimble. Born in 1820.

J82—Minerva Verlinda Trimble. Born in 1822 and died in 1893. Married Reziah Banks.

+**J83—Francis Marion Trimble.** Born in 1823 and died in 1878. Married in 1851 to Mary Ann Long.

J84—Joseph W. Trimble. Born in 1826.

J85—Mary M. Trimble. Born in 1828.

J86—William C. Trimble. Born in 1830.

J87—Thomas J. Trimble. Born in 1833.

J88—Amanda Violet Trimble. Born in 1835 and died in 1860. Married James McGowen.

J89—Peter H. Trimble. Born in 1837. Married Bonner in 1865.

J90—Sarah Trimble. Born in 1839.

J28—Moses Trimble. Son of Moses Trimble and Catherine Lewis. (Third generation of James and Grace Trimble.) Born in 1801 in Franklin County, Georgia and died in 1855 in Cherokee County, Texas. Married Mary "Polly" Lovvorn on July 3, 1823 in Morgan County, Georgia. She was born on September 18, 1803 in Clark, Dodge County, Georgia and died in 1867 in Jacksonville, Cherokee County, Texas.

They moved with his brother Philip Lewis Trimble (J25) to Texas about 1840.

The children of Moses Trimble and Mary "Polly" Lovvorn:

J91—Nancy A. Trimble. Born in 1825.

+**J92—Elisha Lorenzo Trimble.** Born in 1827. Married Jane Tollett.

+**J93—Elijah C. Trimble.** Born in 1827. married Margaret Tollett.

J94—Mary W. Trimble. Born in 1825. She never married.

+**J95—Thomas L. Trimble.** Born in 1831. Mary Jane Bearden.

J96—Martha Washington Trimble. Born in 1833.

J97—Frances C. Trimble. Born in 1834.

J98—Sarah E. Trimble. Born in 1836.

+**J99—William Franklin Trimble.** Born in 1837 in Newton County, Georgia and died June 1868 in Lamar County, Texas. Married Sarah Elizabeth Tollett.

J100—Susan C. Trimble. Born in 1839.

J29—Elisha Trimble. Son of Moses Trimble and Catherine Lewis. (Third generation of James and Grace Trimble.) Elisha was born in 1803 and died on November 11, 1893, in Iredell, Texas. Married on July 15, 1829, to Elizabeth Johnson in Georgia. Elisha was a Methodist minister in both Georgia and Texas.

The children of Elisha Trimble and Elizabeth Johnson:

J101—Sarah Agnes Trimble. Born in 1830 and died on August 10, 1895. Married Hugh Torrance.

J102—Cornelia Catherine Trimble. Born in 1833. Never married.

+**J103—John Howard Trimble.** Born on August 31, 1836. He married two times.

+**J104—Alexander Means Trimble.** Born on January 26, 1839. married Margaret Shaw.

J105—Harriet Elizabeth Trimble. Born in 1842. Never married.

J106—Harrison Summerfield Trimble. Born in 1845 and died in 1855.

+**J107—Lambeth Hopkins Trimble.** Born in 1848. He married two times.

+**J108—Alston Bascom Trimble.** Born in 1852 and died in 1905. Married Media Dudley.

J30—James Trimble. Son of John Trimble and Charity Redwine. (Third generation of James and Grace Trimble.) Married two times. His first wife's name is unknown to us; his second wife was Millie Wood and they married on February 4, 1844.

James Trimble and his first wife had five children:

J109—Sarah Trimble. Born in 1832.

J110—Zebulon Trimble. Born in 1834.

J111—Martha Trimble. Born in 1836.

J112—Prestly Trimble. Born in 1837.

J113—Lavena Trimble. Born in 1840.

James Trimble and Millie Wood had three children:

J114—Georgia A. Trimble. Born in 1844.

J115—Moses Trimble. Born in 1846.

J116—Nancy Trimble. Born in 1848.

This data is from the 1850 Census of DeKalb County, Georgia, of James Trimble and household. Millie Trimble and her children were living in Tennessee in 1871. We know nothing more of this family.

J32—Joseph Trimble. Son of John Trimble and Charity Redwine. (Third generation of James and Grace Trimble.) Born in 1778 in Georgia. He was living in Gordon County, Georgia, in 1860. He married Nancy ——.

The son of Joseph and Nancy Trimble:

J117—Josephus Trimble. Born in 1831. Josephus had a son, Josephus C. Trimble, Married Katherine A. —— and they lived in Washington, D.C.

J44—Isaac Trimble. Son of James Trimble and Margaret Gillispie. (Fourth generation of James and Grace Trimble.) Born on December 4, 1810, in Livingston County, Kentucky, and died on September 5, 1891. He married three times: first, to Jane Hosick in 1833; second, to Mary Barnes in 1851;

and third, to Emily Robinson in 1887. Isaac and Emily had no children.

The children of Isaac Trimble and Jane Hosick:

+J118—**James Alexander Trimble.** Born on November 14, 1834. Married three times.

J119—**Clarissa Trimble.** Born in 1837 and died in 1870. Married William Adcock.

J120—**Narcissa Jane Trimble.** Born in 1838 and died in 1880. Married John D. Jamison.

J121—**William Joseph Trimble.** Born in 1839 and died in 1864. He was unmarried and died of smallpox while serving in the Confederate Army.

J122—**Uriah Berry Trimble.** Born in 1841 and died in 1935. Married two times: first, to Eliza Reynolds, and second, to Ida May. He had no children.

J123—**Sarah Catherine Trimble.** Born in 1843. Married James Anderson Threlkeld.

+J124—**Benjamin Franklin Trimble.** Born in 1845. He married two times.

J125—**Hannah Louise Trimble.** Born in 1847 and died 1939. She was unmarried.

J126—**Rachel Margaret Trimble.** Born in 1849 and died in 1936. She married James A. Love.

The children of Isaac Trimble and Mary Barnes:

J127—**Mary Ellen Trimble.** Born in 1853 and died in 1910. Married Francis Clemens.

J128—**Tempy Luella Trimble.** Born in 1855 and died in 1856.

J129—**Cordelia Trimble.** Born in 1857 and died in 1934. Married Frank Lay.

J45—**Joseph Trimble.** Son of John Trimble and Mary Ann Harris. (Fourth generation of James and Grace Trimble.) Born in 1810 in Morgan County, Georgia, and died in 1864 in Troup County, Georgia. Married Sarah Horton in 1835.

The children of Joseph Trimble and Sarah Horton:

+J130—**John Thomas Trimble.** Born in 1836. Married Mittie Horton.

J131—**Moses Marion Trimble.** Born in 1836 and died on July 1, 1862, in the Civil War in Virginia. He was unmarried.

+J132—**William Sanders Trimble.** Born in 1840 in Troup County, Georgia. He died in 1896. Married Laura Ann Norwood in 1866.

J133—**Winnie Trimble.** Born in 1845 in Troup County, Georgia, and died in 1929. Married her cousin James T. Jones.

J134—**Joseph Trimble.** Born in 1843 and died in 1853.

Trimble Families of America

J47—Moses Trimble. Son of John Trimble and Mary Ann Harris. (Fourth generation of James and Grace Trimble.) Born in 1817 and died in 1895. Married two times: first, to Melinny Horton and they had one child which died young; and second, Moses married Susan S. Robertson.

The three children of Moses Trimble and Susan S. Robertson:

J135—Mary Ann Trimble. Born in 1845.

J136—Delia Trimble. Married John C. Nicholson and they lived near Mount Meigs, Alabama, in 1900.

J137—John E. Trimble. Lived in Montgomery, Alabama, in 1900. He was unmarried.

J51—James Trimble. Son of Moses Trimble and Rebecca Harris. (Fourth generation of James and Grace Trimble.) Born on October 29, 1805 and died on January 12, 1854. Married Clarissa Bigelow in 1821. He was a planter.

The children of James Trimble and Clarissa Bigelow:

+**J138—Julius Bigelow Trimble.** Born in 1842. Married Sally Busbee.

J139—Ella Trimble. Born in 1844.

J140—Willia Ross Trimble. Born in 1845. Married and had seven children.

J141—Clara Trimble. Born in 1847.

J142—James Trimble, Jr. Born in 1849 and died young.

J53—Benjamin Trimble. Son of Moses Trimble and Rebecca Harris. (Fourth generation of James and Grace Trimble.) Born about 1810 and died in 1876. Benjamin married two times: first, to unknown Pace and there were no children in this marriage; second, he married Frances Simms. Benjamin was a merchant and banker in Montgomery, Alabama.

The children of Benjamin Trimble and Frances Simms:

+**J143—Edward Moses Trimble.** Married Annie Griggs.

J144—William Trimble. Lived in Montgomery, Alabama.

J145—Sarah Simms Trimble.

J56—Augustus Crawford Trimble. Son of William Trimble and Harriet Welborn. (Fourth generation of James and Grace Trimble.) Born on December 11, 1818 and died in 1894. He married two times: first in 1839 to Louisa Brogdon and second in 1851 to Loany Fain.

The children of Augustus Crawford Trimble and Louisa Brogdon:

J146—Josephine Melina Trimble. Born on June 6, 1840.

+**J147—William Wiley Trimble.** Born on May 8, 1843.

J148—Virginia Rawles Trimble. Born in 1845 and died in 1894.

The children of Augustus Crawford and Loany Fain Trimble:

J149–John Wesley Trimble. Died in infancy.

J150–Harriet Keron Trimble. Born in 1854 and died in 1889.

J151–Helen Louisa Trimble. Born on May 27, 1856, and married two times: first, to the Reverend Eli Smith and later to his brother, John Smith.

J152–James Augustus Trimble. Died in infancy.

J76–A. Sidney Trimble. Son of John Haddon Trimble and Elizabeth Evans. (Fourth generation of James and Grace Trimble.) Born in 1820 in Georgia. Married Margaret L. Crews. They were living in Gordon County, Georgia, in 1860.

The children of A. Sidney Trimble and Margaret L. Crews:

J153–S. Elizabeth Trimble. Married James H. Stark and they lived in Atlanta, Georgia, in 1916.

J154–John L. Trimble. Born in 1852 in Georgia. He never married.

J77–Milton Conyers Trimble. Son of John Haddon Trimble and Elizabeth Evans. (Fourth generation of James and Grace Trimble.) Born on October 28, 1823 or 1827 and died on July 19, 1898. He married two times: first, to Sarah Ann Lovvorn, and second, to Susan Copeland on May 30, 1850.

The child of Milton Conyers Trimble and Sarah Ann Lovvorn:

J155–John Ethan Trimble. Born on October 20, 1848 and died at age four.

The children of Milton Conyers Trimble and Susan Copeland:

+**J156–William Sidney Trimble.** Born on May 15, 1851 and died on December 23, 1938.

+**J157–Willis Clinton Trimble.** Born on December 12, 1853.

+**J158–Lemuel Shackleford Trimble.** Born on July 23, 1856.

+**J159–Thomas Milton Trimble.** Born on February 16, 1864.

J160–Sarah Jennie Trimble. Born on May 2, 1861. Married a Mr. Johnson.

J161–Jesse Penn Trimble.

J162–Adelk S. Trimble. Born on January 23, 1867. Married Jacob Edmund Lewis on September 29, 1887.

J78–Elisha Newton Trimble. Son of John Haddon Trimble and Elizabeth Evans. (Fourth generation of James and Grace Trimble.) Born in 1825 and married Martha E. Chambers; they lived at Mount Zion, Georgia, in 1910.

The children of Elisha Newton Trimble and Martha E. Chambers:

J163–Rose Trimble. Married a Mr. Martin.

+**J164–Robert Augustus Trimble.**

J - James and Grace Trimble

J165—Lovick Pierce Trimble. He married and had one son, Charles.

J166—Kelle Trimble. Lived in 1910 at Mount Zion, Georgia. She married two times: first, to a Mr. Robinson, and second, to a Mr. Morris and they had a daughter, Bonnie.

J79—John Lewis Trimble. Son of Philip Lewis Trimble. (Fourth generation of James and Grace Trimble.) Born in 1815 and died in 1883. Married Jane Martin Garner.

The children of John Lewis Trimble and Jane Martin Garner:

J167—Martha W. Trimble. Born in 1840 and died in infancy.

J168—James L. Trimble. Born in 1842 and died in 1862. He never married.

J169—George F. Trimble. Born in 1843.

J170—William Kimbrue Trimble. Born in 1846.

J171—Margaret Ann Trimble. Born in 1848 and married Benjamin Hill.

+**J172—Thomas Kerr Trimble.** Born in 1851. Married Joanna Ashworth.

J173—Sarah Clement Trimble. Born in 1851.

J174—Stockton Trimble. Born in 1852 and died in 1868.

J175—Kneel Trimble. Born in 1854 and died in infancy.

J176—Joseph Warren Trimble. Born in 1857.

J80—James M. Trimble. Son of Philip Lewis Trimble. (Fourth generation of James and Grace Trimble.) Born in 1818 and died in 1861. Married Nancy Roark in 1849.

The children of James M. Trimble and Nancy Roark:

J177—Laura Louise Trimble. Born in 1850 and married Richard H. Small.

J178—Margaret Ella Trimble. Born in 1854 and died in 1935. Married Reuben Horton.

J179—Catherine Lewis Trimble. Born in 1856 and died in 1936. Never married.

J180—Evelyn Bell Trimble. Born in 1858 and died in infancy.

+**J181—Frank Roark Trimble.** Born in 1860 and died in 1931. Married Margaret Ramey.

J83—Francis Marion Trimble. Son of Philip Lewis Trimble. (Fourth generation of James and Grace Trimble.) Born in1823 and died in 1878. Married in 1851 to Mary Ann Long.

The children of Francis Marion Trimble and Mary Ann Long:

+**J182—Philip Edward Trimble.** Born in 1852. Married Amanda Wheeler.

J183—Martha Ann Trimble. Born in 1859 and died in 1884. Married in 1879 to Charles McCullough.

J92—Elisha Lorenzo Trimble. Son of Moses Trimble and Mary "Polly" Lovvorn. (Fourth generation of James and Grace Trimble.) Born in 1827. Married Jane Tollett.

The children of Elisha Lorenzo Trimble and Jane Tollett:

  J184—Mary Trimble. Married Alexander Rabb.

  +**J185—Frank Trimble.** Married Emma ——.

J93—Elijah C. Trimble. Son of Moses Trimble and Mary "Polly" Lovvorn. (Fourth generation of James and Grace Trimble.) Born in 1827 and married Margaret Tollett.

The four children of Elijah C. Trimble and Margaret Tollett:

  J186—Thomas Trimble. Never married.

  J187—Ellen Trimble. Married Sam Spears.

  J188—Floyd Trimble. Married Mary Beard.

  J189—Frances Trimble. Married Joseph Fortenberry.

J95—Thomas L. Trimble. Son of Moses Trimble and Mary "Polly" Lovvorn. (Fourth generation of James and Grace Trimble.) Born in 1831 and married Mary Jane Bearden in 1852.

The children of Thomas L. Trimble and Mary Jane Bearden:

  +**J190—Clinton D. Trimble.** Born in 1853 and married —— Greer.

  J191—Jefferson Trimble. Born in 1856.

J99—William Franklin Trimble. Son of Moses Trimble and Mary "Polly" Lovvorn. (Fourth generation of James and Grace Trimble.) Born in 1837 in Newton County, Georgia and died in June 1868 in Lamar County, Texas. Married Sarah Elizabeth Tollett in 1856 in Lamar County, Texas. She was born on January 9, 1836 in Point, Rains County, Texas and died on January 2, 1908 in Point, Rains County, Texas.

The children of William Franklin Trimble and Sarah Elizabeth Tollett:

  J192—Susan Letitia Trimble. Born on December 10, 1857 in Lemar, Texas. Married William McShan.

  J193—Martha Ellen Trimble. Born about in 1858 in Texas and died in February 1893 in Texas.

  +**J194—Moses Wesley Trimble.** Born on February 20, 1859 in Lamar, Texas and died on July 17, 1932 in Lone Oak, Hunt County, Texas. Married Kate Beard in 1884.

  J195—Alice Trimble. Born on December 5, 1860 and died in 1861 as an infant.

  J196—William Edward Trimble. Born on February 11, 1862 and died in 1942.

J197—Mary Catherine Trimble. Born on February 11, 1866 and died in 1943. Married Sam Spears.

J198—Ann Margaret Trimble. Born on March 17, 1868 and died on November 19, 1954 in Wichita Falls, Wichita County, Texas. Married George Kimbrough.

J103—John Howard Trimble. Son of the Elisha Trimble and Elizabeth Johnson. (Fourth generation of James and Grace Trimble.) Born on August 31, 1836 and died April 14, 1904. He married two times: first, to Mary S. Hancock on May 30, 1860, and second, to Sally Johnson on April 4, 1882. John Howard was a Methodist minister.

The children of John Howard Trimble and Mary S. Hancock:

J199—Elizabeth Jane Trimble. Born on November 28, 1861 and died on February 7, 1902. She married James Tidwell.

J200—Lewis Alexander Trimble. Born on November 28, 1863 and died in July 1911. He had no children.

J201—Milton S. Trimble. Born in 1866.

J202—John B. Trimble. Born in 1868. He died young.

The children of John Howard Trimble and Sally Johnson:

J203—Linus Parker Trimble. Born in 1883; married Lucille Tucker in 1907.

J204—Ben Brown Trimble. Born in 1885 and died in 1934. He never married.

J205—Mertie Trimble. Born in 1887. Married F. D. Eskew.

J206—Elbert Lyle Trimble. Born in 1889 and died in 1947. Married Grace Toler.

J104—Alexander Means Trimble. Son of the Elisha Trimble and Elizabeth Johnson. (Fourth generation of James and Grace Trimble.) Born on January 26, 1839 and died on August 10, 1881. He married Margaret Shaw in 1865.

The children of Alexander Means Trimble and Margaret Shaw:

J207—Elisha John Trimble. Born in 1866 and died in infancy.

+J208—Charles Summerfield Trimble. Born on April 6, 1869 and died on October 17, 1911.

J209—Frank Lewis Trimble. Born on June 22, 1871 and died in infancy.

J210—Emmett Lee Trimble. Born on September 5, 1873 and died in infancy.

+J211—William Brown Trimble. Born on May 24, 1876. Married Elizabeth Wickson.

J212—Ethel Trimble. Born on August 11, 1878, and married Charles Richards on November 12, 1899.

Trimble Families of America

J107—Lambeth Hopkins Trimble. Son of the Elisha Trimble and Elizabeth Johnson. (Fourth generation of James and Grace Trimble.) Born in 1848. He was a Methodist minister. He married two times. We do not know his first wife's name; second, he married Mary G. Owen on July 11, 1880.

The child of Lambeth Hopkins Trimble and his first wife:

J213—Oscar Trimble.

The children of Lambeth Hopkins and Mary G. Owen Trimble:

J214—Alston Means Hopkins. Married Bessie Wallace.

J215—Bertha Vivian Hopkins. Married Louis C. Graff.

J216—Buena Vista Hopkins. Married Clarence C. Easley.

J217—Elmer Hopkins. Died unmarried.

J218—La Fetra Elisha Hopkins. Born in 1892. Married Cordelia Games.

J108—Alston Bascom Trimble. Son of the Elisha Trimble and Elizabeth Johnson. (Fourth generation of James and Grace Trimble.) Born in 1852 and died in 1905. He was a Methodist minister and married Media Dudley.

The children of Alston Bascom Trimble and Media Dudley:

+J219—William Dudley Trimble. Born on January 23, 1894. Married Hilda Kaase.

J220—Imogene Trimble. Died young.

J221—Taylor Earl Trimble. Born on August 7, 1897.

J118—James Alexander Trimble. Son of Isaac Trimble and Jane Hosick. (Fifth generation of James and Grace Trimble.) Born on November 14, 1834, in Livingston County, Kentucky, where he died around in 1928. James Alexander married three times: first, to Elizabeth Mary Davis in 1856; second, to Maria Young in 1878; and third, to Drucilla Lowrey.

The children of James Alexander Trimble and Elizabeth Mary Davis:

J222—David E. Trimble. Died in childhood.

J223—Mary A. Trimble. Born in 1858. Married William Thompson.

J224—Iola M. Trimble. Born in 1860.

+J225—Isaac Newton Trimble. Born in 1862. Married Jo Ann Davis.

+J226—William J. Trimble. Born in 1858. Married Lou Rhodes.

J227—Isabella Trimble. Born in 1866.

J228—James R. Trimble. Born on October 17, 1867 and died on December 4, 1900.

+J229—Barney Franklin Trimble. Married Mary Charlotte Davis.

J230—Carlus Trimble. Born in 1872 and died in 1894. He was unmarried.

J - James and Grace Trimble

J231—Johnny Trimble.

The children of James Alexander Trimble and Maria Young:
J232—Katherine Trimble. Born in 1879. Married Levi Tanner.
J233—Maria Trimble.

The children of James Alexander Trimble and Drucilla Lowrey:
J234—Bertie Trimble. Died in her teens.
J235—Ora Trimble. Born in 1884 and died in 1955.
+**J236—Homer Trimble.** Born in 1888 and died in 1953. Married Reba Stallions.

J124—Benjamin Franklin Trimble. Son of Isaac Trimble and Jane Hosick. (Fifth generation of James and Grace Trimble.) Born in 1845 and died in 1895. He married two times: first, to Mary Peters in 1871: the second marriage was to Charlotte Patmor, and they had no children.

The child of Benjamin Franklin Trimble and Mary Peters:
+**J237—Henry Oliver Trimble.** Born in 1874. Married Charlotte Clark.

J130—John Thomas Trimble. Son of Joseph Trimble and Sarah Horton. (Fifth generation of James and Grace Trimble.) Born in 1836 and died in 1865. Married Mittie Horton. John Thomas was a soldier of the Confederacy and died at Petersburg, Virginia.

The children of John Thomas Trimble and Mittie Horton:
J238—Joseph A. Trimble. He was living in Gainesville, Florida, in 1910.
J239—John T. Trimble. Born in 1865. Living in Atlanta, Georgia, in 1931. He had a family, but we have no information.

J132—William Sanders Trimble. Son of Joseph Trimble and Sarah Horton. (Fifth generation of James and Grace Trimble.) Born in 1840 in Troup County, Georgia. He died in 1896. Married Laura Ann Norwood in 1866.

The children of William Sanders Trimble and Laura Ann Norwood:
J240—R. Wilbur Trimble. Born in 1866.
J241—Bunnie P. Trimble. Born in 1869. Married J. C. Johnson.

J138—Julius Bigelow Trimble. Son of James Trimble and Clarissa Bigelow. (Fifth generation of James and Grace Trimble.) Born in 1842. He died in Montgomery, Alabama, in 1899. Married Sally Busbee.

The children of Julius Bigelow Trimble and Sally Busbee:
J242—Lavina Trimble.
J243—Frank Trimble. Living in New Orleans, Louisiana, in 1900.

J143–Edward Moses Trimble. Son of Benjamin Trimble and Frances Simms. (Fifth generation of James and Grace Trimble.) Married Annie Griggs.

The one child of Edward Moses Trimble and Annie Griggs:

J244–William Burwell Trimble. Born on September 27, 1870, at Montgomery, Alabama. In 1921 he was living in New York City. He married Catherine Colvin, and they had one child, a son, Richard Burwell. William Burwell Trimble was a noted physician specializing in skin diseases.

J147–William Wiley Trimble. Son of Augustus Crawford Trimble and Louisa Brogdon. (Fifth generation of James and Grace Trimble.) Born on May 8, 1843 and died in 1907. Married Lou Gray in 1867. He was a large landowner and member of the Methodist church.

The children of William Wiley Trimble and Lou Gray:

J245–Clara Virginia Trimble. Born in 1868. She was unmarried.

J246–Minnie Louisa Trimble. Born in 1870. Married Thomas J. Noland.

J247–Ella Josephine Trimble. Born in 1872. She was unmarried.

J248–Gussie Gray Trimble. Married Robert D. Jackson.

J249–Loulie Ethel Trimble. Married Henry Ezzard.

J250–Maude Trimble. Died in infancy.

J251–William Wiley Trimble, Jr. Married Bessie Hunt.

J156–William Sidney Trimble. Son of Milton Conyers Trimble and Susan Ann Copeland. (Fifth generation of James and Grace Trimble.) Born on May 15, 1851 and died on December 23, 1938. Married Julia Rollins on February 3, 1870.

The children of William Sidney Trimble and Julia Rollins:

J252–Matilda Ann Trimble. Born in 1871 and died at age one year.

+**J253–James Milton Trimble.** Born on February 6, 1873. He married two times.

J254–John Newton Trimble. Born on April 8, 1875.

+**J255–William Franklin Trimble.** Born on March 31, 1877. Married Mary Daniel.

+**J256–Robert Lemuel Trimble.** Born on March 9, 1879. Married Essie Lynch.

J257–Julia Viola Trimble. Born on November 1, 1881 and died on February 5, 1910.

J258–David Sidney Trimble. Born on March 30, 1884.

J259–Jennie Leona Trimble. Born on October 20, 1886.

J260–Jesse Theodore Trimble. Born on May 20, 1890.

J261—Susie Adella Trimble. Born on June 15, 1894.

J262—Mittie Alberta Trimble. Born on March 29, 1899, and married on July 21, 1915, to William Speggle.

J157—Willis Clinton Trimble. Son of Milton Conyers Trimble and Susan Ann Copeland. (Fifth generation of James and Grace Trimble.) Born on December 12, 1853 and died on January 6, 1888.

Willis Trimble married and had two children:

J263—Allie Trimble.

J264—Ann Trimble.

J158—Lemuel Shackleford Trimble. Son of Milton Conyers Trimble and Susan Ann Copeland. (Fifth generation of James and Grace Trimble.) Born on July 23, 1856.

Lemuel Shackleford Trimble married and had six children:

J265—Asa Trimble.

J266—Alice Trimble.

J267—Lee S. Trimble.

J268—Dora Trimble.

J269—Homer Trimble.

J270—Hattie Trimble.

J159—Thomas Milton Trimble. Son of Milton Conyers Trimble and Susan Ann Copeland. (Fifth generation of James and Grace Trimble.) Born on February 16, 1864.

Thomas Milton Trimble married and had six children:

J271—Lilly Trimble.

J272—Pearl Trimble.

J273—Henning Trimble.

J274—Clyde Trimble.

J275—Forrest Trimble.

J276—Ethel Trimble.

J164—Robert Augustus Trimble. Son of Elisha Newton Trimble and Martha E. Chambers. (Fifth generation of James and Grace Trimble.)

The children of Robert Augustus Trimble:

J277—Robert Newton Trimble.

J278—Willie Belle Trimble. She never married.

J279—Martha Trimble. Married a Mr. Templeton.

J280—Elizabeth Trimble. Married a Mr. Flowler.

J172–Thomas Kerr Trimble. Son of John Lewis Trimble and Jane Martin Garner. (Fifth generation of James and Grace Trimble.) Born in 1851 and died in 1920. Married in 1877 to Joanna Ashworth.

The children of Thomas Kerr Trimble and Joanna Ashworth:

+**J281–Carlie Stockton Trimble.** Born in 1880 and died in 1943. Married Zeulla Vincent.

+**J282–Howard Franklin Trimble.** Born in 1882. Married Armenia Burnett.

J283–Anna Lee Trimble. Born in 1884 and died in infancy.

J284–Lou Ella Trimble. Born in 1891 and died in infancy.

J285–Thomas Marvin Trimble. Born in 1894 and died in 1939. He never married.

J181–Frank Roark Trimble. Son of James M. Trimble and Nancy Roark. (Fifth generation of James and Grace Trimble.) Born in 1860 and died in 1931. Married Margaret Ramey in 1896.

The children of Frank Roark Trimble and Margaret Ramey:

J286–Maurice Ramey Trimble. Born in 1897 and died in infancy.

J287–Alice Maurine Trimble. Born in 1899 and never married.

+**J288–Gerald Roark Trimble.** Born in 1901. Married Mae Frances O'Conner.

+**J289–William Ramey Trimble.** Born in 1903. Married Mabel Durrett.

J182–Philip Edward Trimble. Son of Francis Marion Trimble and Mary Ann Long, (Fifth generation of James and Grace Trimble.) Born in 1852 and died in 1899. Married Amanda Wheeler in 1877.

The children of Philip Edward Trimble and Amanda Wheeler:

J290–Cora May Trimble. Born in 1878 and married Eli Boyett in 1902.

+**J291–Elbert Reziah Trimble.** Born in 1882. Married Johnnie B. Reed.

+**J292–Williard Edward Trimble.** Born in 1888. Married Ella Foster.

J293–Lydia Ann Trimble. Born in 1892. Married Almos Thurman.

J185–Frank Trimble. Son of Elisha Lorenzo Trimble and Jane Tollett. (Fifth generation of James and Grace Trimble.) Married Emma ——

The children of Frank and Emma Trimble:

J294–Sarah Trimble. Married Protus Krunk.

J295–Ellen Trimble. Married Henry Murphy.

J296–Elisha Trimble.

J297–Clara Trimble.

J190–Clinton D. Trimble. Son of Thomas L. Trimble and Mary Jane Bearden.

J - James and Grace Trimble

(Fifth generation of James and Grace Trimble.) Born in 1853 and married —— Greer.

The children of Clinton Trimble and —— Greer:

J298—Frances Trimble.

J299—Ruth Trimble.

J300—Elbert Trimble.

J301—Alexander Trimble.

J302—A son name is unknown.

J194—Moses Wesley Trimble. Son of William Franklin Trimble and Sarah Elizabeth Tollett. (Fifth generation of James and Grace Trimble.) Born on February 20, 1859 in Lamar County, Texas and died on July 17, 1932 in Lone Oak, Hunt County, Texas. Married Kate Beaird in 1884. She was born on October 7, 1863 in Arcadia, Bienville Parish, Louisiana and died March 7, 1957 in Lone Oak, Hunt County, Texas

The children of Moses Wesley Trimble and Kate Beaird:

+J303—William Clarence Trimble. Born on July 27, 1886 in Point, Rains County, Texas and died on December 8, 1942 in Greenville, Hunt County, Texas. Married Mary Hughes.

+J304—Elisha Burt Trimble. Born on January 2, 1888 in Texas and died on April 13, 1973 in Ft. Worth, Tarrant County, Texas. Married Dicey Pearl Rainey.

+J305—Robert Dewitt Trimble. Born on December 8, 1890 in Texas and died on February 3, 1974 in Greenville, Hunt County, Texas. Married Winnie A. Corley.

J306—Annie Rose Trimble. Born on May 28, 1892 and died on August 7, 1892 as an infant of 2 months.

+J307—Audrey Beaird Trimble. Born on June 17, 1893 in Point, Rains County, Texas and died on May 28, 1949 in Greenville, Hunt County, Texas. Married Hazel Dell Weatherly.

J308—Moses Ray Trimble. Born on March 20, 1896 in Texas and died September 29, 1926 in Kerr County, Texas.

J309—Little Tot Trimble. Born on March 10, 1898 and died on February 1, 1899.

J310—Sara Lillian Trimble. Born on December 7, 1899 and died on October 10, 1905 as a young child.

J311—Marye Kate Trimble. Born on May 4, 1905 in Point, Rains County, Texas and died on January 26, 1994 in Oklahoma City, Oklahoma County,

Oklahoma. Married Thomas Shelton Aldridge.

J208—Charles Summerfield Trimble. Son of Alexander Means Trimble and Margaret Shaw. (Fifth generation of James and Grace Trimble.) Born on April 6, 1869 and died on October 17, 1911. Married Martha Buchanan in 1898.

The child of Charles Summerfield Trimble and Martha Buchanan:

+**J312—Homer Buchanan Trimble.** Born on October 31, 1900. Married Mary Zella Davidson.

J211—William Brown Trimble. Son of Alexander Means Trimble and Margaret Shaw. (Fifth generation of James and Grace Trimble.) Born on May 24, 1876 and died on May 24, 1942. Married Elizabeth Wickson on December 24, 1909.

The children of William Brown Trimble and Elizabeth Wickson:

J313—William Brown Trimble. Born on September 18, 1910. Died in infancy.

+**J314—Charles Owen Trimble.** Born on May 14, 1912. Married two times.

+**J315—John Raymond Trimble.** Born on October 25, 1915. Married Geraldine Smith.

+**J316—Henry Alexander Trimble.** Born on January 5, 1919. Married Fay Webb.

J317—Wilma Ann Trimble. Born on June 14, 1921. Married Martin Droigk.

J219—William Dudley Trimble. Son of Alston Bascom Trimble and Media Dudley. (Fifth generation of James and Grace Trimble.) Born on January 23, 1894. Married Hilda Kaase.

The one child of William Dudley Trimble and Hilda Kaase:

J318—Lloyd Clinton Trimble. Born on December 24, 1921, and married Nona Leal Vannerson.

J225—Isaac Newton Trimble. Son of James Alexander Trimble and Elizabeth Mary Davis. (Sixth generation of James and Grace Trimble.) Born in 1862 and died in 1949. Married Jo Ann Davis and they moved to Ballard County, Kentucky, where he was president of the First National Bank of Wickliffe, Kentucky.

The children of Isaac Newton Trimble and Jo Ann Davis:

J319—Eunice Trimble. Married Henry P. Newton and lives at Creve Coeur, Missouri.

J320—William Lawrence Trimble. Born in Kentucky. Married Helen —— and had a daughter, Joanne.

J321—Isaac Newton Trimble, Jr. Born in Kentucky. Married and has a child who lived in Phoenix, Arizona.

Trimble Families of America
J - James and Grace Trimble

J226—William J. Trimble. Son of James Alexander Trimble and Elizabeth Mary Davis. (Sixth generation of James and Grace Trimble.) Born in 1858 and died in 1904. Married Lou Rhodes.

The three children of William Trimble and Lou Rhodes:

J322—Lloyd Trimble. Died at age thirty. He had no children.

J323—Lemma Trimble. Married Sterling Murrell and lives at Daytona Beach, Florida.

J324—Marjorie Trimble. Married Byron Brown and lived in Sebastian, Florida, in 1956.

J229—Barney Franklin Trimble. Son of James Alexander Trimble and Elizabeth Mary Davis. (Sixth generation of James and Grace Trimble.) Died in 1912 in Livingston County, Kentucky. Married Mary Charlotte Davis.

The children of Barney Franklin Trimble and Mary Charlotte Davis:

J325—Mary Cornelia Trimble.

+J326—Barney Franklin Trimble, Jr. Born in Kentucky and married Edna Randolph. They live at Golconda, Illinois.

J236—Homer Trimble. Son of James Alexander Trimble and Drucilla Lowrey. (Sixth generation of James and Grace Trimble.) Born in 1888 and died in 1953 at Burna, Kentucky. Married Reba Stallions.

The children of Homer Trimble and Reba Stallions:

J327—James Trimble. He lived in Florida in 1957. He has two daughters: Sandra and Marcia.

J328—Helen Trimble.

J237—Henry Oliver Trimble. Son of Benjamin Franklin Trimble and Mary Peters. (Sixth generation of James and Grace Trimble.) Born in 1874 and died in 1947. Married Charlotte Clark in 1895.

The child of Henry Oliver Trimble and Charlotte Clark:

+J329—Foster Oliver Trimble. Born in 1896. He married two times.

J253—James Milton Trimble. Son of William Sidney Trimble and Julia Rollins. (Sixth generation of James and Grace Trimble.) Born on February 6, 1873. He married two times: first, to Elizabeth Daniel on June 23, 1895; and second, to Annie King in 1911.

The children of James Milton Trimble and Elizabeth Daniel:

J330—Chester Loring Trimble. Married Lois Hancock.

J331—William Alvin Trimble. Married Mabel Watson.

J332—Robert Milton Trimble. Married Dorie Murphy.

J333—Lila Montez Trimble. Married William Nesmith.

J334—J. Gertrude Trimble. Married Adolphus Owen.

J335—Flora Trimble. Married Albert Kempson.

The children of James Milton Trimble and Annie King:

J336—Julia Rebecca Trimble. Married Howard Blocker.

J337—Mary Elizabeth Trimble. Married Andrew Morris.

J255—William Franklin Trimble. Son of William Sidney Trimble and Julia Rollins. (Sixth generation of James and Grace Trimble.) Born on March 31, 1877 and died on January 6, 1939. Married Mary Daniel in 1895.

The children of William Franklin Trimble and Mary Daniel:

+**J338—James Leonard Trimble.** Born on December 27, 1896. Married Sarah Boudlin.

+**J339—Jesse Newton Trimble.** Born on November 21, 1898. Married Minnie Treptau.

J340—Mamie Pearl Trimble. Born on April 28, 1901. Married Robert Bates. In 1950 they were living in Cullman, Alabama.

J341—Mattie Naomi Trimble. Born on June 14, 1903. Married Sterling Clavert.

J342—William Otis Trimble. Born on September 25, 1905.

+**J343—Archie Edward Trimble.** Born on August 15, 1907. Married Elizabeth Reid.

+**J344—Woodrow Vertie Trimble.** Born on June 14, 1912. Married Lila Hancock

+**J345—Erston Daniel Trimble.** Born on July 3, 1917. Married Jessie Knight.

J256—Robert Lemuel Trimble. Son of William Sidney Trimble and Julia Rollins. (Sixth generation of James and Grace Trimble.) Born on March 9, 1879. Married Essie Lynch in 1900. They lived in Cullman County, Alabama.

The children of Robert Lemuel Trimble and Essie Lynch:

J346—Harvey Newton Trimble. Born on November 12, 1901.

J347—Julia Elizabeth Trimble. Born on February 11, 1904. Married a Mr. Pate.

J348—Essie Leona Trimble. Born on October 24, 1906. Married a Mr. Jordan.

J349—Minnie Roberta Trimble. Born on November 27, 1908. Married a Mr. Calvert.

J350—Mary Florine Trimble. Born on September 5, 1910.

J351—William Walter Trimble. Born on February 21, 1913.

J352—Pickney Elton Trimble. Born on September 10, 1916.

J353—Ray Lemuel Trimble. Born on February 2, 1919.

J - James and Grace Trimble

J354—Susan Inez Trimble. Born on December 3, 1922. Married a Mr. McMinn.

J281—Carlie Stockton Trimble. Son of Thomas Kerr Trimble and Joanna Ashworth. (Sixth generation of James and Grace Trimble.) Born in 1880 and died in 1943. Married Zeulla Vincent

The daughter of Carlie Stockton Trimble and Zeulla Vincent:
J355—Sybil Maud Trimble. Born in 1909. Married Bernell Jernigan.

J282—Howard Franklin Trimble. Son of Thomas Kerr Trimble and Joanna Ashworth. (Sixth generation of James and Grace Trimble.) Born in 1882 and married Armenia Burnett.

The children of Howard Franklin Trimble and Armenia Burnett:
J356—Velma Maud Trimble. Born in 1903 and married Robert Bond.
J357—Clara Erma Trimble. Born in 1904. Married Vernon Corley.
J358—Drury Pauline Trimble. Born in 1907. Married John Martin.
J359—Fay Vernora Trimble. Born in 1909. Married Lee Bryant.
J360—Jay Trimble. Born in 1911. He married two times: first, to Lessie Mitchell, and second, to Mouzella Flowers.
J361—Rex Darrah Trimble. Born in 1914. Married Nadine White.

J288—Gerald Roark Trimble. Son of Frank Roark Trimble and Margaret Ramey. (Sixth generation of James and Grace Trimble.) Born in 1901 and died in 1947. Married Mae Frances O'Conner in 1927.

The children of Gerald Roark Trimble and Mae Frances O'Conner:
J362—Gerald Roark Trimble, Jr. Born in 1933.
J363—William Neve Trimble. Born in 1937.

J289—William Ramey Trimble. Son of Frank Roark Trimble and Margaret Ramey. (Sixth generation of James and Grace Trimble.) Born in 1903 and married Mabel Durrett in 1932.

The children of William Ramey Trimble and Mabel Durrett:
J364—James Ramey Trimble. Born in 1934.
J365—Maxine Elizabeth Trimble. Born in 1934.
J366—Ellen Beatrice Trimble. Born in 1936.

J291—Elbert Reziah Trimble. Son of Philip Edward Trimble and Amanda Wheeler. (Sixth generation of James and Grace Trimble.) Born in 1882. Married Johnnie B. Reed in 1904.

The one child of Elbert Reziah Trimble and Johnnie B. Reed:

+J367—Williard Lynn Trimble. Born in 1906. Married Velma Gilbert.

J292—Williard Edward Trimble. Son of Philip Edward Trimble and Amanda Wheeler. (Sixth generation of James and Grace Trimble.) Born in 1888 and died in 1950. Married Ella Foster in 1907.

The child of Williard Edward Trimble and Ella Foster:

J368—John Edward Trimble. Born in 1911. Married Dolores Durman.

J303—William Clarence Trimble. Son Moses Wesley Trimble and Kate Beaird. (Sixth generation of James and Grace Trimble.) Born on July 27, 1886 in Point, Rains County, Texas and died on December 8, 1942 in Greenville, Hunt County, Texas. Married Mary Hughes. She was born about 1890 in Texas and died in Greenville, Hunt County, Texas.

The children William Clarence Trimble and Mary Hughes:

J369—Dr. Orman Hughes Trimble. Born on July 5, 1913 in Point, Rains County, Texas and died on September 8, 1976 in Wichita Falls, Wichita County, Texas. Married Mary Sue Woods on August 1, 1942 in Greenville, Hunt County, Texas.

J370—Moses Wray "Jack" Trimble. Born on December 18, 1919 in Point, Rains County, Texas and died on June 16, 1985 in Henderson County, Texas. Married Louise Pearson.

J304—Elisha Burt Trimble. Son Moses Wesley Trimble and Kate Beaird. (Sixth generation of James and Grace Trimble.) Born on January 2, 1888 in Texas and died on April 13, 1973 in Ft. Worth, Tarrant County, Texas. Married Dicey Pearl Rainey. She was born about 1891 in Texas.

The children Elisha Burt Trimble and Dicey Pearl Rainey:

J371—Robert Lewis Trimble. Born about 1913 in Texas and died in July 1977 in Fort Worth, Tarrant County, Texas, Married Francis Kesterson.

J305—Robert Dewitt Trimble. Son Moses Wesley Trimble and Kate Beaird. (Sixth generation of James and Grace Trimble.) Born on December 8, 1890 in Texas and died on February 3, 1974 in Greenville, Hunt County, Texas. Married Winnie A. Corley. She was born on October 17, 1892 in Texas and died on July 13, 1983 in Dallas, Dallas County, Texas.

The children Robert Dewitt Trimble and Winnie A. Corley:

J372—Robert Derrell Trimble. Born on December 21, 1917 in Lone Oak, Hunt County, Texas and died on June 16, 1996 in Big Sandy, Upshur County, Texas. Married Wylma Elayne Sanford.

J373—Harry Burt Trimble. Born about 1920 in Texas and died on July 16,

2006 in Austin, Travis County, Texas. Married Laura Gean Simpson on August 10, 1942 in Greenville, Hunt County, Texas.

J307—Audrey Beaird Trimble. Son Moses Wesley Trimble and Kate Beaird. (Sixth generation of James and Grace Trimble.) Born on June 17, 1893 in Point, Rains County, Texas and died on May 28, 1949 in Greenville, Hunt County, Texas. Married Hazel Dell Weatherly. She was born on November 2, 1897 in Lone Oak, Hunt, Texas and died in March 1992 in Greenville, Hunt, Texas.

She is the daughter of Thomas Madison Weatherly and Mae Elizabeth Cole. Thomas was born on January 28, 1864 in Georgia and died April 4, 1935 in Lone Oak, Hunt County, Texas. Mae was born on October 1868 in Texas and died on September 15, 1951 in Lone Oak, Hunt County, Texas.

The children of Audrey Beaird Trimble and Hazel Dell Weatherly:

+**J374—Harold Frederick Trimble.** Born on August 15, 1919 in Lone Oak, Hunt County, Texas and died on January 22, 2003 in Dallas, Dallas County, Texas. Married Dorothy Nell Dunn.

J312—Homer Buchanan Trimble. Son of Charles Summerfield Trimble and Martha Buchanan. (Sixth generation of James and Grace Trimble.) Born on October 31, 1900. Married Mary Zella Davidson in 1921.

The children of Homer Buchanan Trimble and Mary Zella Davidson:

J375—David Buchanan Trimble. Born on November 22, 1922.

J376—Charles Edward Trimble. Born on September 3, 1928. Married on December 27, 1956, to Mary Lee Hosea and now lives in Houston, Texas.

J314—Charles Owen Trimble. Son of William Brown Trimble and Elizabeth Wickson. (Sixth generation of James and Grace Trimble.) Born on May 14, 1912. Married two times: first, to Jean Pugh, and second, to Lois Fort.

The child of Charles Owen Trimble and Jean Pugh:

J377—Isaac Doss Trimble. Born on June 13, 1934.

The children of Charles Owen Trimble and Lois Fort:

J378—Lois Laverne Trimble. Born on August 19, 1944.

J379—Mary Ann Trimble. Born on December 31, 1945.

J380—Charles Owen Trimble, Jr. Born om August 4, 1947.

J315—John Raymond Trimble. Son of William Brown Trimble and Elizabeth Wickson. (Sixth generation of James and Grace Trimble.) Born on October 25, 1915. Married Geraldine Smith.

The children of John Raymond Trimble and Geraldine Smith:

Trimble Families of America

J381—Geraldine Esther Trimble. Born on September 19, 1941.

J382—Alexis Raymond Trimble. Born on October 15, 1944.

J383—Victoria Elizabeth Trimble. Born on December 15, 1945.

J384—John William Trimble. Born on October 15, 1949.

J316—Henry Alexander Trimble. Son of William Brown Trimble and Elizabeth Wickson. (Sixth generation of James and Grace Trimble.) Born on January 5, 1919. Married Fay Webb.

The children of Henry Alexander Trimble and Fay Webb:

J385—Dale Ray Trimble. Born on June 23, 1941.

J386—William Ernest Trimble. Born on December 26, 1946.

J387—Henry Alexander Trimble. Born in December 1949.

J326—Barney Franklin Trimble, Jr. Son of Barney Franklin Trimble and Mary Charlotte Davis. (Seventh generation of James and Grace Trimble.) Born in Kentucky and married Edna Randolph. They live at Golconda, Illinois.

The children of Barney Franklin Trimble, Jr. and Edna Randolph:

J388—Barney Franklin Trimble III

J389—John Randolph Trimble.

J329—Foster Oliver Trimble. Son of Henry Oliver Trimble and Charlotte Clark. (Seventh generation of James and Grace Trimble.) Born in 1896. He married two times: first, we do not know the name of his first wife; second, he married Lura Schouse. Foster Oliver had a twin brother, Forrest A., who died December 17, 1897, and is buried in the May and Trimble Family Cemetery near Lola, Kentucky.

The child of Foster Oliver Trimble and his first wife:

J390—Woodrow Trimble.

The children of Foster Oliver Trimble and Lura Schouse:

+**J391—Eugene Earl Trimble.** Born on April 28, 1922. Married Betty Sue Owen.

J392—Glen Allen Trimble. Born on April 7, 1927. He lives in New York City. He is unmarried and an engineer graduate of the University of Kentucky.

+**J393—Lou Ellen Trimble.** Born on April 21, 1929. Married Ralph W. Preston, Jr. This family lives at Bellaire, Texas.

J338—James Leonard Trimble. Son of William Franklin Trimble and Mary Daniel. (Seventh generation of James and Grace Trimble.) Born on December 27, 1896. He was living in 1957 at Signal Mountain, Tennessee. Married Sarah Bouldin in 1921.

Trimble Families of America

The children of James Leonard Trimble and Sarah Bouldin:

J394—James Leonard Trimble. Born on August 11, 1922.

+**J395—William Franklin Trimble.** Born on October 22, 1923. Married Evelyn Hudson.

J396—Myra Elizabeth Trimble. Born on August 8, 1925. Married Charles Conner.

+**J397—Robert Daniel Trimble.** Born on August 7, 1927. Married Alice Kirk.

+**J398—Edwin Ernest Trimble.** Born on November 25, 1931. Married Mary Elizabeth McDougall.

J399—Wanda Azalee Trimble. Born in 1936. Married Sigsbee Jumper and had one child: Sigsbee Benjamin Jumper, Jr.

J400—Wendell Rickey Trimble. Born on October 17, 1945.

J339—Jesse Newton Trimble. Son of William Franklin Trimble and Mary Daniel. (Seventh generation of James and Grace Trimble.) Born on November 21, 1898. Married Minnie Treptau in 1917.

The children of Jesse Newton Trimble and Minnie Treptau:

J401—Oline Trimble. Born on June 15, 1919.

+**J402—Dwight Trimble.** Born on January 29, 1921. Married Nathalee Baxter.

J403—Aline Trimble. Born on August 26, 1923. Married John Tiller.

J404—Newton Trimble. Born on August 20, 1924.

+**J405—Jesse Trimble.** Born on February 25, 1926. Married Lola Laving.

J406—Frances Azalee Trimble. Born on October 18, 1929. Married Richard Waters and lives in Mobile, Alabama.

J407—Judy Marie Trimble. Born on May 30, 1933. Married Doyce Mitchell and lives in Mobile, Alabama.

J408—Shirley Ann Trimble. Born on April 18, 1939.

J409—John Franklin Trimble. Born on January 18, 1945.

J343—Archie Edward Trimble. Son of William Franklin Trimble and Mary Daniel. (Seventh generation of James and Grace Trimble.) Born on August 15, 1907. Married Elizabeth Reid in 1927.

The child of Archie Edward Trimble and Elizabeth Reid:

+**J410—Archie Edward Trimble, Jr.** Born on May 6, 1928. Married Opal Gaar.

J344—Woodrow Vertie Trimble. Son of William Franklin Trimble and Mary Daniel. (Seventh generation of James and Grace Trimble.) Born on June 14,

1912. Married Lila Hancock in 1933.

The children of Woodrow Vertie Trimble and Lila Hancock:

J411–Gary Woodrow Trimble. Born on May 12, 1939.

J412–Nancy Lynn Trimble. Born on April 18, 1951.

J345–Erston Daniel Trimble. Son of William Franklin Trimble and Mary Daniel. (Seventh generation of James and Grace Trimble.) Born on July 3, 1917. Married in 1936 to Jessie Knight.

The children of Erston Daniel Trimble and Jessie Knight:

J413–Erston Daniel Trimble, Jr. Born on November 16, 1937.

J414–Eric Christopher Trimble. Born on November 23, 1944.

J415–Millie Elaine Trimble. Born on November 30, 1949.

J367–Williard Lynn Trimble. Son of Elbert Reziah Trimble and Johnnie B. Reed. (Seventh generation of James and Grace Trimble.) Born in 1906. Married in 1927 Velma Gilbert.

The children of Williard Lynn Trimble and Velma Gilbert:

J416–Mary Lynn Trimble.

J417–Robert Gilbert Trimble.

J374–Harold Frederick Trimble. Son of Audrey Beaird Trimble and Hazel Dell Weatherly. (Seventh generation of James and Grace Trimble.) Born on August 15, 1919 in Lone Oak, Hunt County, Texas and died on January 22, 2003 in Dallas, Dallas County, Texas. Married Dorothy Nell Dunn. She was born in 1917 in Texas and died on October 24, 1997 in Hunt County, Texas.

The child of Harold Frederick Trimble and Dorothy Nell Dunn:

J418–Glenda Ruth Trimble. Born on June 4, 1948 in Greenville, Hunt County, Texas. Married Harold Wayne Wise on May 6, 1994 Las Vegas, Clark County, Nevada. Harold was born on September 30, 1940 in Cottle County, Texas.

J391–Eugene Earl Trimble. Son of Foster Oliver Trimble and Lura Schouse. (Eighth generation of James and Grace Trimble.) Born on April 28, 1922, near Joy, Kentucky. Married Betty Sue Owen from Conway, Arkansas, on April 7, 1950. They live at 5203 Flanders Avenue, Kensington, Maryland. Eugene Trimble is a certified public accountant and a partner in a successful office supply company. He is the author of the book *Trimble Families,* published in 1958, which is the most outstanding work on the Trimble families that this author has seen. Most of our information on the descendents of John and

Trimble Families of America

James and Grace Trimble are exact copies of the Eugene Trimble book. He dealt more extensively with these families than we have. The author has had the pleasure of visiting in Eugene's home and meeting his family.

The children of Eugene Earl Trimble and Betty Sue Owen:

J419—Gary Allen Trimble. Born on October 4, 1955.

J420—Janet Lynn Trimble. Born on September 9, 1958.

J393—Lou Ellen Trimble. Daughter of Foster Oliver Trimble and Lura Schouse. (Eighth generation of James and Grace Trimble.) Born on April 21, 1929. Married Ralph W. Preston, Jr. This family lives at Bellaire, Texas.

The children of Ralph W. Preston, Jr. and Lou Ellen Trimble:

J421—Thomas Glen Preston. Born in 1953.

J422—David Preston. Born in 1956.

J395—William Franklin Trimble. Son of James Leonard Trimble and Sarah Bouldin. (Eighth generation of James and Grace Trimble.) Born on October 22, 1923. Married in 1943 to Evelyn Hudson.

The children of William Franklin Trimble and Evelyn Hudson:

J423—Diane Elizabeth Trimble. Born on October 8, 1944.

J424—Selenda Gail Trimble. Born in 1946.

J397—Robert Daniel Trimble. Son of James Leonard Trimble and Sarah Bouldin. (Eighth generation of James and Grace Trimble.) Born on August 7, 1927. Married Alice Kirk in 1947.

The children of Robert Daniel Trimble and Alice Kirk:

J425—Robert Daniel Trimble, Jr. Born on August 17, 1949.

J426—Debra Lynn Trimble. Born on January 16, 1954.

J398—Edwin Ernest Trimble. Son of James Leonard Trimble and Sarah Bouldin. (Eighth generation of James and Grace Trimble.) Born on November 25, 1931. Married on January 1, 1954, to Mary Elizabeth McDougall.

The child of Edwin Ernest Trimble and Mary Elizabeth McDougall:

J427—Connie Lee Trimble. Born on September 6, 1955.

J402—Dwight Trimble. Son of Jesse Newton Trimble and Minnie Treptau. (Eighth generation of James and Grace Trimble.) Born on January 29, 1921. Married Nathalee Baxter in 1947.

The child of Dwight Trimble and Nathalee Baxter:

J428—Mary Jane Trimble. Born on October 2, 1954.

J405–Jesse Trimble. Son of Jesse Newton Trimble and Minnie Treptau. (Eighth generation of James and Grace Trimble.) Born on February 25, 1926. Married Lola Laving. They live at Daytona Beach, Florida.

The child of Jesse Trimble and Lola Laving:

J429–Dennie Trimble. Born on February 11, 1947.

J410–Archie Edward Trimble, Jr. Son of Archie Edward Trimble and Elizabeth Reid. (Eighth generation of James and Grace Trimble.) Born on May 6, 1928. Married Opal Gaar on April 8, 1951.

The children of Archie Edward Trimble and Opal Gaar:

J430–Archie Edward Trimble III. Born on June 12, 1953.

J431–Steven Winston Trimble. Born on November 26, 1955.

K - James Trimble 1840s

K1—James Trimble was born in 1814 in Enniskillen, Northern Ireland, and died in 1873 in western Pennsylvania. He is buried at Crossroads Presbyterian Cemetery at Gibsonia, Pennsylvania. James married two times. His first wife died in Ireland and James married the second time to Margaret Graham, who died in 1888 at age seventy-eight. James died in an accident while driving a wagon home from Pittsburgh, Pennsylvania, in 1873.

We are gratefully indebted to Vice-Admiral Paul E. Trimble, USCG Ret., Emma Bierline Schriener, and Mrs. Nelson Dean for their excellent genealogy of this Trimble line. This author has in his library a *Trimble History,* published in Enniskillen, Ireland, which states that William Trimble, founder of the *Enniskillen Impartial Reporter Newspaper,* had a younger brother James who migrated to America. Since Enniskillen is a small town and this James Trimble, who is the subject of Part I, is from Enniskillen, it would appear logical to assume that this be the same family, but we have no definite proof of this theory.

The children of James Trimble and Margaret Graham:

+ **K2—John Trimble.** Born on June 16, 1839. Married Mary Ann Robertson.
+ **K3—James Trimble.** Born on August 11, 1841. Married Alice Gardner.
  K4—Elizabeth Margaret Trimble. Born on September 25, 1843, in Enniskillen and died in May 1926. She married Samuel McCush, who was born on January 12, 1837, and they are buried in the Crossroads Cemetery. Samuel and Elizabeth lived in the vicinity of Mars or Valencia, Pennsylvania.
+ **K5—Robert Trimble.** Born on March 24, 1846. Married Emma Alvina Wright.
  K6—Thomas Trimble. Born in 1850 in Pennsylvania. He spent several years with his brother James near Agenda, Kansas (Republic County, U.S. Census of 1880). He later moved to Oklahoma where he died.
  K7—Richard Trimble. Born on May 21, 1852, in Pennsylvania. He died on June 20, 1875 and is buried at Crossroads Cemetery. He did not marry.

K2—John Trimble. Son of James Trimble and Margaret Graham. Born on June 16, 1839, in Enniskillen, Ireland, and died on June 18, 1910. Married Mary Ann Robertson. They are buried in the Ingomar Methodist Church Cemetery, Ingomar, Pennsylvania. John was a private in the Thirty-sixth Regiment of Pennsylvania Volunteers in the Civil War.

Trimble Families of America

The children of John Trimble and Mary Ann Robertson:

K8—Margaret Trimble. Died at birth.

K9—William Trimble.

K10—Byron Trimble.

K11—Annie Trimble.

+ **K12—Harry Lindley Trimble.** Born on November 24, 1881. Married Ellen Harris.

K3—James Trimble. Son of James Trimble and Margaret Graham. Born on August 11, 1841, in Enniskillen, Ireland, and died in 1922 in Kansas. Married Alice Gardner on December 27, 1867, near Pittsburgh, Pennsylvania. Alice was born in 1849 and died in 1889 at Agenda, Kansas. James and Alice are buried in the Agenda Cemetery.

The children of James Trimble and Alice Gardner:

K13—James Trimble. Born on September 10, 1868, in Pennsylvania. Died on August 21, 1949.

K14—John Trimble. Born in Pennsylvania on July 17, 1870 and died on October 13, 1950.

K15—Margaret Trimble. Born in Pennsylvania on March 20, 1873 and died on April 26, 1950.

K16—Alice Trimble. Born in Pennsylvania on October 16, 1876 and died on October 27, 1951.

K17—Robert Trimble. Born in Agenda, Kansas on May 25, 1879, and died on February 4, 1949.

K18—William Trimble. Born near Agenda, Kansas on December 6, 1881, and died on May 2, 1946.

K19—Luella Trimble. Born near Agenda, Kansas on April 24, 1884, and died on January 30, 1958.

+ **K20—Harry Leon Trimble.** Born on August 23, 1886. He married two times.

K21—Eliza Trimble. Born near Agenda, Kansas on March 18, 1889. Married Ira Rock and lived in Rossville, Indiana. He died in 1958. Eliza had a stroke but was living in 1970.

K5—Robert Trimble. Son of James Trimble and Margaret Graham. Born on March 24, 1846, in Enniskillen, Ireland. Robert came to America in his infancy and died on March 5, 1915. Married Emma Alvina Wright, who was born in 1855 and died in 1936.

The children of Robert Trimble and Emma Alvina Wright:

Trimble Families of America

+ **K22—John Edgar Trimble.** Born on November 13, 1878. Married Julia Florence Adams.

+ **K23—Robert M. Trimble.** Born on November 20, 1880. Married Minnie P. Keck.

+ **K24—Margaret Trimble.** Born on June 22, 1884. Married George E. Wagner.

+ **K25—Joseph Omer Trimble.** Born on June 18, 1885. Married Augusta Henrietta McConnell.

+ **K26—Charles Dambach Trimble.** Born on October 8, 1887. Married Emma Matilda Blank.

+ **K27—Della Trimble.** Born on March 8, 1890. Married Thomas File.

+ **K28—Emma Pearl Trimble.** Born on November 19, 1892. Married Frank Ralph Bierline.

+ **K29—Elder McKinley Trimble.** Born on January 22, 1897. Married Elizabeth Mae Phillips.

K12—Harry Lindley Trimble. Son of John Trimble and Mary Ann Robertson. (Third generation of James Trimble and Margaret Graham.) Born on November 24, 1881, in Ingomar, Pennsylvania, and died on January 10, 1957, at Ingomar. Married Ellen Harris in 1918.

The children of Harry Lindley Trimble and Ellen Harris:

+ **K30—Mary Ellen Trimble.** Married Walter F. Calvert. They live in Pittsburgh, Pennsylvania.

+ **K31—Margaret Anne Trimble.** Married Samuel W. Lees, Jr.

K20—Harry Leon Trimble. Son of James Trimble and Alice Gardner. (Third generation of James Trimble and Margaret Graham.) Born on August 23, 1886, near Agenda, Kansas, and died on May 25, 1969. He married twice. First, to Velma Ellen Long.

Velma was born on March 9, 1893, near Agenda, Kansas where she and Harry Leon were married on April 4, 1912. In 1918, towards the end of World War I, they moved to Milaca, Minnesota, and started farming. Eventually they entered the baby chick hatching business. They were divorced during the 1930s and Velma kept the family together. She died in October 1962 at Milaca and is buried in the village cemetery there.

Leon moved to the Pacific Northwest and became a lumberjack. During World War II he was a foreman of a logging gang in Oregon. In the early 1940s he remarried. Interestingly, second, to Ferne Church van Buren. She was also a baby chick hatchery proprietor, in Silverton, Oregon. After the war they moved to Apache Junction, Arizona. No children were born to this union and Harry Leon died in Apache Junction in May 1969. He is buried in the Mountain View Cemetery there.

The children of Harry Leon Trimble and Velma Ellen Long:

+ **K32—Paul Edwin Trimble.** Born on March 24, 1913. Married to the former Iva E. McClaren.

+ **K33—Keith Lawrence Trimble.** Born on February 19, 1915. Married Vina Breberg of Princeton, Minnesota on January 26, 1940.

K34—Shirley Belle Trimble. Born at Milaca on January 24, 1921. Married Paul Golichia of Pittsburg, Kansas on October 27, 1950. They have two children: Paula Jean, born on April 16, 1953 at Pittsburg, and Gayle Ellen, born on October 27, 1950.

K35—Alice Jean Trimble. Born in Milaca on August 1, 1925. Married Kenneth E. Janeksela of Ely, Minnesota on July 9, 1949. Their two children: Tracy Lynn, born on January 25, 1957, at Minneapolis; and James Kenneth, born on March 19, 1960.

K36—Dorothy Anne Trimble. Born in Milaca on May 8, 1928. Unmarried. She was living at Saint Paul in 1971.

K22—John Edgar Trimble. Son of Robert Trimble and Emma Alvina Wright. (Third generation of James Trimble and Margaret Graham.) Born on November 13, 1878, at Butler County, Pennsylvania. Died on November 30, 1938. Married on April 8, 1909, to Julia Florence Adams of Johnstown, Pennsylvania. She was born in 1887 and died in 1929. John was a farmer in Butler County.

The children of John Edgar Trimble and Julia Florence Adams:

K37—John Edgar Trimble. Born on February 24, 1910, at Johnstown, Pennsylvania. He works as a crane man in Aliquippa.

K38—Emma Catherine Trimble. Born on July 21, 1911, at Johnstown. She is married and lives at New Brighton, Pennsylvania.

K39—Ethel Marie Trimble. Born on January 21, 1913, at Johnstown, Pennsylvania. She is married and lives at Freedom, Pennsylvania.

K40—Garnet Louise Trimble. Born on October 23, 1914, at Johnstown, Pennsylvania. She died on December 17, 1942.

K41—Robert Louis Trimble. Born on February 9, 1919, in Butler County, Pennsylvania, and died on July 5, 1944.

K42—Lloyd Wilmer Trimble. Born on January 2, 1922, in Butler County, Pennsylvania. He is married and works as a crane man at Valencia,

Trimble Families of America

Pennsylvania.

K43—Lawrence Lavern Trimble. Born on March 6, 1924, in Butler County, Pennsylvania. He is married and works as a truck driver. He lives at Menomonee Falls, Wisconsin.

K44—Florence Lavada Trimble. Born on March 6, 1924, in Butler County, Pennsylvania. She is married and lives in Centerville, Pennsylvania.

K23—Robert M. Trimble. Son of Robert Trimble and Emma Alvina Wright. (Third generation of James Trimble and Margaret Graham.) Born on November 20, 1880, at Lovi, Pennsylvania died on July 7, 1945. He married Minnie P. Keck on April 6, 1904, and they lived at Mars, Pennsylvania, where he was a farmer and mill worker. Minnie was born in September 1880 and died in March 1966.

The children of Robert M. Trimble and Minnie P. Keck:

K45—Charles A. Trimble. Born on February 9, 1905, at Ogle, Pennsylvania, and died on February 27, 1908.

K46—Goldie P. Trimble. Born on December 20, 1911, at Baden, Pennsylvania. She married and lived at Zelienople, Pennsylvania. Goldie died on October 28, 1937.

K47—Raymond R. Trimble. Born on October 7, 1916, at Baden, Pennsylvania. He married and lived at Aliquippa, Pennsylvania, where he is a mill worker.

K48—Russell W. Trimble. Born on June 29, 1919, at Mars, Pennsylvania. He married and lived at Titusville, Florida, where he is a custodian.

K24—Margaret Trimble. Daughter of Robert Trimble and Emma Alvina Wright. (Third generation of James Trimble and Margaret Graham.) Born on June 22, 1884, at Cranberry Township, Butler County, Pennsylvania. She married George E. Wagner on March 8, 1904. He was born on June 24, 1882, at Marshall Township, Allegheny County, Pennsylvania. George was a carpenter and they lived in Baden, Pennsylvania. Margaret died on March 10, 1925, and George died on October 31, 1940.

The children George E. Wagner and Margaret Trimble:

K49—Arthur E. Wagner. Born on February 3, 1905, at Baden, Pennsylvania. He is a rural mail carrier.

K50—Edna Wagner. Born on August 16, 1906, at Baden. She married Paul Keck in 1928 and they live at Evans City, Pennsylvania, where she is a schoolteacher.

K51—Viola Wagner. Born on November 9, 1908, and married Oliver Boehm. They live at Beloit, Ohio.

K52—Orville R. Wagner. Born on May l, 1911, and died on August 1, 1934. He was a construction worker.

K53—Emma Wagner. Born on June 1, 1913. Married La Verne Lewis in 1932 and they live in Freedom, Pennsylvania.

K54—Harriet Wagner. Born on December 5, 1916. She married Ben Zinkham in 1940 and they live at Baden, Pennsylvania.

K55—Hazel Wagner. Born on December 9, 1918. She is married John Petrus and they live at Beaver, Pennsylvania, where Hazel is a practical nurse.

K56—Herbert L. Wagner. Born on March 28, 1921. He is married and lives at Freedom, Pennsylvania, where he is a steelworker.

K57—Lester R. Wagner. Born on August 3, 1923. He is married and lives at Baden, Pennsylvania, where he is a credit manager.

K25—Joseph Omer Trimble. Son of Robert Trimble and Emma Alvina Wright. (Third generation of James Trimble and Margaret Graham.) Born on June 18, 1885, in Butler County, Pennsylvania. Married on December 27, 1906, to Augusta Henrietta McConnell of Butler County. They lived at Zelienople, Pennsylvania, where Joseph was a molder. Joseph died on July 19, 1960, and Henrietta died on September 8, 1970.

The children of Joseph Omer Trimble and Augusta Henrietta McConnell:

K58—Ethel Marie Trimble. Born on May 3, 1907, at Mars, Pennsylvania. She married a Mr. Tonnes on August 4, 1922, and they live at Cincinnati, Ohio.

K59—Howard Leroy Trimble. Born on June 7, 1908, at Mars, Pennsylvania. He married in 1934 and died on June 27, 1966.

K60—Kenneth Omer Trimble. Born on April 23, 1910, at Mars, Pennsylvania. He married two times and lives at Warren, Ohio, where he is a foreman.

K61—Dorothy Mae Trimble. Born on January 2, 1912, at Zelienople, Pennsylvania. She married a Mr. Curry in 1930 and they live at Zelienople.

K62—Gladys Mohrbacher Trimble. Born on March 28, 1914. She married a Mr. Harter in 1933 and they live at Beaver Falls, Pennsylvania. She is a salesclerk.

K63—Viola Grace Trimble. Born on June 5, 1916, at Zelienople, Pennsylvania. She married a Mr. Boros in 1939 and they live at Zelienople.

K64—Della Pearl Trimble. Born on May 4, 1918, at Harmony, Pennsylvania. She married a Mr. Barton. They live at Scottsdale, Arizona.

K65—Joseph Oscar Trimble. Born on April 22, 1921, at Zelienople, Pennsylvania. He married in 1946 and lives at Zelienople where he is a mill worker.

Trimble Families of America

K66—Ellen Ruth Trimble. Born on July 5, 1923 and died on December 28, 1925.

K67—Kathryn Lorain Trimble. Born on August 29, 1925 and married a Mr. Cunningham in 1946. She is a salesclerk in Zelienople, Pennsylvania.

K68—Alice Lucille Trimble. Born on January 6, 1928 and married a Mr. Mignanelli in 1952.

K69—Betty Lou Trimble. Born on January 13, 1930 and married a Mr. Sapienza in 1952. They live at Harmony, Pennsylvania.

K70—Richard Lee Trimble. Born on September 12, 1931 and married in 1954. Lives at Zelienople, Pennsylvania, where he is a plumber.

K26—Charles Dambach Trimble. Son of Robert Trimble and Emma Alvina Wright. (Third generation of James Trimble and Margaret Graham.) Born on October 8, 1887, in Butler County, Pennsylvania. He married Emma Matilda Blank on June 22, 1910. Charles died on December 29, 1957.

The children of Charles Dambach Trimble and Emma Matilda Blank:

K71—Virgil Gustave Trimble. Born on January 24, 1911, at Monaca, Pennsylvania. He married in 1933 and lives. in Tucson, Arizona, where he is in the appliance repair business.

K72—Leora Trimble. Born on July 28, 1913, in Beaver County, Pennsylvania. She married in 1944 to Chester Rhodes and they live at Beaver Falls, Pennsylvania.

K73—Merl Alvin Trimble. Born on May 15, 1918, in Beaver County, Pennsylvania. He married in 1945 and lives in Tucson, Arizona, where he operated a mobile home court.

K74—Clifford Leroy Trimble. Born on November 12, 1922, in Butler County, Pennsylvania. He married in 1942 and lives in Tucson, Arizona, where he is in the appliance sales.

K75—Doris Trimble. Born on April 16, 1925, in Butler County, Pennsylvania. He married in 1945 to Clair Goehring and they live at New Brighton, Pennsylvania.

K76—Grace Trimble. Born on July 15, 1927, in Butler County, Pennsylvania. She married in 1954 to Wray E. Dennis and they live at Wexford, Pennsylvania.

K27—Della Trimble. Daughter of Robert Trimble and Emma Alvina Wright. (Third generation of James Trimble and Margaret Graham.)

Born on March 8, 1890, in Butler County, Pennsylvania. Married on March 27, 1912, to Thomas File, a farmer in Butler County. He died in 1963 and Delia died on June 19, 1938.

The children of Thomas File and Delia Trimble:

K77—Thomas File. Born on June 18, 1915 and died on August 8, 1916.

K78—Dorothy File. Born on August 18, 1918. She married a Mr. Woods in 1950 and they live at Economy Boro, Pennsylvania.

K79—Chester File. Born on July 18, 1925, in Butler County, Pennsylvania. He died in July of 1925.

K28—Emma Pearl Trimble. Daughter of Robert Trimble and Emma Alvina Wright. (Third generation of James Trimble and Margaret Graham.) Born on November 19, 1892, in Cranberry Township, Butler County, Pennsylvania. She was married on September 14, 1911, to Frank Ralph Bierline of Allegheny County, Pennsylvania. Frank is now a retired carpenter in Freedom, Pennsylvania, and Emma died on October 1, 1968.

The children of Frank Ralph Bierline and Emma Pearl Trimble:

K80—Robert Frederick Bierline. Born on November 7, 1912, at Freedom, Pennsylvania. He married in 1932 and lived at Freedom where he was a carpenter. Robert died on September 30, 1935.

K81—Emma Kathryn Bierline. Born on February 13, 1915, at Freedom, Pennsylvania and married in 1930 to Joseph R. Schreiner. They live at Freedom, Pennsylvania.

K82—Ida Mae Bierline. Born on January 15, 1917, at Rochester, Pennsylvania. She married in 1945 to Melvin Dempsey and they live at Streetsboro, Ohio, where she is a nurse.

K83—Frank Joseph Bierline. Born on April 8, 1919, at Freedom, Pennsylvania. He married in 1960 and lives in East Palestine, Ohio, where he is a steel plant superintendent.

K84—Ralph Edgar Bierline. Born on May 11, 1921, at Freedom, Pennsylvania. He married in 1943 and lives at Zelienople, Pennsylvania, where he is an electrician.

K85—Lowrie McCandless Bierline. Born on January 26, 1924, arid married in 1954. He lives at Rochester, Pennsylvania, where he is a truck driver.

K86—Wilmer Elder Bierline. Born on September 11, 1926. He lives at Freedom, Pennsylvania, where he works in the steel mill.

K87—Infant daughter Bierline. Born on September 12, 1929 and died at birth.

K29—Elder McKinley Trimble. Son of Robert Trimble and Emma Alvina Wright. (Third generation of James Trimble and Margaret Graham.) Born on January 22, 1897, at Cranberry Township, Butler County, Pennsylvania. He married on December 26, 1916, to Elizabeth Mae Phillips, born in 1897 and died on March 30, 1951. Elder died in May 1930. He was a worker on the railroad, and they lived at New Sewickley Township, Pennsylvania. Elizabeth lived at Rochester, Pennsylvania, after Elder's death.

The children of Elder McKinley Trimble and Elizabeth Mae Phillips:

K88—Naomi Mae Trimble. Born on July 10, 1917, at Monaca, Pennsylvania. She married in 1943 to a Mr. Stuck and lives at Beaver, Pennsylvania.

K89—Evelyn Ruth Trimble. Born on March 18, 1919, at Monaca, Pennsylvania. She married in 1947 to a Mr. Schmidt and they live at Rochester, Pennsylvania.

K90—Eleanor Elizabeth Trimble. Born on March 8, 1921, at New Sewickley Township, Pennsylvania. She lived at Rochester, Pennsylvania, where she was a secretary. She died on August 12, 1941.

K91—Mildred Alice Trimble. Born on March 19, 1923, at New Sewickley Township. She was married in 1940 to a Mr. Halfhill and they live at Rochester, Pennsylvania.

K92—Edsel William Trimble. Born on June 7, 1925. He married in 1951 and lives at Dayton, Ohio, where he is an industrial engineer.

K93—Wilbur Rayburn Trimble. Born on May 9, 1927 and married in 1951. He lived at Rochester, Pennsylvania, where he was a plumber. Wilbur died on June 24, 1970.

K94—Robert La Verne Trimble. Born on November 6, 1929. Married in 1956 and lives at Monaca, Pennsylvania, where he is a technical service representative.

K30—Mary Ellen Trimble. Daughter of Harry Lindley Trimble and Ellen Harris. (Fourth generation of James Trimble and Margaret Graham.) Married Walter F. Calvert. They live in Pittsburgh, Pennsylvania.

The children of Walter F. Calvert and Mary Ellen Trimble:

K95—Walter F. Calvert, Jr. Born on January 17, 1947.

K96—William Harry Calvert. Born on April 27, 1949.

K97—John Raymer Calvert. Born on December 28, 1950.

K31—Margaret Anne Trimble. Daughter of Harry Lindley Trimble and Ellen Harris. (Fourth generation of James Trimble and Margaret Graham.) Married Samuel W. Lees, Jr.

The child of Samuel W. Lees, Jr. and Margaret Anne Trimble:

K98—Ellen Jane Lees. Born on March 22, 1953. The Leeses live at Ingomar, Pennsylvania.

K32—Paul Edwin Trimble. (Admiral Retired). Son of Harry Leon Trimble and Velma Ellen Long. (Fourth generation of James Trimble and Margaret Graham.) Born on March 24, 1913, at Agenda, Kansas. This author (John Farley Trimble) has had extensive communication in the past few years with Paul E. Trimble and considers him to be a man of rare intellect and congenial personality. Despite his busy professional schedule, he has found time to research his family history. This he did quite thorough in detail. Paul Edwin and this author (John Farley Trimble), being the same age, spent much of their life curious, without knowledge, of their ancestral background.

Paul Edwin Trimble graduated from Milaca High School, Milaca, Minnesota, ranking near the top of his class. While in high school he was a member of the National Honor Society, and was active on the school paper, in football, basketball, and scout programs.

His military career began with his appointment as cadet to the U.S. Coast Guard Academy at New London, Connecticut, on August 13, 1932. He was graduated with a B.S. degree and a commission as ensign in the Coast Guard on June 8, 1936.

Subsequently he advanced to lieutenant (j.g.) on June 8, 1939, lieutenant, on February 25, 1942, lieutenant commander on December 8, 1942, commander, on April 15, 1949, captain on July 1, 1958, rear admiral on July 1, 1964, and vice-admiral on July 27, 966.

After leaving the academy he served six years of sea duty on board various Coast Guard cutters stationed on the coast of New England: the cutter Mojave, Algonquin, Chelan, Tahoe, and Cayuga. In August in 1940, he was ordered to a postgraduate training course at the Harvard School of Business Administration, where he was graduated with a master's degree (MBA) with distinction in June 1942; he was named a Baker Scholar in 1941.

With the service's World War II expansion program underway, he resumed regular military duties at the Third Coast Guard District office in New York as finance officer. From August 1943 to August 1945 he commanded, respectively, the patrol frigates, U.S.S. Hoquiam, operations. While with the Sausalito he also commanded, Escort Division Twenty-seven, which ultimately was turned over to Russia under the lend-lease program.

After the war he was assigned as assistant chief, Budget Division, at Coast Guard Headquarters, Washington, D.C. From October 1951 to July 1953, he commanded the Starts (WAG-83), a multi-function (search and rescue, logistics, law enforcement, buoy tending, icebreaking) vessel then stationed at Juneau, Alaska. Following that tour of. duty, he was returned to Coast Guard Headquarters to serve, successively, as chief, Budget and Cost Analysis Division, until September 1955, as assistant comptroller until August 1957, and as comptroller of the Coast Guard until August 1959.

After commanding the 327-foot Duane on ocean station patrol and search and rescue in the North Atlantic for two years, he became commanding officer of the Coast Guard base at Boston, Massachusetts, in July 1961.

On July 13, 1966, the president named Rear Admiral Trimble to the post of assistant commandant of the U.S. Coast Guard with the rank of vice-admiral (succeeding retiring VADM William D. Shields, USCG).

In December 1966, VADM Trimble received the Distinguished Service Medal from the secretary of the treasury for his service from June 1964 to November 1966.

In June 1967 he was presented the Legion of Merit Medal by the secretary of transportation, Alan S. Boyd, for his performance as chairman of the Interagency Task Force.

In June 1970, he was presented the Distinguished Service Medal by Secretary John A. Volpe for his performance as assistant commandant of the Coast Guard.

On July 15, 1970, VADM Trimble became president of the Lake Carriers' Association with offices at 1411 Rockefeller Building, Cleveland, Ohio.

VADM Trimble is married to the former Iva E. McClaren of Milaca, Minnesota. They reside at Lakewood, Ohio.

The children of Paul Edwin Trimble and Iva E. McClaren:

+ **K99—Sharrol Lee Trimble.** Born on April 8, 1940, at Saint Paul, Minnesota. Married James E. Foels on July 22, 1960, at Boston, Massachusetts. He is a graduate of the U.S. Coast Guard Academy, class of 1959, and is now operations officer with the Coast Guard at Saint Petersburg, Florida.

K100—James Patton Trimble. Born on June 17, 1946, in Cheverly, Maryland. He married Margaret Elizabeth Moody of Washington, D.C., August 24, 1968. They were married at Chatham, Massachusetts. Margaret was born on September 21, 1945, at York, Pennsylvania.

K33—Keith Lawrence Trimble. Son of Harry Leon Trimble and Velma Ellen Long. (Fourth generation of James Trimble and Margaret Graham.) Born in Agenda, Kansas on February 19, 1915. Married Vina Breberg of Princeton, Minnesota on January 26, 1940.

The children of Keith Lawrence Trimble and Vina Breberg:

K101—Kenneth Gene Trimble. Born on November 9, 1940.

K102—Larry Keith Trimble. Born on August 26, 1944, at Milaca.

K103—Donald Lee Trimble. Born on March 26, 1948.

K104—Judith Ann Trimble. Born on September 14, 1953, at Milaca.

K99—Sharrol Lee Trimble. Daughter of Paul Edwin Trimble and Iva E. McClaren. (Fourth generation of James Trimble and Margaret Graham.) Born on April 8, 1940, at Saint Paul, Minnesota. Married James E. Foels, July 22, 1960, at Boston, Massachusetts. He is a graduate of the U.S. Coast Guard Academy, class of 1959, and is now operations officer with the Coast Guard at Saint Petersburg, Florida.

The children of James E. Foels and Sharrol Lee Trimble:

K105—Christy Lyn Foels. Born on February 14, 1961 in Florida.

K106—Stacy Jean Foels. Born on October 23, 1962, in Alaska.

K107—Craig Steven Foels. Born on January 16, 1964, in Alaska.

K108—Kelly Lee Foels. Born on February 22, 1966, in California.

L - William and Penelope Trimble

L1—William Trimble was born in Ireland on January 1, 1783, and died in Logan County, Kentucky on June 17, 1864. Married Penelope Ivey, born on May 25, 1790, in North Carolina (another source says Nashville, Tennessee) and died in Logan County on September 13, 1884. William was a farmer.

We are gratefully indebted to Mr. and Mrs. Lee Trimble Good of 208 Montclair, Tulsa, Oklahoma, for the extensive data on this William Trimble lineage which they found in the Eli Trimble scrapbook.

The children of William Trimble and Penelope Ivey:

+ **L2—Harvey M. Trimble.** Born on December 31, 1808. Married Matilda Proctor.

  L3—Matilda S. Trimble. Born on January 29, 1811. Married John B. Murray of Simpson County, Kentucky on December 15, 1827.

  L4—Sarah "Sallie" Trimble. Born on September 27, 1813 Married Greenberry Copeland on August 8, 1832.

+ **L5—John C. Trimble.** Born on February 10, 1816. Married Rhoda Ann Proctor.

  L6—Elizabeth "Betsey" Trimble. Born on July 22, 1818 Married on December 24, 1843, to Ambrose Dabney Owen and they lived in Webster County, Missouri.

+ **L7—Aaron D. Trimble.** Born on December 15, 1821 and died December 2, 1879.

  L8—Nancy Trimble. Born on November 14, 1822. Married on March 25, 1850, to Luther Riggan (Riggins) and the lived in Robertson County, Tennessee. She died on July 19, 1905.

  L9—Margaret Trimble. Born on March 21, 1824. Married Spivilly Sivels on December 22, 1844.

+ **L10—Selden Y. Trimble.** Born on September 17, 1827. Married Mary Ellen Morehead.

  L11—Andrew Jackson Trimble. Born on November 3, 1829 and lived and died in California.

+ **L12—James Riley Trimble.** Born on May 20, 1835. Married Letitia Elizabeth C. Hill.

L2—Harvey M. Trimble. Son of William Trimble and Penelope Ivey. Born on December 31, 1808 and died in 1907. Married in 1827 to Matilda Proctor, who was born on September 12, 1813.

The children of Harvey M. Trimble and Matilda Proctor:

L13—Charles Y. P. Trimble. Born on May 6, 1831.

L14—Clifton P. Trimble. Born on February 22, 1833.

L15—Amanda E. Trimble. Born on December 17, 1834.

L16—Robin Francis P. "Bob" Trimble. Born on October 23, 1836. Married Nancy B. Ashoranah on December 8, 1854.

L17—Mary E. Trimble. Born in 1839.

L5—John C. Trimble. Son of William Trimble and Penelope Ivey. Born on February 10, 1816 and died on August 26, 1887. He was born at Adairville, Kentucky. Married Rhoda Ann Proctor, born on February 3, 1818, and died on June 1, 1856. She, too, was born at Adairville.

The children of John C. Trimble and Rhoda Ann Proctor:

+ L18—William Jefferson Trimble. Born on July 18, 1839. Married Martha Jane Brixey.

L19—James H. Trimble. Born on October 5, 1841, and on died January 28, 1858, at Adairville, Kentucky.

L20—Elizabeth Trimble. Born on October 5, 1843, and died on January 21, 1858, at Marshfield, Missouri.

L21—John Montecue Trimble. Born on February 19, 1846 and died on December 25, 1863. He was Born at Marshfield.

L22—Penelope Trimble. Born on February 16, 1848, at Marshfield and died on January 21, 1896.

L23—Charles Samuel Trimble. Born on April 4, 1850, at Marshfield and died on January 25, 1912.

L24—Sarah Jane Trimble. Born on June 1, 1852, at Marshfield and died on February 26, 1905.

L25—Margaret M. Trimble. Born on May 20, 1855, at Marshfield and died on November 10, 1934.

L7—Aaron D. Trimble. Son of William Trimble and Penelope Ivey. Born on December 13, 1820, at Adairville, Kentucky, and died on December 2, 1879.

Aaron D. Trimble married and had a son:

L26—Ed Trimble. Born on July 4, 1876.

L10—Selden Trimble. Son of William Trimble and Penelope Ivey. Born on September 17, 1827, at Adairville, Kentucky, and died on October 4, 1873. He married Mary Ellen Morehead, born in 1832 and died in 1890.

Trimble Families of America

The children of Selden Y. Trimble and Mary Ellen Morehead:

L27—Su Major Trimble. Born on January 1, 1860 and died on June 14, 1918. Married John P. Garnett.

+**L28—Bettie Morehead Trimble.** Born on November 2, 1861. Married Selden Lyne.

+**L29—Grace Martin Trimble.** Born on October 18, 1863. Married two times.

+**L30—Selden Y. Trimble II.** Born on April 19, 1867 Married Mariah Perkins.

+**L31—Henry Leland Trimble.** Born on July 3, 1869. Married Julia Perkins.

L32—Mary M. Trimble. Born on February 15, 1872 and died on August 10, 1872.

L33—Nellie Manly Trimble. Born on December 19, 1873 and died on March 19, 1892. She never married.

L12—James Riley Trimble. Son of William Trimble and Penelope Ivey. Born on May 20, 1835, at Adairville, Kentucky, and died on November 20, 1887. He was married on August 4, 1857, to Letitia Elizabeth C. Hill, who died in 1897.

The children of James Riley Trimble and Letitia Elizabeth C. Hill:

+**L34—Mary E. Trimble.** Married J. A. McClanahan.

+**L35—Anna Trimble.** Married John Harris.

+**L36—Sarah Trimble.** Born on November 20, 1863 and was living in 1956. Married Will Harris.

+**L37—Willie Lena Trimble.** Married John Walton Winkler.

+**L38—Jimmie Trimble.** Married James H. Pritchett.

+**L39—Charles Eugene Trimble.** Married Mattie Dickerson.

+**L40—Elmore (Elmo) Trimble.** Married Sallie Price.

L18—William Jefferson Trimble. Son of John C. Trimble and Rhoda Ann Proctor. (Third generation of William Trimble and Penelope Ivey.) Born on July 18, 1839, at Adairville, Kentucky, and died on October 3, 1920. Married on February 3, 1858, to Martha Jane Brixey, born in 1837 and died in 1925 at Marshfield, Missouri. William served with the Union Army in the Civil War and founded the City National Bank in Tulsa, Oklahoma. For additional details on this family see *The History of Webster County, Missouri.*

The children of William Jefferson Trimble and Martha Jane Brixey:

+**L41—John William Trimble.** Born on December 12, 1861, at Waldo, Missouri (Webster County), and died on June 22, 1923. Married Jincy L. Davis.

+ **L42—Eli Trimble.** Born on February 17, 1867, at Waldo, Missouri. Married Mrs. Stella Blanchard Scott, a widow.

+ **L43—Hulda M. Trimble.** Born on June 13, 1870. Married Albert Bentley Good.

+ **L44—Charles Ira Trimble.** Born on October 4, 1872. Married Lily V. Tunnell.

+ **L45—Sallie Jane Trimble.** Born on September 23, 1881. Married Clyde Maston Williams.

L28—Bettie Morehead Trimble. Daughter of Selden Y. Trimble and Mary Ellen Morehead. (Third generation of William Trimble and Penelope Ivey.) Born on November 2, 1861 and died on August 27, 1921. Married Selden Lyne.

The children of Selden Lyne and Bettie Morehead Trimble:

L46—Selden Trimble Lyne. Born on December 22, 1880. He died on November 17, 1907. He never married.

L47—Mary Nelle Lyne. Born on May 6, 1883. She was living in 1957 at Bowling Green, Kentucky. Mary Nelle did considerable research on her Trimble line and Eugene E. Trimble used much of her information in his book and we, too, are gratefully indebted for this valuable genealogy.

L48—Grace Garnett Lyne. Born in 1886 and married M. D. Browning.

L29—Grace Martin Trimble. Daughter of Selden Y. Trimble and Mary Ellen Morehead. (Third generation of William Trimble and Penelope Ivey.) Born on October 18, 1863 and died on May 28, 1936. Grace married two times: first, to Edward O. Garretson, and second, to Bunyan P. Eubank.

The children of Edward O. Garretson and Grace Martin Trimble:

L49—Mary Neva Garretson. Born on April 14, 1890. She married, first, J. R. Sparks and, second, M. R. Schuster.

L30—Selden Y. Trimble II. Son of Selden Y. Trimble and Mary Ellen Morehead. (Third generation of William Trimble and Penelope Ivey.) Born on April 19, 1867 and died on August 14, 1950. Married Mariah Perkins. He was a lawyer and businessman of Hopkinsville, Kentucky. He was graduated from Bethel College, Russellville, Kentucky, about 1886 and practiced law in that town. He represented Logan County in the legislature of 1892. His wife's father was Ben T. Perkins, a prominent banker and lawyer in Elkton. Selden moved to Elkton in 1898 to form a partnership with his father-in-law. In 1904 he moved to Hopkinsville where he lived the remainder of his life. Selden's father was Reverend S. Y. Trimble, Baptist minister, who was among the first

Trimble Families of America

missionaries that went from America to Africa.

The children of Selden Y. Trimble II and Mariah Perkins:

L50—Selden Y. Trimble III. Born on September 17, 1906. He married Sarah Ridley.

L51—Mary Perkins Trimble. Born on March 2, 1909. Married Lou Byers.

L52—Jane Mariah Trimble. Born on April 6, 1913. Married LeRoy Parker.

L31—Henry Leland Trimble. Son of Selden Y. Trimble and Mary Ellen Morehead. (Third generation of William Trimble and Penelope Ivey.) Born on July 3, 1869 and died on July 5, 1947. Married Julia Perkins, sister of Mariah Perkins, Married Selden Y. Trimble II, Julia Perkins and Mariah Perkins are daughter of Ben T. Perkins.

The children of Henry Leland Trimble and Julia Perkins:

L53—Roxane Weathers Trimble. Born on March 15, 1899. Married Leo McCall.

L54—Selden Y. Trimble. Born on August 22, 1901 and died on June 28, 1906.

L55—Mariah Jane Trimble. Born on August 6, 1903 and died on February 19, 1904.

L56—Flora Trimble. Born on September 14, 1904. Married Dr. Keene Hill of Burkesville, Kentucky.

L57—Henry Leland Trimble, Jr. Born on February 21, 1906. Died on October 30, 1910.

L58—Thornton Perkins Trimble. Born on June 24, 1907. Married Anne Ridings.

L59—Benjamin Perkins Trimble. Born on May 16, 1910. Married Anna Elisa Andres.

L60—Julia Porter Trimble. Born on October 24, 1912. She never married.

Henry Leland Trimble married second Seleta Thompson. This is found in the *Story of Russellville, Kentucky.*

L34—Mary E. Trimble. Daughter of James Riley Trimble and Letitia Elizabeth C. Hill. (Third generation of William and "Penelope Ivey Trimble.) Married J. A. McClanahan of Peoria, Illinois.

The children of J. A. McClanahan and Mary E. Trimble:

L61—Eugene McClanahan.

L62—Ethel McClanahan.

L63—James McClanahan.

L64—Jean McClanahan.

L65—Mignon McClanahan.

Trimble Families of America

L35—Anna Trimble. Daughter of James Riley Trimble and Letitia Elizabeth C. Hill. (Third generation of William Trimble and Penelope Ivey.) Married John Harris of Simpson County, Kentucky.

The children of John Harris and Anna Trimble:

L66—Vera Oma Harris.
L67—Rayburn Harris.
L68—Roy Maynard Harris.
L69—Luther Harris.
L70—Ruth Harris.
L71—James Harris.
L72—Nora Harris.

L36—Sarah Trimble. Daughter of James Riley Trimble and Letitia Elizabeth C. Hill. (Third generation of William Trimble and Penelope Ivey.) Born on November 20, 1863 and was living in 1956. Married Will Harris and they have lived in Franklin County, Kentucky.

The children of Will Harris of Sarah Trimble:

L73—Vada Harris.
L74—Lillian Harris.
L75—Lucy Harris.
L76—Annie Lou Harris.
L77—Cassie Harris.
L78—Hortense Harris. Born in 1897. Married Vincent Taylor.
L79—Selden Harris. Died in 1954. Married Mildred Johns.

L37—Willie Lena Trimble. Daughter of James Riley Trimble and Letitia Elizabeth C. Hill. (Third generation of William Trimble and Penelope Ivey.) Died in 1948. Married John Walton Winkler and they lived in Springfield, Tennessee.

The children of John Walton Winkler of Willie Lena Trimble:

L80—Lillian Winkler.
L81—Belle Winkler.
L82—Charles Winkler.
L83—Josephine Winkler.
L84—Helen Winkler.

L38—Jimmie Trimble. Daughter of James Riley Trimble and Letitia Elizabeth C. Hill. (Third generation of William Trimble and Penelope Ivey.) Married James H. Pritchett and lived in Fullerton, California.

L - William and Penelope Trimble

Their children James H. Pritchett of Jimmie Trimble:

L85—Jessie Ruth Pritchett.

L86—Mary Pritchett.

L87—Ruby Pritchett.

L39—Charles Eugene Trimble. Son of James Riley Trimble and Letitia Elizabeth C. Hill. (Third generation of William Trimble and Penelope Ivey.) Born in Logan County, Kentucky. He died at his home near Adairville, in Logan County, Kentucky on January 26, 1956. Married Mattie Dickerson.

Charles Eugene Trimble spent his entire life in the Logan County area except for a few years that he lived near Dallas, Texas, where he operated a ranch for his uncle, Will Hill. Upon his return to Kentucky, Charles purchased the old John Bailey farm, three miles northeast of Adairville, where he lived until 1926. He was a successful and influential farmer and in 1907 assisted in the organization of the First National Bank of Adairville and was elected to the first board of directors.

The children of Charles Eugene Trimble and Mattie Dickerson:

+ **L88—James Rufo Trimble.** Born on July 18, 1890. Married Neva Kroker.

L89—Mabel Trimble. Born on July 28, 1894. Married Loy B. Moore of Adairville, Kentucky.

L90—C. Hershel Trimble. Born on September 13, 1898. Married Ina Edwards.

L91—unnamed child Trimble. Died young.

L40—Elmo Trimble. Son of James Riley Trimble and Letitia Elizabeth C. Hill. (Third generation of William Trimble and Penelope Ivey.) Married Sallie Price and lived in Barstow, Texas.

The children of Elmo Trimble and Sallie Price:

L92—Virginia Trimble.

L93—Sarah Trimble.

L94—Elmo Trimble, Jr.

L41—John William Trimble. Son of William Jefferson Trimble and Martha Jane Brixey. (Fourth generation of William Trimble and Penelope Ivey.) Born on December 12, 1861, at Waldo, Missouri (Webster County). He died June 22, 1923. Married Jincy L. Davis. She was Born in 1857 in Double-Springs, Arkansas, and died in 1913.

The children of John William Trimble and Jincy L. Davis:

L95—Johnnie Jefferson Trimble. Born on May 20, 1881 and died August 24, 1883. He was born at Waldo, Missouri.

L96—Ella May Trimble. Born on September 14, 1882, at Seymour, Missouri.

L97—Charles Ulysis Trimble. Born on December 30, 1885, at Seymour, Missouri, and died July 3, 1925.

L98—Fred Thomas Trimble. Born on May 6, 1887, at Seymour.

+ **L99—Aaron Ray Trimble.** Born on September 19, 1893, at Seymour.

L100—Lillian Mable Trimble. Born on January 3, 1896, at Seymour, Missouri.

L42—Eli Trimble, Dr. Son of William Jefferson Trimble and Martha Jane Brixey. (Fourth generation of William Trimble and Penelope Ivey.) Dr. Eli Trimble was the son of a prominent pioneer family in the Ozarks. He was born on February 17, 1867, at Waldo, Missouri. He received his preliminary education in the schools of Seymour and then was the Frisco as a telegraph operator in Rogersville. When the decision came to study medicine, he entered the Louisville Medical College in Kentucky, from which he graduated in 1896. For forty-three years he practiced in Seymour.

Dr. Trimble was a member of the Masonic lodge. On February 17, 1907, he was married to Mrs. Stella Blanchard Scott. She was the widow of Dr. Dewitt Clinton Scott of Raymond, Wisconsin. She had a daughter by this first marriage, Blanch Janette Scott, born on March 5, 1888, in East Troy, Wisconsin. Blanch married Fred Martin, and they lived at Chico, California.

Dr. Trimble loved the outdoors, his garden, and his beautiful flowers. He died on January 5, 1940, just one month before his seventy-third birthday. His funeral was held in the Seymour Baptist Church.

L43—Hulda M. Trimble. Daughter of William Jefferson Trimble and Martha Jane Brixey. (Fourth generation of William Trimble and Penelope Ivey.) Born on June 13, 1870, at Waldo, Missouri, and died in 1952. Married on September 25, 1890, to Albert Bentley Good, born on October 7, 1865, and died on September 22, 1937. He was born in Marshfield, Missouri.

The children of Albert Bentley Good and Hulda M. Trimble:

L101—Dora E. Good. Born on September 14, 1891, at Seymour.

L102—Fay Good. Born on March 3, 1894, at Seymour and died June 6, 1897.

L103—Clyde B. Good. Born on May 27, 1901, at Dustin (Native Americans Territory), Oklahoma, and died on April 28, 1938.

+ **L104—Fred Trimble Good.** Born on May 27, 1901, at Dustin and died on October 27, 1967. Clyde and Fred were fraternal twins.

L44—Charles Ira Trimble. Son of William Jefferson Trimble and Martha Jane Brixey. (Fourth generation of William Trimble and Penelope Ivey.) Born on October 4, 1872, at Waldo, Missouri. Married Lily V. Tunnell on April 11,

1894. She was born on July 13, 1875, at Hartsville, Missouri.

The children of Charles Ira Trimble and Lily V. Tunnell:

L105—Iris Trimble. Born on January 1, 1897, at Seymour, Missouri.

L106—Joe Tunnell Trimble. Born on September 30, 1903, at West Plains, Missouri.

L45—Sallie Jane Trimble. Daughter of William Jefferson Trimble and Martha Jane Brixey. (Fourth generation of William Trimble and Penelope Ivey.) Born on September 23, 1881, at Waldo, Missouri. Married on October 15, 1900, to Clyde Maston Williams, born in 1878 at Utica, Missouri.

The daughter of Clyde Maston Williams and Sallie Jane Trimble:

L107—Ruth Williams. Born on November 10, 1902, at Seymour.

L88—James Rufo Trimble. Son of Charles Eugene and Mattie Dickerson Trimble. (Fourth generation of William Trimble and Penelope Ivey.) Born on July 18, 1890, and married Neva Kroker.

The children of James Rufo Trimble and Neva Kroker:

L108—Martha L. Trimble. Born in 1917.

L109—James Trimble. Born in 1919.

L99—Aaron Ray Trimble. Son of John William Trimble and Jincy L. Davis. (Fifth generation of William Trimble and Penelope Ivey.) Born on September 19, 1893, at Seymour, Missouri. He currently lives at Sand Springs, Oklahoma, where he is a dentist.

Aaron Ray Trimble has a son:

L110—Aaron Ray Trimble, Jr. He is a dentist in practice with his father at 300 North Lincoln, Sand Springs, Oklahoma.

L104—Fred Trimble Good. Son of Albert Bentley Good and Hulda M. Trimble. (Fifth generation of William Trimble and Penelope Ivey.) Born on May 27, 1901 and died on October 27, 1967. He was born at Dustin (Native Americans Territory), Oklahoma. Fred married Irene May Carlin. She was born at Tulsa (Native Americans Territory). Irene died in April 1960. Fred was married in 1963 to Minnie Milliken.

The children of Fred Trimble Good and Irene May Carlin:

+L111—Lee Trimble Good. Born on March 9, 1928, at Tulsa, Oklahoma. Married Mary Elizabeth Edwards.

+L112—Owen Carlin Good. Born on July 13, 1932, at Tulsa, Oklahoma. Married Sandra Ackley.

L111—Lee Trimble Good. Son of Fred Trimble Good and Irene May Carlin. (Sixth generation of William Trimble and Penelope Ivey.) Born on March 9, 1928, at Tulsa, Oklahoma. Married on October 9, 1948, to Mary Elizabeth Edwards, born on March 1, 1930, at Tulsa. Lee and Mary Elizabeth Good are co-founders of the Tulsa Muzzle Loading Firearms Matches which are held annually at the John Zink Ranch west of Skiatook, Oklahoma. This is the largest black powder competition west of the Mississippi.

In 1968 they were appointed consultants to the Sites Gun Shop Restoration at Arrow Rock, Missouri. Lee served as president of the Tulsa Archaeological Society as did Mary Elizabeth for two years. She was the first woman to be elected president of this society. Both have served as state representative to the Oklahoma Anthropological Society.

Mary Elizabeth is completing Memoir No. 2 for Central States Archaeological Societies on the "Guebert Site, 1719-1833 ... a Kaskaskia Native Americans Village." She serves on the advisory board (as historian) for the Murrell House, a Cherokee landmark in Oklahoma.

Lee builds mountain dulcimores (a primitive Appalachian folk instrument). He is employed as research specialist for the J. M. Davis Gun Museum in Claremore, Oklahoma. Mary Elizabeth is employed as public relations assistant and assistant editor of *Seis News* for Seismograph Service Corporation, Tulsa.

The children of Lee Trimble Good and Mary Elizabeth Edwards Good:

L113—Alyne Elizabeth Good. Born on December 25, 1952, at Tulsa.

L114—Clyde Lee Good. Born on April 9, 1956, at Tulsa.

L115—Martin Marshall Good. Born on December 26, 1958, at Tulsa.

L112—Owen Carlin Good. Son of Fred Trimble Good and Irene May Carlin. (Sixth generation of William Trimble and Penelope Ivey.) Born on July 13, 1932, at Tulsa. Married Sandra Ackley.

Owen Carlin Good married, second, Donnie Dale Murphree Glossop, born on September 1, 1933. She had three children by her previous marriage to Raymond Glossop: Don, Lou Ann, and Sue Ellen Glossop.

The children of Owen Carlin Good and Sandra Ackley:

L116—Debbie Lee Good. Born on March 12, 1959, at Tulsa, Oklahoma.

Other Trimble Families in America

Despite all efforts, it has been impossible to trace all the Trimble families, with whom we have corresponded, to their immigrant ancestors. However, we feel certain that we have recorded all the early Trimble immigrants to America, and through this book those who proceed to research further into their family ancestry will be able to establish their complete lineage.

M - Thomas Trimble and Sarah Matthews

M1—Thomas Trimble Born on January 7, 1785, was living in Indiana County, Pennsylvania, in 1849. He died on January 9, 1853. He married Sarah Matthews, on December 8, 1812.

The information concerning this Trimble family line was supplied by Richard Dean Trimble, 2057 Arch Drive, Falls Church, Virginia 22043; and his father, Thomas Edward Trimble, Sr., Route 3, Box 55, Marshall, North Carolina 28753.

Thomas Trimble was born in Westmoreland County, Pennsylvania, and migrated to Indiana County in 1849. He lived on land in the Trimble District in Montgomery Township. Sarah Matthews Trimble was born on August 22, 1790 and died June 6, 1875.

The children of Thomas Trimble and Sarah Matthews:

M2—Eliza Trimble. Born on December 2, 1813. Married on March 16, 1838, to Daniel Hill. They had four daughters and four sons. Three others died in infancy.

M3—William Trimble. Born on June 13, 1815 and died on April 28, 1825.

M4—Martha Trimble. Born on December 3, 1816 and died on November 15, 1869. Married John W. Huston, on April 6, 1842. He was born on February 26, 1817 and died on September 28, 1898. They had four daughters and two sons.

+ **M5—Thomas Trimble.** Born on June 9, 1818. Married Mary Ann Bostick.

M6—James Trimble. Born on February 20, 1820. Married Sarah Jane Wallace on April 4, 1849. She was born in 1826. They had five daughters and two sons. They had triplets, which were girls, named: Adah, Carrie, and Emma.

M7—John Trimble. Born on February 9, 1822. Married Mary Ford on February 18, 1851. They had two daughters and seven sons.

M8—Archibald Trimble. Born on March 15, 1824 and died on December 20, 1841.

M9—Unknown Trimble. Born on October 28, 1826 and died on August 5, 1854.

M10—Samuel Trimble. Born on August 3, 1827 and died on December 15, 1854.

M11—Mary Jane Trimble. Born on February 25, 1829. Married James Horrell on October 5, 1859. They had five daughters and three sons.

M12—One child. Died in infancy.

M13—Sarah Ann Trimble. Born on April 23, 1833. Married Francis Ford on

M - Thomas Trimble and Sarah Matthews

December 24, 1856. They had four daughters and six sons.

M5—Thomas Trimble. Son of Thomas Trimble and Sarah Matthews. Born on June 9, 1818 and died in December 1896. Married Mary Ann Bostick. She was Born in 1834 and died in 1928.

The children of Thomas Trimble and Mary Ann Bostick:

M14—John Trimble. Born on March 26, 1853 and died on April 6, 1930. Married Eliza Dye on July 4, 1874. She was born in 1856 and died in 1930.

M15—Ann Trimble. Born on January 26, 1855 and died on January 9, 1908. Married on July 2, 1874, to Alex McCracken. He was born in 1852 and died in 1909.

M16—Sarah Trimble. Born on November 28, 1856 and died on September 3, 1931. Married Bruce Irwin in March 1882.

+ **M17—Samuel Trimble.** Born on November 30, 1858. Married Emma Bliss.

+ **M18—Benjamin Trimble.** Born on April 17, 1861. Married Rose Irwin.

M19—Thomas Trimble. Born on February 17, 1863 and died on May 16, 1933. Married Mary Colmer on October 5, 1884. She was born in 1867 and died in 1949.

+ **M20—Felix Trimble.** Born on March 5, 1865. He married May Powell.

M21—James Trimble. Born on January 31, 1867 and died on February 2, 1941. Married Ada Bennett on June 23, 1891. She was born in 1869.

M22—Mary Trimble. Born on December 5, 1869 and died on February 23, 1892. Married Patrick Smith on September 10, 1887. He was born in 1869.

M23—Margaret Trimble. Born on December 22, 1870 and died on November 16, 1897. Married McClelland Brady.

M17—Samuel Trimble. Son of Thomas Trimble and Mary Ann Bostick. (Third generation of Thomas Trimble and Sarah Matthews.) Born on November 30, 1858 and died on July 11, 1933. Married Emma Bliss on January 1, 1885. She was Born in 1858 and died in 1939.

The children of Samuel Trimble and Emma Bliss:

M24—Cora Blanche Trimble. Born on March 17, 1887.

M25—Celia Kathryn Trimble. Born on February 8, 1889.

M26—Cleave Alline Trimble. Born on May 8, 1891.

M27—John Thomas Trimble. Born on March 8, 1893.

M28—James Ford Trimble. Born on March 18, 1895.

M29—Lucia Moyer Trimble. Born on March 13, 1898.

M30—Sara Jean Trimble. Born on July 20, 1900.

M31—Ora Ruth Trimble. Born on May 10, 1905.

M32—Henrietta Elizabeth Trimble. Born on April 27, 1908.

M18—Benjamin Trimble. Son of Thomas Trimble and Mary Ann Bostick. (Third generation of Thomas Trimble and Sarah Matthews.) Born on April 17, 1861 and died on January 17, 1915. Married Rose Irwin in April 1885. They were married at Hillsdale, Pennsylvania. She died on May 17, 1907. She was born in 1861.

The children of Benjamin Trimble and Rose Irwin:

M33—Bessie Francis Trimble. Born on September 12, 1887 and died on June 1, 1953.

+ **M34—Thomas Edward Trimble.** Born on February 24, 1890. Married Emily Gahagan.

M35—John Irvin Trimble. Born on August 16, 1891 and died on September 20, 1943.

M36—Edna Kate Trimble. Born on August 5, 1893.

M37—Charles Frank Trimble. Born on May 11, 1895 and died on July 8, 1896.

M38—Sallie Estelle Trimble. Born on May 12, 1897 and died on April 5, 1937.

M39—Ida Zoe Trimble. Born on April 4, 1899 and died on March 18, 1968.

M40—Alex A. Trimble. Born on October 4, 1901 and died on February 6, 1960.

M41—Mary Pauline Trimble. Born on September 9, 1903 and died on November 29, 1903.

M42—Helen Christine Trimble. Born on May 6, 1906 and died on June 13, 1906.

M20—Felix Trimble. Son of Thomas Trimble and Mary Ann Bostick. (Third generation of Thomas Trimble and Sarah Matthews.) Born on March 5, 1865. He married May Powell on March 27, 1888. He was born in 1870.

The children of Felix Trimble and May Powell:

M43—Cora Belle Trimble. Born on December 17, 1888 and died on June 22, 1965. Married Allonza K. Sheesley on April 4, 1932. He was born in 1891.

M44—Nellie Mae Trimble. Born on January 7, 1891 and died on December 29, 1960. Married Rex Brickle in 1913. He was born in 1888. They had two sons.

M45—Paul Trimble. Born in 1893 and died in 1894.

M46—Frank Powell Trimble. Born on May 11, 1896. Married Velma Conner on October 7, 1917, and they had two daughters. She was born in 1901.

M47—Porter Samuel Trimble. Born on July 31, 1898. Married Edna Grace

Goss, on December 31, 1918. They had one daughter and two sons. Edna was born in 1901.

M48—Harry Ambrose Trimble. Born on February 6, 1901. Married Winefred Gromley on November 28, 1923. They had one daughter and one son. Winefred was born in 1906.

M49—Chester Arthur Trimble. Born on June 19, 1903. He married two times: first, to Maxie Henry on December 31, 1924, and they had four children; second, to Melvina ——— on January 3, 1963. Maxie died on March 28, 1961.

M34—Thomas Edward Trimble. Son of Benjamin Trimble and Rose Irwin. (Fourth generation of Thomas Trimble and Sarah Matthews.) Born on February 24, 1890. Married Emily Gahagan on December 27, 1914. Thomas Edward Trimble, Sr., was born in the coal mining section of Pennsylvania on February 24, 1890. He was the second child of Benjamin and Rose Trimble. He worked in the mines of Pennsylvania before moving to West Virginia, where he worked in logging camps and then followed the logging operations through Virginia and then into North Carolina where he met and married Emily Gahagan in 1914. After several years of work in logging camps in western North Carolina he then worked in CCC camps. He worked until retirement at Oak Ridge, Tennessee, for the Atomic Energy Commission and the Carbide Carbon Company.

Four of his children are teachers and between them they represent some forty-six years of teaching service. One daughter is a nurse and one a part-time teacher.

The children of Thomas Edward Trimble and Emily Gahagan:

M50—Edna Mable Trimble. Born on December 5, 1915. Married Charlie Martin, born in 1908 and died in 1964. They were married on June 20, 1936. She is a part-time teacher. They had no children.

+ **M51—Blanche Marie Trimble.** Born on December 23, 1917. Married John Wayne Chandler on May 25, 1940. John was born in 1908 and died in 1966.

+ **M52—Thomas Edward Trimble, Jr.** Born on January 24, 1922. Married Bernice Lee on January 3, 1950. She was born on October 14, 1923. Thomas Edward had twenty-two years in the service of the U.S. Navy and is retired. He has taught school for the past six years.

+ **M53—Hazel Beryl Trimble.** Born on January 9, 1920. Married Hampton Guthrie on May 9, 1945. He was born in 1914. They have a daughter, Sandra Ann Guthrie, born on June 10, 1946, who is a teacher. Sandra married Robert Halpin, on May 19, 1968.

+ **M54—Thelma Faye Trimble.** Born on April 14, 1925. Married David M. Ramsey, on September 9, 1944. Thelma is a nurse.

+ **M55—Ann Louise Trimble.** Born on June 24, 1929. She has been a teacher for twenty years. Married Ben Howze on July 7, 1949.

+ **M56—Howard Russell Trimble.** Born on May 15, 1934 and has been a teacher for several years. Married Wilma Reece on May 28, 1959.

+ **M57—Richard Dean Trimble.** Born on June 30, 1942. He has been a teacher for the past seven years. Married in 1963 to Louise Wright.

M51—Blanche Marie Trimble. Born on December 23, 1917. Married John Wayne Chandler on May 25, 1940. John was born in 1908 and died in 1966.

The daughter of John Wayne and Blanche Marie Trimble:

M58—John Wayne Chandler, Jr. Born on November 15, 1942.

M52—Thomas Edward Trimble, Jr. Born on January 24, 1922. Married Bernice Lee on January 3, 1950. She was born on October 14, 1923. Thomas Edward had twenty-two years in the service of the U.S. Navy and is retired. He has taught school for the past six years.

The son of Thomas Edward Trimble, Jr, and Bernice Lee:

+ **M59—Thomas James Trimble.** Born on December 18, 1951.

M53—Hazel Beryl Trimble. Born on January 9, 1920. Married Hampton Guthrie on May 9, 1945. He was born in 1914.

They have a daughter,

M60—Sandra Ann Guthrie. Born on June 10, 1946, who is a teacher. Sandra married Robert Halpin, on May 19, 1968.

M54—Thelma Faye Trimble. Born on April 14, 1925. Married David M. Ramsey, September 9, 1944. Thelma is a nurse.

The daughters of David M. Ramsey and Thelma Faye Trimble:

M61—Lynne Ramsey. Born in 1946 and married to Robert Lombard, they have a son, Robert Lombard, Jr.

M62—Catherine Ramsey. Born on December 18, 1948, a college graduate, Married Robert Edwards.

M55—Ann Louise Trimble. Born on June 24, 1929. She has been a teacher for twenty years. Married Ben Howze on July 7, 1949.

The children of Ben Howze and Ann Louise Trimble:

M63—Karen Howze. Born in 1950.

M64—Christine Howze. Born in 1951.

M65—Kelly Howze. Born in 1953.

M66—Stephen Howze. Born in 1957.

M67—Martin Howze. Born in 1962.

M68—Elizabeth Howze. Born in 1964.

M56—Howard Russell Trimble. Born on May 15, 1934 and has been a teacher for several years. Married Wilma Reece on May 28, 1959.

The children of Howard Russell Trimble and Wilma Reece:

M69—Deborah Trimble. Born in 1961.

M70—Allan Russell Trimble. Born in 1964.

M57—Richard Dean Trimble. Born on June 30, 1942. He has been a teacher for the past seven years. Married in 1963 to Louise Wright.

They have two children:

M71—Leslie Carole. Born on July 6, 1965,

M72—Richard Dean Trimble II. Born on October 14, 1966.

M59—Lynne Ramsey. Born in 1946 and married to Robert Lombard.

The son of Robert Lombard and Lynne Ramsey:

M73—Robert Lombard, Jr.

N - Millard Trimble of Montgomery County, Kentucky

We are gratefully indebted to Henry Price Trimble of Route 1, Jeffersonville, Kentucky 40337, for the genealogy of his Trimble family line. This family is, in all probability, descended from David of the Five Trimble Brothers.

N1–Millard Trimble. Married Lofa Wells. They had eight children.

The children of Millard Trimble and Lofa Wells:

+ **N2–Henry Philmore Trimble.** Born on May 4, 1880. Married Nannie Chany.

N3–Oliver Trimble. Born in 1883 and died in infancy.

N4–Hallie Trimble. Born in 1885 and died in 1950. He married Clemie White. They have two sons and four daughters. They live in Ohio.

+ **N5–Hisele Trimble.** Born in 1887 and died in 1953. Married Nannie Bell Martin.

+ **N6–James Burgin Trimble.** Born in 1889 and died in 1956. He was called "J.B." and married Eddie White. They had four children: James, who died in infancy; Hobert, born in 1911 and married in Tennessee and has five children; Bettie, born in 1913 and has one daughter, Dellia; Jimmie, who is still at home in Montgomery County, Kentucky.

+ **N7–Eddie Trimble.** Born in 1891 and died in 1966. He married Margaret French.

N8–Maggie Trimble. Born in 1893. She married George Coburn and they have one son, Sparks Coburn. He married and had a daughter. Maggie Trimble Coburn died in 1967.

N9–Lula Trimble. Born in 1882 and died in 1955. She married Taulb Parker in 1908. Then later, Lula married a second time to James Willoughby. By this marriage, Lula had one son who died. Lula and Taulb Parker had eight children.

N2–Henry Philmore Trimble. Son of Millard Trimble and Lofa Wells. Born on May 4, 1880 and died on December 10, 1952. Married Nannie Chany in 1900 and they had twelve children. For several years Henry Philmore was a U.S. Mail carrier.

The children of Henry Philmore Trimble and Nannie Chany:

+ **N10-Greenia Trimble.** Born on August 23, 1901. Married Banford Powell. They had two children: Irene, who married Salvator Woosley in

1948 and had four children; and Lillian, who married Tracy Woosley in 1950 and had three children.

+ **N11—Lofa Trimble.** Born in 1903 and died in 1952. She married Clarence Howell.

N12—Jessie Trimble. Born in 1905 and died in infancy.

N13—Mary Kathern Trimble. Born in 1907. She married Fred Henry and had six children: Pauline, Dewie, Mable, Richard, Susie, and Freddie.

+ **N14—Johnny Trimble.** Born on November 2, 1909. Married Fanny Harrison.

N15—Hazel Trimble. Born in 1911. Married Carl Powell and they have six children: Imogene, Dallas, Faye, Henry, Homer, and Elwood. This family lives in Estill County, Kentucky.

N16—Elizabeth Trimble. Born in 1912. Married Harry McDowell and they with their two children live in Estill County.

+ **N17—James William Trimble.** Born in 1914. Married Mildred Moberly.

N18—Flora Trimble. Born in 1916. Married Russell Woosley and they have six children: Delnoe, Wavalene, Henry Walter, JoAnn, Sue, Berna Pearl. This family lives in Oldham County, Kentucky.

N19—Beulah Trimble. Born in 1919. Married Belvie Tipton in 1939. They have five children: Peggy Alice, Wavalene, James Belvie, Benton, and Sherry. This family lives in Estill County, Kentucky.

N20—Vashtie Trimble. Born in 1921 and died in infancy.

N21—Mealie Trimble. Born on December 23, 1923. Married Velvie Noe in 1942. They have six children: Henry Wallace, Barbara, Nancy, Virginia Mae, Theota, and Viola. This family lives in Ohio.

N5—Hisele Trimble. Born in 1887 and died in 1953. Married Nannie Bell Martin. This family lives in Bourbon County, Kentucky.

The children of Hisele Trimble and Nannie Bell Martin:

N22—Bertha Trimble.

N23—Clemmie Trimble.

N24—Clayton Trimble. He had a son, Clayton, Jr., who was killed while serving in the armed forces.

N6—James Burgin Trimble. Born in 1889 and died in 1956. He was called "J.B." and married Eddie White.

They had four children:

N25—James Trimble. Died in infancy.

N26—Hobert Trimble. Born in 1911 and married in Tennessee and has five children.

N27—Bettie Trimble. Born in 1913 and has one daughter, Dellia.

N28—Jimmie Trimble. He is still at home in Montgomery County, Kentucky.

N7—Eddie Trimble. Son of Millard Trimble and Lofa Wells. Born in 1891 and died in 1966. Married Margaret French.

The two children of Eddie Trimble and Margaret French:

N29—Evert Russell Trimble. Married Ruby Stogdale. They have one child, Wilma Jean, Married Dexter Howard. The Howards have two children.

N30—Wavelene Trimble. Married Harold Witt. They have two children: Nellie Fay, Married Robert Greer; and Harold Wayne Witt, Jr., Married —— Walters and they have two children.

N10-Greenia Trimble. Born on August 23, 1901. Married Banford Powell.

They had two children:

N31—Irene Trimble. She married Salvator Woosley in 1948 and had four children.

N32—Lillian Trimble. She married Tracy Woosley in 1950 and had three children.

N11—Lofa Trimble. Born in 1903 and died in 1952. She married Clarence Howell. This family lives in Ohio.

The children of Clarence Howell and Loaf Trimble:

N33—William Trimble.
N34—Ralph Trimble.
N35—Charles Trimble.
N36—Ray Trimble.
N37—Phyllis Trimble.
N38—Patricia Trimble.
N39—Margie Trimble.

N14—Johnny Trimble. Son of Henry Philmore Trimble and Nannie Chany. (Third generation of Millard Trimble and Lofa Wells.) Born on November 2, 1909. Married Fanny Harrison, October 8, 1931. She was born on April 24, 1913.

The children of Johnny Trimble and Fanny Harrison:

N40—Henry Price Trimble. Born on February 22, 1946, at Mount Sterling, Kentucky, Montgomery County. Married JoAnn Persgram in 1965. They have one daughter, Michele Lynn, born on August 23, 1968. Henry is a mechanic for the Queen Chevrolet and Oldsmobile Company in

Trimble Families of America

Jeffersonville, Kentucky.

N41—Elmer D. Trimble. Born on March 19, 1937, in Estill County, Kentucky. Married Anna Lue Cornwell in 1966. They have two children: Dee Ann, born on December 11, 1966; and John Clinton, born on August 31, 1969. Elmer is a construction worker with heavy equipment. He is self-employed.

N42—Stanley William Trimble. Born on December 7, 1943, in Montgomery County, Kentucky. Married Lorena Horn, February 7, 1970. Stanley served with the U.S. Army for three years. He is self-employed in automobile mechanics.

N43—Roy Virgil Trimble. Born on January 30, 1945, Montgomery County, Kentucky. He served the US Army in 1969 in Germany. He is in computer work.

N44—Cecil Chase Trimble. Born on March 5, 1947. Married Brenda Sue Ross, September 4, 1965. He was an assistant manager for J. J. Newberry Company and now is an assistant manager with the Winn Dixie Stores.

N45—Nannie J. Trimble. Born on October 15, 1932, in Estill County, Kentucky. Married Luther Fritt in 1953. They have two children: Judy, born on January 1, 1954, and Colinda Russ, born on October 28, 1960.

N46—Greenia Mae Trimble. Born on October 3, 1934. Married Harold Thomas Craycraft on February 22, 1959. They have two children: Mark Thomas, born on March 22, 1960; and Donna Lynn, born on May 21, 1963.

N47—Ella Clay Trimble. Born on October 15, 1939. Married Steven Ray Trimble on April 21, 1963.

N48—Martha Lee Trimble. Born on September 21, 1942. Martha attended college and worked for the state of Kentucky. She married Robert Lee Parker, and they have two children: Nancy, born on November 13, 1964, and Angela Lynn, born on September 15, 1966.

N17—James William Trimble. Son of Henry Philmore Trimble and Nannie Chany. (Third generation of Millard Trimble and Lofa Wells.) Born in 1914. Married Mildred Moberly in 1944. He served in World War II and was wounded. This family lived in Estill County, Kentucky.

The children of James William Trimble and Mildred Moberly:

N49—Winda Kay Trimble.

N50—Shirley Trimble.

N51—Nancy Trimble.

O - Archibald Trimble of Canada

This family of Trimbles migrated from County Longford, Ireland, to Canada. Around 1870, two brothers, Archibald John and William James Trimble, came to the United States and worked in the borax fields of Nevada. They joined a cousin, Ad Farrington, in the driving of the mule teams transporting the borax from the desert. Cousin Farrington was claimed by Cousin William James Trimble to have been the driver pictured on the Borax box with the 22 Mule Team. They later engaged in ranching and catching wild horses in Nevada. Eventually they returned to the area near Kearney, Nebraska. It is with the descendents of these Trimbles that this part is concerned.

We are gratefully indebted to Mrs. Margaret C. Trimble of Route 3, Glenwood Court, Kearney, Nebraska; Mrs. Hazel B. Cruise of 12 West 32nd Street, Kearney, Nebraska; W. Arch Trimble of Route 2, Box 91, Gothenburg, Nebraska; and Mrs. Elsie Matthews of 375 East 3rd Street, Logan, Utah, for their family line of Archibald Trimble.

O1—**Archibald Trimble.** Born in County Longford, Ireland, in 1779. He died on July 14, 1834, soon after coming to Canada. He is buried near Toronto, Canada. He married Sarah Reynolds, born at Castle Pollard, Westmeath County, Ireland.

　　The child of Archibald Trimble and Sarah Reynolds:

+ O2—**James Trimble.** Born on March 22, 1820, in Ireland. Married Elizabeth Clark.

O2—**James Trimble.** Son of Archibald Trimble and Sarah Reynolds. Born on March 22, 1820, in Ireland. He came to Toronto when he was eight years of age. James married Elizabeth Clark, born in Quebec, Canada on January 29, 1844.

　　The children of James Trimble and Elizabeth Clark:

+ O3—**Archibald John Trimble.** Married Margaret Eveline Marshall.
+ O4—**William James Trimble.** Married —— Marshall.
+ O5—**Ebenezer Belmont Trimble.** Married Marie C. Lawson.
　O6—**Charles Dobbins Trimble.**

O3—**Archibald John Trimble.** Son of James Trimble and Elizabeth Clark. (Third generation of Archibald Trimble and Sarah Reynolds.) Married Margaret Eveline Marshall on January 13, 1885.

　　The children of Archibald John Trimble and Margaret Eveline Marshall:

+ **O7—Walter Archibald Trimble.** Born on September 16, 1889. Married Hazel Sheridan.

+ **O8—Hazel Deane Trimble.** Born on November 22, 1894. Married Clyde William Cruise.

O4—William James Trimble. Son of James Trimble and Elizabeth Clark. (Third generation of Archibald Trimble and Sarah Reynolds.) Married in 1885 to the sister of Margaret E. Marshall, who was the wife of Archibald John Trimble. William James Trimble went to Nevada about 1873 and was naturalized for United States citizenship there. His daughter Elsie Trimble Jacquot has his naturalization papers in her possession.

The children of William James Trimble and Margaret E. Marshall:

O9—Elsie Emma Trimble. Married a Jacquot and lives at 1537 E. Avenue, Casper, Wyoming.

O10—Ella Mable Trimble.

O11—Albert William Trimble.

+ **O12—Frank Trimble.** Married Margaret C. ———.

O13—George Ira Trimble.

O5—Ebenezer Belmont Trimble. Son of James and Elizabeth Clark. (Third generation of Archibald Trimble and Sarah Reynolds.) Born at Burford Township, Ontario, Canada. Married Marie C. Lawson.

The child of Ebenezer Belmont Trimble and Marie C. Lawson:

O14—Lila E. Trimble. Born at Salix, Iowa. Married Lewis C. Matthews and they live at 375 East 3rd North, Logan, Utah.

O7—Walte Archibald Trimble. Son of Archibald John Trimble and Margaret Eveline Marshall. (Fourth generation of Archibald Trimble and Sarah Reynolds.) Born on September 16, 1889, in Phelps County, Nebraska. He died on March 21, 1959, at Gothenburg, Nebraska. Married Hazel Sheridan on November 25, 1914.

The child of Walter Archibald Trimble and Hazel Sheridan:

+ **O15—Walter Archibald Trimble.** Born on July 15, 1919. Married Bernice Anderson.

O8—Hazel Deane Trimble. Daughter of Archibald John Trimble and Margaret Eveline Marshall. (Fourth generation of Archibald Trimble and Sarah Reynolds.) Born on November 22, 1894, in Phelps County, Nebraska. Married on November 22, 1917, at Kearney, Nebraska, to Clyde William Cruise. He was a farmer and raised purebred Angus cattle; was chairman of Phelps County Board of

Supervisors until he retired and moved to Kearney. Clyde died on August 3, 1965. He had been blind for six years.

The children of Clyde William Cruise and Hazel Deane Trimble:

+ **O16—Dean Trimble Cruise.** Born on December 11, 1927. Married Wanda June Simmerman.

+ **O17—Dale Alan Cruise.** Born on July 24, 1931. Married Helen Marie Worthing.

O12—Frank Trimble. Son of William James Trimble and Margaret E. Marshall. (Fourth generation of Archibald Trimble and Sarah Reynolds.) Married Margaret C. ———. Frank died in 1962.

Frank and Margaret C. Trimble had seven daughters and four sons. We have the names of their sons but not the daughters:

O18—Jerry E. Trimble. Captain in the U.S. Air Force.

O19—Wayne Trimble. Works with guided missiles.

O20—Robert Trimble. In the U.S. Air Force.

O21—Bruce Trimble. In the U.S. Air Force.

Four of Frank and Margaret Trimble's daughters are registered nurses, and one is a teacher.

O15—Walter Archibald Trimble. Born on July 15, 1919. Married Bernice Anderson.

The children of Walter Archibald Trimble and Bernice Anderson:

O22—Judith Rose Trimble. Born in 1946 at Gothenburg, Nebraska, and married Keith J. Maurer in 1969.

O23—Walter A. Trimble. Born in 1950 at Gothenburg.

O16—Dean Trimble Cruise. Son of Clyde William Cruise and Hazel Deane Trimble. (Fifth generation of Archibald Trimble and Sarah Reynolds.) Born on December 11, 1927. Married Wanda June Simmerman on February 6, 1949. They have three sons and Dean is in the electrical business. This family lives in Loomis, Nebraska.

The children Dean Trimble Cruise and Wanda June Simmerman:

O24—Robert Dean Cruise.

O25—Russell Alan Cruise.

O26—Richard Wayne Cruise.

O17—Dale Alan Cruise. Son of Clyde William Cruise and Hazel Deane Trimble. (Fifth generation of Archibald Trimble and Sarah Reynolds.) Born on July 24, 1931. Married Helen Marie Worthing on December 27, 1955.

Dale graduated from the University of Nebraska and from the Nebraska Medical School at Omaha. He is in the obstetrics and gynecology field of medicine with his practice in Salem, Oregon.

The children of Dale Alan Cruise and Helen Marie Worthing:

O27—Mark Alan Cruise.

O28—Kevin Dale Cruise.

O29—Jeffery Dean Cruise.

O30—Susan Kay Cruise.

O31—Linda Marie Cruise.

O32—Gregory David Cruise.

P - William and Charity Trimble

P1—William Trimble and their descendants lived in Upstate New York. William was born in the 1820s and died in 1902. Charity was born in 1829 and died in 1908. Married Charity.

The children of William and Charity Trimble:

P2—George Trimble. Married Mary ——. They had one son, Herman Trimble.

P3—John Trimble. He married Viola ——. They have an adopted daughter, Bertha.

+ **P4—Ward Trimble.** Born on November 14, 1869. He married Phoebe Case.

+ **P5—Glen Trimble.** Born in 1871 and died in 1941. Married Myrtie Harris.

+ **P6—Sophronia Trimble.** Married John Fisher.

+ **P7—Belle Trimble.** Married Arthur Scullens.

P8—Sara Trimble. Died in youth.

+ **P9—Mina Trimble.** Married Moses Ketchum.

P4—Ward Trimble. Son of William and Charity Trimble. Born on November 14, 1869 and died on July 5, 1927. He married Phoebe Case.

The children of Ward Trimble and Phoebe Case:

+ **P10—Gordon Trimble.** Born on February 20, 1894. Married Faith Page.

+ **P11—Gladys Trimble.** Born on September 17, 1897. Married Lewis Carr.

+ **P12—Gertrude Trimble.** Born on March 20, 1901. Married Lyle Cartweight.

P5—Glen Trimble. Son of William and Charity Trimble. Born in 1871 and died in 1941. Married Myrtie Harris.

The children of Glen Trimble and Myrtie Harris:

P13—Dewey Trimble. Born in 1898. Married Augusta Moore. They had one child, Robert, who died in infancy.

P14—Hazel Trimble. Born in 1902. She married Adrian Zonneyville. They had no issue.

P15—Elmer Trimble. Born in 1904. Married Marian Heisel. They have two children: Verne and Glen, Jr., who has a son, David.

+ **P16—Luther Trimble.** Born in 1910. Married Beulah De Neef.

P6—Sophronia Trimble. Daughter of William and Charity Trimble. She married John Fisher.

The children of John Fisher and Sophronia Trimble:

Trimble Families of America

P17—Inez Fisher. Married two times: first, to Raymond Cotrell, and second, to George Morse. Inez had three children: Lemon, and twins, Freeman and Grandin.

P18—Marion Fisher. Married Harvey Smith. They had no issue.

P19—Mina Fisher. Married Fred Meinhardt. They had two children: Jack, who was killed in the war; and Bill, who is a doctor and has five children.

P20—Lillian Fisher. Married Paul Nettling. No issue.

P21—Christine Fisher. Married Elmer Holland. They have two children: Dolores, Married G. Waterman; and Theodore, who died on September 26, 1937.

P7—Belle Trimble. Daughter of William and Charity Trimble Married Arthur Scullens.

The two children of Arthur Scullens and Belle Trimble:

P22—Beatrice Scullens. Married Stewart Lettuce and they have two children: Richard and Jane.

P23—Leila Scullens. Married Bernard Patten who died in 1965. They have an adopted son, Jack.

P9—Mina Trimble. Daughter of William and Charity Trimble Married Moses Ketchum.

The children of Moses Ketchum and Mina Trimble:

P24—Burr Ketchum. Born on August 5, 1896. Married Helene —— on September 20, 1930. They have two children: Elizabeth, Married Martin Maloney, and Ben Ketchum, born on December 21, 1930.

P25—Clarence Ketchum. Married Esther ——. They had no issue.

P10—Gordon Trimble. Son of Ward Trimble and Phoebe Case. (Third generation of William and Charity Trimble.) Born on February 20, 1894. Married on February 17, 1915, to Faith Page.

The children of Gordon Trimble and Faith Page:

+ **P26—Marjorie Fern Trimble.** Born on December 16, 1915. Married Harry Wasdorp.

+ **P27—Joyce Trimble.** Born on June 12, 1926. Married Kenneth Rankin.

+ **P28—Keith Trimble.** Born on August 8, 1927. Married Rosanna Quick.

P11—Gladys Trimble. Daughter of Ward Trimble and Phoebe Case. (Third generation of William and Charity Trimble.) Born on September 17, 1897. Married Lewis Carr on October 15, 1919.

The children of Lewis Carr and Gladys Trimble:

P29—Paul Carr. Born on October 24, 1921. Married Marjorie Cornelius on May 21, 1947. They have five children: Sue Ann, Paula, Paul, Robert, and Kimberly.

P30—Jane Carr. Born on January 17, 1925. Married William Bassage and had two children: Lon and Lynn.

P12—Gertrude Trimble. Daughter of Ward Trimble and Phoebe Case. (Third generation of William and Charity Trimble.) Born on March 20, 1901. She married Lyle Cartweight in 1921.

The children Lyle Cartweight and Gertrude Trimble:

P31—Thomas Cartweight. Born on November 21, 1924. Married Alethe ——. They were married on July 15, 1947. They have one child: Alethe, born on April 17, 1948.

P32—Frederick Cartweight. Married Dixie Britton and they have one son, Brent.

P16—Luther Trimble. Son of Glen Trimble and Myrtie Harris. (Third generation of William and Charity Trimble.) Born in 1910. Married Beulah De Neef, on October 31, 1937.

The children of Luther Trimble and Beulah De Neef:

P33—Russell Trimble. Married Anne Dutcher. They have a son, Christopher, born on June 5, 1970. Russell has a master's degree in science and is an engineer. Anne has a B.A. and is a teacher.

P34—Harris J. Trimble. Married Vickie Hill. They have a daughter, Tammy, born on April 18, 1966; and a son, Matthew, born on July 14, 1970.

P35—Wanda K. Trimble. Married Timothy Morris and has two sons: Scott, born on September 27, 1966; and Todd, born on May 29, 1968.

P26—Marjorie Fern Trimble. Daughter of Gordon Trimble and Faith Page. (Fourth generation of William and Charity Trimble.) Born on December 16, 1915. Married Harry Wasdorp on March 19, 1937.

The three children of Harry Wasdorp and Marjorie Fern Trimble:

P36—Janice Wasdorp. Born on February 8, 1938. Married in 1956 to Rodney Van Gee. They have three children: Randy, Daniel, and Candace.

P37—Gordon Wasdorp. Born on October 8, 1937. He is teacher and holds a Ph.D. degree.

P38—Craig Wasdorp.

P27—Joyce Trimble. Daughter of Gordon Trimble and Faith Page. (Fourth generation of William and Charity Trimble.) Born on June 12, 1926. Married

P - William and Charity Trimble

Kenneth Rankin.

The children of Kenneth Rankin and Joyce Trimble:
P39—Mary Ellen Rankin.
P40—Philip Rankin.
P41—Marcy Rankin.
P42—Joanna Rankin.

P28—Keith Trimble. Son of Gordon Trimble and Faith Page (Fourth generation of William and Charity Trimble.) Born on August 8, 1927. Married Rosanna Quick on November 12, 1949.

The six children of Keith Trimble and Rosanna Quick:
P43—Keith Allen Trimble.
P44—John Trimble.
P45—Scott Trimble.
P46—Roger Trimble.
P47—Cheri Trimble.
P48—Anthony Trimble.

We are gratefully indebted to Mrs. Marjorie Wasdorp (P26) and Mrs. Augusta Trimble (P13) of Knickerbocker Road, Ontario, New York 14519, and Russell L. Trimble (P33) of 456 Tivoli Road, Pittsburgh, Pennsylvania 15239, for the genealogy of William and Charity Trimble.

Q - James Emmett Trimble

Q1–James Emmett Trimble was born on September 27, 1851 and died on February 13, 1898. He lived in Carroll County, Arkansas. Married Sarah Ann Nard.

The nine children of James Emmett Trimble and Sarah Ann Nard:

+ **Q2–Matthew Allen Trimble**. Born on June 27, 1870. Married Nancy McFarland.

+ **Q3–Thomas Trimble**. Married Belle ———.

Q4–Robert Trimble. He moved to Oklahoma and was never married.

Q5–Eliza Trimble. Born in 1876 and died in 1939. She married Isaac Howerton. This family lives at Springdale, Arkansas. Their children: Tom, Noah, Grady, Dee, Clyde, and Mose Howerton.

Q6–Sally Trimble. Married Marion Beardon. This family lived near Delmar, Arkansas. Their children: William, Mattie, Nora, Mary, Crate, and Roy Beardon.

Q7–Abraham Trimble. Married Ada ———. They lived at Pueblo, Colorado.

+ **Q8–William Henry Trimble**. Born in April 1882. Married Grace Bishop.

Q9–Lillie Trimble. Born in 1884 and died in 1963. She is buried at Los Angeles, California. Married Leo Fellows. Their children: Gaylord, Lowee, Willard, Harmon, Haldane, and Edra, Married Harold Lee and lives in Los Angeles, California.

+ **Q10–Winfield Trimble**. Married Theo ———.

Q2–Matthew Allen Trimble. Son of James Emmett Trimble and Sarah Ann Nard. Born on June 27, 1870, in Lead Hill, Arkansas. Married to Nancy McFarland in 1893 in Carroll County, Arkansas.

The children of Matthew Allen Trimble and Nancy McFarland:

+ **Q11–James William Trimble**. Born on February 3, 1894 in Osage, Carroll County, Arkansas. Married Ruth Maples on February 14, 1922, in Arkansas.

+ **Q12–Otis Carroll Trimble**. Born on November 17, 1896 and died June 6, 1967. He is buried at Green Forest, Arkansas.

+ **Q13–Flossie Lee Trimble**. Born on November 28, 1898. Married James Sisk.

Q14–Eva Lillie Trimble. Born on December 28, 1900. Married J. dell Mayes. Eva attended the University of Arkansas and taught in rural schools in Arkansas for twenty-five years. They have no children. We are deeply

Trimble Families of America

indebted to Mrs. Clell Mayes for the genealogy of her Trimble family line. It took much time and work. The Mayes live at 208 Douglas Street, Berryville, Arkansas.

+ **Q15—Claude Mack Trimble.** Born on December 8, 1903. Married Ruth Gallagher.

+ **Q16—Violet Beatrice Trimble.** Born on August 19, 1907. Married Joseph Morris Lee.

+ **Q17—Ruby Nell Trimble.** Born on October 21, 1911. Married Vern White.

+ **Q18—Lois Ardena Trimble.** Born on September 27, 1913. Married William Miller.

+ **Q19—Jerry Allen Trimble.** Born on December 28, 1915 Married Juanita Bedell.

Q3—Thomas Trimble. Son of James Emmett Trimble and Sarah Ann Nard. Born in Carroll County, Arkansas. He married Belle ———. They lived at Holdenville, Oklahoma.

The children of Thomas and Belle Trimble:

Q20—Roy Trimble.
Q21—William Trimble.
Q22—Nold Bess Trimble.
Q23—Wesley Trimble.

Q8—William Henry Trimble. Son of James Emmett Trimble and Sarah Ann Nard. Born in April 1882 and died on January 1, 1966. He is buried at Springdale, Arkansas. Married Grace Bishop

The seven children of William Trimble and Grace Bishop:

Q24—Clifford Trimble.
Q25—Halleen Trimble.
Q26—James L. Trimble.
Q27—Kate Trimble.
Q28—Carless Lee Trimble.
Q29—Carroll O. Trimble.
Q30—Mildred Trimble.

Q10—Winfield Trimble. Son of James Emmett Trimble and Sarah Ann Nard. Married Theo ——— and they lived at Pueblo, Colorado.

The children of Winfield and Theo Trimble:

Q31—Herbert W. Trimble. Lives at Pueblo, Colorado.

Trimble Families of America

Q32—Hazel Trimble. Married Pat Johnson.

Q33—Luveta Trimble. Married Jack Smith.

Q34—Kathy Trimble. Married Burley Shockley.

Q11—James William Trimble. Son of Matthew Allen Trimble and Nancy McFarland. (Third generation of James Emmett Trimble and Sarah Ann Nard.) James William graduated from the University of Arkansas at Fayetteville in 1917. Was admitted to the bar in 1925 and commenced practice in Berryville, Carroll County, Arkansas. During the First World War, he served in the United States Army as a private and was assigned to the Adjutant General's Office, Little Rock, Arkansas. He was prosecuting attorney of the fourth judicial circuit of Arkansas 1930-1938 and was circuit judge from 1938 to 1944. He then served in the United States Congress in which he served distinctively for twenty-two years. After his terms in Congress, he was an attorney for the World Bank in Washington, D.C. Later he returned to his home in Berryville, Arkansas.

James William was born on February 3, 1894, in Arkansas. He married Ruth Maples on February 14, 1922, in Arkansas.

Their children of James William and Ruth Maples:

Q35—Margaret Carol Trimble. Born on August 17, 1923 and died May 23, 1925.

Q36—James Kerry Trimble. Born on August 17, 1923. He now lives in Alaska. Married Ann Thomas, on January 30, 1954, in Alaska. Ann is a teacher in Anchorage, Alaska.

Q12—Otis Carroll Trimble. Son of Matthew Allen Trimble and Nancy McFarland. (Third generation of James Emmett Trimble and Sarah Ann Nard.) Born on November 17, 1896 and died on June 6, 1967. He is buried at Green Forest, Arkansas. Otis married Mary Eva Walker on October 24, 1920, in Arkansas. He graduated from the University of Arkansas. Later he was superintendent of Fayetteville, Arkansas, High School then of the schools of Peoria, Illinois. Otis received his Ph.D. at Harvard. At Purdue University, Otis was head of the Department of Psychology. In Washington, D.C., he was assistant in the U.S. Department of Education until 1967 when he retired and moved to Alaska.

The children of Otis Carroll Trimble and Mary Eva Walker:

Q37—A daughter Trimble. Died in infancy.

Q38—Mary Allen Trimble. Born on April 13, 1925, in Arkansas. Married Robert Juillerat on September 19, 1949. They live at Mount Kisco, New

Trimble Families of America

York.

Q13—Flossie Lee Trimble. Daughter of Matthew Allen Trimble and Nancy McFarland. (Third generation of James Emmett Trimble and Sarah Ann Nard.) Born on November 28, 1898, and married James Sisk. They lived at Blue Eye, Missouri, before moving to Berryville, Arkansas.

The children of James Sisk and Flossie Lee Trimble:

Q39—James Woodrow Sisk. Born on September 22, 1925. Married Wilma Stacey and they have two children: Mary Jo and Steven Allen.

Q40—William Joseph Sisk. Born on January 18, 1928. Married Greta Murty and has two daughters: Lee Ann and Rebecca Jo. This family lives at Overland Park, Kansas.

Q15—Claude Mack Trimble. Son of Matthew Allen Trimble and Nancy McFarland. (Third generation of James Emmett Trimble and Sarah Ann Nard.) Born on December 8, 1903. Married Ruth Gallagher on May 30, 1930. Graduated from the University of Arkansas and attended Purdue University. He was coach at the Peoria, Illinois, High School; retired a lieutenant colonel after thirty years in the service of his country; is now coaching in Yucca Middle School in Roswell, New Mexico.

The children of Claude Mack Trimble and Ruth Gallagher:

Q41—A baby Trimble. Died at birth.

Q42—Jerry Pelton Trimble. Born on August 31, 1933. Married Mary Alice Anderson. Jerry received his master's degree from the University of Nebraska and teaches and coaches at the Lincoln High School in Lincoln, Nebraska. Their children: Jerry Scott, Chris Allen, and Ann Elizabeth Trimble.

Q16—Violet Beatrice Trimble. Daughter of Matthew Allen Trimble and Nancy McFarland. (Third generation of James Emmett Trimble and Sarah Ann Nard.) Born on August 19, 1907. Married Joseph Morris Lee who is an engineer with the United States Geological Service. They were married in Arkansas on May 18, 1930.

The son of Joseph Morris Lee and Violet Beatrice Trimble:

Q43—Joseph Trimble Lee. Married Cynthia Croall of California on May 15, 1964. They have two children: Joseph Allen and Rebecca Ann.

Q17—Ruby Nell Trimble. Daughter of Matthew Allen Trimble and Nancy McFarland. (Third generation of James Emmett Trimble and Sarah Ann Nard.) Born on October 21, 1911. Married Vern White.

The children of Vern White and Ruby Nell Trimble:

Q44—David Wendell White. Graduated from the University of Arkansas and married Anna Jean Barnes. They live at High Fill, Arkansas. Their children: Teresa and Travis.

Q45—Robert Vern White. Married Imalee Hayworth and they have two children: Bobbie and Michael. Imalee died on June 12, 1967. Robert married Donna Hayworth. They live at High Fill, Arkansas.

Q46—Phyllis Jane White. Married Harold Whittle of Springdale, Arkansas, and they have a son: Stevie Whittle.

Q18—Lois Ardena Trimble. Daughter of Matthew Allen Trimble and Nancy McFarland. (Third generation of James Emmett Trimble and Sarah Ann Nard.) Born on September 27, 1913. Married William Miller. He died in January 1966.

The children of William Miller and Lois Ardena Trimble:

Q47—Viola Miller. Married a Mr. Powell and they live in Rockford, Illinois.

Q48—Dorothy Louise Miller. Married a Mr. Downs of Baytown, Texas.

Q49—Barbara Miller. Married a Mr. Bellairs of Webb City, Missouri.

Q50—Margaret Miller. Married a Mr. Eppright of Carl Junction, Missouri.

Q19—Jerry Allen Trimble. Son of Matthew Allen Trimble and Nancy McFarland. (Third generation of James Emmett Trimble and Sarah Ann Nard.) Born on December 28, 1915 Married Juanita Bedell. He graduated from the College of the Ozarks in Clarksville, Arkansas. Jerry Allen is now the sales manager for the Mutual of Omaha Insurance Company in Waterloo, Iowa.

The children of Jerry Allen Trimble and Juanita Bedell:

Q51—Patricia Ann Trimble. Born on March 10, 1939. Married James F. Cooper and they live at Des Moines Iowa.

Q52—Richard Allen Trimble. Born on February 28, 1943. Married Sarah Jane Clark of California on February 5, 1965. They live at Ames, Iowa.

R - Walter Trimble of Kanawha County, West Virginia

This Trimble family genealogy was submitted by Mrs. Jacob M. Carter, Jr., 1907 North Third Street, Monroe, Louisiana 71201.

The compiler has done extensive research trying to ascertain from which progenitor this family descended but with no concrete results.

R1—Walter Trimble married Mary Gordon Mitchell on March 19, 1823. Her brother, Dr. Charles B. Mitchell, was a United States senator. Walter and Mary were married in Nashville, Tennessee. Walter was first recorded in Charleston, West Virginia (Kanawha County). By June 1843 they were in Hempstead County, Arkansas. On March 8, 1844, Walter bought a farm in this county but died shortly before 1848. Two of his daughters were still minors. They lived in the home of their uncle, Dr. Charles B. Mitchell.

The children of Walter Trimble and Mary Gordon Mitchell:
+ **R2—Mary Jane Trimble.** Born in 1825. Married John Field.
+ **R3—Almedia Clark Trimble.** Born in 1832. Married David Block.
+ **R4—Martha Gordon Trimble.**

R2—Mary Jane Trimble. Daughter of Walter Trimble and Mary Gordon Mitchell. Born in 1825 in Kanawha County, Virginia (now West Virginia). Died in 1895 in Arkansas. Married on November 29, 1843, to John Field and lived in Arkansas.

The children of John Field and Mary Jane Trimble:
R5—John P. Field. Died in infancy.
R6—Louisa Field. Born in 1845 and married in 1864 to John J. Grinstead in Arkansas.
+ **R7—Mary Field.** Born in 1846. She married two times.
R8—Frances F. Field. Married on June 22, 1870, to John P. Lowry in Hempstead County, Arkansas.
R9—William Field. Born in Arkansas about 1854. He did not marry.

R3—Almedia Clark Trimble. Daughter of Walter Trimble and Mary Gordon Mitchell. Born in Kanawha County in 1832 and died in June 1909 in Texarkana, Arkansas. Married David Block on March 16, 1848.

The children of David Block and Almedia Clark Trimble:
+ **R10—Rosena (Rosa) Block.** Born in 1849 at Washington, Hempstead County, Arkansas, and died in 1908 at Texarkana, Arkansas. Married

December 15, 1870 to Judge Joel Dyer Conway, Jr.

R11—Abraham Block. Born in 1851 and died in 1901. He did not marry.

R12—Walter Block. Born in 1855 and died in New Orleans, Louisiana. He did not marry.

+ **R13—Frances Block.** Born in 1856. Married Dr. William Johnston.

R14—Estelle Block. Born in 1859. Married Elmore Baird and they had no issue. Estelle died in 1886.

R15—Ellen Block. Born in 1862. Married George Alston. No issue.

+ **R16—Juliet Block.** Born on October 3, 1864. Married Paul Booker.

R4—Martha Gordon Trimble. Daughter of Walter Trimble and Mary Gordon Mitchell. Born in 1836 in Kanawha County. She married two times: first, on November 27, 1855, to Dr. Samuel Harrison Harvey, and second, to L. B. Cunningham on September 18, 1866.

The children of Dr. Samuel Harvey and Martha Trimble:

R17—Charles Harvey. Born in 1856.

R18—Robert G. Harvey. Born in 1858.

R19—David B. Harvey. Born in 1860.

R20—Samuel Harrison Harvey, Jr. Born in 1862.

R7—Mary Field. Daughter of John Field and Mary Jane Trimble. (Third generation of Walter Trimble and Mary Gordon Mitchell.) Born in 1846 and died in New Mexico. She married two times: first, in 1866 to William R. Walker, and second, to Captain Thomas H. Simms.

The children of Captain Thomas H. Simms and Mary Field:

R21—Mary Simms. Married William Sels and they have one daughter: Letitia.

R22—Albert G. Simms. Married two times; first, to Mrs. Ruth Hanna McCormick. They had no issue. Albert was a physician in New Mexico.

R23—John F. Simms. Governor of New Mexico in 1954. Married Anne Schluter. Their descendents lived in Albuquerque, New Mexico, in 1954.

R24—Myra Simms. Married Albert Brack of Little Rock, Arkansas. They have a daughter.

R10—Rosena (Rosa) Block. Daughter of David Block and Almedia Clark Trimble. (Third generation of Walter Trimble and Mary Gordon Mitchell.)

The children of Judge Joel Dyer Conway, Jr. and Rosena (Rosa) Block Conway:

R25—Eola Conway. Born in 1871 and died in 1929. Married Thomas Frederick Booker on January 9, 1895. They had no children.

Trimble Families of America

    R26—Bessie Conway. Married in 1903 at Texarkana, Arkansas, to John Thomas. No issue.

    R27—David Block Conway. He did not marry.

    R28—Gray Conway. Married Norma Hill. No issue.

    R29—Josie Conway. Married Adam Offenhauser. They had a daughter: Katrina.

    R30—Charles Mitchell Conway. He did not marry.

    R31—George Taylor Conway. Married May O'Dwyer. They had six children.

    R32—Walter Block Conway. Married Posey Trippett. They had one son, Walter B. Conway, Jr.

    R33—Rose Conway. Married Homer Carpenter. No issue.

    R34—Charlotte Conway. Married Marcus Morgan. No issue.

R13—Frances Block. Daughter of David Block and Almedia Clark Trimble. (Third generation of Walter Trimble and Mary Gordon Mitchell.) Born in 1856. Married Dr. William Johnston.

    The children of Dr. William Johnston and Frances Block:

    R35—Mary "Mamie" Johnston. Married Walter Simms. No children.

  + **R36—Walter Johnston.** Married Winifred Mercer.

    R37—Almedia Johnston. Married Horace Harner. No children.

    R38—Jane Johnston. Married William Harrison and they had two children: Frank, who died young; and William, Married and had children.

    R39—David Johnston. Married Fay Hudgens. No children.

    R40—Fewell Johnston. Did not marry.

    R41—Eugene Johnston. Did not marry.

R16—Juliet Block. Daughter of David Block and Almedia Clark Trimble. (Third generation of Walter Trimble and Mary Gordon Mitchell.) Born on October 3, 1864, and died on February 21, 1914, at Texarkana, Arkansas. Married Paul Booker.

    The children of Paul Booker and Juliet Block:

  + **R42—Leila Estelle Booker.** Married Granville M. McClerkin.

  + **R43—Pauline Almedia Booker.** Married Judge Jacob Monroe Carter, Jr.

  + **R44—Eola Gertrude Booker.** Married Cecil Whitmarsh Watson.

R36—Walter Johnston. Son of Dr. William Johnston and Frances Block. (Fourth generation of Walter Trimble and Mary Gordon Mitchell.) Married Winifred Mercer

    The four children of Walter Johnston and Winifred Mercer:

    R45—Frances Johnston. Married and had children.

R46—Walter Johnston, Jr. Married and had children.

R47—Winifred Johnston. Married and had children.

R48—Alex Johnston. Married and had children.

R42—Leila Estelle Booker. Daughter of Paul Booker and Juliet Block. (Fourth generation of Walter Trimble and Mary Gordon Mitchell.) Married Granville M. McClerkin.

The two children of Granville M. McClerkin and Leila Estelle Booker:

+ **R49—Mary Ellen McClerkin.** Born on November 6, 1920. Married in April 1943 to Collins Gaines, Jr.

+ **R50—Juliet Clem McClerkin.** Born on August 24, 1923. Married Albert Hershel Branson.

R43—Pauline Almedia Booker. Daughter of Paul Booker and Juliet Block. (Fourth generation of Walter Trimble and Mary Gordon Mitchell.) Married Judge Jacob Monroe Carter, Jr.,

The one child of Judge Jacob Monroe Carter, Jr. and Pauline Almedia Booker:

+ **R51—Juliet Nell Carter.** Born on October 20, 1923. Married Joseph Hindman Fenton.

R44—Eola Gertrude Booker. Daughter of Paul Booker and Juliet Block. (Fourth generation of Walter Trimble and Mary Gordon Mitchell.) Married Cecil Whitmarsh Watson.

The one child of Cecil Whitmarsh Watson and Eola Gertrude Booker:

+ **R52—Julie Cecile Watson.** Born on December 15, 1932. Married two times.

R49—Mary Ellen McClerkin. Daughter of Granville M. McClerkin and Leila Estelle Booker. (Fifth generation of Walter Trimble and Mary Gordon Mitchell.) Born on November 6, 1920. Married in April 1943 to Collins Gaines, Jr.

The three children of Collins Gaines, Jr. and Marry Ellen McClerkin:

R53—Mary Susan Gaines. Born on July 1, 1945, at San Mateo, California. Married Richard Allen Coleman on July 20, 1968, at Dallas, Texas.

R54—John Granville Gaines. Born on August 5, 1952, at Temple, Texas.

R55—Jeffrey Collins Gaines. Born on November 11, 1954, at Dallas, Texas.

R50—Juliet Clem McClerkin. Daughter of Granville M. McClerkin and Leila Estelle Booker. (Fifth generation of Walter Trimble and Mary Gordon

Trimble Families of America

Mitchell.) Born on August 24, 1923, in California. Married in June 1943 to Albert Hershel Branson at San Mateo, California.

The two children of Albert Hershel Branson and Juliet Clem McClerkin:

+ **R56—Linda Jean Branson.** Born in 1946. Married James Harrison Byrd.

R57—Paul Michael **Branson.** Born on May 1, 1951, at San Mateo, California.

R51—Juliet Nell Carter. Daughter of Judge Jacob Monroe Carter, Jr., and Pauline Almedia Booker. (Fifth generation of Walter Trimble and Mary Gordon Mitchell.) Born on October 20, 1923, at Texarkana, Arkansas. Married on September 4, 1948, at Texarkana, Texas, to Joseph Hindman Fenton, son of Hode J. and Aimee (Hindman) Fenton.

The one child of Joseph Hindman Fenton and Juliet Nell Carter:

R58—Joseph Hode Fenton. Born on August 4, 1952, at Wichita Falls, Texas.

R52—Juliet Cecile Watson. Daughter of Cecil Whitmarsh Watson and Eola Gertrude Booker. (Fifth generation of Walter Trimble and Mary Gordon Mitchell.) Born on December 15, 1932. Married two times: first, to Thomas Lloyd Naylor on November 20, 1954, at Shreveport, Louisiana, and second, to Philip Randall Bishop on May 2, 1967, at Fort Worth, Texas.

The children of Thomas Lloyd Naylor and Juliet Cecile Watson:

R59—Elizabeth Lloyd Naylor. Born on October 19, 1958, at Shreveport.

R60—Juliet Amadea Naylor. Born on November 5, 1962, at Shreveport.

R56—Linda Jean Branson. Daughter of Albert Hershel Branson and Juliet Clem McClerkin. (Sixth generation of Walter Trimble and Mary Gordon Mitchell.) Born on November 23, 1946, in California. Married James Harrison Byrd on December 26, 1966.

The two children of James Harrison Byrd and Linda Jean Branson:

R61—James Harrison Byrd, Jr. Born on June 30, 1968.

R62—Andrew Clinton Byrd. Born on June 17, 1969.

S - George Ware Trimble

S1—George Ware Trimble was Born in Kentucky in 1787 or 1788. He was living in Haywood County, Tennessee, according to the 1850 Census. George died about 1855. He had a sister, Elizabeth, Married William Neal, and another sister, Anna.

This compiler, against extensive research, cannot connect the early ancestors of George Ware Trimble. His descendents are a prominent line of the American Trimble Families. Detailed research by the Reverend William Bradley Trimble, rector of the Grace Episcopal Church of Monroe, Louisiana, has also been without results. Any reader of this book who has the information needed for George Ware Trimble's line is asked to please contact the author or the Reverend Mr. Trimble.

George Ware Trimble went to Williamson County, Tennessee, where he was married on September 9, 1815, to Miss Elizabeth E. Dyer.

The children of George Ware Trimble and Elizabeth E. Dyer:

+ **S2—John Dyer Trimble.**

S3—Robert Trimble. Moved to Kentucky in 1860.

S4—Will Trimble. Moved to Missouri.

S5—James Trimble. Lived in Brownsville, Tennessee.

S6—Amanda Trimble. She lived in Brownsville with her brother James.

+ **S7—George E. Trimble.** Married Cordelia P. Woolfolk of Georgetown, Kentucky.

S8—Thomas Trimble. Deceased.

S9—Sue Trimble. Deceased. Born in 1830. She was a half-sister of the above children.

S10—Abner Trimble. Born in 1831. He lived in Haywood County, Tennessee, on the little farm George Ware Trimble owned when he died.

These children were born at the home place near Franklin, Tennessee.

S2—John Dyer Trimble. Son of George Ware Trimble and Elizabeth E. Dyer. Born on September 9, 1816 and died on August 29, 1863. He was born in Franklin, Williamson County, Tennessee. Married Adelia Ann Neal on June 7, 1840, at the home place in or near Franklin. Adelia was the daughter of William and Elizabeth Trimble Neal; therefore, they were first cousins. Adelia Ann Neal was born on June 11, 1821 and died on May 13, 1889. John Dyer and Adelia Ann Trimble went to live in Hempstead County, Arkansas, where their home was at Washington, Arkansas. He was a lawyer and farmer.

Trimble Families of America

He graduated from the University of Tennessee and joined the Presbyterian church early in life.

He held many important offices in Hempstead County, during the early part of its history. Among the treasured papers in the possession of his descendants are commissions issued by Governor Archibald Yell in 1842, Governor Samuel Adams in 1844, and by Governor Thomas S. Drew.

He was elected county and probate judge in 1847 and again in 1849.

A clearheaded businessman, he was a model of excellence and clean morals in filling the many important trusts that he so many times did. Judge Trimble's name is indelibly written in the courthouse records of Hempstead County and in the hearts of the generation that followed him.

At the outbreak of the War Between the States, he was too old to bear arms, but like many others of his type, he did all he could to further the cause of the South by giving his talent and his money, with both of which he was abundantly supplied.

The record he left is replete with services well rendered to his family and to his state.

The children of John Dyer Trimble and Adelia Ann Neal:

S11—Charles Edward Trimble. Born on May 16, 1846 and died on September 14, 1877. He never married.

S12—Anna Neal Trimble. Died in 1907 and was never married.

+ **S13—John Dyer Trimble, Jr.**

S14—Waitsell Williams Trimble. Died in infancy.

S15—Henry Johnson Trimble. He was a lawyer and married Nanka Faucett. They had no children.

S16—Elizabeth Adelia Trimble. Born on May 3, 1843 and died on May 12, 1900. Married James W. Williams on July 20, 1864.

S7—George E. Trimble. Son of George Ware Trimble and Elizabeth E. Dyer. He returned to Kentucky and on October 19, 1848, married Cordelia P. Woolfolk of Georgetown, Kentucky, youngest daughter of one of the most respected farmers of Scott County, Kentucky.

In 1873, George E. Trimble stated in his letter to his nephew that three children of his were deceased. George E. lived temporarily in Midland, Kentucky. The compiler has a copy of a fourteen-page letter written by George E. Trimble in 1873. His eloquence was equaled only by his fervent religious overtones.

In 1873 he wrote to his nephew in Washington, Arkansas, and gave the names of his children:

Trimble Families of America

S17—Winston Ware Trimble. In 1873, he was twenty-four years of age according to the letter written by the father, George E. Trimble.

S18—Lenora "Nolie" Trimble. In 1873, she was nineteen years of age.

S19—John Dyer Trimble, Jr. In 1873, he was fifteen years of age.

S20—Gertie Trimble. In 1873, she was almost ten years of age.

S13—John Dyer Trimble, Jr. Son of John Dyer Trimble and Adelia Ann Neal. (Third generation of George Ware Trimble and Elizabeth E. Dyer.) Born on February 10, 1851 and died on April 7, 1897. Married Lillie White Nelson, born on November 20, 1856, and died on December 5, 1923.

The six children of John Dyer Trimble, Jr. and Adelia Ann Neal:

+ **S21—John Dyer Trimble III.** Born on October 13, 1890. Married Lillie White Nelson.

+ **S22—Charles Nelson Trimble.** Born on November 26, 1882. Married Jennie June Williams.

S23—Lenore "Nellie" Trimble. Born on October 25, 1886 and died August 5, 1966. Married James Wetheral Butler on February 12, 1913. They had no children.

S24—Mattie Mae Trimble. Born on August 15, 1888. Married Joseph Algernon Wilson, on November 29, 1911. They had no children. He died on February 28, 1946.

S25—Elizabeth Trimble. Born on April 18, 1881 and died on April 10, 1961. She never married.

+ **S26—Frank Yates Trimble.** Born on December 22, 1893. Married Ruby Etta Conway

S21—John Dyer Trimble III. Son of John Dyer Trimble, Jr. and Lillie White Nelson. (Fourth generation of George Ware Trimble and Elizabeth E. Dyer.) Born on October 13, 1890 and died February 11, 1953. Married Lena Godwin, on October 5, 1921.

The four children of John Dyer Trimble, III and Lillie White Nelson:

+ **S27—Bettie Sue Trimble.** Married Jack Patton Mabray on November 25, 1944.

+ **S28—Lillie Jean Trimble.** Married Thomas Arnold Turner, Jr. on December 31, 1946.

+ **S29—Mary Cooper Trimble.** Born on November 6, 1927. Married John Lewis Maier, Jr., on June 22, 1949.

+ **S30—John Dyer Trimble IV.** Born on May 6, 1931. Married Robin Nelson Berry, on June 11, 1955.

Trimble Families of America

S22—Charles Nelson Trimble. Son of John Dyer Trimble, Jr. and Lillie White Nelson. (Fourth generation of George Ware Trimble and Elizabeth E. Dyer.) Born on November 26, 1882 and died on October 30, 1939. Married Jennie June Williams on June 18, 1912

The five children Charles Nelson Trimble and Jennie June Williams:

+ **S31—William Bradley Trimble, Sr.** Born on August 10, 1913. Married Josephine Prentiss Finch on December 31, 1935.

+ **S32—Charlean Trimble.** Born on August 10, 1913. Married William Henry Etter IV.

+ **S33—Charles Nelson Trimble, Jr.** Born on July 28, 1916. Married Billie Sue Averytt.

+ **S34—Virginia June Trimble.** Born on July 28, 1916. Married Thomas Cobb Wilson III.

S35—Thomas David Trimble. Born on May 3, 1921. He was a pianist and voice critic in New York City.

S26—Frank Yates Trimble. Son of John Dyer Trimble, Jr., and Adelia Ann Neal. (Fourth generation of George Ware Trimble and Elizabeth E. Dyer.) Born on December 22, 1893 and died October 1, 1957. Married Ruby Etta Conway, on December 28, 1920. They had one child. Frank was abstractor, real estate, and county clerk of Hempstead County, Arkansas.

The children of Frank Yates Trimble and Ruby Etta Conway:

+ **S36—Carolyn Conway Trimble.** Born on November 6, 1924. Married Idus Laviga Murphree on September 2, 1950.

S27—Bettie Sue Trimble. Daughter of John Dyer Trimble III and Lillie White Nelson. (Fifth generation of George Ware Trimble and Elizabeth E. Dyer.) Born on February 8, 1923. Married Jack Patton Mabray on November 25, 1944.

The four children of Jack Patton Mabray and Bettie Sue Trimble:

S37—Melinda Mabray. Born on March 30, 1947.

S38—Jack Patton Mabray, Jr. Born on July 11, 1950.

S39—Susan Trimble Mabray. Born on February 23, 1953.

S40—Mary Elizabeth Mabray. Born on November 4, 1958.

S28—Lillie Jean Trimble. Daughter of John Dyer Trimble III and Lillie White Nelson. (Fifth generation of George Ware Trimble and Elizabeth E. Dyer.) Born on September 11, 1925. Married Thomas Arnold Turner, Jr. on December 31, 1946.

The children of Thomas Turner, Jr. and Lillie Jean Trimble:

S41—Rebecca Godwin Turner. Born on December 8, 1947.

S42—Thomas Arnold Turner, III. Born on September 10, 1950.

S43—Susan Trimble Turner. Born on February 23, 1953.

S44—Mary Elizabeth Turner. Born on November 4, 1958.

S29—Mary Cooper Trimble. Daughter of John Dyer Trimble III and Lillie White Nelson. (Fifth generation of George Ware Trimble and Elizabeth E. Dyer.) Born on November 6, 1927. Married John Lewis Maier, Jr. on June 22, 1949.

The three children of John Lewis Maier, Jr. and Mary Cooper Trimble:

S45—Marilyn Maier. Born on June 2, 1950.

S46—John Lewis Maier III. Born on August 15, 1951.

S47—Nancy Cooper Maier. Born on November 29, 1955.

S30—John Dyer Trimble, IV. Son of John Dyer Trimble III and Lillie White Nelson. (Fifth generation of George Ware Trimble and Elizabeth E. Dyer.) Born on May 6, 1931. Married Robin Nelson Berry on June 11, 1955.

The three children of John Dyer Trimble IV and Robin Nelson Berry:

S48—John Dyer Trimble, V. Born on May 5, 1957.

S49—Robin Elizabeth Trimble. Born on May 21, 1959.

S50—James Berry Trimble. Born on May 22, 1962.

S31—William Bradley Trimble, Sr. Son of Charles Nelson Trimble and Jennie June Williams. (Fifth generation of George Ware Trimble and Elizabeth E. Dyer.) Born on August 10, 1913. Married Josephine Prentiss Finch on December 31, 1935. He was a lawyer from 1936 to 1951 and then became a priest in the Episcopal church. At the present he is associated in the clergy with the Grace Episcopal Church of Monroe, Louisiana.

The children of William Bradley Trimble, Sr. and Josephine Prentiss Finch:

+ **S51—William Bradley Trimble, Jr.** Born on October 19, 1940. Married Rebecca Holt Johnstone on June 5, 1965.

S52—Joseph Finch Trimble. Born on December 3, 1942. Married Karen Marie Boudloche on February 15, 1969. They have one child, Joseph Finch Trimble, Jr., born on July 22, 1970. Joseph has a B.A. in political science and was a captain in the U.S. Army, with the 101st Airborne, Green Beret. Has three Silver Stars, and three Bronze USA.

S53—Kathryn Louise Trimble. Born on September 22, 1945. Married James

Graves Theus, Sr. on October 22, 1965. They have two children: James Graves, Jr., born on June 22, 1966; and Kathryn Prentiss, born on November 30, 1969.

S54—Rebecca Jane Trimble. Born on September 13, 1947.

S32—Charlean Trimble. Daughter of Charles Nelson Trimble and Jennie June Williams. (Fifth generation of George Ware Trimble and Elizabeth E. Dyer.) Born on August 10, 1913. Married William Henry Etter IV on June 6, 1934.

The four children of William Henry Etter IV and Charlean Trimble:

S55—Sarah June Etter. Born on December 11, 1935. Married William John Wixon July 9, 1965. They have one child, William Ronald, born on June 20, 1967.

S56—Charlean Trimble Etter. Born on October 8, 1940. Married Thomas Edward Roberts on May 7, 1960. They have two children: Kristen Charlean, born on April 19, 1961; and Susan Kathleen, born on September 13, 1967.

S57—Margaret Anne Etter. Born on January 14, 1947. Married David Wayne Burke, on February 28, 1964. They have one child, Mary Nannette, born on November 30, 1964.

S58—William Henry Etter V. Born on August 16, 1949.

S33—Charles Nelson Trimble, Jr. Son of Charles Nelson Trimble and Jennie June Williams. (Fifth generation of George Ware Trimble and Elizabeth E. Dyer.) Born on July 28, 1916. Married Billie Sue Averytt on October 26, 1946. They have four children. Charles was in the U.S. Navy during World War II and is now a tax accountant.

The children of Charles Nelson Trimble, Jr. and Billie Sue Averytt:

S59—Charles Nelson Trimble III. Born on December 15, 1950.

S60—Thomas Averytt Trimble. Born on October 26, 1952.

S61—James Butler Trimble. Born on November 18, 1956.

S62—Carolyn Sue Trimble. Born on November 8, 1958.

S34—Virginia June Trimble. Daughter of Charles Nelson Trimble and Jennie June Williams. (Fifth generation of George Ware Trimble and Elizabeth E. Dyer.) Born on July 28, 1916. She died on December 30, 1963. Married Thomas Cobb Wilson, III on June 6, 1936.

The two children of Thomas Cobb Wilson, III and Virginia June Trimble:

S63—Thomas Cobb Wilson, IV. Born on June 2, 1939.

S64—Charles Trimble Wilson. Born on June 10, 1940 and died the next day on

June 11, 1940.

S36—Carolyn Conway Trimble. Daughter of Frank Yates Trimble and Ruby Etta Conway. (Fifth generation of George Ware Trimble and Elizabeth E. Dyer.) Born on November 6, 1924. Married Idus Laviga Murphree on September 2, 1950.

The children of Idus Laviga Murphree and Carolyn Conway Trimble:

S65—Kathryn Trimble Murphree. Born on April 10, 1952.

S66—Emily Strough Murphree. Born on February 25, 1954.

S67—Robert Murphree. Born on March 13, 1960.

S51—William Bradley Trimble, Jr. Son of William Bradley Trimble, Sr. and Josephine Prentiss Finch. (Sixth generation of George Ware Trimble and Elizabeth E. Dyer.) Born on October 19, 1940. Married Rebecca Holt Johnstone on June 5, 1965. He was a lieutenant in the United States Navy and is a priest in the Episcopal church.

The children of William Bradley Trimble, Jr. and Rebecca Holt Johnstone:

S68—Rebecca Jane Trimble. Born on October 13, 1967.

S69—Josephine Fields Trimble. Born on November 15, 1969.

T - Elisha Trimble

T1—Elisha Trimble. and his brothers and sisters were born in Virginia in the late 1700s. We do not know the name of their father or mother. Yet, the compiler believes, through the process of elimination as we have made an extensive search of the early records of Virginia, that these were the children of either Thomas Trimble, Married Abigail Gattliff, or John Trimble, who were sons of David of the Five Trimble Brothers. The compiler has been unable to locate records of the descendents of these two brothers and consequently these are the only early Trimbles of Virginia of whom we have no records.

We are gratefully indebted to Hal E. Trimble of Route 2, Bloomington, Illinois 61701, for the Trimble genealogy of the Elisha Trimble family.

The children of Elisha Trimble and Abigail Gattliff:

+ **T2—Elisha Trimble.** Born in 1784 in Virginia and died on June 21, 1857. He is buried at the Phelam Cemetery, Fountaintown, Indiana.

T3—James Trimble. Born on March 13, 1790, in Virginia. Died on April 15, 1860. He is buried at Phelam Cemetery, Fountaintown, Indiana.

T4—John Trimble. Born on September 11, 1794, in Virginia. Died on March 22, 1873. Buried at Phelam Cemetery, Fountaintown, Indiana.

T5—Joseph Trimble.

T6—Elizabeth Trimble. Married a Mr. Johnson.

T7—Stephen Trimble.

T8—Jane Trimble. Married a Mr. Briney.

T9—Nancy Trimble. Married a Mr. Hinkley.

T10—Rebecca Trimble. Married a Mr. Dilly.

T2—Elisha Trimble. Son of Elisha Trimble and Abigail Gattliff. Born in 1784 in Virginia and died on June 21, 1857. Buried in the Phelam Cemetery, Fountaintown, Indiana. In the 1810 Kentucky Census he was in Campbell County, Kentucky. In the 1820 Census he was in Lawrence County, Indiana. Elisha married Hester Hawkins a widow. She was born on July 18, 1780 and died on July 18, 1840. She, too, is buried at Phelam.

The five children of Elisha Trimble and Hester Hawkins:

+ **T11—Ambrose Trimble.**

T12—Robert Trimble. Died and is buried in the Redford Cemetery in Jasper County, Illinois. He married Eliza Kearns of Jasper County.

T13—Sally "Sarah" Trimble. Born on April 14, 1813, in Kentucky and died on May 19, 1899, and is buried in the Phelam Cemetery. She married David

Franklin Ferris of Fountaintown, Indiana, on June 14, 1832.

T14—Priscilla Trimble. Married Hyram Tracy of Rose Hill, Illinois.

T15—Betsy Trimble. Married Caleb Higgins of Wisconsin, Nebraska, and Kelso, Washington.

T11—Ambrose Trimble. Son of Elisha Trimble and Hester Hawkins. Born on February 14, 1814, in Shelby County, Indiana, where he lived all his life. He died on September 10, 1890. Ambrose married three times. We do not know his first wife's name; second, Sarah Roan; and third, Mary Hines. Sarah was the only wife by whom Ambrose had children.

The children of Ambrose Trimble and Sarah Roan:

T16—John R. Trimble. Born on March 7, 1843. He returned from the Civil War and settled in Cloud County, Kansas, at Clasco. He married twice but had children by his first wife only.

T17—Esther Eleanor Trimble. Born on July 23, 1844. They lived in Kansas near John Trimble. She married a Mr. Copple and their oldest son, Adam Copple, lived in Olympia, Washington.

T18—Jane Trimble. Born on October 6, 1846.

T19—Prissa Trimble. Born on April 7, 1848. She married a Mr. Kelley and lived in Rushville, Illinois.

T20—Melissa Trimble. Born on April 7, 1848, and died in 1868, probably of tuberculosis.

+ **T21—Melvin Franklin Trimble.** Born on August 6, 1850 and died on November 7, 1927. He was brought to Illinois by his uncle, Robert Trimble. Married Mary Ann Nichols.

T22—Mary Elizabeth Trimble. Born on August 26, 1852. She died in 1871, probably of tuberculosis.

T23—Marian Trimble. Born on August 26, 1852.

T21—Melvin Franklin Trimble. Son of Ambrose Trimble and Sarah Roan. (Third generation of Elisha Trimble and Abigail Gattliff.) Born on August 6, 1850, in Shelby County, Indiana, and died on November 7, 1927, at Jasper County, Illinois. He is buried at Island Creek. Married on October 2, 1872, to Mary Ann Nichols, born on October 8, 1852, and died on June 20, 1929, in Jasper County, Illinois. She is buried at Island Creek. Mary Ann Nichols Trimble was the daughter of Henry and Jane Dittamore Nichols.

The children of Melvin Trimble and Mary Nichols:

T24—William Marian Trimble. Born on October 8, 1873 and died on April 19, 1954. He married three times: first, to Sonora Bloomfield; second, to Maude

Trimble Families of America

T - Elisha Trimble

Marks: and third, to Hettie Rowell.

T25—Lillie Ellen Trimble. Born on March 7, 1875 and died August 20, 1882.

T26—Edward Ambrose Trimble. Born on November 7, 1876 and died on November 21, 1965. Married Belle Ward, born in 1876 and died in 1965. They were married on March 6, 1901.

T27—Robert Franklin Trimble. Born on November 3, 1878. Married Cora Ellen Newlin, born in 1877.

T28—Hiram Alexander Trimble. Born on October 6, 1880 and died on September 15, 1882.

T29—Laura Jane Trimble. Born on November 1, 1882 and died on June 23, 1965. Married John Spesard, born in 1880 and died in 1958.

T30—Albert Grover. Born on October 12, 1884 and died on November 5, 1962. Married Susan Grisson born in 1887 and died in 1948.

T31—Jessie Trimble. Born on July 27, 1886. Married Phil Isley, who died in 1962.

T32—Maud Trimble. Born on January 25, 1888 and died on January 3, 1947. Married Orville E. Isley, born in 1884 and died in 1957.

T33—Clay Trimble. Born on November 30, 1889 and died on July 24, 1969. Married Lucy Alice Myers on December 18, 1910. She was born in 1889 and died in 1970.

T34—Franc Trimble. Born on October 10, 1891, and married Homer Isley, born in 1890 and died in 1964.

U - Isaac Trimble 1854 — 1903

We are appreciative of the genealogy of the Isaac Trimble family contributed by Walter James Trimble, Sr., of 5532 North Fourth Street, Philadelphia, Pennsylvania 19120. Mr. Trimble wrote in a letter to the compiler, "We knew little about our father except that he was naturalized on October 30, 1893, in Mahoning County, Ohio. The probate judge was E. M. Wilson. My father died in Youngstown, Ohio in February 1903. I do not know if he had any other brothers or sisters in this country. As I was only little when he passed away, I do not even remember him at all. After his death, my mother being left with six children ranging in age from one to ten years found she was unable to provide for us. Through the help of Reverend George Worrell, we were brought to the Orange Home, in Hatboro, Pennsylvania. My father was a member of the Orange Lodge in Youngstown, Ohio. I stayed in the home until I was fifteen years of age. When I left, my youngest brother Richard left with me. The other children had left at different times before this. We were the first family to enter the home as it had just been dedicated and opened for children. It is now a home for the aged."

U1—Isaac Trimble.

The children of Isaac Trimble and Mary Ann Jevens:

U2—Isaac Trimble. Born in 1854 at 51 Mote Street, Dunaghadee, Ireland, and died in 1903. Married Mary Ann Jevens, born in 1861 at Lancashire, England. She died in 1924. Isaac had been married before, but we do not know her name. Isaac and Mary Ann Jevens Trimble had six children:

U3—Grace Elizabeth Trimble. Born in 1893 and died in 1960.

U4—Frances Caroline Trimble. Born in 1895 and died in 1965. Married a Mr. Sultzbach. Their children: Walter, John, Grace Rottmund, Vernon, and Raymond of Lancaster, Pennsylvania.

+ **U5—William Alexander Trimble.**

U6—Fredrick Isaac Trimble. Born in 1897 and died in 1954. His children: Elizabeth Serogo, of 531 Louise Road, Glenside, Pennsylvania; and Fredrick Trimble

+ **U7—Walter James Trimble, Sr.** Born in 1899.

U8—Richard Thomas Trimble, Sr. Born in 1901 and died in 1968. His son: Richard Thomas Trimble, Jr. of 1416 Scottsdale Road, Champaign, Illinois.

U5—William Alexander Trimble. Son of Isaac Trimble and Mary Ann Jevens. Born in 1896. He lives at 117 Woodlawn Avenue, Willow Grove, Pennsylvania.

Trimble Families of America

The children of William Trimble:

U9—William Trimble.

U10—James Trimble. Died in 1947.

U11—Fredrick Trimble. (Twin.)

U12—Walter Trimble. (Twin.)

U13—Katherine Trimble.

U14—Gertrude Trimble.

U15—Robert Bruce Trimble.

U7—Walter James Trimble, Sr. Son of Isaac Trimble and Mary Ann Jevens. Born in 1899. He lives at 5532 North Fourth Avenue, Philadelphia, Pennsylvania.

His child:

U16—Walter James Trimble, Jr. Born in 1923. He lives at 127 Johns Road, Cheltenham, Pennsylvania. His children: Robert Bruce, born in 1951; and Joyce Ann Trimble, born in 1956.

V - Henry Johnson Trimble

V1—Henry Johnson Trimble. Died on September 17, 1907. Married Louella Kennedy.

The children of Henry Johnson Trimble and Louella Kennedy:

+ **V2—William Scott Trimble.** Died on May 25, 1929. He married Sadie Clinton Blair.

+ **V3—Bess Trimble.** Born on October 17, 1879. Married Harry Nelson.

  V4—Edith Trimble. She did not marry and died about 1931.

V2—William Scott Trimble. Son of Henry Johnson Trimble and Louella Kennedy. Died on May 25, 1929. He married Sadie Clinton Blair, also known as Sallie. She was born on December 12, 1867 and died on August 4, 1930. They were married on September 20, 1894.

The children of William Scott Trimble and Sadie Clinton Blair:

  V5—Martha Louella Trimble. Born on March 9, 1899 and died August 13, 1899.

+ **V6—Henry Blair Trimble.** Born on April 21, 1901 and died on March 31, 1951. Married on June 12, 1929, to Eunice Kinkead, born on October 5, 1901.

+ **V7—William Scott Trimble, Jr.** Born on April 21, 1906 and died on February 16, 1958. Married Eleanor Masker on October 24, 1936.

V3—Bess Trimble. Daughter of Henry Johnson Trimble and Louella Kennedy. Born on October 17, 1879 and died on June 10, 1919. Married Harry Nelson on October 11, 1911.

The son of Harry Nelson and Bess Trimble:

  V8—Frank Nelson.

V6—Henry Blair Trimble. Son of William Scott Trimble and Sadie Clinton Blair. (Third generation of Henry Johnson Trimble and Louella Kennedy.) Born on April 21, 1901 and died on March 31, 1951. Married on June 12, 1929, to Eunice Kinkead, born on October 5, 1901.

The children of Henry Blair Trimble and Eunice Kinkead:

  V9—Henry Blair Trimble, Jr. Born on July 27, 1932, and married Rosemary Morris on October 5, 1957. She was born on June 18, 1936.

  V10—Charles Kinkead Trimble. Born on November 15, 1936, and married Virginia Johnson on May 27, 1961. Their children: Charles Kinkead, Jr., born on November 9; 1962; and Marcia Virginia, born on March 28, 1965.

V7—William Scott Trimble, Jr. Son of William Scott Trimble and Sadie Clinton Blair. (Third generation of Henry Johnson Trimble and Louella Kennedy.) Born on April 21, 1906 and died on February 16, 1958. Married Eleanor Masker on October 24, 1936. She was born on February 16, 1912 and died in August 1968.

The children of William Scott Trimble, Jr. and Eleanor Masker:

V11—Josephine Tehune Trimble. Born on August 25, 1940. Married on December 23, 1960, to John Moody Sims. Their children: John Moody, Jr., born on October 8, 1964; and Eleanor, born on December 20, 1968.

V12—William Scott Trimble. Born on April 14, 1942, and married Donna Dukes, on December 22, 1963. She was born in 1944. Their children: Laura Brooks, born on December 22, 1964, and Lisa Trimble.

W - William Franklin Trimble

We are gratefully indebted to Jim Trimble of 4215 North 13th Place, Phoenix, Arizona 85014, for the genealogy of the William Franklin Trimble family.

W1—William Franklin Trimble. He is buried at or near Sherman, Texas. Married Susan Virginia Thompson, born in 1817 and died in 1898.

The five children of William Franklin Trimble and Susan Virginia Thompson:

+ **W2—William Wallace Trimble.** Born on July 24, 1843 and died on January 28, 1928. Married Louise Marshall Savage, born in 1846 and died in 1912.

W3—Samuel Trimble. Born in 1845 and died on March 21, 1927. Married Elizabeth M. Voelkel, born in 1859 and died in 1935.

W4—Albert Edward Trimble. Born on August 1, 1847 and died on September 21, 1918. Married Utopia Case.

+ **W5—Sarah Jane Trimble.** Born on September 10, 1848 and died on April 16, 1910. Married Samuel Barton Smith.

+ **W6—Mary Trimble.** Born on March 29, 1849 and died on June 4, 1880. Married Orlando Milton Van Arsdell.

W2—William Wallace Trimble. Son of William Franklin Trimble and Susan Virginia Thompson. Born on July 24, 1843 and died on January 28, 1928. Married Louise Marshall Savage, born in 1846 and died in 1912. William Wallace is buried at Maysville, Kentucky.

The eight children of William Wallace Trimble and Louise Marshall Savage:

+ **W7—Virginia Roberts Trimble.** Born on November 17, 1873 and died on April 13, 1958. Married Thomas Owen Henderson.

W8—Margaret Savage Trimble. Born on June 16, 1875 and died on February 24, 1905.

+ **W9—Emma Byrd Trimble.** Born on June 28, 1877 and died on March 4, 1939. Married Clarence Perrine Dobyns.

+ **W10—William Edwin Trimble.** Born on April 13, 1879 and died on February 15, 1932. Married Addie Amelia Curtis.

+ **W11—Max Trimble.** Born on August 3, 1881 and died August 20, 1951. Married Mary Sue Lloyd.

+ **W12—Franklin Leroy Trimble.** Born on November 10, 1883 and died on October 23, 1968. Married Evalina Dunn.

Trimble Families of America

+**W13—Robert Malcolm Trimble.** Born on March 3, 1885 and died on October 3, 1948. Married Mary Elizabeth Harrigan.

W14—Grover Cleveland Trimble. Born on May 9, 1888. Married Louise Becker, born on April 18, 1888.

W4—Albert Edward Trimble. Son of William Franklin Trimble and Susan Virginia Thompson. Born on August 1, 1847 and died on September 21, 1918. Married Utopia Case, born in 1857 and died in 1938.

The two children of Albert Edward Trimble and Utopia Case:

W15—Edna Bell Trimble. Born on December 17, 1876 Married James Benjamin Baker, born in 1877 and died in 1931. They had a daughter, Fern Trimble Baker, born on November 28, 1912, Married Mils Elmer Moser, born in 1916.

W16—Clarence Lee Trimble. Born on April 2, 1878.

W5—Sarah Jane Trimble. Daughter of William Franklin Trimble and Susan Virginia Thompson. Born on September 10, 1848 and died on April 16, 1910. Married Samuel Barton Smith, born in 1841 and died in 1901.

The daughter of Samuel Barton Smith and Sarah Jane Trimble:

W17—Ida. B. Smith. Born in 1868, married James M. Greening.

W6—Mary Trimble. Daughter of William Franklin Trimble and Susan Virginia Thompson. Born on March 29, 1849 and died on June 4, 1880. Married Orlando Milton Van Arsdell, born in 1836 and died in 1918.

The daughter of Orlando Milton Van Arsdell and Mary Trimble:

W18—Prudence Ann Van Arsdell. Born in 1870, married Benjamin Wilson, born in 1865.

W7—Virginia Roberts Trimble. Daughter of William Wallace Trimble and Louise Marshall Savage. (Third generation of William Franklin Trimble and Susan Virginia Thompson.) Born on November 17, 1873 and died on April 13, 1958. Married Thomas Owen Henderson, born in 1872 and died in 1952.

The children of Thomas Owen Henderson and Virginia Roberts Trimble:

W19—Adrian Gordo Henderson. Born in 1896 and died in 1911.

W20—William Trimble Henderson. Born in 1903, Married Mary Elizabeth Birks.

W9—Emma Byrd Trimble. Daughter of William Wallace Trimble and Louise Marshall Savage. (Third generation of William Franklin Trimble and Susan

Trimble Families of America

Virginia Thompson.) Born on June 28, 1877 and died March 4, 1939. Married Clarence Perrine Dobyns, born in 1875 and died in 1955.

The children of Clarence Perrine Dobyns and Emma Byrd Trimble:

W21—Marie Jewel Dobyns. Born in 1899.

W22—Owen Trimble Dobyns. Born in 1901.

W23—Frank Perrine Dobyns. Born in 1914.

W10—William Edwin Trimble. Son of William Wallace Trimble and Louise Marshall Savage. (Third generation of William Franklin Trimble and Susan Virginia Thompson.) Born on April 13, 1879 and died on February 15, 1932. Married Addie Amelia Curtis, born in 1880.

The children of William Edwin Trimble and Addie Amelia Curtis:

W24—Emma Ruth Trimble. Born on July 10, 1904. Married George Frank Rohrig, born in 1898.

+**W25—Arvid Riley Trimble.** Born on April 15, 1906. Married Bernice Greeley Michels, born on August 8, 1911.

+**W26—Cecil Hutton Trimble.** Born on August 16, 1908. Married Martha Huntington Woodson, born in 1914.

+**W27—Helen Curtis Trimble.** Born on August 21, 1910. Married John Lyon, born in 1907.

W11—Max Trimble. Son of William Wallace Trimble and Louise Marshall Savage. (Third generation of William Franklin Trimble and Susan Virginia Thompson.) Born on August 3, 1881 and died on August 20, 1951. Married Mary Sue Lloyd, born in 1879 and died in 1953.

The children of Max Trimble and Mary Sue Lloyd:

+**W28—Max Lloyd Trimble.** Born on October 7, 1908 and died in 1963. Married Pauline Mary Pulliam, born in 1912.

W12—Franklin Leroy Trimble. Son of William Wallace Trimble and Louise Marshall Savage. (Third generation of William Franklin Trimble and Susan Virginia Thompson.) Born on November 10, 1883 and died on October 23, 1968. Married Evalina Dunn, born in 1884.

The children of Franklin Leroy Trimble and Evalina Dunn:

+**W29—Riley Weston Trimble.** Born on June 12, 1910. Married Dorothey Eloise Wilhelmy, born in 1916.

+**W30—Roy Lane Trimble.** Born on November 21, 1916 in Bloomington, Illinois and died 1993 in Colfax, Illinois. He married two times: first, to Willia Mae Bien, born in 1927, and second, to Helen Rachel Land, born in 1918.

W13—Robert Malcolm Trimble. Son of William Wallace Trimble and Louise Marshall Savage. (Third generation of William Franklin Trimble and Susan Virginia Thompson.) Born on March 3, 1885 and died on October 3, 1948. Married Mary Elizabeth Harrigan born in 1895.

The children of Robert Malcolm Trimble and Mary Elizabeth Harrigan:

W31—Gravel Robert Trimble. Born on April 20, 1915. Married Leona Loretta Revelle, born in 1914.

W32—Richard Wayne Trimble. Born on September 5, 1917. Married Myla Pauline Hixson, born in 1915. Their children: Barbara Sue, born in 1950; and Richard Lee, born in 1947.

W33—Max William Trimble. Born on September 24, 1921. Married Ruth Alvia Bass, born in 1920. Their children: Gary Robert, born in 1946, married Carol Allison; John Leland, born in 1951, married Mary Lou, Rizzo, born in 1951; and Kim Alan Trimble, born in 1956.

+ **W34—James Adrian Trimble.** Born on September 28, 1924. Married three times: first, to Lenore Beryle Duncan; second, to Agnes Frey; and third, to Mary Bamberger Pacanowski.

+ **W35—Mary Elizabeth Trimble.** Born on March 10, 1937. Married Farrel Rasner, born in 1944.

W25—Arvid Riley Trimble. Son of William Edwin Trimble and Addie Amelia Curtis. (Fourth generation of William Franklin Trimble and Susan Virginia Thompson.) Born on April 15, 1906. Married Bernice Greeley Michels, born on August 8, 1911.

The children of Arvid Riley Trimble and Bernice Greeley Michels:

+ **W36—Richard Edward Trimble.** Born on March 21, 1938. Married Mary Alice Kash, born in 1940.

W37—Robert Arvid Trimble. Born on January 9, 1940 and died on January 19, 1940.

+ **W38—David Joseph Trimble.** Born on June 18, 1945. Married Donna Marie Yeager, born in 1945. Their children: Darin, born in 1967; Dodie Marie, born in 1968; and Danny, born in 1969.

W26—Cecil Hutton Trimble. Son of William Edwin Trimble and Addie Amelia Curtis. (Fourth generation of William Franklin Trimble and Susan Virginia Thompson.) Born on August 16, 1908. Married Martha Huntington Woodson, born in 1914.

The children of Cecil Hutton Trimble and Martha Huntington Woodson:

W39—Carole Jane Trimble. Born on October 8, 1941.

W40—Norman Cecil Trimble. Born on December 18, 1950.

W41—Susan Ann Trimble. Born on January 5, 1952.

W27—Helen Curtis Trimble. Daughter of William Edwin Trimble and Addie Amelia Curtis. (Fourth generation of William Franklin Trimble and Susan Virginia Thompson.) Born on August 21, 1910. Married John Lyon, born in 1907.

The children of John Lyon and Helen Curtis Trimble:

W42—Orland Dwaine Lyon. Born on January 31, 1939.

W43—Myrna Lee Lyon. Born on January 31, 1941.

W28—Max Lloyd Trimble. Son of Max Trimble and Mary Sue Lloyd. (Fourth generation of William Franklin Trimble and Susan Virginia Thompson.) Born on October 7, 1908 and died in 1963. Married Pauline Mary Pulliam, born in 1912.

The children of Max Lloyd Trimble and Pauline Mary Pulliam:

+ **W44—Delores Jean Trimble.** Born on August 18, 1933. Married Francis A. Grice, born in 1930.

W29—Riley Weston Trimble. Son of Franklin Leroy Trimble and Evalina Dunn. (Fourth generation of William Franklin Trimble and Susan Virginia Thompson.) Born on June 12, 1910. Married Dorothey Eloise Wilhelmy, born in 1916.

The children of Riley Weston Trimble and Dorothey Eloise Wilhelmy:

W45—Kent Weston Trimble. Born on February 8, 1945 Married Barbara Jeanne Blair, born in 1944.

W46—Eric Reid Trimble. Born on November 19, 1946, and married Barbara Berry James, born in 1947.

W30—Roy Lane Trimble. Son of Franklin Leroy Trimble and Evalina Dunn. (Fourth generation of William Franklin Trimble and Susan Virginia Thompson.) Born on November 21, 1916 in Bloomington, Illinois and died in 1993 in Colfax, Illinois. He married two times: first, to Willia Mae Bien, born in 1927, and second, to Helen Rachel Land on May 29, 1954 in Cook County, Illinois. She was born in 1918.

The children of Roy Lane Trimble and Willia Mae Bien:

+ **W47—Jeffrey Lane Trimble.** Born on October 16, 1938, Married Mildred

Trimble Families of America

Ann ———. Their children: Michelle Ann Trimble born in 1961; and Linda Ann, born in 1965.

+ **W48—Gary Leroy Trimble.** Born on August 5, 1940 and died on November 10, 1966. Married Kathleen Madeline Casey, born on January 25, 1939. Their children: Michael Joseph born in 1964; Patrick Andrew, born in 1965; and Julie Lynn, born in 1966.

+ **W49—Brian Thomas Trimble.** Born on April 18, 1946. Married Barbara Virginia Parsley, born in 1946. Their child: Brian Thomas Trimble, Jr., born in 1969.

+ **W50—Craig Alan Trimble.** Born on April 18, 1946. Married Diane Lynn Stringfield, born in 1949. Their child Kelly Ann Trimble, born in 1969.

+ **W51—Holly Ann Trimble.** Born on December 9, 1950. Married Lynn Arthur Seism, Born in 1948. Their child Shon Arthur Seism, born on May 28, 1970.

W34—James Adrian Trimble. Son of Robert Malcolm Trimble and Mary Elizabeth Harrigan. (Fourth generation of William Franklin Trimble and Susan Virginia Thompson.) Born on September 28, 1924. Married three times: first, to Lenore Beryle Duncan; second, to Agnes Frey; and third, to Mary Bamberger Pacanowski.

The children of James Adrian Trimble:

W52—Lyndall Duncan. Born in 1947, married William David Brown.

W53—Robert Malcolm Trimble. Born in 1949, married Jimmie Ann Trimble, born in 1954.

W35—Mary Elizabeth Trimble. Daughter of Robert Malcolm Trimble and Mary Elizabeth Harrigan. (Fourth generation of William Franklin Trimble and Susan Virginia Thompson.) Born on March 10, 1937. Married Farrel Rasner, born in 1944.

The children of Farrel Rasner and Mary Elizabeth Trimble:

W54—Marybeth Rasner. Born in 1956.

W55—Farrel Rasner, Jr. Born in 1958.

W36—Richard Edward Trimble. Son of Arvid Riley Trimble and Bernice Greeley Michels. (Fifth generation of William Franklin Trimble and Susan Virginia Thompson.) Born on March 21, 1938. Married Mary Alice Kash, born in 1940.

The children of Richard Edward Trimble and Mary Alice Kash:

W56—Shae Marie Trimble. Born in 1962.

W57—Roland Trimble. Born in 1964.

W58—Rodney Trimble. Born in 1967.

W38—David Joseph Trimble. Son of Arvid Riley Trimble and Bernice Greeley Michels. (Fifth generation of William Franklin Trimble and Susan Virginia Thompson.) Born on June 18, 1945. Married Donna Marie Yeager, born in 1945.

The children of David Joseph Trimble and Donna Marie Yeager:

W59—Darin Trimble. Born in 1967.

W60—Dodie Marie Trimble. Born in 1968.

W61—Danny Trimble. Born in 1969.

W44—Delores Jean Trimble. Daughter of Max Lloyd Trimble and Pauline Mary Pulliam. (Fifth generation of William Franklin Trimble and Susan Virginia Thompson.) Born on August 18, 1933. Married Francis A. Grice, born in 1930.

The three children of Francis A. Grice and Delores Jean Trimble:

W62—Deborah Jean Grice. Born in 1951.

W63—Brent Kell Grice. Born in 1950.

W64—Kevin Lloyd Grice. Born in 1958.

W47—Jeffrey Lane Trimble. Son of Roy Lane Trimble and Willia Mae Bien. (Fifth generation of William Franklin Trimble and Susan Virginia Thompson.) Born on October 16, 1938, Married Mildred Ann ———.

The children of Jeffrey Lane Trimble and Mildred Ann ———:

W65—Michelle Ann Trimble. Born in 1961.

W66—Linda Ann Trimble. Born in 1965.

W48—Gary Leroy Trimble. Son of Roy Lane Trimble and Willia Mae Bien. (Fifth generation of William Franklin Trimble and Susan Virginia Thompson.) Born on August 5, 1940 and died on November 10, 1966. Married Kathleen Madeline Casey, born in 1939.

The children of Gary Leroy Trimble and Kathleen Madeline Casey:

W67—Michael Joseph Trimble. Born in 1964.

W68—Patrick Andrew Trimble. Born in 1965.

W69—Julie Lynn Trimble. Born in 1966.

W49—Brian Thomas Trimble. Son of Roy Lane Trimble and Willia Mae Bien. (Fifth generation of William Franklin Trimble and Susan Virginia Thompson.) Born on April 18, 1946. Married Barbara Virginia Parsley, born

W - William Franklin Trimble

in 1946.

The child of Brain Thomas Trimble and Barbara Virginia Parsley:
W70—Brian Thomas Trimble, Jr. Born in 1969.

W50—Craig Alan Trimble. Son of Roy Lane Trimble and Willia Mae Bien. (Fifth generation of William Franklin Trimble and Susan Virginia Thompson.) Born on April 18, 1946. Married Diane Lynn Stringfield was born in 1949.

The child of Craig Alan Trimble and Diane Lynn Stringfield:
W71—Kelly Ann Trimble. Born in 1969.

W51—Holly Ann Trimble. Daughter of Roy Lane Trimble and Willia Mae Bien. (Fifth generation of William Franklin Trimble and Susan Virginia Thompson.) Born on December 9, 1950. Married Lynn Arthur Seism, Born in 1948.

The child of Lynn Arthur Seism and Holly Ann Trimble:
W72—Shon Arthur Seism. Born on May 28, 1970.

X - Murray Trimble

We are gratefully indebted to A. G. Trimble and his son Malcolm B. Trimble of 4 Wellington Road, Pittsburgh, Pennsylvania 15221, for the genealogy of their Trimble family. A. G. Trimble is the owner of a specialty company in the Jenkins Arcade in Pittsburgh that has made badges for several presidential candidates and other forms of advertisements. Some of these badges are now museum pieces.

X1—Murray Trimble. Born on May 9, 1841 and died on June 1, 1926. Married Harriett Rugg on June 11, 1876.

    The children of Murray Trimble and Harriet Rugg:

+ **X2—Arthur Garfield Trimble.** Born on November 2, 1880. Married Lily May Beltz.

X2—Arthur Garfield Trimble. Son of Murray Trimble and Harriett Rugg. Born on November 2, 1880, at White Station, Armstrong County, Pennsylvania. Married Lily May Beltz.

    The children of Arthur Garfield Trimble and Lily May Beltz:

X3—Arthur Pershing Trimble. Born in 1918. He lives in Webster, New York, and is employed by Eastman Kodak Company.

+ **X4—Malcolm Beltz Trimble.** Born in 1920. Married Mary Alice Garland.

X5—Richard Charles Trimble. Born in 1922. He is in business with his father, A. G. Trimble, in Pittsburgh, Pennsylvania.

X4—Malcolm Beltz Trimble. Son of Arthur Garfield Trimble and Lily May Beltz. (Third Generation of Murray Trimble and Harriett Rugg.) Born in 1920. Married Mary Alice Garland.

    The children of Malcolm Beltz Trimble and Mary Alice Garland:

X6—Bonnie Lee Trimble. Born on January 22, 1950.

X7—Sharon Joyce Trimble. Born on March 12, 1951.

X8—Wayne Malcolm Trimble. Born on November 17, 1952.

X9—Eileen Beth Trimble. Born on September 4, 1954.

X10—Daniel Roger Trimble. Born on May 14, 1959.

Y - Stephen Trimble

We are gratefully indebted to Charles T. Trimble of Vinton, Virginia, for the Trimble genealogy of the Stephen Trimble family.

Y1—Stephen Trimble. Born about 1860 in Virginia. He lived at Hot Springs, Virginia, and married Matilda Rucker.

The two sons of Stephen Trimble and Matilda Rucker:

+ **Y2—John Alexander Trimble.** Born on March 25, 1881. Married Emma McFadden.

+ **Y3—Henry Burton Trimble.** Born on December 26, 1885 in Hot Springs, Virginia and died in 1996 at the age of 103. Married Mattie Cargill.

Y2—John Alexander Trimble. Son of Stephen Trimble and Matilda Rucker. Born on March 25, 1881. Married Emma McFadden.

The two children of John Alexander Trimble and Emma McFadden:

Y4—Porter Alexander Trimble. Born on July 22, 1903 and died on March 6, 1970. Married Gladys ——. They lived at Ocean View, Virginia, and had no issue.

+ **Y5—Charles Arthur Trimble.** Born on January 10, 1906. Married Dicie Cornelia ——. They have four children:

Y3—Henry Burton Trimble. Son of Stephen Trimble and Matilda Rucker. Born on December 26, 1885 and died in 1996 at the age of 103. Married Mattie Cargill in 1914. He received an A.B. from Roanoke College, an M.A. from Columbia University, and a B.D. from both Vanderbilt University and Union Theological Seminary. He then moved to Arkansas where he met and married his wife, Mattie. He later became pastor in Tennessee and North Carolina before becoming Dean of the Candler School of Theology in 1937, a position he held until 1953. He had been the dean of theology at Emory University since 1931 and was the author of books related to Methodism. Henry Burton Trimble is listed in Who's Who as one of our nation's leading theologians. Mattie Cargill was born on April 13, 1893 in Alpha, La and died in 1996 at the age of 103. Graduated from Meridian Female College in Mississippi in 1913. She moved to Leslie, Ark. to become a teacher where she met her future husband. She was an active member of the Glenn Memorial United Methodist Church in Atlanta, Georgia, heading the Women's Missionary Society there as well as the Women's Society of

Christian Service for the North Georgia Conference of the Methodist Church. In 1956 she became a delegate to the General Conference of the Methodist Church, voting that year to allow for full ordination rights for women. In 1962, Trimble became the first woman appointed to the Georgia Commission on Civil Rights. She was also a member of the Emory Woman's Club.

The children of Henry Burton Trimble and Mattie Cargill:

Y6—Mertis Trimble. Married William Pate.

Y7—Martha Marie Trimble.

Y8—Henry Burton Trimble, Jr. Never married.

Y5—Charles Arthur Trimble. Son of John Alexander Trimble and Emma McFadden. (Third generation of Stephen Trimble and Matilda Rucker.) Born on January 10, 1906. Married Dicie Cornelia ———.

The four children of Charles Trimble and Dicie Cornelia ———:

Y9—Dicie Scott Trimble. Born on December 1, 1931. Married Julian Griffin and they have a daughter, Kathy, and a son, Mark. This family lives at Hot Springs, Virginia.

Y10—Charles Thurmond Trimble. Born on August 22, 1933. Married Virginia Hite. Their children: Charles Stephen and Robin Ann. This family lives at Vinton, Virginia.

Y11—Floyd Burton Trimble. Born in November 1941. Married Eleanor Neff. They have three children: Donna Lynn, Michael Burton, and Richard Trimble. This family lives at Millboro Springs, Virginia.

Y12—David Porter Trimble. Born in October 1945. Married Lela Pritt. They have a son, Kevin, and they live at Front Royal, Virginia.

Z - Gilbert K. Trimble

This part deals with the family of Gilbert K. Trimble, one of the leading research chemists in rubber. He lives in Saint Louis, Missouri, and is listed in *Who's Who in America,* 1970-1971. Nothing is known of his ancestry beyond his father. There is a chance that he descended from Alexander Trimble, youngest of the Five Trimble Brothers. Alexander settled in Philadelphia in the 1730s.

Z1—Gilbert K. Trimble. was born in Philadelphia and his family were Presbyterians.

Z2—William McClelland Trimble. Married Anna Frances Quillman. He lived in Philadelphia, Pennsylvania, where he was in the wholesale grocery business.

Their children of William McClelland Trimble and Anna Frances Quillman:

Z3—Gilbert Kohler Trimble. Born on March 11, 1898. Married Florence Nadine Immier on April 2, 1931. They have two daughters: Nancy Ann and Judith Ellen.

Z4—Dorothy Trimble. Married Reese Bender now deceased. She lives at Havertown, Pennsylvania, and has three children: Reese, Carol, and Linda.

Z5—Aline Trimble. Married William McElwee and they live at Cherry Hill, New Jersey. They have three children: William, who is a minister; Robert, who is a graduate of Annapolis Naval Academy where he was a member of the Navy Football Team; and Betsy Trimble.

AA - Warren W. Trimble

Warren W. Trimble along with his brothers, John and Wallace Trimble, settled around 1850 in Ohio after going to Oklahoma where they had participated in the Oklahoma Land Rush. They had disappointing results from their adventures. Wallace settled in Mineral Ridge, Ohio, where he operated a grocery store for years before his retirement. John lived on Charles Street in Warren, Ohio. He worked as gatekeeper for a metal works factory. Warren W. lived next door to John in Warren, Ohio. Warren is the grandfather of Samuel E. Trimble of Route 5, Box 1009, Lakeland, Florida 33801, who compiled his family line for us. One other brother of Warren W. Trimble settled in Lisbon, Ohio, but we do not know his name.

AA1—Warren W. Trimble. Married Mary Koyer of Youngstown, Ohio.

The children of Warren W. Trimble and Mary Koyer:

AA2—George Trimble.

AA3—Charles Trimble.

AA4—Samuel Trimble.

+ **AA5—James Trimble.**

AA5—James Trimble. Son of Warren W. Trimble and Mary Koyer. Married Lula Belle Lewis of Pittsburgh, Pennsylvania.

The children of James Trimble and Lula Belle Lewis:

AA6—Herbert Trimble. Married and lives at Temple Terrace, Florida. He has three sons: Gary and Warren, who live at Temple Terrace, and James, who lives at Fairview Park, Cleveland, Ohio. They are all married.

AA7—Bertha Trimble. Married William A. Dietrich and lives at East Canton, Ohio. They have two sons and one daughter who are all married.

AA8—Justine Trimble. Married John A. Patrick of Paducah, Kentucky. They are both deceased. They had one son and a daughter.

AA9—Samuel E. Trimble. Married Goldie Williams of Sheakleyville, Pennsylvania. Samuel will be seventy-two years of age on November 2, 1972. Their children: Elizabeth, Married Glen F. Reichard of Warren Ohio, they have a daughter, Frances, Married George W. Rowlands and lives at Fort Lauderdale Florida; Julia, Married James Nycum and they live at Warren, Ohio, with their two sons; and Leonard Lewis, who is married and lives at Windermere Florida, with his family of two sons and one daughter.

AB - Thomas Trimble

We are appreciative of the following Trimble family line submitted by Warren A. Trimble of 35185 Holbrook Road, Chagrin Falls, Ohio 44022. Warren Trimble mentions that Thomas Trimble settled in Mineral Ridge, Ohio. In the genealogy of Warren W. Trimble, we note that Wallace Trimble also settled in Mineral Ridge, Ohio. We would therefore feel these families are interrelated.

AB1—Thomas Trimble. Born on March 10, 1807 and died on March 13, 1881. He married Nancia Luman, born on May 22, 1814, and died on December 15, 1883. Thomas was from Pennsylvania, He first met Nancia as she was passing through Pennsylvania on a wagon train going West from New England. We do not know if she left the wagon or if Thomas joined them, at any rate they married and settled at Mineral Ridge, Ohio. Thomas was a farmer.

The children Thomas Trimble and Nancia Luman:
AB2—Austin Trimble.
AB3—James Trimble.
AB4—John Trimble.
AB5— Adel Trimble.
AB6—Wallace Trimble.
AB7—Mary Trimble.
AB8—Albert Warren Trimble. He was the grandfather of Warren A. Trimble.

AC - Green Berry Trimble

AC1—Green Berry Trimble was born in Cole County, Missouri, and married Annie L. Morrow who was also born and reared in Cole County. They moved to Tarrant County, Texas, in; 1866 and lived twelve miles east of the city of Fort Worth, Texas. He served in the Confederate Army during the Civil War.

We know of only one child of Green Berry Trimble and Annie L. Morrow.

AC2—Dr. William Marshall Trimble. Son of Green Berry Trimble and Annie L. Morrow. He was first an educator then later a medical doctor. *The History of Central and Western Texas* contains the following resume: "Dr. Trimble was founder and President of Arlington College, Supt. of Public Schools of Fort Worth, after which he studied: medicine at Baylor University. He became the city physician of Fort Worth. He married February 17, 1897, to Susie Borah." We have record of two children, perhaps there were others.

Two of the children of Dr. William Marshall Trimble and Susie Borah:

AC3—Dr. Green B. Trimble. A retired physician who lives in Fort Worth, Texas. (The compiler had the pleasure of meeting Dr. Trimble at a Trimble reunion in Ashland, Kentucky.)

AC4—J. B. Trimble. An attorney in Corpus Christi, Texas, with whom the compiler has corresponded. We are still doing research on this family. Anyone reading this book who might know the ancestor of the first Green B. Trimble please contact J. B. Trimble, Suite 410 Palm Plaza, North 1801 South Staples Street, Corpus Christi, Texas.

AD - George Trimble

AD1—George Trimble was born in Tyrone, now Northern Ireland in 1760. This the only branch of Trimbles in this book that has a generation that did not live in America. Married Mary Rush. She was born 1775 in Stewartstown, Tyrone, Northern Ireland.

The children of George Trimble and Mary Rush:

AD2—Andrew Trimble. Born about 1804 in Ireland and died on November 11, 1891 in Munderadoe, Tyrone, Ireland.

AD3—George Trimble. Born about 1806 in Northern Ireland.

AD4—John Trimble. Born about 1808 in Northern Ireland.

AD5—Charlotte Trimble. Born about 1810 in Northern Ireland.

AD6—Annie Trimble. Born about 1812 in Northern Ireland.

AD7—Robert Trimble. Born about 1814 in Northern Ireland.

AD8—William Trimble. Born about 1816 in Northern Ireland.

AD9—David Trimble. Born about 1818 in Northern Ireland.

+ **AD10—Samuel Trimble.** Born 1820 in Ireland. Married Lillian Kyle in 1840.

AD10—Samuel Trimble. Son of George Trimble and Mary Rush. Born in 1820 in Ireland. Married Lillian Kyle in 1840. She was born in 1822 in Ireland.

The children of Samuel Trimble and Lillian Kyle:

+ **AD11—John Trimble.** Born in 1842 in Carrickmore, Termonmaguirk, Omagh, Tyrone, Ireland and died on May 17, 1920 in 86 Cliff Street, North Adams, Massachusetts. Married Elizabeth Trimble on June 23, 1876 in Sandholes Presbyterian Church, Desertcreat, Cookstown, Tyrone, Ireland.

AD12—Annie Trimble. Born in 1844 in Northern Ireland.

AD13—Samuel Trimble. Born about 1848 in Northern Ireland.

AD14—Charlotte Trimble. Born on March 23, 1851 in Northern Ireland and died on March 11, 1919 in 73 Cliff Street, North Adams, Massachusetts.

AD15—Robert Trimble. Born about 1854 in Northern Ireland.

AD16—Thomas Trimble. Born about 1856 in Northern Ireland.

AD17—George Trimble. Born about 1859 in Northern Ireland.

AD11—John Trimble. Son of Samuel Trimble and Lillian Kyle. (Third generation of George Trimble and Mary Rush.) Born in 1842 in Carrickmore, Termonmaguirk, Omagh, Tyrone, Ireland and died on May 17, 1920 in 86 Cliff Street, North Adams, Massachusetts. Married Elizabeth

Trimble on June 23, 1876 in Sandholes Presbyterian Church, Desertcreat, Cookstown, Tyrone, Ireland. She was born about 1853 in Gortavale, Desertcreat, Cookstown, Tyrone, Ireland and died on November 29, 1891 in North Adams, Berkshire County, Massachusetts. Elizabeth's father was Robert Trimble born about 1830 in Gortavale, Desertcreat, Cookstown, Tyrone, Ireland and died on November 25, 1895 in Gortavale, Desertcreat, Cookstown, Tyrone, Ireland.

The children of John Trimble and Elizabeth Trimble:

AD18—Samuel Trimble. Born on August 25, 1877 in North Adams, Massachusetts and died on July 16, 1956 in Pinellas, Florida.

AD19—Anna Eliza Trimble. Born on August 3, 1879 in North Adams, Massachusetts and died on July 13, 1948 in Cambridge, Massachusetts.

AD20—Lillian Trimble. Born on January 20, 1882 in North Adams, Pittsfield, Berkshire County, Massachusetts and died in 1955.

AD21—Margaret J. Trimble. Born on June 26, 1884 in North Adams, Massachusetts.

AD22—Robert Trimble. Born in 1886 in North Adams, Massachusetts and died 1928.

AD23—Emma Trimble. Born on February 20, 1889 in North Adams, Massachusetts.

AD24—Infant Trimble. Born and died on February 20, 1889 in North Adams, Berkshire, Massachusetts.

AD25—Female Infant Trimble. Born and died on November 27, 1891 in North Adams, Berkshire, Massachusetts.

AE– Thomas Brogdon Trimble

AE1–Thomas Brogdon Trimble was born on January 31, 1806 and died in November 1833 in Baltimore, Harford County, Maryland. Thomas emigrated to the US arriving in Baltimore, Harford County, Maryland in September of 1827 from Great Britain (Ireland). Married Margaret "Margaretha" B. Wilson on March 2, 1829 in New York, New York. She was born on July 4, 1809 in Baltimore, Harford County, Maryland and died on September 30, 1883 in Baltimore, Harford County, Maryland.[74]

The children of Thomas Brogdon Trimble and Margaret "Margaretha" B. Wilson:

+ **AE2–Henry Clay Trimble.** Born on July 18, 1829 in Baltimore, Harford County, Maryland and died on April 7, 1887 in Baltimore City, Maryland. Married Phoebe D. Carr on May 5, 1853.[75]

+ **AE3–Charles T. Trimble.** Born on September 1, 1831 in Baltimore, Harford County, Maryland and died on April 6, 1892 in Baltimore City, Maryland. Married twice.

AE2–Henry Clay Trimble. Son of Thomas Brogdon Trimble and Margaret "Margaretha" B. Wilson. Born on July 18, 1829 in Baltimore, Harford County, Maryland and died on April 7, 1887 in Baltimore City, Maryland. Married Phoebe D. Carr on May 5, 1853. She was born on June 17, 1838 in Baltimore, Harford County, Maryland and died on July 17, 1914 in Manhattan, New York, New York.[76]

The children of Henry Clay Trimble and Phoebe D. Carr:

+ **AE4–Margareth A. Trimble.** Born on October 15, 1854 in Baltimore City, Maryland and died on July 13, 1949 in Niagara Falls, Niagara County, New York. Married Theodore V. Ryder

+ **AE5–Charles Henry Trimble.** Born on March 2, 1857 in Baltimore City, Maryland and died in 1930 in Havre de Grace, Harford County,

---

[74] Tepper, Michael H. Passenger Arrivals at the Port of Baltimore 1820-1834, From Customs Passenger Lists. Baltimore, MD: Clearfield Company, Inc., 2000. pp. 370-768 Page 683.

[75] 1870 US Federal Census, Baltimore Ward 20, Baltimore, Maryland. Page 270.

[76] 1880, U.S. Federal Census, Baltimore Ward 10, Baltimore, Maryland, Supervisor District 1, Enumeration District 91, Sheet 15.

Maryland. Married Annie L. Carr in 1880.

+ **AE6—Hannah Jane Trimble.** Born on October 21, 1859 in Baltimore City, Maryland and died on November 27, 1926 in Hollis, Queens, New York. Married Candido Francisco Menendez on October 14, 1875.

+ **AE7—Thomas Brogdon Trimble.** Born on September 29, 1861 in Baltimore City, Maryland and died in 1930. Married Ida F. Haskell in 1882.

AE8—Lydia Mary Trimble. Born on March 11, 1864 in Baltimore, Maryland and died on July 25, 1864 as an infant.

+ **AE9—William Dyer Trimble.** Born on December 2, 1865 in Kent County, Maryland. Married Id Mae Sutton on September 24, 1890.

AE10—Florence Trimble. Born about 1870 in Maryland.

AE11—Phebe Trimble. Born about 1873 in Maryland.

AE12—Walter Trimble. Born about 1876 in Maryland.

AE3—Charles T. Trimble. Son of Thomas Brogdon Trimble and Margaret "Margaretha" B. Wilson. Born on September 1, 1831 in Baltimore, Harford County, Maryland and died on April 6, 1892 in Baltimore City, Maryland. The 1880 US Census lists his occupation as Carpenter.

Married first Mary Ensore about 1860. She was born about 1832 in Baltimore, Maryland and died in 1867 in Baltimore, Maryland. [77]

Married second to Sarah E. Price. She was born about 1854 in Maryland.

The children of Charles T. Trimble and Mary Ensore:

+ **AE13—Luke Wesley Marion Trimble.** Born on December 1860 in Maryland and died on February 25, 1951 in Baltimore, Maryland. Married Emma Jane Smith in 1884.

The children of Charles T. Trimble and Sarah E. Price:

+ **AE14—Clarence U. Trimble.** Born about 1872 in Maryland. Married Mary about 1901.

AE15—Sarah E. Trimble. Born about 1878 in Maryland.

AE4—Margareth A. Trimble. Daughter of Henry Clay Trimble and Phoebe D. Carr. (Third generation of Thomas Brogdon Trimble and Margaret "Margaretha" B Wilson.) Born on October 15, 1854 in Baltimore City, Maryland and died on July 13, 1949 in Niagara Falls, Niagara County, New

---

[77] 1880 US Federal Census, District 8, Baltimore, Maryland, Supervisor's District 1, Enumeration District 241, Page 9.

York. Married Theodore V. Ryder on April 20, 1876 in Baltimore, Maryland. He was born on June 20, 1852 in Maryland and died on April 2, 1911 in New York, New York.[78]

The children of Theodore V. Ryder and Margareth A. Trimble:

AE16—Leonora Rachael Ryder. Born on January 13, 1880 and died May 8, 1898. She was only 18.

AE17—Helen Mae Ryder. Born on December 8, 1883 and died in January 1884 as an infant.

AE18—Mary E. Ryder. Born on December 8, 1883 in Washington, DC. She is listed in the 1990 US Census, so she died after 1900.

AE5—Charles Henry Trimble. Son of Henry Clay Trimble and Phoebe D. Carr. (Third generation of Thomas Brogdon Trimble and Margaret "Margaretha" B. Wilson.) Born on March 2, 1857 in Baltimore City, Maryland and died in 1930 in Havre de Grace, Harford County, Maryland. Married Annie L. Carr in 1880. She was born in August 1863 in Harford County, Maryland and died on August 20, 1936 in 110 Conduit St, Annapolis, Maryland. She was the daughter of Mary S. Carr. Mary was born about November 1838.[79]

The children of Charles Henry Trimble and Annie L. Carr:

AE19—George Mulberry Trimble. Born on January 29, 1884 in Harford County, Maryland.

AE20—Susie S. Trimble. Born on October 1886 in Maryland and died in 1971.

+ AE21—Elva L. Trimble. Born on August 1894 in Maryland and died about 1922. Married Noah Sylvester McFadden in 1914 in Hartford County, Maryland.

AE22—Charles Medford Trimble. Born on August 4, 1898 in Maryland and died in March 1993 in Havre De Grace, Harford County, Maryland.

AE6—Hannah Jane Trimble. Daughter of Henry Clay Trimble and Phoebe D. Carr. (Third generation of Thomas Brogdon Trimble and Margaret "Margaretha" B. Wilson.) Born on October 21, 1859 in Baltimore City, Maryland and died on November 27, 1926 in Hollis, Queens, New York.

---

[78] 1900 US Federal Census, Baltimore Ward 12, Baltimore City, Maryland, Supervisor District 1, Enumeration District 148, Sheet 10.

[79] 1990 US Federal Census, Kent County, Maryland, 3rd District, Supervisor District 2, Enumeration District 49, Sheet No 6.

Married Candido Francisco Menendez on October 14, 1875 in Baltimore, Maryland. He was born on October 3, 1854 in Cuba and died on August 10, 1928 in Hollis, Queens, New York. He was a store clerk.

The children of Candido Francisco Menendez and Hanna Jane Trimble:

AE23—Francisco Candida Menendez. Born on June 12, 1876 in Baltimore, Maryland and died on October 18, 1920 in Mattituck, Long Island, New York.

AE24—Carmen Menendez. She was born in 1879 in Baltimore, Maryland and died before 1900 in Baltimore, Maryland.

AE25—Dolores Lolita C. Menendez. Born on June 23, 1885 in Baltimore, Maryland and died on January 29, 1933 in Jamaica, Queens, New York.

AE7—Thomas Brogdon Trimble. Son of Henry Clay Trimble and Phoebe D. Carr. (Third generation of Thomas Brogdon Trimble and Margaret "Margaretha" B. Wilson.) Born on September 29, 1861 in Baltimore City, Maryland and died 1930. Married Ida F. Haskell in 1882. She was born in 1863 in Maryland. [80]

The children of Thomas Brogdon Trimble and Ida F. Haskell:

AE26—Albert Haskell Trimble. Born on January 12, 1884 in Baltimore, Maryland.

AE27—May B. Trimble. Born in 1888 in Baltimore, Maryland.

AE28—Thomas Brogdon Trimble. Born on October 5, 1894 in Baltimore, Maryland and died in January 1971 in Baltimore, Maryland.

AE29—Della G. Trimble. Born in 1906 in Baltimore, Maryland.

AE9—William Dyer Trimble. Son of Henry Clay Trimble and Phoebe D. Carr. (Third generation of Thomas Brogdon Trimble and Margaret "Margaretha" B. Wilson.) Born on December 2, 1865 in Kent County, Maryland. Married Ida Mae Sutton on September 24, 1890 in Harford County, Maryland.

The children of William Dyer Trimble and Ida Mae Sutton:

AE30—William Dyer Trimble, Jr. Born on March 31, 1893 Baltimore, Maryland.

+ **AE31—Earle Stanley Trimble.** Born on March 22, 1895 in Baltimore, Maryland and died in May 1976 in Portsmouth, Virginia. Married Garnet LaReine Fraser.

---

[80] 1910 US Federal Census, Baltimore Ward 12, Baltimore, Maryland, Supervisor District 3, Enumeration District 183, Page 7.

AE32—Thomas Alva Edison Trimble. Born on February 1, 1897 in Baltimore, Maryland.

AE33—Nikola T. Trimble. Born in June 1899 in Baltimore, Maryland. Married Macon L.

AE13—Luke Wesley Marion Trimble. Son of Charles T. Trimble and Mary Ensore. (Third generation of Thomas Brogdon Trimble and Margaret "Margaretha" B. Wilson.) Born in December 1860 in Maryland and died on February 25, 1951 in Baltimore, Maryland. Married Emma Jane Smith in 1884. She was born in August 1865 in Maryland.[81]

The children of Luke Wesley Marion Trimble and Emma Jane Smith:

AE34—Roland Sargent Trimble. Born on July 12, 1884 in Maryland and died on December 16, 1941 in Baltimore, Maryland. Married twice. Married first Susie Smith. Married second to Mary Brady.

AE35, Lee Trimble. Born in November 1886 in Baltimore, Maryland and died in Baltimore, Maryland. Married Ethel Arnell Busick.

AE36—Lillian Irene Trimble. Born in August 1887 in Maryland.

AE37—Frank Elwood Trimble. Born on November 14, 1890 in Maryland and died on May 4, 1970. Married Sarah Emily Price on December 25, 1912.

AE38—Susan Virginia Trimble. Born in August 1893 in Maryland.

AE39—Gladys Ola Trimble. Born in 1902 in Maryland and died in 1984.

AE40—Milton Leroy Trimble. Born on October 25, 1903 in Baltimore, Maryland and died January 1978 in Baltimore, Maryland. Married Loretta Pscherer

AE14—Clarence U. Trimble. Son of Charles T. Trimble and Mary Ensore. (Third generation of Thomas Brogdon Trimble and Margaret "Margaretha" B. Wilson.) Born about 1872 in Maryland. Married Mary about 1901. She was born about 1882.[82]

The child of Clarence U. and Mary Trimble:

AE41—Dorothy Trimble. Born about January 1910.

AE21—Elva L. Trimble. Son of Charles Henry Trimble and Annie L. Carr.

---

[81] 1900 US Federal Census, Baltimore Ward 12, Baltimore City, Maryland, Supervisor District 1, Enumeration District 147, Sheet 19.

[82] 1910, US Federal Census, Baltimore Ward 13, Baltimore City, Maryland, Supervisor District 3, Enumeration District 208, Sheet 10.

(Fourth generation of Thomas Brogdon Trimble and Margaret "Margaretha" B. Wilson.) Born in August 1894 in Maryland and died about 1922. Married first Noah Sylvester McFadden in 1914 in Hartford County, Maryland. He was born on July 31, 1893 in Hartford County, Maryland and died on August 26, 1952 in Chester County, Pennsylvania.

Married second Daniel Wilson. Born about 1894.[83]

The children of Noah Sylvester McFadden and Elva L. Trimble:

AE42—Ann Reese McFadden. Born in Havre de Grace, Harford County, Maryland and died on July 9, 1995.

The children of Daniel Wilson and Elva L. Trimble:

AE43—Patricia Wilson. Born about 1937 in Maryland.

AE31—Earle Stanley Trimble. Son of William Dyer Trimble and Ida Mae Sutton. (Fourth generation of Thomas Brogdon Trimble and Margaret "Margaretha" B. Wilson.) Born on March 22, 1895 in Baltimore, Maryland and died in May 1976 in Portsmouth, Virginia. Married Garnet LaReine Fraser.

The children of Earl Stanley Trimble and Garnet LaReine Fraser:

AE44—Ida Trimble. Born in 1917. Married Saunders.

AE45—Earle Stanley Trimble, Jr. Born on October 17, 1919 in Virginia and February 3, 2012 in Hampton, Virginia. Married Doris R.

AE46—Charles H. Trimble. Born on May 30, 1927 in Virginia and died on April 8, 2009 in Portsmouth, Virginia.

---

[83] 1940, US Federal Census, Harford County, Maryland, Election District 6, Block Number 234, Supervisor District 2, Enumeration District 13-24, Sheet 17.

AF - John Cozzens Trimble

Mary Louise Trimble of 3816 Milan Drive No. 5, Alexandria, Virginia 22305, has contributed a listing of marriages, births, and deaths of descendants of John Cozzens Trimble who migrated from Ireland in the latter part of the nineteenth century.

Marriages:

On July 3, 1873-John Cozzens Trimble to Laura Green.

On September 21, 1873-Sarah Adams to Wesley P. Green.

On December 31, 1915-Wesley Green Trimble to Leslie May Wolfe.

On September 4, 1938-Clifford Samuel Hoover to Elizabeth Joe Trimble.

On June 15, 1939-John Wesley Trimble to Frances Mae Hillard.

On August 26, 1941-Mahlon Gray Eberhart to Susanna Harvey Trimble.

On August 26, 1941-Edward Gensimire to Laura Mae Trimble.

On September 24, 1960-Wesley Green Trimble to Garnet Aurora Wilson.

Births:

John Cozzens Trimble on March 9, 1851.

Laura Green on January 12, 1852.

Wesley P. Green on July 5, 1812.

Sarah Adams on October 26, 1812.

Anna Mary Green on June 29, 1838.

Sarah Margaret Green on April 27, 1840.

Jane Elizabeth Green on March 11, 1842.

Eleanor Green on February 21, 1844.

Juniatta Green on December 24, 1846.

Stillborn child on May 13, 1849.

Sallie M. Trimble on May 15, 1876.

Mary B. Trimble on June 12, 1876.

John C. Trimble on February 6, 1887.

Wesley G. Trimble on September 3, 1881.

Walter A. Trimble in October 1883.

Walter L. Baker on December 27, 1892.

Laura M. Baker on July 26, 1895.

Leslie May Wolfe Trimble born to William Wallace Wolfe and Harriet Elizabeth Willard Wilhide Trimble on September 23, 1893.

John Wesley Trimble born to Wesley Green Trimble and Leslie Wolfe Trimble on October 28, 1916.

Elizabeth Joe Trimble born to Wesley Green Trimble and Leslie Wolfe

Trimble Families of America

AF - John Cozzens Trimble

Trimble on July 25, 1918.

Suzanna Harvey Trimble born to Wesley Green Trimble and Leslie Wolfe Trimble in February 1922.

Laura May Trimble born to Wesley Green Trimble and Leslie Wolfe Trimble on May 8, 1927.

Wesley Green Trimble born to John Wesley Trimble and Frances Mae Hillard Trimble on June 21, 1941.

Mary Louise "Mame" Trimble born to John Wesley Trimble and Frances Mae Hillard Trimble on June 19, 1949.

Elizabeth Ann Eberhart born to Suzanna Trimble Eberhart and Mahlon Eberhart on June 20, 1942.

Tina Marie Trimble Born to Wesley Green Trimble and Garnet A. Wilson on October 3, 1961.

Tammy Jo Trimble Born to Wesley Green Trimble and Garnet A. Wilson on December 2, 1964.

Melissa Sue Trimble born to Wesley Green Trimble and Garnet A. Wilson on July 1, 1968.

Deaths:

John Cozzens Trimble on October 23, 1903.

Laura Green Trimble on February 13, 1930.

Wesley Green Trimble on April 6, 1941.

Laura May Baker on April 11, 1946.

Walter Lee Baker on September 20, 1955.

Charles M. Trimble on April 16, 1890.

Mary Jane Trimble on born March 18, 1831 and died on March 18, 1904.

Sarah Adams Green on October 2, 1906.

Walter Adams Trimble on October 23, 1955.

John C. Trimble on April 8, 1958.

Ann Mary Green on June 15, 1843.

Eleanor Green on January 22, 1848.

Wesley P. Green on September 23, 1856.

Leslie May Wolfe Trimble on March 25, 1958.

Walter Lee Baker died in Covington, Virginia, and is buried at Wilmington, Delaware. He was sixty-two years of age at his death.

AG - Eric Gillespie Trimble

One of the most colorful and dramatically written genealogies that we were privileged to receive came from the pen of one of the most talented modern-day Trimbles, Kenny Trimble. Kenny is the first-chair trombonist in the renowned Lawrence Welk Band of television and supper club fame. Perhaps this statement of Kenny Trimble in a letter written to the compiler in 1971 sums up the feeling many of us have when asked about our family history, "Why didn't I ask my dad more things about our family before he passed away?" Eric Gillespie Trimble was the father of Kenny Trimble, and this is part of his history.

AG1—Eric Gillespie Trimble. Born in Redmon, Illinois, in 1884. When he was a young man, he worked as a lumberjack in northern Minnesota where he met and married a French-Canadian girl. Her maiden name was Renault, but when she was a child, her parents changed it to Reno. On her head stone it is listed as Ada Ruby Roberts. She was born in 1895 and died in 1969. Eric was struck and killed by a bus at the age of seventy-eight in 1962 in Winter Park, Florida.

When Kenny Trimble was born, his father came down with tuberculosis of the spine. It was a result of extreme exposure, roughing it in sub-zero weather in the Canadian timber country. He went to the Mayo Clinic in Rochester, Minnesota, where Dr. Charles Mayo, Sr., performed radical surgery (for that time, 1919). He scraped out all the rotten bone from the spinal column and took bone from Eric's shin and grafted it into his back. They then put a cast on him from the neck to the hips and told him to leave it on for one year. Six months later Eric broke the cast off himself with a hammer and went back to the "Bush." Naturally, a relapse set in this time in the form of an open sore on the hip. "I hope my graphic description won't shock the readers too much, but the Trimbles come from good stock, so I'm not worried," said Kenny Trimble. This time the Mayo brothers told Eric that his impulsive act might result in death. But that a change of climate might solve his problem. They suggested either Florida or California and the old man (God Bless Him) flipped a coin. Our next address was Palm Beach, Florida. Not the Palm Beach of the Kennedy clan, more of a backwoods frame house with chickens scratching in the backyard. Kenny was only four years old at the time, but a brother Rex who lives in Milwaukee often told Kenny of his father's ordeal. Every day Eric walked into the Atlantic Ocean on his crutches and when the

Trimble Families of America

surf finally reached that open sore on his hip, he collapsed in pain.

His favorite saying those days was: "Every day in every way I'm getting better and better." Their walk home was by the way of a rural railroad route. One day on the way home Rex Trimble says that his father Eric threw one of his crutches into the woods. A few weeks later he threw the other crutch into the woods and cut off a branch to use as a cane. Finally, he threw the cane away. He is on record at the Mayo Clinic as being somewhat indestructible. "I'm proud of my father," says Kenny Trimble.

Eric Gillespie Trimble had a sister Ethel Turner.

The children of Eric Gillespie Trimble:

AG2—Ray Trimble. Recently (the printing date of the first edition date 1975) retired from the U.S. Navy as a full commander.

AG3—Rex Trimble.

+ **AG4—Kenny James Trimble.**

AG4—Kenny James Trimble. Son of Eric Gillespie Trimble. He was born March 1, 1919 in International Falls, Koochiching, Minnesota and died May 8, 1991 Reno, Washoe County, Nevada. Married for twenty-eight years to his childhood sweetheart. Her name is Bonnie. Her father was Kenny's scoutmaster and when she was eleven years old Kenny was thirteen. They have a son, Jimmy Trimble, who plays first trombone in the house band at Caesar's Palace in Las Vegas, Nevada. He was with the Harry James Band for a year, but his wife made him quit the road to settle down. Kenny says Bonnie made him do the same thing twenty years ago when he was with the Tex Beneke and Glen Miller Band. Their daughter, Pat Trimble, is a beautiful girl and is married to a college student. They have a son. Kenny served in the Army playing trombone during World War II.

We quote from Kenny Trimble, "I must mention something that may embarrass Ray. We grew up during the depression when things were tough. I sold newspapers on a street corner for spending money. There was a pawnshop on that corner with the most beautiful little cornet I ever saw hanging in the window. I wanted this cornet so much I could taste it, although I didn't know a note of music. I finally saved up five dollars and walked in and asked how much the cornet was. The price was eight dollars, and he wouldn't budge a penny lower. Well, there was an old beat-up trombone hanging from a nail in the hock shop and in desperation I asked how much, and it was four dollars, so I bought it. I learned to play in a Salvation Army band and I'm proud of it. But getting back to my brother Ray, who graduated from high school two years ahead of me. His first job was part time while he was going to college. It paid

AG - Eric Gillespie Trimble

thirteen dollars per week, and he bought me a brand-new Conn trombone for $125. The payments were $7.50 per month. Do you see what I mean about my family? As far as I'm concerned, I have the best job in the country, and I couldn't be happier. Bonnie and I live in a rather small house in North Hollywood but I'm fifteen minutes from the Hollywood Palladium where we play Saturday night and twenty minutes away from ABC-TV where we tape our television show ('The Lawrence Welk Show'). We have a pool in our backyard that's nine feet deep and I mow our lawn in January which is saying a lot for a newsboy who grew up with a cold nose and cold feet and a dream.

Printed in the USA
CPSIA information can be obtained
at www.ICGtesting.com
LVHW082002171123
764248LV00009B/904